I0046910

Liferay Portal 6.2
Enterprise Intranets

A practical guide to adopting portal development best practices in an enterprise world

Navin Agarwal

[PACKT] open source *

PUBLISHING   community experience distilled

BIRMINGHAM - MUMBAI

Liferay Portal 6.2 Enterprise Intranets

Copyright © 2015 Packt Publishing

All rights reserved. No part of this book may be reproduced, stored in a retrieval system, or transmitted in any form or by any means, without the prior written permission of the publisher, except in the case of brief quotations embedded in critical articles or reviews.

Every effort has been made in the preparation of this book to ensure the accuracy of the information presented. However, the information contained in this book is sold without warranty, either express or implied. Neither the author, nor Packt Publishing, and its dealers and distributors will be held liable for any damages caused or alleged to be caused directly or indirectly by this book.

Packt Publishing has endeavored to provide trademark information about all of the companies and products mentioned in this book by the appropriate use of capitals. However, Packt Publishing cannot guarantee the accuracy of this information.

First published: April 2008

Second edition: May 2010

Third edition: August 2015

Production reference: 1240815

Published by Packt Publishing Ltd.
Livery Place
35 Livery Street
Birmingham B3 2PB, UK.

ISBN 978-1-78216-284-1

www.packtpub.com

Credits

Author
Navin Agarwal

Reviewers
Chandan Sharma
Kartikeya Sharma
Shuyang Zhou

Acquisition Editor
Kevin Colaco

Content Development Editor
Athira Laji

Technical Editor
Humera Shaikh

Copy Editors
Sarang Chari
Sonia Mathur

Project Coordinator
Harshal Ved

Proofreader
Safis Editing

Indexer
Mariammal Chettiyar

Graphics
Abhinash Sahu

Production Coordinator
Arvindkumar Gupta

Cover Work
Arvindkumar Gupta

About the Author

Navin Agarwal has been working extensively with Liferay for more than 5 years. This includes work on Java and J2EE technologies. He has executed projects using Liferay in various domains (including retail, insurance, networking, and medical), providing solutions for collaboration, document management, and web content management systems. He also has extensive experience in integrating Liferay with Alfresco and various third-party tools.

He started his career as an intern in portal technology with Sun Microsystems, India. Currently, he is working for IEEE as a senior programmer analyst. He is also an expert in Liferay integration with Ad Server OpenX, different search engines, enterprise content (including video, audio, images, documents, and web content), and other technologies such as Activiti, BPM Intalio, business intelligence, LDAP, and SSO.

Besides development and consulting, he has also delivered training programs on Liferay and Alfresco. He has experience in various software development life cycle (SDLC) models and different technologies, including MongoDB and Pentaho BI, and has worked with numerous frameworks, including Spring, Struts, Hibernate, Apache PDFBox, and ICEfaces.

In his free time, he enjoys writing blogs and reading technical articles. You can send your queries, if any, directly to his e-mail ID at `navin.agarwal11@gmail.com`. You can even go through his blog at `https://navinagarwalmca.wordpress.com/` to learn more about Liferay Portal.

Acknowledgments

I would like to thank all my friends and the team members who work with me. I would also like to thank Rajeeva Lochana, Abhishek Saxena, James Falkner, Jorge Ferrer, Juan Fernández, and Ganesh Samarthyam for their valuable support and guidance.

A special thanks to my parents and family members for their encouragement and support during the writing of this book. I would also like to thank my lovely wife, Neha Agarwal, for supporting and encouraging me during the entire book-writing process and for her contribution in proofreading the chapters.

My sincere thanks and appreciation to the acquisition editor, Kevin Colaco; technical editor, Humera Salim Shaikh; and content development editor, Athira Laji, at Packt Publishing for their valuable support, help, and guidance. My heartfelt thanks to them for filling the communication, visualization, and technical gaps in the book. A very special thanks again to Athira Laji—without her, this book wouldn't have reached the production stage; it was really a joy to work with her.

About the Reviewers

Chandan Sharma is currently a software programmer analyst at Mroads, a company building a next-generation workforce that leverages technology and awareness, located in the U.S. At Mroads, his primary responsibility is designing and implementing solutions that use Liferay, Spring Framework, and Hibernate for portals and RESTful/SOAP web services. Previously, he worked as a senior consultant for CIGNEX Datamatics and TransIT mPower Labs. He also likes to coach people. Throughout his career, he has had hands-on experience in Liferay with Spring Framework, Hibernate, and Liferay integration with other applications, the cloud, and so on. He runs his own technical blog at `http://codingloading.com`.

I would like to thank Packt Publishing for the opportunity to be a technical reviewer for this book. I would also like to thank Gaurav Vaish (the author of *Getting Started with NoSQL*), who inspired me to get into reviewing books. And I would like to thank Meenu Gupta, who is like a sister to me, for her support and encouragement in reviewing this book. I would also like to thank my friends ☺ group (Monalisa Sahu, Manoj Patro, and Debasis Padhi) for their encouragement and support when I do new things in my life. Special thanks to my best friend for helping me in reviewing this book.

Kartikeya Sharma (Kartik) has over 10 years of experience in application architecture, design, development, implementation, and maintenance and the administration of portals and content management systems. He is currently working as a technical architect at Datamatics. His areas of expertise include Java/J2EE, Spring, SOAP, REST, Pega, and various content management and portal technologies, such as Liferay, WebLogic, WebCenter, Vignette, Documentum, SharePoint, and Alfresco.

He can be reached via LinkedIn at https://www.linkedin.com/in/kartiksharma84.

You can find his blog about various ECM and Portal technologies at http://www.ecmpexperts.com.

I would like to thank my wife, Punima Sharma, for her support, understanding, and patience during the long hours of work. I would also like to thank my parents and my manager, Aashish Thakur, for their constant encouragement.

Shuyang Zhou is a software architect focused on performance optimization and infrastructure development. Since joining Liferay in 2009, he has significantly improved Liferay Portal's performance and developed a high-performance benchmark toolset for performance tuning and monitoring. He has developed Liferay Portal's AOP, caching, and cluster infrastructure. He has also developed a set of low-level, high-performance concurrency tools and IO utilities, portlet container separation, and the portal resiliency feature that allows portlets to be executed from separate JVMs to achieve physical process isolation for better stability and better hardware resource utilization on high-end servers. Recently, he has focused on Liferay Portal Continuous Integration testing automation on machines on a large scale.

Shuyang holds a bachelor's degree in electronic and information engineering and a master's degree in communications and information systems from Dalian University of Technology.

www.PacktPub.com

Support files, eBooks, discount offers, and more

For support files and downloads related to your book, please visit www.PacktPub.com.

Did you know that Packt offers eBook versions of every book published, with PDF and ePub files available? You can upgrade to the eBook version at www.PacktPub.com and as a print book customer, you are entitled to a discount on the eBook copy. Get in touch with us at service@packtpub.com for more details.

At www.PacktPub.com, you can also read a collection of free technical articles, sign up for a range of free newsletters and receive exclusive discounts and offers on Packt books and eBooks.

https://www2.packtpub.com/books/subscription/packtlib

Do you need instant solutions to your IT questions? PacktLib is Packt's online digital book library. Here, you can search, access, and read Packt's entire library of books.

Why subscribe?

- Fully searchable across every book published by Packt
- Copy and paste, print, and bookmark content
- On demand and accessible via a web browser

Free access for Packt account holders

If you have an account with Packt at www.PacktPub.com, you can use this to access PacktLib today and view 9 entirely free books. Simply use your login credentials for immediate access.

Table of Contents

Preface

Liferay is one of the leading enterprise open source portals and has been named the leader in Gartner's Magic Quadrant for Horizontal Portals too. Liferay Portal is so flexible that it is in high demand when it comes to enterprise portal solutions.

To develop an intranet portal for an enterprise, Liferay is one of the best open source portal development platforms that has a large-scale graph for the developer to extend any component. Liferay also provides best-in-class support for integration with other applications.

In this book, we have explained easy steps to develop intranet and extranet portals for an organization. You may be a new, experienced, or advanced user of Liferay: this book is organized in such a way that you'll find useful information to take away and apply it in your day-to-day work to develop portals. If you are a Liferay Portal administrator, you will find this book useful to maintain the portal server and keep it running smoothly.

This book covers Liferay features in detail, including new features of Liferay, such as Liferay Sync, Liferay Marketplace, Recycle Bin, Liferay Connected Services, Audience Targeting, and so on. This will help you to integrate Liferay with other key applications, such as LDAP, SSO, and Alfresco 4.x and above. This book has numerous practical examples that will help you to develop an intranet portal on the fly. Most importantly, after going through each chapter, you will be able to understand and develop an intranet portal on your own.

Integration between different applications, such as LDAP, SSO, and Liferay Social Office, with numerous illustrations, diagrams, clear step-by-step instructions, and practical examples with screenshots are provided.

By reading this book, you will understand Liferay and its advance features. There are numerous Tips and Notes to help you understand the discussed ideas better.

What this book covers

Chapter 1, Introducing Liferay for Your Intranet, provides an introduction to the Liferay Portal 6.2 architecture and framework and also briefly explains Liferay's out-of-the-box portlets and features.

Chapter 2, Setting Up a Home Page and Navigation Structure for the Intranet, provides the reader with detailed, step-by-step instructions for the installation of the Liferay Portal server. It also explains the navigation structure for the portal page and helps to understand the different controls/actions for making the portal work for an enterprise.

Chapter 3, Bringing in Users, teaches you the creation of users and managing the users in the portal. It explains different terms, such as Organization, Site, User Groups, and Roles, in brief. It also provides the steps to configure portal settings.

Chapter 4, Forums, Categorization, and Asset Publishing, provides a detailed explanation of forums (Message Boards), Categorization, Tags, and Asset Publisher. It takes you through the steps to create and manage forums. It also covers categorization and tagging to help you manage the content in your portal. Finally, it provides step-by-step instructions to configure Asset Publisher.

Chapter 5, Understanding Wikis, Dynamic Data Lists, and Polls, teaches you about the Wiki, Dynamic Data List, and Polls portlets. It helps you with the creation of a wiki page and also allows you to manage the wiki for the portal. It even teaches you how to create a dynamic data list for your departments. Finally, it briefs you how the Polls portlet works and how you can implement it in your intranet portal.

Chapter 6, Blogs, WYSIWYG Editors, and Social Networking, explains how to create and manage blogs in the intranet portal. It also explains the WYSIWYG editor features and helps you to configure a different look and feel for your intranet portal. This chapter also explains the social networking portlets available within Liferay and how you can make use of all the portlets in creating social networking integrations into your intranet portal.

Chapter 7, Understanding Sites, provides the detailed discussion on Site. It helps you understand the site and how you can manage the site with different settings and controls provided for the site administrator. This chapter describes the advanced settings for the site, such as Application Display Templates, Social Activity, Workflow configurations, and Mobile Device families.

Chapter 8, Document and Media Management, teaches you about documents and media in detail. Here, you will learn about all the features of documents and media and how you can implement it in your enterprise intranet portal. It briefs you on Liferay Sync, which allows you to sync the Liferay document and media files in your local filesystem and access them through mobile devices too.

Chapter 9, Web Content Management, briefs you about the web content management system. This chapter guides you in creating and managing the web content for your intranet portal. Its also covers advanced topics, such as the staging page and publication, which allows you to publish the ready page to live production after you have formatted it in the staging environment.

Chapter 10, Marketplace, Social Office, and Audience Targeting, provides a detailed discussion on Liferay Marketplace, Liferay Social Office, and Audience Targeting, which are new features provided by Liferay.

Chapter 11, Server Administration, teaches you about server and portal administration, performance tuning, Liferay Connected Services, and Liferay Clustering. This chapter will teach you how to manage the Liferay Portal server and manage multiple instances. You will learn about the custom fields and their creation. It will also take you through Liferay Connected Services, which helps you to monitor the server and keep an eye on any fix update from Liferay through `https://lcs.liferay.com`. You will also learn how to create clustering for your Liferay server instance. Finally, it will update you on the new features in Liferay 7.

What you need for this book

Basically, to run the Liferay server, you need to have Java running on your local system. Secondly, you need to download Liferay Tomcat Server CE (liferay-portal-6.2-ce-ga2) from the SourceForge site `http://sourceforge.net/projects/lportal/files/Liferay%20Portal/`. Also, in your local system, you should have the MySQL database server running. For more details on the Liferay setup, refer to *Chapter 2, Setting Up a Home Page and Navigation Structure for the Intranet*.

Who this book is for

Liferay Portal 6.2 Enterprise Intranets is for everyone who is interested in Liferay Portal. This book is for beginners, intermediate, and advanced portal developers who need to create enterprise intranet portals for the business. It will be handy for IT professionals who already know the concepts of portal technologies and need to learn advanced integrations for different open source technologies with Liferay. It is also useful for experienced Liferay Portal developers and Liferay architects as it explains the various technologies used in Liferay Portal.

Conventions

In this book, you will find a number of styles of text that distinguish between different kinds of information. Here are some examples of these styles, and an explanation of their meaning.

Code words in text, database table names, folder names, filenames, file extensions, pathnames, dummy URLs, user input, and Twitter handles are shown as follows: "Suppose we have a set of variables, where `$PORTAL_VERSION` represents the current portal version and `$LIFERAY_PORTAL` represents the working folder containing the portal that we are planning to install."

A block of code is set as follows:

```
terms.of.use.journal.article.group.id=$ARTICLE_GROUP_ID
terms.of.use.journal.article.id=$ARTICLE_ID
```

When we wish to draw your attention to a particular part of a code block, the relevant lines or items are set in bold:

```
permissions.checker=com.liferay.portal.security.permission.Advanced
  PermissionChecker
```

Any command-line input or output is written as follows:

```
$LIFERAY_HOME=$LIFERAY_PORTAL/liferay-portal-$PORTAL_VERSION
```

New terms and **important words** are shown in bold. Words that you see on the screen, in menus or dialog boxes for example, appear in the text like this: "In the Liferay 6.2 control panel, under the **Apps | Store** link section, you will see apps that are stored in the Marketplace portlet."

> Warnings or important notes appear in a box like this.

> Tips and tricks appear like this.

Reader feedback

Feedback from our readers is always welcome. Let us know what you think about this book—what you liked or may have disliked. Reader feedback is important for us to develop titles that you really get the most out of.

To send us general feedback, simply send an e-mail to feedback@packtpub.com, and mention the book title via the subject of your message.

If there is a topic that you have expertise in and you are interested in either writing or contributing to a book, see our author guide on www.packtpub.com/authors.

Customer support

Now that you are the proud owner of a Packt book, we have a number of things to help you to get the most from your purchase.

Downloading the example code

You can download the example code files for all Packt books you have purchased from your account at http://www.packtpub.com. If you purchased this book elsewhere, you can visit http://www.packtpub.com/support and register to have the files e-mailed directly to you.

Downloading the color images of this book

We also provide you a PDF file that has color images of the screenshots/diagrams used in this book. The color images will help you better understand the changes in the output. You can download this file from: `https://www.packtpub.com/sites/default/files/downloads/2841OS_Graphics.pdf`.

Errata

Although we have taken every care to ensure the accuracy of our content, mistakes do happen. If you find a mistake in one of our books—maybe a mistake in the text or the code—we would be grateful if you could report this to us. By doing so, you can save other readers from frustration and help us improve subsequent versions of this book. If you find any errata, please report them by visiting `http://www.packtpub.com/submit-errata`, selecting your book, clicking on the **Errata Submission Form** link, and entering the details of your errata. Once your errata are verified, your submission will be accepted and the errata will be uploaded to our website or added to any list of existing errata under the Errata section of that title.

To view the previously submitted errata, go to `https://www.packtpub.com/books/content/support` and enter the name of the book in the search field. The required information will appear under the **Errata** section.

Piracy

Piracy of copyright material on the Internet is an ongoing problem across all media. At Packt, we take the protection of our copyright and licenses very seriously. If you come across any illegal copies of our works, in any form, on the Internet, please provide us with the location address or website name immediately so that we can pursue a remedy.

Please contact us at `copyright@packtpub.com` with a link to the suspected pirated material.

We appreciate your help in protecting our authors, and our ability to bring you valuable content.

Questions

You can contact us at `questions@packtpub.com` if you are having a problem with any aspect of the book, and we will do our best to address it.

1
Introducing Liferay for Your Intranet

Liferay is an enterprise application solution. It provides a lot of functionalities, which helps an organization to grow and is a one-solution package as a portal and content management solution. This book will help you to create an organization intranet portal solution with Liferay. In this chapter, we will look at the following topics:

- The complete features you want your organization's intranet solution to have by the time you reach the end of this book
- Reasons why Liferay is an excellent choice to build your intranet
- Where and how Liferay is used besides intranet portals
- Easy integration with other open source tools and applications
- Getting into more technical information about what Liferay is and how it works

So, let's start looking at exactly what kind of site we're going to build in this book.

Liferay Portal makes life easy

Over the course of this book, we're going to build a complete corporate intranet solution using Liferay. Let's discuss some of the features your intranet portal will have.

Hosted discussions

Are you still using e-mail for group discussions? Then, it's time you found a better way! Running group discussions over e-mail clogs up the team's inbox — this means you have to choose your distribution list in advance, and that makes it hard for team members to *opt in and out* of the discussion.

Using Liferay, we will build a range of discussion boards for discussion within and between teams. The discussions are archived in one place, which means that it's always possible to go back and refer to them later.

On one level, it's just more convenient to move e-mail discussions to a discussion forum designed for the purpose. But once the forum is in place, you will find that a more productive group discussion takes place here than it ever did over e-mail.

Collaborative documents using wikis

Your company probably has guideline documents that should be updated regularly but swiftly lose their relevance as practices and procedures change. Even worse, each of your staff will know useful, productive tricks and techniques — but there's probably no easy way to record that knowledge in a way that is easy for others to find and use.

We will see how to host *wikis* within Liferay. A wiki enables anybody to create and edit web pages and link all of those web pages together without requiring any HTML or programming skills. You can put your *guideline* documents into a wiki, and as practices change, your frontline staff can quickly and effortlessly update the guideline documentation.

Wikis can also act as a shared notebook, enabling team members to collaborate and share ideas and findings and work together on documents.

Team and individual blogs

Your company probably needs frequent, chronological publications of personal thoughts and web links in the intranet. Your company probably has teams and individuals working on specific projects in order to share files and blogs about a project process and more. By using the Liferay Blog features, you can use HTML text editors to create or update files and blogs and to provide RSS feeds.

Liferay provides an easy way for teams and individuals to share files with the help of blogs. Blogs provide a straightforward blogging solution with features such as RSS, user and guest comments, browsable categories, tags and labels, and a rating system. Liferay's RSS with the subscription feature provides the ability to frequently read RSS feeds from within the portal framework. We will see the detailed features of Liferay Blog in *Chapter 6, Blogs, WYSIWYG Editors, and Social Networking*.

At the same time, **What You See Is What You Get (WYSIWYG)** editors provide the ability to edit web content, including the blogs' content. Less technical people can use the WYSIWYG editor instead of sifting through complex code.

Shared calendars

Many companies require calendar information and share the calendar among users from different departments.

We will see how to share a calendar within Liferay. The shared calendar can satisfy the basic business requirements incorporated into a featured business intranet, such as scheduling meetings, sending meeting invitations, checking for attendees' availability, and so on. Therefore, you can provide an environment for users to manage events and share calendars. We will see the details of calendar features in future chapters.

Document management – CMS

When there is a need for document sharing and document management, Liferay's *Documents and Media library* helps you with lots of features.

The Documents and Media portlet allows you to add folders and subfolders for documents and media files, and also allows users to publish documents. It serves as a repository for all types of files and makes **Content management systems** (**CMSes**) available for intranets. The Documents and Media library portlet is equipped with customizable folders and acts as a web-based solution to share documents and media files among all your team members—just as a shared drive would. All the intranet users will be able to access the files from anywhere, and the content is accessible only by those authorized by administrators. All the files are secured by the permission layer by the administrator.

Web content management – WCM

Your company may have a lot of images and documents, and you may need to manage all these images and documents as well. Therefore, you require the ability to manage a lot of web content and then publish web content in intranets.

We will see how to manage web content and how to publish web content within Liferay. Liferay Journal (Web Content) not only provides high availability to publish, manage, and maintain web content and documents, but it also separates content from the layout. Liferay WCM allows us to create, edit, and publish web content (articles). It also allows quick changes in the preview of the web content by changing the layout. It has built-in functionality, such as workflow, search, article versioning, scheduling, and metadata.

Personalization and internalization

All users can get a personal space that can be either made public (published as a website with a unique, friendly URL) or kept private. You can also customize how the space looks, what tools and applications are included, what goes into Documents and Media, and who can view and access all of this content.

In addition, Liferay supports multiple languages, where you can select your own language. Multilingual organizations get out-of-the-box support for up to 45 languages. Users can toggle among different language settings with just one click and produce/publish multilingual documents and web content. Users can make use of the internalization feature to define the specific site in a localized language.

Workflow, staging, scheduling, and publishing

You can use a workflow to manage definitions, instances, and predetermined sequences of connected steps. Workflow can be used for web content management, assets, and so on. Liferay's built-in workflow engine is called Kaleo. It allows users to set up the review and publishing process on the web content article of any document that needs to end up on the live site. Liferay 6.2 integrates with the powerful features of the workflow and data capabilities of dynamic data lists in Kaleo Forms; it's only available in Liferay Enterprise Edition.

Staging environments are integrated with Liferay's workflow engine. To have a review process for staged pages, you need to make sure you have a workflow engine configured and you have a staging setup in the workflow. We will see how we can achieve the staging environment in *Chapter 9, Web Content Management*.

As a content creator, you can update what you've created and publish it in a staging workflow. Other users can then review and modify it. Moreover, content editors can make a decision on whether to publish web content from staging to live, that is, you can easily create and manage everything from a simple article of text and images to fully functional websites in staging and then publish them live.

Before going live, you can schedule web content as well. For instance, you can publish web content immediately or schedule it for publishing on a specific date.

Social networks and Social Office

Liferay Portal supports social networks—you can easily manage your Google Plus, Facebook, MySpace, Twitter, and other social network accounts in Liferay. In addition, you can manage your instant messenger accounts, such as AIM, ICQ, Jabber, MSN, Skype, YM, and so on smoothly from inside Liferay.

> **Liferay Social Office** gives us a social collaboration on top of the portal—a fully virtual workspace that streamlines communication and builds up group cohesion. It provides holistic enhancement to the way you and your colleagues work together. All components in Social Office are tied together seamlessly, getting everyone on the same page by sharing the same look and feel. More importantly, the dynamic activity tracking gives us a bird's-eye view of who has been doing what and when within each individual site. Using Liferay Social Office, you can enhance your existing personal workflow with social tools, keep your team up to date, and turn collective knowledge into collective action. Note that Liferay 6.2 supports the Liferay Social Office 3.0 current version.

Liferay Sync and Marketplace

Liferay Sync is Liferay's newest product, designed to make file sharing as easy as a simple drag and drop! Liferay Sync is an add-on product for Liferay 6.1 CE, EE, and later versions, which makes it a more raw boost product and enables the end user to publish and access documents and files from multiple environments and devices, including **Windows** and **MacOS** systems, and iOS-based mobile platforms. Liferay Sync is one of the best features, and it is fully integrated into the Liferay platform. We will be go more in-depth in later chapters.

Liferay 6.1 introduced the new concept of the marketplace, which leverages the developers to develop any components or functionality and release and share it with other users. It's a user-friendly and one-stop place to share apps. Liferay Marketplace provides the portal product with add-on features with a new hub to share, browse, and download Liferay-compatible applications.

In Liferay 6.2, Marketplace comes under App Manager, where all the app-related controls can be possible. You will see this in more detail in the upcoming chapters.

More features

The intranet also arranges staff members into teams and sites, provides a way of real-time IM and chatting, and gives each user an appropriate level of *access*. This means that they can get all the information they need and edit and add content as necessary but won't be able to mess with sensitive information that they have no reason to see.

In particular, the portal provides an integrating framework so that you can integrate external applications easily. For example, you can integrate external applications with the portal, such as Alfresco, OpenX, LDAP, SSO CAS, Orbeon Forms, Konakart, PayPal, Solr, and so on.

In a word, the portal offers compelling benefits to today's enterprises — reduced operational costs, improved customer satisfaction, and streamlined business processes.

Everything in one place

All of these features are useful on their own. However, it gets better when you consider that all of these features will be combined into one easy-to-use searchable portal.

A user of the intranet, for example, can search for a topic — let's say *financial report* — and find the following in one go:

- Any group discussions about financial reports
- Blog entries within the intranet concerning financial reports
- Documents and files — perhaps the financial reports themselves
- Wiki entries with guidelines on preparing financial reports
- Calendar entries for meetings to discuss the financial report

Of course, users can also restrict their search to just one area if they already know exactly what they are looking for.

Liferay provides other features, such as tagging, in order to make it even easier to organize information across the whole intranet. We will do all of this and more over the course of the book.

Introducing Palm Tree Publications

In this book, we are going to build an intranet for a fictional company as an example, focusing on how to install, configure, and integrate it with other applications and also implement portals and plugins (portlets, themes, layout templates, hooks, and webs) within Liferay. By applying the instructions to your own business, you will be able to build an intranet to meet your own company's needs.

"Palm Tree Publications" needs an intranet of its own, which we will call bookpub.com. The enterprise's global headquarters are in the United States. It has several departments—editorial, website, engineering, marketing, executive, and human resources.

Each department has staff in the U.S., Germany, and India or in all three places.

The intranet site provides a site called "Book Street and Book Workshop" consisting of users who have an interest in reading books. The enterprise needs to integrate collaboration tools, such as wikis, discussion forums, blogs, instant messaging, mail, RSS, shared calendars, tagging, and so on.

Palm Tree Publications has more advanced needs too: a workflow to edit, approve, and publish books. Furthermore, the enterprise has a lot of content, such as books stored and managed alfresco currently.

In order to build the intranet site, the following functionality should be considered:

- Installing the portal, experiencing the portal and portlets, and customizing the portal and personal web pages
- Bringing the features of enabling document sharing, calendar sharing, and other collaboration within a business to the users of the portal
- Discussion forums—employees should be able to discuss book ideas and proposals
- Wikis—keeping track of information about editorial guidance and other resources that require frequent editing
- Dissemination of information via blogs—small teams working on specific projects share files and blogs about a project process
- Sharing a calendar among employees
- Web content management creation by the content author and getting approved by the publisher
- Document repository—using effective content management systems (CMSes), a natural fit for a portal for secure access, permissions, and distinct roles (such as writers, editors, designers, administrators, and so on)

- Collaborative chat and instant messaging, social network, Social Office, and knowledge management tools
- Managing a site named Book Street and Book Workshop that consists of users who have the same interest in reading books as staging, scheduling, and publishing web content related to books
- Federated search for discussion forum entries, blog posts, wiki articles, users in the directory, and content in both the Document and Media libraries; search by tags
- Integrating back-of-the-house software applications, such as Alfresco, Orbeon Forms, the Drools rule server, Jasper Server, and BI/Reporting Pentaho; strong authentication and authorization with LDAP; and single authentication to access various company sites besides the intranet site

The enterprise can have the following groups of people:

- **Admin**: This group installs systems, manages membership, users, user groups, organizations, roles and permissions, security on resources, workflow, servers and instances, and integrates with third-party systems
- **Executives**: Executive management handles approvals
- **Marketing**: This group handles websites, company brochures, marketing campaigns, projects, and digital assets
- **Sales**: This group makes presentations, contracts, documents, and reports
- **Website editors**: This group manages pages of the intranet—writes articles, reviews articles, designs the layout of articles, and publishes articles
- **Book editors**: This group writes, reviews, and publishes books and approves and rejects the publishing of books
- **Human resources**: This group manages corporate policy documents
- **Finance**: This group manages accounts documents, scanned invoices and checks accounts
- **Corporate communications**: This group manages external public relations, internal news releases, and syndication
- **Engineering**: This group sets up the development environment and collaborates on engineering projects and presentation templates

Introducing Liferay Portal's architecture and framework

Liferay Portal's architecture supports high availability for mission-critical applications using clustering and the fully distributed cache and replication support across multiple servers. The following diagram has been taken from the Liferay forum written by Jorge Ferrer. This diagram depicts the various architectural layers and functionalities of portlets:

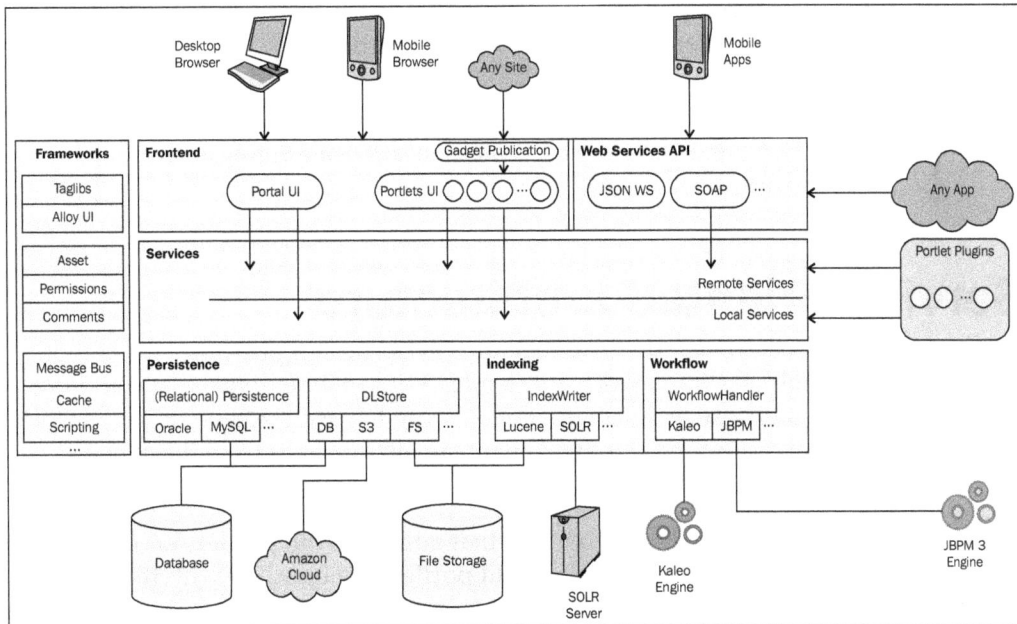

Figure 1.1: The Liferay architecture

> The preceding image was taken from `https://www.liferay.com/web/jorge.ferrer/blog/-/blogs/liferay-s-architecture-the-beginning-of-a-blog-series` site blog.

The Liferay Portal architecture is designed in such a way that it provides tons of features at one place:

- **Frontend layer**: This layer is the end user's interface
- **Service layer**: This contains the great majority of the business logic for the portal platform and all of the portlets included out of the box
- **Persistence layer**: Liferay relies on Hibernate to do most of its database access
- **Web services API layer**: This handles web services, such as JSON and SOAP

In Liferay, the service layer, persistence layer, and web services API layer are built automatically by that wonderful tool called **Service Builder**.

> Service Builder is the tool that glues together all of Liferay's layers and that hides the complexities of using Spring or Hibernate under the hood.

Service-oriented architecture

Liferay Portal uses **service-oriented architecture (SOA)** design principles throughout and provides the tools and framework to extend SOA to other enterprise applications. Under the Liferay enterprise architecture, not only can the users access the portal from traditional and wireless devices, but developers can also access it from the exposed APIs via REST, SOAP, RMI, XML-RPC, XML, JSON, Hessian, and Burlap.

Liferay Portal is designed to deploy portlets that adhere to the portlet API compliant with both JSR-168 and JSR-286. A set of useful portlets are bundled with the portal, including Documents and Media, Calendar, Message Boards, Blogs, Wikis, and so on. They can be used as examples to add custom portlets. In a word, the key features of Liferay include using SOA design principles throughout, such as reliable security, integrating the portal with SSO and LDAP, multitier and limitless clustering, high availability, caching pages, dynamic virtual hosting, and so on.

Understanding Enterprise Service Bus

Enterprise Service Bus (ESB) is a central connection manager that allows applications and services to be added quickly to an enterprise infrastructure. When an application needs to be replaced, it can easily be disconnected from the bus at a single point. Liferay Portal uses Mule or ServiceMix as ESB.

Through ESB, the portal can integrate with SharePoint, BPM (such as the jBPM workflow engine and Intalio | BPMS engine), BI Xforms reporting, JCR repository, and so on. It supports JSR 170 for content management systems with the integration of JCR repositories, such as Jackrabbit. It also uses Hibernate and JDBC to connect to any database. Furthermore, it supports an event system with synchronous and asynchronous messaging and a lightweight message bus.

Liferay Portal uses the Spring framework for its business and data services layers. It also uses the Spring framework for its transaction management. Based on service interfaces, *portal-impl* is implemented and exposed only for internal usage — for example, they are used for the extension environment. *portal-kernel* and *portal-service* are provided for external usage (or for internal usage) — for example, they are used for the Plugins SDK environment. Custom portlets, both JSR-168 and JSR-286, and web services can be built based on *portal-kernel* and *portal-service*.

In addition, the Web 2.0 Mail portlet and the Web 2.0 Chat portlet are supported as well. More interestingly, scheduled staging and remote staging and publishing serve as a foundation through the tunnel web for web content management and publishing.

Liferay Portal supports web services to make it easy for different applications in an enterprise to communicate with each other. Java, .NET, and proprietary applications can work together easily because web services use XML standards. It also supports REST-style JSON web services for lightweight, maintainable code and supports AJAX-based user interfaces.

Liferay Portal uses industry-standard, government-grade encryption technologies, including advanced algorithms, such as DES, MD5, and RSA. Liferay was benchmarked as one of the most secure portal platforms using LogicLibrary's Logiscan suite. Liferay offers customizable single sign-on (SSO) that integrates into Yale CAS, JAAS, LDAP, NTLM, CA Siteminder, Novell Identity Manager, OpenSSO, and more. Open ID, OpenAuth, Yale CAS, Siteminder, and OpenAM integration are offered by it out of the box.

In short, Liferay Portal uses ESB in general with an abstraction layer on top of an enterprise messaging system. It allows integration architects to exploit the value of messaging systems, such as reporting, e-commerce, and advertisements.

Understanding the advantages of using Liferay to build an intranet

Of course, there are lots of ways to build a company intranet. What makes Liferay such a good choice to create an intranet portal?

It has got the features we need

All of the features we outlined for our intranet come built into Liferay: discussions, wikis, calendars, blogs, and so on are part of what Liferay is designed to do.

It is also designed to tie all of these features together into one searchable *portal*, so we won't be dealing with lots of separate components when we build and use our intranet. Every part will work together with others.

Easy to set up and use

Liferay has an intuitive interface that uses icons, clear labels, and drag and drop to make it easy to configure and use the intranet.

Setting up the intranet will require a bit more work than using it, of course. However, you will be pleasantly surprised by how simple it is—no programming is required to get your intranet up and running.

Free and open source

How much does Liferay cost? Nothing! It's a free, open source tool.

Here, being *free* means that you can go to Liferay's website and download it without paying anything. You can then go ahead and install it and use it. Liferay comes with an enterprise edition too, for which users need to pay. In addition, Liferay provides full support and access to additional enterprise edition plugins/applications.

Liferay makes its money by providing additional services, including training. However, the standard use of Liferay is completely free. Now you probably won't have to pay another penny to get your intranet working. Being open source means that the program code that makes Liferay work is available to anybody to look at and change. Even if you're not a programmer, this is still good for you:

- If you need Liferay to do something new, then you can hire a programmer to modify Liferay to do it.
- There are lots of developers studying the source code, looking for ways to make it better. Lots of improvements get incorporated into Liferay's main code.
- Developers are always working to create plugins—programs that work together with Liferay to add new features.

Probably, for now, the big deal here is that it doesn't cost any money. However, as you use Liferay more, you will come to understand the other benefits of open source software for you.

Grows with you

Liferay is designed in a way that means it can work with thousands and thousands of users at once. No matter how big your business is or how much it grows, Liferay will still work and handle all of the information you throw at it.

It also has features especially suited to large, international businesses. Are you opening offices in non-English speaking countries? No problem! Liferay has internationalization features tailored to many of the world's popular languages.

Works with other tools

Liferay is designed to work with other software tools — the ones that you're already using and the ones that you might use in the future — for instance:

- You can hook up Liferay to your LDAP directory server and SSO so that user details and login credentials are added to Liferay automatically

- Liferay can work with Alfresco — a popular and powerful Enterprise CMS (used to provide extremely advanced document management capabilities, which are far beyond what Liferay does on its own)

Based on "standards"

This is a more technical benefit; however, it is a very useful one if you ever want to use Liferay in a more specialized way.

Liferay is based on standard technologies that are popular with developers and other IT experts and that confer the following benefits on users:

- **Built using Java**: Java is a popular programming language that can run on just about any computer. There are millions of Java programmers in the world, so it won't be too hard to find developers who can customize Liferay.

- **Based on tried and tested components**: With any tool, there's a danger of bugs. Liferay uses lots of well-known, widely tested components to minimize the likelihood of bugs creeping in. If you are interested, here are some of the well-known components and technologies Liferay uses — Apache ServiceMix, Mule, ehcache, Hibernate, ICEfaces, Java J2EE/JEE, jBPM, Activiti, JGroups, Alloy UI, Lucene, PHP, Ruby, Seam, Spring and AOP, Struts and Tiles, Tapestry, Velocity, and FreeMarker.

- **Uses standard ways to communicate with other software**: There are various standards established to share data between pieces of software. Liferay uses these so that you can easily get information from Liferay into other systems. The standards implemented by Liferay include AJAX, iCalendar and Microformat, JSR-168, JSR-127, JSR-170, JSR-286 (Portlet 2.0), JSR-314 (JSF 2.0), OpenSearch, the Open platform with support for web services, including JSON, Hessian, Burlap, REST, RMI, and WSRP, WebDAV, and CalDAV.

- **Makes publication and collaboration tools Web Content Accessibility Guidelines 2.0 (WCAG 2.0) compliant**: The new W3C recommendation is to make web content accessible to a wide range of people with disabilities, including blindness and low vision, deafness and hearing loss, learning disabilities, cognitive limitations, limited movement, speech disabilities, photosensitivity, and combinations of these. For example, the portal integrates CKEditor-standards support, such as W3C (WAI-AA and WCAG), 508 (Section 508).

- **Alloy UI**: The Liferay UI supports HTML 5, CSS 3, and Yahoo! User Interface Library 3 (YUI 3).

- **Supports Apache Ant 1.8 and Maven 2**: Liferay Portal can be built through Apache Ant by default, where you can build services; clean, compile, and build JavaScript CMD; build language native to ASCII, deploy, fast deploy; and so on. Moreover, Liferay supports Maven 2 SDK, providing **Community Edition** (**CE**) releases through public maven repositories as well as **Enterprise Edition** (**EE**) customers to install maven artifacts in their local maven repository.

- **Bootstrap**: Liferay 6.2 provides support for Twitter Bootstrap out of the box. With its fully responsive UI, the benefit of bootstrap is that it will support any device to render the content. Even content authors can use bootstrap markup and styles to make the content nicer.

Many of these standards are things that you will never need to know much about, so don't worry if you've never heard of them. Liferay is better for using them, but mostly, you won't even know they are there.

Other advantages of Liferay

Liferay isn't just for intranets! Users and developers are building all kinds of different websites and systems based on Liferay.

Corporate extranets

An intranet is great for collaboration and information sharing within a company. An extranet extends this facility to suppliers and customers, who usually log in over the Internet.

In many ways, this is similar to an intranet—however, there are a few technical differences. The main difference is that you create user accounts for people who are not part of your company.

Collaborative websites

Collaborative websites not only provide a secure and administrated framework, but they also empower users with collaborative tools, such as blogs, instant e-mail, message boards, instant messaging, shared calendars, and so on. Moreover, they encourage users to use other tools, such as tag administration, fine-grained permissions, delegable administrator privileges, enterprise taxonomy, and ad hoc user groups. By means of these tools, as an administrator, you can ultimately control what people can and cannot do in Liferay.

In many ways, this is similar to an intranet too; however, there are a few technical differences. The main difference is that you use collaborative tools simply, such as blogs, instant e-mail, message boards, instant messaging, shared calendars, and so on.

Content management and web publishing

You can also use Liferay to run your public company website with content management and web publishing.

Content management and web publishing are useful features in websites. It is a fact that the volume of digital content for any organization is increasing on a daily basis. Therefore, an effective CMS is a vital part of any organization. Meanwhile, document management is also useful and more effective when repositories have to be assigned to different departments and groups within the organization. Content management and document management are effective in Liferay. Moreover, when managing and publishing content, we may have to answer many questions, such as "who should be able to update and delete a document from the system?". Fortunately, Liferay's security and permissions model can satisfy the need for secure access and permissions and distinct roles (for example, writer, editor, designer, and administrator). Furthermore, Liferay integrates with the workflow engine. Thus, users can follow a flow to edit, approve, and publish content in the website.

Content management and web publishing are similar to an intranet; however, there are a few technical differences. The main difference is that you can manage content and publish web content smoothly.

Infrastructure portals

Infrastructure portals integrate all possible functions, as we stated previously. This covers collaboration and information sharing within a company in the form of collaborative tools, content management, and web publishing. In infrastructure portals, users can create a unified interface to work with content, regardless of source via content interaction APIs. Furthermore, using the same API and the same interface as that of the built-in CMS, users can also manage content and publish web content from third-party systems, such as Alfresco, Vignette, Magnolia, FatWire, Microsoft SharePoint, and so on.

Infrastructure portals are similar to an intranet; there are a few technical differences though. The main difference is that you can use collaborative tools, manage content, publish web content, and integrate other systems in one place.

Why do you need a portal? The main reason is that a portal can serve as a framework to aggregate content and applications. A portal normally provides a secure and manageable framework where users can easily make new and existing enterprise applications available. In order to build an infrastructure portal smoothly, Liferay Portal provides an SOA-based framework to integrate third-party systems.

Out-of-the-box portlets and features

Liferay provides **out-of-the-box** (OOTB) portlets that have key features and can be used in the enterprise intranet very efficiently. These portlets are very scalable and powerful and provide the developer with the tools to customize it very easily.

Let's see some of the most frequently used portlets in Liferay Portal.

Content management

Content management is a common feature in any web-based portal or website:

- The **Web Content** portlet has the features of full web publishing, office integration, and the asset library, which contains documents, images, and videos. This portlet also has the structure and templates that help with the designing of the web content's look and feel. Structure can be designed with the help of a visual editor with drag and drop. It has the integrated help feature with tooltips to name the attributes of the fields. You will see more details in *Chapter 9, Web Content Management*.

- The **Asset Publisher** portlet provides you with the feature to select any type of content/asset, such as wiki pages, web content, calendar events, message board messages, documents, media documents, and many more. It also allows us to use filter on them by types, categories, tags, and sources. The display settings provide configurable settings, which helps the content to be displayed to the end users perfectly. In *Chapter 4, Forums, Categorization, and Asset Publishing*, you will see this in more detail.

- The **Document and Media** portlet is one of the most usable portlets to store any type of document. It allows you to store and manage your documents. It allows you to manage Liferay documents from your own machine's filesystem with the help of WebDAV integration. It has lots of new, built-in features, such as the inline document preview, image preview, and video player. Document metadata is displayed in document details, which makes it easier for you to review the metadata of the document. Also, Document and Media has features named **checkin** and **checkout** that helps editing the document in a group very easily. The Document and Media portlet has the multi-repository integration feature, which allows you to configure or mount any other repository very easily, such as SharePoint, Documentum, and Alfresco, utilizing the CMIS standard. In *Chapter 8, Document and Media Management*, you will come to know how to achieve such features in your corporate intranet.

Collaboration

Collaboration features are generally ways in which users communicate with each other, such as the ones shown in the following list:

- The **Dynamic data list** portlet provides you with the facility of not writing a single line of code to create the form or data list. Say, for example, your corporate intranet needs the job posting done on a daily basis by the HR administrator. The administrator needs to develop the custom portlet to fulfill that requirement. Now, the dynamic data list portlet will allow the administrator to create a form for job posting. It's very easy to create and display new data types. You will see more on this in *Chapter 5, Understanding Wikis, Dynamic Data Lists, and Polls*.

- The **Blog** portlet is one of the best features of Liferay. Blog portlets have two other related portlets, namely Recent Bloggers and Blogs Aggregator. The blog portlet provides the best possible ways for chronological publications of personal thoughts and web links in the intranet. Blog portlets can be placed for users of different sites/departments under the respective site// department page.

- The **Calendar** portlet provides the feature to create the event and schedule the event. It has many features that help the users in viewing the meeting schedule.

- The **Message Board** portlet is a full-featured forum solution with threaded views, categories, RSS capability, avatars, file attachments, previews, dynamic lists of recent posts, and forum statistics. Message Board portlets work with the fine-grained permissions and role-based access control model to give detailed levels of control to administrators and users. You will find more details about this in *Chapter 4, Forums, Categorization, and Asset Publishing*; you will see how to work on message boards.

- The **Wiki** portlet, like the Message Boards portlet, provides a straightforward wiki solution for both intranet and extranet portals that provides knowledge management among the users. It has all of the features you would expect in a state-of-the-art wiki. Again, it has the features of a file attachment preview, publishing the content, and versioning, and works with a fine-grained permission and role-based access control model. This again takes all the features of the Liferay platform. In *Chapter 5, Understanding Wikis, Dynamic Data Lists, and Polls*, you will find more about the Wiki portlet.

- The **Social Activity** portlet allows you to tweak the measurements used to calculate user involvement within a site. The contribution and participation values determine the reward value of an action. It uses the blog entry, wiki, and message board points to calculate the user involvement in the site.

- The **Marketplace** portlet is placed inside the control panel. It's a hub for the applications provided by Liferay and other partners. You can find that many applications are free, and for certain applications, you need to pay an amount. It's more like an app store. This feature was introduced in Liferay Version 6.1. In *Chapter 10, Marketplace, Social Office, and Audience Targeting*, it has been described in detail.

> In the Liferay 6.2 control panel, under the **Apps** | **Store** link section, you will see apps that are stored in the Marketplace portlet. Liferay 6.2 comes with a new control panel that is very easy to manage for the portal's Admin users. We will discuss this in more detail in *Chapter 10, Marketplace, Social Office, and Audience Targeting*. **Liferay Sync** is not a portlet; it's a new feature of Liferay that allows you to synchronize documents of Liferay Document and Media with your local system. Liferay provide the *Liferay Sync* application, which has to be installed in your local system or mobile device. In *Chapter 8, Document and Media Management*, you can see detailed examples of Liferay Sync.

News

RSS portlets provide RSS feeds. RSS portlets are used for the publishers by letting them syndicate content automatically. They benefit readers who want to subscribe to timely updates from their favorite websites or to aggregate feeds from many sites into one place. A Liferay RSS portlet is fully customizable, and it allows you to set the URL from which site you would like to get feeds.

Social

Activities portlets display portal-wide user activity, such as posting on message boards, creating wikis, and adding documents to Documents and Media. There are more portlets for social categories, such as **User Statistics** portlets, **Group Statistics** portlets, and **Requests** portlets. All these portlets are used for the social media.

Tools

The **Search** portlet provides faceted search features. When a search is performed, facet information will appear based on the results of the search. The number of each asset type and the most frequently occurring tags and categories as well as their frequency will all appear in the left-hand side column of the portlet. It searches through Bookmarks, Blogs Entries, Web Content Articles, Document Library Files, Users, Message Board, and Wiki.

Finding more information on Liferay

In this chapter, we looked at what Liferay can do for your corporate intranet and briefly saw why it's a good choice.

If you want more background information on Liferay, the best place to start is the Liferay corporate website (`http://www.liferay.com`) itself. You can find the latest news and events, various training programs offered worldwide, presentations, demonstrations, and hosted trails. More interestingly, Liferay eats its own dog food; corporate websites within forums (called message boards), blogs, and wikis are built by Liferay using its own products. It is a real demo of Liferay Portal's software.

Liferay is 100 percent open source and all downloads are available from the Liferay Portal website at `http://www.liferay.com/web/guest/downloads/portal` and the **SourceForge** website at `http://sourceforge.net/projects/lportal/files`. The source code repository is available at `https://github.com/liferay`.

The Liferay website's wiki (`http://www.liferay.com/web/guest/community/wiki`) contains documentation, including a tutorial, user guide, developer guide, administrator guide, roadmap, and so on.

The Liferay website's discussion forums can be accessed at `http://www.liferay.com/web/guest/community/forums` and the blogs at `http://www.liferay.com/community/blogs/highlighted`. The official plugins and the community plugins are available at `http://www.liferay.com/marketplace` and are the best place to share your thoughts, get tips and tricks about Liferay implementation, and use and contribute community plugins.

If you would like to file a bug or know more about the fixes in a specific release, then you must visit the bug-tracking system at `http://issues.liferay.com/`.

This book will tell you more about a new trend in the portal world with respect to user needs, functionalities, and what we can achieve with the Liferay Portal 6.2 features.

Summary

In this chapter, we looked at what Liferay can offer your intranet and what we should consider while designing the company's enterprise site. We saw that our final intranet will provide shared documents, discussions, collaborative wikis, and more in a single, searchable portal. Well, Liferay is a great choice for an intranet because it provides so many features and is easy to use, free and open source, extensible, and well-integrated with other tools and standards. We also saw the other kinds of sites Liferay is good for, such as extranets, collaborative websites, content management, web publishing, and infrastructure portals. For the best example of an intranet and extranet, you can visit `www.liferay.com`. It will provide you with more background information.

In the next chapter, we're going to install Liferay and continue building the intranet.

2
Setting Up a Home Page and Navigation Structure for the Intranet

This chapter will assist administrators and normal users with implementing a portal page with portlets, in the Palm Tree Publications enterprise. It will guide you through setting up the portal, building pages, setting up portal pages, and customizing portlets. It will also address the topic of navigating the structure of intranet websites. In addition, it will provide guidance on configuring the portals, as well as bringing pages together in action. And finally, it will show us how to share portlets within a portal page and how to configure the Control Panel settings through the properties file. By the end of this chapter, you will have learned the following:

- Using a portal page with portlets, basic knowledge about portlets, and how the portal works
- Setting up the portal, building pages, and setting up portal pages
- Customizing portlets
- Navigating the structure of the intranet
- Configuring the portal
- Bringing pages together in action
- Sharing portlets within a portal page
- Configuring the Control Panel

Experiencing the portal

Liferay provides unique interface for the portal. It makes the portal unique by providing everything customizable. The Palm Tree Publications enterprise administrator, say "Palm Tree", will experience the portal locally. After starting up the portal by typing the `http://localhost:8080` URL in a browser, you will able to see the Liferay Portal home page. Now, log in as "Palm Tree" Admin to see the portal page interface similar to the following screenshot. Generally speaking, a portal page is made up of a set of portlets — for example, **Web Content Display**, the navigation portlet, breadcrumb portlet, and the default pages.

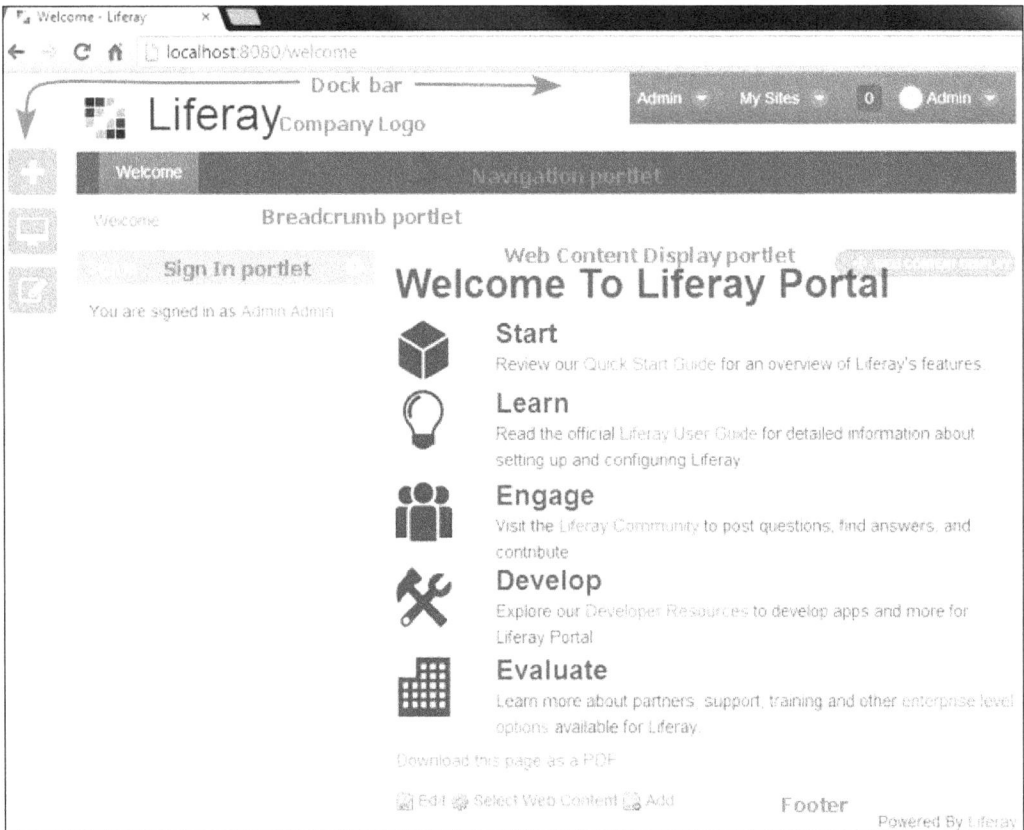

Figure 2.1: Guest home page

The preceding screenshot is the default welcome page of Liferay Portal.

Getting portal pages

Suppose we have a set of variables, where $PORTAL_VERSION represents the current portal version and $LIFERAY_PORTAL represents the working folder containing the portal that we are planning to install. Logically, you can have a different folder name. But for simplicity, we will use a folder named Liferay-Portal. More specifically, you will have a value for $LIFERAY_PORTAL — that is, C\:Liferay-Portal in Windows, and /Liferay-Portal in Linux, Unix, and Mac OS. In addition, we use a variable $LIFERAY_HOME to represent the current folder where the portal is installed. Therefore, we would have the following expression:

$LIFERAY_HOME=$LIFERAY_PORTAL/liferay-portal-$PORTAL_VERSION

In order to get the preceding portal page with portlets, install the portal in your local machine using the following steps:

1. Download the latest Liferay Portal Standard Edition bundled with Tomcat 7.x from the website http://www.liferay.com/downloads/liferay-portal/available-releases. It is a large file of about 291.1 MB. You have to wait for a while in order to download it.

2. Unzip the downloaded file into $LIFERAY_PORTAL.

> Make sure that you have downloaded the latest version of JDK. It is available at http://www.oracle.com/technetwork/java/javase/downloads/jdk7-downloads-1880260.html for every OS.

3. You need to install JDK in your local machine and set the JAVA_HOME variable as well. Also, make sure that the MySQL database is running in your local system. This is the only thing you need in order to run the portal properly. Run $TOMCAT_AS_DIR/bin/startup.bat for Windows or $TOMCAT_AS_DIR/bin/startup.sh for Linux. Note that you may need to wait for about 60 seconds for it to start up.

4. Open your browser and type http://localhost:8080 if it doesn't open automatically. You will get the **Basic Configuration** wizard/interface, where you have to set up the **Portal Name, Administrator User**, and database setting. While you start with the portal pages, you'll have to set up the basic configuration or it will just take the default settings.

5. In the **Basic Configuration** wizard, keep the default settings. For the portal name, let's keep the default name **Liferay**, which is the guest site. We will be creating a new site **Palm Tree**, which will be called the Palm Tree portal.

> Setting up the database is optional. If you don't select a specific database, Liferay will use the default database and map it to the **hypersonic database** automatically.
>
> Create a database in MySQL with the database name `lportal`, before setting up the database configuration. You can use the MySQL command `create database lportal character set utf8;` for creating the database.

6. Now, click on the **Change** link below the database; the **Database** section will expand and you will able to set up the database settings.

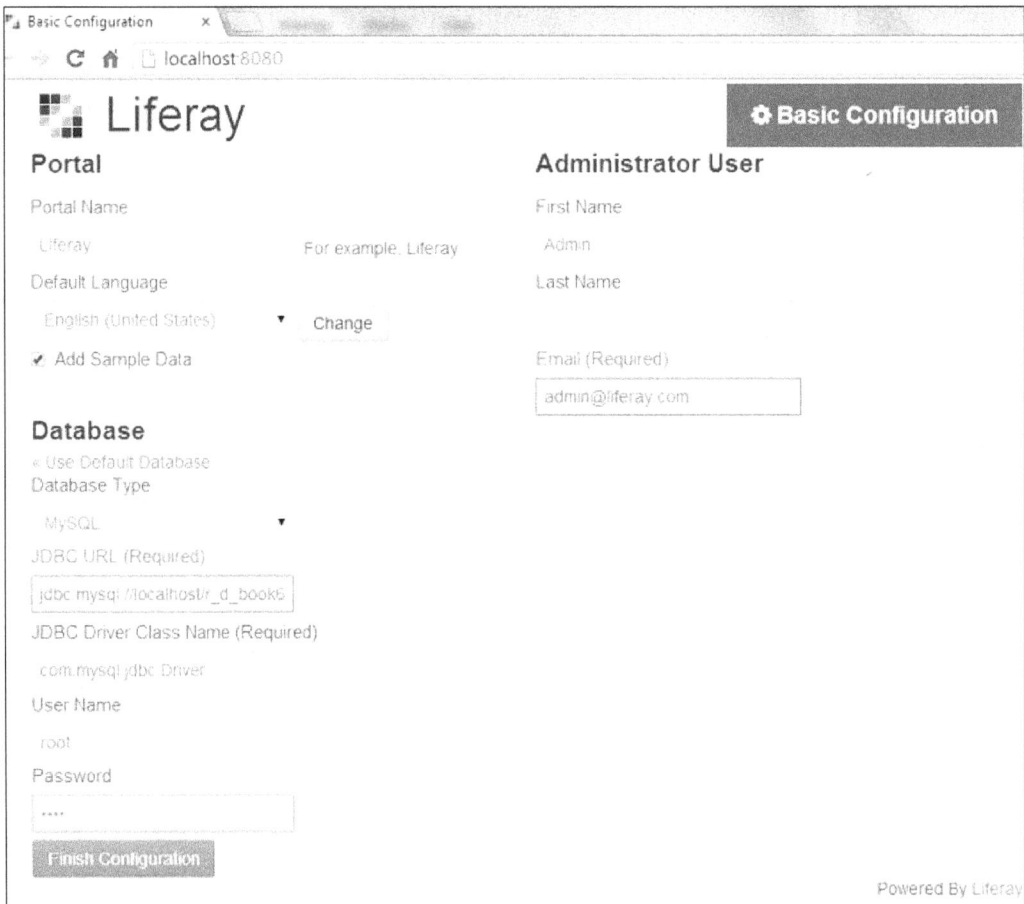

Figure 2.2: The basic configuration

The preceding screenshot shows the basic configuration for the database.

7. In the database setup, you have to select the database vendor, that is, **MySQL** or any other database provider, and automatically, the respective JDBC class name and JDBC driver will be taken. You just need to pass the database name and the database username and password.

> For MySQL, the database URL must be like the following line of code, where `databaseName` will be say `lportal`:
>
> ```
> JDBC URL - jdbc:mysql://localhost/<databaseN
> ame>?useUnicode=true&characterEncoding=UTF-
> 8&useFastDateParsing=false
> ```

8. In the previous screenshot, we selected **MySQL** as the database. As **Administrator User**, you can set any user name such as `Admin`; by default, the user name is `Test`. For this example, let us take the **First Name** as `Admin`, **Last Name** as `Admin`, and **Email** as `admin@liferay.com`.

> Liferay comes with sample data (optional) for the portal; while configuring the portal, it will set up the sample data. But this is optional and if you don't want the sample data, you can uncheck the checkbox for sample data. Then finish the configuration.

9. Then click on **Finish Configuration**.

10. You will get a success message in the next page. Click on **Go to my Portal**.

11. Now the agreement page for terms and conditions appears; just click on the **I Agree** option. Then you need to change the password for the **Administrator User** which is `Admin` in our case. After that, answer the remainder questions on the page.

Consequently, you will see a portal interface like the one shown in the preceding screenshot. The portal page shows different content after you have logged in. It consists of portlets such as, **Web Content Display** portlet, a dock bar menu, navigation bar, and breadcrumb bar.

In Liferay 6.2, the look and feel of the portal has been changed with extensive use of responsive features and the **Alloy User Interface** (**AUI**) components.

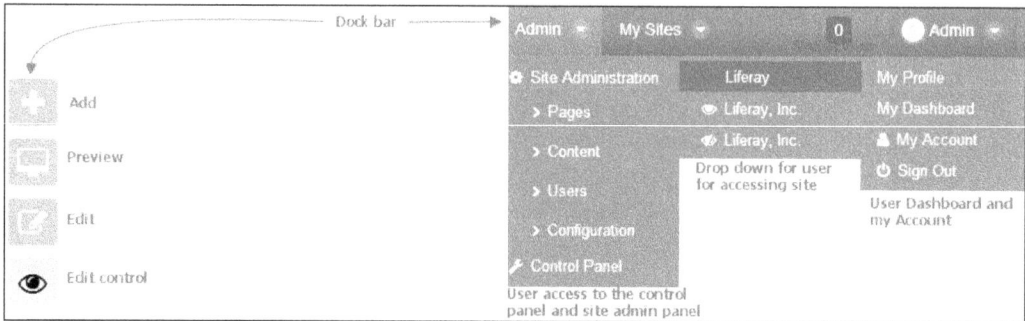

Figure 2.3: The Dock bar menu

The preceding screenshot shows different actions in the dock bar menu.

The dock bar menu in Liferay 6.2 has been changed with a new look and improved functionality. The screenshot shows the three drop-down menus of the dock bar. Let's look at each of these links in detail:

- **Add** allows the user to add pages, content, and applications.
  - **Page**: This link allows the user to add a new page
  - **Content**: The user can add new content
  - **Applications**: This link allows the user to add a new application to the page
- **Preview** allows the user to preview the page in different resolutions(by customizing the size in pixels) and devices such as smartphones, tablets, desktops, and so on.
- **Edit** allows the user to edit all page-related settings or example:
  - **Page**: This allows editing of pages
  - **Page Layout**: This allows changing of the page layout
- **Edit control** helps the user to enable and disable the portlet configuration and settings.
- **Admin**:
  - **System Administration**: This link redirects to the Site Administrator Panel for site page and content. It has sublinks such as Pages, Content, Users, and Configuration. Clicking on any of these links will take you to the respective section in Site Administrator Panel. It works like the manage site content feature in Liferay 6.1

- ° **Control Panel**: This link redirects to the **Control Panel**

- **My Sites**:
  - ° **My public pages**: This redirects to the public page of the site
  - ° **My private pages**: This redirects to the private page of the site

- **User Avatar**:
  - ° **My Profile**: This redirects to the user's public page
  - ° **My Dashboard**: This redirects to the user's private page
  - ° **My Account**: This pops up the user's **My Account** detail page and also provides the **My Pages**, **My Workflow Tasks**, and **My Submissions** options as tabs
  - ° **Sign Out**: This is a logout button to exit

Congratulations! You now have a running copy of the portal. The remainder of this section will explain what a portal is, and how to implement a portal page with a set of portlets.

What you have previously seen is a portal page with the name *Welcome*. The portal page has a dock bar menu, a logo, a navigation bar, a breadcrumb bar, a set of portlets, and a footer. When you have logged in, the portal will generate this page automatically.

An intranet website is made up of a set of pages such as Welcome. The portal can be used to build and manage these pages smoothly.

The working of the portal

The following is a typical sequence of events, initiated when you access a portal page, for example, the **Welcome** page in the portal:

- A client (for example, **Liferay**), after being authenticated, makes an HTTP request to the portal.
- The request is received by the portal (for example, the Liferay Portal).
- The portal determines if the request contains any kind of action targeted to the portlets; if not, it simply renders it on the page. For example, Web Content Display is associated with the portal page such as **Liferay**.
- If there is an action targeted to a portlet, for example, **Web Content Display**, then the portal requests the portlet container to invoke the portlet to process the action.

- The portal invokes portlets such as **Web Content Display**, and so on through the portlet container.

- The portal aggregates the output of portlets in the portal page and sends it to the client (for example, Liferay).

Experiencing portlets

A portal page is made up of a set of portlets. For example, the **Welcome** portal page contains portlets like the **Web Content Display** portlet, and others. Moreover, the **Web Content Display** portlet has many controls icons (such as **Look and Feel**, **Configuration**, **Export / Import**, **Maximize**, **Minimize**, and **Remove**), the **Move** icon and title.

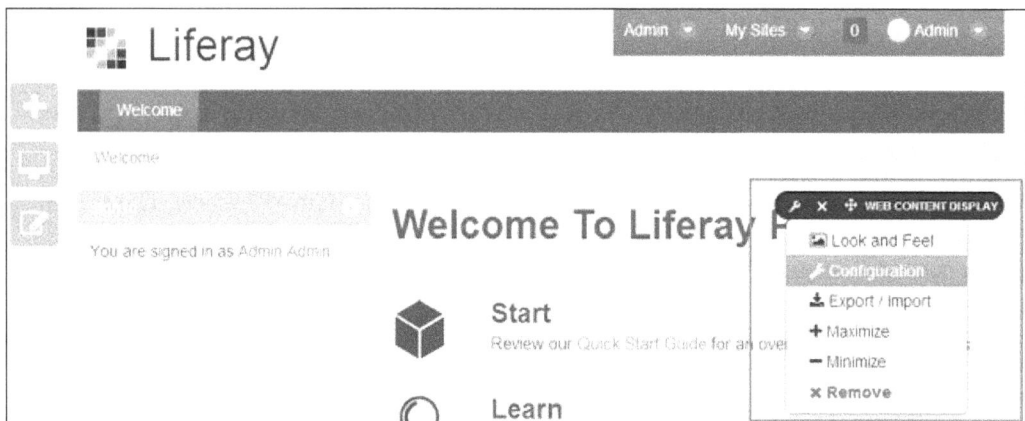

Figure 2.4: Portlet control (setting)

Each portlet has control settings (**Gear** icon), as seen in the preceding screenshot.

Normally, a portlet is an application that provides a specific piece of content (such as information or a service) to be included as a part of a portal page. It is managed by a portlet container that processes requests and generates dynamic content. Actually, portlets are used by portals as pluggable user interface components that provide a presentation layer to information systems.

Loosely speaking, portlets are fragments of an HTML page—pieces of markup (such as HTML, XHTML, WML, and so on). The content of a portlet is normally aggregated with the content of other portlets to form the portal page. The life cycle of a portlet is managed by the portlet container. The content generated by a portlet may vary from one user to another, depending on the user's configuration for the portlet.

The portal comes with several useful bundled portlets and also fully supports JSR-168 / JSR-286 standards, which allow the portal to deploy third-party portlets.

> **What's JSR-168 and JSR-286?**
>
> JSR-168 means Portlet Specification 1.0/1.1 and JSR-286 means Portlet Specification 2.0. Refer to `http://jcp.org/en/jsr/detail?id=168` and `http://jcp.org/en/jsr/detail?id=286` for more details.
>
> JSR-362 means Portlet Specification 3.0. Refer to `http://jcp.org/en/jsr/detail?id=362`. It is likely to be released soon.

Using the portlet container

The **Web Content Display** portlet runs in the portal page. It requires a runtime environment, that is, a portlet container.

Generally, a portlet container provides portlets with persistent storage for preferences and the required runtime environment. A portlet container manages a portlet's life cycle and receives requests from the portal to execute requests on the portlets. A portlet container is mostly the responsibility of the portal handling the aggregation.

Portlet applications are responsible for providing the user interface of the portal by accessing distinct applications, systems, or data sources and for generating markup fragments to present the content to the portal users.

The life cycle of a portlet

A portlet has a life cycle that defines how it is loaded, instantiated, and initialized, as well as how it handles requests from clients, and how it's taken out of service. The life cycle of a portlet includes the `Init()`, `processAction()`, `render()`, and `destroy()` methods of the portlet interface, as shown in the following figure:

- **Loading and instantiation**: The loading and instantiation can occur when the portlet container starts the portlet application, or it can be delayed until the portlet container determines that the portlet needs to service a request.

- **Initialization**: Portlets can initialize resources and perform other one-time activities.

- **Request handling**: The portlet container may invoke the portlet to handle client requests. The portlet handling request can be an action request, event request, or a render request.

- **Requests**: These are the `processAction` method and the `render` method, as shown in the next figure. Generally speaking, during a render request, portlets such as language generate content based on their current state.

- **End of service**: When the portlet container determines that a portlet should be removed from service, it calls the `destroy` method of the portlet interface in order to allow the portlet to release any resource it is using and save any persistent state.

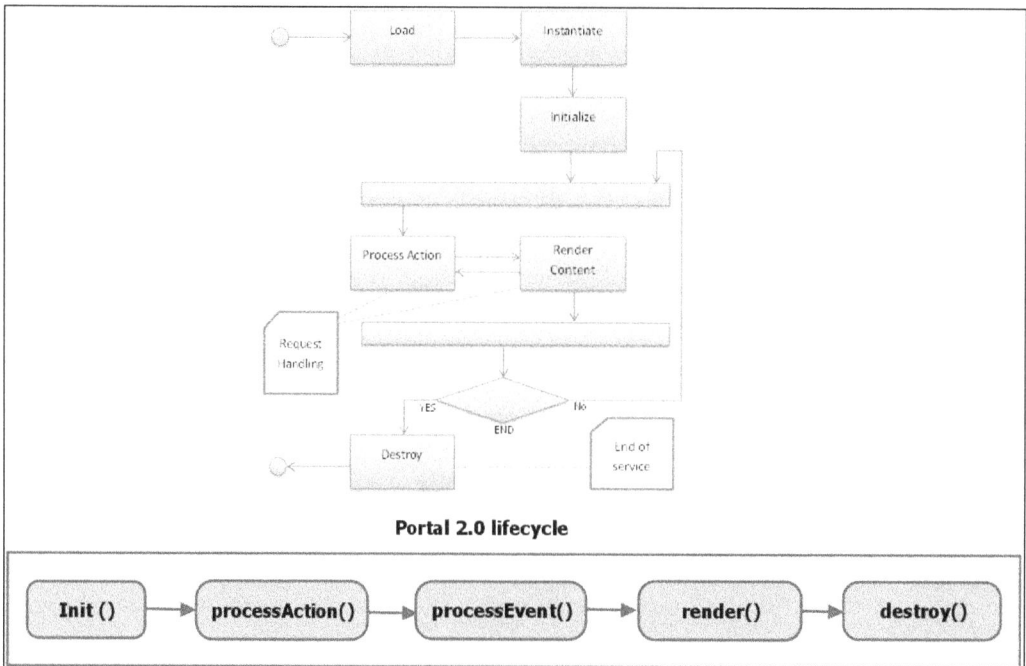

Figure 2.5: Portlet life cycle

In the preceding figure, you can see the portlet 2.0 life cycle, along with an explanation on the flow of each process. In JSR 286, that is portlet 2.0, a few methods have been introduced to make the portlet application more robust. For more information, you can refer to the JSR 286 official documentation.

Let's suppose that there are three portlets in a portal page: A, B, and C. Now suppose that the end user initiates an action on the page, which demands that the content of the portlets A, B, and C to be modified. The processes that take place during the interaction are illustrated in the following sequence diagram:

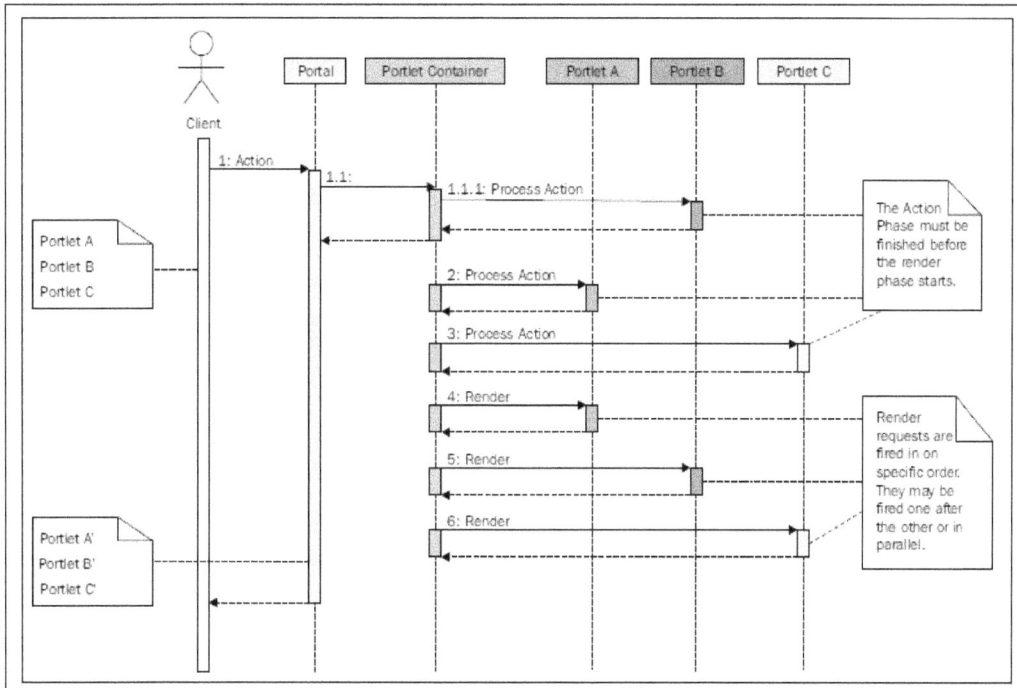

Figure 2.6: Portlet sequence diagram

The portlet sequence diagram illustrates the processes that take place during interactions between users and portlets.

Terminologies, scope, and hierarchy within the portal

We have discussed portal, pages, and portlets. What are the relationships between them? Let's take a high-level overview of the terminologies, scope, and hierarchy within the portal. As shown in next figure, the portal is implemented by portal instances. The portal can manage multiple portal instances in one installation. Of course, you can install multiple portal instances in multiple installations, separately.

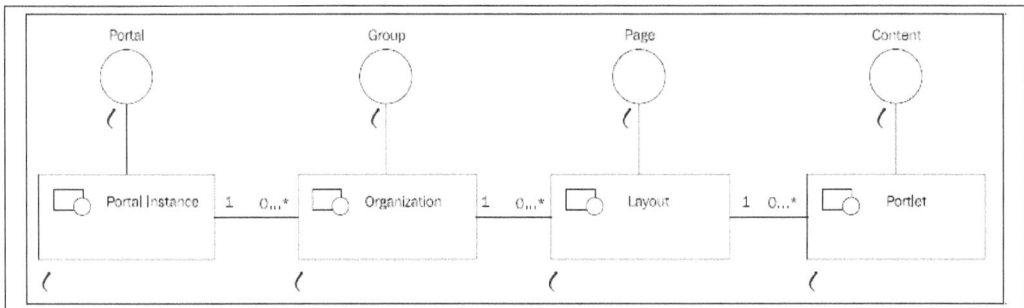

Figure 2.7: Portal-Group-Page-Content

The portal as a whole, broken down into different layers, is shown in the preceding figure.

Each portal instance can have many groups, which may be implemented as organizations, sites, user groups, and users. Note that each user can be represented as a group by itself. For example, if a user is a power user, then the user will have access to public pages and private pages, like any other group. Here, we can use the term organization to represent organizations (or locations), sites, user groups, and users (only one user in a group). Each portal instance has complete isolation of the users, organizations, locations, and user groups. There is a hierarchy in organizations, for example, the parent organization, child organizations, and locations.

Each group has two sets of pages (that is public and private, called portal pages) implemented as layouts. There is a hierarchy in layouts, for example, parent pages and child pages.

Each page may contain different content implemented as portlets. Therefore, the content will have different scopes. For example, the content would be *scoped* into a page, group, portal instance, or portal. This pattern is called **Portal-Group-Page-Content**.

Note that from **Liferay 6.1** onwards, the **Communities** have been named as **Sites**.

Setting up the portal

As an administrator at the enterprise Palm Tree Publications, you will need to undertake many administrative tasks such as installing the portal, installing and setting up databases, and so on.

You can install the portal in different ways based on your needs. Normally, there are three main installation options:

- **Using an open source bundle**: The easiest and fastest installation method is to install the portal as a bundle. By using a Java SE runtime environment with an embedded database (that is, **hypersonic** database), you can simply unzip and run the bundle just as we had done in the beginning. You may configure the database and other settings by using the Basic Configuration wizard.
- **Detailed installation procedure**: You can install the portal in an existing application server. This option is available for all the supported application servers.

We will consider the second installation option, *the detailed installation procedure*, later. In the previous section, we have used the first installation option.

Installing Liferay on an existing application server

We will be installing Liferay Portal using its `.war` file on an existing application server. Liferay supports a wide combination of application servers and databases.

1. Download the `liferay-portal-6.2-ce...war` and `liferay-portal-dependencies-6.2-ce...zip` files.
2. Check and undeploy any application listening at the root (/) of the server.
3. Make sure that the application server is down.
4. Unzip the dependencies to the global classpath of your server so that both Liferay and the plugins can access them.
5. Deploy the Liferay `.war` file and start the application server.

Let us assume that the database installed in your system is MySQL, and that the database has already been created. Your application server is already installed and running successfully.

> Note that Liferay uses the UTF-8 character encoding. So, make sure that your application server has the `Java-Dfile.encoding=UTF-8` parameter set before you proceed. Different application servers have different setting for this parameter.

Using the Liferay Portal bundled with GlassFish 3.1.x in Windows

Firstly, let's consider one scenario—you, as an administrator, need to install the portal in Windows with a MySQL database, and your local Java version is Java SE 7.0. Let us install the portal, bundled with GlassFish 3.1.x in Windows, through the following steps:

1. Download the latest Liferay Portal Standard Edition bundled with GlassFish 3.1.x from the website `http://www.liferay.com/downloads/liferay-portal/available-releases`.

2. Unzip the downloaded file into `$LIFERAY_PORTAL`.

3. Now start the server by running start `serv.bat`, which is located at `C:\Liferay_Home\liferay-portal-6.1.1-ce-ga2\glassfish-3.1.2\bin`.

4. Create a database named `lportal` in MySQL as follows:

   ```
   drop database if exists lportal;
   create database lportal character set utf8;
   ```

5. You need to wait for couple of minutes to start the server. Once the server is running, type `http://localhost:8080` in the browser if it doesn't open automatically. You will get the **Basic Configuration** wizard/interface, where you have to setup the **Portal Name**, **Administrator User**, and database setting. As you start with the portal pages, you will have to set up the basic configuration, or it will just take the default settings. You can refer to the *Figure 2.2*.

6. After setting up the basic configuration, click on **Finish**. You will be redirected to the confirmation page, where you should click on **Go to my portal**.

7. Now you have to change the password for the **Administrator User**, that is, `Admin` in our case. Answer the remaining questions. And last, but not the least, when the terms and conditions **Agreement** page appears, just click the **I Agree** option.

> If you have already set up the database that you want to map with your portal instance, you can set your existing its details of in the Basic configuration.
>
> If you don't want the Basic Configuration wizard to appear, just disable it by adding the `setup.wizard.enabled=false` setting in `portal-ext.properties`. You will need to create the `portal-ext.properties` file under `$LIFERAY_HOME` or at `$TOMCAT_AS_DIR/webapps/ ROOT/WEB-INF/classes`. Note that you should only have one file in either location.

Using Liferay Portal bundled with Tomcat 6.x in Linux

Let's consider another scenario in which you, as an administrator, need to install the portal in Linux with a MySQL database, and your local Java version is JDK 6.0. Let's install the portal bundled with Tomcat 6.x in Linux as follows:

1. Download the latest Liferay Portal Standard Edition bundled with Tomcat 7.x from the website http://www.liferay.com/downloads/liferay-portal/available-releases.

2. Unzip the downloaded file into `$LIFERAY_PORTAL`.

3. Configure the database details in the portal-ext. properties file.

4. Create a database `lportal` and an account `root`/`root` in MySQL as follows:

```
drop database if exists lportal;
create database lportal character set utf8;
grant all on lportal.* to 'root'@'localhost' identified by
  'root' with grant option;
grant all on lportal.* to 'root'@'localhost.localdomain'
  identified by 'root' with grant option;
```

5. Add the following lines at the end of `portal-ext.properties`.

```
## MySQL
jdbc.default.driverClassName=com.mysql.jdbc.Driver
jdbc.default.url=jdbc:mysql://localhost:3306/lportal?useUni
  code=tr ue&characterEncoding=UTF-8&useFastDateParsing=
  false
jdbc.default.username=root
jdbc.default.password=root
```

6. If you don't want to go through the basic configuration wizard, then paste the following line in `portal-ext.properties`:

   ```
   setup.wizard.enabled=false
   ```

   This will disable the basic configuration.

7. Run `$TOMCAT_AS_DIR/bin/startup.sh`. Note that you may need to wait for about 60 seconds for it to start up.

8. Open your browser, and type `http://localhost:8080` if it doesn't open automatically. Now you will not get the Basic configuration wizard/interface.

9. Now you have to change the password for the **Administrator User** to `Admin`. After that, answer the remaining questions. When the terms and conditions agreement page appears, just click on the **I Agree** option.

10. You have successfully installed Tomcat in Linux.

> Note that `JAVA_HOME` should be set before you run the server.

Setting up production servers

If the portal was used for production, then you may need to reset the JVM parameters as follows:

1. Locate the `setenv.sh` file in `$TOMCAT_AS_DIR/bin`.

2. Remove all current lines, and add the following lines in the `setenv.sh` file:

   ```
   JAVA_OPTS="$JAVA_OPTS –Xms2048m -Xmx2048m -XX:MaxPermSize=
     1024m -Dfile.encoding=UTF8 -Duser.timezone=GMT -Djava.
     security.auth. login.config=$CATALINA_HOME/conf/jaas.
     config -Dorg.apache. catalina.loader.WebappClassLoader.
     ENABLE_CLEAR_REFERENCES=false"
   ```

The previous code shows the JVM parameters and reasonable values for a production environment.

Setting up domains

Additionally, if the portal was used for production, you may need to test the domain (a real domain or a virtual domain) instead of *localhost*. As mentioned earlier, we can type the URL `http://www.bookpub.com:8080` in a browser. How to make it happen?

1. Locate the hosts file in the `etc` folder and open it. Note that in a Windows environment, the `etc` folder would be something like `C:/Windows/System32/drivers/etc`.

2. Add the following line at the end of the host file and save it:

    ```
    127.0.0.1          www.bookpub.com
    ```

The preceding code maps the IP address `127.0.0.1` to the domain `www.bookpub.com`. Note that you should use the real IP address of your production system and the real domain. Therefore, a portal with a real domain name in this box will be available on the Internet.

Shortening the URL

As you can see, there is a port number `8080` in the URL. You may want to remove the port number and make the URL shorter to something like `http://www.bookpub.com`. You can do this by following these steps:

1. Locate `server.xml` at `$TOMCAT_AS_DIR/conf` and open it.

2. Replace the port number `8080` with `80` and save it. Make sure you don't have any other processes running on port `80` such as the Apache server.

3. The preceding code resets the port number. Normally, the number `80` gets hidden in the URL. This is an option we can use to shorten the URL. There are other options that we can use to make the URL even shorter, such as friendly URL mapping and virtual hosting. These options will be addressed in the coming chapters.

More options for portal installation

You can use one of following options for servlet containers and full Java EE application servers in order to install the Liferay Portal:

*   Bundled with Geronimo: `liferay-portal-geronimo-6.2-ce-ga2`

*   Bundled with GlassFish 3: `liferay-portal-glassfish-6.2-ce-ga2`

*   Bundled with JBoss: `liferay-portal-jboss-6.2-ce-ga2`

*   Bundled with Jetty: `liferay-portal-jetty-6.2-ce-ga2`

- Bundled with Resin: `liferay-portal-resin-6.2-ce-ga2`
- Bundled with Tomcat 7.x: `liferay-portal-tomcat-6.2-ce-ga2`

You can choose the preferred bundle according to your requirements, and directly download it from the official download page (refer to `http://www.liferay.com/downloads/liferay-portal/available-releases`). The examples in this book are based on the Liferay Portal bundled with Tomcat 7.x and GlassFish 3.

A flexible deployment matrix

As an administrator, you can install Liferay Portal on all major application servers, databases, and operating systems. There are over 700 ways to deploy Liferay Portal. Therefore, you can reuse your existing resources, stick with your budget, and get an immediate return on an investment that everyone will be happy with. In general, you can install the portal on Mac, Linux, Unix, or Windows with any one of the following application servers (or servlet containers), and by selecting any one of the following database systems:

Application server	Borland ES, Apache Geronimo, Sun GlassFish 2 UR1, JBoss, JOnAS, JRun 4 Updater, Oracle AS, Orion, Pramati, RexIP, SUN JSAS, WebLogic, WebSphere, Jetty, Resin, Tomcat
Database	Apache Derby, IBM DB2, Firebird, Hypersonic, H2 (Hypersonic 2), Informix, InterBase, JDataStore, MySQL, Oracle, PostgreSQL, SAP, SQL Server, Sybase
Operating system	LINUX (Debian, RedHat, SUSE, Ubuntu, and so on.), Unix (AIX, FreeBSD, HP-UX, OS X, Solaris, and so on), Windows, and Mac OS X

Building the Palm Tree Publications site

Let's create a site for our example with the name Palm Tree, which will help us understand the portal concept clearly.

Follow these steps to create a new site:

1. Click on the **Admin** link; a drop-down menu will appear (see *Figure 2.3*).
2. Click on **Control Panel** and select **Sites**.

3. Now, click on **Add** and select **Blank Site**.

4. Fill in the site name and site description keeping all other settings default. We will be discussing this in detail in the coming chapters.

5. Finally, click on the **Save** button. The Palm Tree site is created successfully and it will redirect to the site admin page.

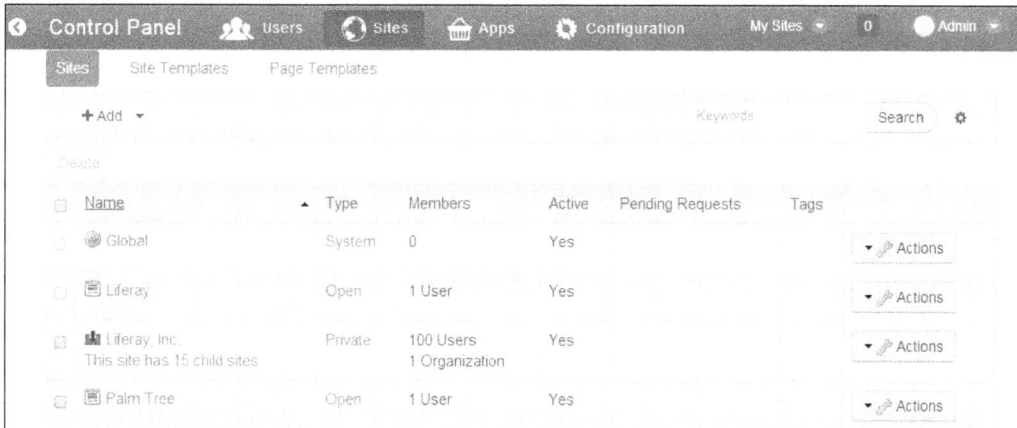

Figure 2.8: Control Panel sites

The preceding screenshot shows the list of sites displayed by the Sites section in the **Control Panel**.

6. Now create a page for the site. Click on the **Pages** link and select **Site Pages** from the drop-down menu on the left-hand side. Under **Public page**, add a new page with the name **Home**. See the detailed steps given in the following section.

Finally, you have created the Palm Tree site with the **Home** page.

Building pages

As a Palm Tree administrator of the enterprise Palm Tree Publications, you may be expected to build more pages like the home page that you see when you are signed-in by default.

Generally, the pages could be public pages or private pages of different sites. Before building a page, you must take a look at the dock bar menu. As shown in following screenshot, you can see some items in the dock bar menu under **My Sites**:

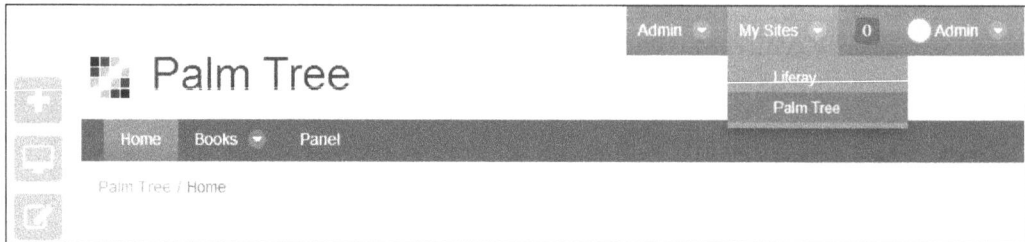

Figure 2.9: The Palm Tree site

Finally, after the entire configuration, the **Home** page of Palm Tree gets loaded.

As you might have noticed, while setting **Basic Configuration**, we have set the portal name as Liferay. Under **My Sites**, you will see the list of active sites; *Liferay* and *Palm Tree* are the current active sites.

As you can see, every user will have his/her own public pages and private pages. Furthermore, you will see a set of pages with a set of portlets in both public pages and private pages. After logging in successfully, you are ready to build pages in the Palm Tree site for carrying out the following tasks:

- Add or remove or update pages
- Add or remove portlets in newly created pages
- Change layout templates for newly added pages

In general, registered users who have the appropriate permissions will have access to their own public pages and private pages, and then they may have the ability to build pages in the site also.

Adding pages

Let's add two pages say **Books** and **Departments** in the Palm Tree site. Follow these steps for adding the Books page:

1. Click on the **Add** link (plus icon) on left side of the dock bar panel. In the following screenshot, you can see the **Add** link marked with a red box.

2. Once you click the **Add** link, it will open the **Add** panel on the left-hand side. The **Add** panel allows you to add content, applications, and pages. For adding pages, click on the **Page** link.

3. Simply enter the page name as Books, and select the language (the default is US English).

4. Select the page type from the following: **Empty Page**, **Blog**, **Content Display Page**, **Wiki**, **Panel**, **Embedded**, **Link to URL**, **Link to a page to this Site**, and **Copy of a page to this Site**. The default option is **Empty Page** and the layout is **2 Columns (30/70)**.

5. Finally, click on the **Add Page** button.

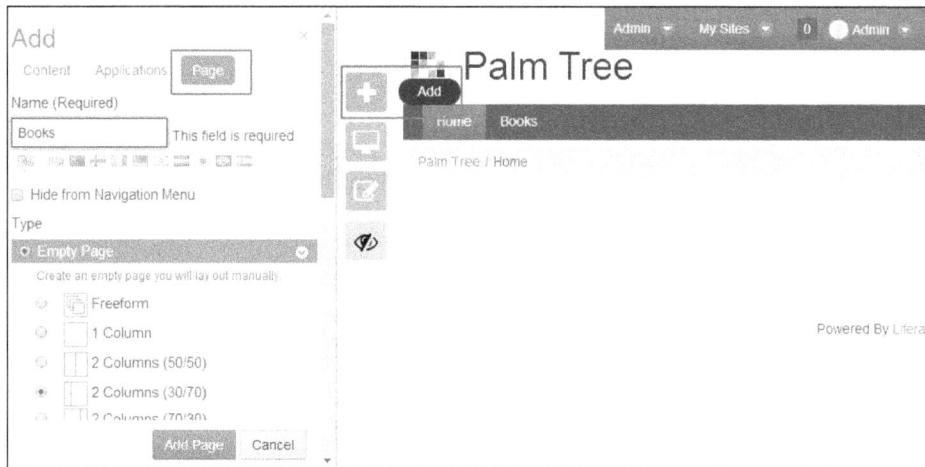

Figure 2.10: Adding pages

The preceding screenshot shows how to add pages in the portal.

Repeat this process to add another page called *Departments*. Of course, you can add as many pages as you want. After adding a set of pages, you can add different portlets.

Removing pages

If you decide that you do not need the **Departments** page and want to remove it, we can do this by following these steps:

1. Move the mouse to the page named **Departments**. If the page isn't the current page, then the delete icon will appear.

2. Click on the **Delete** icon next to the page name. A message, **Are you sure you want to delete this page?** with the **OK** and **Cancel** buttons will appear.

3. Click the **OK** button if you want to remove the page.

As you can see, you can remove other pages as well. Removing a page is a simple but dynamic process. You can delete the page by visiting **Site Admin | Pages | Site Pages** and delete the page.

> Note that there is no delete icon for the current page. If you want to delete the current page, then you need to click on another page and make that page a normal page first. Then you can delete it, as previously stated. Furthermore, any instance of portlets on this page would be removed if the page is deleted.

Adding portlets

It is now time to add portlets to the newly created pages. Let's say, we need to add the **Language** portlet to the page **Home**. Let's do it in the following way:

1. Click on the **Home** page link in the navigation bar, which you've just created.

2. Click on the link **Add link | Applications** in the **Add** panel on the left. This will bring up the add application panel on your screen (follow *Figure 2.11*).

3. Enter the portlet name Language in the search text box, and locate the **Language** portlet from the menu. You will find the portlet under the tools category.

4. Click on the **Add** button to the right of the portlet named **Language**.

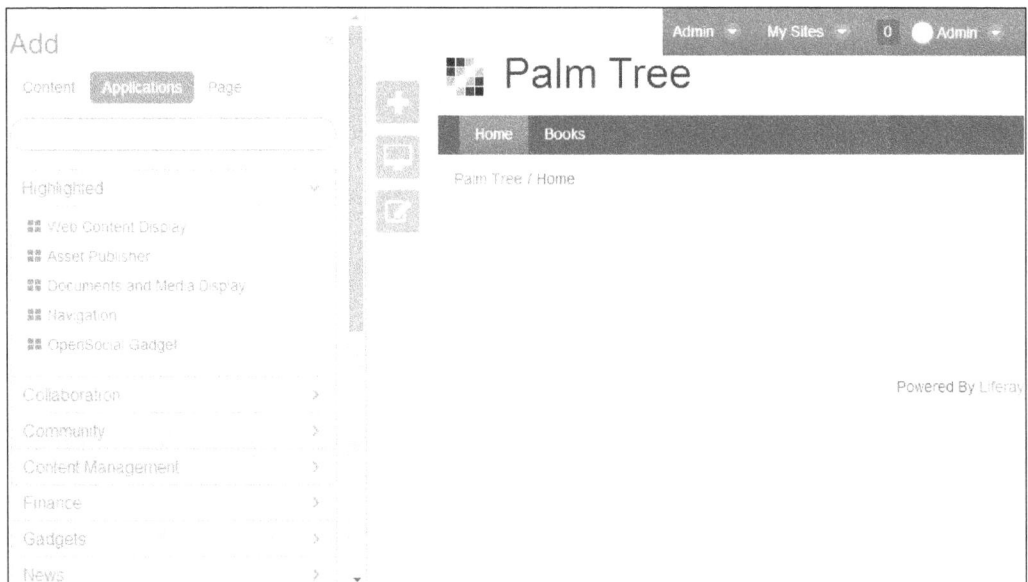

Figure 2.11: Adding a portlet

The edit panel interface on the left allows adding a portlet on the page.

You will see that the **Language** portlet has been added to the top of your page. Now, you are ready to change the portlet placement. Click on the title bar of the portlet, and drag it to wherever you like. You can add many portlets, just as you can add many pages.

Removing portlets

If we decide that we no longer need the **Language** functionality on the Home page, we can remove the portlet by following these steps:

1. Locate the **Language** portlet.
2. Click on the remove link from the **Gear** (icon) on the upper-right corner of the portlet.
3. A message, **Are you sure you want to remove this component?** with the **OK** and **Cancel** buttons will appear.
4. Click on the **OK** button.

Of course, you can remove any portlet from any page, but only if you have the proper permissions.

> Note that portlet preferences related to the portlet in the page would be removed if the portlet was removed from the page. You cannot recover these after deletion. By the way, if you remove a portlet, such as Web Content Display from a page, it will not remove the portlet content such as the web content itself.

Changing the layout templates

You can also change the layout templates for pages. A layout template allows us to arrange the portlets in one, two-two, or one-two-one columns as well as designate the width of the columns. You can add and arrange all the portlets that you would like on the pages, using the layout templates.

Let us follow the steps for changing the layout of the page:

1. First, select the page for which you want to change the layout. You can change the layout for the parent page, which will make changes in all its child pages. In our example, let's select the **Home** page.

2. Click on the **Edit** (icon) | **Edit Page** link. The **Edit Page** section will appear in the panel on the left, as seen in the following screenshot.

3. Now, under the **Layout** page type, you can select any layout such as **Freeform**, **2 columns**, **3 columns**, and so on.

4. Click on the **Save** button.

> If you want to have a common layout for all the pages, just you need to select the parent page and change the page layout. In the column on the left, you can see the page hierarchy. It will create a common page layout for all the child pages.

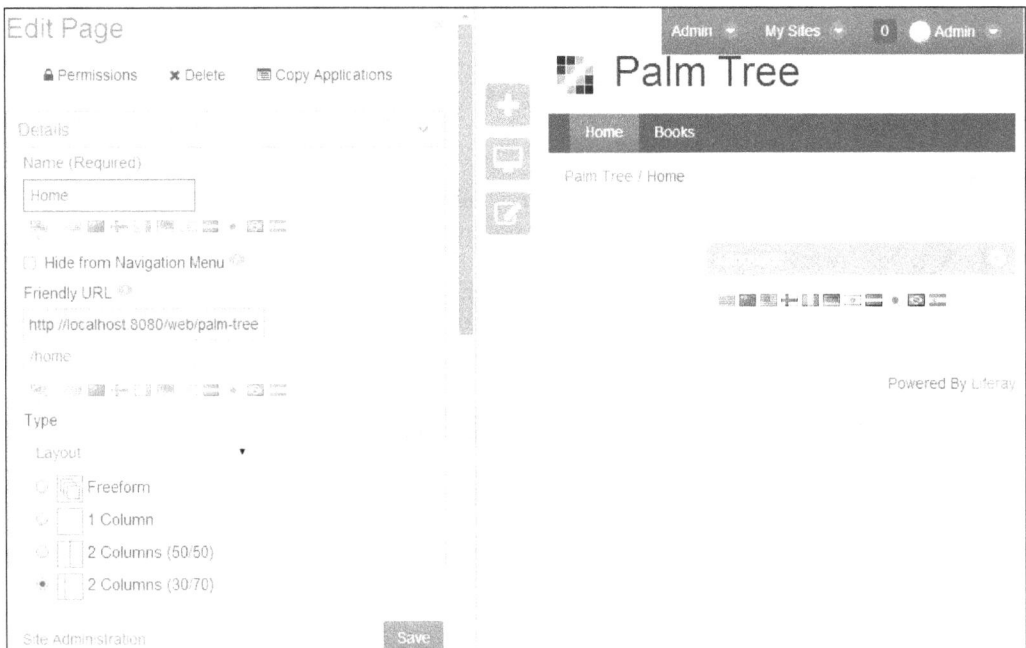

Figure 2.12: The page layout

The **Edit Page** feature allows you to edit the page layouts, set a friendly URL, and so on. The preceding screenshot shows the **Edit Page** layout screen.

Note that you can change the layout from **Site Admin | Pages | Site pages**, under the Palm Tree site administration panel.

Generally speaking, layout templates define the areas where you can place portlets on a page. Normal users or administrators can choose different layout templates for each portal page.

You might need a very specific custom layout as per the business needs. For organizations that develop website games /videos/ playlists, each home page will be very different. The portal provides maximum flexibility to deploy extra layout templates.

Setting up portal pages

As an administrator or a website editor, you are required to set up pages of any site. Let's say that you're expected to set up the public pages for the Palm Tree site with the following tasks.

Adding a child page

1. Let us add a child page under the Books page. Select **Admin | Site Administration | Pages** under the dock bar menu.

2. Click on **Add Child Page** button; an **Add Child Page** popup will appear to allow you to fill in the new child page name and page type.

3. Enter the page name as Stories, keep the page type **Empty Page**. Click on **Add page** to complete the task.

4. A child page **Stories** has been created under the **Books** page, as seen in the following screenshot.

5. Finally, save the child page.

Public pages: These are accessible to anyone, even to users who are not signed-in(guests). Pages can be restricted at any page level for different users through the permission system.

Private pages: These are accessible only to users who are members of the site that owns the pages.

That means that the private pages of an organization's site would be viewable only to members of the organization.

Note that both set of pages, public and private, have different URLs, which will have different themes, layouts, content, and applications.

The whole purpose of private pages and public pages is to allow users to create and maintain their own portal pages for different sites.

For an intranet site, it allows the user to establish an environment that works for them (adding and deleting the portlets that they use).We will see this in more detail in the *Exploring Social Networking* section of *Chapter 6, Blogs, WYSIWYG Editors, and Social Networking*.

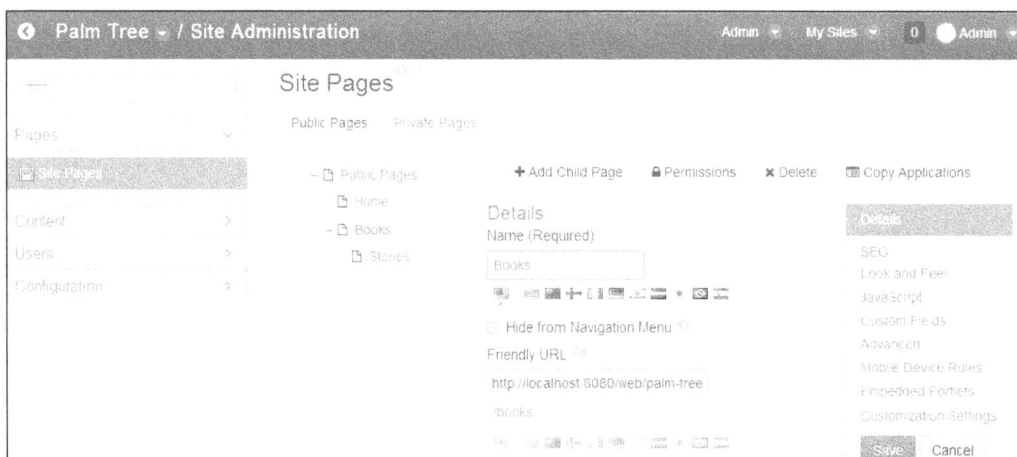

Figure 2.13: Site Pages

The **Site Pages** interface in the site administration panel allows more page configuration options.

Page type / template

The Liferay 6.2 portal provides different type of page templates like **Empty page**, **Blog**, **Content display page**, **Wiki**, **Panel**, **Embedded**, **Link to URL**, **Link to a page of this Site**, and **Copy of a page of this site**.

Whenever you create a page, it always, by default, selects the page type as **Empty page**. In some business requirements you might want to use one of the other options.

- **Empty page** will always have the layout defined as two columns (30/70) and it allows you to drag and drop portlets onto the page.
- **Blog** will have three applications related to blogging on the page, which are **Blog** portlet, **Tag Cloud** portlet, and **Recent Bloggers**. This template has two columns with the **Blog** portlet placed in the main, left column and the **Tag Cloud** and **Recent Bloggers** portlets in the right column.

- **Content display page** allows you to have a page that is preconfigured to display content. This page will have three auxiliary applications (**Tags Navigation**, **Categories Navigation**, and **Search**) and an **Asset Publisher**. The Asset Publisher is preconfigured to display any web content associated with this page. You can select this page for a web content article when creating a new web content article or when editing an existing one.

- **The Wiki** page template will have three applications related to a wiki. This too has two columns, the main left column with the **Wiki** portlet and the right column with **Tags** and **Categories** portlets for navigating.

- **Panel** pages can have any number of portlets on them as selected by an administrator, but only one will be displayed at a time. Users select which portlet they want to use from a menu on the left side of the page. The selected portlet is displayed on right-hand side of the page.

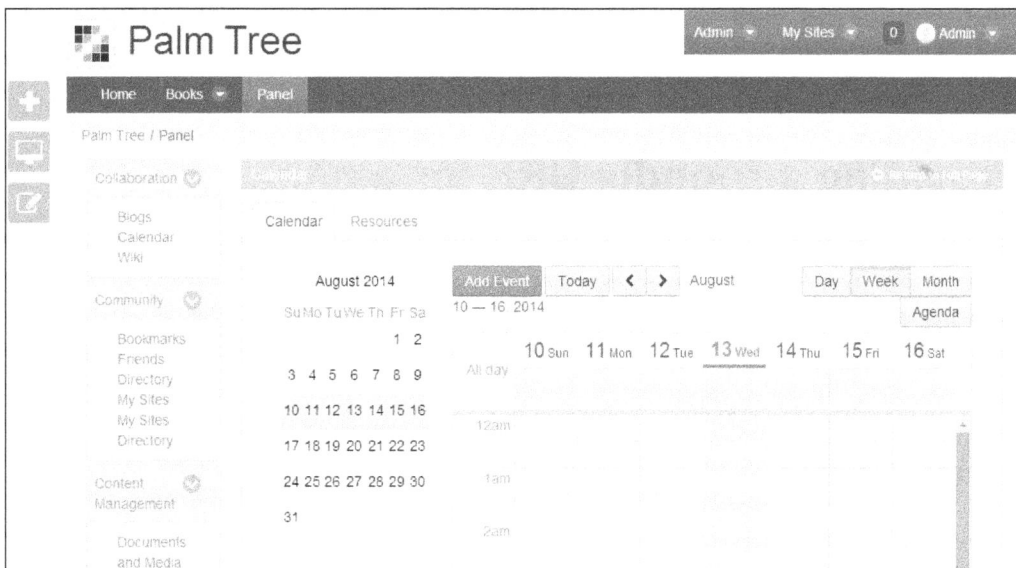

Figure 2.14: The Panel page type

The Panel page type allows end users to navigate and experience different applications on portal.

- **Embedded** page template allows the administrator to set a URL for an external website or application, and it displays content from another website inside your portal page using an Iframe. It's great for quick integration of external applications. The Iframe helps in automatically resizing the page to avoid unnecessary scrolling.

- **Link to URL** redirects the user to any URL specified by an administrator. The URL can be set to another website such as www.google.com.

- **Link to a page of this site** is used for an immediate redirect to another page within the same site. You can select the page to be link from a dropdown in the page management interface. It can be used as a link to a page to place a deeply nested page in the primary navigation menu of your site.

- **Copy of a page of this site** allows you to copy an existing page of the current site page, including the portlets, to a new page.

Changing the display order

You can change the display order of the child pages under **Admin | Site Administration | Pages** within the dock bar menu.

Refer to *Figure 2.13*. From the page list on the left, select the page for which you want to change the display order with the mouse pointer and drag and drop it at the required position.

Providing a friendly URL for a page

You can provide a **friendly URL** for a page as well. For example, you could have the URL for the **Books** page as http://localhost:8080/web/guest/books.

As many parameters are passed in through the URL, the portal URL is very long and difficult to read. However, you can give your page a friendly URL to make it easier to read and access.

The portal provides a friendly URL for each group (including sites, organization, and user). Therefore, you just type in a friendly URL for a page (this too must start with "/") /books. If there is no duplication, you can now access your page using the following URL pattern:

```
http://${server-name}/${group-friendly-url}/${page-friendly-url}
```

Copying pages or portlets

You already have a page named **Stories**, which is the child page of **Books** in the Palm Tree site. Now, suppose you would like to copy other page portlets to this **Stories** page. In such a case, you can use the **Copy** portlets from page function.

1. Select **Admin | Site Administration | Pages** under the dock bar menu.

2. Just select the page (like Stories) and click on **Copy Applications** present right at the top of the site pages. The **Copy Applications** dialog box popup will appear.

3. Select the page from which you want to copy the portlets to the **Stories** page. Select the **Home** page.

4. Save the setting. You can now see the **Stories** page as an exact copy of the **Home** page.

Furthermore, you can specify SEO, meta tags, and JavaScript for a given page. For example, if you need to add a function to redirect to an external website on a page, you could directly add JavaScript code in the JavaScript part of that page as shown in the following line:

```
Window.location="http://google.com";
```

Deleting a page

Let's see how we can delete a page. Say that you want to delete the **Stories** page, which is the child page of the **Books** page.

1. Select the **Stories** page and click on the **Delete** button in the manage page dialog popup.

2. A message, **Are you sure you want to delete this page?**, with the **OK** and **Cancel** buttons will appear.

3. Click on the **OK** button if you want to delete the page.

> Note that deleting a page will delete all child pages related to that page and remove all portlet instances that the page owns.

Multiple languages

The portal is designed to handle as many languages as you want to support. By default, it supports most of the popular languages. When a page is loading, the portal will detect the language it should use, pull up the corresponding language file, and display the text in the correct language.

> You can modify the language list by inserting `locales.enabled=`, followed by your preferred languages in your `portal-ext.properties` file. For example, `locales.enabled=ar_SA,nl_NL,hi_IN` offers Arabic (Saudi Arabia), Dutch (Netherlands), and Hindi (India).

For the page **Books**, the default language is English (United States). If you select a localized language—say, for example, German (Germany)—then you have the capability to enter the **Name** and **HTML Title** in German.

Changing the look and feel – themes

You can change the *look and feel* of the portal or a particular page, that is, your private page. Let's change the look and feel of the **Books** page.

1. Go to **Admin | Site Administration | Pages** under the dock bar menu and select the **Books** page on the left side of the screen.

2. Now to select the look and feel, you will get the option to select the theme on the right side of the screen. Select **Define a specific look and feel for this page** option.

3. In this dialog box, you will find the details about the current theme with different color schemes and the available new themes. In the following screenshot, we don't have any new themes available.

4. Let's select the color scheme **Orange**. Save the setting.

There are more features and settings to change the theme for your page.

- You can switch the bullet style between dots and arrows for the portlets

- You can select whether or not to show portlet borders by default

- The CSS section allows you to enter your custom CSS that will be a part of your theme to reflect on the page, overriding the existing ones:

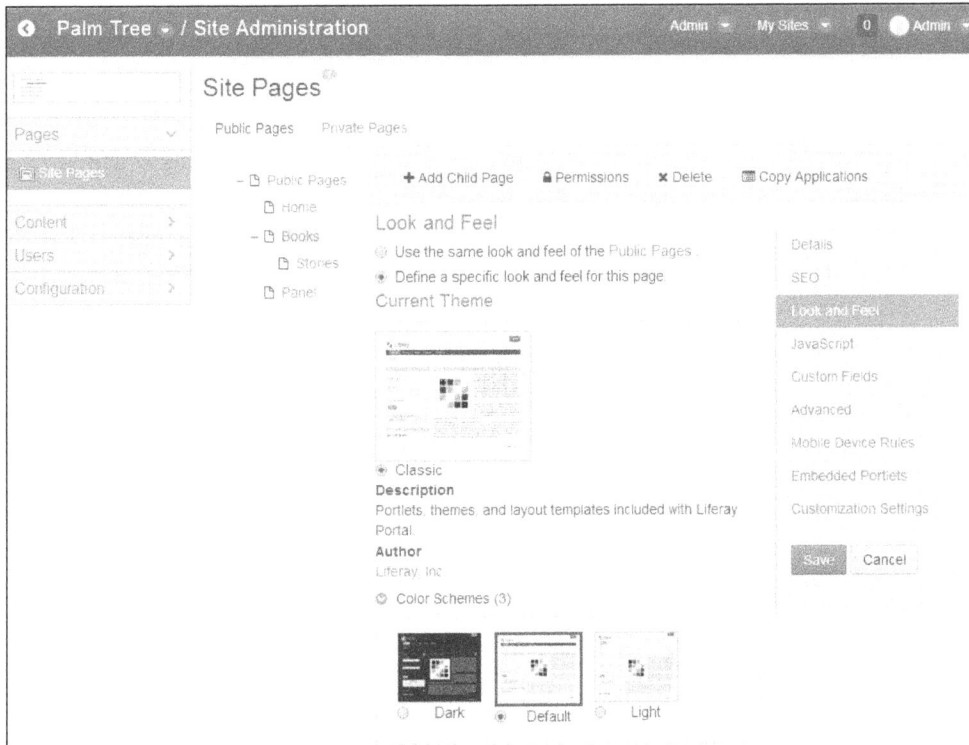

Figure 2.15: Look and Feel

The Site Pages allows look and feel (theme) settings for each page.

Now the theme is changed to orange color for the **Books** page.

Managing other settings on a page

You have more settings for managing page interfaces such as **Custom Fields**, **Advanced**, **Mobile Device Rules**, **Embedded Portlets**, and **Customization Settings**. Let's go through the details:

- **Custom Fields**: In Liferay, you can set the custom field, which are the metadata about the page and can be anything like author name, creation date, and so on. At the page level, you can set the custom field from the Control panel.

- **Advanced**: This is a unique feature for setting up the page with Setting up the query string to provide parameters to the page. This query string helps you with the web content templates.

  You can set the target for the page so that it either pops up in a particularly named window, or appears in a frameset. Also you can change the page icon, which appears in the navigation bar menu.

- **Mobile Device Rules**: Liferay has mobile support. Mobile Device Rules allow you to apply the rules for pages for different mobile devices. It's basically for rendering of the page in mobile devices.

- **Embedded Portlets**: In Liferay 6.2, a new feature called Embedded Portlets has been implemented. Embedded Portlet allows embedding a portlet into a particular page, using the UI.

- **Customization Settings**: It's one of the best features of Liferay for allowing the users to customize the page according to their requirement.

If you see the top menu, you will see some actions like **Add Child Page**, **Permissions**, **Delete**, and **Copy Applications**. Let's click on the permission action to set the permissions on the page.

Liferay gives us the best way to control role-based permission. On clicking on the **Permissions** button, the permission dialog box pops up. Here you can define which specific role should perform a view, update, delete, and so on. A **Guest** user has only **View** permission. The **Owner** has all permissions, whereas a **Site Member** has only **Add Discussion**, **Customize**, and **View** permissions:

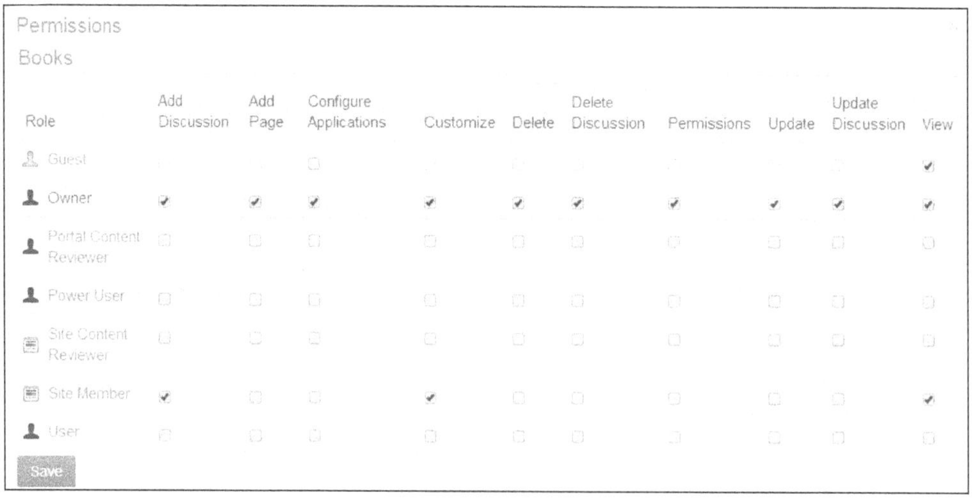

Role	Add Discussion	Add Page	Configure Applications	Customize	Delete	Delete Discussion	Permissions	Update	Update Discussion	View
Guest			☐							✔
Owner	✔	✔	✔	✔	✔	✔	✔	✔	✔	✔
Portal Content Reviewer	☐	☐	☐	☐	☐	☐	☐	☐	☐	☐
Power User	☐	☐	☐	☐	☐	☐	☐	☐	☐	☐
Site Content Reviewer	☐	☐	☐	☐	☐	☐	☐	☐	☐	☐
Site Member	✔	☐	☐	✔	☐	☐	☐	☐	☐	✔
User	☐	☐	☐	☐	☐	☐	☐	☐	☐	☐

Permissions
Books

Save

Figure 2.16: The interface for portlet permission setup for setting different permission for users

If you navigate to the parent-page level by clicking on public pages, you will able to see the **Export** and **Import** action buttons:

- **Export**: You can export the page content and all the settings to a **Liferay Archive (LAR)** file. This LAR file can be imported to any page to get the same content and portlet into the page. LARs help you to take backups of your site content.

> Note that LAR files depend on the versions, so you have to take care while importing the LARs. You can import the old version of the Liferay LAR file to new version of Liferay.

Customizing portlets

As a Palm Tree administrator of the enterprise Palm Tree Publications, you may be needed to customize the portlet.

Liferay provides us with a feature to customize the portlet through options/controls like **Look and Feel**, **Configuration**, **Export/Import**, **Maximize**, **Minimize**, and **Remove.**

- **Look and Feel**: This is used to change the portlet display by using the CSS and JavaScript. It even allows enabling and disabling the portlet border among many other settings.

Figure 2.17: The popup interface for portal look and feel (CSS) setting

As you can see in the preceding screenshot, there are many links for settings like **Portlet Configuration, Text Styles, Background Styles, Border Styles, Margin and Padding**, and **Advance Styling**:

- ○ **Portlet Configuration**: In this, you can change the portlet title, define a custom title, link portlet URLs to different internal pages, and you can show the border of the portlet

- ○ **Text Styles**: This allows you to change the text style of the portlet

- ○ **Background Styles**: This allows you to change the background style of the portlet

- ○ **Border styles**: This allows you to change the border style of the portlet

- ○ **Margin and Padding**: This allows you to change the margin and padding of the portlet

- ○ **Advanced Styling**: This allows to you configure your own custom CSS styling

- • **Configuration**: In some businesses, there might be a requirement for configuring the portlet with the default values. These values will be used in portlet action. In the Sign In portlet configuration, we can see the **Setup, Permission**, and the **Sharing** setting.

The portlet administrator and other super users have the right to access the configuration dialog popup. They can change the setting for the portlet.

Setup allows setting the default values for the portlet. **Permission** allows setting for the role-based user; the user is able to view and take action on the portlet. **Sharing** allows the setting for sharing the application with external social websites such as Facebook, OpenSocial Gadget, Netvibes, and so on.

In **Sign In - Configuration** | **Setup** | **General**, you can set the value for **Authentication Type**. Also, you can change the setting for **Email Notifications**:

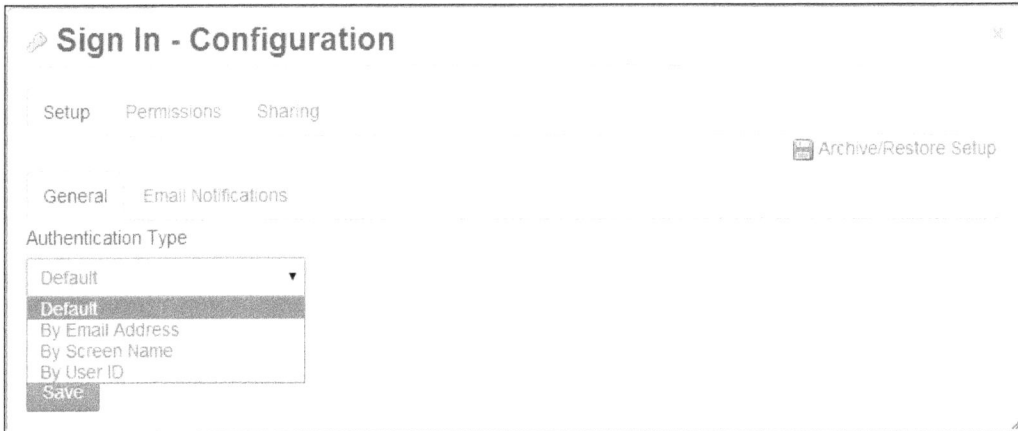

```
Sign In - Configuration                                              x

  Setup    Permissions    Sharing

                                                     Archive/Restore Setup

  General    Email Notifications
Authentication Type

  Default                        ▼

  Default
  By Email Address
  By Screen Name
  By User ID
  Save
```

Figure 2.18: The popup interface for portlet configuration allows setting preference value for portlet

Navigating the structure of an intranet site

Let's customize the **Home** page by placing the portlets and providing the following functions:

- Show the structured directory of links to all the pages in the portal. You simply add the **Site Map** portlet (portlet ID 85) in a page if the portlet isn't there.

- Display a directory of links by reflecting the page structure, which helps to drill down into the current page. You can add a **Navigation** portlet (portlet ID 71) in a page.

- Display a trail of parent pages for the current page. You just add the **Breadcrumb** portlet (portlet ID 73) in a page.

The **Breadcrumb** portlet displays a trail of parent pages for the current page. It can be placed on public portal pages as a navigational aid for publishing websites. It helps the user visualize the structure of a website and quickly move from a page to a broader grouping of information. Note that the breadcrumb portlet is embedded within the **Classic** theme.

A **Navigation** portlet provides a directory of links to reflect page structure, with drill down into the current page. Style and appearance are adjustable. The **Navigation** portlet displays links to other pages outside the current page's trail of parent pages. It helps users visualize the structure of a website and provides links to quickly move from one page to another. Moreover, it displays more information about the current page.

The **Site Map** portlet provides us with the ability to display a structured directory of links to all the pages of a website. Furthermore, it can be configured to display the entire site or a sub-section of pages.

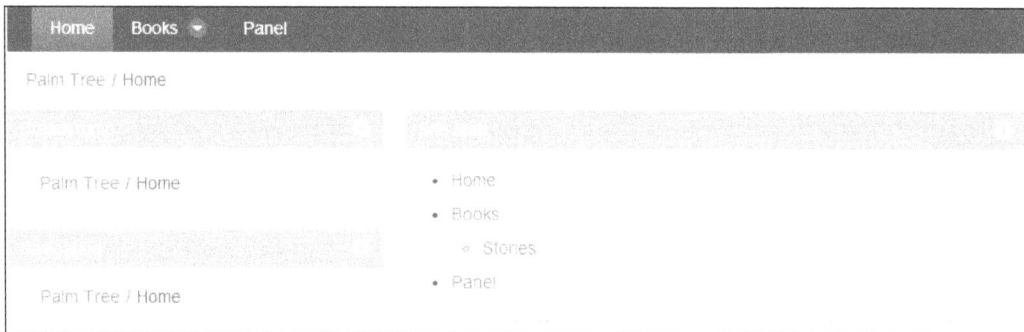

Figure 2.19: Navigation, Breadcrumb, and Site Map

The preceding screenshot displays **Navigation**, **Breadcrumb**, and **Site Map** portlets.

On the other hand, you can change the **Display Style** of the **Breadcrumb** portlet by clicking on the **Gear** (icon) | **Configuration** | **Setup**. Similarly, you can change **Display Style** and **Bullet Style** for the **Navigation** portlet, which can be changed by clicking on the **Gear** (icon) | **Configuration** | **Setup**. You can also configure **Root Layout**, **Display Depth**, **Include Root** in **Tree**, **Show Current Page**, **Use HTML Title**, and **Show Hidden Pages** of the portlet **Site Map** by clicking on the **Gear** (icon) | **Configuration** | **Setup**.

Configuring a portal

As an administrator at the enterprise Palm Tree Publications, you may need to customize the portal through configuration files in order to satisfy your own requirements.

Let's see an example for customizing the portal's configuration. As you can see, the default language is English (United States) and the default time zone is (**Coordinated Universal Time (UTC)** when the portal starts. Now, we plan to set the default language as German (Germany) and the default time zone as **Central European Time (CET)** when the portal starts. We can implement it as follows:

1. Shut the portal down if it is still running, by running `$TOMCAT_AS_DIR/bin/shutdown.sh`.

2. Clean Tomcat by deleting the files and directories inside temp and work folders.

3. Create the properties file `system-ext.properties` in `$TOMCAT_AS_DIR/webapps/ROOT/WEB-INF/classes` and open it.

4. Add the following line to the beginning of the properties file `system-ext.properties` and save it:

   ```
   user.country=DE
   user.language=de
   user.timezone=Europe/Paris
   ```

5. Restart the portal by running `$TOMCAT_AS_DIR/bin/startup.sh`.

Configuring portal paths

Before customizing the configuration files at the server level, it is better to review and adjust the values of the following properties in `portal.properties`, shown with their default values at the time of writing:

- `auto.deploy.deploy.dir=${liferay.home}/deploy` for auto-deploy
- `jdbc.default.url=jdbc:hsqldb:${liferay.home}/data/hsql/` for Hypersonic SQL scripts
- `lucene.dir=${liferay.home}/data/lucene` for search and indexing
- `jcr.jackrabbit.repository.root=${liferay.home}/data/jackrabbit` for JCR jackrabbit

What's the `liferay.home` variable? What are the `/data` and `/deploy` folders used for? By default, the portal has the following settings:

```
liferay.home=$LIFERAY_HOME
```

For this reason, after installing the portal, you will see following folders under `$LIFERAY_HOME`:

- `deploy`: This is a folder for hot deploy

> Hot deployment allows you to place the war file in the configured directory, and the application server picks up that artifact and deploys it within the application server with any server restart.
>
> Auto deployment works in conjunction with the hot deployment capabilities of your application server. Executing `ant deploy` invokes both deployment and auto deployment tasks, which inject the required JAR files and descriptors into your application archive file.

- `data`: This is a folder for runtime data
- `license`: This is a folder for license information, used only for **Community Edition (CE)**
- `$APPLICATION_SERVER_DIR`: This is a folder for the application server

As shown in the previous code, you will have the default `/deploy` and `/data` folders for the properties such as `auto.deploy.deploy.dir`, `lucene.dir`, and so on. Of course, you can set the `liferay.home` variable to any folder you desire.

Adding extended properties files

We can override the settings through properties files and determinately configure the portal through the properties files `portal-ext.properties` and `system-ext.properties`. These properties files are stored in the global classpath of application servers, presented as a variable `$PORTAL_EXT_PROPERTIES_HOME`. That is, you can create these properties files and store them at `$PORTAL_EXT_PROPERTIES_HOME`. Moreover, let's introduce another variable `$PORTAL_ROOT_HOME`, presenting the global `portal ROOT` path. Therefore, you will have the following expression:

```
$PORTAL_EXT_PROPERTIES_HOME=$PORTAL_ROOT_HOME/WEB-INF/classes
```

Obviously, the value of `$PORTAL_ROOT_HOME` is different from the application server as compared to the application server. Moreover, the variable `$AS_WEB_APP_ HOME` presents the global web apps folder of the application servers. For example:

- **Tomcat**:

```
$AS_WEB_APP_HOME=$TOMCAT_AS_DIR/webapps;
$PORTAL_ROOT_HOME=$TOMCAT_AS_DIR/webapps/ROOT
```

- **JBoss**:

  `$AS_WEB_APP_HOME=$JBOSS_AS_DIR/standalone/deployments; $PORTAL_`
  `ROOT_HOME=$JBOSS_AS_DIR/standalone/deployments /ROOT.war`

- **GlassFish**:

  `$AS_WEB_APP_HOME=$GLASSFISH_AS_DIR/domains/domain1/ applications;`

  `$PORTAL_ROOT_HOME=$GLASSFISH_AS_DIR/domains/ domain1/applications/`
  `liferay-portal`

- **Other application servers**: For these, check the documentation provided with them.

As shown in the previous example, `$TOMCAT_AS_DIR` represents the `Tomcat` folder under `$LIFERAY_HOME` and `$JBOSS_AS_DIR` represents the `JBoss` folder under `$LIFERAY_HOME`. Therefore, we could use `$APPLICATION_SERVER_DIR` to present the previously mentioned values–`$TOMCAT_AS_DIR`, `$JBOSS_AS_DIR`, and so on.

Portal structure

The portal has the following structure or folders under `$PORTAL_ROOT_HOME`.

- **dtd**: This contains XML document type definitions such as data types, display, hook, layout templates, look and feel, portlet application, service-builder, and ext
- **errors**: This contains an error page `404.jsp`
- **html**: This is a main folder for the website
- **layouttpl**: This contains standard or custom layout templates
- **wap**: This is a main folder for the WAP site including common themes, portal layout, themes mobile, and so on
- **WEB-INF**: This contains web specification such as `web.xml`, including the folders classes, lib, and tld

The `html` folder has the following subfolders:

- `common`: This contains common themes
- `css`: This contains a set of CSS for the portal
- `icons`: This contains a set of icon images
- `js`: This is a JavaScript for both portal and portlets
- `portal`: This contains portal layout and enterprise edition pages
- `portlets`: This contains default portlet views, including activities, admin, and so on

- `taglib`: This contains taglib for portlet, theme, and UI
- `themes`: This contains default theme folders such as `_style`, `_unstyle`, `classic`, and `control_panel`
- `VAADIN`: This contains a set of VAADIN themes and widgetsets

One of the biggest aspects of implementing the portal is, of course, customization of the user experience.

Portal context

As you have seen, a browser was automatically launched to a URL `http://localhost:8080` when the portal was fully initialized. Why did this happen? How can you customize this? The property `browser.launcher.url` has been set by default in `portal.properties` as follows:

```
browser.launcher.url=http://localhost:8080
```

The previous code specifies a URL to automatically launch a browser to that URL when the portal is fully initialized. You can set this property at the end of the `portal-ext.properties` file as a blank URL if you want to disable this feature.

Besides the URL (that is, `http://localhost:8080`), it also adds the context path `/web/guest`. This behavior is related to the property `company.default.home.url`. The property `company.default.home.url` has been set by default in `portal.properties` as:

```
company.default.home.url=/web/guest
```

The previous code sets the default home URL of the portal. Similarly, you can customize this feature in the properties file `portal-ext.properties`.

You may have noticed that the portal remembered your last visited path upon a successful login. How does it work? The property `auth.forward.by.last.path` has been set by default in `portal.properties` as follows:

```
auth.forward.by.last.path=true
```

The previous code shows that users are forwarded to the last visited path upon successful login. If you set it to false in the properties file `portal-ext.properties`, then users will be forwarded to their default layout page.

Terms of use page settings

The portal provides the ability to force all users to accept some *terms of use* text before using the portal for the first time. For example, before using the portal for the first time, the portal forces the user admin@bookpub.com/admin to accept the terms of use. The reason is that the terms.of.use.required property has been set by default in portal.properties as follows:

```
terms.of.use.required=true
```

The previous code shows that all users are required to agree to the **Terms of Use** before using the portal for the first time. If you set the property false in the properties file portal-ext.properties, then every user is not required to accept some terms of use text before using the portal for the first time.

Default text is included within the portal. However, in most of the installations where this feature is used, this text will need to be customized. Fortunately, you can use a **Web Content** article to change the text of **Terms of Use** with the following settings in the properties file portal-ext.properties:

```
terms.of.use.journal.article.group.id=$ARTICLE_GROUP_ID
terms.of.use.journal.article.id=$ARTICLE_ID
```

The previous code shows the group ID ($ARTICLE_GROUP_ID) and the article ID ($ARTICLE_ID) of the **Journal (Web Content)** article that will be displayed as the Terms of Use. The default text will be used if no **Journal** article is specified. Therefore, all administrators can manage the terms of use instead of the developers.

Session settings

As you can see, the default browser was automatically launched to the URL http://localhost:8080, when the portal was fully initialized. More interestingly, the session ID value will be different from time to time. The property session.enable.url.with.session.id has been set to false by default in the portal.properties file as follows:

```
session.enable.url.with.session.id=false
```

The previous code sets the `session.enable.url.with.session.id` property to `false` in order to disable sessions. To enable it, you can set the `session.enable.url.with.session.id` property to `true` in the `portal-ext.properties` properties file.

Figure 2.20: Session time-out

For security purpose, session time-out is essential for any portal.

Of course, you can configure session-related features as well. For instance, you may override the following properties in the properties file `portal-ext.properties`:

```
session.timeout=30
session.timeout.warning=1
session.timeout.auto.extend=false
session.timeout.redirect.on.expire=false
session.enable.persistent.cookies=true
```

As shown in the previous code, the property `session.timeout` specifies the number of minutes before a session expires. This value is always overridden by the value set in `web.xml` under the folder `$PORTAL_WEB_INF_HOME`. The `session.timeout.warning` property specifies the number of minutes before a warning is sent to the user, informing the user of the session expiration. You can specify `0` to disable any warning.

For the property `session.timeout.auto.extend`, you can set auto-extend mode to true in order to avoid having to ask the user whether to extend the session or not. Instead, the session will be extended automatically. The purpose of this mode is to keep the session open as long as the user's browser is open, with a portal page loaded. It is recommended to use this setting along with a smaller `session.timeout`, such as 5 minutes, *for better performance.*

You can set the property `session.timeout.redirect.on.expire` to `true` if the user is redirected to the default page when the session expires. By default, the user isn't redirected to the default page. Furthermore, you may set the property `session.enable.persistent.cookies` to `false` to disable all persistent cookies, so that features like automatic login don't work.

Default admin

As you have seen, the default admin account is `test@liferay.com/test`. The screen name of the default account is `test`, its default first name is `Test`, and its default last name is `Test` as well. This default account has been specified in `portal.properties` as follows:

```
default.admin.password=test
default.admin.screen.name=test
default.admin.email.address.prefix=test
default.admin.first.name=Test
default.admin.middle.name=
default.admin.last.name=Test
```

The previous code sets the default admin account password, screen name prefix, e-mail address prefix, first name, middle name, and the last name. Of course, you can override these properties in the properties file `portal-ext.properties`.

Guest layouts

The Guest group must have at least one public page. The settings for the initial public page are specified in following properties:

```
default.guest.public.layout.name=Welcome
default.guest.public.layout.template.id=2_columns_ii
default.guest.public.layout.column-1=58
default.guest.public.layout.column-2=47
default.guest.public.layout.column-3=
default.guest.public.layout.column-4=
default.guest.public.layout.friendly.url=/home
```

The previous code sets the name of the public layout, the default layout template ID, the portlet IDs for the columns specified in the layout template, and the friendly URL of the public layout. This is the reason that the default public page of Guest has the name `Welcome`, layout template ID `2_columns_ii`, portlet IDs `58` (Sign In portlet) and `47` (Hello World portlet), and the friendly URL `/home`.

Friendly URLs

As you can see, private pages (My Dashboard) for the user `admin@liferay.com/`
`admin` have friendly URLs such as `/user/admin/home`, and public pages (My Profile)
for the user `admin@liferay.com/admin` have friendly URLs such as `/web/admin/`
`home`. The public pages of Guest have friendly URLs such as `/web/guest` and the
private pages of Guest have friendly URLs such as `/web/guest/welcome`. Why is
this so? This is because the following properties are set in `portal.properties`.

```
layout.friendly.url.private.group.servlet.mapping=/group
layout.friendly.url.private.user.servlet.mapping=/user
layout.friendly.url.public.servlet.mapping=/web
```

The previous code shows that the friendly URLs for users and groups can be set at
runtime. When typing keywords for a friendly URL, you should not use reserved
keywords. The property `layout.friendly.url.keywords` specifies a set of reserved
keywords in the properties file `portal.properties`.

```
layout.friendly.url.keywords=\c,\group,\web,\image,\page,\public,\
    private,\rest,\tunnel-web
```

The preceding code sets reserved keywords that cannot be used in friendly URLs.
You can reset the value of the `layout.friendly.url.keywords` property in the
properties file `portal-ext.properties`.

Mail configuration

In general, there are three parts involved in configuring a mail system integrated
with the portal:

1. Installing the mail systems.
2. Configuring the portal to read and to send e-mails.
3. Integrating the portal and the mail system for the creation of new accounts.

Usually, installing mail systems involves installing an SMTP server and an
IMAP server. This is not related to the portal, so for that, you should check the
documentation provided with the mail server software.

The portlet Mail allows us to visualize all our e-mails from several e-mail accounts.
It can be used to integrate the portal and the mail system for the creation of
new accounts.

This section will introduce you to the way to configure the portal in order to
read and send e-mails. Normally, there are two options: by JNDI name `mail/`
`MailSession` and by `Java mail`.

Mail session

Liferay 6.1 looks for the default configuration for the mail server and tries to communicate with the server and send mail to the user. It always looks for it in the same install system where Liferay is installed. Now let's change the setting for the mail session in Liferay, and set the JNDI name to look up the Java mail session. In order to enable the JNDI name, you need to add the following line at the end of `portal-ext.properties` first:

```
mail.session.jndi.name=mail/MailSession
```

If no name is set, then the portal will attempt to create the Java Mail session based on the properties prefixed with `mail.session`.

Then you need to set the **Global JNDI** Lookup. This process differs from one application server to another. For Tomcat, add the following lines after the line `<Context path="" crossContext="true">` in `$TOMCAT_AS_DIR/conf/Catalina/localhost/ROOT.xml` (or `domain.xml` for GlassFish):

```
<Resource name="mail/MailSession"
auth="Container"
type="javax.mail.Session"
mail.imap.host="imap.gmail.com"
mail.imap.port="993"
mail.pop.host="pop.gmail.com"
mail.store.protocol="imap"
mail.transport.protocol="smtp"
mail.smtp.host="smtp.gmail.com"
mail.smtp.port="465"
mail.smtp.auth="true"
mail.smtp.starttls.enable="true"
mail.smtp.user="${username}"
password="${password}"
mail.smtp.socketFactory. class="javax.net.ssl.SSLSocketFactory"/>
```

Note that the preceding code is a sample code that uses Gmail as an example. You need to replace the mail servers (IMAP, SMTP, and POP), domain names, port numbers, and user accounts.

Java-mail

The portal has unified the configuration of Java-mail in a properties file so that it's the same for all application servers, that is, *Geronimo, JOnAS, Resin, Jetty, GlassFish, JBoss, Tomcat,* and so on. Add the following lines at the end of `portal-ext.properties`:

```
mail.session.mail.pop3.host=pop.gmail.com
mail.session.mail.pop3.password=
mail.session.mail.pop3.port=110
mail.session.mail.pop3.user=
mail.session.mail.imap.host=imap.gmail.com
mail.session.mail.imap.port=993
mail.session.mail.store.protocol=imap
mail.session.mail.transport.protocol=smtp
mail.session.mail.smtp.host=smtp.gmail.com
mail.session.mail.smtp.password=${password}
mail.session.mail.smtp.user=${username}
   mail.session.mail.smtp.port=465
   mail.session.mail.smtp.auth=true
mail.session.mail.smtp.starttls.enable=true mail.session.mail.
   smtp.socketFactory.class= javax.net.ssl.SSLSocketFactory
```

The previous code sets the properties used to create the Java mail session. The property prefix `mail.session.` will be removed before it is used to create the session object. These properties will only be read if the `mail.session.jndi.name` property isn't set.

By default, the portal has Java Mail specified in `portal.properties` in this way:

```
mail.session.mail.pop3.host=localhost
mail.session.mail.pop3.password=
mail.session.mail.pop3.port=110
mail.session.mail.pop3.user=
mail.session.mail.smtp.auth=false
mail.session.mail.smtp.host=localhost
mail.session.mail.smtp.password=
mail.session.mail.smtp.port=25
mail.session.mail.smtp.user=
mail.session.mail.store.protocol=pop3
mail.session.mail.transport.protocol=smtp
```

According to the properties in the previous code, the same features are provided in the Web UI of the **Control Panel**.

You could use the Web UI by going to **Control Panel** | **Configuration** | **Server Administration** | **Mail**, and also by configuring the mail server settings such as POP and SMTP. Fortunately, the Web UI provides us with the ability to set up **Advanced Properties**, where you would be able to manually specify additional Java-mail properties to override the preceding configuration. Therefore, you could configure the same main configuration through the Web UI, in a way similar to the mail configuration that you performed earlier in `portal-ext.properties`.

Mail hook

Besides the previously discussed settings, you could override the following properties in `portal-ext.properties`:

```
mail.mx.update=true
mail.audit.trail=
    mail.hook.impl=com.liferay.mail.util.DummyHook
```

The preceding code sets the `mail.mx.update` to `true` property.

You could set it to `false` if the administrator is not allowed to change the mail domain via **Server** | **Server Administration** | **Mail** or via **Portal** | **Settings** | **General** in the **Control Panel**. Through the property `mail.audit.trail`, you could enter a list of comma-delimited e-mail addresses that will receive a BCC of every e-mail sent through the mail server.

Moreover, using this property, you could set the name of a class that implements `com.liferay.mail.util.Hook` such as `CyrusHook`, `DummyHook`, `FuseMailHook`, `GoogleHook`, `SendmailHook`, and `ShellHook`.

> By using a hook, you can change the existing code for the service layer or change the portlet properties and even change the look and feel of some existing application. It is something like hooking the code with your changes.

Note that the mail server will use this class to ensure that the mail and portal servers are synchronized with user information. The portal will know how to add, update, or delete users from the mail server only through this hook.

Additionally, you would be able to configure the following properties in `portal-ext.properties`:

```
google.apps.username=
google.apps.password=
```

As shown in the preceding code, you will be able to set the default username and password for Google Apps integration. The domain used by Google Apps is retrieved from the portal's mail domain. Note that Google Apps integration isn't used unless the property `mail.hook.impl` is set with the value `com.liferay.mail.util.GoogleHook`.

Bringing pages together in action

Let's place some portlets on the page and perform some action on each.

Adding comments on a page

The Page Comments portlet (portlet ID `107`) allows users to easily add comments to a page. By using this portlet, you can easily add, edit, or delete comments. Let's do it as follows:

1. Add the **Page Comments** portlet to the **Home** page of the Palm Tree site where you want to add comments, if the portlet isn't there.

2. Click on the **Add Comment** link if you want to add comments.

3. Input your comments—click on the **Reply** button to save the comments or the Cancel button to cancel them.

4. You can edit comments by clicking on the **Edit** button first. Then update the comments. Click on the **Update** button to save the changes, or **Cancel** button to cancel the changes, as shown in the next screenshot.

5. You can delete page comments by clicking on the **Delete** button. A screen will appear asking you if you want to delete this. Click on the **OK** button to confirm deletion, or the **Cancel** button to cancel deletion.

6. Or you can go to the top of the **Page Comments** portlet by clicking on the **Top** button, if there are a lot of page comments and you are not at the top of the list.

7. The **Page Comments** portlet is scoped into the current page of that particular site. As the **Page Comments** portlet isn't *instanceable*, one page can have only one **Page Comments** portlet.

Figure 2.21: Page Comments

This screenshot shows the **Page Comments** portlet.

> How do you add a UI tag to incorporate comments to a portlet? You can simply use a `<liferay-ui: discussion>` taglib, which allows users to discuss any type of content or pages in any portlet.

Rating a page

The Page Ratings portlet (portlet ID `108`) allows users to rate a page with 1 to 5 stars. You can add the Page Ratings portlet to a page to receive page ratings.

The Page Ratings portlet can be placed in any portal page to allow users to rate the contents available on that page as a whole. It can be used in a user profile page too, as a way to allow the end users to rate the user. As shown in the following screenshot, the Page Ratings portlet uses Ajax-based ratings that avoid a full-page reload — the rating belongs to an authenticated user and it doesn't allow the same user to rate a page more than once. However, the rating can be changed at any time, and it has a nice appearance based on graphical stars.

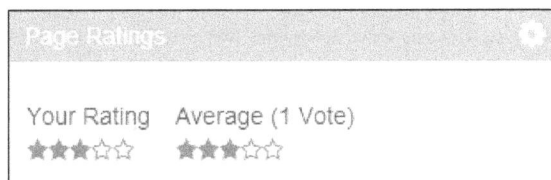

Figure 2.22: Page Rating

The preceding screenshot shows the Page Rating portlet.

Similar to the Page Comments portlet, the Page Ratings portlet is scoped into the current page. The Page Ratings portlet isn't *instanceable*; one page can have only one Page Ratings portlet.

> How can I add a UI tag to incorporate ratings into a portlet? You can simply use a `<liferay-ui: ratings>` UI taglib that allows users to rate any type of content or pages in any portlet.

Flagging content on a page

The Page Flags portlet (portlet ID 142) can be placed in any portal page to allow the users to flag content in the current page as inappropriate. It will enable a user to flag some content as inappropriate for a reason and warn the administrator about it. As shown in the next screenshot, the flags are Ajax-based that avoid a full-page reloading; it will send an e-mail to the administrators so that they can take appropriate action.

The portlet Page Flags normally appears as a small icon of a red flag close to the content (for example, blogs and message boards), which will enable users to flag some content as inappropriate.

There are several properties in `portal.properties` that can be overridden in `portal-ext.properties`:

```
flags.reasons=sexual-content,violent-or-repulsive-content,hateful-
   or-abusive-content,harmful-dangerous-acts,spam,infringes-my-
   rights
flags.email.from.name=Joe Bloggs
flags.email.from.address=test@liferay.com
flags.guest.users.enabled=false
```

As shown in the previous code, you can enter a list of questions used for flag reasons, override e-mail notification settings, and set `flags.guest.users.enabled` to `true` in order to enable guest users to flag content.

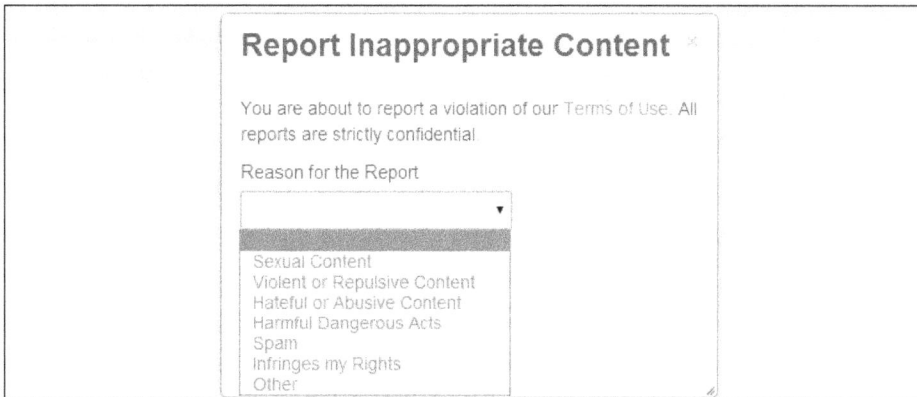

Report Inappropriate Content

You are about to report a violation of our Terms of Use. All reports are strictly confidential.

Reason for the Report

Sexual Content
Violent or Repulsive Content
Hateful or Abusive Content
Harmful Dangerous Acts
Spam
Infringes my Rights
Other

Figure 2.23: Page Flag

The preceding screenshot shows the **Page Flag** portlet.

> Programmatically, you can use a `<liferay-ui:flags>` UI taglib that allows you to flag any type of content or page in any portlet. How does it work? You can refer to the `$PORTAL_ROOT_HOME/html/portlet/flags/edit_entry.jsp` JSP file.

Sharing portlets within a portal page

Within the portal, especially the Sharing portlet with the portlet ID `133`, you can share as many portlets as you want. All portlets will have the **Sharing** tab at **Gear** (icon) | **Configuration**. You can share any portlet (for example, **Sign In**) with any website such as **Facebook**, **Google Gadget**, **Netvibes**, and **Friends**.

It's possible to use any portlet in any website, including these built-in scripts with static HTML pages. For example, to share the **Site Map** with any website, just copy the following code, paste it into your web page and this application will show up:

```
<script src=" http://www.bookpub.com:8080/html/js/
   liferay/widget.js" type="text/javascript"></script>
<script type="text/javascript">
   Liferay.Widget({ url: http://www.bookpub.com:8080/widget/
     web/palm-tree/home/-/85_INSTANCE_K76kRysf5LoG' });
</script>
```

> **Downloading the example code**
>
> You can download the example code files for all Packt books you have purchased from your account at `http://www.packtpub.com`. If you purchased this book elsewhere, you can visit `http://www.packtpub.com/support` and register to have the files e-mailed directly to you.

The preceding code uses a **Widget** to display the **Site Map** portlet of the **Home** page.

By the way, if you select the checkbox **Allow users to add Site Map to any website**, you will see an icon plus a link **Add to any Website** under **Configuration**.

It's also possible to use any portlet as a Facebook application. The Facebook integration is implemented through an IFrame (It is also possible to use FBML.). Each portlet in the portal is automatically exposable to Facebook. Simply go to **Gear** (icon) | **Configuration** | **Sharing** | **Facebook**, first set your **Facebook API key** (for example, `136be69d497ed2688fc853a651c81f17`) and **Canvas Page URL** (for example, `test`). Then copy the following **callback URL** and specify it in Facebook. This application will be exposed to Facebook via an IFrame:

```
http://www.bookpub.com:8080/widget/web/guest/home/-/85
```

Similarly, you can use the following **Google Gadget** URL to create a Google Gadget:

```
http://www.bookpub.com:8080/google_gadget/web/guest/home/-/85
```

Note that the preceding URLs are generated automatically in the portal. You have to use the real URLs of servers in order to make them work properly. In case the URL `http://www.bookpub.com:8080` does not work, try out with `http://localhost:8080`.

How does it work? You can refer to the JavaScript details in `$PORTAL_ROOT_HOME/html/js/liferay/portlet_sharing.js`.

Configuring Control Panel

As mentioned earlier, we have managed a logged-in user's private pages (My Dashboard) and public pages (My Profile) through **Admin | Site Administration | Page**. Now, let's go further and see how to manage a logged-in user's public pages.

Generally speaking, the **Control Panel** is a feature of the portal that allows us to modify portal settings and controls. As shown in the next screenshot, **Control Panel** provides a centralized administration for all content, users, organizations, site, roles, server resources, and more.

Liferay 6.2 control panel has been divided into four main sections **Users**, **Sites**, **Apps**, and **Configuration**.

Liferay 6.2 Control Panel

The **Control Panel** is a unified way to access all portal administration tools within the portal. It provides access to four categories: **Users**, **Sites**, **Apps**, and **Configuration**, as shown in the next screenshot.

- **Users**: The portal administrator can administrate all portlets related to users, organizations, roles, users groups as well as password policies.

- **Sites**: The portal administrator has access to manage sites as well as the tools to build the sites (site templates and page templates). Admin can manage any site (as long as the user has the permission access) simply by clicking on the site name. Through the Control panel, managing a site becomes very user friendly.

- **Apps**: Apps is one place for all types of plugin. New trends gave Liferay a term *Apps*, which will have all sorts of extensions to a product. In Liferay 6.1 Marketplace was being used. The admin could install the app from the Marketplace. Here, a store link provides the same feature.

- **Configuration**: The portal administrator can handle the entire portal level configuration. All kinds of configuration at server level such as handling memory uses, cache, log levels, plugins, and so on are also done here.

Once inside the **Control Panel**, the logged-in user will only be able to see the control section at the top of the page, for which he/she has permissions. A regular user with no administration permissions will not be able to see the control panel link in the dock bar.

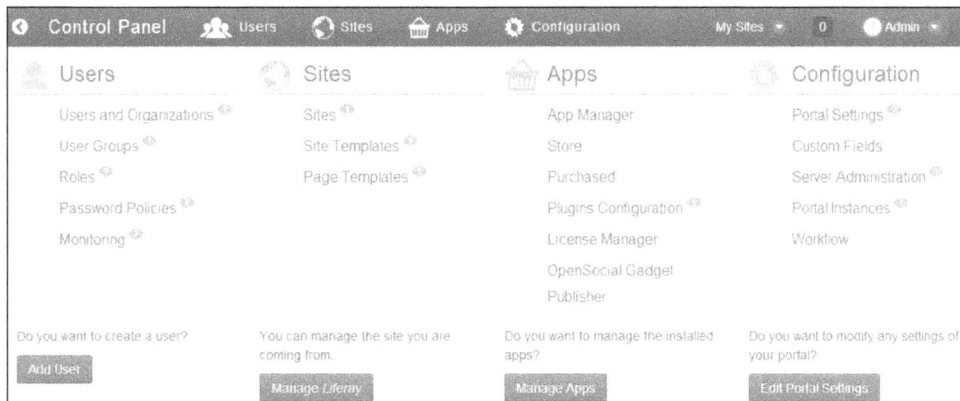

Figure 2.24: Liferay 6.2 Control Panel has different categories for different purposes

We will take a more detailed look at working with different controls and applications inside the control panel in the upcoming chapters.

> Liferay 6.1 came with a new concept of "Marketplace". Marketplace is a small hub of collected applications which the user can install anytime.
>
> Marketplace leverages the entire Liferay ecosystem to release and share apps with the users, through a user-friendly environment and a one-stop site. We will discuss this in detail in *Chapter 10, Marketplace, Social Office, and Audience Targeting*.

My Account

Finally, the user section in the dock bar shows the user's name and provides links to the user's **My Profile** (user's publicly-accessible pages), **My Dashboard** (user's private pages), **My Account** settings, and a **Sign out** link.

As an administrator, you are now running the portal and you see a set of portlets in the default page. It is ready for you to update your profile anytime, to update the screen name, e-mail address, first name, last name, icon, language, display settings, and so on. A user can click on **My Account** right under the user name in the dock bar. The **My Account** popup has links to **Account Settings**, **My Pages**, **My Workflow Tasks**, and **My Submissions**. We will look at each of them in detail in later chapters.

In short, the **My Account** link is useful for a logged-in user in the enterprise Palm Tree Publications to update their profile.

> In Liferay 6.2, the **My Account** link has moved from the **Control Panel** to the dock bar.

Now, in Liferay 6.2, **My Account** provides an easy way to handle a user's information and the related/associated workflow at one place.

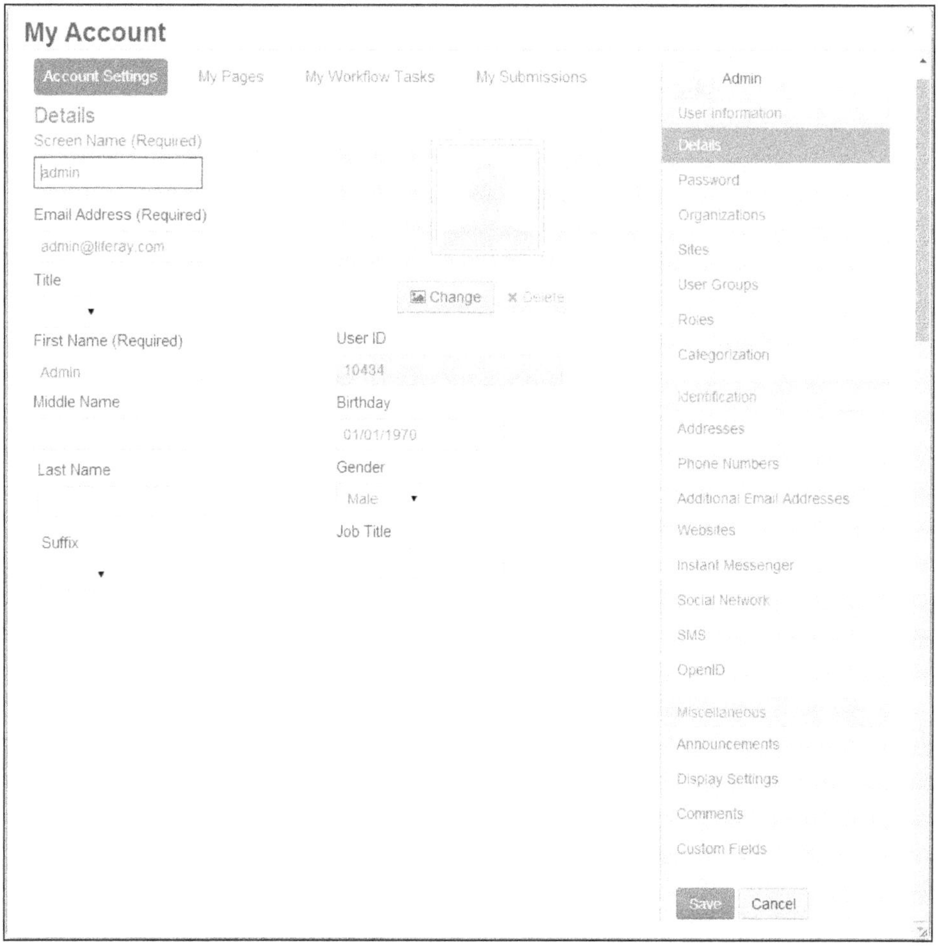

Figure 2.25: A user's My Account popup with many new configuration settings

My Profile

My Profile is especially a public page, which can be viewed by different users in the portal. Here, the logged-in users have the ability to update their public pages by placing the portlets. The users can also change the look and feel of the page by clicking on **My Account | My Pages**.

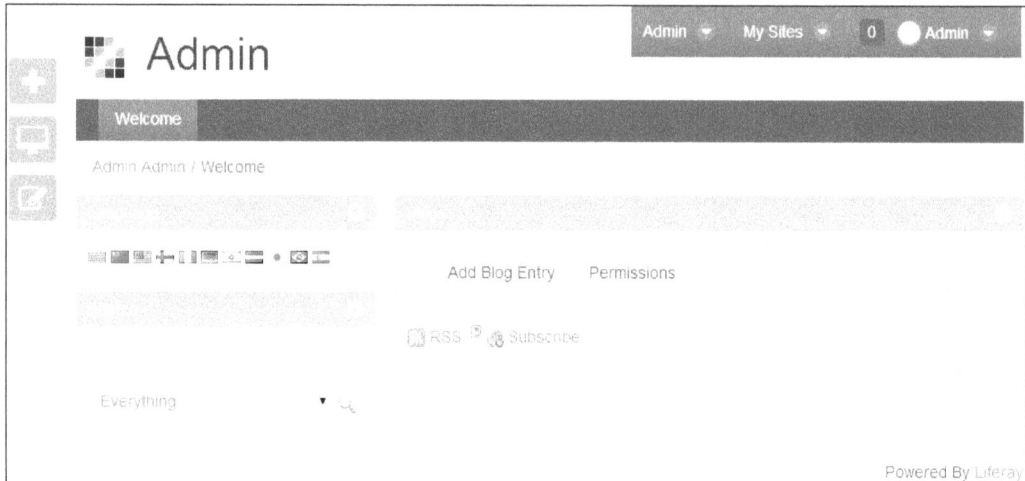

Figure 2.26: A user's public page as My Page

My Dashboard

My Dashboard is essentially the private page of the logged-in user, which can be viewed only by the users logged into the portal. Here, the logged-in users have the ability to update their dashboard pages by placing the portlets. The users can also change the look and feel of the page by clicking on **My Account | My Pages** and then selecting the **My Dashboard** tab.

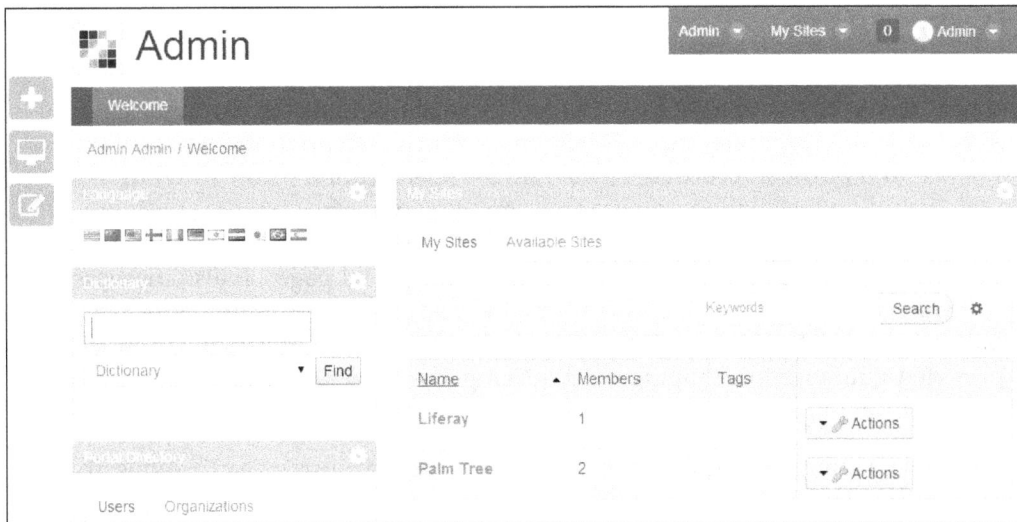

Figure 2.27: A user's private page as My Dashboard

Configuration and settings

The **Control Panel** settings and configuration can be changed through the `portal-ext.properties` file. Generally, the layout name that is named.

The properties `control.panel.layout.name` and `control.panel.layout.friendly.url` are specified by default in `portal.properties` as follows:

```
control.panel.layout.name=Control Panel
control.panel.layout.friendly.url=/manage
```

The preceding code sets the name of the layout as **Control Panel** and it sets the friendly URL of the layout as `/manage`. Of course, you can override these properties in `portal-ext.properties`.

The **Control Panel** comes with a default theme, `controlpanel`, as shown in `portal.properties`.

```
control.panel.layout.regular.theme.id=controlpanel
```

The preceding code sets the theme of the layout to **Control Panel**. It's possible to configure it to use any custom theme. To that end, the property `control.panel.layout.regular.theme.id` can be overridden in `portal-ext.properties`.

Summary

This chapter discussed how to implement a portal page with portlets. It also showed how to customize the look and feel of pages and portlets through themes and the look and feel preferences. It helped us to understand the portal, portlet container, and portlets according to the JSR-286 specification — how to set up the portal, including installation options and deployment matrix, how to configure the home page and all the other pages of the intranet website. Then it introduced us to building basic pages, as well as setting up the portal pages. It also discussed how to navigate the structure of the intranet via portlets, for example, **Site Map**, **Breadcrumb**, and **Navigation**. It also showed us how to configure the portal. Finally, it provided guidance for bringing the pages together in action, sharing any portlet within a portal page, and for customizing the **Control Panel**.

In the next chapter, we're going to bring in users, user groups, organizations, roles, and permissions.

3
Bringing in Users

In the previous chapter, we discussed in detail the pages of the Portal-Group-Page-Content pattern. In this chapter, we're going to open the book group and take a deeper look into it. The portal provides a powerful yet highly configurable, full-security model to control resources, permissions, roles, users, organizations, locations, sites, and user groups. This full security model incorporates fine-grained permissions and role-based access control to give administrators full control over access and privileges to portlets, layouts, groups, and content within the portal. With role-based access control, users can assign permissions to other users, sites, organizations, and user groups via roles. Moreover, users can control permissions scoped up to the portal or down to the page or the content.

This chapter begins with enterprises, departments, and locations, the hierarchy, and the role-based access control model. Then, it proceeds to how to bring in users, organizations, locations, user groups, and roles together. Furthermore, it will discuss all the ways to assign users to organizations, sites, user groups, and roles. In addition, it introduces authentications related to managed accounts, **Lightweight Directory Access Protocol (LDAP)**, **Single Sign-on (SSO)**, Central Authentication Service (CAS), **OpenID**, **OpenSSO**, and **SiteMinder**. Finally, it gives details about how to manage permissions, use permission algorithms, and assign permissions to different resources via roles.

In this chapter, you will learn the following things:

- Building a hierarchy of enterprises, departments, and locations
- Setting up organizations and locations
- Building user groups
- Bringing in users
- Establishing authentication
- Managing roles
- Assembling authorization

Enterprise, departments, and locations

The enterprise Palm Tree Publications has its global headquarters in the U.S. with several departments (such as editorial, engineering, marketing, website, and so on). Each department has staff in the United States, Germany, and India. As shown in following figure, the enterprise, departments, and locations form a hierarchy. In this chapter, we will build this hierarchy with a model called **role-based access control (RBAC)**.

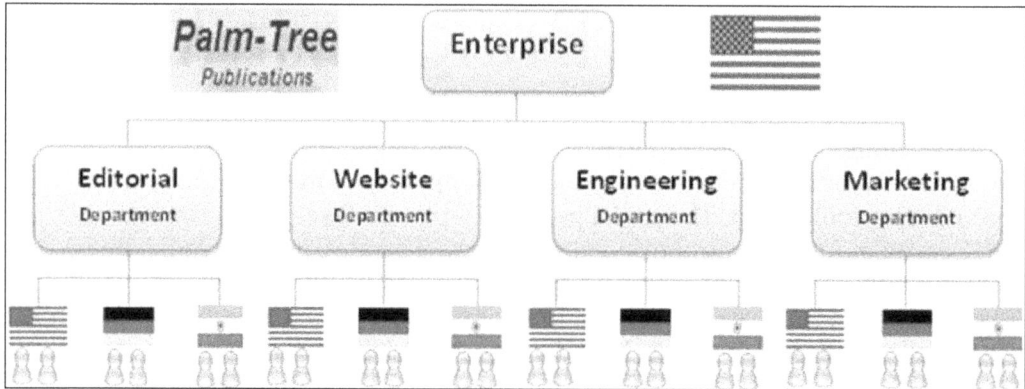

Figure 3.1: The Palm Tree enterprise structure

Before starting, let's assume that we have a set of users in the enterprise Palm Tree Publications. We will plan to bring the following users into the portal; briefly, a user is an individual who performs tasks using the portal:

Full name	Screen name	E-mail	Organization	Location
Palm Trees	bookpubadmin	admin@bookpub.com	Enterprise	US
David Berger	david	david@bookpub.com	Editorial	US
Lotti Stein	lotti	lotti@bookpub.com	Editorial	US
Rolf Hess	rolf	rolf@bookpub.com	Editorial	
Julia Maurer	julia	julia@bookpub.com	Editorial	Germany
Sachin Agarwal	Sachin	sachin@bookpub.com	Editorial	India
James Masse	james	james@bookpub.com	Website	US
John Stucki	john	john@boobpub.com	Website	Germany
Sunil Goyal	Sunil	sunil@bookpub.com	Website	India
Martin Gall	martin	martin@bookpub.com	Editorial	Germany

Let's suppose that as an administrator of the enterprise Palm Tree Publications, you are planning to create a set of users, as listed in the preceding table, and a set of organizations and locations to represent the preceding hierarchy. Moreover, you are planning to set up authentication and authorization, and you are also planning to do more with user administration and organization administration as well.

Role-based access control

Traditional membership security models address two basic criteria: *authentication* (who has access) and *authorization* (what they can do):

- **Authentication** is a process of determining whether someone or something is, in fact, who or what it is declared to be

- **Authorization** is a process of finding out whether the person, once identified, is permitted to have access to a resource

The portal extends the preceding security model using terminologies: resources, users, organizations, locations, user groups, sites, roles, permissions, and so on. The portal provides a role-based, fine-grained permission security model — a full access control security model. At the same time, it also provides a set of administrative tools (which we will discuss later), which can be used to configure and control membership.

The remainder of this section will explore these concepts and relationships among these terminologies, as shown in the following figure. Without a doubt, it will be useful to provide the big picture on how to bring in users. For example, as a user in the engineering department, you may plan to develop a number of portlets to satisfy the enterprise's, Palm Tree Publications, current requirements or even plan for future requirements. The following figure gives a view of the big picture of the security model.

This diagram illustrates the relationship mapping between **Organization**, **Site**, **Users**, and **Role** in Liferay:

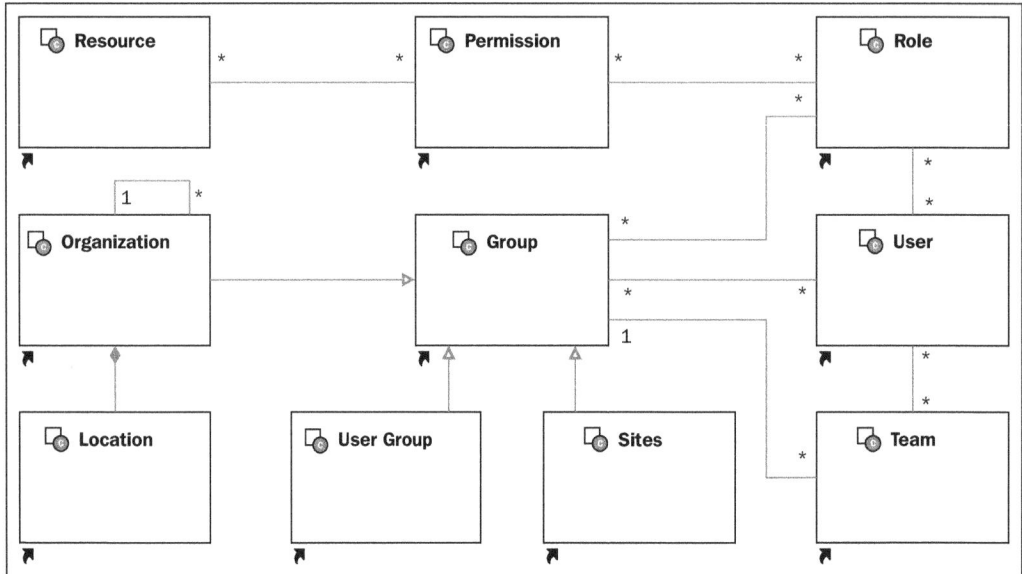

Figure 3.2: The Liferay organization structure with User, Sites, Role, and Permission

Role and permission

As shown in the preceding figure, **Resource** is a base object. It can be a portlet (for example, Message Boards, Calendar, Document Library, and so on), an entity (for example, Message Board Topics, Calendar Event, the Documents and Media library folder, and so on), or a file (for example, documents, images, applications, and so on). Resources are scoped into portals, groups, pages, and content—model resources and application (or portlet) types.

A **permission** is an action on a resource. Portal-level permissions can be assigned to the portal (for example, users, user groups, organizations, and sites) through roles. Organization-level permissions can be assigned to organizations. Site-level permissions can be assigned to sites. Page-level permissions can be assigned to page layouts. Model permissions can be assigned to model resources (for example, blogs entries, web content, and so on). Portlet permission can be assigned to portlets (for example, view, configuration, and so on).

A **role** is a collection of permissions. Roles can be assigned to users, sites, organizations or organizations based on location. If a role is assigned to a site, organization, or location, all users who are members of that entity receive permissions of the role.

User

A **user** is an individual who performs tasks using the portal. Depending on the permissions that have been assigned via roles, the user either has the permission or doesn't have the permission to perform certain tasks.

Additionally, each user can have public pages and private pages. More interestingly, a user's private pages and public pages do have the ability to use page templates that can be used to customize a set of pages. All the Liferay Portal pages belong to group called "site".

Organization and location

An **organization** represents the enterprise-department-location hierarchical structure, such as those of organizations, schools, universities, nonprofit organizations, and government organizations. Organizations can contain other organizations as suborganizations in a hierarchy to unlimited levels. In detail, a suborganization acting as a child organization of a top-level organization can also represent departments of a parent corporation/organization. Moreover, users can be assigned to one or many organizations. Organizations and suborganizations can all reside in a single hierarchy or cut across different hierarchies. For example, a bank organization wants to have an employee portal with respect to different branches, where each branch represents a suborganization.

A **location** is a special organization, with one and only one parent organization associated and with no child organization associated. In simple words, a location organization is based on the location, for example, India, Germany, and so on. Organizations can have any number of locations and suborganizations. Both roles and users can be assigned to organizations (locations or suborganizations).

> Note that the organization administrator's rights apply to both their organization and the suborganization.
>
> By default, a member of a suborganization is a member of the parent organizations. We can customize this setting in the `portal-ext.properties` configuration file.
>
> By default, locations and suborganizations inherit permissions from their parent organization via roles.

User groups and sites

Site is a special group with a flat structure. It can hold a number of users who share common interests. Thus, we can say that a site is a collection of users who have a common interest. Both roles and users can be assigned to a site.

Actually, sites are special groups that have a set of users or a set of user groups. Thus, a site can have a set of users associated. Normally, a site is used to represent a set of users who share common interests. An organization can be associated and unassociated to an existing site whenever required for business needs.

All users of the organization will become members of the site automatically. This means that they will have access to the private pages of the site and will be able to do any action that has been configured to be doable only by members.

How is a site different from an organization?

There is very thin line between both. Sites are mainly about pages and organizations are about user management. Sites can have members and can be hierarchical too. Sites can be open, restricted, or private based on the privacy needs of the site, whereas organizations don't have such features. They are always considered to be centrally maintained. Most importantly, both organizations and sites will have their own private pages and public pages. They also have the ability to apply site templates to easily customize websites.

Last but not least, **user group** is a special group with no context, which may hold a number of users. In other words, users can be gathered into user groups. Users can be assigned to user groups.

In addition, each user group can have public pages and private pages. Thus users in a user group can share private pages and public pages. More interestingly, a user group's private pages and public pages do have the ability to apply page templates in order to quickly customize a set of pages. All the Liferay Portal pages belong to group called "site".

Organizations

As mentioned earlier, we can use organizations to represent the enterprise Palm Tree Publications and its department's hierarchy. In the preceding chapter, we created the organization Palm Tree under the topic "*Building the Palm Tree Publications site*", which we will be treating as the top-level organization. Palm Tree will represent the whole company and will have different departments under it as a set of suborganizations. Now we can create an organization hierarchy under "Palm Tree".

Therefore, the enterprise can be represented as a regular organization of the type **Regular Organization**.

On the right-hand side, you can see the **Organization Site** link, where you can select the checkbox to create the site for the organization. The name and description of the site will be automatically synced with those of the organization (to save the administrator time).

As you can see, there is a toolbar used for top-level navigation. This toolbar is located at the top of the New Organizations title, providing quick access to the most used functions when working with organizations:

- **Add**: This has a dropdown with **User**, **Regular Organization**, and **Location**.
- **Export Users**: By this action, you can export all the users in the **CVS format**. And it will download to your local system.

So, after you save the organization successfully, the **Organization Details** page opens, with many more configurations. Settings are of the type **Organization Information**, **Identification**, and **Miscellaneous**.

The Palm Tree organization settings details provide different headings for settings.

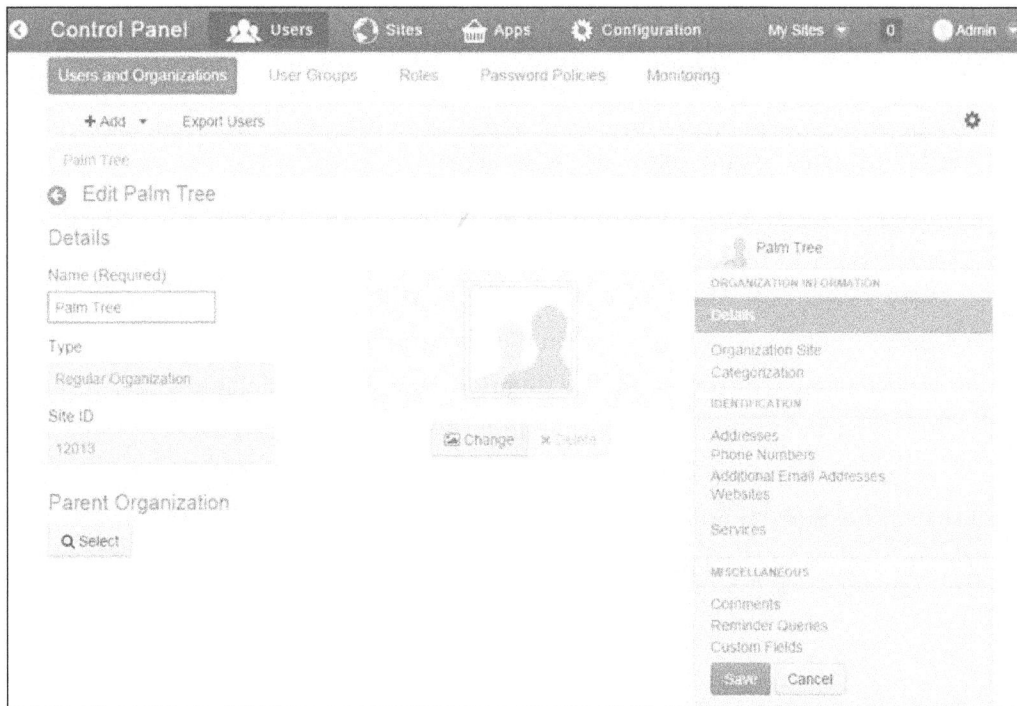

Figure 3.3: Palm Tree organization details

Let's see in brief details of the right-hand side controls with different headings:

- **Organization Information**: This tells us about the details of the organization, such as name, type, site IS, parent organization (if it exists), organization site, and finally categorization

- **Identification**: This helps administrators to save all the details related to the organization, such as organization addresses, phone numbers, additional email addresses, websites, and services

- **Miscellaneous**: This contains comments for the organization, reminder queries, and custom fields

We will discuss this in detail in the *Editing an organization* section.

So, you have created a top-level organization. Now, we need to create organizations for the main departments in the enterprise.

Managing organizations

Organizations can contain other organizations as suborganizations. This is useful in large companies, where each department might almost be a separate company, with little interaction among them.

Adding child organizations

Let's create two departments within the "Palm Tree" Enterprise, **Editorial**, and **Marketing** departments by following these steps:

1. Click on **Users and Organizations** under the Users category.
2. Click on **Add button** and select the **Regular Organizations** link in the same way you did for **Adding a top-level Organization**.
3. Enter `Editorial Department` in the **Name** field.
4. Select a value for type—use the **Regular Organization** default value:
   1. Click on the select button under **Parent Organization**.
   2. A pop-up dialog box will appear; select the parent organization, say **Palm Tree**.
5. Click on the **Save** button.

Adding a child organization in Liferay is as simple as this:

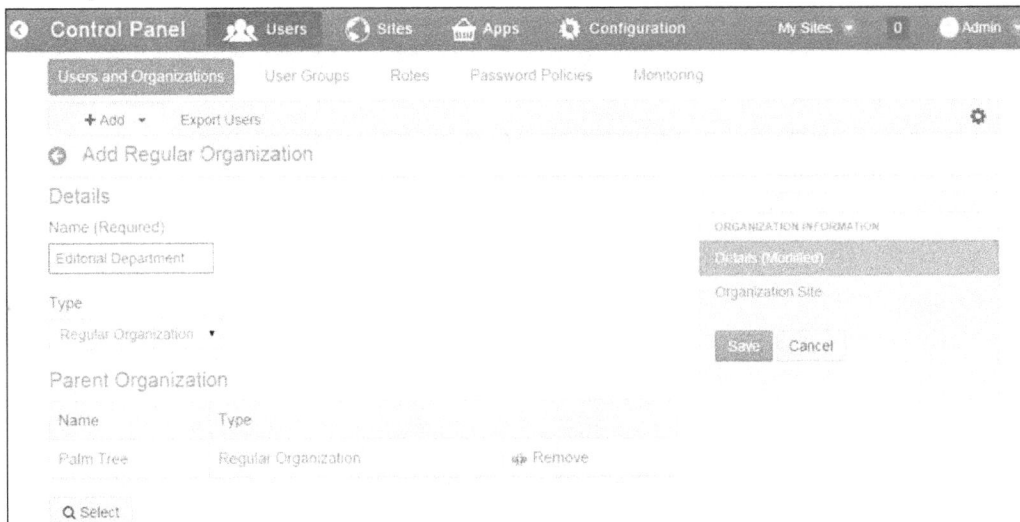

Figure 3.4: Adding a child organization

You can add as many as child organizations under a parent organization as you want. Optionally, you can add the child organization **Marketing Department** from the parent organization Palm Tree by following these steps:

1. Click on **Users and Organizations** under the **Users** category of **Control Panel**.

2. Locate the desired parent organization from the top level organization list, for example, **Palm Tree**.

3. Click on the **Add Regular Organization** icon from **Actions** to the right-hand side of the organization.

4. Enter the enterprise information in the **Name** input field, say `Marketing Department`.

5. Leave **Regular Organization** as the default value of **Type**.

6. Leave **Palm Tree** as the default value of **Parent Organization**.

7. Click on the **Save** button to save the inputs, or click on the **Cancel** button to discard the inputs.

Of course, you can create other departments in most organizations similarly. After adding child organizations, for example, **Engineering Department** and **Website Department**, you can view organizations.

Creating a site with private and public pages

In Liferay, you can create a site while creating **Organization**. Let's create a site for Palm Tree that will have public pages (as a community site) and private pages (as an intranet site):

1. Upon clicking on the **Organization Site** link, a checkbox with Create Site will appear.

2. Check in to the Create Site checkbox.

3. It will ask you for the public and private pages for the sites, which will have Site Templates for selection, that is, **Community site** and **Intranet site**.

4. Now you can select the site template with the community site and intranet site for public pages and private pages respectively.

5. Save the changes.

It will create Site with the same name as that of an organization. The name and description of the Site will be automatically synced with those of the organization (to save the administrator time). You can manage the site pages by clicking on **Manage Site** in **Action** on the right-hand side of the organization. All the Liferay Portal pages belong to this group called "site".

The following screenshot shows how to create an organization's public and private pages:

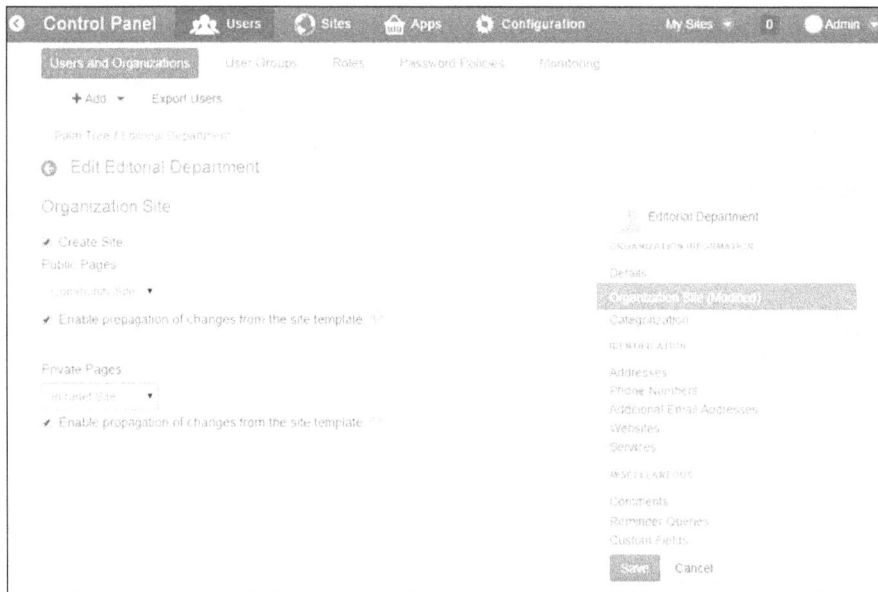

Figure 3.5: Organization Site creation

Viewing organizations

As compared to adding child organizations, viewing organizations is much simpler. This is explained as follows:

1. Click on **Users and Organizations** under the **Users** category of **Control Panel**. It displays sets of top-level organizations and users without an organization. Now, in the top level organization, you will be able to see the parent organization with the field's name and type of organization.

2. Locate an organization, for example, Palm Tree, which you want to view first, and then click on the organization from the link, for example, Palm Tree.

3. You will be redirected to the organization details page, where you can see the set of child organizations.

Searching organizations

You can find organizations using either a basic search or an advanced search. To search for organizations, click on **Users and Organizations**, and then input search criteria for a basic search.

For an advanced search, you need to click on the **All Organizations** tab, and beside the search text button, you will find the **gear** icon for advanced search. Now, click on the icon, input the organization's information in the input fields (for example, name, street, city, zip, country, and region), select the Type value **Regular Organization** for advanced search, and click on the **Search** button. A list of organizations matching the search criteria appears at the bottom of the organization screen.

A basic search will search both organizations and locations. Using the advanced search, you can search organizations with the Type value **Regular Organization**, and locations with the **Type** value **Location**, or both with the **Type** value **any**.

Similarly, you can do an advanced search for users by clicking on the **All Users** tab and filling the required fields for the search criteria, that is, First name, Middle **Name**, **Last name**, **Screen name**, **Email**, and **Status**. Using advanced search will help to find the actual users from all of the organization throughout the portal.

Editing an organization

After adding organizations, you are ready to manage them. For example, you want to update the organization's **Website department** information (for example, changing name, parent organization, and logo). Let's do it by following these steps:

1. Click on **Users and Organizations** and then locate the organization (for example, the Website department with the **Type** value **Regular Organization**, which you want to edit).

2. Click on the **Edit** icon from **Actions** to the right-hand side of the organization or click on any links of the organization, for example, the Website department.

3. Type the changes in the **Name** input field.

4. Remove the current parent organization through the **Remove** link, or select an organization as the parent organization through the **Select** link.

5. Click on the **Change** link and upload an image, for example, `Organization-logo.png`.

6. Click on the **Save** button to save the changes.

> Note that one organization can have one and only one parent organization. When you select an organization as the parent organization of an organization that already has a parent, the current parent organization will get overridden by the selected one. Of course, an organization should not select itself as its parent organization.

As you can see, the portal provides a menu on the right-hand side of the screen, which shows all sections of forms, thereby allowing faster navigation through them in a way that doesn't require a page reload. Forms for adding and editing organizations are different, which allows a fast and easy way to create organizations and a deeper personalization afterwards. Items in the menu are grouped into three sections: **Organization Information**, **Identification**, and **Miscellaneous**. By default, when creating an organization, only the organization's details are visible. When editing an organization, you would be able to see the rest of the enabled sections by following these steps:

- **Organization Information**:
    - **Organization Site**: You can create a site associated with your organization. Once you select the Organization Site link and select the **Create Site** checkbox, it will ask you the public and private pages for the sites, and it will create the Site with the same name as that of the organization. The name and description of Site will be automatically synced with those of the organization.

        ° **Categorization**: You can categorize your organization by adding tags. Each organization can have multiple tags.

- **Identification**:
  - ° **Address**: This holds the mail address information; each organization can have multiple addresses.
  - ° **Phone number**: This manages phone numbers; each organization can have multiple phone numbers.
  - ° **Additional Email Address**: This manages e-mail addresses; each organization can have multiple e-mail addresses.
  - ° **Organization websites**: This manages websites; each organization can have multiple websites, either intranets or public.
  - ° **Services**: This manages services; each organization can have multiple services.

- **Miscellaneous**:
  - ° **Comments**: This manages comments; each organization can have one comment box.
  - ° **Reminder Queries**: This manages reminder queries in different languages. An administrator can set a predefined reminder question for specific organizations for the users to retrieve their forgotten password.
  - ° **Custom Fields**: This manages values of custom attributes if custom attributes have been added to the current organization. The administrator can add additional fields to existed models/entries. Say, for example, **Palm Tree** needs additional entries for different suborganizations. Using custom fields, you can achieve it very easily.

[Note that no changes are applied until the **Save** button is clicked.   ]

Deleting an organization

For some reason, a department (for example, Website Department) does not exist anymore. You need to delete this organization in the portal. We will do it by following these steps:

1. Click on **Users and Organizations**.

2. Locate the organization that you want to delete (for example, **Website Department**).

3. Click on the **Delete** icon from **Actions** on the right-hand side of the organization, or select the checkbox on the left-hand side of the organization and press the **Delete** button.

4. A screen will appear asking whether you want to delete the selected organizations. Click on the **OK** button to confirm, or click on the **Cancel** button to cancel.

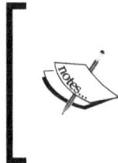

[
Note that you can't *delete an organization* that has *child organizations*, *locations*, or *users* associated with it. In order to delete this organization, you need to remove child organizations, locations, or users from this organization first, and only then will you be able to delete it.
]

Assigning users to an organization

Users can be assigned to an organization by following these steps:

1. Click on **Users and Organizations**.

2. Locate an organization (for example, **Editorial Department**).

3. Then, click on the **Assign Users** icon from **Actions** on the right-hand side of the organization.

4. Click on the **Available** tab to display a list of all available users in the portal. Search for the desired users using the search form (by either a basic search or an advanced search). Tick the checkboxes on the left-hand side of the desired users. If you would like to select all of the users on the current page, then check the checkbox next to the name column.

5. Click on the **Update Associations** button to assign users to an organization. Optionally, to confirm that desired users were successfully associated with the organization, click on the current tab.

Additionally, you can view users by clicking on the **View Users** icon from Actions on the right-hand side of the organization. Moreover, each organization that has the **Site** associated with it has its own public pages and private pages. You can manage these pages by clicking on the **Manage Site** icon from Actions on the right-hand side of the organization. Otherwise, you can assign user roles by clicking on the **Assign User Roles** icon from Actions on the right-hand side of the location.

Using organizations in an effective way

Organizations represent the enterprise and department hierarchy. Each organization has a set of basic properties, such as name, parent organization (not for top-level organizations), status, country, and so on. It can also have a set of optional properties, such as, e-mail addresses, mail addresses, websites, phone numbers, services, comments, custom fields, and so on.

An organization can represent a parent corporation. An example would be the enterprise Palm Tree Publications.

An organization that acts as a child organization of a top-level organization can also represent departments of a parent corporation. Examples would be Editorial Department, Marketing Department, and so on.

Logically, users can be members of more than one organization. For best practice, it is better to make a user belong to only one organization. So, make sure your organizations don't overlap. For example, if you have a department called Marketing Department and another department called Engineering Department, then the marketing manager can be in one department or the other, but not in both.

This might seem limiting, but there is an answer—Sites with user groups. A user can be a member of any number of user groups, and "managers" is a common user group. Now we can associate a user group with Sites. We'll see how to work with them later.

Location-based organizations

A company can have several locations, just as it has many departments. Palm Tree Publications has one location in California, United States, one in Berlin, Germany, and one in Mumbai, India. Let's go ahead and create them.

Adding a location for the enterprise

First of all, we need to add a location for the enterprise Palm Tree Publications, that is, the organization **Palm Tree US**. Let's do that now:

1. Click on **Users and Organizations**.
2. Then, click on the **Add** button and select the **Location** link.
3. Enter the enterprise information in the **Name** input field (for example, Palm Tree US), Select **Type** with the **Location** value, select a country from the **Country** menu (for example, United States), and a region from the **Region** menu (for example, California).

4. Click on the **Select** button to select **Parent Organization**. In the organization selection page, choose **Palm Tree Enterprise**.

5. Click on the **Save** button to save the inputs.

So we've added a location for a top-level organization. Now, we need to create locations for Editorial Department.

Let's create a location-based organization in Liferay for the parent organization Palm Tree. The following screenshot shows the addition of locations to organizations:

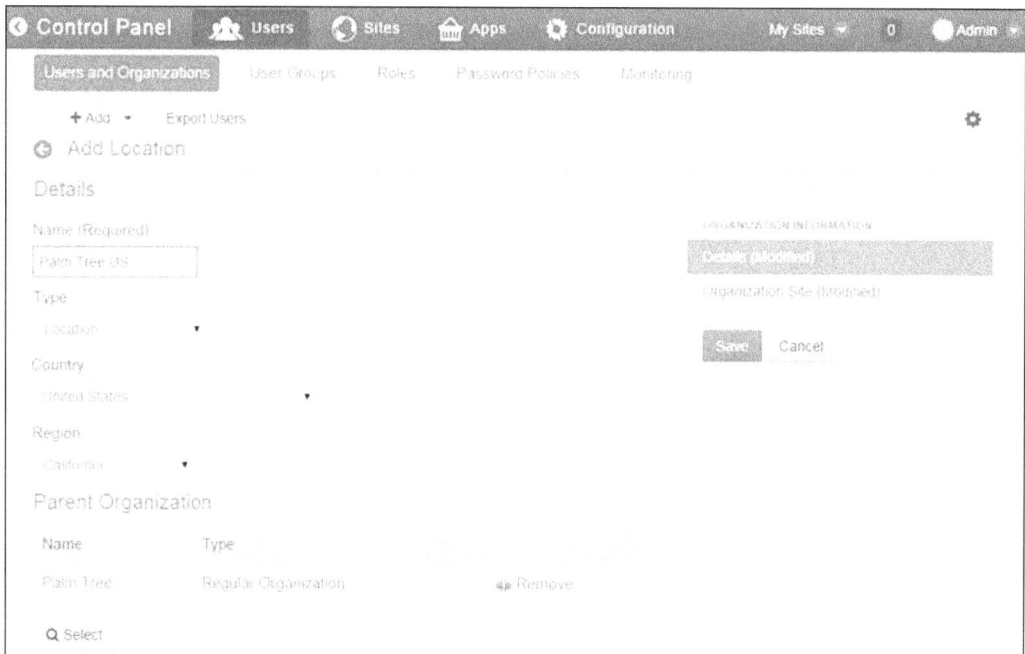

Figure 3.6: Adding Location organization

Generally speaking, a location is a special organization, which associates with a parent organization. Most importantly, locations can't have any child organizations associated with them. Locations can usually be distinguished by their geographic position. An organization can have any number of suborganizations and locations. Obviously, locations are the leaves of organizations.

Adding locations for suborganizations

Let's create a location called Editorial US for the "Editorial" department by following these steps:

1. Click on **Users and Organizations**. Then, click on the **Add** button and select the **Location** link.

2. Enter the enterprise information in the Name input field (for example, **Editorial US**, select **Type** with the value **Location**, select a country from the **Country** menu, for example, **United States** and a region from the **Region** menu, for example, **California**.

3. Click on the **Select** button to select a value for **Parent Organization**. In the organization selection page, choose the **Editorial Department**.

4. Click on the **Save** button to save the inputs.

Similarly, we can add another location called **Editorial Germany** for the **Editorial Department** or we can add it directly as follows:

1. Click on **Users and Organizations** and locate a parent organization.

2. Click on the **Add Location** icon from **Actions** on the right-hand side of the organization.

3. Enter enterprise information in the **Name** input field (**Editorial Germany**), Select **Type** with the value **Location**, select a country from the **Country** menu (Germany) and a region from the **Region** menu (Berlin).

4. Keep the default value of **Parent Organization**.

5. Click on the **Save** button to save the inputs.

You can create other locations for most organizations in the same way, after which, you can view them.

Creating a site with private and public pages

Just as with the Palm Tree organization, we will create a site for the Palm Tree US location organization, which will have public pages (as a community site) and private pages (as an intranet site):

1. Click on the **Organization Site** link; you will able to see a checkbox with create site. Enable the checkbox for **Create Site**.

2. It will ask you for the public pages and private pages for the sites, which will have **Site Templates** for selection, that is, the **Community site** and the **Intranet site**.

3. Now, you can select the site template with **Community site** and **Intranet site** for public pages and private pages, respectively.

4. Save the changes.

It will create the site with the same name as that of an organization. The name and description of the Site will be automatically synced with those of the organization (to save the administrator time). You can manage the site pages by clicking on **Manage Site** in **Action** on the right-hand side of the organization. All the Liferay Portal pages belong to the group called "site".

Note: **Site Templates** can be created and managed by the site administrator.

Viewing locations

Compared to adding locations, viewing them is much simpler. It is done by following these steps:

1. Click on **Users and Organizations** under the **Users** category of **Control Panel**. You will be able to see a list of top-level organizations and the list of Users.

2. Locate an organization in the top-level organization list, and select the organization you want to view first. See the following screenshot.

3. Now, if you want to view the specific organization, let's say Editorial department. You just need to select the organization link, that is, the organization name.

4. Then, you will be able to view all the suborganization of that particular organization.

5. In the following screenshot, you will see the location-based organization "**Palm Tree US**".

A list of suborganizations, users under the Palm Tree organization, and location-based organizations is given here too.

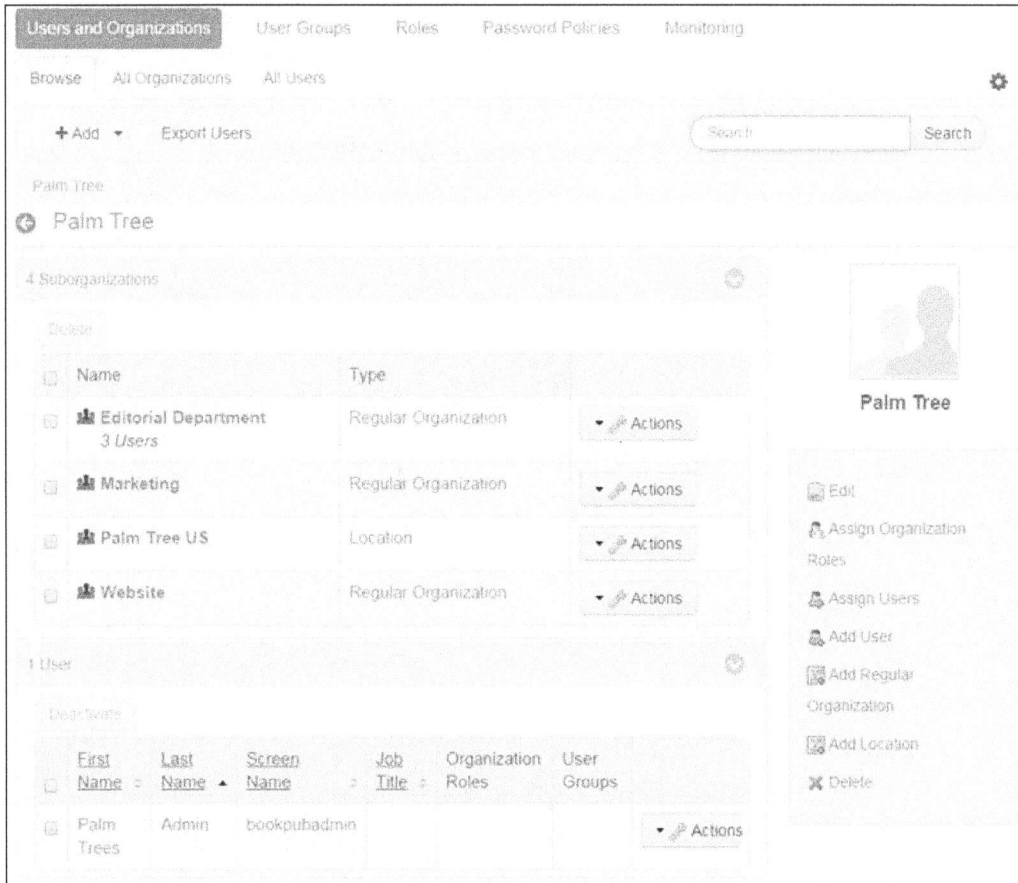

Figure 3.7: Viewing location-based organizations

Searching locations

Locations are searchable either by **advanced search** or by **basic search**. To search for locations, simply click on **Users and Organizations** under the **Users** category of **Control Panel** first, then input the organization information in the search input fields, and then click on the **Search** button. You will get the particular searched organization as a list below the search button.

Now for the advanced search, click on the **All Organizations** link. Once you click on this, you will get all the parent organizations, suborganizations, and organizations by location as a list. Now you can see the **gear** icon beside the **Search** button. Click on the **gear** icon and advance search criteria (see the following screenshot), select the **Type** value as **Location**, and click on the **Search** button. It will provide the searched list with organization type value as **Location**.

Here's an advanced search for a location-based organization list:

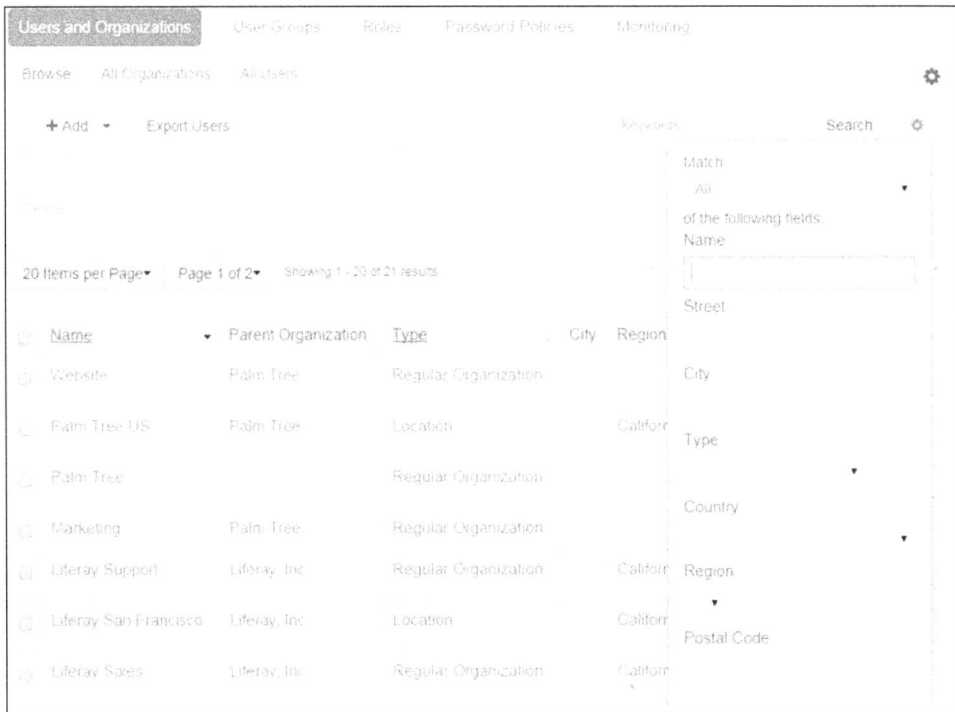

Figure 3.8: Advanced search criteria

Editing a location

After adding locations, we are ready to manage them. Consider that we want to update the location information of Website US (for example, changing parent organizations and adding e-mail addresses and comments). We can do this by following these steps:

1. Click on **Users and Organizations** under the **Users** category of **Control Panel**.

2. Find the location (for example, **Website US**) with the **Type** value as **Location** that you want to edit.

3. Click on the **Edit** icon from **Actions** on the right-hand side of the location, or click on links of the location (for example, the name **Website US**).

4. Then, in the editing page, type the changes in the **Name** input field and select values from the **Country** and **Region** menus to make changes. Otherwise, click on links on the right-hand side, such as **Email Addresses**, **Addresses**, **Websites**, **Phone Numbers**, **Services**, **Comments**, **Custom Fields**, and so on.

5. Click on the **Save** button to save the changes.

Deleting a location

For some reason, a location, say **Website US**, doesn't exist anymore. Therefore, we need to delete this location in the portal. We can do it by following these steps:

1. Click on **Users and Organizations** under the **Users** category of **Control Panel**.

2. Locate the location you want to delete, for example, **Website US**.

3. Click on the **Delete** icon from **Actions** on the right-hand side of the location, or select the checkbox on the left-hand side of the location and press the **Delete** button.

4. A screen will appear that asks whether you want to delete the selected locations. Click on the **OK** button to confirm.

> Note that you can't delete a location that has users associated with it. In order to delete this location, you need to remove all users from it first.

Assigning users to a location

Users can be assigned to a location as follows:

1. Click on **Users and Organizations** under the **Users** category of **Control Panel**.

2. Locate a particular location (for example, **Editorial US**).

3. Then, click on the **Assign Users** icon from **Actions** on the right-hand side of the location.

4. Click on the **Available** tab to display a list of all available users in the portal.

5. Select users by checking in the checkbox, click on the **Update Associations** button to assign users to the current location. Optionally, to confirm that the desired users were successfully associated with the current location, click on the **Current** tab.

In addition, you can view a location's users by clicking on the **Location** link (Editorial US), which will provide you with the suborganization and user list associated with that organization. Now, each organization that is **Location**-based can have its own **Site**, which will again have private pages and public pages. Fortunately, you can manage these private and public pages by clicking on the **Manage Site** icon from **Actions** on the right-hand side of the location.

Using locations in an effective way

Locations are special organizations associated with a parent organization and have no child organizations. A location can be used to represent a child corporation of an organization and is usually distinguished by its geographic location. An organization can have any number of sub organizations and locations, while a location must belong to one and only one organization. Some examples would be Editorial US, Editorial Germany, and Editorial India.

Each location has a set of basic properties (for example, name, parent organization, country, and so on). As a special organization, each location can also have a set of optional properties as well as the properties of a regular organization, for example, e-mail addresses, addresses, websites, phone numbers, services, comments, custom fields, and so on.

Organization settings

As you have seen, there are two ways of adding and editing organizations: regular organization and location. When adding an organization, the default value of type would be **Regular Organization**, whereas when adding a location for a regular organization, the default value of type would be **Location**.

When you choose the type **Regular Organization**, the drop-down menus **Country** and **Region** are invisible. However, when you choose the type **Location**, the drop-down menus **Country** and **Region** are visible again. How does it work?

As you can see, there is a difference between the forms to add or edit organizations. When adding a regular or a location organization, you will see only one section—**Organization Information with Details**. When editing an organization or location, you will be able to see the rest of the enabled sections, such as **Identification**, **Miscellaneous**, and the **Organization Information** section. Under the **Organization Information** section, **Details** and **Organization Site** are visible. Under the **Identification** section, you would see **Addresses**, **Phone Numbers**, **Additional Email Addresses**, **Websites**, and **Services**. Under the **Miscellaneous** section, you will have **Comments**, **Reminder Queries**, and **Custom Fields**. How can we customize it?

The portal provides the *organization administration* tool with the following design patterns to achieve better usability and more flexibility. You can customize the preceding features using the overriding properties.

Organization types

Organization types are configurable. By default, the following properties are set in `portal.properties`:

```
organizations.types=regular-organization,location
organizations.rootable[regular-organization]=true
organizations.children.types[regular-organization]=regular-
organization,location
organizations.country.enabled[regular-organization]=false
organizations.country.required[regular-organization]=false
organizations.rootable[location]=false
organizations.country.enabled[location]=true
organizations.country.required[location]=true
```

The preceding code shows the configuration of organization types. The `organizations.types` property specifies two organization types: `regular-organization` and `location`. This configuration mandates that a `regular-organization` can be a root at the top level with no parents, and it can have a `regular-organization` and a `location` as children, whereas a `location` must always have a `regular-organization` as a parent and it can't have any children.

The `country` is disabled for the `regular-organization` as it isn't required for the `regular-organization`. However, it is enabled and required for the `location`. This is the reason that when you choose the **Regular Organization** type, the drop-down menus **Country** and **Region** are invisible. When you choose the type **Location**, the drop-down menus **Country** and **Region** are visible.

You can override these properties in `portal-ext.properties`.

Organization forms

The kinds of organization forms are `add` form and `update` form. The following properties have been set for the `add` form by default in `portal.properties`:

```
organizations.form.add.main=details,organization-site
  organizations.form.add.identification=
  organizations.form.add.miscellaneous=
```

As shown in the preceding code, you can input a list of sections that will be included as part of the organization form when you add an organization. For the add form, only the `main` section has two items, `details` and `organization site`. Thus, when adding an organization or location, you will see only one section, **Organization Information**.

The following properties have been set for the `update` form, by default, in `portal.properties`:

```
organizations.form.update.main=details,organization-
  site,categorization
organizations.form.update.identification=addresses,phone-
  numbers,additional-email-addresses,websites,services
organizations.form.update.miscellaneous=comments,reminder-
  queries,custom-fields
```

As shown in the preceding code, you can input a list of sections that will be included as part of the organization form when updating an organization. For the `update` form, three sections (**Organization Information**, **Identification**, and **Miscellaneous**) are available. Therefore, when editing an organization or location, you will be able to see all sections, including **Identification**, **Miscellaneous**, and **Organization Information** (that is, `main`).

These properties can be overridden in `portal-ext.properties`. For example, you can hide some items in any sections or add new items to a given section.

Overriding assignment and membership

In addition, you can override properties related to assignment and membership. By default, the following properties have been set in `portal.properties`:

```
organizations.assignment.strict=true
organizations.membership.strict=false
```

As shown in the preceding code, you can set the `organizations.assignment.strict` property to `false` if you want any administrator of an organization to be able to assign any user to that organization. By default, the administrator will only be able to assign the users of organizations and suborganizations that they can manage.

In the same way, you can set the `organizations.membership.strict` property to `true` if you want users to only be members of the organizations to which they are assigned explicitly. By default, they will also become implicit members of the ancestors of those organizations. For example, if a user belongs to Editorial US, then they will implicitly be a member of the ancestors Editorial Department and Palm Tree Enterprise, and they will be able to access their private pages. These properties can be overridden in `portal-ext.properties` instead.

Hierarchy tree and Shared Global

As mentioned earlier, organizations and locations are the mechanisms to organize users and websites just as a portal following a hierarchical structure. Each attached website can have a team and a dedicated workflow. That is the only way to have a hierarchical structure of websites. An organization represents the logical structure of the company or institution where the portal is going to be used. It has a hierarchical structure with as many levels as required. A location represents a physical location where the company or the institution users can work. Each location belongs to an organization.

The organization hierarchy

A regular organization can be a root, with no parent organization. A regular organization can even have a parent organization and many child organizations or locations. A location must have a regular organization as a parent and have no child organizations. Therefore, organizations and locations form a hierarchical structure: regular organizations form the root and trunk, while locations form leaves.

How can you benefit from the organization hierarchy? The first benefit you can get is inherited permissions. Each user can be assigned to at the most one organization inheriting the permissions and associations of that organization. The user will also inherit all permissions and associations of parent organizations of that organization that have been marked as inherited. Each user can be assigned to at the most one location. That location must belong to an organization that the user is assigned or to one of the inherited parent organizations of that organization.

The second benefit you can get is content sharing in the organization hierarchy. As mentioned in the previous chapter, content could be scoped into pages. Organizations and locations have their own content. Through a hierarchical structure, the content in parent organizations can be shared in child organizations. For example, the content in Palm Tree enterprise would be accessible in "Editorial Department". Furthermore, content in both Palm Tree enterprise and Editorial Department would be accessible in the location "Editorial US".

Shared Global

The portal provides a global space called **Shared Global** that only the administrator can manage. Any content in the global space will be publishable in any organization or site pages. In addition, web content structures and templates will be reusable all across the portal. It's very useful to share a Dictionary (categories/tags) as well. Vocabularies are often shared between organizations for normalization purposes.

> Note that Shared Global is not portal-wide. It is limited to the portal instance in which it resides, that is, Shared Global is associated with a portal instance. You would have one unique shared global scope for each portal instance.

User groups

Like many departments, a company might have several user groups. Palm Tree Publications has *Julia Maurer*, an *Editorial manager* in the Germany office and *John Stucki*, a *website manager* also in the Germany office. Both are managers but belong to different departments, thanks to the user group called *Managers* that contains a number of users belonging to different departments. Let's go ahead and create them.

User groups provide a way to group users independently of the organizations to which they belong. Administrators can define a user group and assign the user group as a member of a site to make all of its users members automatically.

User groups give some of the best solutions. They help to simplify the mapping of several roles to a group of users. They helps us to simplify membership to one or more sites by specifying a group of users. And they help us to provide predefined public or private pages to the users who belong to the user group.

Adding a user group

First of all, we will create a user group "Managers", which contains users Julia Maurer and John Stucki, by following these steps:

1. Click on **User Groups** under the **Users** category of **Control Panel**.
2. Then click on the **Add** button.
3. Enter a name for the user group in the **Name** input field (for example, **Managers**).
4. Enter the description of the user group. Leave the default User Group Site.
5. Click on the **Save** button to save the inputs.
6. Then, click on the **Assign Members** icon from **Actions** on the right-hand side of the user group **Managers**.
7. Click on the **Available** tab to display a list of all the available users in the portal. Check the checkboxes on the left-hand side of the desired users. Note that these users don't exist at the moment. We'll learn about adding users in the next section.

8. Click on the **Update Associations** button to assign users to a user group. Optionally, to confirm that the desired users were successfully associated with the user group, click on the **Current** tab.

Other user groups can be created in a similar fashion. After adding one more user group, **Developers**, we can view user groups, as shown in following screenshot:

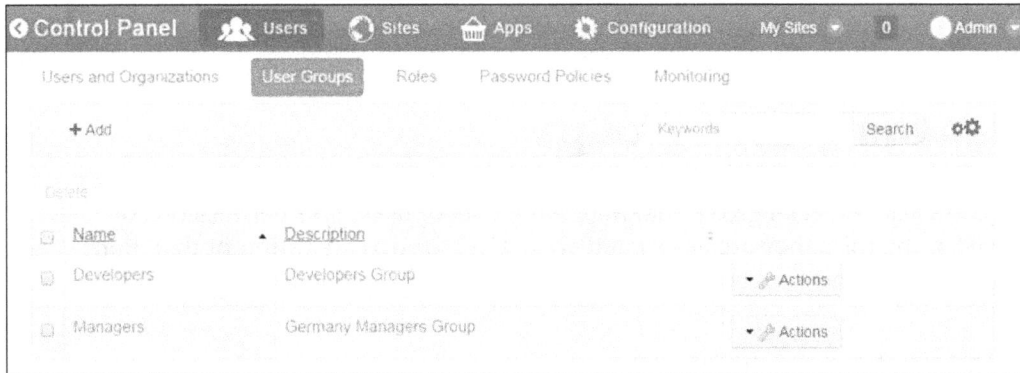

Figure: 3.9: A list of the current user groups

As you can see, there is a toolbar for top-level navigation. The toolbar is located at the top of the user groups section just below the **User Groups** title.

Note: If the users with the permission are able to see the action in the toolbar, the **Add** button allows them to add user groups.

Creating User Group Site with public pages and private pages

In Liferay, **Site** is one of the cool features. Whenever we need public pages and private pages, there will be sites for each of them. Now, you can create a site for **User Group**, with respect to public pages (as a **Community site**) and private pages (as an **Intranet site**).

Let's edit **Managers Group** and create the site with public and private pages:

1. Click on the **Action** button on the right-hand side and click on **Edit**.

2. Now, select the public pages as **Community site** and private pages as **Intranet site** under the heading **User Group Site**.

3. Save the changes by clicking on the **Save** button.

Now, you have successfully created the site for the respective user group. You can manage the site pages by clicking on **Action** and selecting **Manage site pages**.

The name and description of Site will be automatically synced with those of the User Group (to save the administrator time).

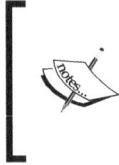

[

The site of a user group cannot be accessed directly by end users. The pages of a user group will be shown automatically as part of the public or private pages of the personal site of each user who belongs to the user group. To allow users to make changes, enable the customization options of each page.

]

Managing user groups

As mentioned earlier, a user group can hold any number of users. In fact, a user group is also a special group that may have a set of users and permissions by virtue of the roles they are associated with. User groups are different than both organizations and sites because they have no context associated with them.

Viewing user groups

To view user groups, click on **User Groups** under the **Users** category of **Control Panel**. A list of user groups appears at the bottom of the screen. Click on the user group that you want to view (for example, **Managers**). The portal will display **Name** and **Description** of that user group.

Searching user groups

User groups are searchable. To search user groups, click on **User Groups** under the **Users** category of **Control Panel**. Then, type a user group name as search keywords, and click on the **Search** button. For an advanced search, click on the **gear** icon beside the search button. A drop-down search form will appear, where you can search by Name and Description of the group.

Editing a user group

You might need to edit a user group. Click on **User Groups** under the **Users** category of **Control Panel**, and then locate the user group that you want to edit. Click on the **Edit** icon from the **Actions** button on the right-hand side of the user group, or click on any links of the user group. In the **Edit** page, type the changes in the **New Name** input field and the **Description** input field. Then, click on the **Save** button to save the changes.

Deleting user groups

For some reason, the **Developers** user group does not exist anymore. We need to delete this user group in the portal. We will delete the **Developers** user group as follows:

1. Click on **User Groups** under the **Users** category of **Control Panel**.

2. Locate the user group that you want to delete (that is, Developers).

3. Then, click on the **Delete** icon from the **Actions** button on the right-hand side of the user group, or check the box on the left-hand side of the user group and click on the **Delete** button.

4. A screen will appear asking you if you want to permanently delete the selected user groups.

5. Click on the **OK** button to delete the selected user group.

Similarly, you can delete multiple user groups by checking the checkboxes located on the left-hand side of the user groups that you want to delete first and then click on the **Delete** button. All user groups can be deleted at one go by checking the checkbox located next to the Name column and then clicking on the **Delete** button. A screen will appear asking whether you want to permanently delete the selected user groups. Click on the **OK** button to delete or the **Cancel** button if you do not want to delete the selected user groups.

Assigning users to a user group

Users can be assigned to a user group by following these steps:

1. Click on **User Groups** under the **Users** category of **Control Panel**.

2. Locate the user group to which you want to assign members and click on the **Assign Members** icon from the **Actions** button on the right-hand side of the user group.

3. Click on the **Available** tab to display a list of all available users in the portal. To assign users to the current user group, select the users and click on the **Update Associations** button. Optionally, to confirm that the desired users were successfully associated with the current user group, click on the **Current** tab.

As you can see, each user group has its own public pages and private pages. Of course, you can manage these pages by clicking on the **Manage Site Pages** icon from the **Actions** button on the right-hand side of the user group. Note that users who belong to the current user group will have these pages copied to their user pages when the user is first associated with the current user group. User groups can cross organizational boundaries and can be used to assign all members to other collections, such as sites or roles. User groups may also be used to customize personal site templates for members.

Users

Users are individuals who perform tasks using the portal. Administrators can create new users or deactivate existing users. Users can join sites, be placed into organization hierarchies, be delegated permissions in roles, or be collected into user groups.

As stated earlier, a user is an individual who performs tasks using the portal. Users can belong to a regular organization, special organization, location, or user group. Before adding new users, let's suppose we log in with the admin account Palm Tree to add new users in the portal.

Adding users

Let's add Martin Gall, who works in the editorial department in the Germany office.

1. Click on **Users and Organizations** under the **Users** category of **Control Panel**.

2. Then click on the **Add** button. Select **User** from the drop-down menu.

3. Enter the user's information in the input field. Most importantly, **Screen Name**, (for example, **Martin**) and **Email Address**, (for example, martin@ bookpub.com) are required, along with the **First Name** and the **Last Name**, since both act as unique identifiers for this user. When this user logs in, the **Screen Name**, **Email Address**, or **User Id** will be used as the login ID.

4. A location can be selected by clicking on **Organizations** in the menu on the right-hand side (such as **Editorial Germany**, to which the new user belongs).

5. Click on the **Save** button to save the inputs; after you save the inputs, you will see the message, **Your request completed successfully**.

Adding users in Liferay Portal with all the details, such as organization, sites, user group, private and public pages, and so on. The following screenshot shows the users setting page:

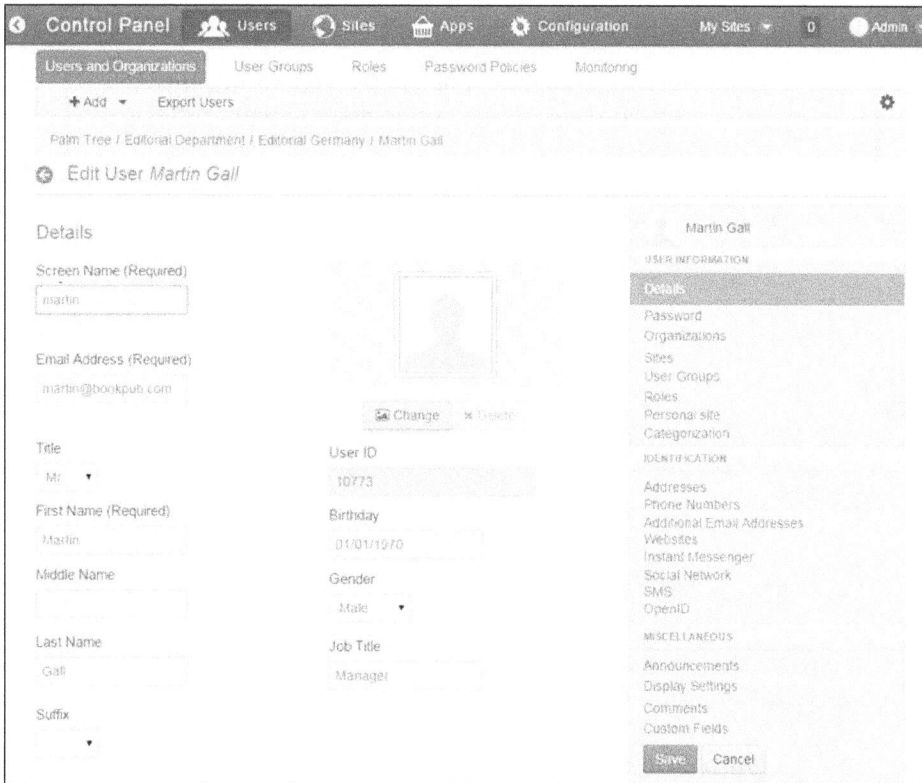

Figure 3.10: Adding a user

As shown in the previous screenshot, there is a toolbar used for top-level navigation. This toolbar is located at the top of the **Users** section and below the **Users** title, which provides quick access to the most used functions when working with users:

1. **Add** shows a drop-down menu with three options: **User, Regular Organization**, and **Location**. Once you click on **User**, the adding user form will appear; only users with proper permissions will be able to see this in the toolbar.

2. **Export** is a very simple export functionality to download a CSV file that contains **User ID** and **Email Address** of all the users. It is available only to users with the Administrator role.

What's happening?

You added the first user to the portal. When we create the new account, the portal will send an e-mail to the specified e-mail address that notifies the user that they can log in and start using the portal.

> Note that the e-mail will only be sent successfully if you have specified an SMTP server in the mail portlet for the portal to use.

Here's an example of the e-mail that Martin will receive:

Dear Martin,

Welcome! You recently created an account at http://bookpub.com/. Your password is ********. Enjoy!

Sincerely,

Palm Tree

admin@bookpub.com

http://bookpub.com

Figure 3.11: E-mail notification settings

When the user clicks on the link, he will be taken to a page that displays signing in as a regular account. After inputting his e-mail address and password and clicking on the **Sign in** button, they will be taken to a page that displays terms and conditions, including the terms of use.

> Note that you would be able to change the e-mail notification (for example, the "account created" notification and "password changed" notification). This will be discussed in detail in a later chapter.

Adding more users

We will add a few more users, David Berger and Lotti Stein, in the way we just mentioned. Both belong to the editorial department in the US offices.

Fortunately, there are two more options to add users — to add a user for a given organization and to add a user from scratch, as mentioned in the following paragraph:

You can add David Berger from scratch by following these steps:

1. Click on Users and Organizations under the **User** category of **Control Panel**.

2. Then click on the **Add** button. And select **User** from the drop-down menu.

3. Enter the user's information in the input fields, select the organization link from the right-hand side menu, and select the organization location (**Editorial US**).

4. Click on the **Save** button to save the inputs.

Let's add Lotti Stein through a given organization by following these steps:

1. Click on **Users and Organizations**. Select a location (**Editorial US**) to which you want to add a new user.

2. Click on the **Add User** icon from the **Actions** located on the right-hand side of the organization to which you want to add a user. You will see that the selected organization has been selected by default.

3. Enter the user information in the input fields.

4. Click on the **Save** button to save the inputs.

Creating a personal site with public and private pages

Users can have a personal site with the help of public pages and private pages. While creating users, we can assign Personal sites for the user.

Let's create a personal site for David Berger with Public pages and Private pages:

1. Select the user (David Berger), click on **Action** on the right-hand side, and select **Edit** action.

2. Click the personal site link on the right-hand side panel. You will be able to see the Personal site's heading with the public pages options: **Default**, **Community site**, and **Intranet site**, and the same is true for private page too.

3. Select one option for each public page (**Community site**) and private page (**Intranet site**).

4. Save the changes by clicking the **Save** button.

Now, the personal site for David Berger has been created successfully. The name and description of the Site will be automatically synced with those of the User's (to save the administrator time).

Adding users in bulk

It won't be long before you're bored of manually adding users. Fortunately, you don't need to type them all in one at a time. There are several options to add users in bulk:

- **Lightweight Directory Access Protocol (LDAP)**: For example, Apache Directory Server, Fedora Directory Server, Microsoft Active Directory Server, Novell eDirectory, OpenLDAP, and so on.

- **Single Sign-On (SSO)**: This is a method of access control that enables a user to authenticate once and gain access to the resources of multiple software systems. For example, CAS, NTLM, OpenSSO, SiteMinder, SAML and so on.

- **OpenID**: This is a decentralized single sign-on system.

Creating an account on the fly

As an administrator at Palm Tree Publications, you can set up the portal allowing users to create an account on the fly. For example, Rolf Hess accesses the portal's login page and clicks on the **Create Account** tab. He inputs the user information and text verification and then clicks on the **Save** button. How do you do this?

Go to **Control Panel** | **Configuration** | **Portal Settings** (under the Configuration category) | **Authentication** link on right-hand side, and now, under the **General** tab, check the **Allow strangers to create accounts?** box.

The portal will create an account for the user **Rolf Hess** and send an e-mail to him with a new password.

> Note that there is no organization or location selected for the new account created on the fly. In order to set the proper organization and location to the new account, administrators have to update this account on the portal.

Fortunately, as an administrator, you can set up **Default User Associations** on **Sites**, **Roles**, and **User Groups**. You can find this feature at **Control Panel** | **Configuration** | **Portal Settings** | **Users** | **Default User Associations**.

The portal's default users association helps to directly associate the users with the respective sites, organization sites, roles, and user groups.

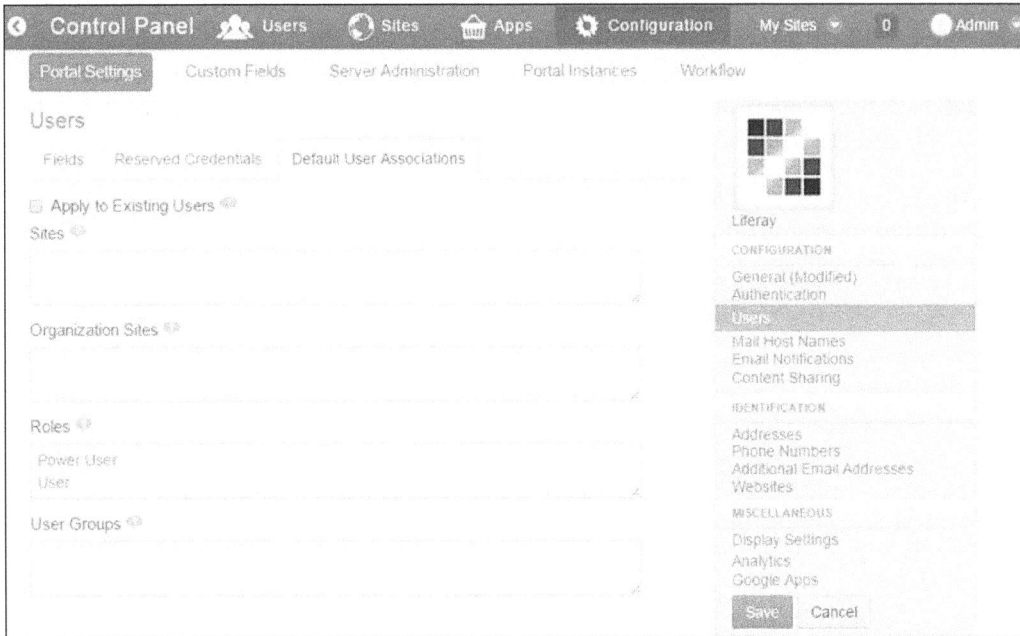

Figure 3.12: Portal settings for default user associations

What to do when a user forgets the password?

If a user forgets their password, they can access the portal's login page and can click on the **Forgot Password** tab. They need to input their e-mail address and text verification and then press the **Send New Password** button. The portal will create a new password for the user and mail it to them. As mentioned in the previous chapter, you can configure this feature.

Managing users

You can add users of others departments in most organizations in a similar fashion. After adding more users, we can view the users.

Viewing users

Users could either be **Active** or **Inactive** on the portal. It is simple to view active users. Click on **Users and Organizations** under the category **User** of **Control Panel**. You will be able to see the top-level organization list and the **Users** list, which are not associated with any organization. To view all the active users on the portal, click on **All users**. A list of users appears on the other page. Locate the user that you want to view first, and click on the user's name (for example, **David**).

The following screenshot display the list of users on the portal, which are associated with a different organization:

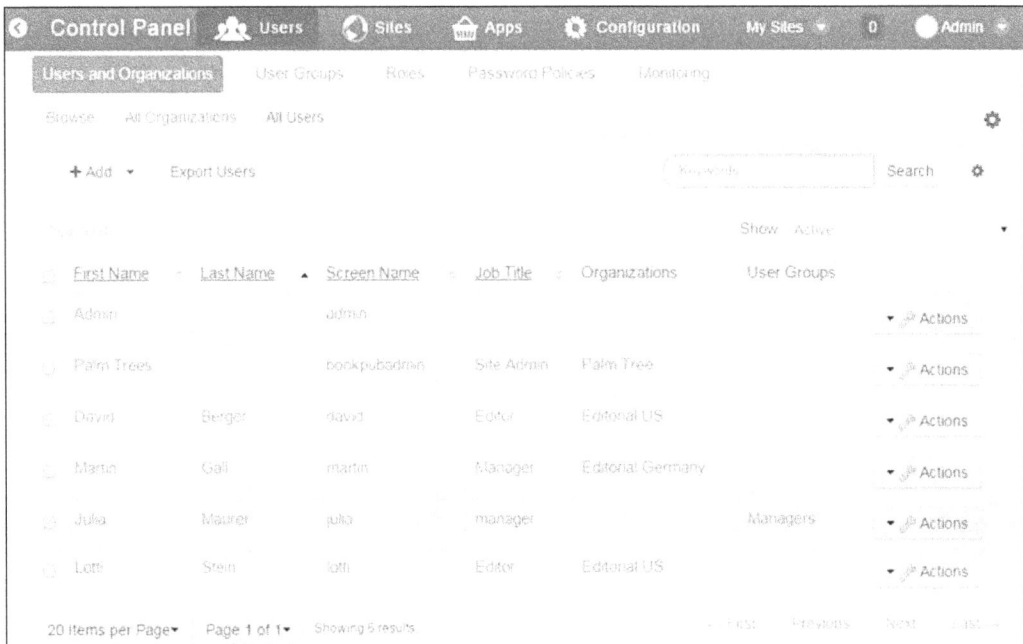

Figure 3.13: View all users

Optionally, we can view users for a specific organization or location. To view users that belong to a specific organization, simply click on the **Organizations** section. You will be able to see the **Suborganization** list and the **Users** list belong to the same **Organization**. Now, you want to view **Users**, **Suborganization** and **Location Organization**. Then, drill down to **Suborganization**. Refer to *Figure 3.7*.

Similarly, you can view users that belong to a specific user group by clicking on the **User Groups** section and then clicking on **Assign Members** icon from the **Actions** button on the right-hand side of a user group. Under the current tab, you will be able to see the list of users associated with that particular group. Most interestingly, you can view users associated with a specific role by clicking on the **Roles** tab in the **Users** category and then clicking on the **View Users** icon from the **Actions** button on the right-hand side of the role.

To view deactivated users, select **Inactive** from the show selection box. Otherwise, click on the **gear** icon beside the search box for an advanced search and select the **Inactive** status. Click on the **Search** button to display a list of deactivated users.

Searching for users

Users are searchable. First, you can search users by clicking on **Users and Organization** under the **Users** category of **Control Panel**. Click on the **gear** icon beside the search box for an advanced search. Input the user's information in the input fields and select a value of the status (**Any Status**, **Active**, and **Inactive**) for an advanced search. Finally, click on the **Search** button. A list of users matching the search criteria appears at the bottom of the user's screen.

> Note that the basic search is only useful for active users. To find inactive users, just select the show selection box value as Inactive. Otherwise, you can use the advanced search option and select **Inactive** from the **Status** options.

Editing a user profile

After adding users, we are ready to manage them. For example, we want to update the profile of Lotti Stein (such as changing the name, parent organizations, and adding e-mail addresses and comments). Let's do it by following these steps:

1. Click on **Users and Organizations** under the **User** category of **Control Panel**.

2. Search the user whose record you want to update, and click on the user (in our case **Lotti Stein**).

3. Click on the **Edit** icon from the **Actions** button on the right-hand side of the user and click on any links of the user.

4. A screen will appear that displays the user's information. Type the changes in the **First Name**, **Middle Name**, **Last Name**, **Email Address**, **Screen Name**, and **Job Title** input fields, and select from the **Title**, **Suffix**, **Birthday**, and **Gender** menus to make the changes.

5. Optionally, you can change the icon, **Display Settings** (including **Display Language**, **Time Zone**, and **Greeting**), **Password**, **Role**, **Organization**, **Additional Emails Addresses**, **Addresses**, **Comments**, **Custom Attributes**, and so on.

6. Click on the **Save** button to save the changes.

> Note that the functions to edit a user are the same as that of updating the profile in **My Account**. In **My Account**, you can only update your own information (as a logged-in user).

As can be seen, the portal provides a right-hand side menu for users, showing sections of forms that allow navigating through them in a fast way that doesn't require page reload. Forms to add and edit users are different, allowing an easy and fast way to create users and a deeper personalization afterwards. Similar to other forms of organizations, items in the right-hand side menu are grouped into three sections: **User Information**, **Identification**, and **Miscellaneous**. By default, when creating a user, only **Details**, **Organizations**, and **s** are visible. Refer to the right-hand side menu in *Figure 3.11*. The following are the items in the right-hand side menu:

- **Password**: This changes the user's password.

- **Organizations**: This changes the membership in organization (or locations) associations. Each user can be a member of multiple organizations (or locations).

- **Sites**: This changes membership in sites. Each user can be a member of multiple Sites.

- **User Groups**: This changes the membership in user groups. Each user can be a member of multiple user groups.

- **Roles**: This changes associations of roles. Each user can be associated with multiple roles, such as **regular roles**, **inherited roles**, **organization roles**, and **site roles**.

- **Personal Site**: This manages a user's private pages and public pages. If site templates are available, then you would be able to apply existing site templates on both private pages and public pages.

- **Categorization**: This adds tags. Each user can have multiple tags.

- **Addresses**: This holds mail address information. Each user can have multiple addresses.

- **Phone Numbers**: This manages phone numbers. Each user can have multiple phone numbers.

- **Additional Email addresses**: This manages e-mail addresses. Each user can have multiple e-mail addresses.

- **Websites**: This manages personal websites. Each user can have multiple websites — either intranets or public ones.

- **Instant Messenger**: This manages instant messengers, such as **YIM**, **Skype**, and **Windows Live Messenger**.

- **Social Network**: This manages Social Networks, such as **Facebook**, **Myspace**, and **Twitter**.

- **SMS**: This manages SMS.

- **OpenID**: This manages OpenID.

- **Announcement**: This manages announcements by **Email** and **SMS** notification.

- **Display Settings**: This manages display settings using **language setting**, **time zone**, and **greetings**.

- **Comments**: This manages comments.

- **Custom Fields**: This manages values of custom attributes if custom attributes have been added to the current user.

Note that no changes are applied until the **Save** button is clicked. Obviously, the right-hand side menu shows at all times which sections have been modified and whether a save is pending. It allows us to make changes to different sections and to save everything at once. Therefore, clicking on the **Save** button will save all the changes at any point in time.

Deactivating a user

Imagine that "Lotti Stein" has become inactive, and we need to deactivate their user account. To deactivate a user, just follow these steps:

1. Click on **Users and Organizations** under the **Users** category of **Control Panel**.

2. Search for the user that you want to deactivate.

3. Then, click on the checkbox next to the user you want to deactivate, and click on the **Deactivate** button. Alternatively, you can also deactivate a user by clicking on the **Deactivate** icon from the **Actions** tab next to a user.

4. A message will pop up asking **Are you sure you want to deactivate the selected users?**. Click on **OK** to deactivate them or on **Cancel** if you don't want to deactivate the selected users.

To deactivate all users listed on a page, click on the checkbox next to the **Name** column (which will select all the users), and click on the **Deactivate** button.

Activating a user

If we want to make an inactive user active again on the portal, we need to restore or activate that user account. Just follow these steps:

1. Click on **Users and Organizations** under the **Users** category of **Control Panel**.

2. Select Show value as Inactive below the search box, or click on the **gear** icon beside the search box and select the status as **Inactive** in the search form. Then click on the **Search** button to display a listing of deactivated users.

3. Click on the checkbox located next to the user you want to reactivate, and then click on the **Restore** button. Alternatively, you can also reactivate a user by clicking on the **Activate** icon from the **Actions** tab on the right-hand side of the user.

To restore all users listed on a page, click the checkbox next to the Name column (which will select all the users), and click on the **Restore** button.

Deleting a user

If a user doesn't exist anymore, we need to delete him/her from the portal as follows. User accounts must be deactivated before they can be deleted.

1. Click on **Users and Organizations** under the **Users** category of **Control Panel**.

2. Select **Show** value as **Inactive** below the search box. Or click on the **gear** icon beside the search box and select the status as **Inactive** in the search form. Then, click on the **Search** button to display a listing of deactivated users.

3. Click on the checkbox located next to the user you want to delete, and click on the **Delete** button. Another way to delete a user is by clicking on the **Delete** icon from the **Actions** tab on the right-hand side of the user.

4. Messages will pop up asking **Are you sure you want to permanently delete the selected users?**. Click on the **OK** button to delete, or click on the **Cancel** button if you don't want to delete the selected users.

5. To delete all users listed on a page, click the checkbox located next to them in the **Name** column. Then, click on the **Delete** button.

Impersonating a user

Administrators and normal users with the **Impersonate User** function can conveniently review updates performed by other users. For example, the administrator gives permissions to the user Lotti Stein to edit all users in the Palm Tree Publications US location. To verify that the edit permission has been correctly given to a user, the administrator can sign in as that user. Alternatively, the administrator can search for the user in **Users and Organizations** under the category **User** of **Control Panel** and click on the **Impersonate User** icon from the **Actions** tab on the right-hand side of the user. By using the **Impersonate** function, the administrator can impersonate the user to review updates without having to sign in as the user.

Using the Actions tab

As mentioned earlier, each user has their public pages and private pages. These pages can be managed by clicking on the **Manage Pages** icon from the **Actions** tab on the right-hand side of the user. In addition, you can set up permissions for a specific user by clicking on the **Permissions** icon from the **Actions** tab on the right-hand side of the user.

User settings

As you can see, forms to add and edit users are different. When adding a user, you will see the **User Information** section where **Details, Organizations**, and **Personal Site** are visible, whereas when editing a user profile, you will also be able to see the rest of the enabled sections, such as **Identification**, **Miscellaneous**, and **User Information**.

For example, while editing the user profile, you would be able to assign roles, organizations, and sites to the user without leaving the form. Any changes will be saved, along with the rest of the form, when the **Save** button is clicked.

The portal provides a user administration tool following design patterns to achieve better usability and more flexibility. You can customize the preceding features by overriding properties.

User forms

User forms can be configured easily. Two kinds of forms are identified: `add` form and `update` form.

- The following properties are set for the `add` form by default in `portal.properties`:

```
users.form.add.main=details,organizations,personal-site
users.form.add.identification=
users.form.add.miscellaneous=
```

  As shown in the previous code, you can input a list of sections that will be included as part of the user form when adding a user. For the add form, the main section has the item details, organizations, and personal site. This is the reason that when adding a user, you will see only one section: **User Information**, with details, organizations, and personal site.

- The following properties have been set for the `update` form by default in `portal.properties`:

```
users.form.update.main=details,password,organizations,sites
   ,user-groups,roles,personal-site,categorization
users.form.update.identification= addresses,phone-
   numbers,additional-email-addresses,websites,instant-
   messenger,social-network,sms,open-id
users.form.update.miscellaneous= announcements,display-
   settings,comments,custom-fields
```

  As shown in the previous code, you can input a list of sections that will be included as part of the user form when updating a user. For the `update` form, three sections (User Information, Identification, and Miscellaneous) are available. For this reason, you'll see these sections when editing a user profile.

These properties can be overridden in `portal-ext.properties`. For example, you can hide or add new items to a given section.

Overriding user-related properties

User-related properties can be overridden. By default, the following properties have been set in `portal.properties`:

```
users.delete=true
users.screen.name.allow.numeric=false
users.screen.name.always.autogenerate=false
users.email.address.required=true
```

```
users.image.max.size=307200
users.update.last.login=true
users.search.with.index=true
```

As shown in the previous code, you can set the `users.delete` property to `false` if the users cannot be deleted. Similarly, you can set the `users.screen.name.allow.numeric` property to `false`. Then, the screen name will always non-numeric. You can set the `users.screen. name.always.autogenerate` property to `true` to always autogenerate user screen names even if the user gives a specific user screen name.

In the same way, you can set the `users.email.address.required` property to `false` if you want to be able to create users without an e-mail address. Note that not requiring an e-mail address would disable some features that depend on an e-mail address being provided.

Again, you can set the maximum file size for user portraits using the `users.image.max.size` property. You can use a value `0` for the maximum file size to indicate unlimited file size. The `users.update.last.login` property is set to `true` by default to record the last login information for a user. The `users.search.with.index` property is set to `true` by default to search users from the index. Set this to `false` to search users from the database. Note that setting this to `false` will disable the ability to search users based on **Custom Attributes**.

> Note that **Custom Attributes** is a good feature of Liferay that allows you to add additional fields to existing models/entries to meet new requirement out of the box. Liferay provides custom fields for many things that are out of the application, such as Blogs, Message Boards, Users, Organizations, Roles, Sites, and so on, you can visit the **Control Panel | Configuration | Custom Fields** for more details.
>
> In the case of users, you might need to add additional fields, such as a User's bank details or credit card details for a shopping cart application; custom fields is the best solution.

Alternatively, you can override these properties in `portal-ext.properties`.

Sites

Sites are a set of pages that display content and provide access to specific applications. Sites can have members, which are given exclusive access to specific pages or content.

Actually, sites are special groups that have a set of users or a set of user groups. That is, a site can have a set of users associated. Sites are used to represent a set of users who share common interests. An organization can be associated and unassociated to an existing site whenever required for business needs.

In Liferay, the **site** idea allows the user to perform the task easily and faster using predefined site templates:

- We can work on multiple sites with respect to WCM, Documents and Media, and so on.
- Enhanced staging includes automatic versioning with history and undo for sites and pages.
- Content display based on user profile attributes offer higher levels of personalization.
- Simplified site management via hierarchical site templates is also offered.

If you have not created the site while creating the Organization, you can create the site separately and map the site with the organization manually.

There may be different possibilities, where an Organization is not required for a simple site, such as a site for program event advertisement.

From Site Control Panel, you can set the settings of multiple sites. This is accessed only by the portal's Administrator.

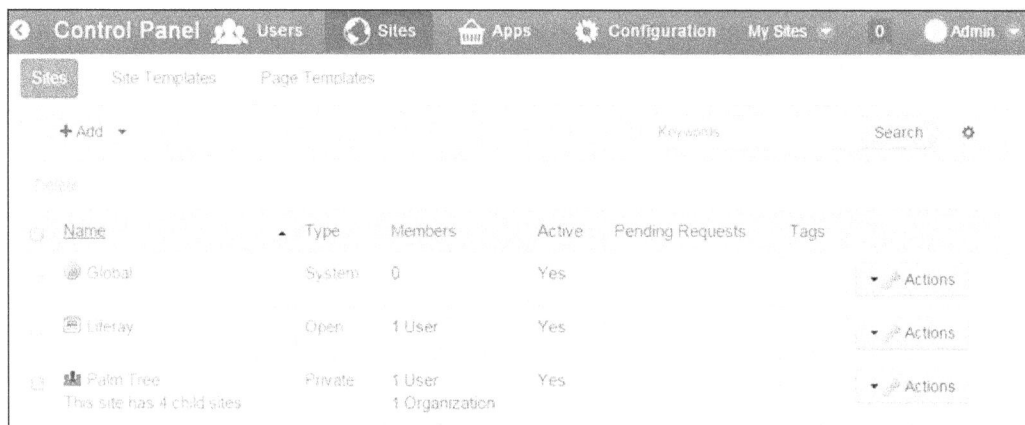

Figure 3.14: Sites

In Liferay 6.2, Sites has been defined in a different section. Once you click on **Control Panel | Sites | Sites**, this will display all the sites under the portal. You can see in the preceding screenshot that Palm Tree is a private site. It has one user and one Organization mapped with it. Also, there are four child sites under it.

> Note that we created the sites while creating the organization. Created sites have the same name as per the organization name. It has taken the same hierarchical structure as that of organization. You would notice that Palm Tree has four child sites. In the preceding screenshot see Palm Tree's **This site has 4 child sites** link, which will redirect you to the list of child site pages.

Let's click on the **This site has 4 child sites** link. You can see the right-hand side menu with the actions **Site Administrations**, **Add Child Site**, **Go to Public Pages**, **Deactivate**, and **Delete**. Each child site has actions that allow you to add another child site under it.

The following screenshot shows all the child sites under Palm Tree:

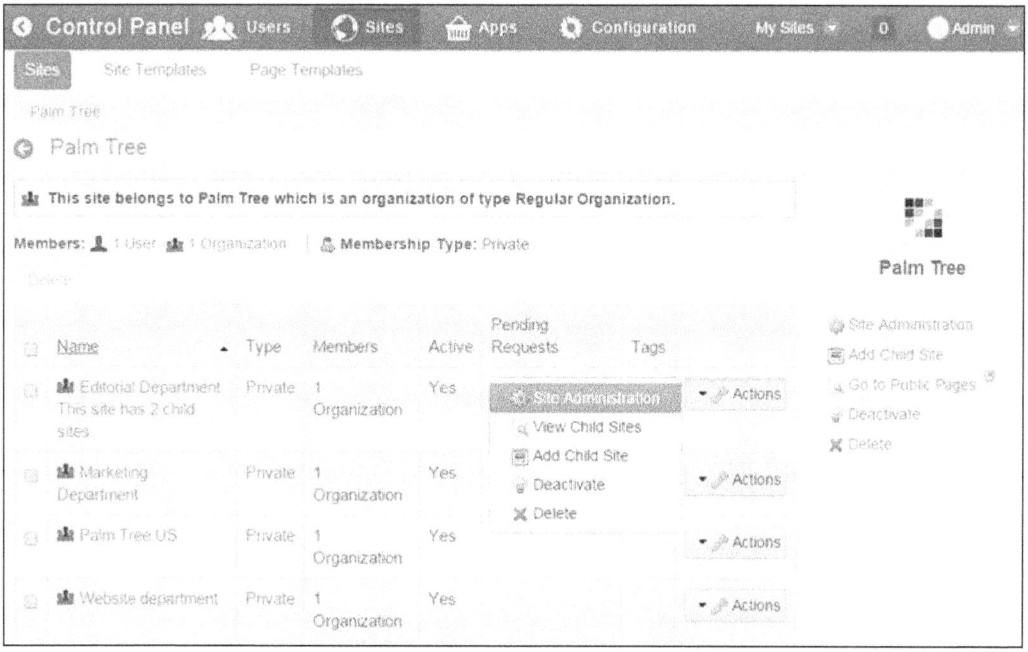

Figure 3.15: View all sites under Palm Tree

Let's create an **Engineering department** site under the **Palm Tree** site:

1. Click on **Sites** under the **Sites** category of **Control Panel**.

2. Click on the **Add child site** link in the **Action** tab of the Palm Tree site.

3. Fill in **Site Name** (**Engineering department**) and **Description**, and select the **Membership Type** as **Open** from the options (**Open**, **Restricted**, and **Private**). Select Public pages and enable the propagation of changes from the site template.

4. Finally, **Save** the changes and go by the following screenshot.

This screenshot shows the site settings page for the engineering department:

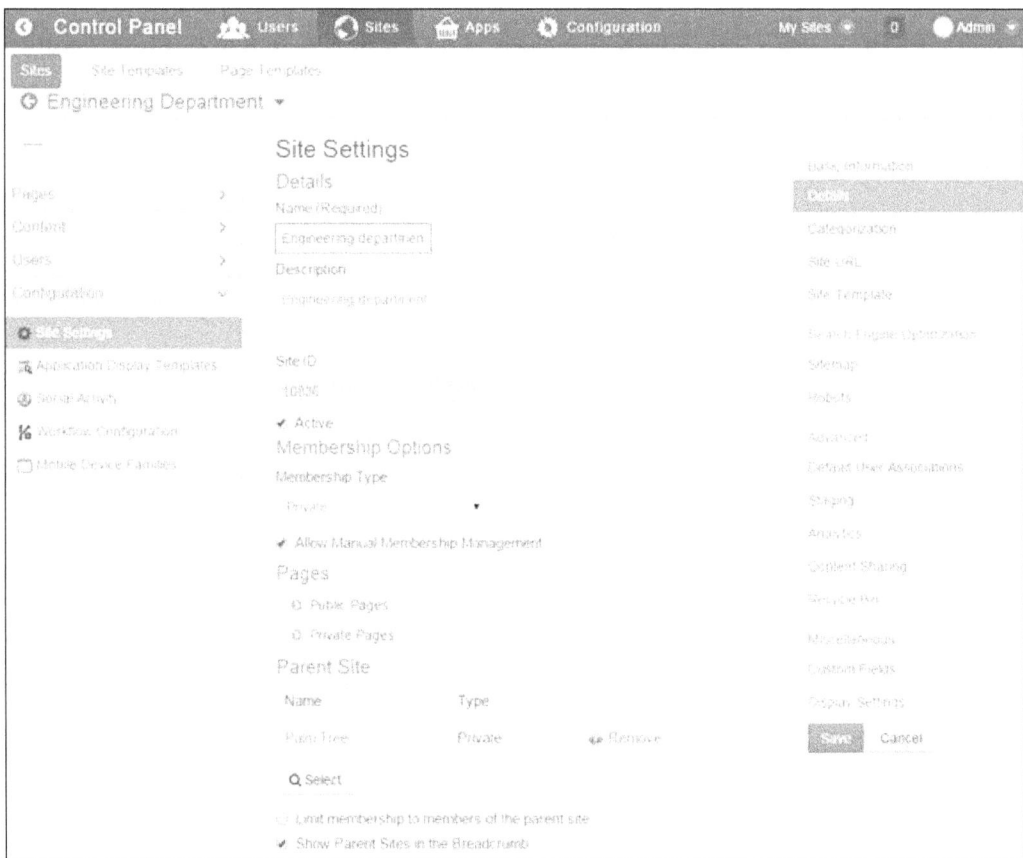

Figure 3.16: Creating a new site

Now, after saving the site, you need to map/associate the site with the organization. For that, you need to configure the site memberships and map the engineering department.

As mentioned, a site can be open, restricted, or private:

- **Open**: This allows portal users to join immediately.
- **Restricted**: The user can't join the site directly; only the site Administrator can add the user. However, a User can request for membership.
- **Private**: It is not visible to nonmembers of the site, membership requests are not possible, and the user is only added by a private Site Administrator.

Site Memberships

Site Memberships allows you to add members to the particular site, which you have selected in the **Site Content** category.

Let's add organization to the site:

1. Click on **Site Memberships** from the left-hand side menu. Refer to the following screenshot.
2. Click on the **Organizations** tab, and then click on the **Assign Organization** link.
3. Select the organization from the list, say **Engineering Department**, by ticking in the checkbox beside the organization name.
4. Save the change. You have successfully associated the organization with a Site.

This screenshot shows the assigning of Users, Organizations, and User Groups to the site:

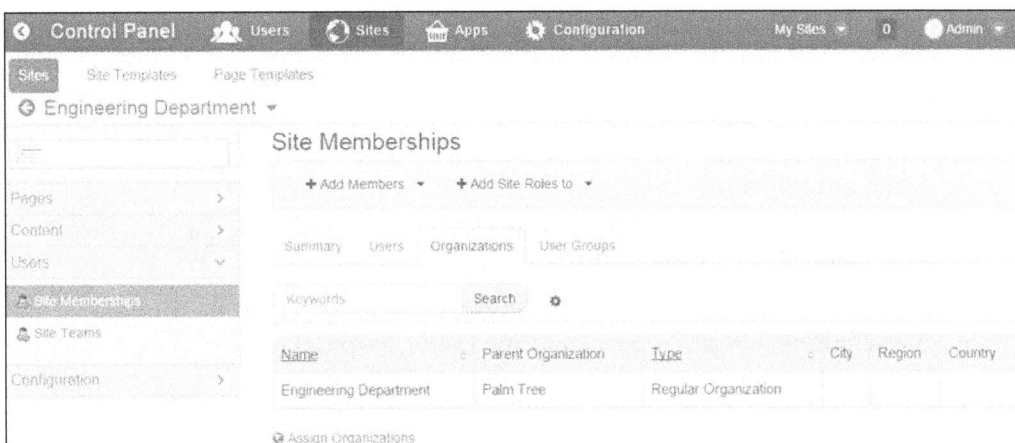

Figure 3.17: Adding organization to site

Site Memberships allows you to add individual **Users**, **Organizations**, and **User Groups** in the selected site in the left-hand side panel. In the preceding screenshot, the engineering department is selected.

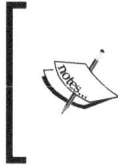

> **Site Administrator** or **Organization Administrator** can't create **Role** anew; however, they can create **Team**. A **Team** role is similar to **Site** and **Organization** role. The purpose of the team is to empower site and organization administration to delegate responsibility without giving them the ability to create roles.

Team

Team provides great flexibility to the site administrator to create various sets/teams of users and permissions for site-specific functions. It provides the feature of permission to specific set of users, for particular functionality in the site. Teams can be scoped to collecting permission within a single site.

Let's create a team—Engineering Team—for the Engineering Department site, the permission defined for it will be only available to the Engineering department site only; no other site can have the same permission.

Creating Team

Let's create a team—"Engineering team"; follow these steps:

1. Click on **Site Teams** under the Engineering department.
2. Click on **Add Team**.
3. Enter the name and description of the team.
4. Click on the **Save** button to save the changes.
5. Now, you can assign the user/members to the Team.
6. Click on the action button on the right-hand side of the team name and select **Assign Members**.
7. Now, you will be able to see two tabs, **Users** and **User Groups**. And below that other tabs—**current** and **available**.
8. Click on the available tab and select users. Finally, click on the **Update Associations** button. You can add the User group too.

Now, you can add the permission for Team by just clicking on action and selecting permissions.

Site Teams give an advantage to the site administrator to create a group within the site. The following screenshot shows the site team list in the engineering department:

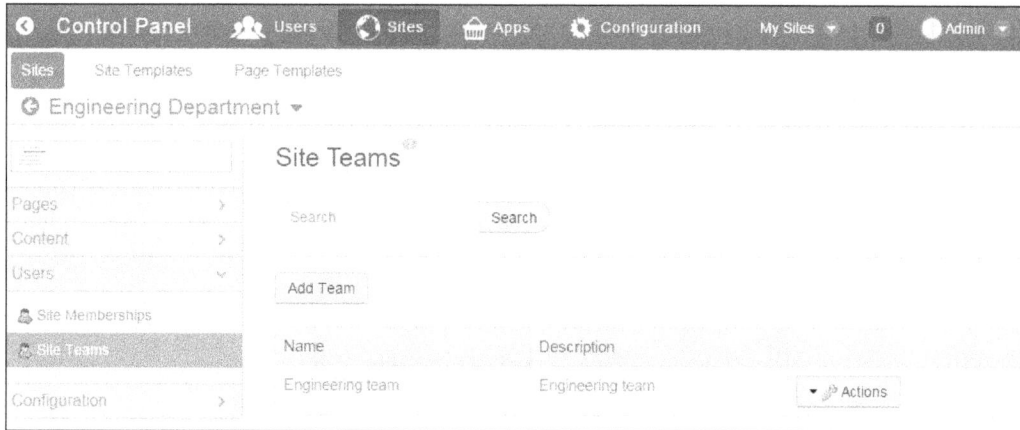

Figure 3.18: Team creation for the Engineering Department site

Site Templates

Site Templates allow you to define a hierarchical set of pages and web content that can be used as a template to create sites. Administrators have the right to define and edit site templates as well as their permissions.

Site Templates can be used when creating Users, Organizations, and Sites. The creation form will show select boxes to use a site template for either public pages or private pages (or both).

When a site template is applied, a copy of its pages and contents is performed. There is no link to the original template, so any change to the site template will not have any effect on the pages that originated from it.

It's also possible to apply a site template to users and organizations as long as they don't have any existing public/private page (otherwise, there could be conflicts).

You can create your own templates as per organization requirement. The following screenshot shows the two default site templates:

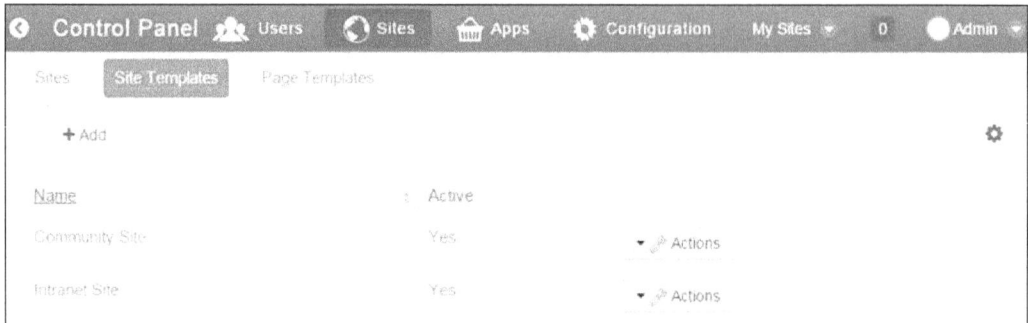

Figure 3.19: Default Site Templates

Let's create a **Palm Tree Community Site** template:

1. Click on **Site Templates** under the **Sites** category in **Control Panel**.
2. Click on the **Add** button.
3. Fill the input fields' name and description, check in the **Active** checkbox, and the **Allow Site Administrators to Modify the Pages Associated with This Site Template** checkbox.
4. Save the changes.

This screenshot displays the creation of a new site template with the name **Palm Tree Community**.

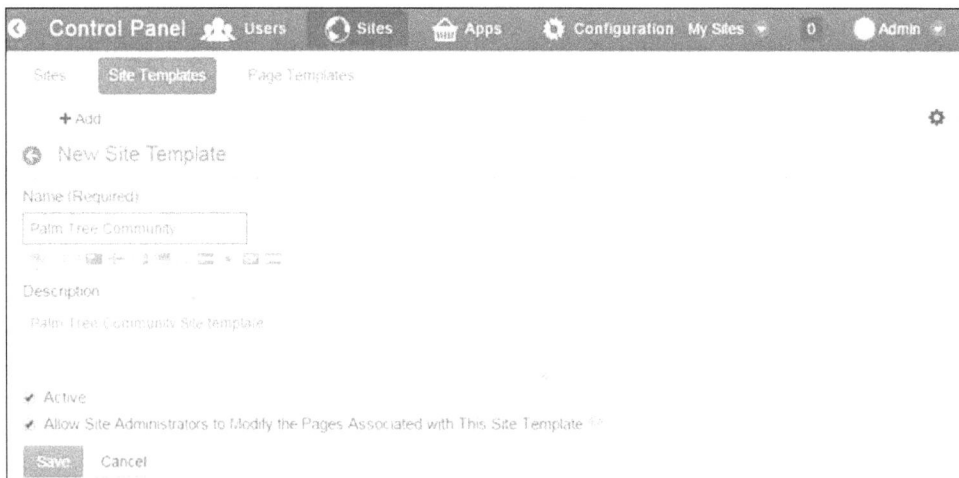

Figure 3.20: Adding a new site template

Authentications

As mentioned earlier, you don't need to type users all at a time. You can add users in bulk via LDAP and SSO. At the same time, you might require the facility for strangers to create accounts and for the users to then request their password via the **Forgot Password** function. How can you customize these features? Let's take a deeper look at authentications.

General configuration

Generally speaking, user login functions are configurable in the portal. By default, authentication is based on the portal database. However, as an administrator, you would be able to set up authentications based on LDAP and SSO other than that on the portal database.

As shown in the following screenshot, you could set up the portal so that users can authenticate by e-mail address, screen name, or user ID. You could allow users to automatically log in, request forgotten passwords, and request password reset links. You could also allow strangers to create accounts and create accounts with a company e-mail address (for strangers) and require them to verify their e-mail address.

Portal settings allows you to do settings for the whole portal. The following screenshot shows the **Authentication** settings for the portal:

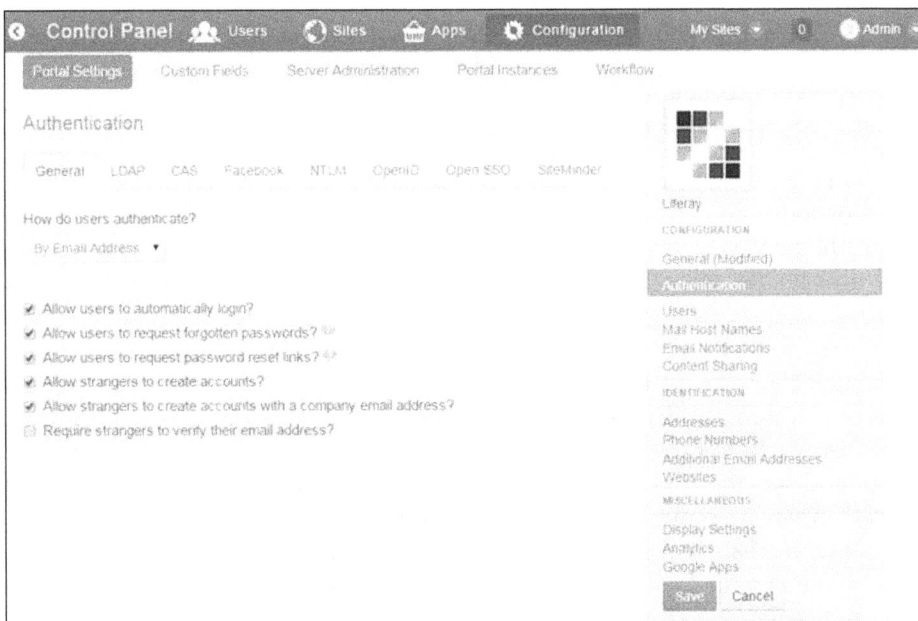

Figure 3.21: Portal Settings and Authentication

For example, imagine that you are planning to set authentication by screen name. You can do it as follows:

1. Navigate to **Control Panel** | **Configuration** | **Portal Settings** | **Authentication**.

2. Select **By Screen Name** from the **How do users authenticate?** drop-down menu. There are other options, such as **By Email Address** and the **By User ID** drop-down menu.

3. Click on the **Save** button.

What's happening?

As you can see, the following items are set to **true**: Allow users to automatically log in? Allow users to request forgotten passwords? Allow users to request password reset links? Allow strangers to create accounts—only the item, that is? Allow strangers to create accounts with a company e-mail address? Require strangers to verify their email address? This is all set to `false` by default.

The portal has the following settings by default in `portal.properties`:

```
basic.auth.password.required=true
company.security.auth.type=emailAddress
company.security.auth.requires.https=false
company.security.auto.login=true
company.security.send.password=true
company.security.send.password.reset.link=true
company.security.strangers=true
company.security.strangers.verify=false
```

As shown in the previous code, the portal sets the `basic.auth.password.required` property to `true` to require a password when using basic authentication. Moreover, the portal can authenticate users based on their e-mail addresses, screen name, or user ID. By default, the `company.security.auth.type` property is set as `emailAddress`. You can set the `company.security.auth.requires.https` property to `true` to ensure that users log in with HTTPS. The portal sets the `company.security.auto.login` property to `true` to allow users to select the "remember me" feature to automatically log in to the portal, sets the `company.security.send.password` property to `true` to allow users to ask the portal to send them their password, and sets the `company.security.strangers` property to `true` to allow strangers to create accounts and register themselves on the portal. In addition, if strangers who create accounts need to be verified via e-mail, you can set the `company.security.strangers.verify` property to `true`.

Auto login

The portal has specified auto login as follows in `portal.properties`:

```
auto.login.hooks=com.liferay.portal.security.auth.CASAutoLogin,com
    .liferay.portal.security.auth.FacebookAutoLogin,com.liferay.
    portal.security.auth.NtlmAutoLogin,com.liferay.portal.security.
    auth.OpenIdAutoLogin,com.liferay.portal.security.auth.
    OpenSSOAutoLogin,com.liferay.portal.security.auth.
    RememberMeAutoLogin,com.liferay.portal.security.auth.
    SiteMinderAutoLogin
auto.login.ignore.hosts=
auto.login.ignore.paths=
```

As shown in the preceding code, the `auto.login.hooks` property inputs a list of comma delimited class names, such as CAS, OpenID, OpenSSO, NTLM, SiteMinder, and so on, that implement `com.liferay.portal.security.auth.AutoLogin`. These classes will run in consecutive order for all unauthenticated users until one of them returns a valid user ID and password combination. If no valid combination is returned, then the request continues to process normally. If a valid combination is returned, then the portal will automatically log in that user with the returned user ID and password combination.

In addition, the `auto.login.ignore.hosts` property sets the hosts that will be ignored for auto login, and the property `auto.login.ignore.paths` sets the paths that will be ignored for auto login.

LDAP authentication

The portal supports LDAP authentication. The portal provides support, by default, for Apache Directory Server, Fedora Directory Server, Microsoft Active Directory Server, Novell eDirectory, OpenLDAP, OpenDS, and so on.

This section will show you how to set up LDAP authentication by examples. For instance, the enterprise, Palm Tree Publications, is planning to store and manage all users in an LDAP server (that is, Apache Directory Server). The LDAP server, in this example, has the following information:

```
Base Provider URL: ldap://docs.palmtree.com:10389
Base DN: ou=book,ou=system
Principal: uid=admin,ou=system
Credentials: secret
```

Thus, you can set authentication through the previous LDAP server. Let's do it by following these steps:

1. Navigate to **Control Panel** | **Configuration** | **Portal Settings** | **Authentication** | **LDAP** tab.

2. In the following settings, check **Enabled** and **Required**. Note that when the required checkbox is selected, the authentication will be done only on LDAP servers.

3. Click on the **Add** button under the **LDAP Servers** section.

4. Input `LDAP-DOCS` as the server name.

5. Select the default value **Apache Directory Server**.

6. Under the **Connection** section, enter the Base Provider URL: `ldap://docs. palmtree.com:10389`; Base DN: `ou=book, ou=system`; Principal: `uid=admin,ou=system`; Credentials: `secret`.

7. Use default values in the **Users**, **Groups**, and **Import/Export** sections.

8. Select the **Import Enabled** checkbox under the **Import/Export** section if you want to import users in bulk.

9. Select the **Export Enabled** checkbox under the **Import/Export** section if you want to synchronize LDAP servers with the portal database.

10. Select the checkbox and use **LDAP Password Policy** under the **Password Policy** section if you are going to use the LDAP password policy.

11. Click on the **Save** button when you are ready.

> **Lightweight Directory Access Protocol** (**LDAP**) is an application protocol used to query and modify directory services running over TCP/IP. A **Directory Information Tree** (**DIT**) is data represented in a hierarchical, tree-like structure consisting of the **distinguished names** (**DNs**) of the directory entries.

LDAP settings for the portal allow the portal Administrator to set the LDAP properties. The following screenshot illustrates the LDAP settings pages:

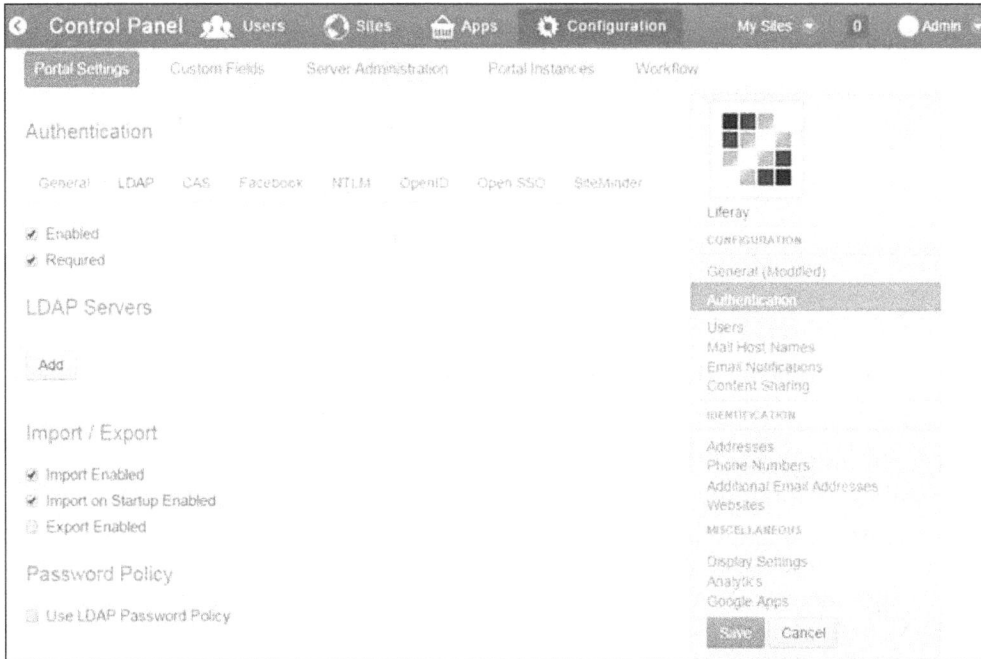

Figure 3.22: LDAP setting

Using LDAP effectively

It is very important to choose a suitable security model at the beginning of the portal implementation. The authentication mechanism, storage for user data, security settings, and business rules are based on the security model that you choose.

The portal imposes authentication through the login ID of the user (e-mail address or user ID) and password. This is where you choose a security model (for example, database-based managed accounts, **Single Sign-on** (**SSO**), or LDAP).

The portal imposes authorization by assigning a role to a specific user on a specific group. This is going to be the same, irrespective of which model you choose.

The security model that you choose (either database-based managed account or external systems, such as LDAP and SSO) will be based on the requirements of your enterprise.

In any case, you can't authenticate the portal against SSO and/or LDAP. Therefore, you will have to remove LDAP and SSO settings from the portal. Fortunately, you could run the following query:

1. Shut down the portal.
2. Run the following SQL script:

```
Delete from PortletPreferences where portletId = 'LIFERAY_PORTAL';
```

3. Restart the portal.

The previous query removed all settings related to the LIFERAY_PORTAL portlet ID.

LDAP authentication chain

There are two kinds of authentication chains supported in the portal: LDAP with portal database and multiple LDAP servers.

When configuring an LDAP server, you would have the ability to enable the LDAP server and make it required. If the LDAP server was marked as required, then authentication only goes through the LDAP server. If the LDAP server wasn't marked as required, then authentication goes through the LDAP server first and then goes through the portal database. Suppose that you have a lot of users on an LDAP server and a set of users existing in the portal database, then you could mark the LDAP server as nonrequired, building an authentication chain. Authentication first goes through the LDAP server and then through the portal database. In this example, you integrated two-pool users both in LDAP and in the portal database.

The portal allows authentication from multiple LDAP servers. Multiple LDAP servers can be specified in **Control Panel** under **Configuration** section | **Portal Settings** | **Authentication** | **LDAP**. The portal will try to authenticate them from top to bottom in order.

CAPTCHA

A **CAPTCHA** is a program that can generate and grade tests that humans can pass but current computer programs cannot. CAPTCHA have several applications for practical security, including, but not limited to, preventing comment spam in blogs, protecting website registration, online polls, preventing dictionary attacks, search engine bots, worms, and spam. Refer to http://www.google.com/recaptcha/intro/index.html.

The portal has specified a set of properties for CAPTCHA in `portal.properties`.

```
captcha.max.challenges=1
captcha.check.portal.create_account=true
captcha.check.portal.send_password=true
captcha.check.portlet.message_boards.edit_category=false
   captcha.check.portlet.message_boards.edit_message=false
```

As shown in the previous code, the `captcha.max.challenges` property sets the maximum number of CAPTCHA checks per portlet session. Set this value to **0** to always check. Set this value to a number less than 0 to never check. Unauthenticated users will always be checked on every request if CAPTCHA checks are enabled.

By default, the portal sets whether or not to use CAPTCHA checks for portal actions, creating an account via the property `captcha.check.portal.create_account` and sending a password via the property `captcha.check.portal.send_password`. In addition, the portal sets whether or not to use CAPTCHA checks for portlet actions, editing a category in the portlet Message Boards via the `captcha.check.portlet. message_boards.edit_category` property and editing a message in the portlet Message Boards via the `captcha.check.portlet.message_boards.edit_message` property.

You would be able to override the mentioned properties in `portal-ext.properties`.

SSO authentication

The portal also supports SSO integration. The portal provides integration with CAS, NTLM, OpenID, OpenSSO, and SiteMinder by default.

This section will show you how to set up SSO authentication with the help of examples. Suppose that the enterprise Palm Tree Publications has a CAS server with the URL **http://docs.palmtree.com/cas-web** and it is planning to set authentication through the SSO CAS server directly, as shown in the following screenshot. Let's do it by following these steps.

1. Go to **Control Panel | Configuration | Portal Settings | Authentication**.
2. Click on the **CAS** tab.
3. Select the **Enabled** checkbox.
4. Select the **Import from LDAP** checkbox. If this is checked, then users authenticated from CAS, who do not exist in the portal, will be imported from LDAP. Note that LDAP must be enabled.

5. Input the following values as an example:

   ○ **Login URL**: `http://docs.palmtree.com/cas-web/login`

   ○ **Logout URL**: `http://docs. palmtree.com/cas-web/logout`

   ○ **Server name**: `www.bookpub.com:8080`

   ○ **Server URL**: `http://docs. palmtree.com/cas-web`

6. Click on the **Save** button.

Now, you are ready to use the SSO CAS. Similarly, you can integrate OpenID, NTLM, OpenSSO, and SiteMinder with the portal.

Portal Administrator has permissions to set the **Central Authentication Service (CAS)** settings; here's the screenshot for the CAS settings page:

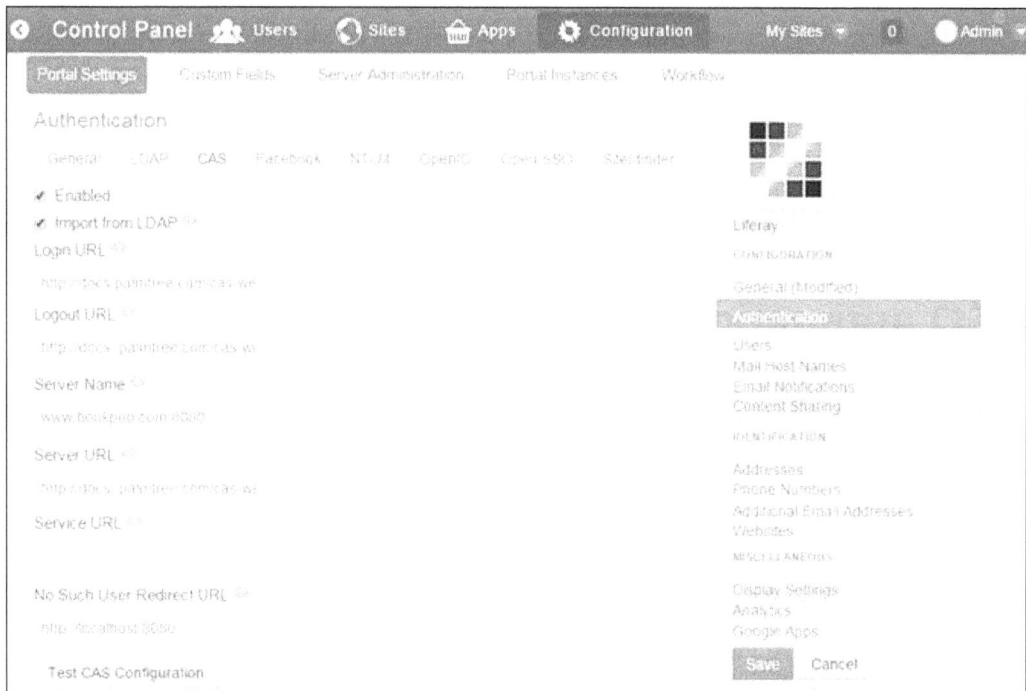

Figure 3.23: The CAS SSO configuration

OpenID authentication

We can also use **OpenID** as authentication. Let's enable OpenID authentication by following these steps:

1. Go to **Control Panel | Configuration | Portal Settings | Authentication**.

2. Click on the **OpenID** tab.

3. Select the checkbox to enable OpenID.

4. Click on the **Save** button to save the changes.

Now, it is ready for users to log in through OpenID. OpenID is a decentralized single sign-on system. Refer to `http://openid.net`.

By default, the portal has the following configuration in `portal.properties`:

```
open.id.auth.enabled=true
```

As shown in the preceding code, the portal sets the property `open.id.auth.enabled` to `true` to enable OpenID authentication. If this property is set to `true`, then the `auto.login.hooks` property must contain a reference to the `com.liferay.portal.security.auth.OpenIdAutoLogin` class. OpenID authentication can be disabled by setting the following property in `portal-ext.properties` instead of the preceding Web UI:

```
open.id.auth.enabled=false
```

Once we set `open.id.auth.enabled` to `false`, either by property or by Web UI, OpenID authentication gets disabled, and the OpenID sign-in link will get hidden in the Sign In portlet.

Open SSO authentication

Sun Open SSO Enterprise (short for **Open SSO** — renamed **OpenAM**) is the single solution for web access management, federation, and web services security. Refer to `http://opensso.dev.java.net`.

The portal has specified the following properties to integrate Open SSO into `portal.properties` and the corresponding web UI:

```
open.sso.auth.enabled=false
open.sso.ldap.import.enabled=false
open.sso.login.url=http://openssohost.example.com:8080/opensso/UI/
    Login?goto=http://portalhost.example.com:8080/c/portal/login
    open.sso.logout.url=http://openssohost.example.com:8080/
    opensso/UI/Logout?goto=http://portalhost.example.com:8080/
    web/guest/home
```

```
open.sso.service.url=http://openssohost.example.com:8080/opensso
open.sso.screen.name.attr=uid
open.sso.email.address.attr=mail
open.sso.first.name.attr=givenname
open.sso.last.name.attr=sn
```

As shown in the preceding code, Open SSO is disabled by default since the `open.sso.auth.enabled` property is set to false. You could set this to **true** to enable Open SSO. If the property is set to true, then the `auto.login.hooks` property must contain a reference to the `com.liferay.portal.security.auth.OpenSSOAutoLogin` class.

When enabling Open SSO, you need specify the properties login URL `open.sso.login.url`, logout URL `open.sso.logout.url`, and service URL `open.sso.service.url`. You need to override these properties in `portal-ext.properties`.

For example, let's say that Open SSO has been installed at a service URL, `http://liferay.palmtree.com:8090/opensso`, and the Liferay Portal is installed at `http://liferay.palmtree.com:8080`. If so, then you would have the following values:

- **Login URL**:

    `open.sso.login.url=http://liferay.palmtree.com:8090/opensso/UI/Login?goto=http://liferay.palmtree.com:8080/c/portal/login`

- **Logout URL**:

    `open.sso.logout.url=http://liferay.palmtree.com:8090/opensso/UI/Logout?goto=http://liferay.palmtree.com:8080/web/guest/home`

In addition, the following attributes are configurable: `firstName=cn, lastName=sn, screenName=givenName, emailAddress=mail` via properties `open.sso.screen.name.attr, open.sso.email.address.attr, open.sso.first. name. attr`, and `open.sso.last.name.attr`.

> Note that if Open SSO and Liferay are installed in the same domain with a default configuration, such as `Encode Cookie Value = True`, then it works fine. If Open SSO and the portal are installed in different domains with the same settings, then it will get the redirect loop. However, anyway Open SSO and the portal should work well across domains. This issue is still open at the time of writing this.

General settings

Let's also say that the admin Palm Tree changed **Main Configuration Name** and **Mail Domain** to bookpub.com and updated the company logo to PalmTree_logo.png under **Portal Settings**, as shown in the following screenshot:

1. Go to **Control Panel** | **Configuration** | **Portal Settings** | **Display Settings**.

2. You will find the **Language and Time Zone** section. Below that, you will find the **Logo** section.

3. Navigate to the logo file from the local system and save it.

Portal **Display Settings** allow the portal Administrator to set the settings for the whole portal. If any change in settings affects the whole portal, you will get a screenshot displaying the **Display Settings** page:

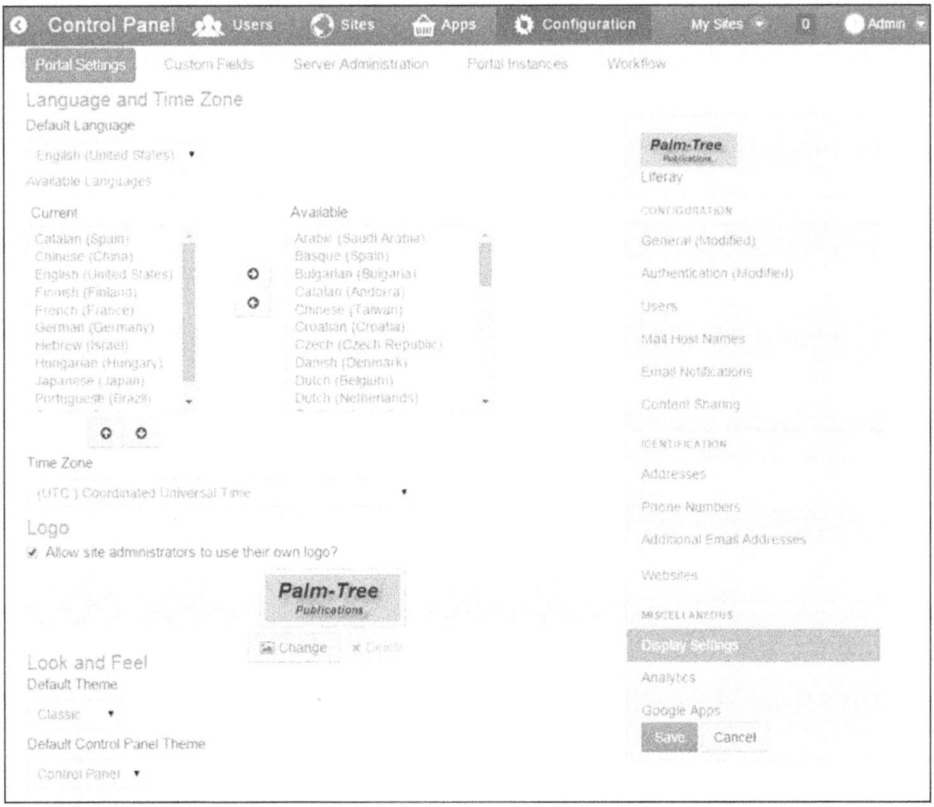

Figure 3.24: Portal Settings

Roles

Roles are groupings of users that share a particular function within the portal according to a particular scope. Administrators can add roles that can be granted permissions to various functions within portlet applications.

Roles in Liferay define permissions according to their scope. Liferay has roles with respect to **Portal**, **Organization**, and **Site**. Its roles are more drilled down and frame the bigger scope for Liferay Portal.

Let's see a role with a different scope. Roles have a lot of emphasis all over the portal. We need to make sure all the roles have the right entitlements for each and every activity. The following screenshot shows this:

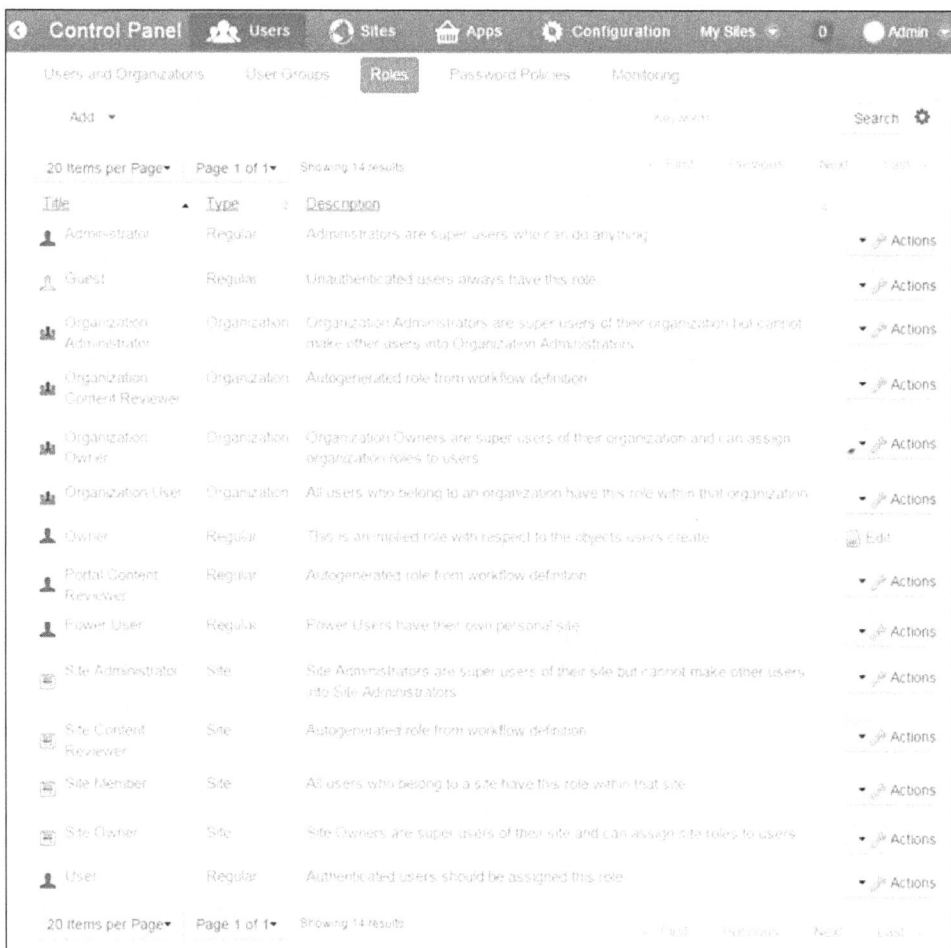

Figure 3.25: Roles

As you can see, out-of-the-box roles are defined for different scopes with respect to **Portal**, **Organization**, and **Site**:

- **Portal (Regular User):**
    - ◦ **Administrator**: Administrators are the super users – they have the right to do anything
    - ◦ **Power user**: A power user has their owner personal site and can be distinguished from normal users
    - ◦ **User**: Authenticated users should be assigned this role
    - ◦ **Guest**: Unauthenticated users always have this role

- **Organization:**
    - ◦ **Organization Administrator**: These are the super users of their Organization but cannot give the right to other users as organization administrators.
    - ◦ **Organization Owner**: These are owners and super users of their organization. They can also assign organization roles to users.
    - ◦ **Organization User**: All users who belong to an organization have their role within that organization.

- **Site:**
    - ◦ **Site Administrator**: These are super users of their site but can't assign other users as site administrators.
    - ◦ **Site Owner**: These are owners and super users of the site and can assign site roles to users.
    - ◦ **Site Members**: All users who belong to a site have this role within that site.

The preceding roles cannot be removed. Well, in Liferay, you can create your own role as per organization requirement. Let's say Palm Tree Publications needs roles for users to handle the Message Board portlet in their page. Let's name these roles `MB Topic Admin` and `MB Category Admin`.

Adding a role

First of all, we need to create a role called `MB Topic Admin`. Let's do that now:

1. Click on **Roles** under the **Users** category of **Control Panel**.

2. Click on the **Add** button and select a type with the **Regular User** value from the options: **Regular User**, **Organization**, and **Site**.

3. Enter an `MB Topic Admin` value in the **Name** input field as well as that of the **Title** input field and the **Description** input field.

4. Click on the **Save** button if you are ready.

Other roles can be created in a similar way. After adding roles, we can view them.

Editing a role

To edit a role, click on **Roles** under **Users** of **Control Panel** first. Then, locate the role you want to edit. Click on the **Edit** icon from the **Actions** tab on the right-hand side of the role, or click on any links of the role. In the edit page, type changes in the **Name**, **Title**, and **Description** input fields. Then, click on the **Save** button to save the changes.

Deleting roles

For some reason, a role does not exist anymore. We can delete this role from the portal by following these steps:

1. Click on **Roles** under the **Users** category of **Control Panel** first.

2. Locate the role (for example, **MB Category Admin**) that you want to delete.

3. Then click on the **Delete** icon from the **Actions** tab on the right-hand side of the role. A screen will appear that asks whether you want to permanently delete the selected roles.

4. Click on the **OK** button.

Note that you can delete a customized role whether it has members associated with it or not. When a customized role gets deleted, membership and permission definitions would get removed permanently.

Assigning members

We can assign a particular role to a specific user. This can be done by following these steps:

1. Click on **Roles** under the **Users** category of **Control Panel**.

2. Click on the **Assign Members** icon from the **Actions** tab next to the role that you want to assign members to.

3. Since the **Current** tab is selected by default, there are no users associated with this role. Therefore, click on the **Available** tab in order to search for the user of your choice.

4. Check the checkbox next to the user.

5. Click on the **Update Associations** button. If you need to verify this, it can be done by clicking on the **Current** tab to confirm that the association was set successfully.

6. If you as an administrator decided that this association should be discarded, then you can uncheck the checkbox next to the user's name and click on the **Update Associations** button again.

Similarly, we can assign other entities, (such as site, organization, location, or user group), to a regular, customized role or system roles (such as Administrator, Power User, and so on). To do so, we just need to repeat the preceding steps. In fact, an identical result would have been achieved by associating the previously selected role with an appropriate entity, instead of directly to the user, if they were a member of an entity.

Authorization

As mentioned earlier, authorization is a process of finding out whether the user, once identified, is permitted to access a resource. This process is implemented by assigning and checking permissions (using roles).

Permission

Permission is an action on a resource. The portal provides a full security model incorporated into fine-grained permissions and role-based access control. It will give administrators full control over access and privileges to portlets, layouts, and groups within the portal. This means that there are two main features on permissions. First of all, permissions are fine-grained in the portal. For example, for a given page, permissions could be **Add Discussion**, **Delete Discussion**, **Update**, **Update Discussion**, **Permissions**, **Delete**, and **View**.

The following table shows the permission actions on pages:

Permission name	Permission functional description
Add Discussion	This provides the ability to add discussions (comments) on a page
Delete Discussion	This provides the ability to delete discussions (comments) on a page
Update	This provides the ability to update the current page
Update Discussion	This provides the ability to update discussions (comments) on a page
View	This provides the ability to view the current page
Permissions	This provides the ability to assign permissions on a page
Delete	This provides the ability to delete a page

Secondly, permissions are always assigned through roles in the portal. For example, the user Rolf Hess is a member of the role MB Topic Admin. As mentioned in the previous chapter, we have the **Welcome** page in the Guest community. Now, we are going to assign the permission **View** on that page for Rolf Hess.

Defining permissions on a role

A role is the set of collection of permission to be assigned to users who belong to it. So, you have to assign the members to the role and define the permission.

Let's define the permission for **MB Topic Admin**. To do that, perform the following steps:

1. Click on **Roles** under the **Users** category of **Control Panel**. You will be shown a list of all the roles.

2. Choose the role for which you want to define the permission, say **MB Topic Admin**.

3. Click on the **Action** button and select **Define Permissions**; you will see a list of all the permissions defined for the role. However, for MB Topic Admin, no roles are defined. So, no list will appear and this message will be shown: **This role does not have any permission.**.

4. On the left-hand side, all the categories of permission are listed with respect to portal components.

5. Select Message Boards from **Site Administration | Applications**. You will be able to see the different permissions for the particular role.

6. Now, select the permission from the list in Message Boards, such as Messages, Message Boards category, Message Board Message, and Message Board Threads. This has several permission options, such as add, delete, view, add file, and so on.

7. Finally click on **Save** to save the selected permission option.

> In Liferay, these permissions fall under various categories, such as **Control Panel: Users, Sites, Apps and Configuration**; **Site Administration: Pages, Content, Users, Configuration, Applications**; **My Account: Account Settings, My Pages, My Workflow Task**, and **My Submissions**. For scoped roles, you need to click on the **Options** link on **individual portlets**.

Site Content permissions cover the content the installed portlets create. If you pick one of the portlets from this list, you'll get options to define permissions on its content. For example, if you pick Message Boards, you'll see permissions to create categories and threads or delete and move topics.

Application permissions affect the application as a whole. So, using our Message Boards example, application permissions might define who can add the Message Board portlet to a page.

The control panel permissions affect how the portlet appears to the user in the control panel. Some control panel portlets have a **Configuration** button, so you can define who gets to see that as well as who gets to see an application in the control panel. The following screenshot shows this:

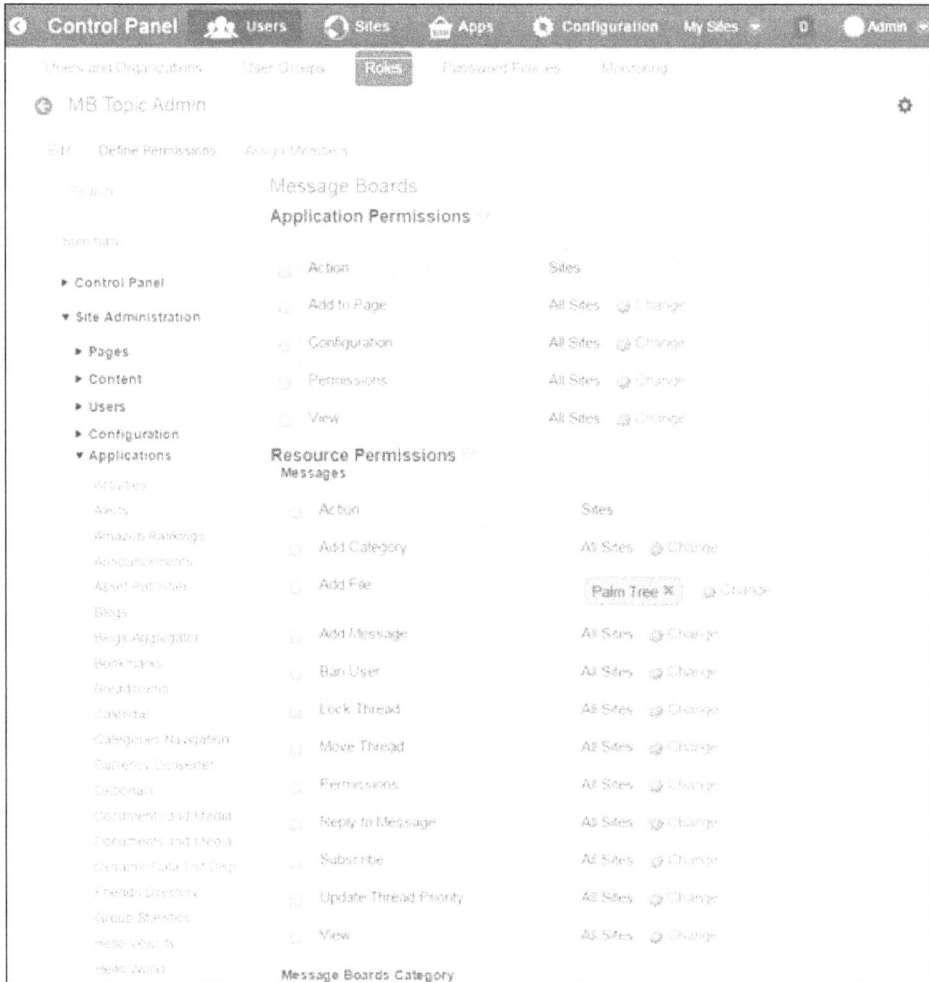

Figure 3.26: Permission defined for the Message Board

You can also limit the scope of the permission to a particular user role by clicking on the limit scope of the user with respect to application permission. As you can see in the preceding screenshot, in which the **MB Topic Admin** role is defined for the message board with the portal scope and the Palm Tree organization, you can easily change the scope and add multiple scopes.

Permission algorithms

The portal includes a pretty flexible permission system based on the concepts of roles, permissions, and resources, which provide several different implementations for the algorithm used to check whether a given user has permissions to perform certain actions or not.

RBAC stands for **Role Based Access Control**. It is a permission system, in which permissions are always assigned through roles. The RBAC implementation was started in Portal 5.1 as a way to improve the existing system, especially in terms of ease of use and performance. There are two algorithms for RBAC implementation at the time of writing this:

- Algorithm 5 was introduced for Portal 5.1 or above. It uses a regular normalized implementation.

- Algorithm 6 was introduced for Portal 5.3 or above. Algorithm 6 is an improved version of Algorithm 5. It provides exactly the same functionality as that of Algorithm 5, but it uses bitwise operations for even faster speed.

In particular, it's possible to assign permissions not only through roles, but also directly to organizations, sites, and individual users. However, this flexibility has a cost in performance and UI complexity.

What's happening?

The portal has set a default permission algorithms in `portal.properties`. The default value of the permission algorithm for Version 5.0 or below is 2. The default value of the permission algorithm for versions 5.1 and 5.2 is 5. Starting from Version 5.3, the default value of the permission algorithm is 6. This is as follows:

```
permissions.user.check.algorithm=6
```

This code sets the algorithm used to check permissions for a user. This is useful so that you can optimize the search for different databases. Of course, depending on the data, you can use different algorithms. To do so, just override the property `permissions.user.check.algorithm` in `portal-ext.properties`:

```
permissions.checker=com.liferay.portal.security.permission.
AdvancedPermissionChecker
```

If you see `portal.properties`, then `permissions.checker` is mapped with `com.liferay.portal.security.permission.AdvancedPermissionChecker` by default to check permissions for actions on objects. This class can be overridden with a custom class that implements `com.liferay.portal.security.permission.PermissionChecker`.

```
permissions.view.dynamic.inheritance=true
```

As shown in the preceding code, the portal sets the `permissions.view.dynamic.inheritance` property to `true` to automatically check the view permission on parent categories or folders when checking the permission on a specific item. For example, if the property was set to `true` to be able to have access to a document, a user must have the View permission on the document's folder and all its parent folders.

Configuration of portal navigation

Once you have completed all the settings, you can configure the portal navigation. In *Chapter 2, Setting Up a Home Page and Navigation Structure for the Intranet*, we configured the domain with `http://www.bookpub.com:8080`, so whenever you trigger the URL in the browser, it lands on the site page by default. Let's change the configuration for the Palm Tree site by following these simple steps:

1. Log in as the portal administrator and go to **control panel | configuration | portal settings**. You will see the **Main Configuration** page; in the same page, locate the **Navigation** section.

2. For **Home URL**, set the value `/web/palmtree/home`.

3. For **Default Landing Page** set value `/web/palmtree/home`.

4. Change the value for **Mail Domain** with `bookpub.com`.

5. Change the value of **Virtual Host** with `www.bookpub.com`.

6. Finally, save the changes by clicking on the **Save** button.

Follow this screenshot to complete the configuration for the portal navigation of Palm Tree site.

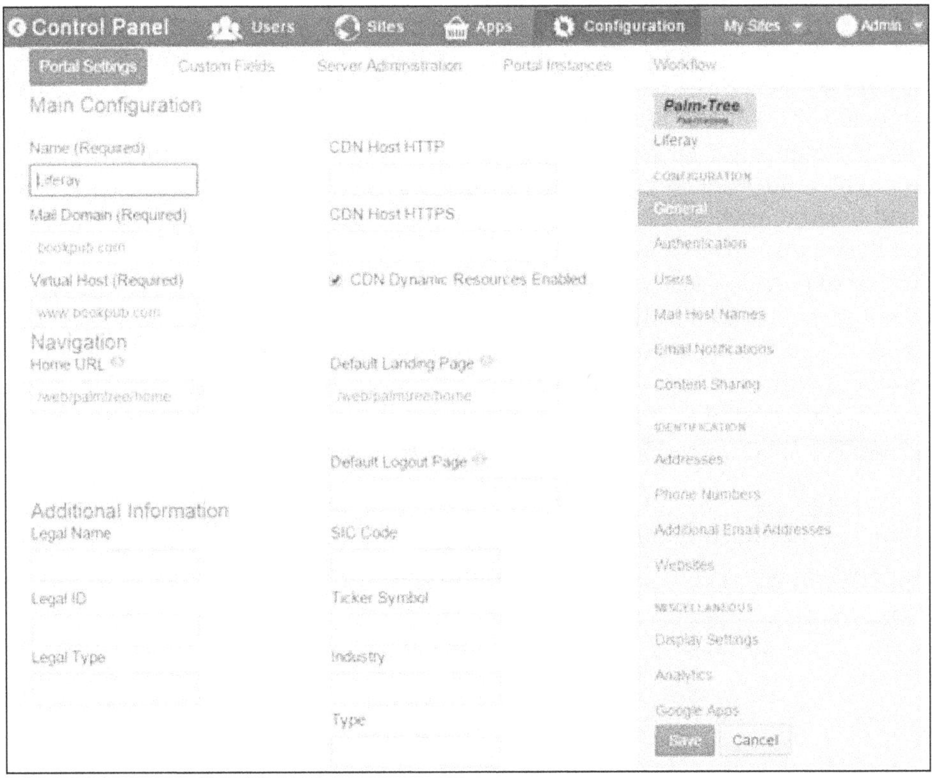

Figure 3.27: Portal Settings for navigation

Now when you trigger the URL http://www.bookpub.com:8080 in the browser, you will land on the Palm Tree home page. Note that on getting the Palm Tree home page URL, you need to copy the URL from /web until the end.

Summary

This chapter first introduced you to creating and managing organizations and locations. We saw how we can add and manage users (for example, view, search, update, deactivate, restore, delete, and impersonate) and how we can add and manage user groups (for example, view, search, update, delete, and assign). It also introduced you to sites, site membership, and site templates. Then, it introduced integration into different authentication servers, such as LDAP, CAS, NTLM, OpenID, and Open SSO. Furthermore, it introduced you to managing permissions and showed how to add roles and manage roles (for example, view, search, update, delete, and assign). You learned that: a resource is a base object, a permission is an action on a resource, a role is a collection of permissions, roles can be assigned to a user, user group, site, location, or organization, a user is an individual who perform tasks using the portal, organizations represent the enterprise-department-location hierarchy, a location is a special organization, with one and only one parent organization associated and with no child organization associated, a community is a special group with a flat structure, and a user group is a special group with no context, which may hold a number of users.

In the next chapter, you will go through the forums (Message Board), categorization, tags, and Asset Publishing, where you will learn more about content and communication between users in a portal through Message Board.

4
Forums, Categorization, and Asset Publishing

In the intranet website bookpub.com of the enterprise Palm Tree Publications, it would be nice to provide an environment for employees to discuss book ideas and proposals. It would also be nice to share important and interesting content with other users inside or outside of the intranet website, content tagging, and publishing. The Message Boards portlet (also called discussion forums) provides a full-featured discussion forums solution. Tags and taxonomies provide a way of organizing and aggregating content. The Asset Publisher portlet allows us to publish any type of content, including Message Boards messages as if it were web content—filtering either through a set of publishing rules dynamically or by manual selections.

In the preceding chapters, we revealed the page and group boxes in the portal-group-page-content pattern. In this chapter, we're going to open the content box and first introduce you to the item "Message Boards" in the content box. This chapter will introduce you to Message Boards first and focus on how to use Message Boards, how to configure the portlet, and how to implement the preceding requirements within Message Boards. Then, we will address taxonomies to aggregate content—for example, Message Boards threads and posts. Finally, it will introduce us to the Asset Publisher portlet to publish any type of content, including Message Boards messages through Categories or Tags.

By the end of this chapter, you will have learned how to:

- Manage categories, threads, and posts of Message Boards
- Set permissions on Message Boards categories, threads, and posts
- Manage tags, tag content, and display tags
- Set permissions on tags

- Manage categories, tag content, and display categories
- Set permissions on categories
- Configure Asset Publisher via Tags and Categories to publish the Message Board

Message Boards

In brief, Message Boards (portlet ID 19) is a full-featured forum solution with threaded views, categories, RSS capability, avatars, file attachments, previews, dynamic list of recent posts, and forum statistics. Message Boards work with the fine-grained permissions and role-based access control model to give detailed levels of control to administrators and users. This section will give examples of how to use, configure, and implement Message Boards.

In order to provide an environment for employees to discuss book ideas and proposals, we could use the Message Boards portlet of the Guest public pages as an example. In this section, suppose that we're using the Message Boards portlet for a page of Guest public pages. A category called will be created. The category **Book Category** contains four categories — **Book Category A**, **Book Category B**, **Book Category C**, and **Book Category D**.

As an administrator of the enterprise Palm Tree Publications, you would be able to create a page called **Forums** in the Guest public pages and then add the Message Boards portlet to the page **Forums**. Then, you are ready to create a category called Book Category. After doing that, add four subcategories to the category Book Category; they are "Book Category A", "Book Category B", "Book Category C", and "Book Category D".

Of course, you can customize Message Boards in **Control Panel** instead of doing the same on a specific page. You may refer to the scope of Message Boards in the coming section. Message Boards are one of the most widely used collaboration features and are called discussion forums. They allow us to post messages (threads and posts) on a website for others to read. These messages are sorted within categories.

You can configure Message Boards by clicking on the **gear** icon beside the portlet title bar and clicking on **Configuration**. You will be able to see the **Setup** tab and a few other tabs. Under the **Setup** tab, you will be able to configure for the Message Boards e-mail features, thread priorities, and user ranking.

Managing categories

As discussed previously, you can create categories and subcategories. Let's see the steps to create categories for Message Boards. Log in as Site Administrator of the enterprise Palm Tree Publications. Now, you will be able to create the category Book Category and subcategories Book Category A, Book Category B, Book Category C, and Book Category D. These subcategories will hold messages related to book ideas and proposals.

Adding categories

First of all, we are going to create a category called **Book Category**:

1. Go to the **Home** public pages, that is, Palm Tree.
2. Add a page called Forums if the page isn't there and change **Layout Template** to 1 Column by clicking on **Edit | Page** under the dock bar menu.
3. Add the **Message Boards** portlet to the Forums if the **Message Boards** portlet isn't already there.
4. Click on the **Add Category** button.
5. Enter the name **Book Category** and the description Books.
6. Permissions settings keep default settings. In order to configure additional permissions, click on the **More option** link, as shown in the next screenshot (*Figure 4.1*).
7. Configure **Mailing List**. We just use the default settings where no options are selected.
8. Click on the **Save** button to save the inputs.

You can definitely add other categories. Generally speaking, Message Boards can have many categories, and each category can have many categories called subcategories within it. That is, a category has a hierarchical structure. For example, the category **Book Category** contains four categories — Book Category A, Book Category B, Book Category C, and Book Category D. Let's create the category Book Category A by following these steps:

1. Locate the newly created category "Book Category", and then click on its name.
2. Click on the **Add Subcategory** button.
3. Enter the name **Book Category A** and the description Liferay books.
4. Permissions settings keep default settings. In order to configure additional permissions, click on the **More option** link.

5. Configure **Mailing List** — leave it at its default value where no option is selected.

6. Click on the **Save** button to save the inputs.

Adding **Category** is illustrated in the following screenshot; follow the screenshot to create a category inside Message Board:

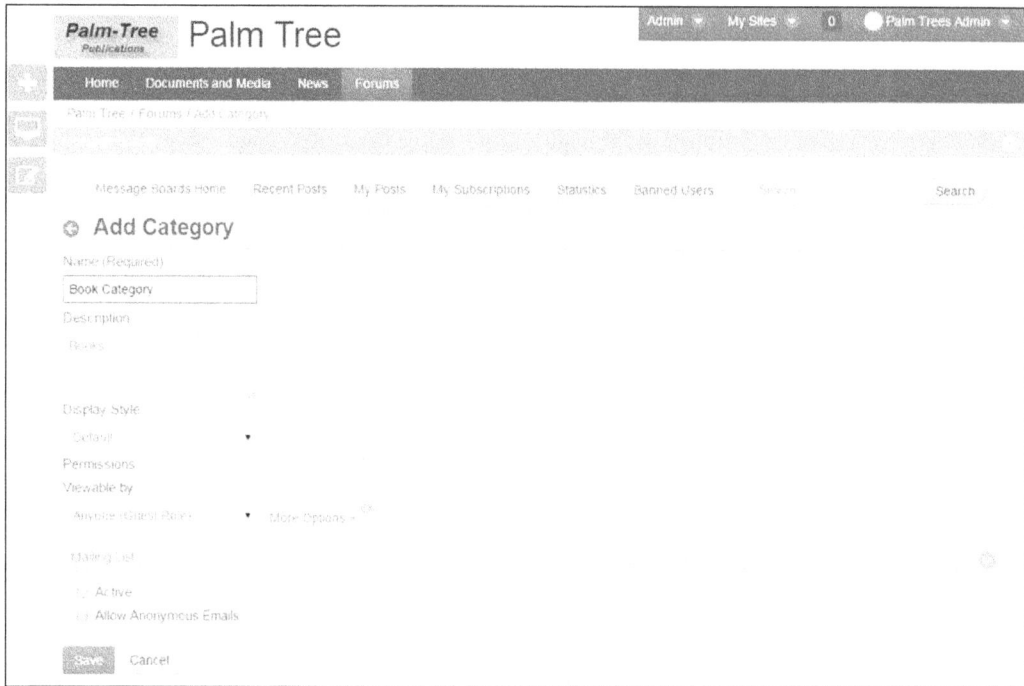

Figure 4.1: Adding a category to Message Board

Of course, you can add as many other categories or subcategories as you want. After creating subcategories, such as Book Category B, Book Category C, and Book Category D, we can view the subcategories, as shown in the following screenshot. In particular, Book Category B and Book Category C use the default permission setting, whereas Book Category D uses only the View permission in the role's **Site Member** column.

Highlights: In Liferay 6.2, parent category option, which appears while creating a category, has been removed. A new action "move" has been implemented on the category, which will allow you to move the particular category under another, different category. This feature gives the flexibility to move any category or subcategory to another category (as a parent).

The following screenshot shows the list of subcategories under the Book category:

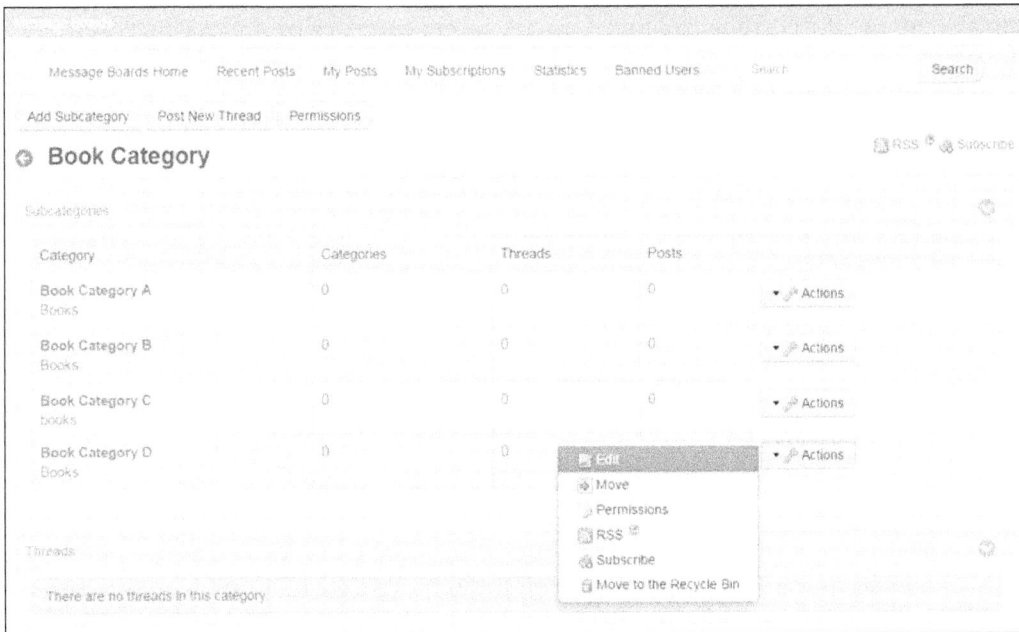

Figure 4.2: View subcategories

Move allows you to move the category under another category. You even get the option to merge the two categories. **Move to the Recycle Bin** allows you to move the category to Recycle Bin.

Editing categories

Categories or subcategories are editable. For example, you may need to change the description of the "Book Category" category from "Books" to "Books discussion category". Let's do it this way:

1. Locate a category, for example, "Book Category", which you want to edit.

2. Click on the **Edit** icon from the **Actions** button next to the category.

3. Keep the name value as is and update the description of the selected category, that is, "Book Category" with a value "Books discussion category".

4. Click on the **Save** button to save the changes.

Also, you can update the name. For example, we can update the name "Book Category" with a value "Books". Similarly, we can edit a subcategory, for example, Book Category C, by updating the name with the value "Liferay books".

Optionally, with the help of **Move**, you can change the parent category of a specific category or subcategory by selecting a particular category as its parent category. You can also merge the current category with its parent category or remove its parent category. If you remove the parent category, the current category will become a category at the root level.

Removing categories

Categories and subcategories are removable. You can't delete a category directly. You will have to move the unwanted category to the recycle bin. For instance, as the subcategory Book Category B doesn't exist anymore, you should remove it. Let's do it by following these steps:

1. Locate the "Books" category in order to list its subcategories.

2. Locate a subcategory, say Book Category B, which you want to delete.

3. Then click on the **Move to the Recycle Bin** icon from the **Actions** next to the category.

4. You will get message **The Message Boards Category Book Category B was moved to the Recycle Bin.** with an undo button. If you don't want to remove it, just click on **Undo**. It will revert back to its previous position.

> Note that removing the category will remove all related subcategories, threads, and posts that belong to this category. Also note that Recycle Bin is in the site scope. So, each site has its own recycle bin.

Viewing RSS feeds

You can view the RSS feeds of all Message Boards, categories, and subcategories. Suppose that you need to view RSS feeds of the "Books" category, you can do this as follows:

1. Select a category, for example, "Books".

2. Click on the **RSS** icon from the **Actions** next to the category.

Refer to the instructions in *Chapter 6, Blogs, WYSIWYG Editors, and Social Networking*.

Managing threads

After adding categories and subcategories, we are ready to post new threads. Generally speaking, a forum can have many categories, and each category may have many subcategories and threads.

Adding threads

Let's say we're going to post new thread **Let's discuss the book Liferay** under the **Liferay books** category. We'll do it by following these steps:

1. Select the **Books** category where you want to find the **Liferay books** subcategory.

2. Select the **Liferay books** subcategory where you want to add a thread by clicking on the subcategory name.

3. Click on the **Post New Thread** button.

4. Enter the subject **Let's discuss the book Liferay** and the body **Liferay Portal 6.1 Enterprise Intranets Book is one of the best Books for learning Liferay** through the default WYSIWYG editor.

5. Keep the checkbox **Mark as a Question** as default—if this is selected, then subsequent replies to this message can be marked as answers.

6. Keep the **Anonymous** checkbox as default—if this is selected, then this message will be posted anonymously.

7. Select the checkboxes **Subscribe Me** and **Allow Pingbacks**; it is selected by default. **Subscribe Me** will subscribe the post with mail notification to the poster. **Allow pingbacks** helps users to trackback the posts.

8. Permissions settings keep default settings. In order to configure additional permissions, click on the **More Options** link. We just use the default settings, as shown in the following screenshot.

9. You can click on the **Attachments** link, which will allow you to add files to the particular thread post. In this example, we won't attach any documents.

10. You can click on the **Categorization** link, which allows you to input **Tags**. Input tags **book** and **Liferay**, or select tags from existing tags by clicking on the **Suggestions** button.

11. You can link the related assets with this post by clicking on **Related Assets** and assigning the respective assets to a particular thread post.

12. You save the post or preview it before publishing the post by clicking on the **Save as Draft** and **Preview** buttons. Finally, you can publish the post by clicking on the **Publish** button.

There are some more actions, which make Message Board more effective for the business use case. In addition, you can attach files by clicking on the **Attach Files** button and upload files afterwards. Similarly, you can preview the thread before publishing it by clicking on the **Preview** button.

In particular, adding a new thread with a subject, for example, **Let's discuss the book Liferay**, will add a post automatically with the same subject as that of the thread. Refer to the following screenshot to create a new thread:

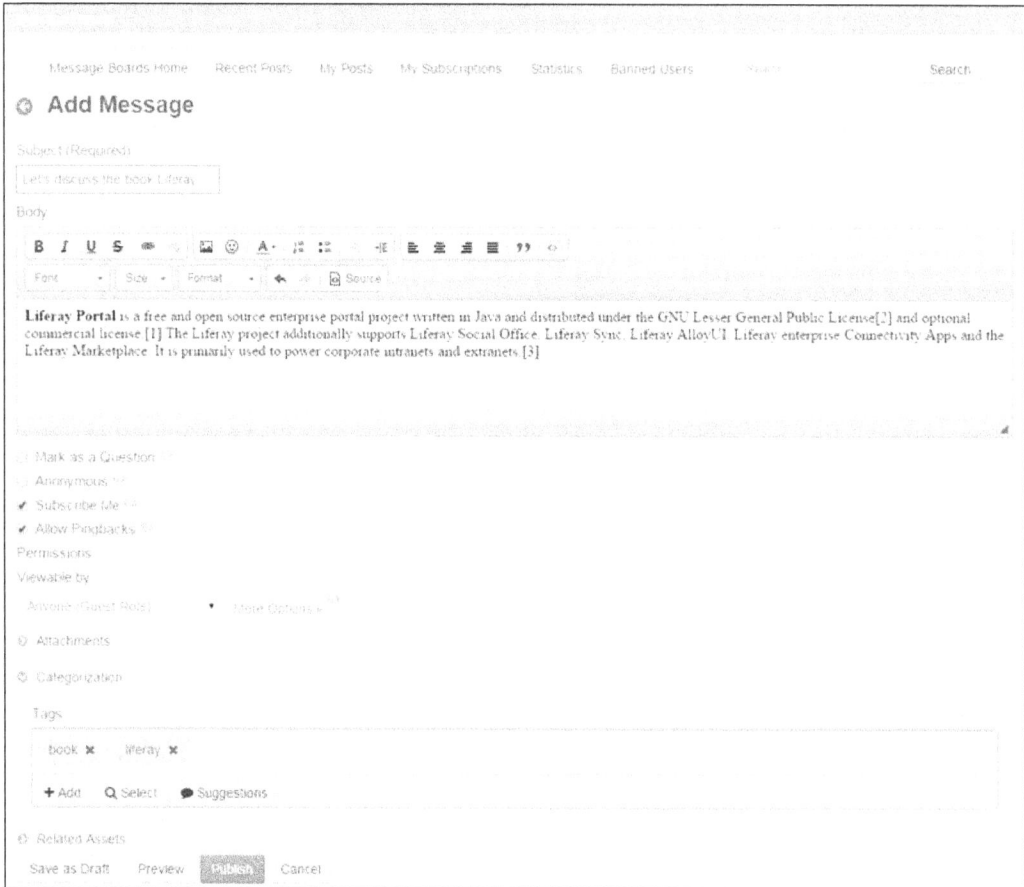

Figure 4.3: Adding a new thread

Refer to the tags instructions in the next section for information on tags.

Likewise, you can add other threads. Note that there's a breadcrumb at the top of the page that eases navigation. After adding the thread **Where is the outline of the Liferay book?**, navigate through the breadcrumb to the **Liferay Books** category, which will list the threads, as shown in the following screenshot:

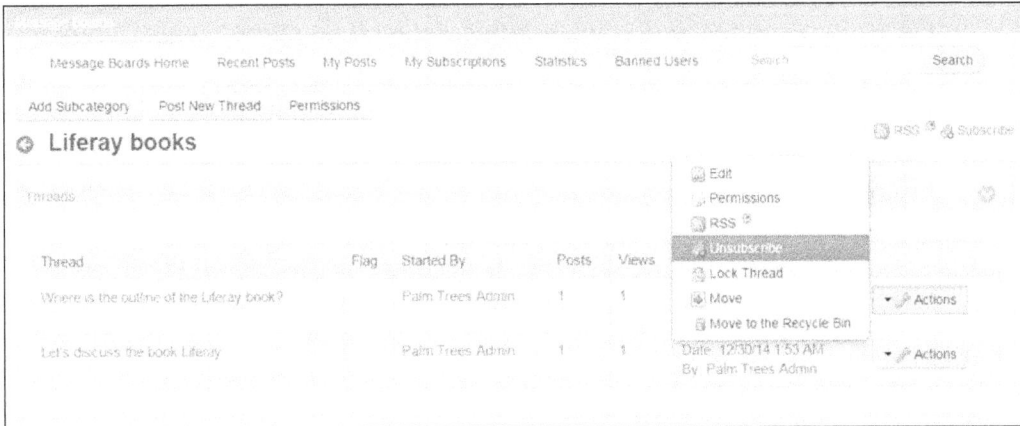

Figure 4.4: Performing an action on a thread

In the preceding screenshot, you can see many more links associated with the action button, which are **Edit**, **Permissions**, **RSS**, **Unsubscribe**, **Lock Thread**, and **Move to the Recycle Bin**. These links allow users to do certain jobs on **Thread Post**. Let's discuss them in brief:

- **Edit**: This allows you to edit the thread post
- **Permissions**: This allows you to set the access permissions for the thread
- **RSS**: This generates RSS for the particular thread
- **Unsubscribe**: This allows you to unsubscribe from the particular thread
- **Lock Thread**: This allows you to lock the thread so that people can view but cannot post. Conversely, you can unlock the thread by clicking on **Unlock Thread** if the thread is locked
- **Move**: This allows you to move the thread post from one category to another
- **Move to the Recycle Bin**: This allows you to move the subcategory to Recycle Bin

Let's discuss editing threads in detail.

Editing threads

Threads are editable too. You may need to change the subject of the thread **Where is the outline of the Liferay book?** to **Did you find the outline of the Liferay book?** Let's do this by following these steps:

1. Locate the thread **Where is the outline of the Liferay book?**, which you want to edit.

2. Click on the **Edit** icon from **Actions** next to the thread.

3. Update the subject of the selected category **Where is the outline of the Liferay book?** with the value **Did you find the outline of the Liferay book?**.

4. Click on the **Publish** button to publish the changes.

Of course, you can update the body and tags and select the checkbox **Mark as a Question** as well. Updating the subject of the thread, that is, **Let's discuss the book Liferay?** will automatically update the subject of the top-level post with the same subject as that of the thread.

Removing threads

Threads are removable too. For example, if the thread "Where is the outline of the Liferay book?" doesn't exist anymore, and you are required to remove it, do it by following these steps:

1. Locate the "**Did you find the outline of the Liferay book?**" thread, which you want to remove.

2. Then, click on the **Move to the Recycle Bin** icon from **Actions** next to the thread.

3. A screen will appear asking you whether you want to undo the action with the message **The Message Boards Thread Did you find the outline of the Liferay book? was moved to the Recycle Bin.** Click on the undo button to undo the action, else do nothing.

> Note that removing a thread will delete all related posts that belong to that thread.

Viewing RSS feeds

You can view RSS feeds of threads as well as categories. Suppose that you need to view RSS feeds of the thread **Let's discuss the book Liferay**. Let's do it by following these steps:

1. Navigate the **Books** category and the **Liferay books** subcategory.

2. Locate the thread **Let's discuss the book Liferay**.

3. Click on the **RSS** icon under **Actions** located next to the thread.

Managing posts

Finally, we are ready to add more posts. As you can see, a forum can have many categories. Each category can have many subcategories and threads, and each thread can have a lot of posts associated with it. Fortunately, you are able to manage posts easily by editing posts, replying to posts, deleting posts, viewing posts, and so on. For instance, if the user **David Berger** is a member of Guest Site, then he can easily reply to posts and edit posts.

Adding posts

The user **David Berger** wants to reply to the thread **Let's discuss the book Liferay** with the message **OK**. Let's do it as follows:

1. Log in as **David Berger**, go to the Palm Tree Publications site, and then go to the **forums** page.

2. Locate the **Books** category and the Liferay books subcategory.

3. Click on the thread with the name **Let's discuss the book Liferay**.

4. Locate the post—for example, **Let's discuss the book Liferay**, to which you want to reply first.

5. Then click on the **Reply** icon in the top-right corner of the post.

6. Keep the default subject **Re: Let's discuss the book Liferay**. Input the value of the body "Liferay 6.2 has lot many functions and features" via an editor and also the select tags or input tags.

7. Permissions settings keep default settings. In order to configure additional permissions, click on the **More Options** link—here, we will use the default settings.

8. Keep anonymous as the checkbox's default state.

9. Click on the **Publish** button to publish the change.

In addition, you can attach a file by clicking on the **Attach Files** button and preview the post by clicking on the **Preview** button. Moreover, you can reply with a quote by clicking on the **Reply with Quote** icon in the top-right corner of the post.

> Note that if Rolf Hess or any other user does not have the permission to access Message Board, then you have to provide the permissions by setting the permission in roles. Refer to the previous chapter for roles and permissions.

Editing posts

Posts are editable. To edit a post, click on the **Edit** icon in the bottom-right corner of the post. You can change the subject and body via a **WYSIWYG** editor and tags. Then, you simply have to click on the **Publish** button to publish the changes or click on the **Cancel** button to cancel those changes. Optionally, you can attach a file by clicking on the **Attach Files** button or preview the post by clicking on the **Preview** button. You can save the post too by clicking on the **Save as Draft** button.

In particular, updating the subject of the top-level post, for example, **Let's discuss the book Liferay**, will automatically update the subject of the thread (that the top-level post belongs to) with the same subject as that of the top-level post.

In addition, you would be able to split the current post into a new thread as well as add an explanation post to the source thread. To do this, first log out, and then log in as an administrator to get the permission to split threads and ban users. Then, locate a post, click on the **Split Thread** icon, followed by selecting the checkbox **Add explanation post to the source thread**. Add a subject and a body to the explanation, and then click on the **OK** button. Optionally, you will be able to reply to the current post with a quote by clicking on the **Reply with Quote** icon. See the following screenshot (*Figure 4.5*). You can even click on **Quick Reply** to replay any post, which provides the **WYSIWYG** editor just below the post, and you can reply and publish it.

Message Board also provides voting and flag features for each post, where users are able to vote for the post and also raise a flag for each post.

Banning users

In addition, you can ban a user if you have proper permissions. As previously stated, **David Berger** has a post called **OK** under the category **Book—Liferay Books**. As an administrator, you will see icon **Ban this user** under the logo of the user **David Berger**. If you need to ban this user, then simply click on the **Ban this user** icon. See the following screenshot (*Figure 4.5*). Then, you will see that the icon **Ban this user** becomes **Un-ban this user**.

When the user **David Berger** is logged in, he will see the message on Message Board: "**You have been banned by the moderator**".

As an administrator, you can unban the user **David Berger** simply by clicking on **Un-ban this user**. Then, you will see that the **Un-ban this user** label becomes **Ban this user** again.

Deleting posts

Posts are removable, too. For example, as the post **Re: Let's discuss the book Liferay** doesn't exist anymore, you can remove it. Let's do it by following these steps:

1. Locate the post **Re: Let's discuss the book Liferay**, which you want to delete.

2. Click on the **Delete** icon in the bottom-right corner of the post.

3. A screen will appear asking you whether you want to delete this. Click on **OK** to confirm the deletion, or on **Cancel** to cancel the deletion.

More interestingly, if the top-level post—for instance, **Let's discuss the book Liferay**, was deleted, the thread that the top-level post belongs to will be linked to the low-level post, such as **Re: Let's discuss the book Liferay**. If the top-level post, for example **Let's discuss the book Liferay**, is the only post in the thread, and if it is deleted, then the thread that the top-level post belongs to will also be deleted.

> Note that only the current post will be deleted when deleting a post inside a thread. The lower-level posts related to the current post will have a link to the top-level post of the current thread.

Viewing posts

All posts of a given thread can have different views, such as **Combination View**, **Flat View**, or **Tree View**. For example, the default view mode is **Combination View**. In order to change the current view mode to flat view, simply click on the **Flat View** button in the top-right corner, next to the navigation. Without a doubt, you can use **Tree View**.

You can also change the thread by clicking on the **Previous** or **Next** links, next to **Threads**. Moreover, you can change the categories by clicking on the category name on the breadcrumb bar.

Searching posts

You can easily find messages by searching. For instance, in order to search for posts that contain "book" in Message Boards, simply input that text as your search criterion. For example, enter "book" and then click on the **Search** button. A list of categories that contain the keywords as messages appears with the following columns: serial number, categories, messages (thread subject), thread posts, and thread views.

Search is scoped by category. For example, if you just need to search for messages, which contain the word "book" in the category **Categories | Books | Liferay books**, simply navigate to the category "Liferay books" first. Then, input the message keyword, for example, "book", and click on the **Search** button.

> What are "messages" in a search? Messages here refer to the content of threads and posts. The content contains the subject and body of threads and posts.

Viewing my posts

You can view your own posts by clicking on the **My Posts** tab in Message Boards. A list of your posts will appear with the **Thread**, **Started by**, **Posts**, **Views**, **Last Post**, **Status**, and **Actions** menus with a set of options, such as **Edit**, **Permissions**, **RSS**, **Subscribe/Unsubscribe**, **Lock Thread**, and so on.

Viewing recent posts

Similarly, you can view recent posts by clicking on the **Recent Posts** tab of Message Boards. A list of recent posts will appear with thread, started by, posts, views, last post, and actions with the **Thread**, **Started by**, **Posts**, **Views**, **Last Post**, and **Actions** menus with a set of options, such as **Edit**, **Permissions**, **RSS**, **Subscribe/Unsubscribe**, **Lock Thread**, **Move Thread**, and **Move to the Recycle Bin**.

Viewing statistics

Furthermore, you can view general statistics by clicking on the **Statistics** tab of Message Boards. On doing so, statistical data, such as the number of categories, posts, and participants, will appear. In addition, click on the **Top Posters** subtab to display a list of the most active users.

Viewing banned users

You can view a list of banned users if you have proper permissions. To do this, simply click on the **Banned Users** tab in Message Boards. A list of banned users will appear with their name, ban date, unban date, and the **Un-ban this user** icon. In order to unban this user, you just click on the **Un-ban this user** icon next to the unban dates.

The following screenshot shows the major actions in the thread post view screen. These actions help you to perform actions on the particular threads:

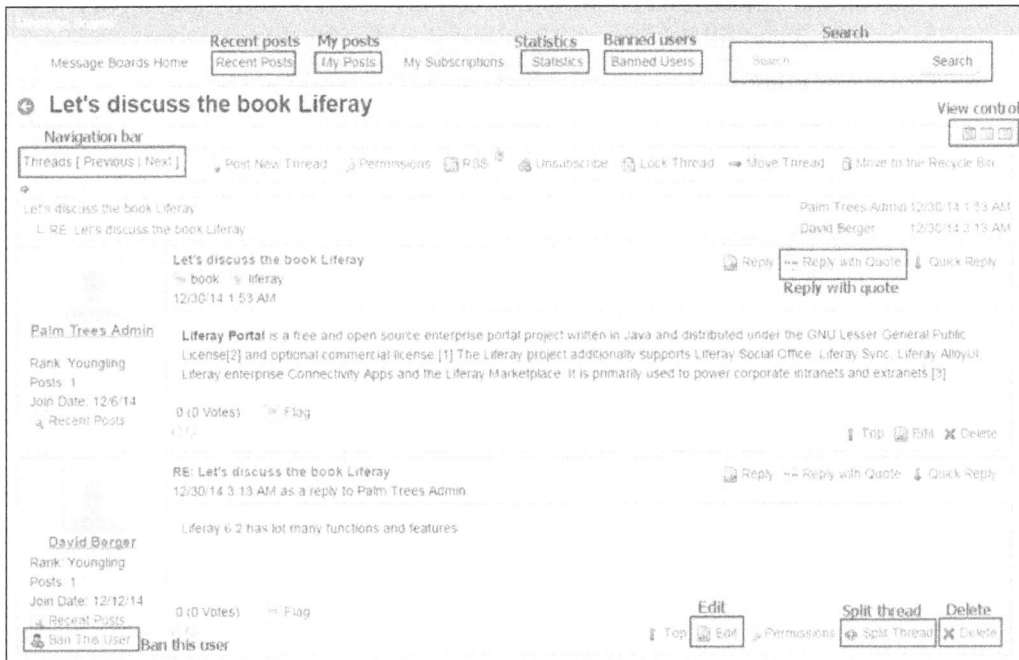

Figure 4.5: The Message Board thread screen

Subscribing to categories and threads

As users of Message Boards, you may be interested in the changes to messages in specific categories and threads. For example, as the "Palm Tree" administrator, you may be interested in the messages in the "Liferay Books" category. You want to watch out for any changes of the messages in this category. You can certainly use the subscription function in the "Liferay Books" category. Let's do it by following these steps:

1. Locate the "Liferay Books" category.

2. Click on the **Subscribe** icon from the **Actions** menu next to the category. The **Subscribe** icon will become an **Unsubscribe** icon for this category.

3. Of course, you can subscribe to other categories. You may be interested in the message of the thread **Let's discuss the book Liferay**. Therefore, you can subscribe to it as follows:

    1. Locate the "Liferay books" category and the thread **Let's discuss the book Liferay**.

    2. Click on the **Subscribe** icon from **Actions** next to the thread. The **Subscribe** icon will become **Unsubscribe**.

Obviously, you can subscribe to other threads. In addition, you can view your subscriptions by clicking on the **My Subscriptions** tab. You will find lists of subscribed categories and threads; refer to the following screenshot:

Figure 4.6: My Subscriptions

Unsubscribing from categories and threads

In addition, you can unsubscribe from the categories, subcategories, or threads that you are currently subscribed to. For example, you may need to unsubscribe from the thread **Let's discuss the book Liferay**. Let's do it by following these steps:

1. Click on the **My Subscriptions** tab in Message Boards.

2. Locate the thread **Let's discuss the book Liferay**.

3. Click on the **Unsubscribe** icon from **Actions** located next to the thread. The thread **Let's discuss the book Liferay** will disappear from the **My Subscriptions** view.

You can also unsubscribe from the thread **Let's discuss the book Liferay** from the Categories view by following these steps:

1. Locate the "Liferay books" category and the thread **Let's discuss the book Liferay**.

2. Click on the **Unsubscribe** icon from the **Actions** menu next to the thread. The **Unsubscribe** icon will become **Subscribe**.

In brief, there are two options to subscribe to and unsubscribe from Message Boards:

- Subscribe/unsubscribe through categories or subcategories
- Subscribe/unsubscribe through threads

Thus, the Message Boards portlet supports e-mail both as a means of sending new posts to users and as a way for those users to answer to posts or create new threads.

What's happening?

If you have subscribed to categories or threads, and the messages of subscribed categories or threads have changed, then you will be notified of those changes.

Subscription is, generally speaking, an agreement to receive electronic text or services, especially over the Internet. Thread subscription provides a useful function, that is, to be notified by e-mail when a new message has been posted or updated. On the one hand, you can subscribe to a thread for a given category or subcategory. Whenever a message has been posted or updated, you will be notified by e-mail. On the other hand, you can unsubscribe from a thread of a given category or subcategory if it has been subscribed to already. On doing this, you wouldn't be notified by e-mail even if a message has been posted or updated.

Moreover, category subscription provides a useful function for notification by e-mail when a category has been updated. As with thread subscription, you can subscribe to a category or subcategory. Whenever a category or subcategory has been updated, you will be notified by e-mail. To learn how to set up mail notifications, refer to the next section.

Customizing Message Boards

As an administrator of the Palm Tree Publications enterprise, you can set up Message Boards. For example, you can configure subscription e-mails.

Setting up

To configure Message Boards to include the subscription function, click on the **Gear** (icon) | **Configuration** on Message Boards title bar. When the **Setup** | **Current** tab is selected, it shows a set of subtabs: **General**, **Email From**, **Message Added Email**, **Message Updated Email**, **Thread Priorities**, **User Ranks**, and **RSS**.

As shown in following screenshot, the **Allow Anonymous Posting**, **Enable Flags**, and **Enable Ratings** checkboxes are checked by default. This means that, by default, the portal allows anonymous posting and enabling of flags and ratings. The following screenshot illustrates the **Message Board** configuration:

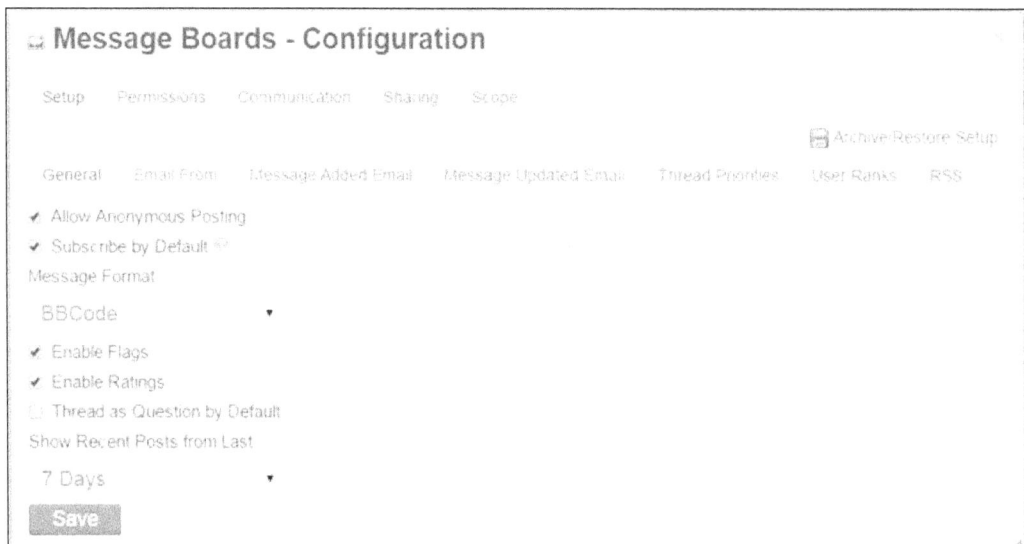

Figure 4.7: Configuration setup

What's happening? The portal sets the following property in `portal.properties` by default:

```
message.boards.anonymous.posting.enabled=true
```

The preceding code snippet sets the `message.boards.anonymous.posting.enabled` property to `true` in order to allow anonymous posting. Of course, you can override the value of the property in `portal-ext.properties` if you want. In addition, you would like to see the UI taglibs. You can find `<liferay-ui:ratings>` and `<liferay-ui:flags>` UI taglibs in `$PORTAL_ROOT_HOME/html/portlet/message_boards/view/view_thread_message.jspf`.

With the **Email From** tab selected, you can change the name and address of the e-mails being sent.

The **Message Added Email** tab allows us to edit the e-mail that is sent whenever a post is added. For disabling e-mail alerts, deselect the **Enabled** box first and then click on the **Save** button after making changes.

Similarly, the **Message Updated Email** tab allows us to edit the e-mail that is sent whenever a post is updated. As mentioned in the previous paragraph, you can disable e-mail alerts by deselecting the **Enabled** box first and then clicking on the **Save** button after making changes.

As you can see, there are default values for **Email From**, **Message Added Email**, and **Message Updated Email**. How? The portal sets the following properties in `portal.properties`:

```
message.boards.email.from.name=
message.boards.email.from.address=
message.boards.email.html.format=true
message.boards.email.message.added.enabled=true
message.boards.email.message.updated.enabled=true
```

The preceding code configures e-mail notification settings. Obviously, you could override these properties in `portal-ext.properties` if necessary.

With the **Thread Priories** tab selected, you can manage the thread priorities profiles. By the way, as an administrator, you can change the name, image, and priority requirements by making changes directly and clicking on the **Save** button. The following table depicts default settings:

Name	Image	Priority	Description
Urgent	`/message_ boards/ priority_ urgent.png`	3.0	Enter the name, image, and priority level in descending order. Threads with a higher priority are displayed before threads with a lower priority.
Sticky	`/message_ boards/ priority_ sticky.png`	2.0	The name is the display name of the priority. The image is the display image of the priority and can be a complete URL or a path relative to the theme.
Announcement	`/message_ boards/ priority_ announcement. png`	1.0	

Note that you need to enter the name, image, and priority level in descending order. Threads with a higher priority are displayed before threads with a lower priority. The name is the display name of the priority, while the image is the display image of that priority and can be a complete URL or a path relative to the theme. More interestingly, localized languages are supported as well.

With the **User Ranks** tab selected, as an administrator, you can manage the ranking profiles. Of course, you can change the ranking names and posting number requirements by making changes directly and then clicking on the **Save** button. The following table shows the default settings:

Rank	Minimum posts	Description
New Member	0	Enter the rank and minimum post pairs per line. Users will be displayed with a rank based on their number of posts.
Junior Member	25	
Regular Member	100	
Master	250	
Expert	500	
Legend	1000	

> Note that you can enter the rank and minimum post pairs per line, while users will be displayed with a rank based on the number of posts. You can definitely use a language other than English.

With the **RSS** tab selected, you can manage the RSS settings. Of course, as an administrator, you can change "Maximum Items to Display", "Display Style", and "Format". Having done that, click on the `Save` button. As you might have noticed, the RSS abstract is limited to 200 characters. Why? This is because the portal sets the following property in `portal.properties`:

```
message.boards.rss.abstract.length=200
```

The preceding code sets the `message.boards.rss.abstract.length` property's value to `200`. You can override the value of the property in `portal-ext.properties`.

> Note that it is also possible to activate SMTP events to allow users to respond to mails sent by Message Boards. In order to avoid HTML problems when posting through replies, the mails are now sent in plain text.

In addition, the portal allows messages to post pingbacks to blogs or any other pingback consumer. The portal has defined the following property to `true` in `portal.properties`:

```
message.boards.pingback.enabled=true
```

As you can see, the portal sets this property to `true` by default to enable pingbacks. Of course, you could disable pingbacks by setting the `false` property in `portal-ext.properties`.

What's happening?

As you can see, you would be able to configure the portlet Message Boards with Threads, Priorities, and User Ranks as portlet preferences. What's happening? The portal has specified the portlet preferences Threads, Priorities, and User Ranks after the line `<portlet-name>19</portlet-name>` in `$PORTAL_ROOT_HOME/WEB-INF/portlet-custom.xml`:

```
<portlet-preferences>
  <preference>
    <name>priorities</name>
    <value>Urgent,/message_boards/priority_urgent.png,3.0</value>
    <!-- ignore details -->
  </preference>
```

```
  <preference>
    <name>ranks</name>
    <value>Youngling=0</value> <!-- ignore details -->
  </preference>
</portlet-preferences>
```

As shown in the preceding code, the portal specifies portlet preferences *priorities* and *ranks*. Of course, you can override the values of the portlet preferences for *priorities* and *ranks* if you need to.

Banning and unbanning users

As mentioned earlier, the portal provides the capability to ban and unban users. In the case of banning users, you may ask questions such as style?

The portal has the following default settings in `portal.properties`:

```
message.boards.expire.ban.job.interval=120
message.boards.expire.ban.interval=10
```

The preceding code sets the time in minutes for how often this job is run with the `message.boards.expire.ban.job.interval` property. For example, if a user's ban is set to expire at 12:05 PM and the job runs at 2 PM, then the expiration will occur during the 2 PM run. The code also sets the time in days to automatically expire bans on users. You can set the `message.boards.expire.ban.interval` property to `0` to disable autoexpiry in `portal-ext.properties`.

Thread views

As stated earlier, a thread can have different views—combination view, flat view, or tree view. The default view is the combination view. The thread view and default view are set through the following properties in `portal.properties`:

```
message.boards.thread.views=combination,flat,tree
message.boards.thread.views.default=combination
```

The preceding code sets thread views to allow and then sets the default thread view. Of course, you can override these properties in `portal-ext.properties`.

Using Message Boards as a mailing list

You may have noticed that you can activate mailing lists when creating a new category or subcategory. In this scenario, you are able to input a default e-mail address, an incoming mail configuration, and an outgoing mail configuration. Once a mailing list gets activated, users are allowed to subscribe to threads of that category or subcategory, and the portal will store a list of all users in the database that have subscribed. When a new post is added to Message Boards, the portal will query the database asynchronously in order to retrieve the users that have subscribed to the thread where the post is attached and also retrieve the hierarchy of categories to which it belongs. Moreover, it sends each of them an e-mail with the contents of the post.

Going deeper, the portal allows users to answer to these e-mails or even write their own new threads using e-mail. How to achieve it? As stated earlier, the portal assigns an e-mail address to each category/subcategory in Message Boards. Such an e-mail address is automatically added to the reply-to headers of the e-mail sent to subscribers so that a reply to e-mails received from Message Board will result in a new post in the appropriate category/subcategory and thread.

Message Boards in scope

One of the most powerful characteristics of Message Boards is the fact that when they are added to different groups, they act as completely independent portlets, each with its own data. By default, any portlet, such as Message Boards, is scoped into a group. That is, when portlets are added to a group, either public pages or private pages, they act as the same portlet.

For instance, when the Message Boards portlet is added to a page, for example, "Forums" of the Guest site, it will use the default scope. If you add the Message Boards portlet to a second page, say "Welcome", it will show the same data as that of the first page. When the Message Boards portlet is added to a page, it will immediately get scoped into the group to which the current page belongs.

As you can see, the Message Boards portlet was scoped into the Palm Tree group when it was added to a page of the Palm Tree site. You don't have flexibility of switching sites in this case. But this limitation can be solved through **Control Panel**. In **Control Panel**, you are able to switch the content of the Message Boards portlet to different sites. You can implement this by following these steps:

1. Click on **Admin | Content**.
2. Locate Message Boards under the Content category and click on **Message Boards**. You would see the same categories and threads as that of the page "Forums" because, by default, the content of the **Message Boards** portlet is scoped into the Palm Tree group.
3. Switch sites by selecting different sites from the sites drop-down menu.

A portlet such as Message Boards could get scoped into a page. How do we scope the Message Boards portlet into a page? To make the **Message Boards** portlet use a different data scope, follow these simple steps:

1. Locate a page such as "Forums" and the Message Boards portlet on the current page.
2. Click **Gear** (icon) | **Configuration** of the Message Boards portlet.
3. Click on the **Scope** tab.
4. Choose **Current page (Forums)** from the **Scope** selection menu and click on the **Save** button.

If you previously entered data in the default scope and then switched to the page scope, don't be afraid if you see all of your categories vanish. They will still remain in the site scope and can be retrieved using the **Control Panel** or by switching back to the default scope. Note that you shouldn't implement the steps we discussed in **Control Panel**; otherwise, you will scope the portlet message. However, scoping the content of the Message Boards portlet into the "Current Page (**Control Panel**)" page will be of no use.

Considering the Portal-Group-Page-Content pattern, the content of the Message Boards portlet could be scoped into a group, for example, by default content, such as all pages including both private pages and public pages. Moreover, it could be scoped into an individual page—this means that a set of data, for example, forum categories and threads, is isolated from other data of the same portlet.

The portal has default settings for the Message Boards portlet in $PORTAL_ROOT_ HOME/ WEB-INF/liferay-portlet.xml as follows:

```
<scopeable>true</scopeable>
```

The preceding code shows that the Message Boards portlet is *scope-able*, that is, you are able to use the **Scope** tab and change the scope from the default page to the current page.

In addition, you may be interested in the **Edit Scope** page. You can find more information about scope editing at `$PORTAL_ROOT_HOME/html/portlet/portlet_configuration/edit_scope.jsp`.

The friendly URL

When you view categories or subcategories, you will see a URL such as `/web/guest/forums/-/message_boards/category/12024`. Similarly, when you view messages (thread and posts), you would see a URL such as `/web/guest/forums/-/message_ boards/message/12024`. This is a short and friendly URL. In fact, the portlet Message Boards supports friendly URL mapping as follows in `$PORTAL_ROOT_HOME/ WEB-INF/liferay-portlet.xml`:

```
<friendly-url-mapper-class>com.liferay.portal.kernel.portlet.
  DefaultFriendlyURLMapper</friendly-url-mapper-class>
<friendly-url-mapping>message_boards</friendly-url-mapping>
<friendly-url-routes>com/liferay/portlet/messageboards/message-
  boards-friendly-url-routes.xml</friendly-url-routes>
```

The preceding code shows that the content inside a portlet needs a friendly URL via the `friendly-url-mapper-class` tag.

Archive, Export, and Import

As stated earlier, you have set up the portlets **Message Boards, displaying general information, E-mail notification, user ranking, RSS**, and so on. It would be nice if you could save these settings, and moreover, revert these changes later. This feature can be achieved through **Archive Setup**. You can set up archives using the following steps:

1. Locate the Message Boards portlet in a page.
2. Click on the **Gear** icon | **Configuration** | **Setup** | **Archive / Restore Setup** (📋).
3. Input the archive name for the current setup, for example, "**My MB**", and click on the **Save** button.

After creating an archive, you will be able to see archives with the **Name, User, Modified Date**, and the icon **Actions** with the **Restore** and **Delete** subicons. Obviously, you can restore the setup via an archive or delete an archive.

Note that this feature is available for portlets for which the **Setup** tab is visible because the portal specifies this function in the portlet configuration file `archived_setup_action.jsp` and `edit_archived_setups.jsp` under `$PORTAL_ROOT_HOME/html/portlet/portlet_configuration`. More details and archives are stored in portlet preferences of the portal instance. Therefore, you shouldn't use this feature to back up data from one portal instance to another portal instance. Refer to the following screenshot for the Archive list:

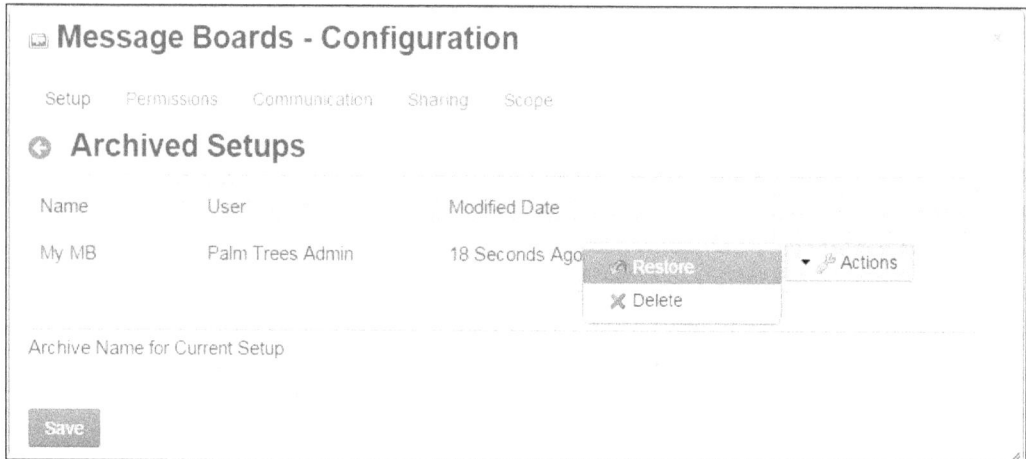

Figure 4.8: Archived setups

Fortunately, you can use the **Export/Import** feature for backup functions. The portal provides the capability to export and import portlet-specific data to a LAR file. You can export the portlet Message Boards-specific data to a LAR file:.

1. Locate the Message Boards portlet in a page.
2. Click on **Gear** (icon) | **Export / Import** and select the **Export** tab.
3. Specify the LAR filename in order to export the selected data.
4. Set what you would like to export.
5. Click on the **Export** button.

Similarly, you can import LAR with the following steps:

1. Click on **Gear** (icon) | **Export / Import** and select the **Import** tab.
2. Choose the LAR file in order to import the data.
3. Set what you would like to import.
4. Click on the **Import** button when you are ready.

> Note that the selection of what you would like to import should be the same as that of what you would like to export.

Why does a portlet such as **Message Boards** have export / import capability, whereas others portlets such as Hello World don't have such a capability? The reason is that the Message Boards portlet has the following setting that the Hello World portlet doesn't have:

```
<portlet-data-handler-class>com.liferay.portlet.messageboards.lar.
    MBPortletDataHandlerImpl</portlet-data-handler-class>
```

The preceding code shows that the content could be backed up as a LAR file via the `portlet-data-handler-class` tag.

> Note that in order to export / import data properly, the versions of the source portal instance and target portal instance should be completely identical. Otherwise, you might meet migration issues.

What're the differences between archives and Export / Import?

Using the feature of Export / Import, you can export LAR from one portal server and import it into another portal server as long as the two portal servers are running the same version. On the other hand, when you use the Archive feature, only one portal instance is involved. The main difference is that archives back up setup configurations, whereas LAR contains data.

Configuring portlets

As you can see, there is a **Setup** tab under **Gear** (icon) | **Configuration** of the Message Boards portlet similar to that of the **Sign In** portlet. However, the Hello World portlet doesn't have this tab. A portlet will have the **Setup** tab under **Gear** (icon) | **Configuration** if the `configuration-action-class` tag is specified in `$PORTAL_ROOT_HOME/WEB-INF/liferay-portlet.xml`, as follows:

```
<configuration-action-class>com.liferay.portlet.messageboards.
    action.ConfigurationActionImpl</configuration-action-class>
```

The preceding code shows that the `configuration-action-class` tag allows users to configure the portlet at runtime. If the `configuration-action-class` tag isn't specified in the portlet configuration, then there will be no **Setup** tab under **Gear** (icon) | **Configuration**. As mentioned in *Chapter 2, Setting Up a Home Page and Navigation Structure for the Intranet,* all portlets have tabs **Permissions** and **Sharing** under **Gear icon** | **Configuration**. Therefore, you may ask: how many tabs are available for a specific portlet? The following are the possible tabs for portlet configuration (portlet ID `86`):.

- Setup: This is specified through the tag configuration-action-class. Refer to `$PORTAL_ROOT_HOME/html/portlet/portlet_configuration/edit_configuration.jsp` to see how it works.

- Supported Clients: This is specified by the tag supports and multiple subtags, such as mime-type in `$PORTAL_ROOT_HOME/WEB-INF/portlet-custom.xml`. Refer to `$PORTAL_ROOT_HOME/html/portlet/portlet_configuration/edit_supported_clients.jsp` to see how it works.

- Permissions: This tab is available for all portlets. Refer to `$PORTAL_ROOT_HOME/html/portlet/portlet_configuration/edit_permissions.jsp` to see how it works.

- Communication: This is specified via the `supported-public-render-parameter` tag in `$PORTAL_ROOT_HOME/WEB-INF/portlet-custom.xml`. Refer to `$PORTAL_ROOT_HOME/html/portlet/portlet_configuration/edit_public_render_parameters.jsp` to see how it works.

- Sharing: This tab is available for all portlets. Refer to `$PORTAL_ROOT_HOME/html/portlet/portlet_configuration/edit_sharing.jsp` to see how it works.

- Scope: This is specified by the tag scope-able in `$PORTAL_ROOT_HOME/WEB-INF/portlet-custom.xml`. Refer to `$PORTAL_ROOT_HOME/html/portlet/portlet_configuration/edit_scope.jsp` to see how it works.

As shown in the tabs discussed previously, all portlets have the **Permissions** and **Sharing** tabs by default. You can find detailed specification in `$PORTAL_ROOT_HOME/html/portlet/portlet_configuration/tab1.jsp`.

Assigning permissions

We have used the default settings for the Message Boards portlet in the "Forums" page of the page. When you're logged in as a "Palm Tree" administrator, you can manage Message Board. As you know, the user "Lotti Stein" is a member of Palm Tree. While trying to log in as "Lotti Stein", you would see Message Boards on the "Forums" page, but you will find out that there is no button called "Add Category" in Message Boards, which you can see in the following screenshot:

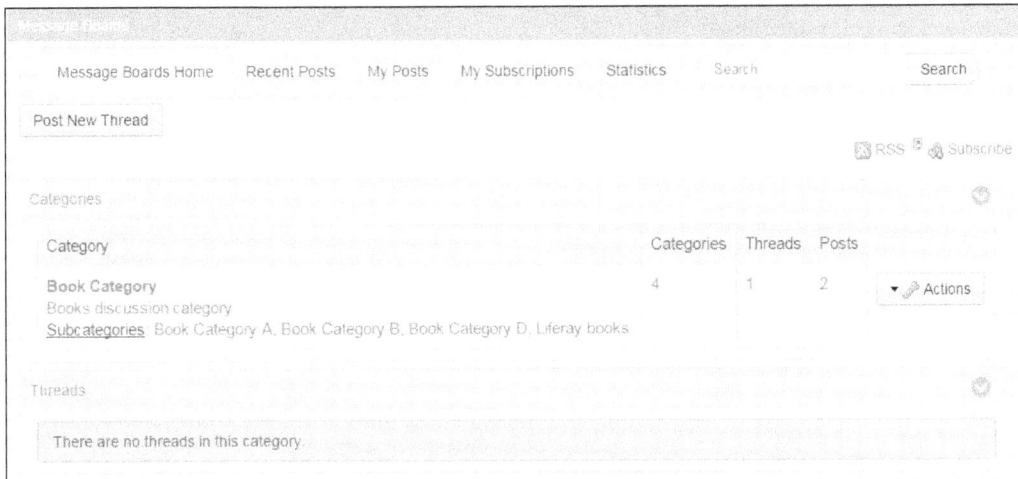

Figure 4.9: The Message Board view for user having limited permission

What's happening? This is something related to permissions. Permissions for Message Board can be assigned under **Site Administration | Content | Message Board** and another one is **Site Administration | Application | Message Board**. Moreover, each has a different set of permission levels:

- **Site Administration | Content | Message Board**: General Permissions, Resource Permissions (Messages, Message Boards category, Message Boards Thread, Message Boards Message)

- **Site Administration | Application | Message Board**: Application Permissions, Resource Permissions (Messages, Message Boards category, Message Boards Thread, Message Boards Message)

Let's discuss each of them one by one in detail.

Site Administration | Content | Message Board | Messages

Entitlements for the messages, which you can select for specific roles, is listed in the following screenshot:

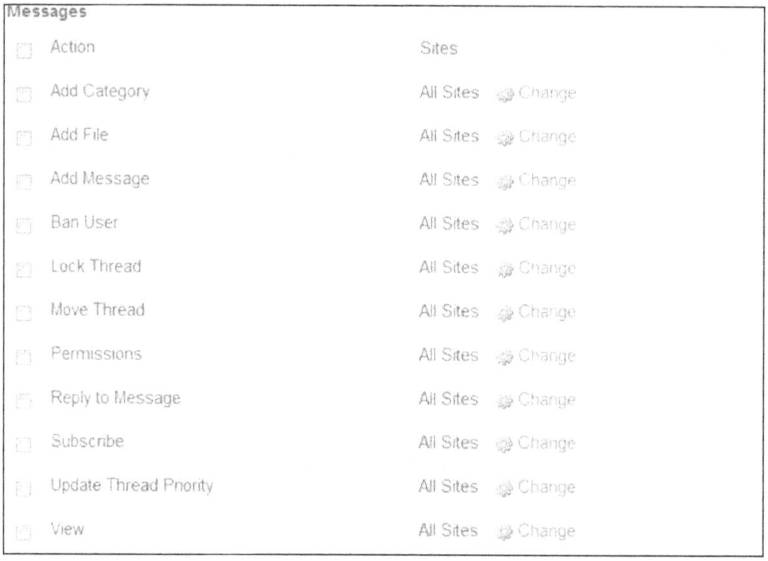

Figure 4.10: Permission for Message Boards

The previous screenshot (*Figure 4.10*) shows permissions on Message Boards. **Portal Admin** has the ability to set up the permissions. By default, **Site Member** has limited permissions given. **MB Topic Admin** may have the ability to set up following permissions (marked as 'X'). By default, a **MB Topic Admin** and **Site Member** user has the view action permission (marked as '*'). The following table shows this:

Action	Description	MB Topic Admin	Site Members
Add Category	This permission provides the ability to add top-level category	X	
Add File	This permission provides the ability to add a file as attachment at the root category	X	
Add Message	This permission provides the ability to add a message	X	
Ban User	This permission provides the ability to ban or unban users	X	

Action	Description	MB Topic Admin	Site Members
Lock Thread	This permission provides the ability to lock the thread	X	
Move Thread	This permission provides the ability to move thread at the root category	X	
Permissions	This permission provides the ability to set up the permissions	X	
Reply to Message	This permission provides the ability to reply to message at the root category	X	
Subscribe	This permission provides the ability to subscribe at the root category	X	
Update Thread Priority	This permission provides the ability to set up the thread priority	X	
View	This permission provides the ability to view the Message Board	X, *	*

As you can see, as a site member, "Lotti Stein" doesn't have the **Add Category** and **Ban User** permissions on the Message Boards content by default. Of course, "Lotti Stein" could get these permissions by assigning permissions via roles. It is an example that shows how permission actions **Add Category** and **Ban User** are assigned.

1. Log in as an admin, say the "Palm Tree" portal.
2. First click on **Roles** under the **Users** category of **Control Panel**.
3. Then, locate a role, say "MB Topic Admin". If the role does not exist, create a new role with the name "**MB Topic Admin**".
4. Then click on the **Define Permissions** icon from **Actions** on the right-hand side of the role.
5. From the left-hand side tree menu, select, **Site Administration | Content | Message Board: Resource Permissions | Messages** and check the **Add Category** and **Ban User** checkboxes.
6. Finally, click on the **Save** button when you are ready.

That's it! From now on, the user "Lotti Stein" has the **Add Category** and **Ban User** permissions on Message Boards content via the "MB Topic Admin" role.

Site Administration | Content | Message Boards Category

Entitlements for the Message Boards category, which you can select for specific roles, is listed in the following screenshot:

Figure 4.11: Site content permission for Message Boards category

As you can see, the previous screenshot (*Figure 4.11*) shows the permission on Message Boards. By default, **site member** has limited permissions given. **MB Topic Admin** may have the ability to set up following permissions (marked as 'X'). By default, **MB Topic Admin** and **Site Member** users have the view action permission (marked as '*'). This is shown in the following table:

Action	Description	MB Topic Admin	Site Members
Add File	This permission provides the ability to add a file as attachment at the root category	X	
Add Message	This permission provides the ability to add a message	X	
Add Subcategory	This permission provides the ability to add subcategory	X	

Action	Description	MB Topic Admin	Site Members
Delete	This permission provides the ability to delete the message	X	
Lock Thread	This permission provides the ability to lock the thread	X	
Move Thread	This permission provides the ability to move thread at the root category	X	
Permission	This permission provides the ability to set up permissions	X	
Reply to Message	This permission provides the ability to reply to message at the root category	X	
Subscribe	This permission provides the ability to subscribe at the root category	X	
Update	This permission provides the ability to update the message	X	
Update Thread Priority	This permission provides the ability to set up the thread priority	X	
View	This permission provides the ability to view the Message Board	X,*	*

Obviously, as a site member, "Lotti Stein" has only **View**, **Add File**, **Add Message**, **Reply to Message**, and **Subscribe** permissions for the subcategories Book Category A, Book Category B, and Book Category D. You can add this permission as we did earlier.

> Note that you need to map **Lotti Stein** with the **MB Topic Admin** role. Once it's done, Lotti will have all the permissions defined. These permissions are defined for existing categories and newly created ones.

Now, let's discuss the individual site members who do not have the **MB Topic Admin** role and only have the Site Member role with the default settings. The Book Category D has only **View** permissions because, while creating the category, we defined only View permissions for the Site Member role.

As an administrator, you may need to set up users of the Site Member role with the default permissions setting (**View**, **Add File**, **Add Message**, **Reply to Messages**, and **Subscribe**) for the Book Category D category. Thus, you need to add the permission actions **Add File**, **Add Message**, **Reply to Messages**, and **Subscribe** to the category **Book Category D** via the Site Member role. Let's do it by following these steps:

1. Click on the parent category **Books** in order to list its subcategories.
2. Locate the subcategory **Book Category D** where you want to change permissions.
3. Then, click on the **Permissions** icon from **Actions** next to the category.
4. Select the **Add File**, **Add Message**, **Reply to Message**, and **Subscribe** permissions to the **Site Member** role.
5. Click on the **Submit** button.

From now on, all the site members will have the following permissions: **View**, **Add File**, **Add Message**, **Reply to Messages**, and **Subscribe** on the subcategory Book Category D.

The preceding steps provide a way to update permissions for an individual resource, for example, Book Category D. How about permissions on categories—existing ones or newly created ones? Let's consider a use case: the user "Lotti Stein" should have the permission **Update** on categories, including subcategories—both existing ones and newly created ones. How to implement this use case? By assigning permissions via roles in **Control Panel** as an example, we give the answer in the following steps:

1. Log in as an admin, say **Palm Tree**.
2. First, click on **Roles** under the **Users** section of **Control Panel**.
3. Then locate a role, say MB Topic Admin.
4. Then click on the **Define Permissions** icon from **Actions** on the right-hand side of the role.
5. From the left-hand side tree menu, select **Site Administration** | **Content** | **Message Board: Resource Permissions** | **Message Boards Category** and check the **Update** checkboxes.
6. Finally, click on the **Save** button.

As shown in the preceding steps, the user is assigned the **Update** permission on the Message Boards category across all sites in which Lotti Stein is a member. The user "Lotti Stein" is mapped to the "MB Topic Admin" role. Therefore, the user "Lotti Stein" got the Update permission on the Message Boards category across all sites in the current portal instance.

Site Administration | Content | Message Boards Messages

Entitlements for **Message Boards Messages** is listed in the following screenshot, which you can select for specific roles:

Figure 4.12: Site content permission for Message Boards message

The previous screenshot (*Figure 4.12*) shows permissions on Message Boards. **MB Topic Admin** may have the ability to set up the following permissions (marked as 'X' by default, **MB Topic Admin** and **Site Member** users have the view action permission (marked as '*'):

Action	Description	MB Topic Admin	Site Member
Delete	This permission provides the ability to delete messages	X	
Permissions	This permission provides the ability to assign permissions	X	
Subscribe	This permission provides the ability to subscribe to the thread	X	
Update	This permission provides the ability to update messages	X	
View	This permission provides the ability to view the details of messages	X, *	*

> Note that the **Owner** role is able to set up all permissions and, by default, has all permission actions. Of course, as a portal administrator, you can create a new role and assign any permission based on the role to different users.

Site Administration | Content | Message Boards Thread

Entitlements for the Message Boards thread, which you can select for specific roles, is listed in the following screenshot:

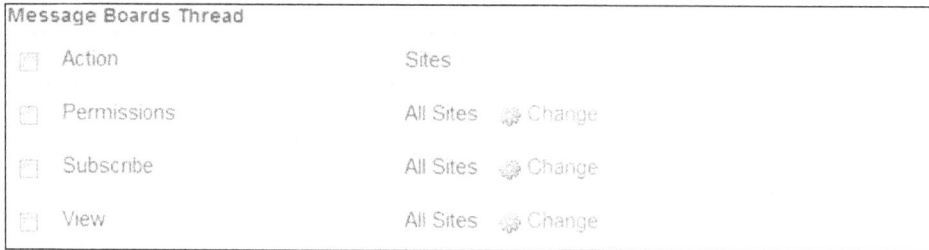

Figure 4.13: Site content permission for Message Boards thread

Message Boards Thread permission settings allow the users to set the permissions in the thread level. It even allows subscribing the thread to the users. This is shown in the following table:

Action	Description	MB Topic Admin	Site Member
Permissions	This permission provides the ability to assign permissions	X	
Subscribe	This permission provides the ability to subscribe to the thread	X	
View	This permission provides the ability to view the details of messages	X, *	*

Site Administration | Content | Message Boards General Permissions

Entitlements for Message Boards to general permissions, which you can select for specific roles, is listed in the following screenshot:

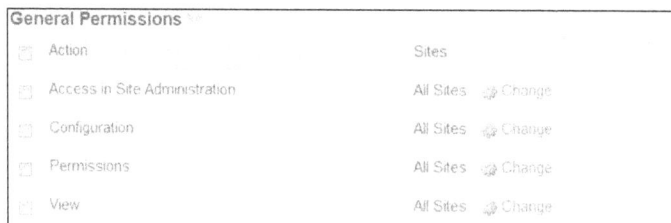

Figure 4.14: Site application permission for Message Boards

Action	Description	MB Topic Admin	Site Member
Access in Site Administration	This permission provides the ability to access the portlet Message Boards in site administration	X	
Configuration	This permission provides the ability to configure portlet	X	
Permissions	This permission provides the ability to set up the permissions	X	
View	This permission provides the ability to view the content of the portlet	X, *	X, *

Obviously, as a site member, "Lotti Stein" only has the **View** permission on the Message Boards portlet by default. As the **Site Member** role doesn't have the **Configuration** and **Access in Site Administration** permissions, "Lotti Stein" wouldn't have the **Configuration** and **Access in Site Administration** permissions too. That is, "Lotti Stein" doesn't have the ability to configure the portlet Message Boards in the "Forums" page or to access the Message Boards portlet in **Site Administration**.

What's the permission action **Access in the Site Administration**? This permission action represents the ability to access the Message Boards portlet in Site Administration. By default, the user "Lotti Stein" doesn't have the ability to access the Message Boards portlet in Site Administration. But the requirement is that the user "Lotti Stein" should have the ability to access the Message Boards portlet in Site Administration.

Simply check the box beside **Access in the Site Administration** and save it. All users who have MB Topic Admin will have the ability to access the Message Boards portlet in site administration.

Site Administration | Application | Message Board | Application Permissions

Entitlements for the application permissions, which you can select for specific roles, are listed in the following screenshot:

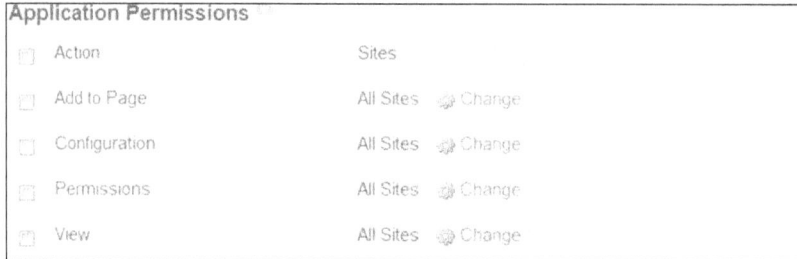

Figure 4.15: Message Board application permission

Site Application permissions affect the application with respect to the portal. So, let's see with the Message Boards example that application permission allows us to define who can add the Message Boards portlet to a page. This is shown in the following table:

Action	Description	MB Topic Admin	Site Member
Add to Page	This permission provides the ability to add the portlet Message Boards portlet in page	X	
Configuration	This permission provides the ability to configure portlet	X	
Permissions	This permission provides the ability to set up permissions	X	
View	This permission provides the ability to view the content of the portlet	X, *	*

As you can see, as a site member, "Lotti Stein" only has the permission actions **View** and **Subscribe** on messages (threads and posts). That's because we have added them through the Site Member role as the default settings. Now, suppose that we're going to add the **Update** permission on message (both thread and post) in following scopes:

- Individual thread or post
- A set of threads and posts belonging to a category such as Book Category D
- All threads and posts in a site
- All threads and posts in a portal instance, such as the current portal instance

How do we implement the preceding use cases? For individual threads or posts, you can assign permissions in the Message Boards portlet through custom regular roles or a custom site role (or Site Member) for site pages or a custom organization role (or Organization Member) for organization pages.

For all threads and posts in a site scope, you can assign permissions in the configuration through a custom site role (or Site Member) for site pages or a custom organization role (or Organization Member) for organization pages.

For all threads and posts in a portal instance, you can assign permissions in **Control Panel** through custom regular roles. For a set of threads and posts belonging to a category, you can use a category hierarchy structure.

In practice, when you assign any permission on a message to a role, make sure that you assign the related permissions, at least *View*, on both the Message Boards portlet and the message's subcategories and category. Otherwise, you wouldn't be able to view the portlet and the related categories. Moreover, the message would be invisible to people with the role.

Using Message Boards effectively

The following figure depicts a forum structure overview of Message Boards. A forum is made up of a set of categories. Each category can have many subcategories and threads. Furthermore, each thread may have many posts (in the form of replies). The thread refers to the collection of messages.

A thread itself is a post too. The posts may be displayed in a flat chronological order by the date of posting or in a question-answer order. The figure shows a thread of one question followed by all the answers in a hierarchy. Actually, threads can be regarded as the root level posts. Subposts are also supported, which enable comments in one of the replies to start another thread that remains linked to the original. Moreover, you can enable flags, thereby allowing users to flag content as inappropriate. In addition, you can subscribe to categories/subcategories and threads. Refer to the following screenshot for more details on relationships:

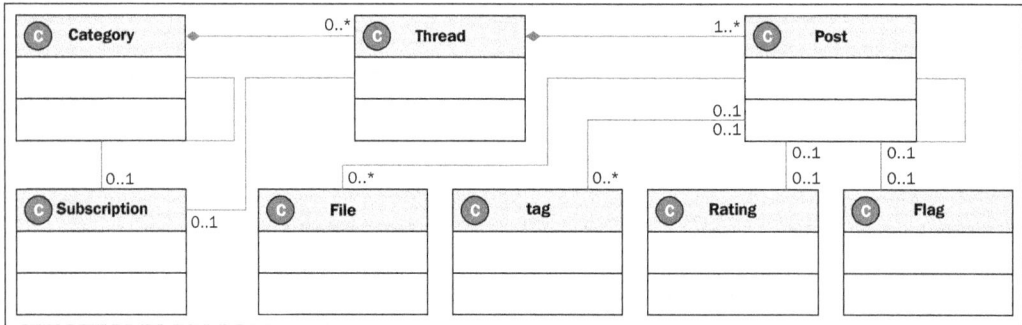

Figure 4.16: Message Board design

As shown in the preceding figure, you are able to attach a set of files to posts (and threads because a thread itself is a post). In addition, you are able to select existing tags or add new tags to posts.

The category hierarchy

As you can see, there are top-level categories with the **Add Category** permission action. A top-level category forms a root, that is, a message container. Each category can have many subcategories with the **Add Subcategory** permission action. Therefore, categories and subcategories form a hierarchical structure—categories form the root, while subcategories form the trunk and leaves.

How can you benefit from the category hierarchy? The main benefit you can get is inherited permissions. Another benefit you can get is content sharing within a category hierarchy. As mentioned earlier, when you assign any permission on a message to a role, you must make sure that you assign related permissions—at least **View**—on the message's subcategories and categories. Therefore, we can use the category hierarchy to assign permissions for a set of threads and posts belonging to a category or a subcategory.

Semantics and ontology

When a message has been created, the portal will check for spelling. Thus, the message does have a specific syntax, but it doesn't involve semantics. **Semantics** is the study of the meanings of linguistic expressions (as opposed to their sound, spelling, and so on.). Moreover, it would be useful if messages could be managed through semantics.

As previously mentioned, you can tag messages through folksonomy. Later, you would be able to apply taxonomy on messages. Folksonomy is a user-generated taxonomy that is used to categorize and retrieve web content using open-ended labels called tags. On the other hand, taxonomy is the practice and science of classification— hierarchical in structure and commonly displaying parent-child relationships.

This is a good way to approach a semantic classification of content, such as messages. Moreover, it would be possible to build a complete ontology based on the concepts of folksonomy and taxonomy. In this way, content can be classified as instances, and properties of content can be used to navigate through concepts declared in the ontology.

Categorization and tags

Sooner or later, you will have a lot of posts on Message Boards. Therefore, it is useful to allow users to generate content post and classify that content post in their own unique way. Let's first experience tagging assets.

Tagging assets

As an administrator at the enterprise Palm Tree Publications, you may need to add the tags "Liferay" and "book" in the post "**RE: Let's discuss book Liferay**". Let's do it by following these steps:

1. In a post-updating page, locate the **Tag** box.

2. In the **Tag** text box, simply start typing the tag name and a list of tags will appear. For example, when "li" is typed into the textbox, a list of available tags is populated. Select the tag you want, say "liferay", and that tag should show up at the top of the box.

3. Similarly, when bo is typed into the textbox, a list of available tags is populated. Select the tag you want, say "book", and the tag should show up at the top of the box too.

4. Click on the **Save** button when you are ready.

5. For some reason, let's say you need to remove a tag "Book" from the tag list. To remove the "Book" tag, simply click on the mark "[x]" located next to the tag first and then click on the **Save** button when you are ready.

6. Similarly, you can tag content including Bookmark entries, Blog entries, Document and Media portlets, Wiki articles, Web Content articles, Message Board messages, and so on.

Tags and Categorization can be defined for any assets using the Tags field, which is shown in the following screenshot:

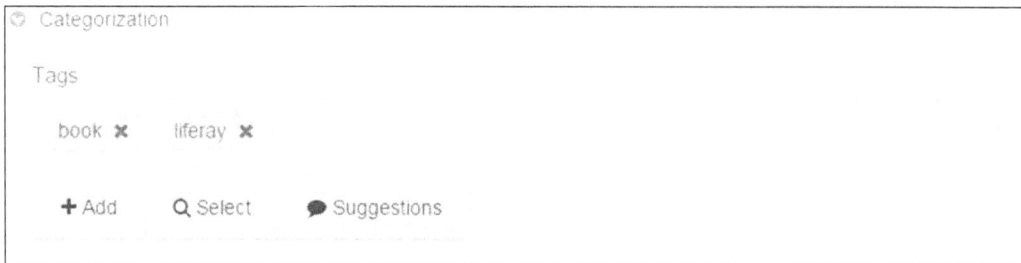

Figure 4.17: Categorization and tags

Folksonomies

As you can see, there is an open set of tags called *Folksonomies* that can be extended by end users. In general, as a user, you are able to carry out the following tasks based on the tags:

- Extend tags by entering a tag and press *Enter*
- Select tags by clicking on the **Selected Tags** button, where it displays a set of existing tags for you to select multiple tags
- Find tags by clicking on the **Suggestions** button, where it uses advanced search techniques to find out tags

In short, the portal provides the meta tag *Folksonomies*, which is a tagging system that allows us to tag web content, documents, Message Board messages, and more. It also dynamically publishes content by tags. The meta tags can later be used to classify assets and search and aggregate them.

Taxonomies

Besides the meta tag *Folksonomies*, you could use another kind of tag called *Taxonomies*. In general, taxonomies are a way of organizing and aggregating content—a closed set of categories (tags by a different name) of the vocabulary, which are created and organized in a hierarchical structure.

Categories are displayed in a hierarchical structure. You are able to choose as many categories as you expected. You could search and find your favorite categories in a quick way when the number of categories is huge. Let's see how to build a category hierarchy in the next section.

Tags administration

The following is a summary of tags and their related portlets in the portal:

- **Administration**:
  - ○ **Tags**: This manages folksonomies—tags
  - ○ **Categories**: This manages taxonomies—vocabulary, categories, and their properties
- **Tag different types of assets in the portal**: These include Bookmark entries, Blog entries, Wiki articles, Document and Media portlets, Web Content articles, and Message Board messages
- **Aggregate assets in the portal**: This is Asset Publisher
- **Display tags**:
  - ○ **Tag Cloud**—This is a visual depiction of user-generated tags
  - ○ **Tags Navigation**—This is used to display user-generated tags in multiple styles
  - ○ **Categories Navigation**—This is used to display predefined tags in a hierarchical structure

The Tags portlet

To manage tags, you should go to **Tags** under the Content category of **Site Administration**. Using the Tags portlet (portlet ID 99), you can add tags. As shown in the following screenshot, the Tags portlet provides the capabilities to manage tags with the **Actions** and **Add Tag** options and Search.

Tags enable categorization of content through flexible groups of terms and preset vocabularies. Administrators can manage all tags, assign permissions, and set advanced options. Users can manage their tags and define tag sets and categories to use when categorizing content.

To search for tags, you can simply input a search criterion, say "chapter" first and then click on the **Search** button. The search results will appear dynamically.

To add a tag, simply click on the **Add Tag**, **Add Tag** button and the pop-up dialog window will appear, and input the tag name, say "Chapter". Then click on the **Save** button to save inputs or the **Cancel** button in order to discard inputs. If the tag doesn't exist in the current group, the tag will be added by associating it with the current group, and it will bring us to the **Tag** view. Otherwise, it will display a message stating "**That tag already exists**".

Suppose that you want to change the "chapter" tag to "Chapter details", how would you do this? The process is simple; just click on the tag "chapter" using the edit button in the tag details section. In the **Edit Tag** view, the tag name is displayed. In the tag name "chapter", you can type "Chapter details " and click on the **Save** button. Optionally, you can click on the **Close** button or the close icon to cancel the current process.

Don't forget that you can merge tags. For example, after you can select multiple tags, say "book" and "liferay", in the top menu, the **Actions** drop-down link will be visible. Now, click on the **Merge** link. The **Merge Tags** window will pop up. Select the tags and click on **Ok**, and then you would see a pop-up message that says: **Are you sure you want to merge the chosen tags into "book"?** This will change all items tagged with "book" to be tagged with "liferay".

Creating Tags for a specific site scope is done through the Site Administrator panel; refer to the following screenshot:

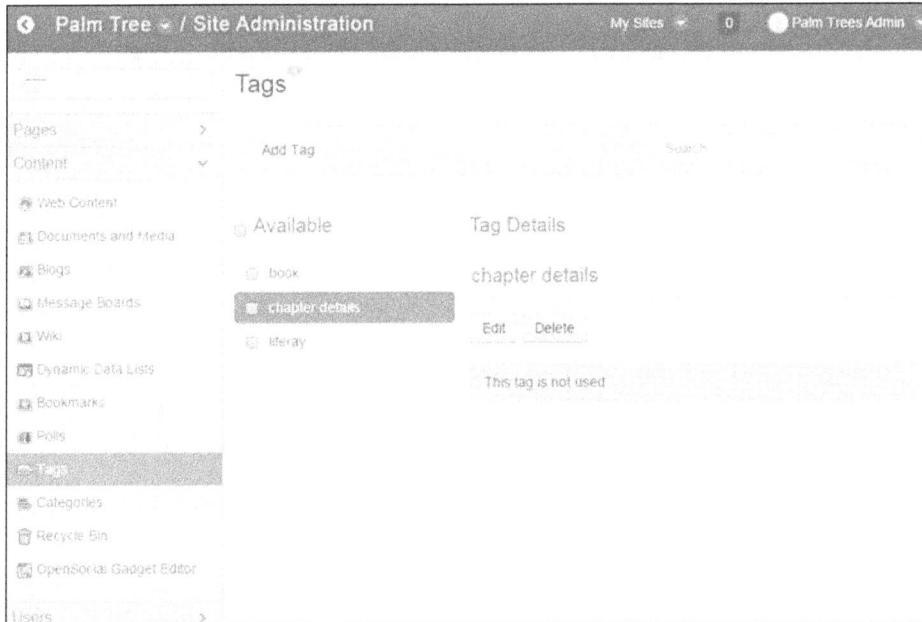

Figure 4.18: The Tags portlet—adding a new tag

The Categories portlet

Categories describe a set of vocabulary terms to tag content items. Administrators can create vocabularies and populate them with categories that users can choose from when authoring content.

In order to manage vocabularies and categories, you can go to **Categories** under the **Content** category of **Site Administration**. Using the Categories portlet (portlet ID 147), you can add vocabularies and categories and also manage categories' properties. As shown in the following screenshot, the Categories portlet provides capabilities to manage tags, including **Search**, **Add Vocabulary**, **Add Category**, **Permissions**, and **Actions**.

As you may have noticed, the **Topic** vocabulary was created by default, and it was shown under the **Vocabularies** column. Of course, you can search vocabularies and categories in a convenient way. In order to do so, you can simply input a search criterion, say "book", first, then select types—either Categories or Vocabularies—and then click on the **Search** button. The search results will appear dynamically.

To add a vocabulary, simply click on the **Add Vocabulary** button, input the vocabulary name, for example, "Book", and change the default permission settings first. Then, click on the **Save** button to save inputs or the **Cancel** button to discard inputs. If the vocabulary doesn't exist in the current group, then the vocabulary will be added associated with the current group. Otherwise, it will show **That vocabulary already exists**. Thus, vocabulary names must be unique in the current group.

Suppose that you want to change the vocabulary from "Book" to "Books". In order to implement it, click on the "Book" vocabulary using the edit link. In the **Edit** view, the vocabulary name will be editable. Where the vocabulary name is "Book", you can type "Books" and click on the **Save** button. Again, the updated vocabulary name must be unique in the current group.

If needed, you can delete a vocabulary. You can first locate a vocabulary, say "Book" and click on the **Delete** button under **Actions**. As you can see, a vocabulary could have many categories associated with it. Therefore, when a vocabulary gets deleted, the categories that belong to the current vocabulary will get removed too.

After adding vocabularies, you are ready to add categories, as shown in the following screenshot:

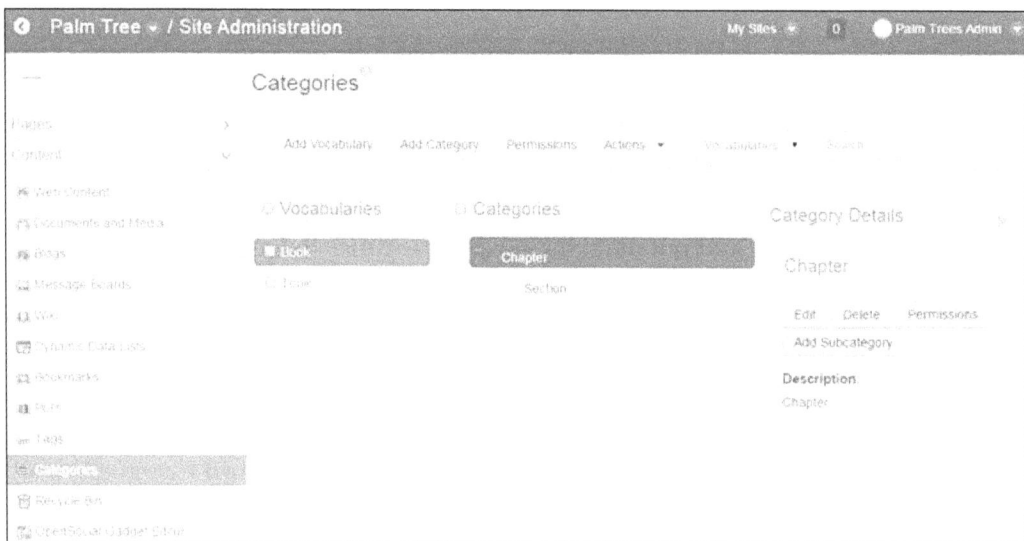

Figure 4.19: Categories portlet

In order to add a category, simply locate a vocabulary, for example "Book", click on the **Add Category** button, input a tag name, say "Chapter", and change the default permission settings. Optionally, you are able to select different vocabularies from the drop-down list. Then, click on the **Save** button to save inputs or the **Cancel** button to discard inputs. If a category doesn't exist in the current vocabulary, then the category will be added to the current vocabulary, and it will bring us to the Edit Category view. Otherwise, it will throw an error message **That category already exists**.

In cases where you want to change the category "Chapter" to "Main Chapter", click on the category using the edit links, say "Chapter". In the **Edit Category** view, the category name and properties are displayed. In the category name "Chapter", you can type "Main Chapter", and click on the **Save** button. Optionally, you can press the **Close** button or close icon to cancel the current process. Again, the updated category name must be unique in the current vocabulary.

A category can have another category as its parent category. That is, categories support a hierarchical structure. In order to build the hierarchy, you can add categories, such as "Chapter" and "Section" first, and then you can drag and drop a category called "Section" to a correct parent category, say "Chapter". That's it!

To delete a property of a given category called "Chapter", locate the property first. After locating it, click on the delete icon next to the property. In order to add one more property of a given category, say "Chapter", just click on the add icon first. Then, simply input the name and value. Finally, click on the **Save** button to save the changes or the **Cancel** button to cancel the changes.

As you can see, a category can have many properties associated with it. Note that when a category gets deleted, the properties that belong to the current category will get removed too.

As stated earlier, a vocabulary may have many categories associated with it, where each category may have other categories as its child categories, and where each category may, in turn, have many properties.

Configuring tags

As you have noticed, when you click on **Categories** under the **Content** category of **Site Administration**, the **Topic** vocabulary is created by default. However, when you add categories, there is no default property for a newly created category. Moreover, when you click on **Tags** under the **Content** category of **Site Administration** and add tags, you will see that there is no default tag property for newly created tags. The portal has the following settings by default in `portal.properties`:

```
asset.categories.properties.default=
asset.tag.properties.default=
asset.vocabulary.default=Topic
```

As shown in the preceding code, you can input a list of comma-delimited default properties for newly created categories via the `asset.categories.properties.default` property. Note that each item of the list should have the `key: value` format. You can also input a list of comma-delimited default tag properties for newly created tags via the `asset.tag.properties.default` property. Again, each item on the list should have the `key:value` format. Moreover, you can set a name, other than **Topic**, to the default vocabulary. Of course, you can override these properties in `portal-ext.properties` if required.

In addition, the portal has the following settings by default in `portal.properties`:

```
asset.categories.search.hierarchical=true
```

The preceding code shows that the `asset.categories.search.hierarchical` property is set to `true`; thus, the child categories are also included in the search. Of course, you can set it to `false` in order to specify that searching and browsing using categories should only show assets that have been assigned the selected category explicitly.

Publishing tags

There are several portlets available to publish tags. These portlets include **Tag Cloud** (portlet ID `148`), **Tags Navigation** (portlet ID `141`), and **Categories Navigation** (portlet ID `122`). How do we get these portlets in one place? As an example, you can simply create a page called "Tags" in the Guest public pages and add these three portlets using **Add | Application** under **dock bar menu**.

The Tag Cloud portlet provides a visual depiction of user-generated tags, shown with varying font size. Note that there is the **Communication** tab under **Gear** (icon) | **Configuration** and that the shared parameter tag can be mapped to `categoryId` because the portlet has the following configuration in `$PORTAL_ROOT_HOME/WEB-INF/portlet-custom.xml`:

```
<supported-public-render-parameter>tag</supported-public-render-
  parameter>
```

Set up communication among the portlets that use public render parameters. For each of the public parameters in this portlet, it is possible to ignore the values coming from other portlets or to read the value from another parameter.

The Tags Navigation portlet gives us the capability to navigate user-generated tags in different ways. Just as with the Tag Cloud portlet, there is a **Communication** tab under **Gear** (icon) | **Configuration**, and the shared parameter tag can be mapped into `categoryId` using it. Additionally, the portlet has the **Setup** tab under **Gear** (icon) | **Configuration**. Therefore, you can configure views of user-generated tags via the **Setup** tab. Using **Setup**, you will be able to show the asset count, select the asset type (for example, **Any**, **Blogs Entry**, **Bookmarks Entry**, **Document and Media Document**, **Web Content**, **Message Boards Message**, **Wiki Page**, and so on), select the display type (for example, **Number**, **Cloud**), and show tags with no assets.

What happens when we map `Tag` to `CategoryId` or vice versa? `Tag` and `CategoryId` are defined as **Public Render Parameters**. With the **Public Render Parameters** feature, the render parameters set in the `processAction` method of one portlet will be available in the `render` parameter of other portlets as well. Using public render parameters instead of **Events** avoids the additional process event call. In the portlet section, each portlet can specify the public render parameters it would like to share via the `supported-public-render-parameter` element.

The Categories Navigation portlet provides the capability to navigate categories in a hierarchical structure. Just as with the Tag Cloud portlet, but in reverse order, there is a **Communication** tab under **More...** | **Configuration**. The shared parameter `categoryId` can be mapped to a tag because the portlet has the following configuration in `$PORTAL_ROOT_HOME/WEB-INF/portlet-custom.xml`:

```
<supported-public-render-parameter>categoryId</supported-public-
  render-parameter>
```

Asset Publisher

As stated earlier, we discussed how to build assets, for example, Message Board messages. We have also introduced you to adding tags and categories on assets such as Message Board messages. Now it is time to investigate how to publish assets with tags and categories. Asset Publisher is a flexible tool to publish many types of assets within the portal. It allows the showing of lists of web content, blog entries, images, documents, bookmarks, wiki pages, and so on. Each element on the list can be displayed as a title, a summary (abstract), in full detail, and much more.

Main features

Let's say that you have a page named "Asset Publishing" in the Guest public pages, and you are going to publish any assets including a Message Boards message in this page. How will you publish any assets on a page? Obviously, the Asset Publisher portlet is the key! First, you can create a page named "Asset Publishing" under the Guest public pages via **Add | Page** of the dock bar menu. Then, you can add Asset Publisher via **Add | Asset Publisher**.

After adding Asset Publisher, you would see that assets, especially Message Boards messages in this example, get published as shown in following screenshot:

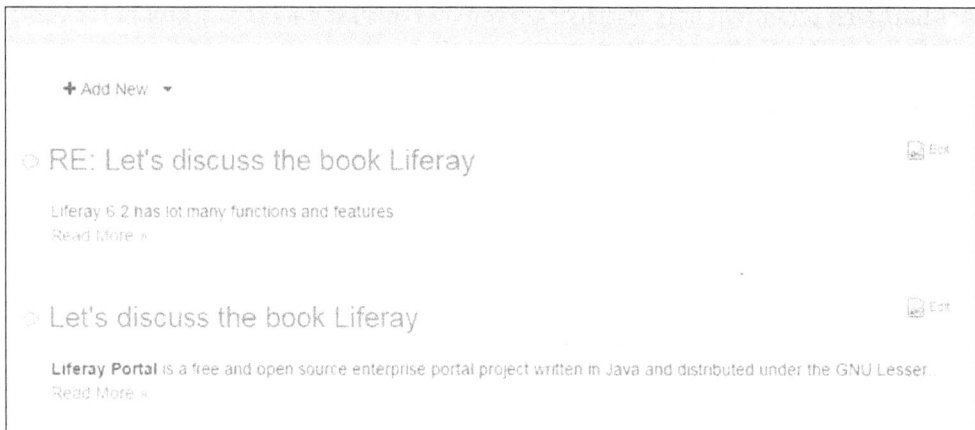

Figure 4.20: The Asset Publisher portlet

What are the main features of the Asset Publisher portlet? The following are the main features. However, the Asset Publisher has many other features too:

- It includes the ability to add new assets, including Web Content, Documents and Media Document, Blog Entry, and Bookmark Entry, all in one place.

- The features include the capability to publish many types of assets within the portal.

- Other features include the ability to edit different types of assets in one place.

- It can also show lists of web content, blog entries, images, documents, bookmarks, wiki pages, and Message Boards messages as a title, a summary, or even in full detail through publishing rules. Note that this summary doesn't support multiple languages.

- It can support pagination in different styles.

- It allows users to click an asset in order to see it in full detail.

- It supports both manual and dynamic selection of asset types.

In short, the Asset Publisher portlet allows users to publish any type of asset in the portal as if it was web content, either filtering through a set of publishing rules or by manual selection.

The Asset Publisher portlet provides a way to display tagged assets — Bookmark entries, Blog entries, Document and Media documents, Wiki articles, Web Content articles, and Message Board messages. Given a set of tags or categories, assets "tagged" with specific tags or categories will be displayed in the Asset Publisher portlet.

In addition, you can easily add assets (Bookmark entries, Blog entries, Document and Media documents, and Web Content articles) within the portlet.

> For Bookmark entries, Blog entries, Document and Media documents, Wiki articles, and Web Content articles, refer to the instructions given in the coming chapters.

Configuration

Generally speaking, the Asset Publisher portlet is highly configurable. You can select assets manually or dynamically. Using the **Gear** (icon) | **Configuration** | **Setup** navigation, you will be able to set up publishing rules — **Asset Selection Manual** and **Asset Selection Dynamic**. By the way, you are able to save the current setup in the archives by navigating to the **Gear** (icon) | **Configuration** | **Setup** | **Archive/Restore Setup** link. This process is the same as that of the Message Boards archives setup.

Selecting assets manually

Once you've chosen the **Manual** option under **Asset Selection**, as shown in the following screenshot, you will be able to select assets manually. In general, there are three sections for manual asset publishing: the **Asset Selection** tab, the **Display Settings** tab, and the **Show metadata** section under the **Display Settings** tab.

- **Asset Selection**: You are able to choose what will be published in Asset Publisher

- **Display Settings**: You are able to set up how to display assets in Asset Publisher

- **Show metadata**: You are able to select the metadata field to display under each published content in Asset Publisher

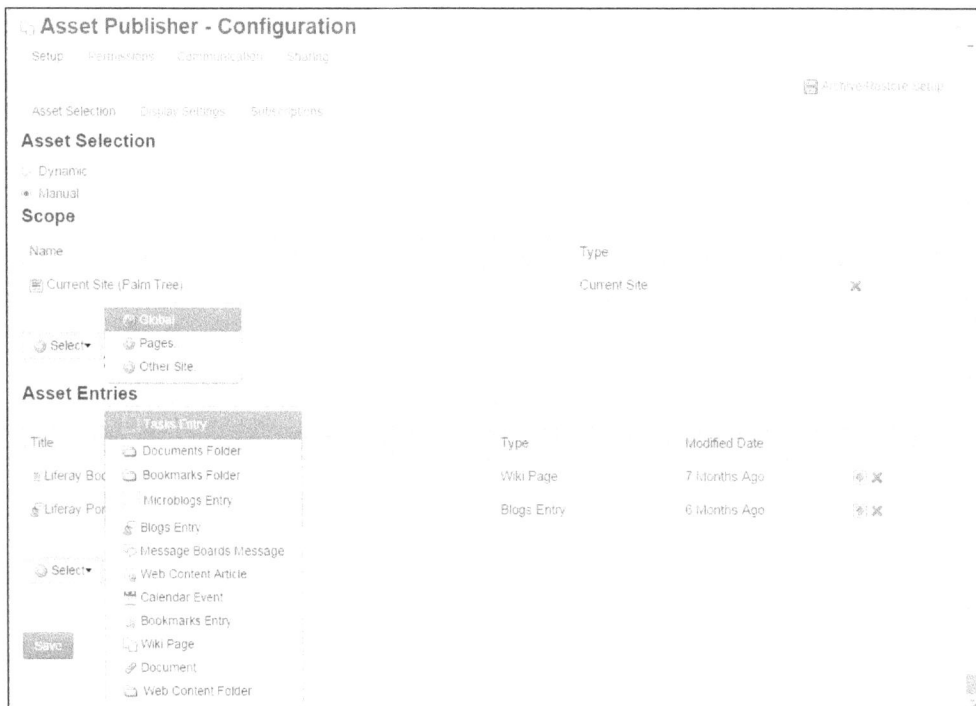

Figure 4.21: The Asset Publisher configuration

In **Asset Selection**, you will be able to select **Scope** and **Asset Entries**. **Scope** allows you to define the scope for Asset Publisher as to which site scope the asset will be picked up for display. By default, it's **Current Site**, but you can add multiple scopes to Asset Publisher, such as **Global**, **Sites**, and **Pages**. Selecting **Asset Entries** allows you to select the assets that you have already created in the scope, such as Tasks Entry, Document Folder, Bookmarks Folder, Microblogs Entry, Blogs Entry, Message Boards Message, Web Content Article, Calender Event, Bookmark Entry, Wiki Pages, and Document and Web Content Folder. You can select multiple **Assets Entries** one by one by clicking on the **Select** button.

Once you've selected multiple assets, you are able to view the selected assets with the **Type** and **Title** columns plus the **Move Up / Move Down** and **Delete** icons. If needed, you can change the order of assets by clicking on **Move Up / Move Down** next to the asset or remove an asset from the list by clicking on the **Delete** icon next to the asset.

The configuration has been differentiated by **Asset Selection**, **Display Settings**, and **Subscription**, which are in the form of tabs. See the previous screenshot.

- **Asset Selection**: The selection of assets needs to be done here, for example, with Message Board as the asset type or by filtering the Asset categories or tags
- **Display Setting**: All the display settings will be done here
- **Subscription**: Setting for subscription

As shown in the next screenshot, Display Settings specifies the style in which selected assets will be displayed. For assets in Asset Publisher, you can specify the following styles:

- **Display Style**: This has **Table**, **Title List**, **Abstracts**, and **Full Content** as options.
- **Abstract Length**: This specifies the number of characters to display for abstracts; the default is 200 and the maximum number is 500.
- **Asset Link Behavior**: This can either be set to **Show Full Content** or **View in a specific portlet** and gives you options to decide what happens when a user clicks on an asset—showing the content right where you are or by taking you to the page where the content was originally published.
- **Number Items to Display**: This is a number used for dynamic selection only.
- **Pagination Type**: The types are **None**, **Simple**, or **Regular**. This is used for dynamic selection only.

- **Show metadata Descriptions**: This is a checkbox for content related to tags.

- **Show Available Locales**: This enables the display of available locales.

- **Set as the Default Asset Publisher for This Page**: The default asset publisher will be used to display web content associated with this page.

- **Enable Conversion To**: Enabling OpenOffice integration provides the document conversion functionality. The possible formats involved are DOC, ODT, PDF, RTF, SXW, and TXT, but this list is not limited.

- **Enable Print**: This checkbox enables print capability on assets.

- **Enable Flag**: This checkbox enables flag capability on the assets.

- **Enable permissions**: This checkbox enables permission capability on the assets.

- **Enable Related Asset**: This checkbox enables related assets to be mapped.

- **Enable Ratings**: This checkbox enables the ratings capability on assets.

- **Enable Comments**: This checkbox enables the comments capability on assets.

- **Enable Comments Ratings**: This checkbox enables ratings capabilities on comments of assets.

- **Enable social Bookmarks**: This checkbox enables the following social bookmarks features:
  - **Display style**: This allows you to define the position of the social bookmarks on the assets page, for example, **Simple**, **Horizontal**, and **Vertical**.
  - **Display position**: This allows you to position the social bookmarks on the assets page, for example, **Top** or **Bottom**.

- **Show Metadata**: This shows the metadata of assets, and the available metadata includes **Author**, **Categories**, **Create Date**, **Expiration Date**, **Modified Date**, **Priority**, **Publish Date**, **Tags**, and **View Count**. You can also add metadata by clicking on the **Add** icon from **Available** to **Current**, remove metadata by clicking on the **Remove** icon from Current to Available, or change the order of metadata in Current by clicking on the **Move Up** or **Move Down** icons for selected metadata in Current.

Asset Publisher - Configuration

Setup   Permissions   Communication   Sharing

Archive/Restore Setup

Asset Selection   Display Settings   Subscriptions

☑ Show Add Content Button

Display Template

Abstracts   ▼   Manage Display Templates for Palm Tree

Abstract Length

200   ▼

Asset Link Behavior

Show Full Content   ▼

Number of Items to Display

20   ▼

Pagination Type

None   ▼

☑ Show Metadata Descriptions
☐ Show Available Locales
☐ Set as the Default Asset Publisher for This Page
Enable Conversion To

DOC   ODT   PDF   RTF   SXW   TXT

☐ Enable Print
☐ Enable Flags
☑ Enable Related Assets
☐ Enable Ratings
☐ Enable Comments
☐ Enable Comment Ratings
☑ Enable Social Bookmarks

Display Style

Horizontal   ▼

Display Position

Bottom   ▼

Show Metadata

Metadata Fields

Current	Available
	Author
	Categories
	Create Date
	Expiration Date
	Modified Date
	Priority
	Publish Date
	Tags
	View Count

Save

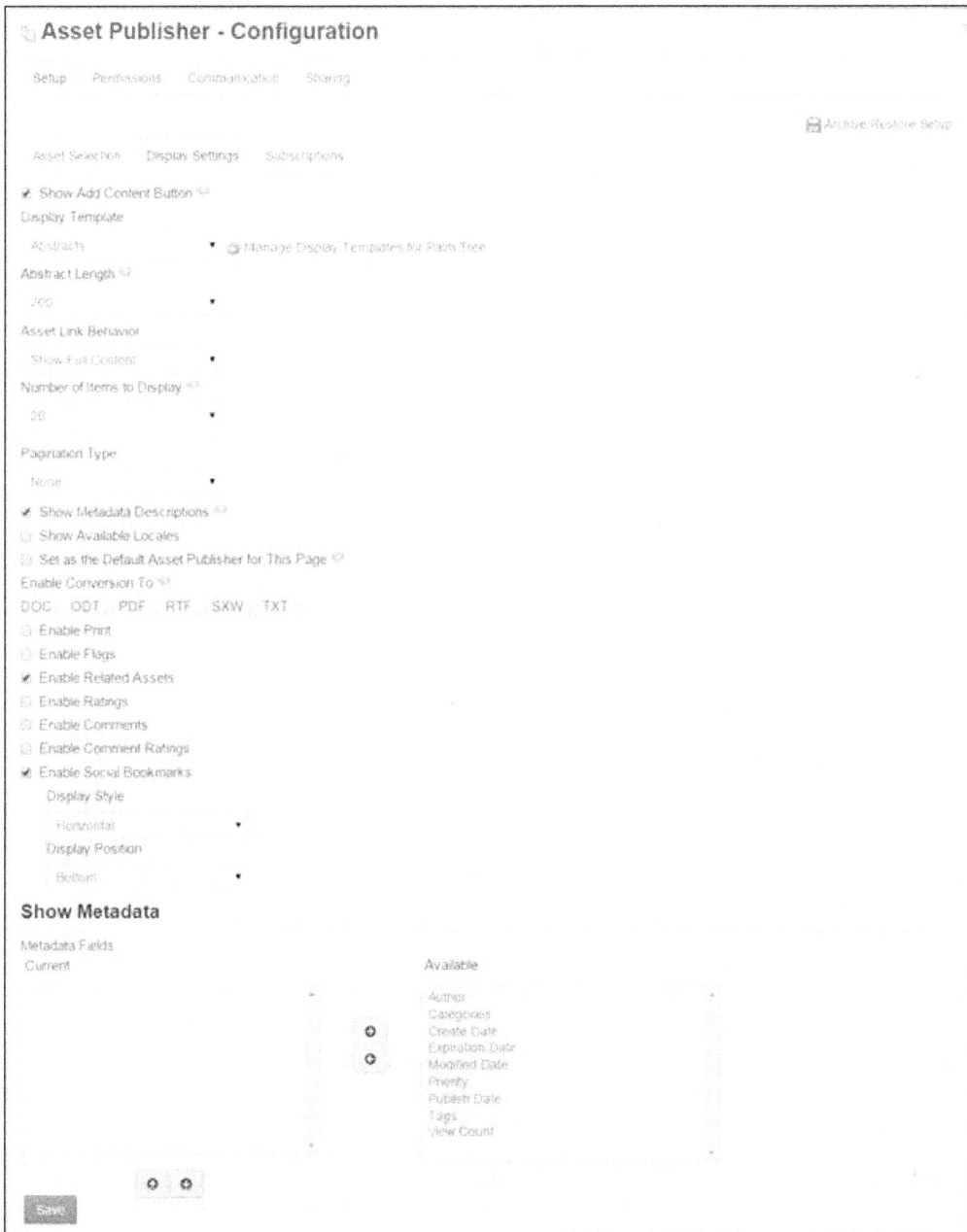

Figure 4.22: Display settings of Asset Publisher

Selecting assets dynamically

Once you've chosen **Asset Selection Dynamic**, you are able to select assets dynamically. In general, there are four sections of dynamic asset publishing: **Source**, **Filter**, **Custom User Attribute**, **Ordering** and **Grouping**, **Display Settings** and **RSS**.

In the **Source** section, there are two options, one to select **Scope** and another to select **Asset Type**.

The default **scope** is the current group. As Asset Publisher was added to the "**Asset Publisher**" page of the Guest public pages, the default scope is the group Guest. If Asset Publisher was added to the "Asset Publishing" page of the "Palm Tree Enterprise" organization's public pages, the default scope would've been the group organization "Palm Tree Enterprise".

Besides the default scope, there is another group called Shared Global available in the portal. Therefore, you will have three options for scope: default scope only, Shared Global only, or both default scope and Shared Global. Using any of these options, you will be able to add a scope by clicking on the Add icon from Available to Current, or remove a scope by clicking on the **Remove** icon from Current to Available. Moreover, you can change the order of scopes in Current by clicking on the Move Up or Move Down icon for a selected scope in Current.

The default asset type would be "any". Thus, the assets that you would be able to include are Wiki Pages, Calendar Event, Bookmark Entry, Message Board Messages, Web Content, Documents and Media Document, and Blog Entry. Of course, you can choose more than one asset type. You will be able to add an asset type by clicking on **Add** icon from Available to Current, remove an asset type by clicking on the **Remove** icon from Current to Available, or even change the order of asset types in Current by clicking on the **Move Up** or **Move Down** icon for a selected asset type in Current.

In the **Filter** section, there are two options, that is, selecting display rules and checkboxes with **Show only assets with Asset Publishing as its display page**, **Include Tags specified in the URL**, and **Include tags set by other applications?**. The displayed assets must follow these rules. The display rule has an expression: find assets which "contain / don't contain" "any/all" "tags/categories". Moreover, you can have as many of these expressions as you want.

By default, "tags" was selected and not "categories". In order to input tags that will be displayed, the content must "contain / not contain" "any/all"; simply start typing the tag and a list of tags will appear. Pick up a tag where the displayed content must **contain / not contain**, and click on the Add Tags button. The selected tags will appear at the top of the input box. Optionally, simply click on the **Select Tags** button, and then pick up one or more tags. To remove a tag, click on the [x] mark located next to the tag.

To use categories instead of tags, select "categories" first, and then click on the **Select Categories** button. Pick up one or more categories. To remove a category, click on the [x] mark located next to the category.

The **Show only assets with Asset Publishing as its display page**. checkbox shows only assets related to Asset Publisher in the display.

The **Include tags specified in the URL** checkbox shows whether the portal includes tags specified in the URL or not. By default, this checkbox is selected, which means that the portal will include tags specified in the URL. Of course, you can deselect this checkbox to disable this functionality if you want.

The **Include tags set by other applications?** checkbox allows certain applications, such as Blogs or Wiki, share the tags of their entries within the page. Asset Publisher can use them to show other assets with the same tags.

In the **Ordering and Grouping** section, there are three options, namely **Order by**, **And Then By**, and **Group by**. The metadata for **Order by** and **And Then By** would be **Title**, **Create Date**, **Modified Date**, **Published Date**, **Expiration Date**, **Priority**, **View Count** and **Ratings** — the order can be ascending or descending.

The metadata of **Group by** would be Asset Type or Vocabulary. That is, you would be able to group assets by asset type (Web Content, Documents and Media Document, Blogs, Wiki, Message Boards, and Bookmarks) or vocabulary (for example, "Book", and "Topic").

In the **Display Settings** section, you can specify the style in which selected assets will be displayed. The processes would be the same as, or similar to, those of the Asset Selection Manual.

In the **RSS** section, you will find the checkbox, **Enable RSS Subscription**. Once you select the checkbox, It allows you to perform setting for RSS, such as "RSS feed Name", "Maximum item to display", "Display style", and Format.

Finally, you can click on the **Save** button to save the changes if you are ready or click the **Cancel** button to cancel the changes.

Customization

As you can see, there are four display styles—**Tables**, **Title List**, **Abstracts**, and **Full Content**. The portal has the following setting by default in `portal.properties`:

```
asset.publisher.display.styles=table,title-list,abstracts,full-
    content
```

As shown in the preceding code, you can input a list of comma-separated display styles that will be available in the configuration screen of the Asset Publisher portlet. Of course, you can override this property in `portal-ext.properties`.

In addition, there is one more property related to the tag, which is, "Include tags specified in the URL" as follows:

```
tags.compiler.enabled=true
```

The preceding code sets the `tags.compiler.enabled` property to `true` in order to provide the ability to compile tags from the URL. This is the reason that the **Include tags specified in the URL** checkbox was selected by default. Note that disabling this feature can speed up performance.

What's happening?

As you can see, Asset Publisher can publish any of the assets from the portal's core part, such as Wiki Pages, Calendar Event, Bookmark Entry, Message Board Messages, Web Content, Documents and Media Document, and Blog Entry. In addition, Asset Publisher can publish any assets from plugins, such as the Knowledge Base portlet.

What's happening? The portal provides a framework called **Asset Renderer Framework** with the tag `asset-renderer-factory` at `$PORTAL_ROOT_HOME/ dtd/ liferay-portlet-app_6_1_0.dtd`. This framework allows us to register custom asset types so that generic portlets, such as Asset Publisher, can be used to publish them. Note that the `asset-renderer-factory` value in the custom asset types must be a class that implements `com.liferay.portlet.asset.model. AssetRendererFactory` and is called by Asset Publisher.

A configurable look and feel

Now, you can implement the views through templates. CSS and JavaScript should be available as templates as well. It would be easy for end users, not developers, to customize velocity templates (including CSS and JavaScript) directly.

It would be a good idea to add velocity templates to views in the Asset Publisher portlet. The following is a brief proposal:

1. Define a set of templates (for different views: table, title list, abstracts, full content) in the / `vm` folder (or in some other folder) in Asset Publisher.

2. In the *Render* action, pick up a proper template to generate the view. In addition, variables of velocity templates should consider fields of web structures in order to make summaries localizable.

Summary

This chapter first introduced you to how we can add categories and subcategories in Message Boards. Then, it discussed how to add a tag and manage (add, delete, and update) categories and vocabularies as well as how to tag assets and display tags. Finally, it addressed how to publish assets through the Asset Publisher portlet and how to configure and customize the Asset Publisher portlet.

In this chapter, you learned how to manage the categories, threads, and posts of Message Boards; set permissions on Message Boards categories, threads, and posts; manage tags, tag content, and display tags; set permissions on tags; manage categories, tag content, and display categories; set permissions on categories; and publish Assets through tags and categories.

In the next chapter, we're going to introduce other important content, such as Wiki, Web Forms, and Polls.

5
Understanding Wikis, Dynamic Data Lists, and Polls

On the intranet website bookpub.com of the enterprise Palm Tree Publications, it would be useful to keep track of information about editorial guidance and other resources that require frequent editing, for example, to keep track of votes on the topic "Is this book on Liferay a proper book?" and to collect suggestions on subjects such as "Liferay books". A wiki is a social collaborative encyclopedia that allows users to come together and share knowledge in an area. Administrators can add and edit wiki pages, change permissions, and set advanced options. The Wiki portlets provide a straightforward wiki solution, while the Polls portlets provide surveys to assess public opinion. Also, we are going to see a new feature of Liferay 6.2, "Recycle Bin".

This chapter is going to introduce you to wikis, Dynamic Data Lists, and the Polls portlet and show how to configure them and implement requirements based on them.

By the end of this chapter, you will have learned how to:

- Manage (view, update, and delete) nodes of wikis
- Manage (view, update, delete, and search) pages of a given node in a wiki
- Assign permissions on wiki nodes and pages
- Publish wiki pages
- Convert documents
- Use dynamic data lists

- Configure the Polls portlet
- Display polls
- Recycle Bin

Understanding Wikis

In order to provide an environment for employees at the Palm Tree Publications enterprise that keeps track of information about editorial guidance and other resources that require frequent editing, we can use the Wikis portlet (portlet ID 36) in Palm Tree (public pages).

Now, log in to the palm tree site as a site administrator (admin@bookpub.com). Select the Palm Tree site from the dock bar (**My Sites**) drop-down list. Once you have landed on the Palm Tree site, you can create the "Wiki" page and add the Wiki portlet in the **Wiki** page. Then, you are ready to create the "Liferay" and "Alfresco" nodes.

Managing nodes

As an administrator of the enterprise Palm Tree Publications, we're going to create nodes called "Liferay" and "Alfresco". As we discussed before, Liferay Portal maintains different content for multiple sites, that is, **site scope**. For example, Palm Tree, Global, and a default page called "FrontPage" for the node "Main" was also created with empty content. First, navigate to **Admin | Content** under the dock bar menu, and then select **Wiki**. Here, you will see the wiki **main**, which will have pages within it. To see all the pages, click on **main**. You will see something similar to the following screenshot. How does the portal implement these? This is answered in the next section.

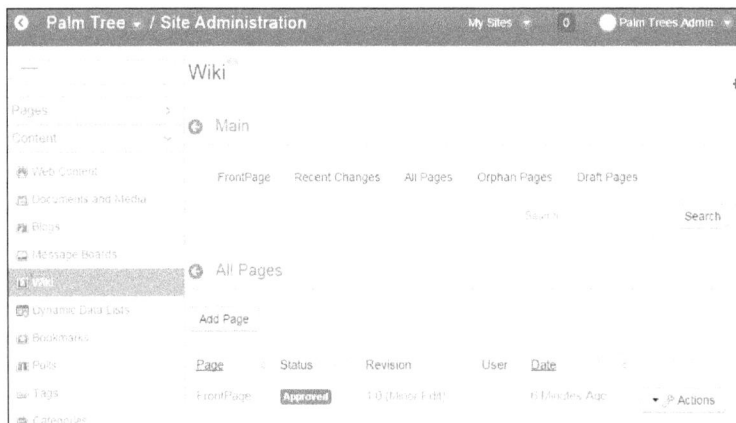

Figure 5.1: Wiki Control Panel

Adding nodes in a Wiki

First of all, we need to create a node called "Liferay". Let's create a node as follows:

1. Log in as a site administrator, for example, "Palm Tree".

2. Select **Admin | Content** under the dock bar menu.

3. Click on **Wiki** under the category **Content (Palm Tree)** of the site's control panel.

4. By default, the node "Main" is created.

5. Click on the **Add Wiki** button at the top of the nodes list.

6. Enter the name "Liferay" and the description "Liferay root".

7. Permissions settings keep default settings. In order to configure additional permissions, click on the **More Options** link.

8. Click on the **Save** button to save the inputs. Refer to the following screenshot to create a new wiki node.

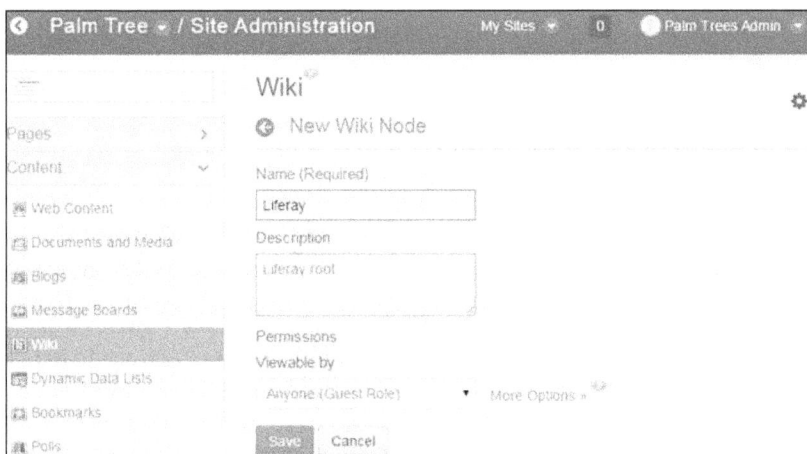

Figure 5.2: Creating a new Wiki node

Of course, you can add other nodes as expected. After creating the node called "Alfresco", we can view Wiki nodes. Nodes are displayed via node names, number of pages, last post date, and the Actions menu next to the node with a set of actions (that are, **Edit, Permissions, Import Pages, RSS, Subscribe, Move to the Recycle Bin**, and **View Removed Attachments**). The following screenshot displays the Wiki node list.

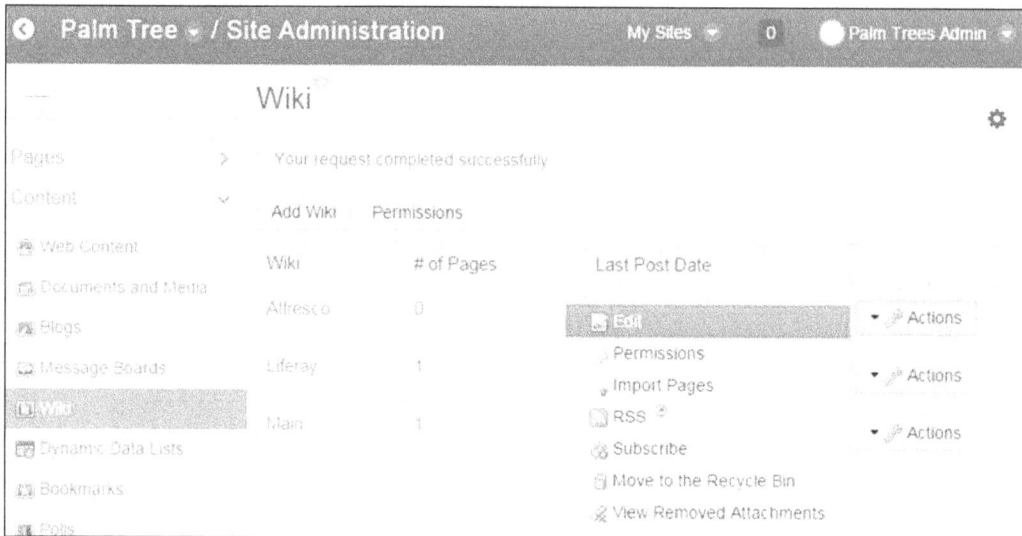

Figure 5.3: The Wiki node list

In short, we can create a node by clicking on the **Add Wiki** button and filling the name and, optionally, the description. An initial page called **FrontPage** (called a wiki article or a wiki page) is created when a new node is created inside the front page.

Generally speaking, a set of pages in groups is called **nodes**. Each node acts as a whole wiki. Nodes can have their own set of permissions and recent changes list and a listing of all pages. After creating nodes, we can manage wiki nodes easily.

Editing a node

Nodes are editable. For example, we plan to change the description of the node "Liferay" from the value "Liferay root" to the value "Liferay Wikis Root". Let's do it by following these steps:

1. Locate the "**Liferay**" node.
2. Click on the **Edit** icon from the **Actions** menu next to the node.
3. Update the description with the value "**Liferay Wikis Root**".
4. Click on the **Save** button to save the changes.

Remove a node

Nodes are removable. For instance, the node "Alfresco" doesn't exist anymore as per our requirement. We have to remove this from the Wiki portlet by following these steps:

1. Locate the "**Alfresco**" node that you want to remove.

2. Click on the "**Move to the Recycle Bin**" icon from the **Actions** menu located next to the node.

3. You will get the message "**The Wiki Node Alfresco was moved to the Recycle Bin.**" with an undo button. If you don't want to remove it, just click undo. It will revert back to its previous position.

> Note that removing a node will remove all related pages that belong to this node. Moreover, any comments related to the pages of this node will also get removed.

Viewing RSS feeds

You can view RSS feeds of nodes. If you need to view RSS feeds of the node "Liferay", you can do so by following these steps:

1. Locate the "Liferay" node.

2. Click on the **RSS** icon from the **Actions** menu next to the node.

Importing pages

In addition, the portal provides the capability to import pages from MediaWiki. **MediaWiki** is a free-software Wiki package written in PHP, originally for use on Wikipedia (refer to www.mediaWiki.org for more details).

Suppose that you are going to import pages from MediaWiki to the "Liferay" node; you can do so by following these steps:

1. Locate the "**Liferay**" node.

2. Click on the **Import Pages** icon from the **Actions** menu next to the node.

3. In **Import Pages**, specify the required or optional items, as shown in the following points and the next screenshot:

    ° **Pages File:** Submit an XML file exported by MediaWiki through the "Special: Export" page at http://www.mediawiki.org/wiki/Manual:Parameters_to_Special:Export.

- ○ **Users File (Optional)**: Submit a CSV file along with the e-mail addresses of the users to match with those in the portal. The file should have two columns: username and email address. This file can be obtained using SQL directly from MediaWiki's database.

- ○ **Images File (Optional)**: Submit a ZIP file of the images to import. You can zip the images folder of MediaWiki directly (sometimes it's called "upload"), removing the directories called "archive", "temp", and "thumbs" to reduce the ZIP size since they will be ignored.

- ○ **FrontPage (Optional)**: The default name is "Main Page".

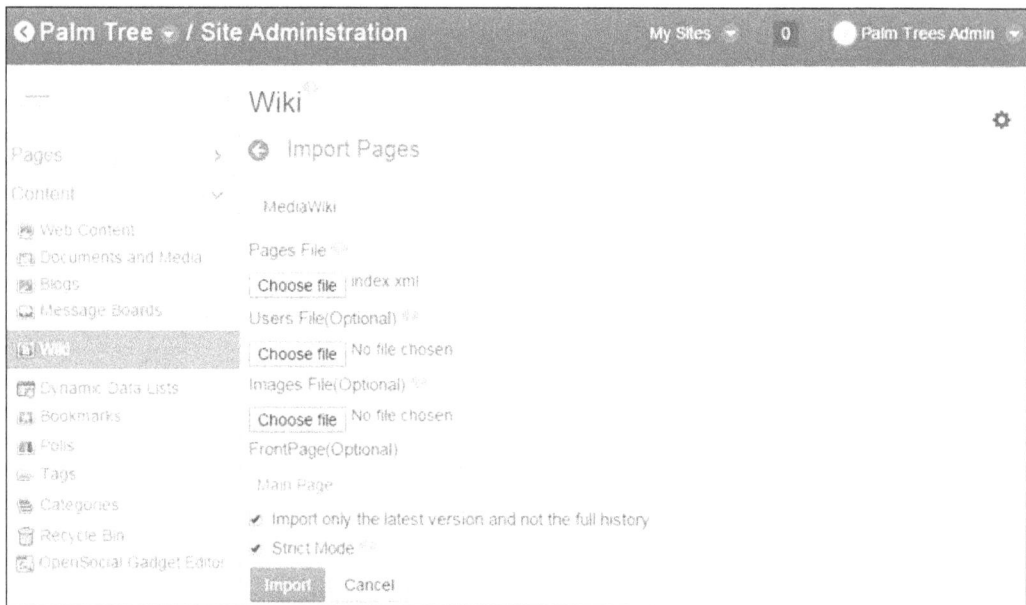

Figure 5.4: The Wiki import page

- ○ Keep the checkbox enabled for **Import** — only the latest version and not the full history. By default, it's checked — even for **Strict Mode**, which allows you to remove every unrecognizable MediaWiki markup from the imported page.

4. Click on the **Import button** to import, or click on the **Cancel** button to cancel the importing process.

Managing pages

As you can see, the default page FrontPage has been created, which is an entry point. Through the FrontPage page, you can add and manage as many pages as you can imagine.

Adding pages

As an administrator of the enterprise Palm Tree Publications, you would like to add more pages under the **Liferay** node, namely "Liferay and Alfresco Integration" and "Liferay Book". Let's do it by following these steps:

1. Click on **Wiki** under the **Content** category (Palm Tree) of the site's **control panel**.

2. Click on the name of the "Liferay" node.

3. Click on the **Edit** icon next to the page "FrontPage".

4. Select the format "Creole".

5. In editing mode, input "[[Liferay and Alfresco Integration]]" and "[[**Liferay Book**]]", or you can just link the words using the link icon.

6. Type a summary for the current edit if required. Check the checkbox that says this is a minor edit (if it is indeed a minor edit) — note that there is no configuration link as it is an action to an edit.

7. Click on **Categorization** and on select **Category** to add categories. Also, input a tag and click on the **Add Tags** button if you need to add tags, and click on **Suggestions** to get suggestions for tags.

8. Click on the **Publish** button when you are ready.

In brief, the most common way to create wiki pages (wiki articles) is usually by creating a link from another article, for example, [[my new page]]. Then, when you click on the link, it will pop up the editing view and ask you to create the new page. The benefit of doing it this way is that we'll interconnect related pages so that it's easier for users to navigate through them. Refer to the screenshot given here for the wiki front page.

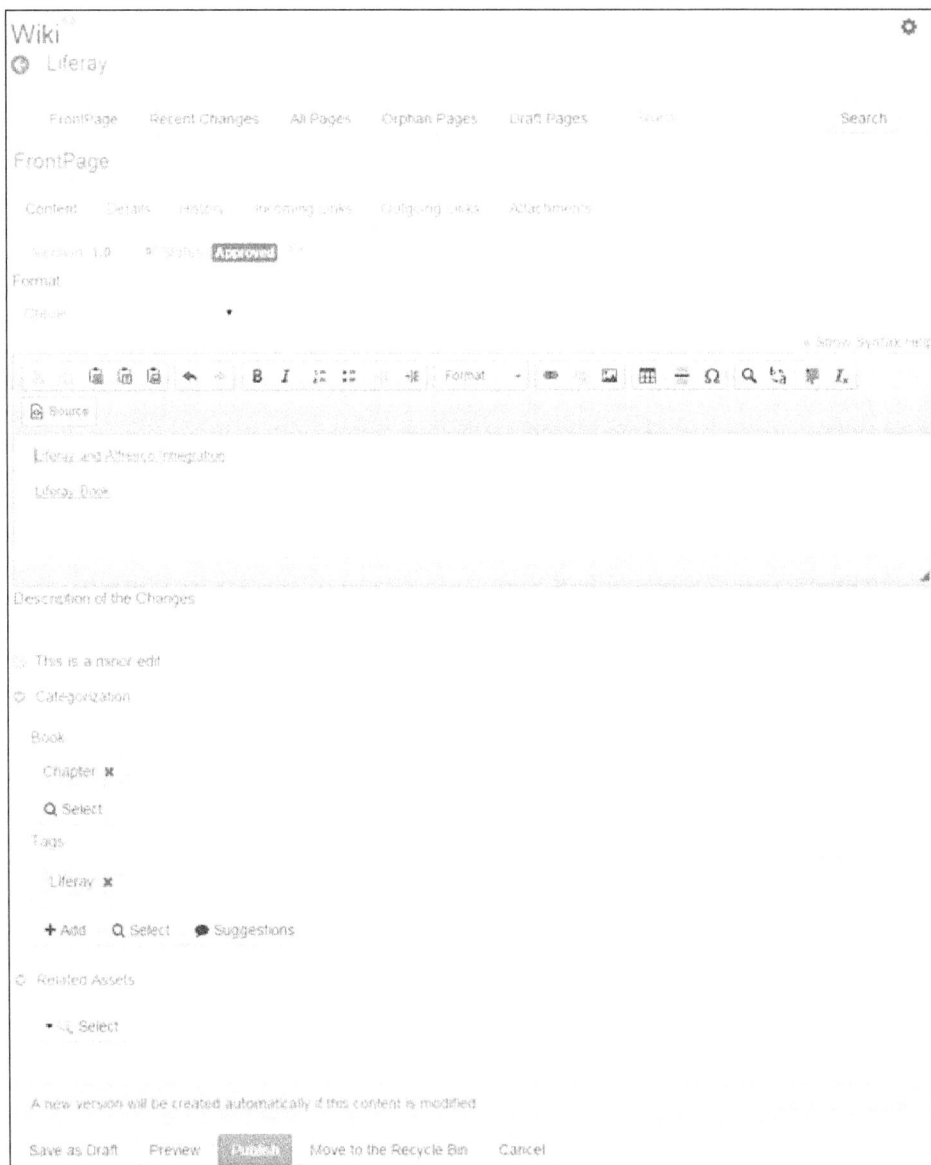

Figure 5.5: The Wiki front page

Of course, you can add pages directly. Let's say that you want to add a page called "My Page" under the node "Liferay". Let's add this page by following these steps:

1. Click on **Wiki** under the category **Content (Palm Tree)** of the site's **control panel**.

2. Click on the name of the "**Liferay**" node.

3. Click on the **Add Page** icon under the "**All Pages**" page.

4. Enter the page title "**My Page**" — note that there is a configuration link here because we add a page instead of editing it.

5. Permissions settings keep default settings. In order to configure additional permissions, click on the **More Options** link.

6. Click on the **Publish** button to publish the changes.

The following screenshot illustrates the Wiki All Pages where you can see the list of pages.

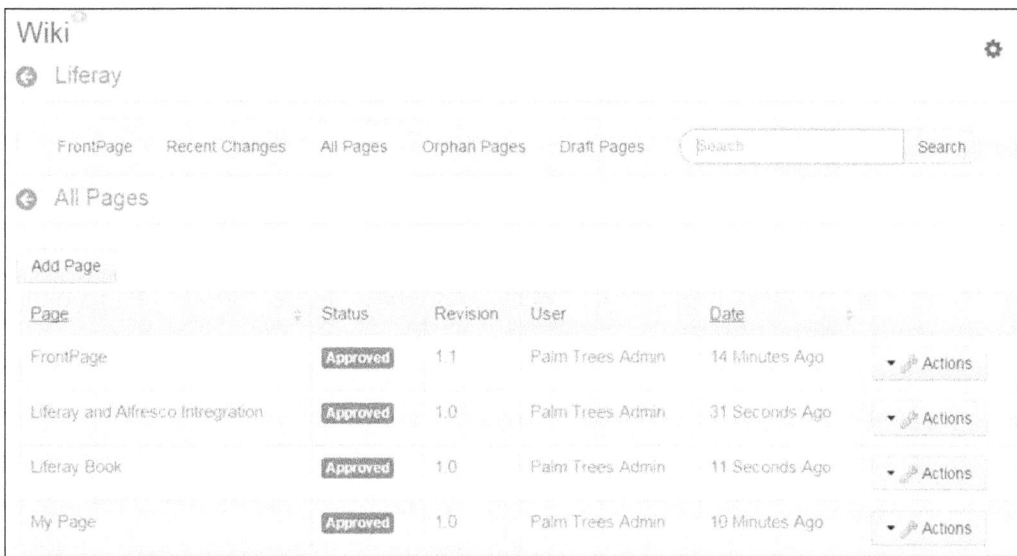

Page		Status	Revision	User	Date	
FrontPage		Approved	1.1	Palm Trees Admin	14 Minutes Ago	▼ Actions
Liferay and Alfresco Intregration		Approved	1.0	Palm Trees Admin	31 Seconds Ago	▼ Actions
Liferay Book		Approved	1.0	Palm Trees Admin	11 Seconds Ago	▼ Actions
My Page		Approved	1.0	Palm Trees Admin	10 Minutes Ago	▼ Actions

Figure 5.6: The Wiki All Pages

As mentioned earlier, there are three editing modes in the current version, that is, formats to edit wiki pages — Creole, HTML, and MediaWiki. Select one of the editing modes. By default, the Creole editing mode is selected. After selecting the mode, the body section editor will change from Classic to Plain Text. In the following section, you will come to know how to configure it.

Liferay wiki is more advanced with the introduction of the FCK editor in the Creole and HTML formats. Most of the wiki Creole syntax will be written easily by the editor.

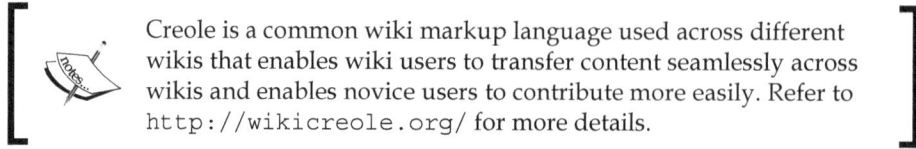

> Creole is a common wiki markup language used across different wikis that enables wiki users to transfer content seamlessly across wikis and enables novice users to contribute more easily. Refer to `http://wikicreole.org/` for more details.

You can definitely follow the wiki Creole mode syntax to edit wiki pages. For example, represent internal links by beginning with double brackets ([[), with the page display name in the middle, and ending with double brackets (]]). On the other hand, you can represent external links by beginning with double brackets ([[), then the URL, a vertical bar (|), the display name, and ending with double brackets (]]), or using the URL directly.

You can simply start typing a tag in the tag textbox, and you will see a list of tags. Just select the tags you want, and you will see the tag showing up adjacent to the box. You can remove a tag by clicking on the mark "[x]" located next to the tag.

Of course, you can create others pages that you need. Let's say that we need to add a page called "Book Wiki" under the "Liferay Book" page. Let's do it by following these steps:

1. Locate the "**Liferay**" node.
2. Click on the name of the "**Liferay**" node.
3. Find the "**Liferay Book**" link by clicking on the front page and clicking on the name "**Liferay Book**".
4. Click on the **Edit** icon next to the page "**Liferay Book**".
5. Select the format, for example, "**Creole**".
6. In the editing page, input "[[**Book Wiki**]]" or other content.
7. Type the summary of the current edit if required in the description textbox. Check the checkbox that says this is a minor edit (if it is a minor edit indeed).
8. Click on **Categorization** and on select **Category** to add categories. Also, input a tag and click on the **Add Tags** button if you need to add tags, and click **Suggestions** to get the tags suggestions.
9. Permissions settings keep default settings. In order to configure additional permissions, click on the **More Options** link.
10. Click on the **Publish** button when you are ready.

Viewing pages

As shown in the following screenshot, the Wiki portlet provides rich messages about wiki pages. This message is grouped into different sections: Content, Details, History, Incoming Links, Outgoing Links, and Attachment. As you have noticed, while editing a wiki page, it will bring you to the **Details | Content** tab, where "Details" is an icon next to the **Edit** icon.

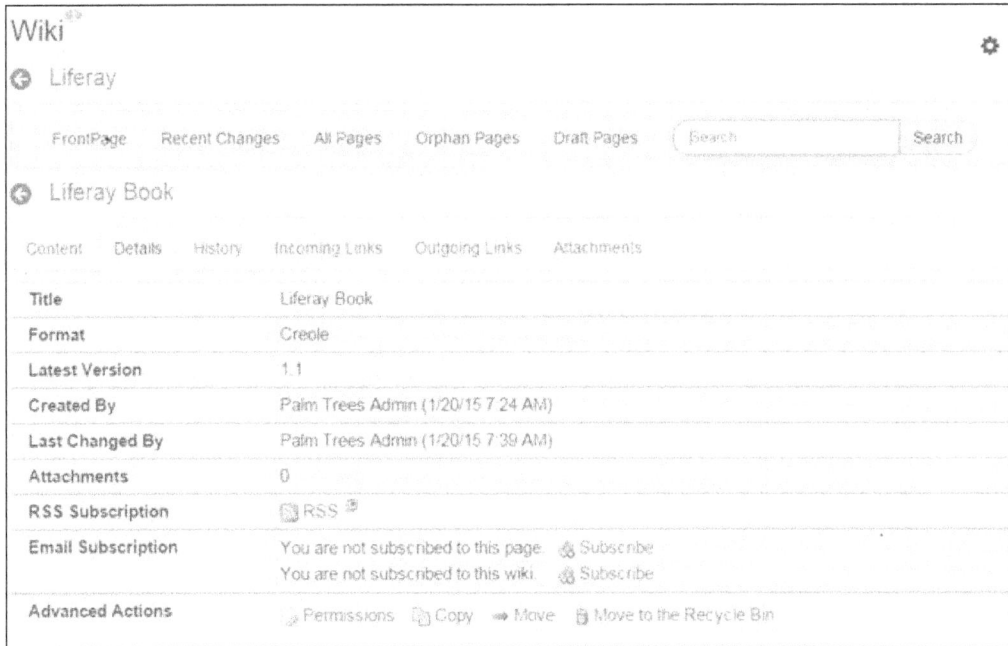

Figure 5.7: The Wiki front page details

In order to create new pages (Wiki Article), you need to edit an existing page and use the syntax to create a link to the new page. When the page is created instead of being converted to a link, the name of the new page is identified by the link. When you click on the name, the portlet will create the page automatically. Furthermore, you can edit it regularly once the page is created. At the same time, the name of the page on the original page will be converted to a link.

You may need to view Page Links—either outgoing links or incoming links for the page "Liferay Book". You can do it by following these steps:

1. Locate and click on the "**Liferay**" node.

2. Locate the "**Liferay Book**" link from the front page, and click on the name "**Liferay Book**".

3. Click on **Details | Incoming** Links or **Details | Outgoing** Links. A list of pages with the current page as incoming links or outgoing links will appear, that is, for "**Liferay Book**", an incoming link is "**Front Page**" and an outgoing link is "**Book wiki**".

A wiki page can have many attachments, which can be managed by clicking on **Details | Attachments**. The functionality related to the attachments' management includes the dragging and dropping of the files that you want to attach but isn't limited to adding attachments, viewing attachments, downloading attachments, and removing a specific attachment. To have a clear picture on **Wiki Outgoing Link**, you can refer to the following screenshot:

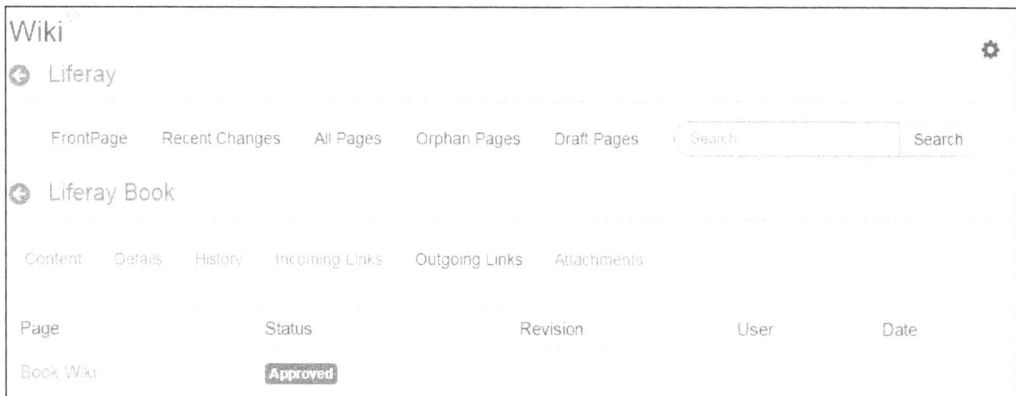

Figure 5.8: Wiki outgoing links

You may need to view the page history of the "**Liferay Book**" page. You can do it as shown in the preceding screenshot by following these steps:

1. Locate and click on the "**Liferay**" node.

2. Find and click on the name "Liferay Book".

3. Click on **Details | History**. You will find the **Activities** and **Versions** tabs. Click on the **Versions** tab, and a list of pages with their histories (different versions with minor edits or major edits) will appear.

As you can see, you can compare versions by selecting different versions and clicking on the **Compare Versions** button. Alternatively, you can bring the content of a page back to a specific version by clicking on the **Revert** icon.

> Printing the wiki page is very simple: click on the print icon on the wiki page, which is in the top-right corner.

Searching pages

Searching a page in the Wiki portlets provides you with a list of search results, as shown in the following screenshot for a specific node. The node here could represent an entire wiki. To search wiki pages, first locate a node, say "Liferay". Then, input a search criterion, say "book", and click on the **Search** button on the wiki menu bar. A list page, wiki name (Node name), and page title will appear below the **Search** button. Additionally, you will have the ability to create a new page on this topic as well.

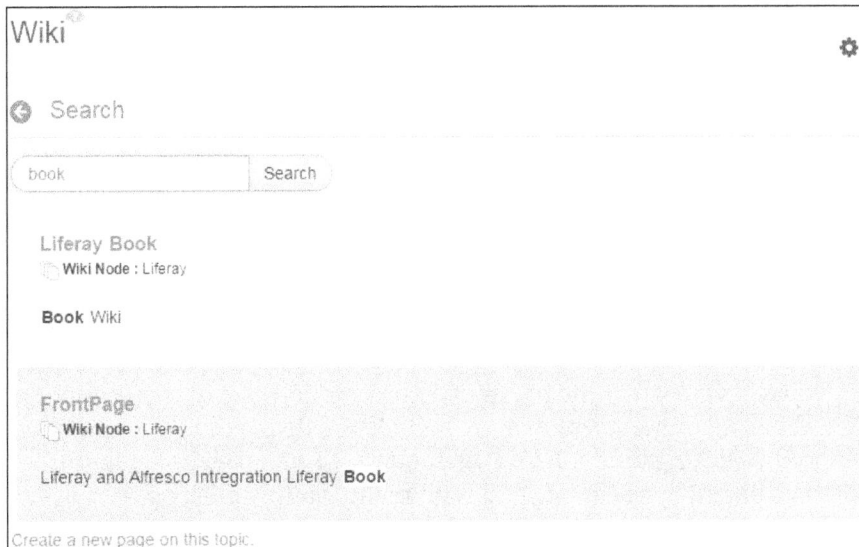

Figure 5.9: Search

In the Wiki menu, you will see few useful links, such as **FrontPage**, **Recent Changes**, **All Pages**, **Orphan Pages**, and **Draft Pages**, even including the **Search Box**. FrontPage is the entry point of the node and contains the message "This page is empty. Edit it to add some text".

As an administrator, you may be interested in the recent changes of all the pages in a given node. To do so, you can use **Recent Changes**. When you click on the **Recent Changes** link, a list of pages with columns (**Page, Status, Revision, User, Date, Summary**, and a set of actions—**Edit, Permissions, Copy, Move, Subscribe**, and **Move to the Recycle Bin**) will appear and be ordered by their modified dates. As you can see, you can manage these pages in order to edit a page, assign permissions on the page, copy a page, move a page, subscribe or unsubscribe a page, and even remove a page. Moreover, you may be interested in **RSS** feeds, such as **Atom 1.0, RSS 1.0**, and **RSS 2.0**. Note that RSS feeds are used for pages with recent changes to a given node. The following screenshot shows this:

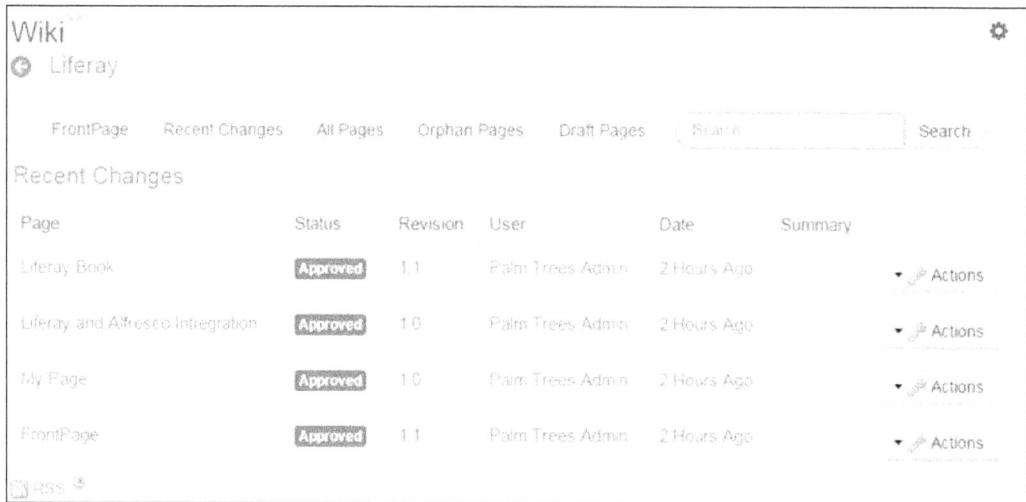

Figure 5.10: Recent changes

Similarly, you can view all of the pages of a given node. Simply click on the **All Pages** link. When all of the pages of a given node are displayed, you would be able to add a page by clicking on the **Add Page** button. To view **orphan pages** (the pages that don't have parent pages associated with them), simply click on the **Orphan Pages** link.

Adding comments

As stated previously, the administrator has created a page called "Liferay Book". As a user of the enterprise Palm Tree Publications, say "Lotti Stein", if you want to review this page and add comments, such as "This is a good book", you can do it just by following these steps:

1. Log in as "Lotti Stein".

2. Navigate to the "**Wiki**" Page as mentioned earlier in the Palm Tree site.

3. Locate the "Liferay" node and click on it.

4. Locate the **Add Comments** link at the bottom of the page. If there is no comment, you will see this message with a link "No Comments yet. Be the first." Refer to the following screenshot.

5. Input the comment "This is a good book".

6. Finally, click on the **Reply** button to save the inputs.

For further reference, you can follow this screenshot, which gives you a clear picture of **Wiki Comments**:

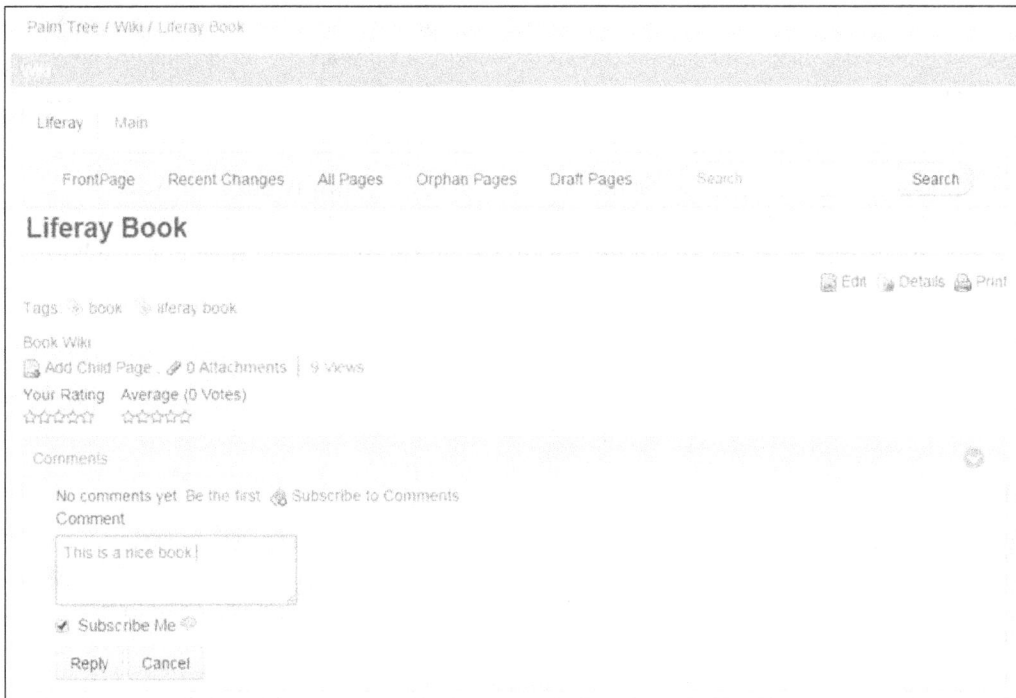

Figure 5.11: Wiki comments

As an administrator, you can view comments from "Lotti Stein" for the page "Liferay Book" through the "Liferay" node.

As you can see, you can add as many comments as possible and manage comments (perform update, delete, and add vote on comments) if you have the proper permissions. Note that a user can only vote once on a specific comment.

To reply to a comment, first locate the comment that you want to reply to. Then, click on the **Post Reply** icon in the bottom-right corner of the comment. Input comments, and then click on the **Reply** button to save the inputs, or click on the **Cancel** button to cancel.

To delete a comment, click on the **Delete** icon in the bottom-right corner of the comment. A screen will appear asking you whether you want to delete this. Click on **OK** to confirm the deletion or on **Cancel** to cancel the deletion.

> Note that only the current comment has been deleted in action. The low-level comments related to the current comment will have a link to the parent comment of the current comment.

To go to the top of the comments, simply click on the **Top** button in the bottom-right corner of any comment.

Generally, to add discussions for the current page, first simply click on **Add Comments** at the bottom of the page. Then, simply input comments and finally, click on the **Reply** button to save the comments or on the **Cancel** button to cancel the comments.

Additionally, to edit a comment, first simply click on the **Edit** icon at the bottom of the post if you have proper permissions. Then, change the comments by clicking on the **Publish** button to save the changes or on the **Cancel** button to cancel the changes.

Adding ratings

In addition, users can add ratings for wiki pages. As an end user, you may have different options on pages, thus you can rate the content of a specific page. The Wiki portlet provides the ability to allow the end user to rate the contents of wiki pages— rating a wiki page from one to five stars. Note that a user can only vote once on a specific page. A user can vote for each comment on the same page. However, it will be counted as one vote in the statistics. This allows users to change their vote. For a clearer picture, refer to *Figure 5.11*.

Subscribing to nodes and Wiki pages

Being users of wiki pages, you would be interested in the wiki pages' changes in a specific node. For example, as a member of the Palm Tree group, you may be interested in the pages in the "Liferay" node. You expect to watch out for any changes in the pages in this node. Therefore, you can use a subscription function on the "Liferay" node. Let's do it by following these steps:

1. Locate the "Liferay" node.
2. Click on the **Subscribe** icon from the **Actions** menu next to the node. The **Subscribe** icon will become the **Unsubscribe** icon for this node.

Of course, you can subscribe to other nodes. You may be interested in any changes to the "Liferay and Alfresco Integration" page. Thus, you can subscribe to it by following these steps:

1. Click on the "Liferay" node—you would see the page "FrontPage".
2. Click on the **All Pages** link.
3. Locate the page "**Liferay and Alfresco Integration**".
4. Click on the **Subscribe** icon from the **Actions** menu next to the page. The **Subscribe** icon will become **Unsubscribe**.

Obviously, you can subscribe to other pages. Optionally, you can go to **Details | Email subscription** in order to either subscribe to, or unsubscribe from, the current page or even current node.

If you have nodes or pages you've subscribed to and the content of the subscribed node or page gets changed, then you will receive notifications for these changes. Moreover, node subscription provides the useful function of notifying by e-mail when the node and its pages have been updated. Page subscription provides the useful function of notifying by e-mail when the content of the page has been updated.

Assigning permissions

We have used the default settings for the Wikis portlet in the page "Wikis". When you're logged in as a "Palm Tree" administrator, you can manage Wiki. As you know, the user "Lotti Stein" is a member of Palm Tree. When Lotti logs in, Lotti sees the nodes "Liferay" and "Main", but Lotti doesn't have the ability to add new nodes or update existing nodes.

What's happening? This is something related to permissions. Permissions for Wiki can be assigned under **Site Administration**. Under **Site Administration | Content | Wiki**, another one is **Site Administration | Application | Wiki**. Moreover, each has a different set of permission level.

To set the permission entitlements for wiki, the portal administrator needs to define permissions in roles. Under the **User** section, click on **Roles** in **Control Panel** and locate **MB Topic Admin**. Select define permissions from the **Action** button beside MB Topic Admin. Search for Wiki. You will get the entitlements settings for wiki:

- **Site Administration | Content | Wiki**: General Permissions, Resource Permissions (Wiki Nodes, Wiki Node, and Wiki Page).

- **Site Administration | Application | Wiki**: Application Permissions, Resource Permissions (Wiki Nodes, Wiki Node, and Wiki Page).

Let's discuss each of them one by one in detail.

Wiki Nodes

Wiki Nodes has two entitlements, that is, **Add Node** and **Permissions**. Refer to the following screenshot:

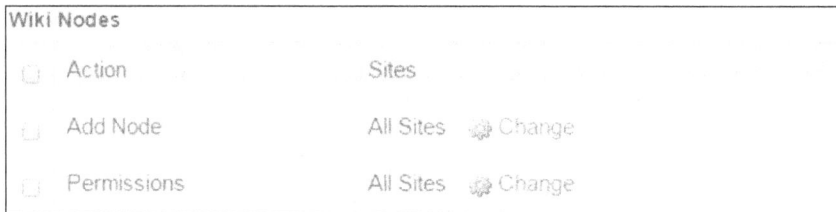

Figure 5.12: Permission for Wiki nodes

Portal Admin has the ability to set up permissions. By default, only the portal administrator and site administrator have these permissions enabled. Let's provide **MB Topic Admin** with the ability to use Add Node:

Action	Description	MB Topic Admin	Site Members
Add Node	This provides the ability to add a top-level category		
Permissions	This provides the ability to set up permissions		

Obviously, as a member of the Palm Tree site, "Lotti Stein" doesn't have the permission to use **Add Node** on Wikis by default. Note that the **Add Node** permission is scoped to a group or portal instance. If you want the user "Lotti Stein" to have the ability to add nodes for all groups in the current portal instance, how will you implement it? The following is an example of how to assign the permission action **Add Node**:

1. Log in as an admin of the "Palm Tree" portal.

2. First, click on **Roles** under the **Users** category of **Control Panel**.

3. Then, locate a role, say "**MB Topic Admin**".

4. Then, click on the **Define Permissions** icon from **Actions** on the right-hand side of the role.

5. From the left-hand side tree menu, select **Site Administration | Content | Wiki: Resource Permissions |Wiki** Nodes and check the **Add Node** checkbox.

6. Finally, click on the **Save** button when you are ready.

That's it! From now onwards, the user "Lotti Stein" has the **Add Node** permissions on Wiki via the "MB Topic Admin" role.

Note that "Lotti Stein" should have access to **Site Administrator | Content | Wiki**. Here she will have access to **Add Wiki** (Node).

Wiki General Permissions

Wiki General Permissions has four entitlements, which are, Access in Site Administrator, Configuration, Permissions, and View. Refer to the following screenshot:

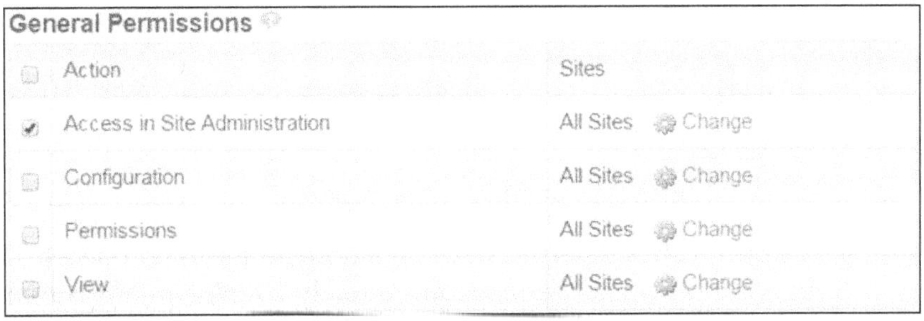

Action	Sites	
✓ Access in Site Administration	All Sites	Change
Configuration	All Sites	Change
Permissions	All Sites	Change
View	All Sites	Change

General Permissions

Figure 5.13: Site content permission for the Wiki portlet

If any Role needs access to the wiki portlet inside Site Administrator, the Access in Site Administration permission helps with the setting.

The permission action Access in Site Administration represents the ability to access the Wiki portlet in Site Administration. By default, the user "Lotti Stein" doesn't have the ability to access the Wiki portlet in Site Administration. Let's provide MB Topic Admin with the permission action **Access in Site Administration**.

What's the permission action **Access in the Site Administration**? This permission action represents the ability to access the Wiki portlet in Site Administration. By default, the user "Lotti Stein" doesn't have the ability to access the Wiki portlet in Site Administration. But the requirement is that the user "Lotti Stein" should have the ability to access the Wiki portlet in Site Administration.

Simply check the box beside **Access in the Site Administration** and save it. All users who have MB Topic Admin will have the ability to access the wiki portlet in site administration.

Wiki Node

Wiki Node permission entitlements are basically permissions for each node action, such as, Add Attachment, Add Page, Delete, Import, Permissions, Subscribe, Update, and View. Refer to the following screenshot:

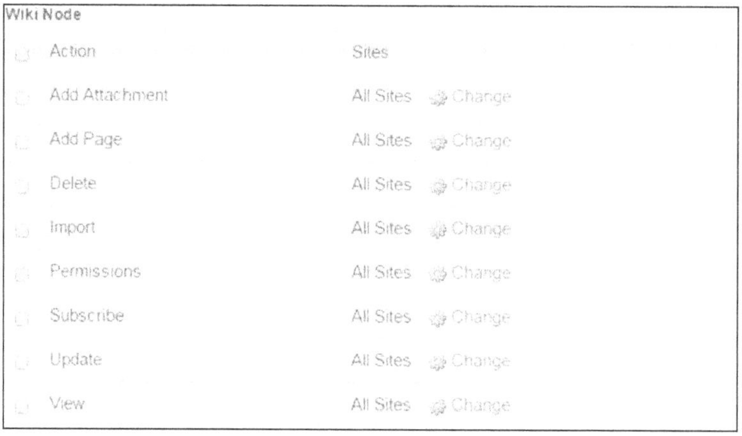

Figure 5.14 Site content permission for Wiki Node

The preceding screenshot shows permissions on a node in the Wiki portlet. The role **MB Topic Admin** is able to set up permissions, namely **View**, **Update**, **Subscribe**, **Permissions**, **Import**, **Delete**, **Add Page**, and **Add Attachments**. On the other hand, the role Guest can set up permissions with **View**, **Delete**, **Permissions**, **Import**, and **Add Attachments**.

Let's add the **View** permission to **MB Topic Admin** so that "Lotti Stein" has the permission to view the Node and allow more actions, such as **Delete**, **Permissions**, and **Update**.

Follow these steps to set the permissions:

1. Log in as an admin, say "Palm Tree".
2. Click on **Roles** under the **Portal** category of **Control Panel**.
3. Then, locate a role, say "**MB Topic Admin**".
4. Then, click on the **Define Permissions** icon from the **Actions** menu next to the right of the role.
5. From the left-hand side tree menu, select **Site Administration | Content | Wiki: Resource Permissions |Wiki** Node, and check the Delete, Permissions, Update, and View checkboxes.
6. Finally, click on the **Save** button when you are ready.
7. Now "Lotti Stein" will be able to view, update, delete, and set the permission for the Node "Liferay".

> Note that you need to map **Lotti Stein** with the **MB Topic Admin** role. Once it's done, Lotti will have all the permissions defined.

Wiki Page

Wiki Page permission entitlements are basically provided on pages such as Add Discussion, Delete, Delete Discussion, Permissions, Subscribe, Update, Update Discussion, and View. Refer to the following screenshot:

	Action	Sites	
	Add Discussion	All Sites	Change
	Delete	All Sites	Change
	Delete Discussion	All Sites	Change
	Permissions	All Sites	Change
	Subscribe	All Sites	Change
	Update	All Sites	Change
	Update Discussion	All Sites	Change
	View	All Sites	Change

Figure 5.15: Site content permission for Wiki Page

The screenshot shows permissions on a page of a given node. The **MB Topic Admin** Member role can set up permissions such as **View**, **Delete**, **Permissions**, **Update**, **Subscribe**, **Add Discussion**, **Delete Discussion**, and **Update Discussion**, whereas the role site member can set up permissions including **View**, **Delete**, **Add Discussion**, and **Subscribe**. By default, the **MB Topic Admin** member role has permission actions, such as **View**, **Update**, and **Add Discussion**, whereas the role site member only has the **View** permission.

As you can see, as a site member, "Lotti Stein" only has the permissions **View**, **Update**, **Add Discussion**, and **Subscribe** on the pages. This is because the pages under the "Liferay" node have been added by default settings. She doesn't have permissions such as **Delete** and **Permissions**, among others.

In general, you are able to assign permissions on pages on two levels: individually or in groups. As shown in the preceding screenshot, you can locate a page first, go to **Details | Permissions**, and assign permission on individual pages via the roles. Furthermore, you can assign permissions in pages through roles in **Control Panel**. If the role is a regular role, you can assign permissions on pages scoped into the current portal instance. On the other hand, if the role is either an organization role or a site role, you can assign permissions on pages scoped into a group, either an organization or site.

Application Permissions

Application Permissions has two entitlements, that is, Add Display Templates and Add to Page, Configuration, Permissions and View. Refer to the following screenshot:

Application Permissions		
Action	Sites	
Add Display Template	All Sites	Change
Add to Page	All Sites	Change
Configuration	All Sites	Change
Permissions	All Sites	Change
View	All Sites	Change

Figure 5.16: Wiki Application Permissions

Site Application permissions affect the application with respect to the portal. So, let's see, with a Wiki example, how application permission allows us to define who can add the Wiki portlet to a page. You can provide permission to **the MB Topic Admin** member. Otherwise, you can provide permission to either the organization or site admin.

Action	Description	MB Topic Admin	Site Member
Add Display Template	This provides the ability to add display templates		
Add to Page	This provides the ability to add the portlet wiki portlet in page	X	
Configuration	This provides the ability to configure the portlet	X	
Permissions	This provides the ability to set up permissions	X	
View	This provides the ability to view the content of the portlet	X, *	*

Permissions on the Wiki portlet

Wiki portlets have configuration links that allow the setting of permissions for different roles on a particular instance of wiki. The administrator can set permissions on a Wiki portlet very easily. Refer to the following screenshot:

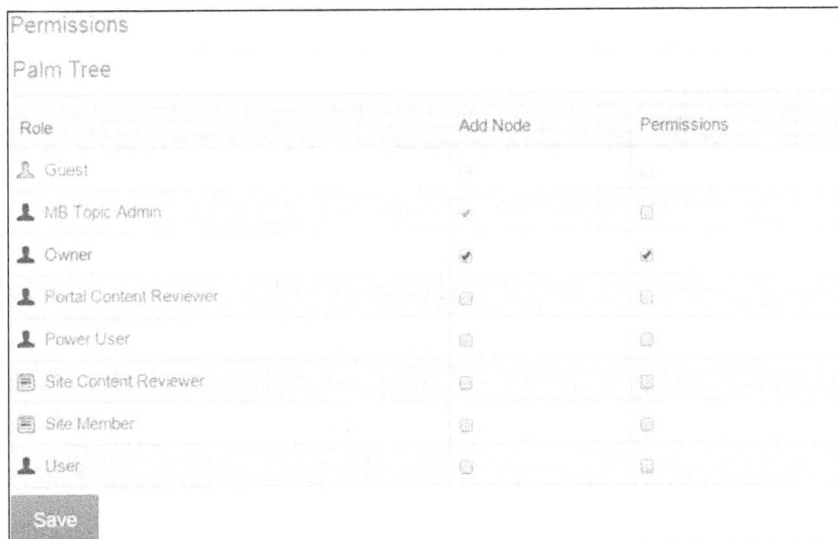

Figure 5.17: Permissions on the Wiki portlet

The permission on the Wiki portlet allows the configuration of actions performed by the different roles in the portal. This permission will be set for specific site content only.

Using the Wiki portlet effectively

Wiki was originally described as a simple online database. Actually, a Wiki is a web-based collaboration platform that lets any user write, place pictures, and post links anywhere on any page so that anyone can edit anything on any page. You can do it through the web interface without the need for any additional software. Certainly, you don't need to learn HTML or wait for a designated webmaster to upload your files.

Understanding the characteristics of Wikis

You can write Wiki documents collaboratively in a simple markup language using a web browser. Here, a single page in Wiki is called a Wiki page, while the entire body of pages, which are usually highly interconnected via hyperlinks, is the Wiki. Basically, a wiki is a database to create, browse, and search information.

A Wiki page can be created and updated simply. However, there is no review before modifications are accepted for a Wiki page. On the one hand, certain Wikis may be open to the general public without the need to register any user account. In order to acquire a Wiki-signature cookie for auto-signing edits, you need to log in for a session. However, many edits on a Wiki page can be made in real time and appear online almost instantaneously. This can lead to abuse of the system. On the other hand, private Wiki pages require user authentication to edit pages, add new pages, and even read pages.

Understanding the pros and cons of Wikis

Wikis have their own advantages and disadvantages. The advantages include the following:

- There is no need to install HTML authoring tools
- Minimal amount of training is required
- It can help develop a culture of sharing and working together
- It's useful to work jointly when there are shared goals you have agreed upon

The disadvantages of Wikis include the following:

- The success of one wiki (such as Wikipedia) may not necessarily be replicated by another.
- A collaborative Wiki may suffer from the lack of a strong vision.
- There may be copyright and other legal issues about collaborative content.
- It can be ineffective when there is a lack of consensus and when navigation is less efficient than in a really collaborative website. This is because there are no real pages, tree views, menus, or breadcrumbs. When using a wiki, we often use the search engine instead of navigating naturally in a tree. That gives the feeling that pages are not organized.

> **Wikipedia** (`http://www.Wikipedia.org/`) is the biggest multi-lingual free-content encyclopedia on the Internet.

Wiki uses

Wikis are useful for a number of purposes. We just list some of them as follows:

- Wikis enable users to contribute information on public websites easily
- Wikis provide an opportunity to learn about teamwork and trust in teaching
- Wikis make it easier to develop collaborative documents for researchers
- Wikis provide the ability to manage departmental content on intranets and are useful for departmental administrators with minimum HTML experience
- Wikis can also be used as knowledge centers
- Wikis are useful at events for note-taking in discussion groups

Using Liferay wikis

Liferay wikis allow the creation of content in a collaborative style. It is based on Wiki Creole with the features discussed here as well as those that are commonly found in good wikis, including content parsing, **Access Control List** (**ACL**) security style, easy-to-use macros, easy-to-adapt security, versioning, and managing all content and security with console tools.

> For more information on Wiki engine, you can visit
> `http://www.wikicreole.org/wiki`.

Pages are considered as groups, which again have multiple connections called nodes in Liferay. Each node can act as a whole wiki. It has its own set of permissions, recent changes list, and listing of all pages, such as Wiki articles. The wiki in Liferay has a very powerful functionality with its robust security model. For example, users can use the wiki in the traditional way (open to public) or as a tool to organize private information for certain organizations or user groups of people.

The following diagram depicts the Liferay wiki structure overview. Liferay Wiki is made up of a set of nodes. Each node can have many pages. Each node has at least one page called "Front Page" by default. Each page can have many comments. In addition, each wiki page can have many versions, ratings, and attachments. Moreover, each page can have subscriptions, tags, and categories associated with it. For further details, refer to the following diagram:

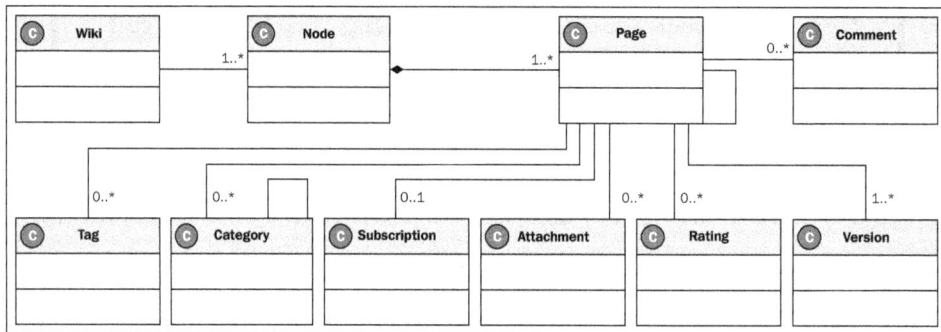

Figure 5.18: The Liferay Wiki structure overview

In general, Wiki comes with three editing modes: Creole, HTML, and MediaWiki.

Understanding the Creole mode

Syntax helps you to get the following details on the Creole mode:

- **Text Styles**: Italics (should begin with double slashes (//), followed by text, and end with double slashes), bold (should begin with two asterisks (**), followed by text, and end with two asterisks).
- **Headers**: Large headings should begin with two equals signs (==), followed by text, and end with two equals signs. Medium headings should begin with three equals signs, followed by text, and end with triple equals signs (===). On the other hand, small headings should begin with quadruple equals signs (====), followed by text, and end with quadruple equals signs.
- **Links**: Internal links should begin with double brackets ([[), followed by the page title, and end with double brackets (]]). External links should begin with double brackets ([[) followed by the URL, optionally the vertical bar (|), followed by the display name, and end with double brackets (]]).

- **Lists**: Items should begin with an asterisk (*) and end with text. Sub-items should begin with double asterisks (**) and end with text, ordered items should begin with a number sign (#) and end with text, whereas ordered sub-items should begin with double number signs (##) and end with text.

- **Images**: The attached image should begin with double brackets ({{), followed by an attached image filename, and end with double brackets (}}). The page image should begin with double brackets ({{), page name, slash (/), page image filename, optionally vertical bar (|), followed by a label, and end with double brackets (}}).

- **Table of contents**: This should begin with double brackets (<<), followed by the keyword **Table Of Contents**, and end with double brackets (>>).

- **Preformatted**: It should begin with triple brackets ({{{), the keyword **Preformatted**, and end with triple brackets (}}}).

Understanding the HTML mode

The text area incorporates an embedded HTML text editor in the HTML mode. The HTML mode allows the user to write the document in a WYSIWYG editor, which is similar to how users work in MS Word or OpenOffice. What's an HTML text editor? How to use the WYSIWYG editor? Refer to the instructions given in *Chapter 6, Blogs, WYSIWYG Editors, and Social Networking*.

Understanding the MediaWiki mode

Currently, MediaWiki is the text area that incorporates pure plain text. It is the same as editing the source in an HTML text editor. For more help, you can visit `http://www.mediawiki.org`.

Configuration

As an administrator of the enterprise Palm Tree Publications, you can set up the Wiki portlet as well. For example, you can configure subscription e-mails. Let's say that the Wiki portlet was added to the page "Wiki" of the Guest group and you are going to configure the portlet in this way.

To configure the Wiki portlet, include the subscription function in the following way: click on **Gear** (icon) | **Configuration** in the upper-right corner of the Wiki portlet. With the **Setup** | **Display Setting** tab selected, there is a set of sub-tabs, namely **Email from**, **Page added email**, **Page updated email**, and **RSS**.

In addition, under the tab **Display Settings**, you can see the following settings:

- **Enable Related Assets**: This enables the display of related assets
- **Enable Page Ratings**: This enables the display of page ratings
- **Enable Comments**: This enables comments
- **Enable Comment Ratings**: This enables comment ratings
- **Visible Wikis**: This enables multiple selection of Wiki nodes

The **Email From** name is `Admin` and the **From-Address** is `admin@liferay.com` by default. This means that the portal will use the name and address as e-mail **From-Name** and **From-Address**. You can change the settings as per your requirement and save it.

Setting properties for Wikis

As you saw, when the portal started, the default node "Main" and page "FrontPage" were created for the Guest group. "What's happening?", you may ask. The portal has the following default settings in `portal.properties`:

```
wiki.front.page.name=FrontPage
wiki.initial.node.name=Main
```

As shown in the preceding code, it sets the name of the default page for a Wiki node as *FrontPage*. Note that the name for the default page must be a valid Wiki word, that is, the first letter should be in uppercase. A Wiki word follows the format of upper Camel case or Pascal case letters. It also sets the name of the default node as *Main*, and that will be automatically created when the Wiki portlet is first used in a group, such as an organization or as a. Of course, you can override these properties in `portal-ext.properties`.

Moreover, when you input a value for the Wiki page title, the portal will validate the title. Similarly, when viewing the Wiki page, you will be able to add ratings and comments. In fact, the portal has the following settings in `portal.properties`:

```
wiki.page.titles.regexp=([^\\\\\\\[\\]\\|:;%<>]+)
wiki.page.titles.remove.regexp=([\\\\\\\[\\]\\|:;%<>]+)
wiki.page.ratings.enabled=true
wiki.page.comments.enabled=true
wiki.formats=creole,html,mediawiki
wiki.formats.default=creole
```

As shown in the preceding code, it specifies validation for the names of Wiki pages via the `wiki.page.titles.regexp` property. By default, only a few characters are forbidden. You can uncomment the preceding regular expression to allow only Camel case titles. It also specifies the characters that will be automatically removed from the titles when importing Wiki pages using the `wiki.page.titles.remove.regexp` property. This should remove any characters that are forbidden in the `regexp` specified in the `wiki.page.titles.regexp` property.

In addition, it sets the `wiki.page.ratings.enabled` property to `true` to enable ratings for Wiki pages and the `wiki.page.comments.enabled` property to `true` to enable comments for Wiki pages. It sets the list of supported Wiki formats via the `wiki.formats` property and the default wiki format via the `wiki.formats.default` property. You can definitely customize these properties in `portal-ext.properties`.

More interestingly, Wiki importers, e-mail notifications, and RSS abstracts are configurable. The portal has specified the following properties in `portal.properties`:

```
Wiki.importers=MediaWiki
Wiki.email.from.name=
Wiki.email.from.address=
Wiki.email.page.added.enabled=true
Wiki.email.page.updated.enabled=true
Wiki.rss.abstract.length=200
```

As shown in the preceding code, the portal sets the list of supported wiki importers via the `wiki.importers` property. By default, *MediaWiki* is supported. It configures e-mail notification settings via the `wiki.email.from.name`, `wiki.email.from.address`, `wiki.email.page.added.enabled`, and `wiki.email.page.updated.enabled` properties. Finally, the portal sets the maximum length of the RSS abstract to `200` via the `wiki.rss.abstract.length` property.

Of course, you can override this property in `portal-ext.properties` depending on your requirements.

Wikis in scope

More interestingly, one of the most powerful characteristics of the Wiki portlet is the fact that when wikis are added to different groups, they act as completely independent portlets—each with its own data. By default, the Wiki portlet is scoped into a group—when portlets are added to a group, be they public or private pages, they act as the same portlets.

For instance, when the portlet Wiki is added to a page — for example — "Wikis" of the Site A, the default scope will be used for Site A. If you add the Wiki portlet to a second page, say "Welcome", it will show the same data as that of the first page. As you can see, the Wiki portlet is scoped into Site A, and when it is added to any pages of the same site, it seems that you don't have the flexibility to switch sites in this case. Fortunately, this limitation could be overcome through the settings. In the configuration, you are able to shift the content of the Wiki portlet to a different site. You can do this by following these simple steps.

The Wiki portlet could get scoped into a page. How to scope a Wiki portlet into a page? The following is just a sample:

1. Click on the "**Wiki**" page, where the Wiki portlet is displayed.
2. Go to **Gear** (icon) | **Configuration** of the Wiki portlet.
3. Click on the **Scope** tab.
4. Choose **Wiki (Create New)** from the **Scope** select menu, and click on the **Save** button.

Considering the pattern Portal-Site-Page-Content, the content of the Wiki portlet could be scoped into a group — for example, all pages, including both private and public pages by default. It could also be scoped into an individual page — this means that a set of data, for example, nodes and pages, is isolated from other data of the same portlet.

How can we customize the scope feature? The portal has default settings for the Wiki portlet in $PORTAL_ROOT_HOME/WEB-INF/liferay-portlet.xml:

```
<control-panel-entry-category>site_administration.content
  </control-panel-entry-category>
<control-panel-entry-weight>7.0</control-panel-entry-weight>
<scopeable>true</scopeable>
```

As shown in the preceding code, the Wiki portlet will appear in the Site Administration category content in position 7, and it is scope-able. This means that you are able to use **Gear** (icon) | **Configuration** | **Scope** and change the scope from default to the current page.

Wikis in communication

Note that there is a **Communication** tab under **Gear** (icon) | **Configuration**, and the shared parameters could be mapped into `categoryId`, `nodeId`, `tag`, `nodeName`, `resetCur`, and `title` because the portlet has the following configuration in `$PORTAL_ROOT_HOME/WEB-INF/portlet-custom.xml`:

```
<supported-public-render-parameter>categoryId</supported-public-
   render-parameter>
<supported-public-render-parameter>nodeId</supported-public-
   render-parameter>
<supported-public-render-parameter>nodeName</supported-public-
   render-parameter>
<supported-public-render-parameter>resetCur</supported-public-
   render-parameter>
<supported-public-render-parameter>tag</supported-public-render-
   parameter>
<supported-public-render-parameter>title</supported-public-render-
   parameter>
```

As shown in the preceding code, there are six parameters, namely `-categoryId`, `nodeId`, `tag`, `nodeName`, `resetCur`, and `title`. You can set mapping among these parameters or even ignore some or all of them in the **Gear** (icon) | **Configuration** | **Communication** tab. You can add Tags and Category Navigation portlets in the wiki page so that you can see by yourselves all the benefits of using this configuration.

Enhancement

As you can see, the portal provides the capability to display recent changes on pages. It would be nice if the time period could be configurable, such as a day, week, month, and so on. Of course, you can have other expectations from the Wiki portlet.

Publishing wiki pages

We have discussed how to create nodes and how to add pages in order to keep track of information about editorial guidance and other resources that require frequent editing. As an administrator at the Palm Tree Publications enterprise, you have created the node **Liferay**. Now, you can publish Wiki articles for the node **Liferay**, as shown in the following screenshot:

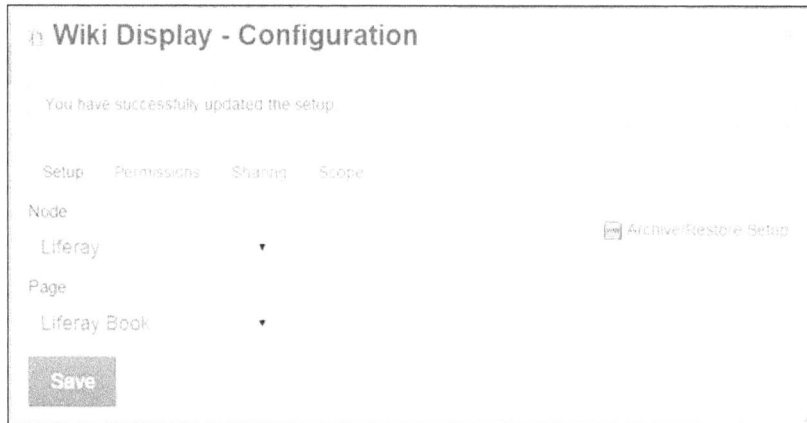

Figure 5.19: Wiki Display portlet configuration

Let's add **Wiki Display** in the page "Wiki". Follow these steps to configure the Wiki display:

1. Click on **Gear** (icon) | **Configuration** | **Setup** | in the upper-right corner of the Wiki display portlet.

2. Select a node name "**Liferay**" that you want to publish as a Wiki in your page and the page "**Liferay Book**".

3. Click on the **Save** button to save the changes.

Obviously, the Wiki Display portlet (portlet ID 54) provides a way to publish Wiki articles in a page of a site. The following screenshot depicts the Wiki display portlet in a Wiki page.

As a member of the Palm Tree site, "Lotti Stein" can have the proper permission to edit the current Wiki page by clicking on the Edit link next to the Wiki page title, add comments on the current Wiki page, and add ratings to the current Wiki page. Note that users can only rate once on a specific page. The vote will be counted once, but users can change their rating later.

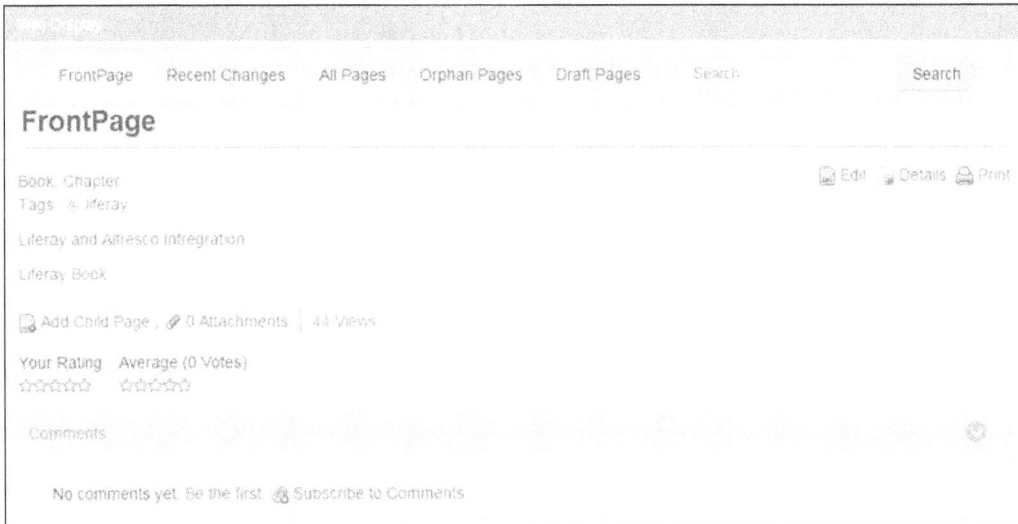

Figure 5.20: Wiki Display portlet

Additionally, you will also be able to change permissions on wiki pages if you have the proper access rights to do so. By clicking on the Details link, you would be able to view Content, Details, History, Incoming Links, Outgoing Links, and Attachments, and the same functions as that of the Wiki portlet. Last but not least, you can print the current wiki page by clicking on the print icon next to the wiki page title.

Benefit of the Wiki Display portlet

The Wiki Display portlet allows the publishing of specific Wiki nodes, while hiding a lot of administration options.

Firstly, the Wiki Display portlet is configurable—you can configure a specific node and Wiki page to be published. Secondly, the Wiki Display portlet is *instanceable*. Therefore, you can add more than one Wiki Display portlet to a given page. Thirdly, it hides a lot of administration options, such as managing Wiki nodes.

Assigning permissions

As a user at the Palm Tree Publications enterprise, say "Lotti Stein", you have the permission to edit the current Wiki page and add comments on the current Wiki page. However, you can't change page permissions because you don't have proper access rights to do so. This is something related to permissions.

Obviously, as a site member, "Lotti Stein" only has the permissions **View** and **Add Discussion** on the pages because the pages under "Liferay" have been added by default settings. Thus, she doesn't have permissions such as **Delete**, **Permissions**, **Delete Discussion**, and **Update Discussion**. Refer to the following screenshot:

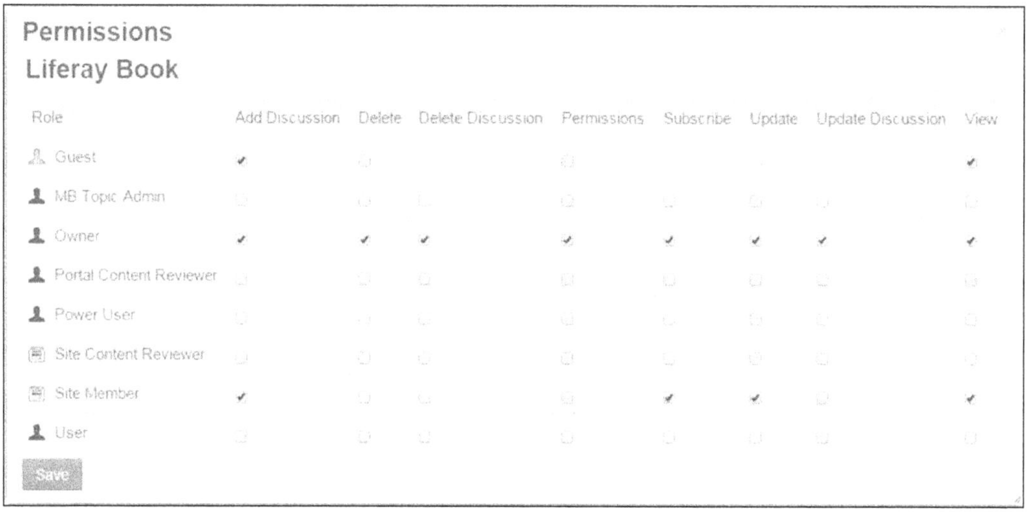

Figure 5.21: Wiki Display portlet permissions

As an administrator, you may need to set up the Site Member role with the permissions **View** and **Update** only on the page "Liferay Book" of the node "Liferay". That is, you need to remove the **Add Discussion** and **Subscribe** permissions on the page "Liferay Book" of the node "Liferay" for the site Palm Tree. Let's do it by following these steps:

1. Click on the **Details| Permissions** icon next to the page "Liferay Book".
2. Uncheck the permissions **Add Discussion** and **Subscribe** under the role "**Site Member**".
3. Click on the **Save** button if you are ready.

Now, as a site member, "Lotti Stein" has the **View** and **Update** permissions on the "Liferay Book" page of the node "Liferay". If you try to log in as "Lotti Stein", you will see the "Liferay Book" page of the node "Liferay" without the "Add Comments" icon. You can go to **Details | Details**, but you wouldn't see the "Subscribe" icon for the current page.

Note that you can only assign permissions on individual pages using the Wiki Display portlet. If you want to assign permissions at the group level or at the portal instance level, you need to define permissions of roles under **Users** in **Control Panel**.

In addition, there are **View** and **Configuration** permissions on the portlet. By default, the Site Member and Guest roles have the **View** permission on the Wiki Display portlet.

Setting properties for the Wiki Display portlet

As you can see, you can add more than one Wiki Display portlet in a given page, while there is only one Wiki portlet in the page. Why are they different? The Wiki Display portlet was specified as being *instanceable* in `$PORTAL_ROOT_HOME/WEB-INF/liferay-portlet.xml`. This is as follows:

```
<configuration-action-class>com.liferay.portal.kernel.portlet.
  DefaultConfigurationAction</configuration-action-class>
<portlet-url-class>com.liferay.portal.struts.StrutsAction
  PortletURL</portlet-url-class>
<instanceable>true</instanceable>
<scopeable>true</scopeable>
```

As shown in the preceding code, the Wiki Display portlet specified the tag `instanceable` with the value `true`. This is the reason why you can add more than one Wiki Display portlet to a given page. Moreover, the portlet Wiki Display has specified the tag `configuration-action-class` with a value `com.liferay.portlet.Wikidisplay.action.ConfigurationActionImpl`. Therefore, after clicking on **Gear** (icon) | **Configuration** in the upper-right corner of the portlet, you can see **Setup**, **permission**, **sharing**, and **scope**, that is, the Wiki Display portlet is configurable.

As you can see, the Wiki Display portlet is scopeable. The Wiki Display portlet is scoped into the site Palm Tree when it is added to any pages of the site. Moreover, the portlet Wiki Display could get scoped into a page. How can we customize this? To make the Wiki Display portlet using a different data scope, you can follow these simple steps:

1. Locate a page, say "**Wiki**", and the Wiki Display portlet in the current page.

2. Go to **Gear** (icon) | **Configuration** of the Wiki Display portlet.

3. Click on the **Scope** tab.

4. Choose "**Wiki (Create page)** from the **Scope** select menu and click on the **Save** button.

Considering the Portal-Site-Page-Content pattern, the content of the Wiki Display portlet could be scoped into a site—for example, all pages, including both private and public pages, by default. Furthermore, it could be scoped into an individual page—this means that a set of data, for example, Wiki pages, is isolated from other data of the same portlet.

Converting documents with OpenOffice

It would be useful to convert documents of different office formats. For example, in Display Settings of the Asset Publisher portlet, we have the ability to convert current documents to different document formats, for example, DOC, ODT, PDF, RTF, SXW, and TXT. Likewise, we are able to convert Wiki articles to different document formats—for example, DOC, ODT, PDF, RTF, SXW, and TXT. When clicking on the link, for example, PDF, the portal will convert the current Wiki article to that format, that is, PDF. How to achieve this? Let's integrate OpenOffice into our portal.

Integrating OpenOffice

OpenOffice.org is a multiplatform and multilingual office suite and an open source project. First of all, you need to download the latest version of OpenOffice. It is available at `http://www.openoffice.org` for every OS. The installation instructions can also be found here. When you install it, make a note of the location because you will need it when setting your `OPENOFFICE_HOME` variable.

To start OpenOffice as a service, go to `$OPENOFFICE_HOME/program` and run the following command:

```
Soffice-headless-accept="socket,host=127.0.0.1,port=8100;urp;"
```

As shown in the preceding code, we start OpenOffice as a service with the host `127.0.0.1` and the port `8100`.

Configuring OpenOffice

Then, we need to enable OpenOffice integration by providing the document conversion functionality. How do we do this? We could implement this using Server Administration, as shown in the following screenshot:

1. Log in as a portal administrator, for example, "Palm Tree", and then go to **Go To | Control Panel** under the dock bar menu.

2. Go to **Server Administration| External Services** under the **Configuration** section of **Control Panel**.

3. Check the **Enabled** checkbox.

4. Finally, click on the **Save** button.

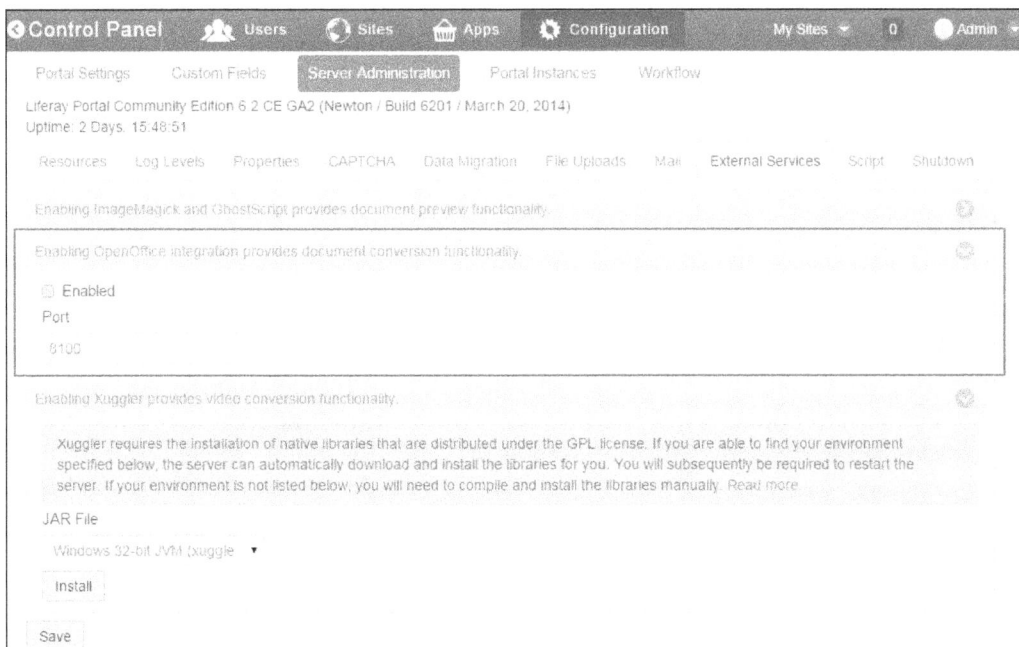

Figure 5.22: OpenOffice integration for document conversion functionality

> Note that if OpenOffice was installed on a remote machine, we would have to change the host and port accordingly. How do we implement it?

Properties settings for OpenOffice

The portal provides the capability to enable OpenOffice integration and allows the Document and Media portlet and the Wiki portlet to provide the conversion functionality. The following are the default settings in `portal.properties`:

```
openoffice.server.enabled=false
openoffice.server.host=127.0.0.1
openoffice.server.port=8100
openoffice.cache.enabled=true
```

The preceding code sets the OpenOffice server by default. As you can see, the property `openoffice.server.enabled` has the value `false`, and the property `openoffice.cache.enabled` has the value `true`. Therefore, by default, the OpenOffice server is disabled and the cache is enabled. The host was specified via the property `openoffice.server.host`, while the port was specified via the property `openoffice.server.port`. By default, OpenOffice was installed in the same machine (`127.0.0.1`) as that of the portal with port `8100`. If OpenOffice was installed on a remote machine, you could override the host using the property `openoffice.server.host` and also the port using the property `openoffice.server.port` in `portal-ext.properties`.

Converting documents

Through OpenOffice, documents can be converted automatically to multiple formats. For example, the document "Full RESTful integration of Liferay and Alfresco" is originally provided in the plain text format. Thus, we can download it as a text file. At the same time, it can be converted into DOC, ODT, PDF, RTF, SXW, and so on.

Dynamic Data List

In Liferay 6.1, Dynamic Data List is one of the new features. Dynamic Data List provides a very nice feature that helps the portal administrator to create a form and store the data without writing a single line of code, which he can display on the portal page.

Say the organization wants to post a job opening on the portal, they want to list all the best employees of the month, or perhaps the users are allowed to maintain a notebook or To-Do list on their private pages. For such requirements, you have to create a custom plugin portlet, but using the Dynamic Data Lists, an administrator can create a custom form anytime and store the data and display using the Dynamic Data List Display portlet.

Creating new Dynamic Data List

Let's create Dynamic Data List for the Best Employee of the Month. A Dynamic Data List's content is specific to the Site. The Dynamic Data List link will be available under Site Content. Follow the steps to create the Dynamic Data List for Best Employee of the Month.

1. Log in to the Palm Tree site as Site Administrator.

2. Click on **Admin | Site Administration | Content** from the dock bar menu. Under site content, click on **Dynamic Data List**.

3. You can view **Dynamic Data List** that is already created.

4. Click on the **Add** button; now you can create New List. Fill the details for the new list name as "Employee List" and description as "Best Employee of the Month".

5. Click on **Data Definition** and select the data definition. If you don't find your required data definition, you can create one by clicking on the **Add** button at the top.

6. A new pop-up window will appear for **New Data Definition**, where you can create the new form to enter employee details. Here, you need to define the name as "**Employee Listing**" and the description as "**Best employee of the month**".

7. The screen provides you with the drag and drop option to add fields and controls. In the following panel, you can see the left-hand side section for fields and the right-hand side section with a blank panel. You just need to drag the fields and drop them on to the blank panel. In this example, **Text**, **Date**, **Text box**, and **Select fields** have been used. Refer to the following screenshot:

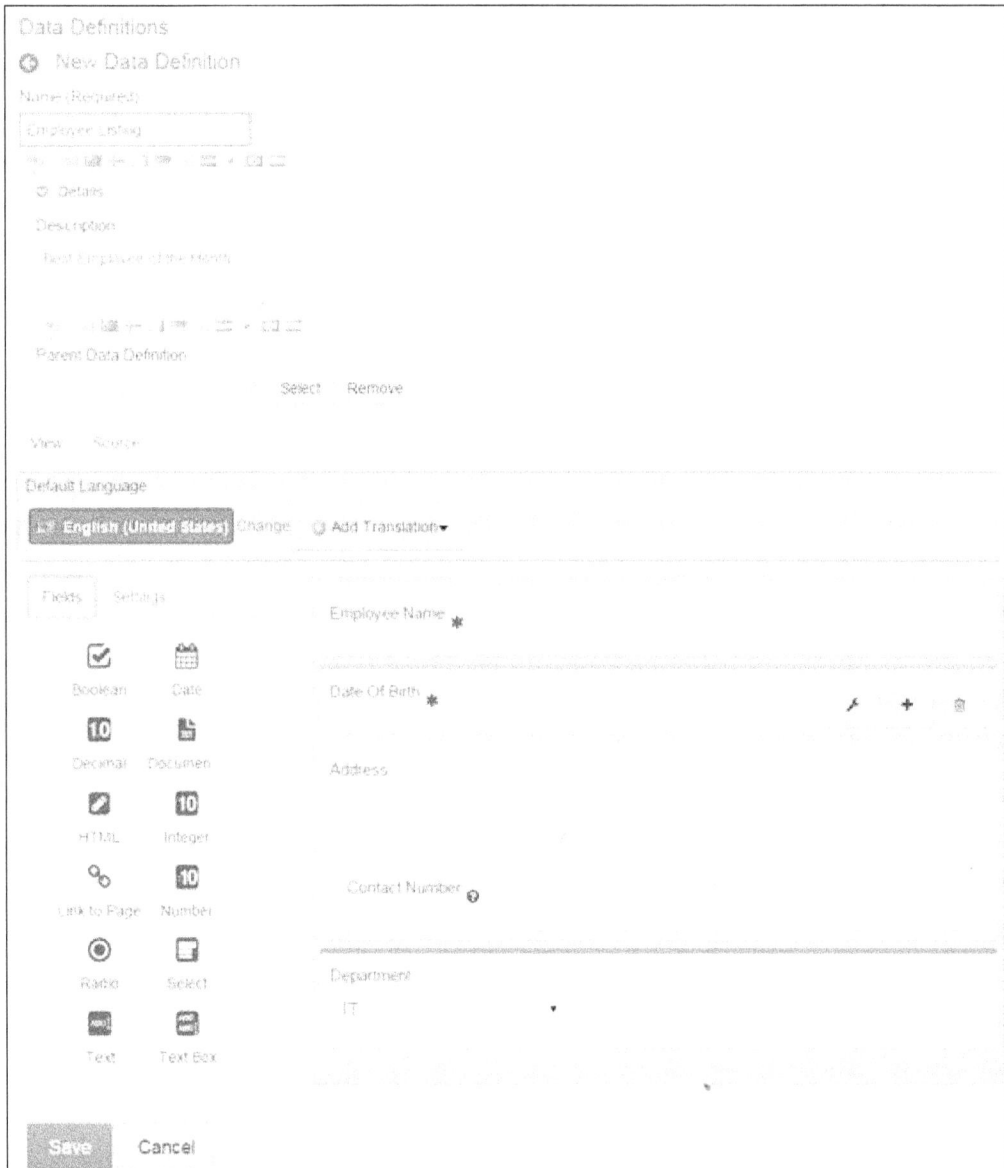

Figure 5.23: New data definition

For every field, you can set properties such as **Field Label**, **Show Label**, **Required**, **Name**, **Predefine Value**, **Tip** and **width**. For the **Select** field, you can set options as shown in the following screenshot. You can also set the select option values for **Select** fields by simply entering the values in the options box. You can even make the **Select** field allow multiple selections by setting the value yes for multiple field in the **Settings** tab.

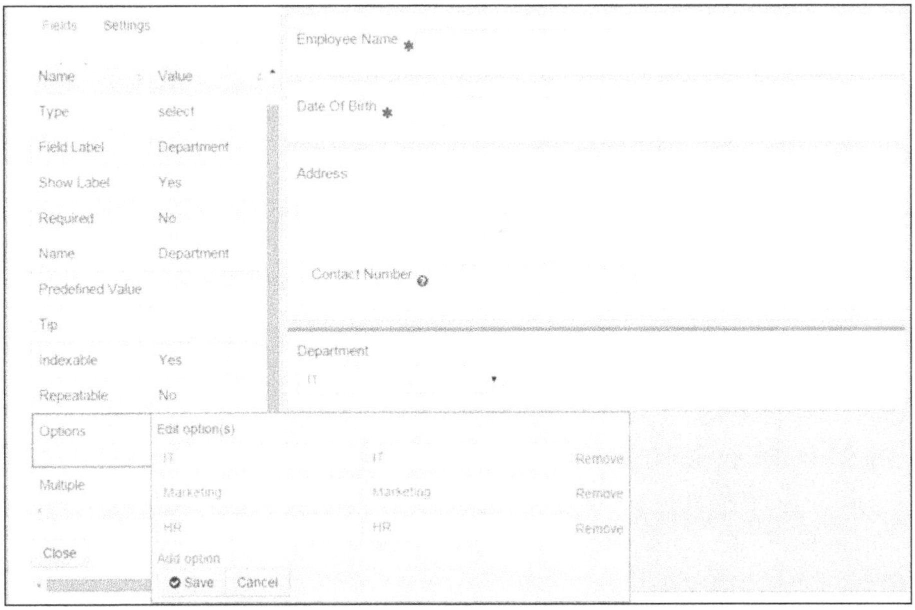

Figure 5.24: Settings for each field

8. Now you can save Data Definition. It will return you to the previous page where it has been listed. You can select it by clicking on **Name**.

9. If you select the workflow option, it will allow you to set the workflow process. Now, we will keep the default value (no workflow).

10. You can save Dynamic Data List by clicking on the **Save** button.

Adding a new record

The Dynamic Data List view option will display "Employee List". Once you click on Employee List, you can use "Add Employee Listing" with the form that you just created.

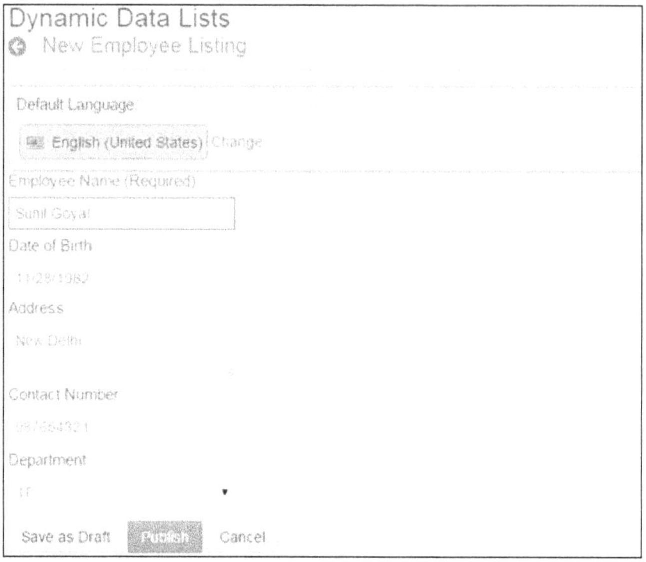

Figure 5.25: Adding a new record

Finally, click on the **Publish** button to publish the data. Refer to the preceding screenshot for further details.

Viewing data in Dynamic Data List

Now, you will be able to see the data in Dynamic Data Lists for Employee List. See the following screenshot:

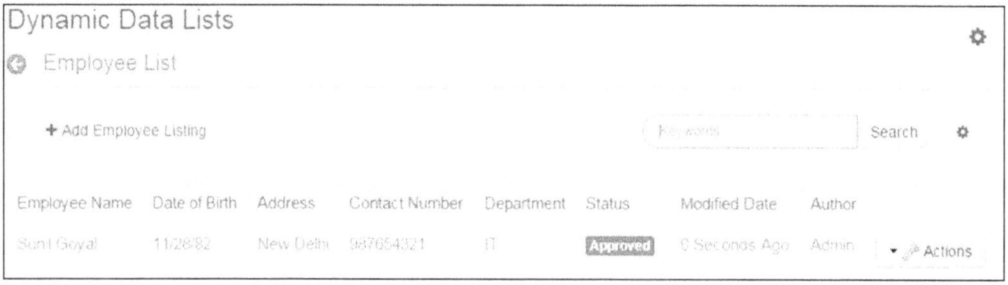

Figure 5.26: Data in Dynamic Data List

Editing the data

You can change values by clicking on edit from the **Action** button. Once you edit the value, it creates a version each time. So, the change in the data can be captured with regard to a particular entry. Even you can retrieve the previous data anytime.

[Changing Data Definition and the form is possible anytime.]

Dynamic Data List Display

Dynamic Data List Display (portlet 169) is an instanceable portlet that allows you to add multiple portlets on the page. This portlet allows you to display Dynamic Data List to the user.

So, you can place this portlet on a page, where users can access it. Let's place this portlet in the Palm Tree public page.

1. On Palm Tree, create a page with the name **Data List**.

2. Add the **Dynamic Data List Display** portlet on the **Data List** page. This portlet is under the **Collaboration** category.

3. Now you need to configure the portlet by selecting the **Data List** name that you want to display. Click on the portlet configuration, select **Employee List**, and **Save** it.

4. Once you save it, you get a configuration pop-up window. Follow this screenshot:

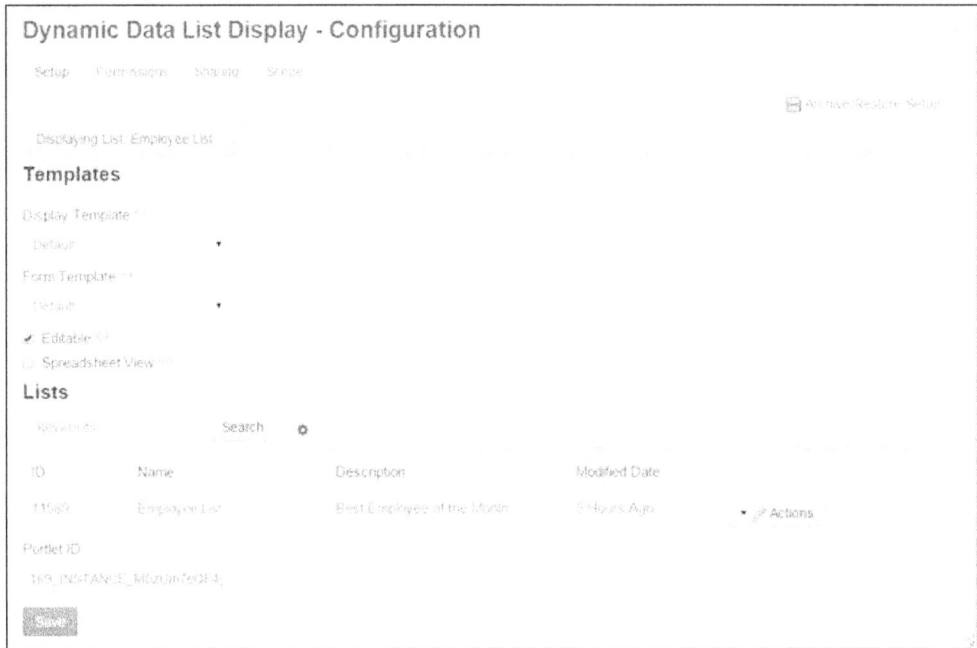

Figure 5.27: Dynamic Data List Display configuration

Templates provide the feature of selecting the list template and the default template with two checkboxes: **Editable** and **Spreadsheet** view.

- **Editable**: This allows the end user to edit the data on the data list table
- **Spreadsheet**: This displays the data in the full length of the spreadsheet

Dynamic Data List is shown in the portlet as follows:

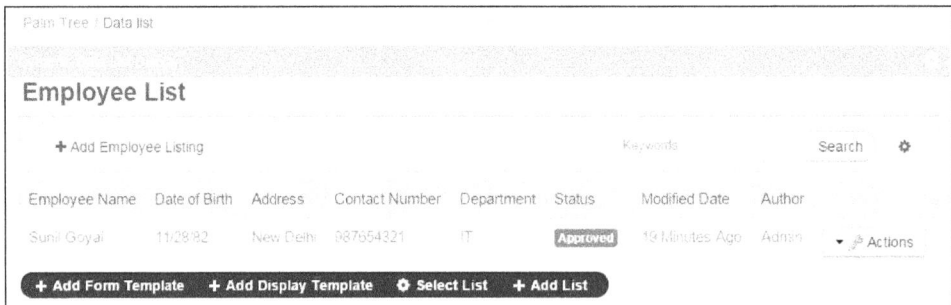

Figure 5.28: Employee list on the Palm Tree page

In the preceding screenshot, you can see actions below the table. These actions are **Add form Template**, **Add Display Template**, **Select List**, and **Add List**. These controls are visible since you are logged in as Administrator. If you don't want to show them to any other users, then you need to set the permissions.

Assigning permissions

We used the default settings for the Dynamic Data List portlet in the "Data List" page. As a user, "Lotti Stein" should be able to perform a few actions on Dynamic Data List; for that, you have to restrict permissions for Lotti accordingly.

Permissions for **Dynamic Data List** can be assigned under **Site Administration | Content | Dynamic Data Lists**.

For the **Dynamic Data List Display** portlet, permissions can be set under **Site Administration | Application | Dynamic Data List Display**. Moreover, each has a different set of permission levels.

To set the permission entitlements for **Dynamic Data List**, the portal administrator needs to define permissions in roles. Under the User section, click on **Roles** in **Control Panel** and locate **MB Topic Admin**. Select define permissions from the Action button beside MB Topic Admin. Search for **Dynamic Data List**. You will able to see the different permission entitlements for **Dynamic Data List**:

- **Site Administration | Content | Dynamic Data List**: General Permissions, Resource Permissions (Lists, Dynamic Data Lists Record Set).
- **Site Administration | Application | Dynamic Data List Display**: Application Permissions, Resource Permissions (Dynamic Data Mapping Structure, Dynamic Data Mapping Template).

Let's discuss each of them one by one in detail.

Site Administration | Content | Dynamic Data List | Lists

The **MB Topic Admin** role is able to set up all permissions for Dynamic Data List: Add Record Set, Add Structure, Add Template, and Permissions.

These actions can be set for MB topic Admin, of which Lotti is a member. For further reference, follow this screenshot:

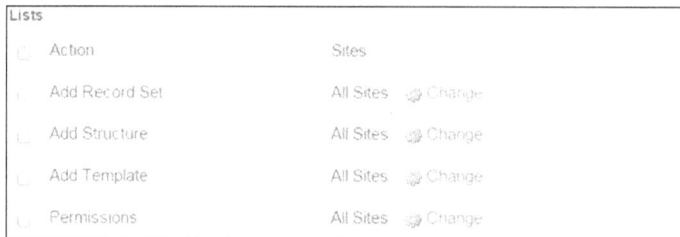

Figure 5.29: Site content permission on Dynamic Data List

Site Administration | Content | Dynamic Data List | Dynamic Data Lists Record Set

The record set allows the users access to Add Record, Delete record, Set permission on records, Update the records, and View the records. For further details, follow this screenshot:

Figure 5.30: Site content permission on Dynamic Data List Record Set

Site Administration | Content | Dynamic Data List | General Permissions

General permissions allows the users to operate the application in the Site Administration panel. Once a User is granted this permission, they will be able to access the application in the Site Administration panel to perform the configuration and set the permission for Dynamic Data List. See the following screenshot for further details:

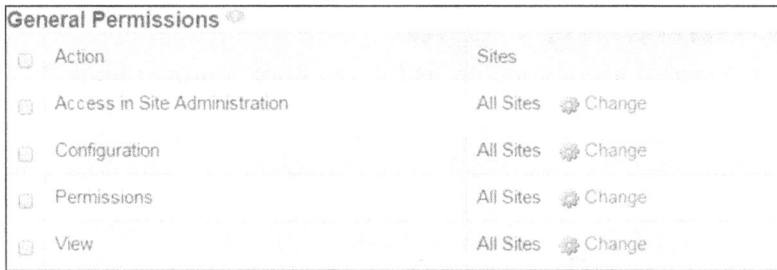

Figure 5.31: Control Panel permissions on the Dynamic Data List

Site Administration | Applications | Dynamic Data List Display | Application Permissions

Application Permissions allows the users access to the portal page. You can grant this permission to MB topic Admin so that the user has access to the Add Dynamic Data List Display portlet on the page, along with the ability to configure the portlet. View is, by default, granted to all the users.

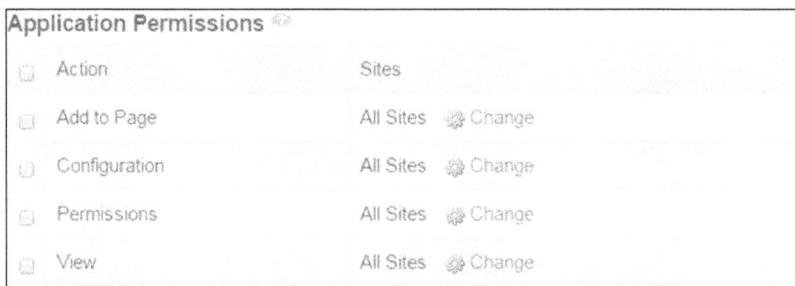

Figure 5.32: Site Application Permissions on the Dynamic Data List Display

For the Dynamic Data List Display portlet, there are two more sections of permission setting, which are, Dynamic data mapping structure and Dynamic data mapping template. Both have the same set of permissions (Delete, Permissions, Update, and View). If you set the permission for Dynamic data mapping structure for any role, generally all the users that have that role will have access to delete the structure, set permission on the structure, update the structure, and view the structure.

As mentioned earlier, the Dynamic data mapping template has the same set of permissions (Delete, Permissions, Update, and View). It's basically there to control the template for Dynamic Data List.

Understanding Polls

Do you want to keep track of votes on "**Is Liferay Book a proper book**"? The Polls portlet (portlet ID 25) and the Polls Display portlet (portlet ID 59) are useful tools. The Polls portlet allows us to create multiple choice polls that keep track of votes and display results on a page where a lot of separate polls can be managed and that is configurable to display a specific poll's results, while the Polls Display portlet allows us to vote for a specific poll's question and view the results.

The Polls portlet

First of all, we plan to add questions. As an administrator, you might need to create a lot of questions for polls, such as "Will Liferay be the best portal solution for this year 2015?" and "Do you plan to buy a Liferay book next month?" and then manage these questions as well as the votes on these questions. Refer to the following screenshot for more details.

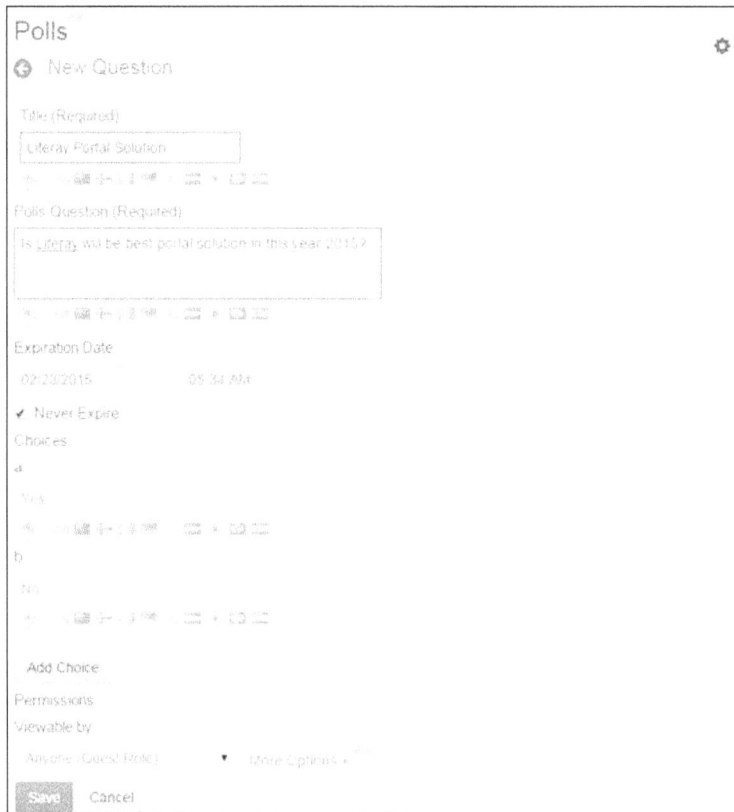

Figure 5.33: Poll New Question

1. Log in as a site admin, say "Palm Tree". Then, click on **Admin | Content** from the dock bar menu, and then select **Polls** from the left-hand side menu.

2. Click on the "**Add Question**" button under the Polls portlet.

3. Input Title "**Liferay Portal Solution**" and Poll Question "Will Liferay be the best portal solution in this year 2015?" You can input the title and poll question in other languages too.

4. Type values for the choices a. and b., for example, "**Yes**" and "**No**". There must be at least two choices—these can't be deleted.

5. Check the **Never Expire** checkbox using default settings, but you can uncheck the checkbox and also set an expiration date.

6. Add more choices by clicking on the **Add Choice** button. After clicking on the **Add Choice** button, you can delete a choice by clicking on the **Delete** button located next to the choice name input box.

7. Permissions settings keep default settings. In order to configure additional permissions, click on the **More Options** link.

8. Click on the **Save** button to save the input.

Of course, you can add other questions. After adding the question "**Do you plan to buy a Liferay book next month?**", you can view the questions:

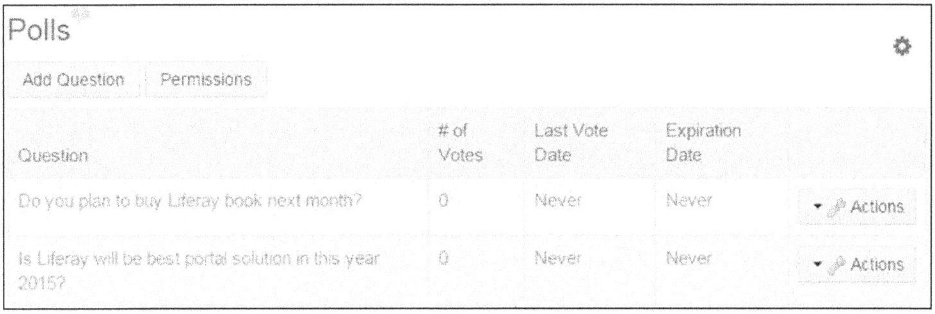

Polls					⚙
Add Question	Permissions				
Question		# of Votes	Last Vote Date	Expiration Date	
Do you plan to buy Liferay book next month?		0	Never	Never	▾ ⚙ Actions
Is Liferay will be best portal solution in this year 2015?		0	Never	Never	▾ ⚙ Actions

Figure 5.34: Polls Question

As shown in the preceding screenshot, poll questions are displayed as question name, numbers of votes, last vote date, expiration date, and actions, with a set of icons: edit, permissions, and delete. By default, this portlet will display all questions scoped into the current site for the current user who has proper permissions.

> Note that the **Polls** portlet is only visible in **Site Administration** under the category **Content**.

Editing a question

All questions are editable. Suppose that we want to change the title of the questions "Do you plan to buy a Liferay book next month?" to "Liferay Book publishing next month?", we need to update it. Let's do it by following these steps:

1. Locate the question, say **Do you plan to buy Liferay book next month?** in the Polls portlet, and click on the **Edit** icon from **Actions** next to the question.

2. Type the value of the title, such as `Liferay Book publishing next month?`.

3. Click on the **Save** button to save the inputs.

Deleting a question

All questions are removable. Let's say that the question "Do you plan to buy a Liferay book next month?" does not exist anymore. Then, we need to delete it. Let's delete it by following these steps:

1. Locate **Do you plan to buy a Liferay book next month?**, which you want to delete.

2. Click on the **Delete** icon from **Actions** located next to the question.

3. A screen will appear that asks whether you want to delete this. Click on the **OK** button to confirm the deletion.

Viewing votes

Suppose that you want to view votes for the question "Will Liferay be the best portal solution in this year 2015?" in different ways. You can simply click on the name of the question and then click on **View Results**. You will see votes in percentage or other charts, such as Area, Horizontal Bar, Line, Pie, and Vertical Bar. Furthermore, you can view actual voters if you have proper permissions.

There are three votes on the question "Will Liferay be the best portal solution in this year 2015?". You could see votes in percentage, by actual voters displayed together with their choice and vote date, and in a Pie chart as an example.

Setting properties for Polls

As you can see, the Polls portlet is located at position 10 under the **Content** category of the Site Administrator panel. At the same time, you will have the capability to export/import polls under the **Gear** (icon) | **Export/Import**. "Why?" you may ask.

The portal has default settings for the Polls portlet in `$PORTAL_ ROOT_HOME/WEB-INF/liferay-portlet.xml`:

```
<portlet-data-handler-class>com.liferay.portlet.polls.lar.Polls
    PortletDataHandler</portlet-data-handler-class>
<control-panel-entry-category>site_administration.content</control
    -panel-entry-category>
<control-panel-entry-weight>10.0</control-panel-entry-weight>
```

The preceding code shows that the Polls portlet will appear in the Content category via the `control-panel-entry-category` tag and at position 10 via the `control-panel-entry-weight` tag. Meanwhile, the polls content can be backed up as an LAR file via the `portlet-data-handler-class` tag.

Features of Polls portlets

As you can see, we can summarize the following features of the Polls portlet:

- The Polls portlet manages (add, delete, and update) questions with multiple choices
- The Polls portlet creates a graph showing the votes automatically
- The Polls portlet expires the poll automatically
- There are fine-grained permissions and role-based access control for polls
- In the Polls portlet, each user can vote on a specific question only once
- In the Polls portlet, you can export and import data, for example, questions, votes, and permissions, for a given group
- The Polls portlet scopes polls into different groups (sites and organizations) and portal instances

The Polls Display portlet

Do you want to display a specific poll's results in the intranet? The Polls Display portlet can be a useful tool. The Polls Display portlet allows users to vote for a specific poll's questions and see the results of votes. Note that the question must be created from the Polls portlet in the **Control Panel** under the **Content** category. Refer to the following screenshot for further details:

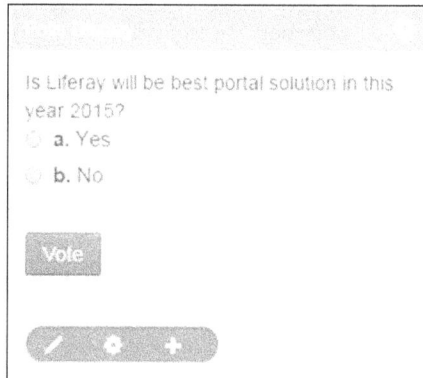

Figure 5.35: The Polls Display portlet

As shown in the preceding screenshot, we're going to put votes on the question "**Will Liferay will be the best portal solution in this year 2015?**" in a page of the Guest public pages. Afterwards, users can vote on this question and view the vote results.

As an administrator, you can create the "Polls" page in the site public pages first and then add the Polls Display portlet by clicking on **Add | Application...** under the dock bar menu. Afterwards, you can select different poll questions by simply clicking on the **Gear** (icon) | **Configuration** icon in the upper-right corner of the Polls Display portlet. Then, you can select a title from a list of poll titles to be published in the website by selecting **Setup**.

Of course, you can archive the current settings by selecting the **Setup | Archive Restore setup** link. Furthermore, you can configure permissions if you have proper access rights by selecting the **Permissions** tab and setting up sharing by selecting the **Sharing** tab.

In this example, you can select the question "Do you plan to buy a Liferay book next month?" under **Gear** (icon) | **configuration** | **Setup** | **Question**. Then, you can click on the **Save** button when you are ready.

When a user such as "Lotti Stein", as a member of the site, signs in and views the page "Polls", she would see the vote page with a button "Vote" and a set of selections with radio buttons, such as "yes" and "no", first. After choosing an answer and clicking on the **Vote** button, she would be able to see the vote results.

Setting properties for the Poll Display portlet

As the Poll Display portlet is instanceable, you can add more than one Polls Display portlet in a given page, while there is only one Polls portlet in the Content category of **Control Panel**. Why are they different? The Polls Display portlet was specified as being instanceable in `$PORTAL_ROOT_HOME/WEB-INF/liferay-portlet.xml`, as follows:

```
<configuration-action-class>com.liferay.portal.kernel.portlet.
    DefaultConfigurationAction</configuration-action-class>
<instanceable>true</instanceable>
```

The preceding code sets the instanceable value to true, that is, the Polls Display portlet can appear multiple times on a page. Of course, you can set it to false so that the portlet can only appear once on a page. The default value is `false`. The Polls portlet doesn't have the aforementioned settings, thus it uses the default value—the Polls portlet can only appear once on a page.

In addition, the preceding code shows that the `configuration-action-class` tag allows users to configure the portlet at runtime. This is the reason that the Polls Display portlet has the capabilities to be configured at runtime. If the tag `configuration-action-class` isn't specified in the portlet configuration, then there would be no *configuration* mode. As you can see, the Polls portlet doesn't have this setting. Therefore, it uses the default value—the Polls portlet doesn't have the **Setup** tab under **Gear** (icon) | **Configuration**.

Features of the Polls Display portlet

As you can see, the Polls Display portlet has the following features:

- The portlet can easily configure the questions and change the question to be displayed.

- The portlet is instanceable, that is, the portlet can appear multiple times on a page. Therefore, you can publish more and more questions on a page with multiple portlet instances.

- The portlet allows you to publish questions across groups—for example, the default site and Shared Global.

- One user can only vote once for a given question.

Assigning permissions

As stated previously, upon logging in as a site administrator of Palm Tree and clicking **Admin | Content**, you will see Polls under the **Content** category of **Site Administrator Panel**. As mentioned earlier, the user Lotti Stein is also a member of the Palm Tree site. Log in as Lotti Stein and go to **Site Administrator Panel**. You will see that **Polls** under the category is invisible.

Permission for **Polls** can be assigned under **Site Administration | Content | Polls**.

For the **Polls Display** portlet, permissions can be set under **Site Administration | Application | Polls Display**.

To set the permission entitlements for **Polls**, the portal administrator needs to define permissions in roles. Under the **User** section, click on **Roles** in **Control Panel** and locate **MB Topic Admin**. Select define permissions from the **Action** button beside **MB Topic Admin**. Search for **Polls**. You will be able to see the different permission entitlements for **Polls**.

Moreover, each has a different set of permission levels:

- **Site Administration | Content | Polls**: General Permissions, Resource Permissions (Poll Questions, Polls Question)
- **Site Administration | Application | Polls Display**: Application Permissions, Resource Permissions (Poll Questions, Polls Question)

Let's discuss each of them one by one in detail.

Poll Questions

You can set permission entitlements for the Poll Questions for users to be able to use **Add Question** and **Permissions** for specific roles, as shown in the following screenshot:

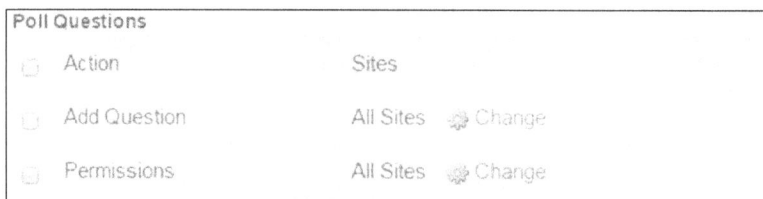

Figure 5.36: Site content permissions on Polls

Site Content permissions are effected on the content of the portlet. If the user is provided with Add Question and Permission, they will be able to add questions and assign permissions to other users. Refer to the preceding screenshot for further details:

Polls Question

The Polls Question permission entitlements allow users to perform different actions on Polls Questions, such as Add Vote, Delete, Permissions, Update, and View. Refer to the following screenshot for further details:

Polls Question		
Action	Sites	
Add Vote	All Sites	Change
Delete	All Sites	Change
Permissions	All Sites	Change
Update	All Sites	Change
View	All Sites	Change

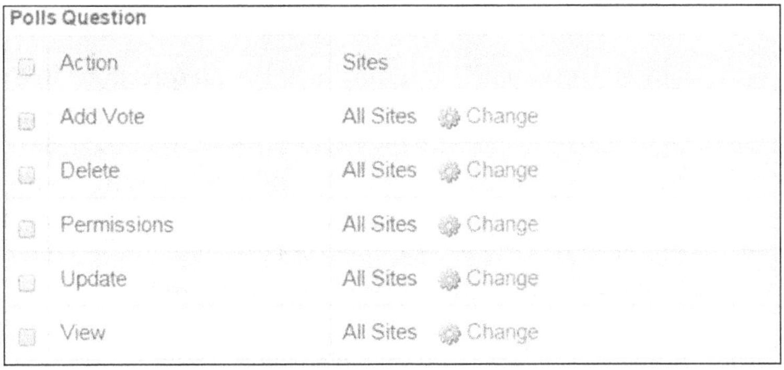

Figure 5.37: Site content permissions on Polls Question

As a user at the Palm Tree Publications enterprise, such as Lotti Stein, you have proper permissions to use **View** and **Add Vote** on the question "**Will Liferay be the best portal solution in this year 2015?**". However, you do not have permissions such as **Update** and **Delete**.

As you can see, as a site member, Lotti Stein only has the permissions to use **View** and **Add Vote** on the question.

As an administrator, you may need to set up the user "Lotti Stein" to have permissions to use **View**, **Add Vote**, **Delete**, and **Update** on the question "Will Liferay be the best portal solution in this year 2015?". Let's do it by following these steps.

1. Log in as a site administrator, say "Palm Tree".
2. Locate the question "**Will Liferay be the best portal solution in this year 2015?**".
3. Click on the **Permissions** button from the **Actions** menu next to the question.
4. Select the **Delete** and **Update** functions under the "**MB Topic Admin**" role.
5. Click on the **Save** button.

From now onwards, as a member of "MB Topic Admin", "Lotti Stein" finally has permissions to use **View**, **Add Vote**, **Update**, and **Delete** on the question "Will Liferay be the best portal solution in this year 2015?". Try to log in as "Lotti Stein" and you will see the **Actions** menu with the **Edit** and **Delete** icons next to the question.

As stated earlier, we have added the **Delete** and **Update** permissions on an individual question. Now, we're going add the **Delete** and **Update** permissions on questions in the following scopes:

- All questions in a site, such as Palm Tree site.
- All questions in a portal instance, such as the current portal instance.

"How to implement these use cases?", you may ask. For all questions in a site, you will be able to assign permissions in the Site Administration panel through the custom site role (or Site Member) for Site pages, or custom organization role (or Organization Member) for organization pages. For all questions in a portal instance, you will be able to assign permissions in the Site Administration panel through custom regular roles. The following is a sample process — assigning **Delete** and **Update** permissions on questions in the current portal instance:

1. Log in as a portal admin.
2. Click on **Roles** under the **User** category of **Control Panel** first.
3. Then, locate a role, say "**MB Topic Admin**".
4. Then, click on the **Define Permissions** icon from **Actions** to the right-hand side of the role.
5. Click on the **Content | Polls** link under **Add Permissions** and select the **Delete** and **Update** checkboxes under Polls Questions.
6. Click on the **Save** button.

Polls | General Permissions

Access to Site Administration Panel Permission on Poll has the following permission on the Poll portlet. For further details, refer the following screenshot:

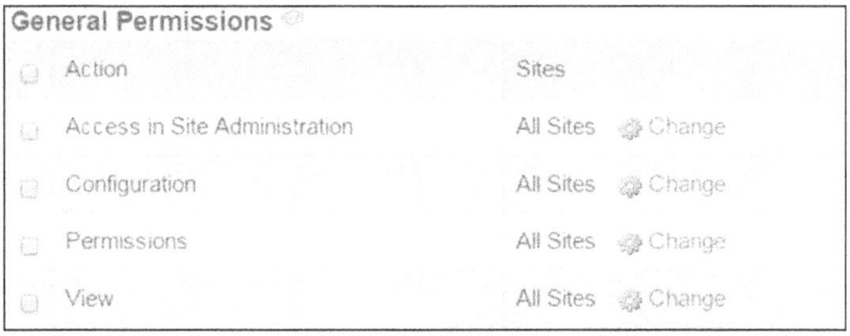

Figure 5.38: Site content permission on General Permissions

Site Administration | Applications | Polls Display | Application Permissions

The Site Application permission on the Poll Display portlet provides the following access to the user. You can assign MB Topic Admin for the Add to page permission. So, Lotti will be able to add the portlet on the page. Refer to the following screenshot:

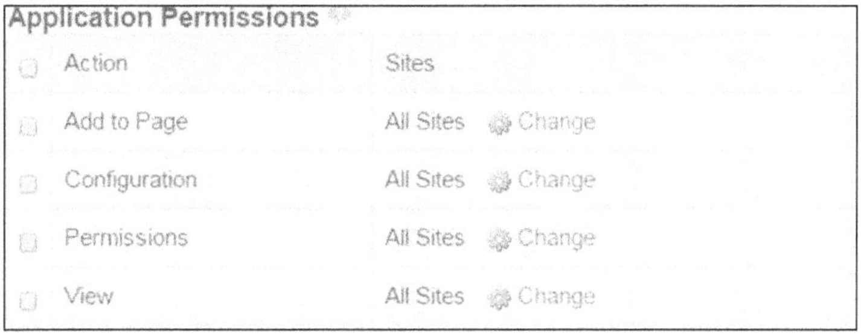

Figure 5.39: Site Application Permissions on the Polls Display portlet

Using polls effectively

Generally speaking, users (who have proper permissions) or administrators can create multiple-choice polls that keep track of votes and display results on the page in the Polls portlet. On the one hand, the Polls portlet manages many separate polls. On the other hand, a separate portlet, such as the Polls Display portlet can be configured to display a specific poll's results.

Actually, the Polls portlet acts as a voting application in order to take public opinion. It provides users with scientifically sampled surveys to assess public opinion. Meanwhile, it effectively uses the portal's customization and personalization features. Furthermore, it also allows an end user to customize the results that will be displayed.

As poll administrators, you can easily add and delete poll topics. You can customize portlets by changing the result title, reordering the poll options, and specifying whether the user can select multiple options.

As shown in following screenshot, polls are made up of questions. Thus, polls will have many questions associated with them. Each question must have two or more choices. In other words, a question would have at least two or more choices associated with it. In turn, each choice may have many votes associated with it. Note that a given user on a specific question can have at the most one vote.

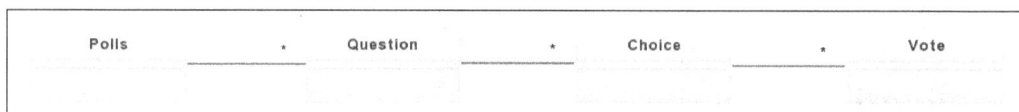

Polls	.	Question	.	Choice	.	Vote

Figure 5.40: Polls structure

Understanding Polls versus surveys

In theory, polls are scheduled to open and close at a given time. As poll administrators, you can view previous poll results if you want to make use of this information for your statistical analysis. At the same time, you can configure the portlet instance to determine what poll is to be shown in the portlet.

In a word, there are differences between surveys and polls. A **survey** is a multiple-page survey questionnaire, whereas a poll is a one-page questionnaire and is replaced by poll results after voting. Either by way of multiple choices or by text, polls consist of straightforward lists related to questions and potential responses. When information-gathering requirements are simple and you don't require the identification of the respondents, then you could use polls. Otherwise, you should use surveys.

Understanding Polls in scope

Considering the `Portal-Group-Page-Content` pattern, the content questions of the Polls portlet could be scoped into a group, for example, all pages, including both private pages and public pages by default. The content questions of the Polls portlet in the Shared Global group would be scoped into the portal instance. This would be the current portal instance—the content questions of the Polls portlet in the Shared Global group would be visible across all groups in the current portal instance.

As you can see, one of the most powerful characteristics of the Polls Display portlet is the fact that when they are added to different groups, they act as completely independent portlets, each with their own default group. By default, the Polls Display portlet is scoped into a group, that is, when one or more Polls Display portlets are added to a group of either public or private pages, they act as completely identical portlets but with their own portlet preferences, for example, **Gear** (icon) | **Configuration** | **Setup**.

When the Polls Display portlet is added to a page, for example, "Polls" of the Guest site, it will use the default scope—the group Guest. If you add the Polls Display portlet to a second page, let's say Welcome, it will show the same questions as those shown in the first page of the Guest group. When the Polls Display portlet is added to a page, it will immediately get scoped into the group to which the current page belongs.

Obviously, the Polls Display portlet is scoped into the Guest group when it is added to any of the pages of this group. You don't have the flexibility to switch groups in this case. However, you can solve this limitation through **Control Panel**. In **Control Panel**, you are able to switch the content of the Polls portlet between different groups. How do you implement it? You will be able to do it by following these steps:

1. Go to **Control Panel** under the dock bar menu.

2. Locate Polls under the **Content** category and click on **Polls**. You will see the same questions because, by default, the content of the Polls portlet is scoped to the Guest group.

3. Switch groups by selecting different groups from the drop-down menu.

Using Polls through JSON services

The portal provides services that allow invoking its methods directly through HTTP using **JavaScript Object Notation (JSON)** as a data serialization mechanism. The JSON API is automatically generated by Service Builder from a remote service interface. Of course, you can use polls through JSON services.

In general, you can use any HTTP client and JSON services to access the service. Alternatively, you can use JavaScript plus Velocity templates to access the JSON Service API. The following is an example of using JavaScript plus Velocity templates:

```
<script type="text/javascript">
Liferay.Service.Polls = {
  servicePackage: "com.liferay.portlet.polls.service."
};
// ignore details
</script>
```

As shown in the preceding code, we used the JSON API (for example, `com.liferay.portlet.polls.service`) and Velocity templates (for example, `$poll`) to form JavaScript functions: vote and add Vote. You may refer to the JavaScript `service.js` in `$PORTAL_ROOT_HOME/html/js/liferay`. Of course, you can use the preceding code with article templates for different purposes.

In addition, you may need to add polls as a type of Web Content Structure, just as that of Image Gallery images and Document and Media documents. Moreover, you can build dynamic articles with polls.

Summary

This chapter introduced you to adding and managing (view, update and delete) nodes of wikis, adding pages at the nodes in wikis, and managing (view, update, delete, and search) the pages for a given node in wikis. We also saw how you can use permissions of the Wiki portlet and permissions on nodes and how to publish wiki articles in the intranet first. Then, it introduced you to how to configure polls and displaying surveys in order to assess public opinion. In addition, it briefly introduced you to how a Dynamic Data List will help the user to create Forms without a single line of code. This chapter has taught you how you can convert the document using OpenOffice and make use of it in different places. We learned about Polls, which allows you to set up polls in your enterprise intranet portal for your employees. It also covered all the possible configurations and permissions for the Polls portlet.

In the next chapter, we're going to introduce blogs, RSS, and the WYSIWYG editor.

6
Blogs, WYSIWYG Editors, and Social Networking

In the intranet website, bookpub.com of the Palm Tree Publications enterprise, it would be nice to let small teams work together on specific projects, share files and Blogs about project processes, use WYSIWYG editors to create or update files and Blogs, and also employ RSS feeds. The Blogs portlet provides a straightforward Blogs solution with features such as RSS support, user and guest comments, browse able categories, tags and labels, and an entry-rating system. The RSS portlet with subscription provides the ability to frequently read RSS feeds from within the portal framework. At the same time, **What You See Is What You Get (WYSIWYG)** editors provide the ability to edit web content, including Blog content. Less technical people can use WYSIWYG editors without sifting through complex code.

This chapter will first introduce you to working with WYSIWYG editors, how to build Blog content with WYSIWYG editors, and how to configure different WYSIWYG editors. We will discuss how to work with RSS and related portlets as well as how to implement them for different requirements. It will talk about Blogs — how to customize and publish Blogs. Finally, it will talk about Social Networking and how to implement it in the portal.

By the end of this chapter, you will have learned how to:

- Use WYSIWYG editors extensively and configure WYSIWYG editors.
- Use RSS, including the RSS portlet, the Alert portlet, and the Announcement portlet.
- Work with blogs, manage (add, update, and delete) entries on blogs. Add comments and ratings on blog entries.
- Assign permissions on the Blogs portlet and blog entries.

- Publish blogs using the Recent Bloggers portlet and the Blogs Aggregator portlet.
- Create the Social Media portal using Liferay.

Exploring WYSIWYG editors

WYSIWYG is an acronym for **What You See Is What You Get**. The WYSIWYG editor helps users to create content with text and graphics using an interface that allows the user to view something very similar to the end result of the document that is being created.

The portal integrates CKEditor as the default HTML text editor. Of course, it is possible that as an administrator, you can integrate other WYSIWYG editors into the portal. Here, we will first use CKEditor as an example in order to build the contents of our portal.

> Liferay has used WYSIWYG everywhere, including web content, blogs, Message Boards, and so on, to make users work easily.

CKEditor provide us with a lot of features, such as the source for HTML and image access from the image portal.

Figure 6.1: A WYSIWYG editor

> CKEditor is web-based HTML text editor with powerful formatting capabilities. It brings to the Web much of the power of desktop editors, such as MS Word. Moreover, it is the most used rich HTML editor on the Web. It's also lightweight and doesn't require any kind of installation on the client's computer. In the year 2009, this product was renamed to CKEditor. Refer to `http://ckeditor.com` for more details.

Let's consider the following use cases of the WYSIWYG editor:

- Upgrade CKEditor to the latest version.
- Use general functions on text, namely font, size, alignment, color, background color, copy, paste, list, and so on. You would be able to use them easily.
- Insert images.
- Insert links.
- Insert flash, tables, smileys, and special characters.
- Edit a source directly.
- Customize WYSIWYG editors.

Upgrading CKEditor

First of all, let's upgrade the WYSIWYG text editor (CKEditor) to the latest version. By default, the portal has bundled CKEditor with a specific version. The version of CKEditor that comes along with the Liferay bundle might not be the latest version. Let's upgrade CKEditor to the latest version by following these steps:

1. Download the latest version of CKEditor from `http://ckeditor.com`. In my example, I have used the builder at `http://ckeditor.com/builder` and created my own editor with the Office 2013 skin.

2. Rename the `editor` folder under the `$PORTAL_ROOT_HOME/html/js to editor.backup` folder.

3. Unzip the ZIP file to the `$PORTAL_ROOT_HOME/html/js/editor.` folder.

4. Restart the server. That's it! From now onwards, you can enjoy the latest version of CKEditor.

> Note that you can use SDK plugins and do this in the `ext` plugin. This tutorial works only for CKEditor 2, and with CKEditor 4.2 and higher.

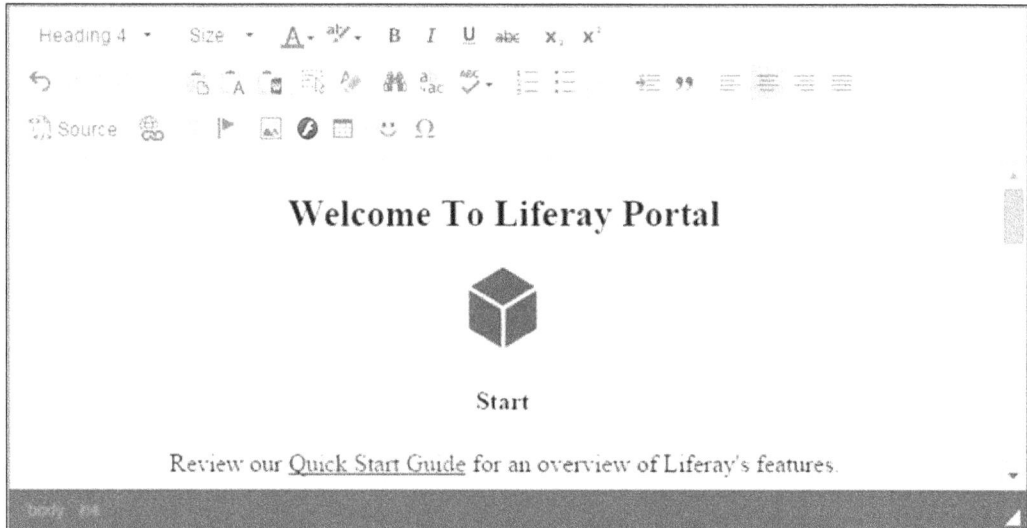

Figure 6.2: CKEditor with the latest version

End user features

CKEditor isn't only functional, flexible, and fast, but it's also innovative, smart, and user friendly. The following are end user features, but it's not limited to them.

The formatting features include:

- **Basic and advanced styling**: This feature allows rich styles under the **Control** tab

- **Real block-quoting**: This feature properly quotes text using the appropriate and semantics-aware `<blockquote>` tag

- **Colors**: This feature makes it easy to apply colors to text, which is a matter of a few clicks with the color selector

- **Advanced paste from Word**: This makes it easy to convert these texts using the powerful **Paste from Word** feature

- **Advanced linking**: This builds advanced links that can open popups, links to anchors, e-mails, and any kind of web resource
- **E-mail linking**: This makes it easy to insert the desired e-mail address—even the message subject and text

The user interface features include:

- **Visual link anchors**: You can use this feature by inserting page *anchors* so that other pages (or even the same page) can link to them, thus positioning the reader in the right place
- **Maximize**: With a single click, you can fill the entire space available in the page, and with another click, it returns to its original size
- **Visible Blocks**: With this feature, you can outline every single block of text, making it easy to control the semantics and the quality of the edited content
- **Resizable**: Through a simple drag operation, this makes it possible to have the perfect fit
- **Right-to-left interface**: Renders from right to left to make the end users feel at home
- **Elements selector**: Showing the hierarchy of HTML tags around the current cursor position makes it easy to manage them
- **Find and Replace**: Finding words in the text is simple and effective using this feature, and replacing words is also easy, including massive replacement operations

The rich content features of CKEditor include the following:

- **Images**: This helps to insert images into the content and is easily configurable
- **Flash content**: This enables inserting flashes on pages and easily controlling the playback features of Flash movies
- **Easy tables**: The creation of tables plays well with accessibility and designing them presents their contents in a better way
- **Smiles**: This feature comes with a set of exclusively designed smiley graphics that can be freely and easily used to display smileys
- **Print breaks**: This feature precisely controls the printing breakpoints inside the contents
- **Templates**: This makes pieces of HTML reusable again and again
- **Form creation tools**: This enables bringing all necessary tools to proper "create and manage" forms and fields

The usability features include:

- **Interface usability**: This feature makes it intuitive to be understood and used by bringing the best editing experience to the hands of our end users.

- **Strong accessibility**: This brings about compliance with worldwide accessibility standards, such as the W3C, WCAG, and the US Section 508.

- **Spellcheck as you type**: This brings a *zero installation* spellcheck based on the quality spellchecking services provided by `SpellChecker.net`.

- **Keyboard navigable**: The keyboard is *totally* keyboard navigable, which means that you don't need a mouse to use its features, and you will never be limited as a result of it.

- **Tab-key friendly**: Using the *Tab* key to navigate through pages, this special form is quite common and intuitive. CKEditor respects it. It does not interfere in the way users would expect pages to behave and makes navigation very natural.

- **Intuitive context menu**: Context menus are easy and intuitive ways to add functionality to applications.

- **Safely undo**: Every single action can be safely reverted, which guarantees that you'll never break things or lose your text.

Inserting images from CKEditor

You can insert an image as an internal image (from the document and image libraries) or an external image (a URL outside of the portal). For example, imagine that you need to insert an image using the `http://cdn.www.liferay.com/osb-community-theme/images/custom/heading.png` URL in the entry **Welcome To Liferay Portal** web content title. Let's do it by following these steps:

1. Click on the **Edit** icon below the **Welcome To Liferay Portal** title of some web content.

2. Locate the position where you want to insert an image.

3. Click on the **Image** icon in CKEditor.

4. For the external image, enter the `https://cdn.lfrs.sl/www.liferay.com/osb-community-theme/images/custom/heading.png` URL and add the other properties, such as width, height, and alignment. Refer to the following screenshot.

5. Click on the **OK** button.

The following screenshot illustrates how to include the image through CKEditor:

Figure 6.3: CKEditor image URL

As shown in the preceding screenshot, you can configure the following items related to **Image Info**:

- **URL**: This is the URL of images
- **Alternative Text**: This is about using the *alt* setting
- **Width**: These are the dimensions in terms of the width of the image
- **Height**: These are the dimensions in terms of the height of the image
- **Border**: This removes the visible border around images
- **HSpace**: This is the horizontal space between the image and surrounding text
- **VSpace**: This is the vertical space between the image and surrounding text
- **Alignment**: This shows whether the image is left-aligned or right-aligned

The size of the dimensions (**Height** and **Width**) of the image can be reset, and the ratio of these dimensions of the image can be locked. You can find the two icons next to **Width** and **Height**—namely, **Lock Ratio** and **Reset Size**.

Of course, you can insert an image as an internal image (from the image gallery). You can do it by following these steps:

1. Click on the **Edit** icon appearing below the **Welcome To Liferay Portal** title of the web content.

2. Select the position where you want to insert an image.

3. Click on the **Image** icon in the WYSIWYG editor.

4. Click on the **Browse Server** (internal image) button.

5. Click on a folder, say `Palm Tree`.

6. Click on **Create New Folder** to add the `Images` folder under the current folder.

> Any folder and image added here will be placed in the document and image library. The document and image library provides a centralized repository for images to be stored and given a unique URL.

7. Type the name of the new folder `Images` and click on the **OK** button.

8. Navigate to the `Images` folder.

9. Click on the **Choose File** button to select an image, `muppets.png`, from your local machine.

10. Click on the **Upload** button to add the image to the folder.

11. Click on the `muppets.png` image and click on the **OK** button to add the image to the document.

12. Click on the **Save** button to save the updates.

> In addition, you can insert an image, flash, or document link from the Alfresco repository. It is called full RESTful integration between Liferay and Alfresco. In this case, Alfresco is used as a repository for Liferay.

As you can see, you can select an existing image from the image gallery or create a folder, upload an image, and select the newly uploaded images.

Configuring CKEditor

The `fckconfig.jsp` JSP file provides an integration of CKEditor and the portal.

First, its customized toolbar sets `liferay` (for Wiki pages, blog entries, and so on), `liferay-article` (for web content), `edit-in-place`, and `e-mail` at `$PORTAL_ROOT_HOME/html/js/editor/fckeditor/fckconfig.jsp`. For example, the `liferay` toolbar set has been specified as follows:

```
FCKConfig.ToolbarSets["liferay"] = [
    ['Style', 'FontSize', '-', 'TextColor', 'BGColor'],
    ['Bold', 'Italic', 'Underline', 'StrikeThrough'],
    ['Subscript', 'Superscript'],
    '/',
    ['Undo', 'Redo', '-', 'Cut', 'Copy', 'Paste', 'PasteText',
      'PasteWord', '-', 'SelectAll', 'RemoveFormat'],
    ['Find', 'Replace', 'SpellCheck'],
    ['OrderedList', 'UnorderedList', '-', 'Outdent', 'Indent'],
    ['JustifyLeft', 'JustifyCenter', 'JustifyRight', 'JustifyFull'],
    '/',
    ['Source'],
    ['Link', 'Unlink', 'Anchor'],
    ['Image', 'Flash', 'Table', '-', 'Smiley', 'SpecialChar']
];
```

As shown in the preceding code, the style and font size are grouped as one tab, and the image, flash, and table are grouped as another tab.

Then, it sets the CSS and links it to the themes. The following is some sample code:

```
String cssPath = ParamUtil.getString(request, "cssPath");
String cssClasses = ParamUtil.getString(request, "cssClasses");
FCKConfig.BodyClass = 'html-editor <%= cssClasses %>' ;
FCKConfig.CustomStyles = {};
FCKConfig.StylesXmlPath = FCKConfig.EditorPath + 'fckstyles.xml' ;
FCKConfig.EditorAreaCSS ='<%= HtmlUtil.escape(cssPath)
    %>/main.css' ;
```

Most importantly, it specifies the image browser URL as follows:

```
long plid = ParamUtil.getLong(request, "p_l_id");
String mainPath = ParamUtil.getString(request, "p_main_path");
String doAsUserId = ParamUtil.getString(request, "doAsUserId");
String connectorURL = HttpUtil.encodeURL(mainPath +
    "/portal/fckeditor?p_l_id=" + plid + "&p_p_id=" +
    HttpUtil.encodeURL(portletId) + "&doAsUserId=" +
    HttpUtil.encodeURL(doAsUserId) + "&doAsGroupId=" +
    HttpUtil.encodeURL(doAsGroupId));
```

Inserting links to content

Links can be internal and external. You can insert internal links and external links into content, such as blog entries. For example, you are going to insert a link with a URL in the **Welcome To Liferay Portal** entry. Let's do it by following these steps:

1. In the WYSIWIG editor text area, locate the position where you want to insert a link.

2. Input some text, for example, `Liferay Portal 6.2 Portal System Development has very cool features`, and then select the text that you want to make a link for.

3. Click on the **Link** button in the WYSIWYG editor:

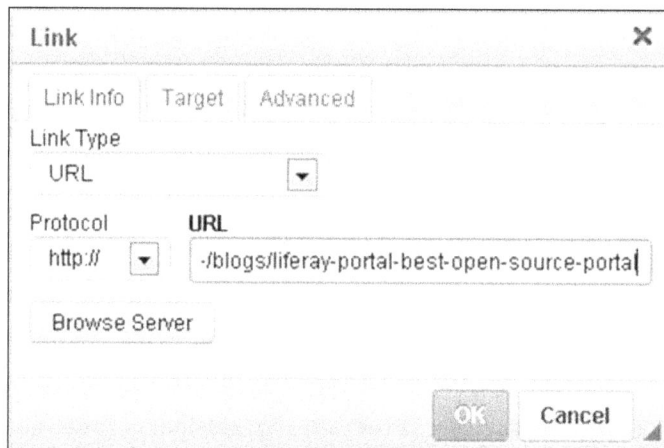

Figure 6.4: CKEditor adding link

4. Now, in the pop-up link window, input the URL for the external link.

5. Finally, click on the **OK** button.

As shown in the preceding screenshot, you can configure the following items related to **Link Info**:

- **Link Type**: This includes the URL, link to anchor in this page, and e-mail
- **Protocol**: This can be `http://`, `https://`, `ftp://`, `news://`, or `<other>`
- **URL**: This is the URL of the links

As you can see, external links refer to any links outside of the portal where link types would be a URL, link to the anchor in the text, and e-mail. Protocols can be `http`, `https`, `news`, `ftp`, and `<other>`. Besides the **Link Info** tab, you can also use the functions from the **Target** and **Advanced** tabs.

The internal links refer to any links in the portal, for example, links to images in the image or documents in the document and image library and links to pages of the current group. In short, there are two types of resources related to internal links: document and page.

Linking text to documents

As previously mentioned, you may need to link to a document. To link text to a document, follow these steps:

1. In the WYSIWIG editor text area, locate the position where you want to insert a link.

2. Select text, such as `Liferay Portal 6.1 Portal System Development has very cool features.`

3. Click on the **Link** button in the WYSIWYG editor.

4. Click on the **Browse Server** button in the **Link Info** tab, that is, internal link.

5. In the **Resource Type** menu, select **Document** — note that the default value of the resource type is **Document**.

6. Select the document from its respective folder. If the document is not uploaded in the portal, then you may have to upload the document and link it.

7. Click on the **Save** button to save the updates.

> Any folders and documents that are added here will be placed in the document and image library. The document and image library provides a centralized repository where documents and images can be stored and given a unique URL.

Linking text to pages

We have discussed how to link text to documents. However, you may need to link text to a page, for example, `web/guest/home`. We can do it by following these steps:

1. In the WYSIWIG editor text area, locate the position where you want to insert a link.

2. Select text, such as `Liferay Portal 6.1 Portal System Development has very cool features.`

3. Click on the **Link** button in the WYSIWYG editor.

4. Click on the **Browse Server** button in the **Link Info** tab, that is, **internal link**.

5. Select the group, say **Palm Tree**, in which the page is located.

6. Click on the page that you want to link the selected text to, for example, `/ web/guest/home`.

7. Click on **OK** to link the page with the selected text.

As you can see, the value that links text to a page would be something similar to `/web/ guest/home` if the link type is URL.

Configuring resource types

As mentioned previously, there are two resource types for links — document and page. The default resource type is document.

In the file `$PORTAL_ROOT_HOME/html/js/editor/fckeditor/editor/ filemanager/browser/liferay/frmresourcetype.html`, we overrode the value of resource types as follows:

```
var defaultTypes = [
    ['Document','Document'],
    ['Page','Page'],
    ['Attachment', 'Attachment'],
    ['Audio', 'Audio'],
    ['Video', 'Video']
] ;
```

The preceding code shows that there would be two resource types, namely, Document and Page. Similarly, in the `$PORTAL_ROOT_HOME/html/js/editor/ fckeditor/editor/ filemanager/browser/liferay/browser.html` file, we overrode the value of the default resource type as follows:

```
if( oConnector.ShowAllTypes )
    oConnector.ResourceType = 'Document';
```

The preceding code sets the default resource type to `Document`.

Most importantly, the configuration file `$PORTAL_ROOT_HOME/html/js/editor/ fckeditor/fckconfig.jsp` specifies the link browser URL as follows:

```
FCKConfig.LinkBrowserURL = FCKConfig.BasePath +
    "filemanager/browser/liferay/browser.html?Connector=<%=
    HtmlUtil.escapeJS(connectorURL) %>";
```

> Note that in WYSIWYG (CKEditor) editor, we can insert flash (`.SWF`) files, tables, smileys, and special characters too.

Understanding RSS

As an administrator, you may need to include formatted data (news) from external **Really Simple Syndication (RSS)** feeds. For example, you're going to add New York Times news feeds (for example, `http://partners.userland.com/nytRss/technology.xml`), BBC news feeds (for example, `http://feeds.bbci.co.uk/news/technology/rss.xml`), and Yahoo! news feeds (`http://news.yahoo.com/rss/tech`) in the **RSS** page of the Palm Tree site. Whenever an RSS XML file is updated on the remote site, the page will reflect those updates on the next portal page reload, as shown in the following screenshot:

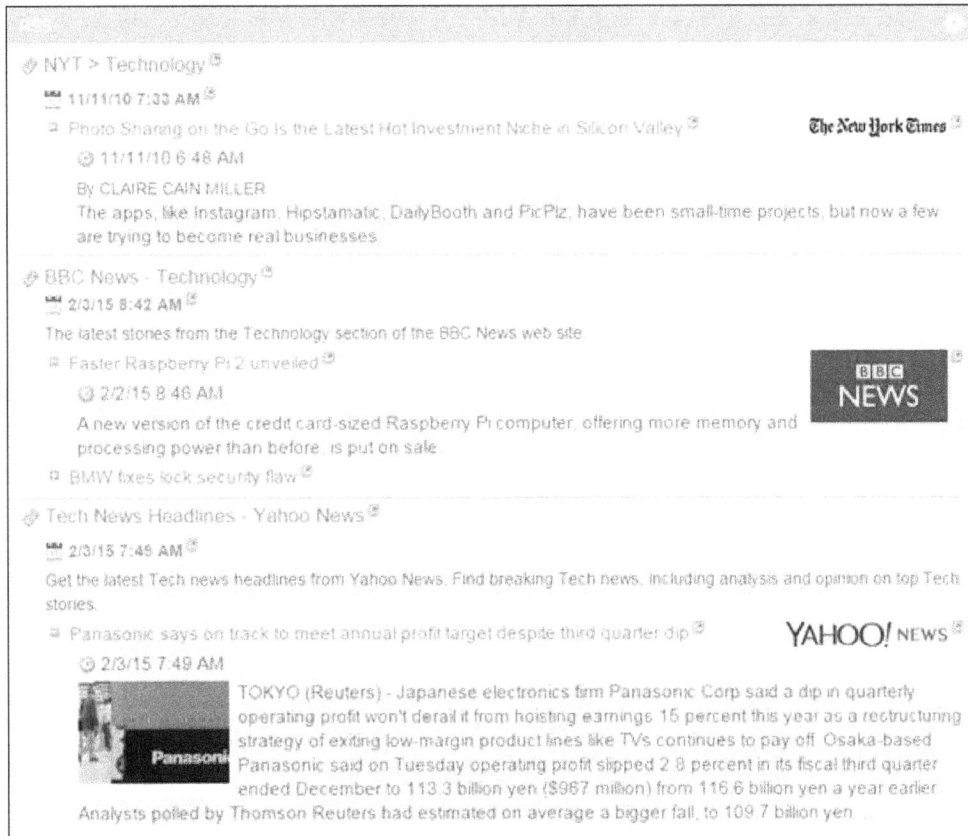

Figure 6.5: The RSS portlet

Let's add the RSS portlet to the **RSS** page first by following these steps:

1. Add a page called RSS in the Palm Tree site's public pages by clicking on **Add** | **Page** under the dock bar menu.

2. Add the RSS portlet in the RSS page of Palm Tree where you want to manage RSS news by clicking on **Add** | **Applications** under the dock bar menu.

The RSS portlet

How do we get RSS news? You need to configure the RSS portlet (portlet ID 39) by following these steps:

1. To set the feeds that you want to display, click on **Gear** (icon) | **Configuration** first in the top-right corner of the RSS portlet.

2. By default, the **Setup** tab is selected.

3. To add a feed, first click on the **Add** icon and then enter a title, say `Yahoo`, and a URL, say `http://news.yahoo.com/rss/tech`.

4. To add another feed, click on the **Add** icon first and then enter a title, for example, `BBC`, and a URL, say `http://feeds.bbci.co.uk/news/technology/rss.xml`.

5. To add another feed, click on the **Add** icon first and then enter a title, for example, `New York Times`, and a URL such as `http://partners.userland.com/nytRss/technology.xml`.

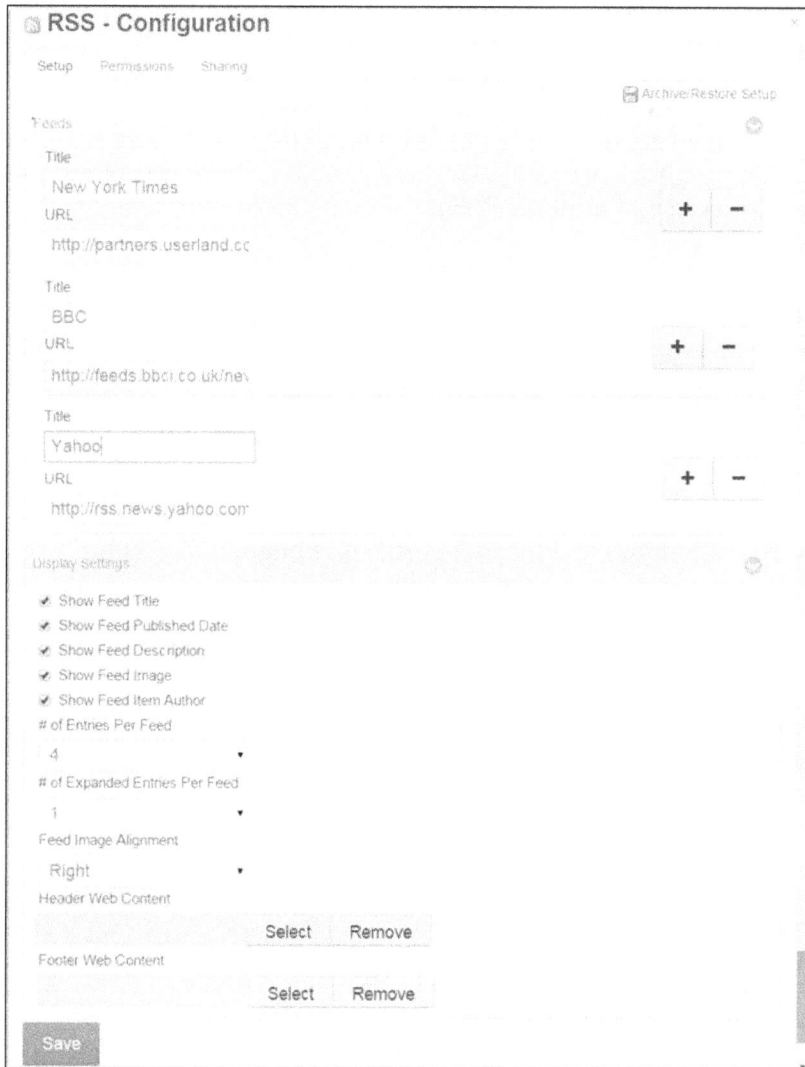

Figure 6.6: RSS feed configuration

6. To delete a feed, locate the feed first and then click on the **Delete** icon on the right-hand side of the feed.

7. To edit a feed, locate the feed, click on the title and/or URL, and then change the title and URL to what you want.

8. Configure the following items as expected. Here, we use the default settings, as shown in the next screenshot.

9. Click on the **Save** button to save the changes.

Of course, you can use other news feeds. In short, to add a feed, simply click on the **Add** icon first and then input the title and the URL. In order to remove a feed, first locate the feed and then click on the **Delete** icon.

As you can see, there are three different news feed URLs by default, three items per channel, and three entries per feed. Moreover, the RSS portlet is configurable and instanceable; you can add multiple RSS portlets in a page.

Configuring RSS

The RSS portlet was specified as being instanceable and configurable as follows in `$PORTAL_ROOT_HOME/WEB-INF/liferay-portlet.xml`:

```
<configuration-action-class> com.liferay.portlet.rss.
  action.ConfigurationActionImpl </configuration-action-class>
<instanceable>true</instanceable>
```

The preceding code shows that the RSS portlet is configurable via the `configuration-action-class` tag and *instanceable* via the `instanceable` tag.

In addition, the RSS portlet has a set of preferences specified in `$PORTAL_ROOT_HOME/WEB-INF/portlet-custom.xml` as follows:

```
<portlet-preferences>
  <preference>
    <name>entriesPerFeed</name>
    <value>4</value>
</preference>
  <preference>
    <name>urls</name>
    <value>http://www.liferay.com/community/blogs/-
      /blogs_stream/community/rss</value>
    <value>http://rss.news.yahoo.com/rss/tech</value>
    <value>http://partners.userland.com/nytRss/technology.
      xml</value>
  </preference>
  <preferences-validator>com.liferay.portlet.rss.RSSPreferences
    Validator</preferences-validator>
</portlet-preferences>
```

As shown in the preceding code, the portlet preference URL has three values. On the other hand, the portlet preference `items-per-channel` has the value 4. This is the main reason that there are three news feed URLs.

Understanding announcements and alerts

Announcements and Alerts are two separate portlets that are responsible for broadcasting messages to a list of users within a scope. Essentially, these portlets provide a mass messaging engine and one-way messaging. All Announcement and/or Alert entries are tracked so that they can be *read* by each individual user and each user can individually hide an entry.

Managing entries

In both the Announcements and Alerts portlets, entries are manageable. If you are going to add an entry in the Announcements portlet on the RSS page of the Palm Tree site, you would be able to do it as shown in the following steps and the next screenshot:

1. Add the **Announcements** portlet in the **RSS** page of the Palm Tree site where you want to manage entries.

2. Select the **Manage Entries** tab and select **Distribution Scope**; the scope would be a portal site or role similar to the following items:
    - Site: Palm Tree and other sites
    - Roles: Regular, organization, and site roles

3. Now click on **Add Entry**.

4. Type a title, such as Book Review, a URL, such as https://www.packtpub.com/web-development/liferay-62-intranet-portal-development-guide, and enter content, such as Liferay Portal 6.2 Systems Development.

5. Select **Type** from the drop-down list: **General**, **News**, and **Test**. We use the default value **General**.

6. Select **Priority** from the drop-down list: **Normal** and **Important**. We use the default value **Normal**.

7. Enter the display date and expiration date—note that the display date and the expiration date should be different.

8. Click on the **Save** button when you are ready.

9. You can preview the entry before saving by clicking on the **Preview** button.

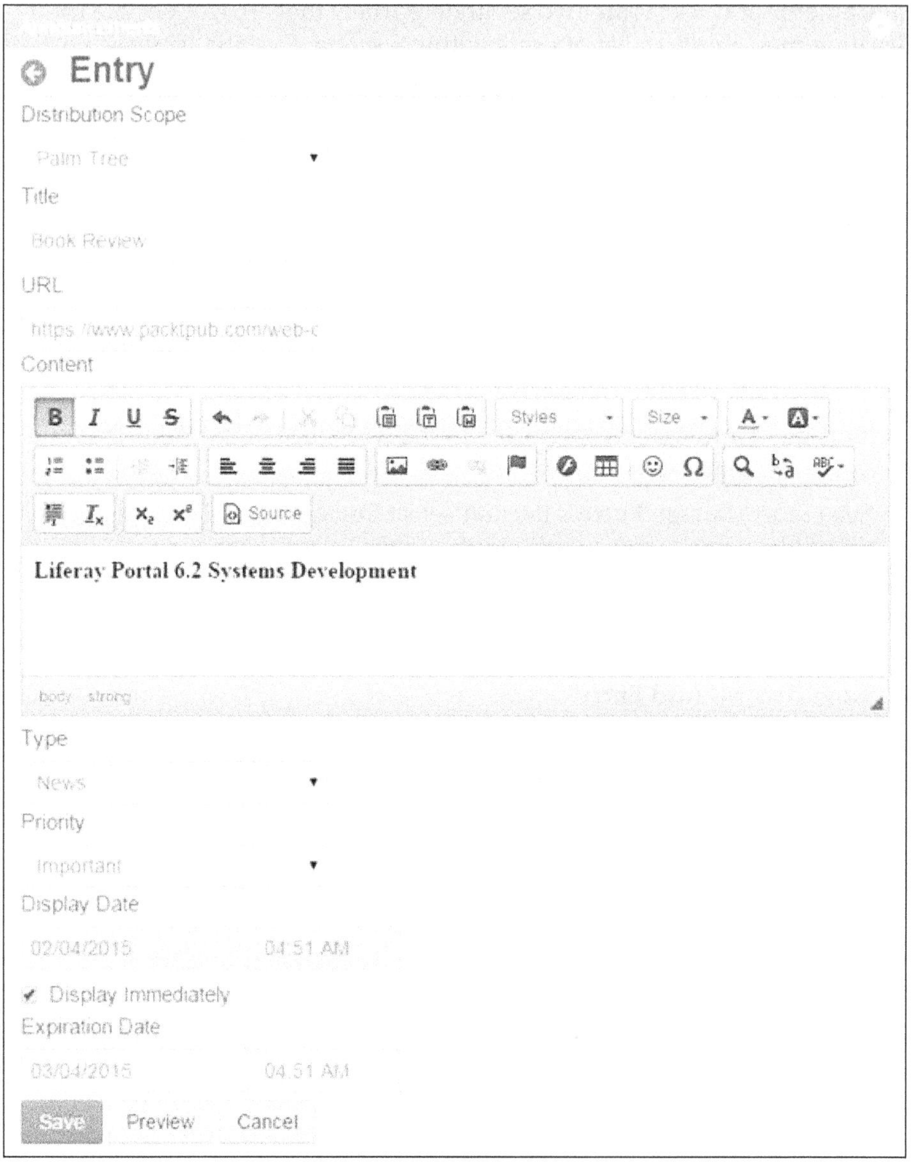

Figure 6.7: New entry in Announcements

Of course, you would be able to add more entries if you have proper permissions. After adding the `Book Review` entry, you are able to view and manage entries, as shown in the following screenshot. You can update an entry by clicking on the **Edit** icon next to the entry, or you can delete an entry by clicking on the **Delete** icon next to the entry. In addition, you could mark an entry as *read* by clicking on the **Mark as Read** link next to the entry. Afterwards, the **Mark as Read** link will be changed to **Show**.

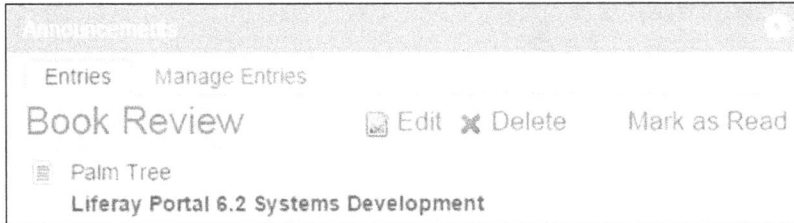

Figure 6.8: The Announcements portlet

In addition, you would be able to configure remote delivery of alerts and announcements. As shown in the next screenshot, remote delivery would be enabled through e-mail and SMS. Each user will have an opportunity to individually configure delivery in the user profile for each configured "type" of announcement entry. Normally, by going to **My Account | Miscellaneous | Announcements**, you would be able to configure your own remote delivery of alerts and announcements.

As a normal user, if you have proper permissions, you would be able to configure other users' remote delivery of alerts and announcements. The following are simple steps to show you how it's done:

1. Click on **Admin | Control Panel** under the dock bar menu.
2. Select **Users and Organizations** under the **Users** category of **Control Panel**.
3. Locate a user, say "Lotti Stein", and click on the **Edit** icon of the **Actions** menu next to the user.

4. Go to **Miscellaneous | Announcements** and you would be able to configure the user's remote delivery of alerts and announcements.

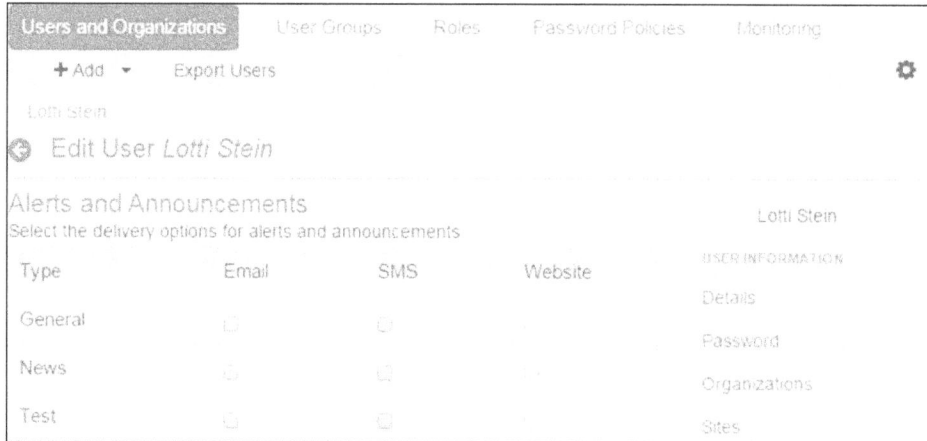

Figure 6.9: Announcements sitting in Users and Organizations

Features of the Announcements portlet

The following are the main features of the **Announcements** portlet:

*   First, there is the feature of being configurable and supporting an unlimited number of announcement types.
*   Then, there is the delivery to scopes, including general (that is, portal instance), communities, and role.
*   The portlet has the feature of delivery mechanisms include e-mail, SMS, and website. Note that website delivery is achieved simply by adding the portlet to any page accessible to the user.
*   Scheduled delivery—each entry has a display date and an expiration date.
*   Readable tracking—each entry has a website delivery that tracks the timestamped read status per user.
*   There is subscription control per user and per announcement type.
*   Broadcast control of announcements is another feature.

Configuring the Announcements portlet

The portal sets the following items for e-mail notification announcements by default in `portal.properties`:

```
announcements.email.from.name=
announcements.email.from.address=
announcements.email.to.name=
announcements.email.to.address=noreply@liferay.com
```

As shown in the preceding code, e-mail notification settings are configured. The e-mail *from* name and the e-mail *from* address can be configured. The e-mail *to* name and the e-mail *to* address is `noreply@liferay.com`, which you can configure. You will definitely be able to override these settings in `portal-ext.properties`.

In addition, the portal has some specified types of announcements as default settings, as shown in the following lines in `portal.properties`:

```
announcements.entry.types=general,news,test
announcements.entry.check.interval=15
```

As shown in the preceding code, the default types of announcement entries are *general*, *news*, and *test*. The `announcements.entry.types` property sets the list of announcement types, while the `announcements.entry.check.interval` property sets the interval at which `Check-Entry-Job` will run. The value `15` is set in 1-minute increments.

Exploring blogs

The Blogs portlet includes full WYSIWYG editing capability and publication date, RSS support, threaded user and guest comments, tags and labels, social bookmarking links, e-mail notifications of blog replies, and an entry rating system. In order to let small teams work on specific projects and share files and blogs about project processes, we should use the Blogs portlet at the **Palm Tree** site member.

Let's look at an example on the Blogs portlet. As an administrator of the enterprise Palm Tree Publications, create a page called **Blogs** at the Palm Tree site, and then add the Blogs portlet (portlet ID `33`) in the **Blogs** page . Then, you are ready to create blog entries named `Liferay Portal Best Open Source Portal` and `How to create best Intranet portal`.

Adding entries

First of all, we need to create an entry called `Liferay Portal Best Open Source Portal`. Let's create the entry, as shown in the following screenshot.

1. On the Blogs portlet, click on the **Add Blog Entry** button.

2. Input a title, say `Liferay Portal Best Open Source Portal`, which can be duplicated.

3. Input a display date; the default date and time are the current date and time respectively.

4. Input content — text, graphics, and any links using the WYSIWYG editor.

5. Enabling the **Allow Pingbacks** checkbox will automatically notify the users when a link has been created to a person's blog post from an external website, allowing a reciprocal link to that website to be created.

6. Check the **Allow Trackbacks** checkbox. Note that in order to allow trackbacks, you must also ensure that the entry's guest view permission is enabled.

7. Input an e-mail address for **Trackbacks to Send**; here, we use the default settings.

8. Set **Permissions**; by default, it's anyone (Guest Role). In order to configure additional permissions, click on **More Options**. Here, we just use the default settings.

9. Input the **Abstracts** description on the content. Even you can upload small images with respect to content.

10. Click **Categorization**, and select proper categories by clicking on the **Select Categories** button. Input the proper **Tags**; if you need help, you can click on the **Suggestions** button.

11. You can set the related assets for the blog. Related assets can be web content, Message Board messages, calendar events, wiki pages, or any documents.

12. Save inputs by clicking on the **Publish** button or the **Save Draft** button. Only published blogs will be visible to users.

The following screenshot illustrates the new blog entry:

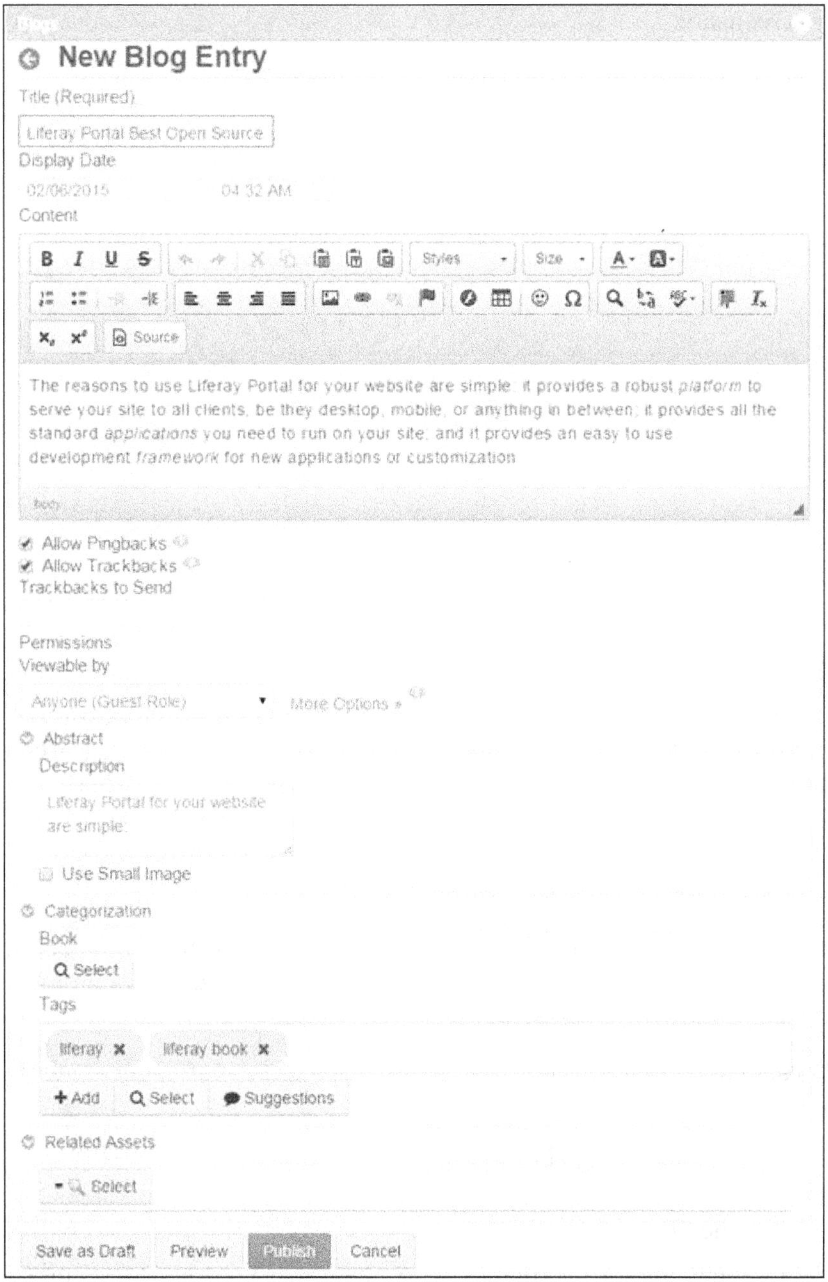

Figure 6.10: Adding a blog entry

Of course, you can create other entries as desired. After creating the entry called `How to create best Intranet portal`, we can view entries, as shown in the following screenshot:

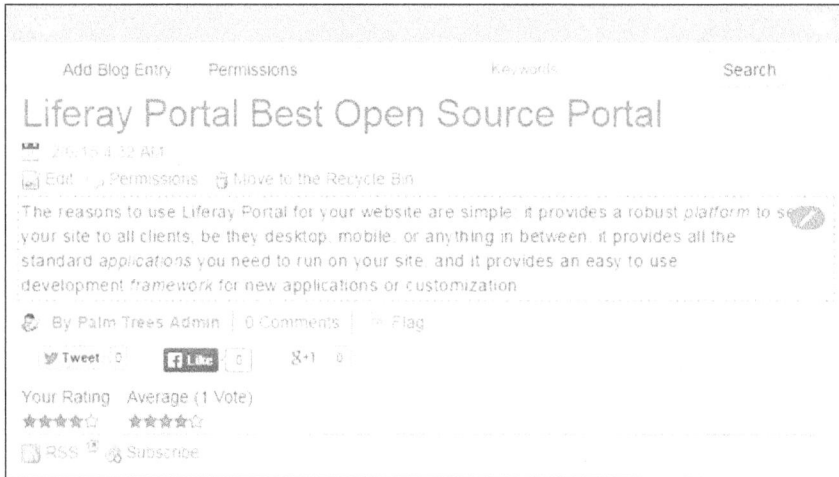

Figure 6.11: The blog entry view

Managing entries

After adding entries, we can manage them smoothly via the Blogs portlet. Blog entry management would involve, but is not limited to, editing, removing, searching, rating, commenting, bringing RSS feeds, bringing entries into third-party blog systems, and so on.

Editing blog entries

Entries are editable. For example, let's change the title of the entry `How to create best Intranet portal` to `Developing Enterprise Intranet with Liferay`. Let's do that by following these steps:

1. Locate the entry, say `How to create best Intranet portal`, that you want to edit.

2. Click on the **Edit** icon appearing below the title `How to create best Intranet portal`.

3. Update the title with `Developing Enterprise Intranet with Liferay`.

4. Retain the values of the display date, content, categories, tags, and so on. If required, you can update them.

5. Now, publish it by clicking on the **Publish** button.

Note that in the edit page, you can update the title, display date, trackbacks, categories, and tags—everything except assigning permissions. In order to change permissions, you have to use functions of permission assignment.

Liferay 6.2 provides an inline editing feature for blog content. In *Figure 6.11*, as an administrator, you can see in the top-right corner of the content a green pencil icon. Once you click on the green pencil icon, it will allow you to edit the content inline. It will pop up the edit controls for content writing.

Removing blog entries

Entries are removable and moved to Recycle Bin. For instance, the entry `Developing Enterprise Intranet with Liferay` is not needed anymore. Let's delete it by following these steps:

1. Locate the entry `Developing Enterprise Intranet with Liferay` that you want to remove.

2. Click on the **Move to the Recycle Bin** icon appearing below the title `Developing Enterprise Intranet with Liferay`.

3. A message will appear saying **The Blogs Entry Developing Enterprise Intranet with Liferay was moved to the Recycle Bin.** with an **Undo** button next to it.

Note that removing an entry will remove all related comments that belong to this entry.

Searching entries

The content of entries is searchable. Let's say that, as an administrator, you want to search entries by the keyword `Liferay`. Let's perform a search as follows:

1. In the **Blog** portlet search box, input the search criterion (that is, keyword) for example, `liferay`.

2. Click on the **Search** button.

A list of entries appears with the content search too. The search displays the blog entries with their respective content. It searches within the content and highlights it.

You can search for entries using any keyword. In short, there is only one condition, that is, you need to have the proper **View** permission for the entries. This means that if you don't have the proper **View** permission for the entries, then you won't be able to view them using search.

Now, log in as "Lotti Stein", just input the search criterion `liferay`, and click on the button **Search**. You will see the entry that has the view permission to "Lotti Stein".

By default, the Blogs portlet has the guest view permission set and the site member view permission set, due to which you will be able to view all the blogs entries.

> What's happening? This is something related to permissions on the entries. Refer to the *Assigning permissions* section.

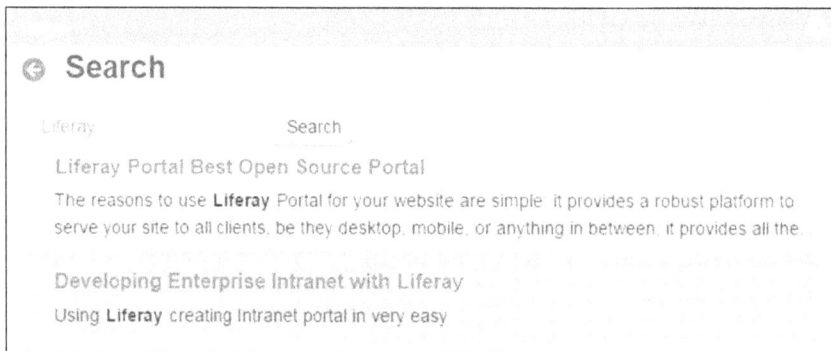

Figure 6.12: Search result

Ratings for blog entries

You can give your own rating to any entries if you are logged in and if you have proper permissions to view them. For instance, as an administrator, you find the blog entry `Liferay Portal Best Open Source Portal` useful and nice and want to give your rating, for example, four stars. You simply have to click on the fourth star under **Your Rating** of the entry `Liferay Portal Best Open Source Portal`.

Each user can give their own ratings for their respective blogs entries. So, when "Lotti Stein" logs in, she can provide her own ratings to blog entries. Now, you will find the calculated average value voted by two people for same blog entry.

> Note that a guest can view the rating but can't vote; users can vote only once on a given blog entry. More interestingly, you, as a user with proper permissions, can change your vote on a specific blog entry anytime.

Why does each entry have ranks? There is a taglib called `<liferay-ui:ratings>` that allows you to rate any type of content or pages in any portlet. Meanwhile, you can find the UI taglib `<liferay-ui:ratings>` at $PORTAL_ROOT_HOME/html/ portlet/blogs/view_entry_content.jsp. To associate any object with ranks, all you need is its `Class-Name` and `Primary-Key`. Note that $PORTAL_ROOT_HOME represents the root folder of the portal (refer to *Chapter 2*, *Setting Up a Home Page and Navigation Structure for the Intranet*, for more details).

RSS feeds for blog entries

You can export blog entries as RSS feeds. Let's do it by following these steps:

1. Click on the **RSS Feed** ( ) icon at the bottom of the entries.

2. The RSS feeds page appears on the next window. All entries are displayed with brief content in the form of XML.

3. Now, you use this XML for the feed using different applications, such as the RSS portlet.

Flagging inappropriate content

As you can see, you can flag the content of a Blog entry as inappropriate. For each entry, you will see a small icon of a flag that will enable a user to flag the content of a blog entry as inappropriate for a reason and warn the administrator about it.

Why does each entry have a flag? There is a taglib called `<liferay-ui:flags>` that allows you to flag any type of content or pages in any portlet. If you are interested in details, you can also find the implementation of the `<liferay-ui:flags>` flags at $PORTAL_ROOT_HOME/html/taglib/ui /flags/page.jsp. On the other hand, you can find the UI taglib `<liferay-ui:flags>` at $PORTAL_ROOT_HOME/html/portlet/ blogs/view_entry_content.jsp.

Understanding social bookmarks

The feature of social bookmarking on blog entries is very cool because it allows the posting of entries to various popular social bookmarking sites, such as Twitter, Facebook, and Google+. Why does each entry have social bookmarks? There is a taglib called `<liferay-ui:social-bookmarks>` that allows the posting of entries to various popular social bookmarking sites. You can find the UI taglib `<liferay-ui:social-bookmarks>` at $PORTAL_ROOT_HOME/html/portlet/blogs/view_ entry_content.jsp.

If you are interested in more details, you can also find the implementation of the social bookmarks `<liferay-ui:social-bookmarks>` at `$PORTAL_ROOT_HOME/html/taglib/ui/ social_bookmarks/page.jsp` and the implementation of the social bookmark `<liferay-ui:social-bookmark>` at `$PORTAL_ROOT_HOME/html/taglib/ui/social_bookmark/page.jsp`.

What's happening? How can we configure social bookmarks for Blog entries? The portal has the following settings by default in `portal.properties`.

```
social.bookmark.types=twitter,facebook,plusone
social.bookmark.jsp[facebook]=/html/taglib/ui/social_bookmark/face
    book.jsp
social.bookmark.jsp[plusone]=/html/taglib/ui/social_bookmark/pluso
    ne.jsp
social.bookmark.jsp[twitter]=/html/taglib/ui/social_bookmark/twitt
    er.jsp
```

As shown in the preceding code, the `social.bookmark.types` property specifies the types of social bookmarks, whereas the `social.bookmark.jsp[facebook]`, `social.bookmark.jsp[plusone]`, and `social.bookmark.jsp[twitter]` properties specify the URL and title for a given bookmark using the type as a parameter. You can override these properties in `portal-ext.properties`.

Adding comments

As stated, being an administrator, you created an entry called `Liferay Portal Best Open Source Portal`. Being a user of the enterprise Palm Tree Publications, "Lotti Stein" wants to review the entry and add a comment to say `Nice Post!`. Let's do it by following the next set of steps:

1. Log in as "Lotti Stein" and navigate to the Blog's page.

2. Locate an entry and click on the entry by title, for example, `Liferay Portal Best Open Source Portal`.

3. Click on the **Comments** link under the content of the Blog entry.

4. Under the **Comments** tab, click on the **Be the first** or **Add Comment** link if you want to add a new comment.

5. Input text, for example, `Nice Post!`.

6. Check in the checkbox **subscribe me**. It will subscribe you to the mail notification if anyone replies to your comments.

7. Click on the **Reply** button to save the input.

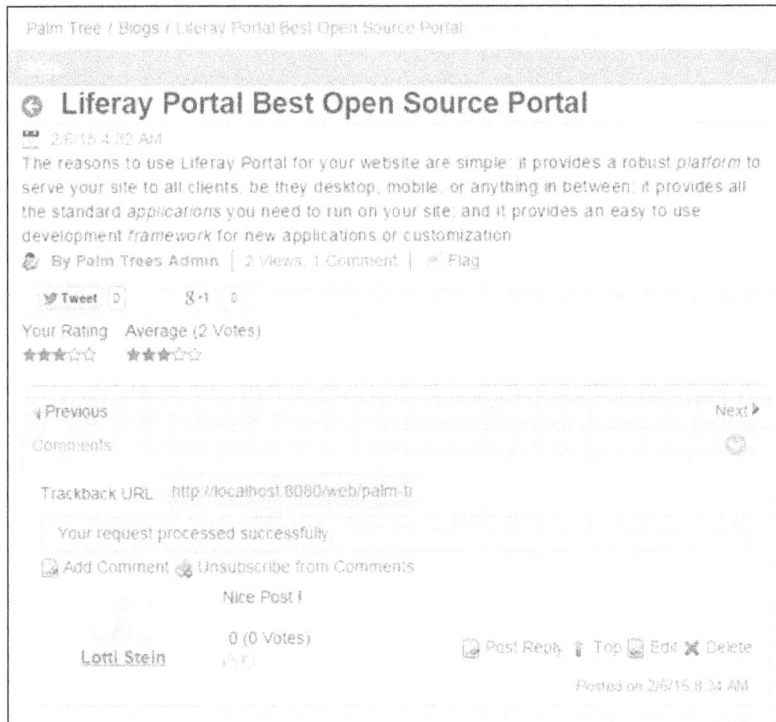

Figure 6.13: Blog comments by a user

As a normal user or a guest user, you can view comments from "Lotti Stein" for the entry Liferay Portal Best Open Source Portal if you have proper permissions, as shown in the following screenshot.

Other users can also comment with very simple steps:

1. Click on the title of this entry.

2. Click on the **Comments** link under the content of the Blog entry.

3. Under the **Comments** tab, click on **Add Comment** or click on the **Post Reply** link.

In addition, you can reply to a comment. You can locate the comment that you want to reply to first, and then click on the **Post Reply** icon in the bottom-left corner of the comment. Enter the comments and then click on the **Reply** button to save the inputs, or click on the **Cancel** button to cancel the changes.

Furthermore, you can edit a comment by simply clicking on the **Edit** icon in the bottom-left corner of the comment, and you will be able to change the body and click on the **Publish** button to save the changes or the **Cancel** button to cancel the changes.

Moreover, you can delete a comment if you have proper permissions. First, click on the **Delete** icon, and in the bottom-left corner of the comment, a message will appear that asks whether you want to delete this and tells you to click on **OK** to confirm the deletion or on **Cancel** to cancel the deletion.

> Note that only the current comment has been deleted by the following action. The low-level comments will link to the parent comment of the current comment.

Finally, in order to go to the top of the comments, simply click on the **Top** button in the bottom-right corner of any comment.

Understanding comment settings

Why does each entry have comments? There is a taglib called `<liferay-ui:discussion>` that allows us to comment on any type of content or pages in any portlet. If you are interested in more details, you can also find the implementation of comments `<liferay-ui:discussion>` at `$PORTAL_ROOT_HOME/html/taglib/ui/discussion/page.jsp`.

Meanwhile, you could find the UI taglib `<liferay-ui:discussion>` at `$PORTAL_ROOT_HOME/html/portlet/blogs/view_entry.jsp`. All you need is `Class-Name`, `Primary-Key`, `user-Id`, `subject`, and other keywords of any object to associate it with comments.

Assigning permissions

We used the default settings for the Blogs portlet on the **Blogs** page. When you're logged in as a Palm Tree administrator, you can manage blogs. As you know, the user "Lotti Stein" is a member of Palm Tree. When Lotti logs in, she can see that there is no **Add Entry** button in the Blogs portlet. Furthermore, Lotti can see the entry `Liferay Portal Best Open Source Portal` without any action icons (such as Edit, Permissions, and Move to the Recycle Bin).

What's happening? This is something related to permissions. The permission for Blogs can be assigned under **Site Administration**. Under **Site Administration | Content | Blogs**, another one is **Site Administration | Application | Blogs**. Moreover, each has a different set of permission levels.

To set the permission entitlements for blogs, portal administrators need to define permissions in roles. Under the **User** section, click on **Roles** in **Control Panel** and locate **MB Topic Admin**. Select **define permissions** from the **Action** button beside **MB Topic Admin**. Search for Blogs. You will get the entitlement settings for blogs:

- **Site Administration | Content | Blogs**: General Permissions, Resource Permissions (Blog Entries, Blogs Entry)
- **Site Administration | Application | Blogs**: Application Permissions, Resource Permissions (Blog Entries, Blogs Entry)

Let's discuss each of them one by one in detail.

Blog entries

For permission entitlements, that is, **Add Entry**, **Permissions**, and **Subscribe**, for Blog Entries, refer the following screenshot:

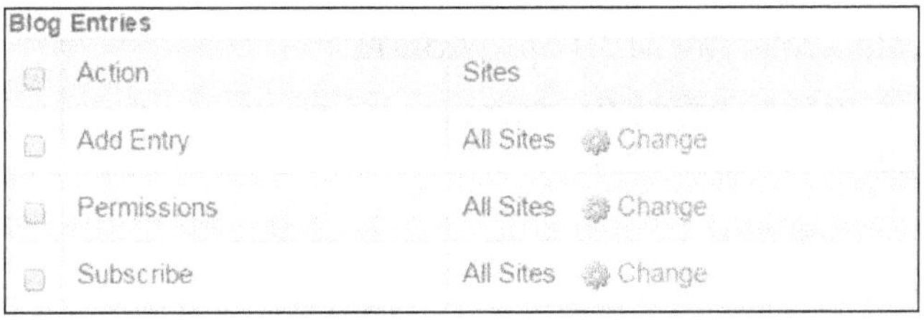

Figure 6.14: Site content permission on the blog entries

Permissions on Blog Entries

The preceding screenshot (*Figure 6.14*) shows permissions on **Blog Entries**. The **MB Topic Admin** role can be set up for all permissions: **Add Entry**, **Permissions**, and **Subscribe**, whereas the role site member doesn't have this capability.

Action	Description
Add Entry	This provides the ability to add an entry to the Blogs portlet
Permissions	This provides the ability to set permissions on the Blogs portlet
Subscribe	This provides the ability to subscribe to the Blogs portlet

Obviously, as a member of the Palm Tree site, "Lotti Stein" doesn't have the permission to add an entry on blogs by default. Note that the **Add Entry** permission is scoped to a group or portal instance. If you want, the user "Lotti Stein" can have the ability to add an entry for blogs to all the sites where Lotti is a member with **MB Topic Admin**. Let's follow this simple set of steps—assigning the **Add Entry** permission action:

1. Log in as the portal administrator (since **Roles** are only accessible by the Portal administrator).

2. Click on **Roles** under the category **Users** of **Control Panel** first.

3. Then, locate a role, say **MB Topic Admin**.

4. Then, click on the **Define Permissions** icon from the **Actions** menu on the right-hand side of the role. Now, search for blogs.

5. Click on the **Content | Blogs** link and check the **Add Entry** checkbox.

6. Click on the **Save** button.

As shown in the preceding steps, the user "Lotti Stein" will get access rights to use the **Add Entry** action via the **MB Topic Admin** role. As the **MB Topic Admin** role is a regular role, the user "Lotti Stein" will get access rights for **Add Entry** scoped to the current portal instance. If the role is an organization or site role, then the user "Lotti Stein" gets access rights on **Add Entry** scoped to the organization or site.

Permissions on Blogs Entry

The following screenshot show the permissions on **Blogs Entry**; this permission is especially for control on the blog entry and discussions on the blogs entry. The role **MB Topic Admin** is able set up permissions, namely **Add Discussion**, **Delete**, **Delete Discussion**, **Permission**, **Update**, **Update Discussion**, and **View**. On the other hand, the roles Guest and site member cannot set up permissions with **View** and **Add Discussion**. Refer to the following screenshot for Blogs Entry entitlements.

Figure 6.15: Site content permission on blog entries

Let's add the **Add Discussion**, **Delete Discussion**, **Update**, **Update Discussion** and **View** permissions to **MB Topic Admin** so that "Lotti Stein" will have the permission.

Follow these steps to set the permissions:

1. In **Define Permissions** of the role "**MB Topic Admin**", search for blogs.
2. Click on the **Site Content | Blogs** link and check the checkbox **Add Discussion**, **Delete Discussion**, **Update**, **Update Discussion**, and **View** under **Blogs Entry**.
3. Click on the **Save** button.

Now, "Lotti Stein" will be able to use **Add Discussion**, **Delete Discussion**, **Update**, **Update Discussion**, and **View** for the blog entry. If you notice, "Lotti" can update comments posted by other users.

Blogs general permissions

If any role needs access to the Blogs portlet inside the **Site Administration** panel, then the **Access in Site Administration** setting needs to be done.

The **Access in Site Administration** permission action represents the ability to access the Blogs portlet in the **Site Administration** panel. By default, the user "Lotti Stein" doesn't have the ability to access the Blogs portlet in the **Site Administration** panel. Suppose that you want the user "Lotti Stein" to have the ability to access the Blogs portlet in the **Site Administration** panel, how would you implement it? The following is an example of assigning the **Access in Site Administration** permission action; refer to the following screenshot:

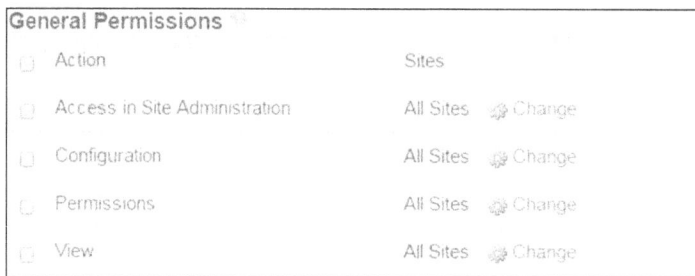

Figure 6.16: General permissions on blogs

1. In **Define Permissions** of the **MB Topic Admin** role, search for blogs.
2. Click on the **Content | Blogs** link, check **Access in Site Administration**, and **View from** checkboxes under **General Permissions**.
3. Click on the **Save** button.

Application permissions

If permission entitlements for the Blogs application/portlet, as shown in the following screenshot are applied to **Add to Page**, they will allow the user to add the Blogs portlet on the page:

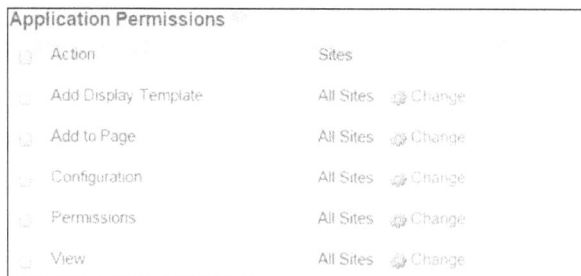

Figure 6.17: Site application permissions on blogs

Site application permissions affect the application as a whole. So, using our blogs example, application permission might define who can add the Blogs portlet to a page. You can provide the permission to the **MB Topic Admin** member or either organization or site admin.

Using blogs effectively

Generally speaking, a **blog** (short for web-log) is personal online content that is frequently updated for general public consumption. Blogs are a series of entries posted to a single page in reverse-chronological order. Generally, they represent the author's personality or reflect the purpose to host the blog on the website.

The author of a blog is called a blogger. Bloggers can syndicate their blog content to subscribers using RSS. In general, blogs are frequent chronological publications of personal thoughts and web links.

Exploring the Blogs portlet

The Blogs portlet can help you to publish information on the Web easily. It helps in the rapid development of your site and, furthermore, gives your enterprise a platform to easily share information among different departments.

The Blogs portlet allows users of the enterprise to manage web-log entries in a portal page. You can create, edit, and delete web-log entries and change permissions on entries. In addition, it provides a simplified interface to create web-logs and publish them as RSS feeds.

The following *Figure 6.18* depicts the blog structure overview. Blogs are made up of a set of entries and each entry can have many comments. In turn, each entry can have many ratings. Of course, users can rate an entry only once. Moreover, each entry enables flags, allowing users to flag content as inappropriate, and enables the capability of trackbacks. In addition, an entry can have many tags and/or categories.

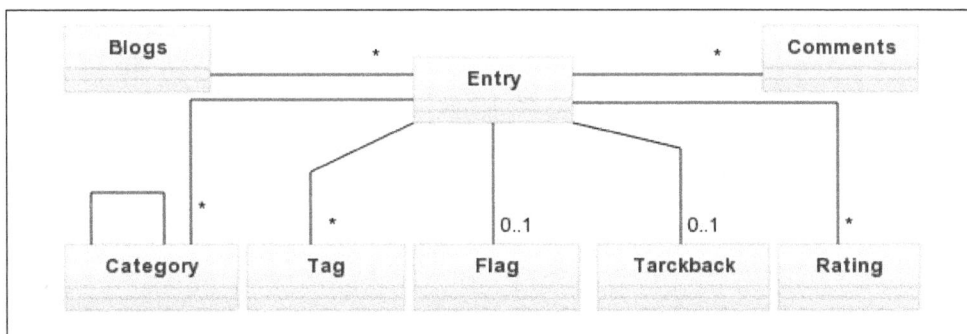

Figure 6.18: The blog structure overview

Configuring the Blogs portlet

As you can see, the Blogs portlet is highly configurable. To configure blogs, including RSS feeds and e-mail settings, click on the **Gear** (icon) | **Configuration** link in the top-right corner of the Blogs portlet. The subtab of the **Setup** tab have the following tabs with the names **Display Setting**, **Email from**, **Entry Added Email**, **Entry Updated Email**, and **RSS**.

As shown in the following screenshot, you can set the display styles used to display settings for blogs. For regular pages, you can set the following items:

- **Maximum Items to Display**: This is the number of displayed blog entries.

- **Display Template**: This determines the visibility of the display of content to end users. It has settings with **Full Content**, **Abstract**, or **Title**. Also, you can configure **Application Display Template** (**ADT**). We will discuss ADT more in the coming chapters.

- **Enable Flags**: This is a checkbox to enable flags on blog entries.

- **Enable Related Assets**: This is a checkbox to enable related assets.

- **Enable Ratings**: This is a checkbox to enable ratings on blog entries.

- **Enable Comments**: This is a checkbox to enable comments on blog entries.

- **Enable Comment Ratings**: This is a checkbox to enable ratings on comments.

- **Enable Social Bookmarks**: This is a checkbox to enable social bookmarks:

    ○ **Display Style**: Social bookmarks display style—**Horizontal** or **Vertical**.

    ○ **Display Position**: This displays the social bookmark's position—**Top** or **Bottom**.

    ○ **Social Bookmarks**: There are three checkboxes for different social media, such as Twitter, Facebook, and Google+.

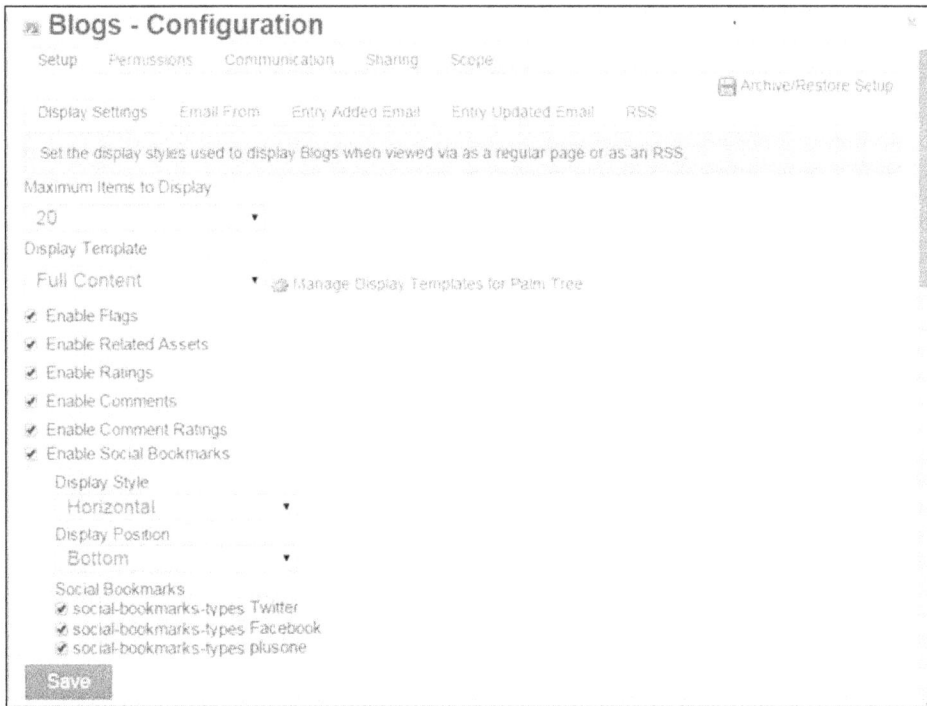

Figure 6.19: Blog configuration setup

Email From allows the setting of the name and the e-mail address for the blog to send messages.

Entry Added Email allows the setting of the e-mail body for the message to be sent to the user for the blog that has been added. You can customize the message as per your requirement.

Entry Updated Email allows the setting of the e-mail body for the message to be sent to the user for the blog that has been updated. You can customize the message as per your requirement.

RSS allows the setting for the RSS feed.

Setting the properties of the Blogs portlet

The portal sets the following properties in `portal.properties` by default:

```
blogs.email.from.name=
blogs.email.from.address=
blogs.email.entry.added.enabled=true
blogs.page.abstract.length=400
blogs.rss.abstract.length=200
blogs.ping.google.enabled=true
blogs.entry.comments.enabled=true
```

As shown in the preceding code, you can configure the e-mail from name and e-mail from address settings via the properties `blogs.email.from.name` and `blogs.email.from.address` respectively. Even the e-mail notification settings are done via the property `blogs.email.entry.added.enabled`. The default abstract length of the page is set to `400`, and the default abstract length of RSS is set to `200`.

You can set the property `blogs.ping.google.enabled` to `true` in order to enable pinging Google on new and updated blog entries. You can also set the property `blogs.entry.comments.enabled` to `true` to enable comments for blog entries. Of course, you can override these properties according to your own requirements in `portal-ext.properties`.

Asset Renderer Framework, search, indexing, and social activity

The framework via the `asset-renderer-factory` tag, called **Asset Renderer Framework**, will allow the registering of custom asset types so that generic portlets, such as the Asset Publisher portlet, can be used to publish them. This is the reason that we can publish blog entries through the Asset Publisher portlet. In fact, the Blogs portlet supports the Asset Renderer Framework in `$PORTAL_ROOT_HOME/WEB-INF/ liferay-portlet.xml` as follows:

```
<indexer-class>
  com.liferay.portlet.blogs.util.BlogsIndexer
</indexer-class>
<open-search-class>
  com.liferay.portlet.blogs.util.BlogsOpenSearchImpl
</open-search-class>
<social-activity-interpreter-class>
  com.liferay.portlet.blogs.social.BlogsActivityInterpreter
</social-activity-interpreter-class>
<asset-renderer-factory>
  com.liferay.portlet.blogs.asset.BlogsEntryAssetRendererFactory
</asset-renderer-factory>
```

As shown in the preceding code, besides the `asset-renderer-factory` tag, the portlet also specifies the `indexer-class`, `open-search-class`, and `social-activity-interpreter-class` tags. The `social-activity-interpreter-class` tag adds social activity tracking to a portlet, and recorded social activities will appear on the Activities portlet.

Meanwhile, the `indexer-class` tag value is called to create or update a search index for the Blogs portlet, whereas the `open-search-class` tag is called to get search results in the Open-Search standard.

Understanding tags and categories

As you can see, when displaying an entry, a set of categories and tags of the current entry are also displayed next to the flag. Why? There are taglibs called `<liferay-ui:asset-categories-summary>` and `<liferay-ui:asset-tags-summary>` that allow us to tag any type of content or pages in any portlet. Of course, you can find UI taglibs `<liferay-ui:asset-categories-summary>` and `<liferay-ui:asset-tags-summary>` in `$PORTAL_ROOT_HOME/html/portlet/blogs/view_entry_content.jsp`. All you need is `Class-Name`, `Primary-Key`, and `portlet-URL` of any object to associate it with tags and categories as follows:

```
<span class="entry-categories">
  <liferay-ui:asset-categories-summary className="<%=
    BlogsEntry.class.getName() %>" classPK="<%= entry.getEntryId()
    %>"
  portletURL="<%= renderResponse.createRenderURL() %>"/>
</span>

<span class="entry-tags">
  <liferay-ui:asset-tags-summary className="<%= BlogsEntry.
    class.getName() %>"
  classPK="<%= entry.getEntryId() %>"
  portletURL="<%= renderResponse.createRenderURL() %>"/>
</span>
```

As you can see, you can tag blog entries with tags and categories. The portal has specified the following code in `$PORTAL_ROOT_HOME/html/portlet/blogs/edit_entry.jsp`:

```
<aui:input name="categories" type="assetCategories" />
<aui:input name="tags" type="assetTags" />
```

As shown in the preceding code, it uses the tag `<aui:input>` with the types `assetTags` and `assetCategories`. Of course, you can find similar code for Message Boards messages, Wiki articles, and so on.

Blogs in scope

Considering the pattern `Portal-Site-Page-Content`, entries of the blogs portlet can be scoped into a site, for example, all pages, including both private and public pages, by default. In addition, blog entries can be scoped into an individual page—a set of data isolated from the other data of the same portlet.

For instance, when the Blogs portlet is added to a page, for example, *blogs* of the Palm Tree site public page, it will use the default scope to the site. If you add the Blogs portlet to a second page, say *welcome*, it will show the same data as that of the previous page. This means that the Blogs portlet is scoped into the Palm Tree when it is added to any page of the same site. Fortunately, you are able to switch the content of the Blogs portlet to a different site. How can you achieve this? The following is an example:

1. Click on **Admin** | **content** and the site administration panel will open.
2. Locate **Blogs** under the category content of the site administration panel and click on Blogs.
3. Switch sites by selecting different sites from the drop-down menu from the dock bar. You will notice blog entries of different sites.

The Blogs portlet can be scoped into a page. How do we scope the Blogs portlet to a page? The following is an example:

1. Locate a page, say **Blogs**, and go to the Blogs portlet in the current page.
2. Go to **Gear** (icon) | **Configuration** of the Blogs portlet.
3. Click on the **Scope** tab.
4. Choose **Blogs** from the **Scope** select menu and click on the **Save** button.

How do you customize the scope feature? The portal has default settings for the Blogs portlet in `$PORTAL_ROOT_HOME/WEB-INF/liferay-portlet.xml` as follows:

```
<scopeable>true</scopeable>
```

The preceding code shows that the Blogs portlet is scopeable—giving it the capability to use the **Gear** (icon) | **Configuration** | **Scope** tab and change the scope from default to the current site.

Friendly URLs

When you view blog entries, you will see URLs, such as `/web/palm-tree/ blogs/-/ blogs/11201` and `/web/palm-tree/blogs/-/blogs/11214`. Similarly, when you view RSS feeds, you will see URLs, such as `/web/palm-tree/blogs/-/blogs/ rss`. These are short, friendly URLs. In fact, the Blogs portlet supports friendly URL mapping in `$PORTAL_ROOT_HOME/WEB-INF/liferay-portlet.xml` as follows:

```
<friendly-url-mapper-class>
   com.liferay.portal.kernel.portlet.DefaultFriendlyURLMapper
</friendly-url-mapper-class>
```

As shown in the preceding code, the content inside a portlet will use a friendly URL via the `friendly-url-mapper-class` tag.

Blogs in communication

There is a tab called **Communication** under **More | Configuration** in the Blogs portlet, and shared parameters can be mapped into `categoryId`, `resetCur`, and `tag` because the portlet has the following configuration in `$PORTAL_ROOT_HOME/WEB-INF/ portlet-custom.xml`:

```
<supported-public-render-parameter>categoryId</supported-public-
   render-parameter>
<supported-public-render-parameter>resetCur</supported-public-
   render-parameter>
<supported-public-render-parameter>tag</supported-public-render-
   parameter>
```

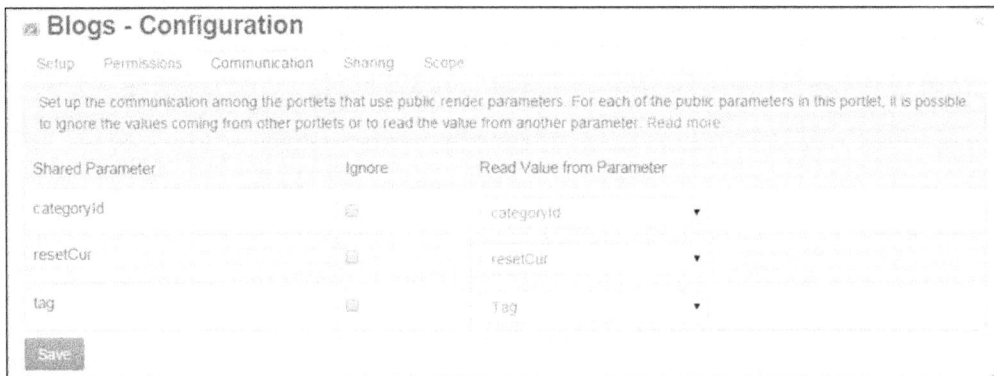

Figure 6.20: Blog setup for communication

As shown in the preceding code, there are three parameters, namely `categoryId`, `resetCur`, and `tag`. Of course, you can set mapping between these parameters or even ignore some or all of them in the **Gear** (icon) | **Configuration** | **Communication** tab. You can simply change the mapping and/or ignore it and click on the **Save** button when you are ready.

Publishing blogs

As stated earlier, we discussed how to create entries in order to let small teams work on specific projects and share files and blogs about the project process. As a user at the enterprise Palm Tree Publication, you may have created a lot of entries, which will be needed to show a list of the latest users from a given department and the latest posts for a given department too.

The Recent Bloggers portlet

The Recent Bloggers portlet (portlet ID `114`) shows a list of the latest users who have posted a blog entry. In practice, you may ask the question *Do you want to show a list of the last users from the Editorial department in the Palm Tree site?* The Recent Bloggers portlet would be useful to show a list of the latest users who have posted a blog entry. Let's do it by following these steps:

1. Navigate to the **Blogs** page.
2. Go to **Add** | **Applications** under the dock bar menu and add the **Recent Bloggers** portlet to the **Blogs** page.

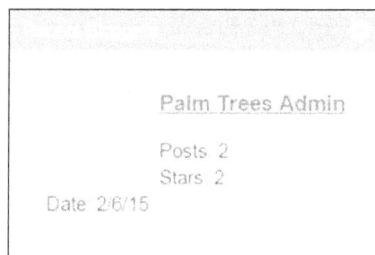

Palm Trees Admin

Posts 2
Stars 2
Date 2/6/15

Figure 6.21: Recent bloggers

You can do the configuration for display settings and a recent blogger in the Palm Tree site from a different organization. Let's do it:

1. Click on **Gear** (icon) | **Configuration** | **Setup** of the portlet.
2. Choose **Select Method** from **Users** and **Scope** using the **Users** default value.
3. Select an organization, for example, **Editorial Department**, using the default value in this example.

4. Select the display style, for example, **User Name and Image**, using the default settings.

5. Select **Maximum Bloggers to Display**, in this case, `10`.

6. Click on the **Save** button when you are ready.

Of course, you can select other organizations, for example, **IT Department**. The Recent Bloggers portlet will show a list of the latest users from the **IT Department** in the Palm Tree site. You can also remove the organization if required. In this case, the portlet will show a list of the latest users from any of the departments in the Palm Tree site.

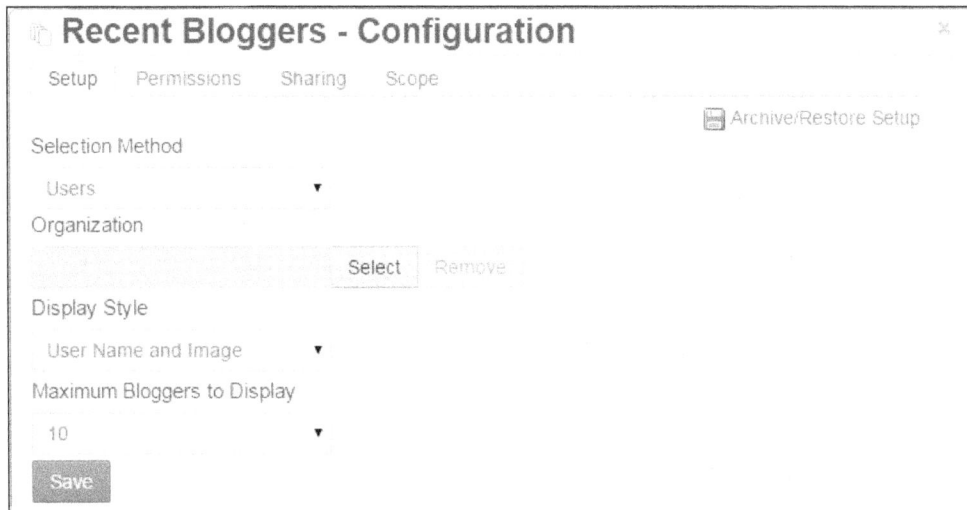

Figure 6.22: Recent bloggers configuration

As you can see, the Recent Bloggers portlet grabs blog entries from the current portal instance or by specific organizations. As shown in the previous screenshot, the Recent Bloggers portlet is configurable. You can configure it with the following items:

- **Selection Method**: **Users** or **Scope**
- **Organization**: Select or remove organizations when users are selected
- **Display Style**: **User Name and Image** and **User Name**
- **Maximum Bloggers to Display**: Number of bloggers

In a word, the Recent Bloggers portlet allows us to show a list of the latest users of the portal instance who have written a blog entry.

Settings for the Recent Bloggers portlet

As you can see, the Recent Bloggers portlet is configurable and scopeable. Why? The portal has default settings for the Recent Bloggers portlet in `$PORTAL_ ROOT_HOME/WEB-INF/liferay-portlet.xml` as follows:

```
<configuration-action-class>
  com.liferay.portal.kernel.portlet.DefaultConfigurationAction
</configuration-action-class>
<scopeable>true</scopeable>
```

The preceding code shows that the Recent Bloggers portlet is *scopeable* — it has the capability to use the **More | Configuration | Scope** tab and the ability to change the scope from default (current group) to the current page. The Recent Bloggers portlet is configurable with the `configuration-action-class` tag, which allows users to configure the portlet at runtime.

In addition, the look and feel of the portlet can be changed in the theme. Therefore, you can change the theme as you want to. Furthermore, you can change the view of the portlet directly at `$PORTAL_ROOT_HOME/html/portlet/recent_bloggers/view.jsp`.

For example, you can configure the portlet by selecting a display style from either of the two options, **User Name and Image** and **User Name**. In the previous file, you only have permission to update and set the display style as image.

The Blogs Aggregator portlet

The Blogs Aggregator portlet (portlet ID 115) grabs blog entries from the entire portal or by specific organizations. Do you want to show the latest posts from the Editorial department in the Palm Tree site? Let's do it by following these steps:

1. Add the **Blogs Aggregator** portlet to the **Blogs** page from the dock bar.

2. Click on **Gear** (icon) | **Configuration** | **Setup**.

3. From the **Select Method** menu, choose from the **Users** and **Scope** options; use the default value **Users**.

4. Select an organization, for example, **Editorial Department**, using default settings.

5. Select display styles, such as **Abstract**. Other display styles are available, such as **Body and Image**, **Body**, **Abstract without Title**, **Quote**, **Quote without Title**, and **Title**. Use the default settings.

6. Choose **Maximum Items to Display**, say 20.

7. Select the **Enable RSS Subscription** checkbox.

8. Click on the **Save** button when you are ready.

The following screenshot shows the Blogs Aggregator configuration screen:

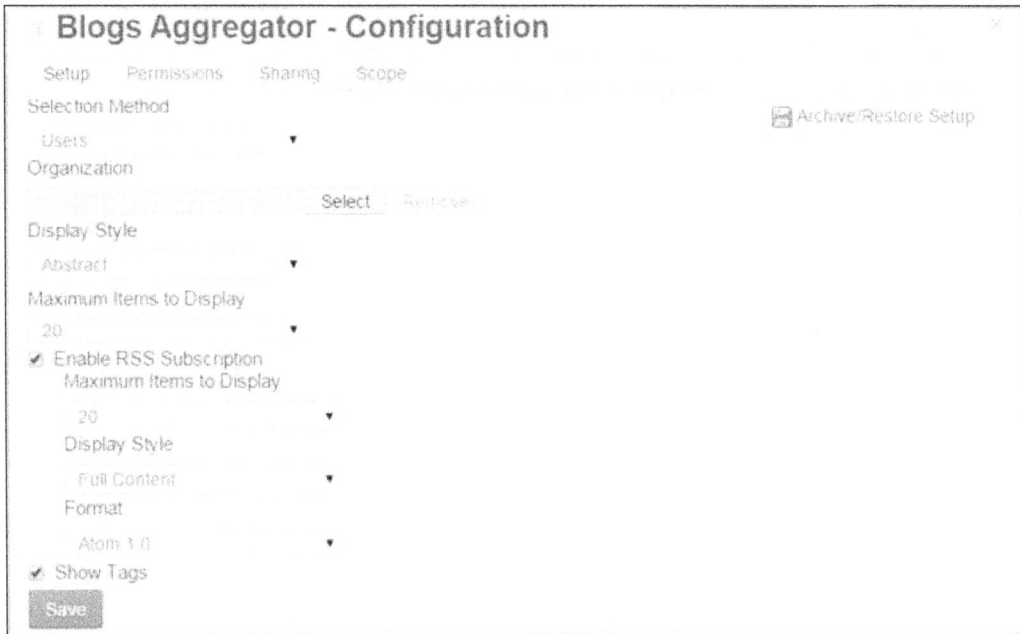

Figure 6.23: Blogs Aggregator configuration

Of course, you can select other organizations, for example, IT department. The Blogs Aggregator portlet will show the latest entries from all the entries of the IT department in the Palm Tree site. Also, you can remove the organization if required and select **Scope** as the value of **Select Method**. In this case, the Blogs Aggregator portlet will show the latest entries from all the entries of any department in a group, such as the Palm Tree site.

As you can see, the Blogs Aggregator portlet grabs blog entries from the current portal instance or from a specific organization. As shown in the preceding screenshot, the Blogs Aggregator portlet is configurable, and you can configure it using the following items:

- **Selection Method**: **Users** or **Scope**
- **Organization**: This is used to select or remove organizations when users are selected; this aggregates blogs from only specific organizations

- **Display Style**: **Body and Image**, **Body**, **Abstract**, **Abstract without Title**, **Quote**, **Quote without Title**, and **Title**

- **Maximum Items to Display**: This is the number of blogs

- **Enable RSS Subscription**: This is a checkbox that allows users to subscribe using RSS

In general, the Blogs Aggregator portlet shows the latest posts from all the entries of any department in a group, such as the Palm Tree site, which specifies the blogs that should be aggregated. It specifies a set of display styles and, moreover, it has the ability to expose an aggregated RSS feed.

What's happening?

Similar to the Recent Bloggers portlet, the Blogs Aggregator portlet is `configurable` and `scopeable`.

In addition, all the look and feel of the portlet can be changed in the theme. Therefore, you can change the theme as you want. Furthermore, you can change the view of the portlet directly at `$PORTAL_ROOT_HOME/html/portlet/ blogs_aggregator/view_entry_content.jsp`.

Exploring Social Networking

Social networking became a new trend in web portals. It allows us to be connected with our loved ones, family, friends, and colleagues. There are many ways by which individuals can be connected with other individuals.

Nowadays in the organization portal, social networking plays an important role, which leverages their employees to connect with each other through social interaction, such as chat, personalized pages, adding friends, viewing friends' activities, and much more.

Liferay Portal 6.2 provides you with lots of features for social activities. Let's discuss each of them in detail.

In Liferay, as we know, all users have their private and public pages. Now, Liferay provides many portlets for social interaction by which you can achieve social interaction among users with respect to organization and site permissions.

Let's try to design a social interaction among the users/employees of the Palm Tree organization. First, you need to install the Social Networking portlet from Marketplace. Liferay provides a new feature to install any application from one place called Marketplace. It's a kind of hub for all the community edition and enterprise edition portlets.

Installing the Social Networking portlet

Here, in this section, you will see how to install portlets from Marketplace:

1. Log in as the portal admin.

2. Navigate to **Admin | Control Panel**, click on **Apps**, and then click on **Store**.

3. Log in with Liferay site credentials and the **Market Place** page will load.

4. Search for **Social Networking CE**, set the **Communication** category, and select the Portal version (which is run currently). Keep the price blank. Finally, click on the **Search** button.

5. The **Social Networking CE** app will be listed. Click on **Social Networking CE**; you will be redirected to a different page, from where you can purchase it. Click on the **Free** button, which will again redirect you to another page called **Purchase**. Here, select the project or select for personal use only; then, check the agreement checkbox. Finally, click on the **Purchase** button.

6. Once you purchase, it will be available inside the **Purchased** link under **Marketplace**.

7. Now, you can **Install** the particular app.

Follow this screenshot for **Social Networking CE**:

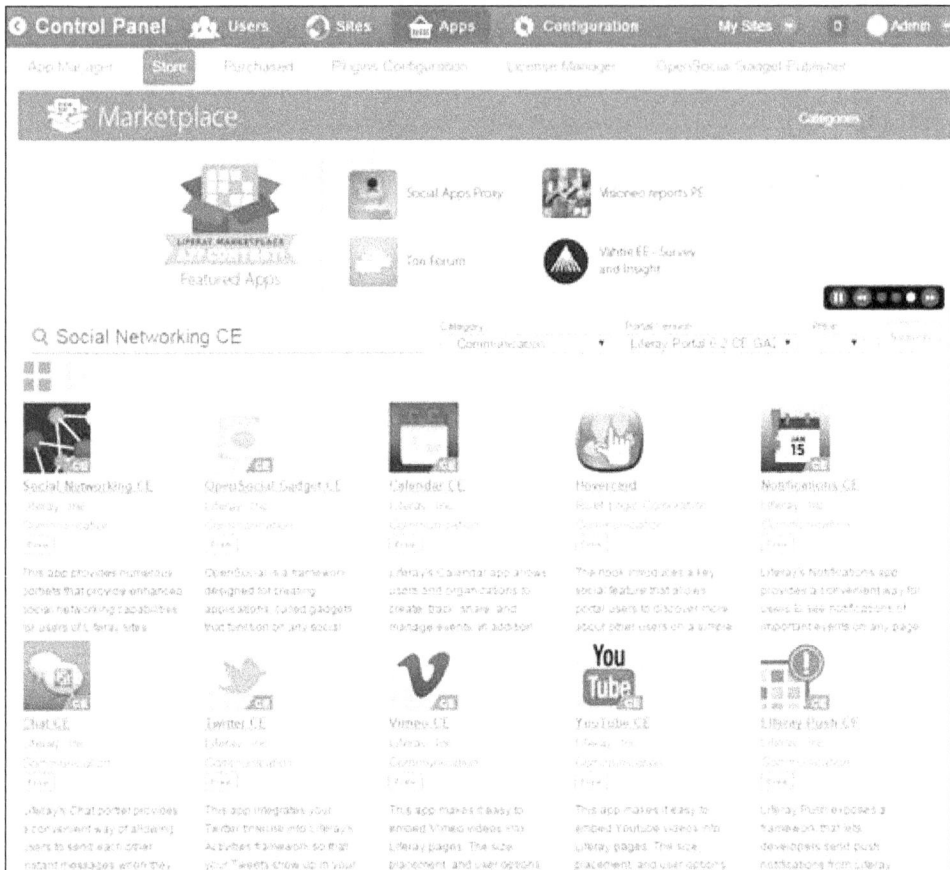

Figure 6:24: The Marketplace store

> Note that Marketplace works on the Internet. If you are not connected to the Internet, you will get an error message. So, for the store and the purchase, we need to be connected to the Internet. Most of the apps with Community Edition (CE) and Enterprise Edition (EE) are free to purchase.

The Members portlet provides you with a list of the members in the particular organization. It helps all the users to know who are associated with the current organization. Refer to the following screenshot for detailed understanding.

Note that if the users are only members of the site and not the organization, then the Member portlet will not display those users.

You can do the setting for the permission in the configuration option and place the portlet in the home page of the site. The following screenshot shows the Members portlet:

Figure 6.25: The Members portlet

The Activities portlet is the one that provides you with the activity/event list. It captures all the activities of the users on the portal, including the events, documents uploaded, and comments on blogs and displays it on the Activities portlet, as shown in the following screenshot. It generally focuses on the entire portal.

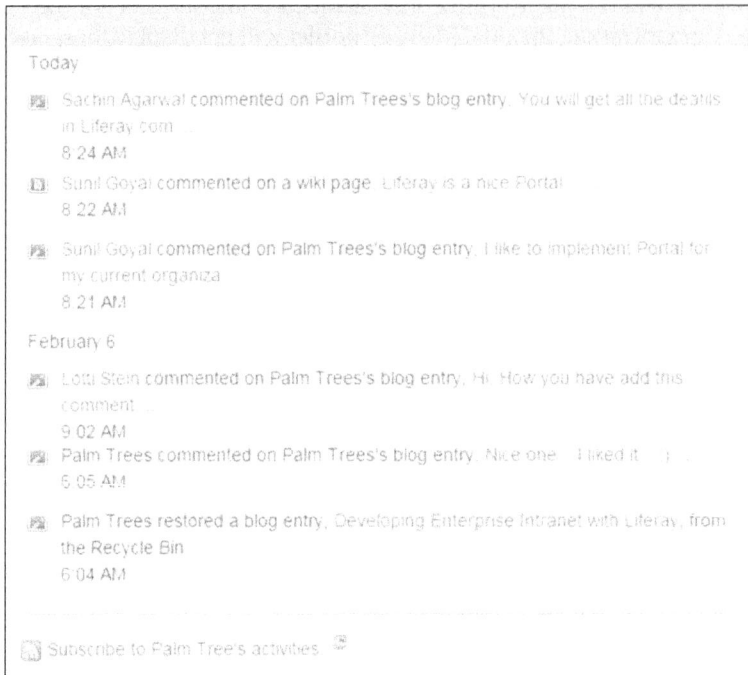

Figure 6.26: The Activities portlet

In the preceding screenshot, you can see that Sachin has created the latest comment on the blogs. The comments are displayed using the activities portlet with tags provided to it.

The Activities portlet is a kind of news feed similar to the one on Facebook, and it also allows you to have an RSS URL to use on external sites.

In the configuration option, you can set the limit on the display list by setting the value for **Maximum Activities to Display**. It will restrict the list to be displayed on the portlet. You will also be able to set up the permissions too.

The Members Activities portlet acts as a feed similar to the one on the Activities portlet, but it provides a more detailed member activities list of a particular site, as shown in the following screenshot:

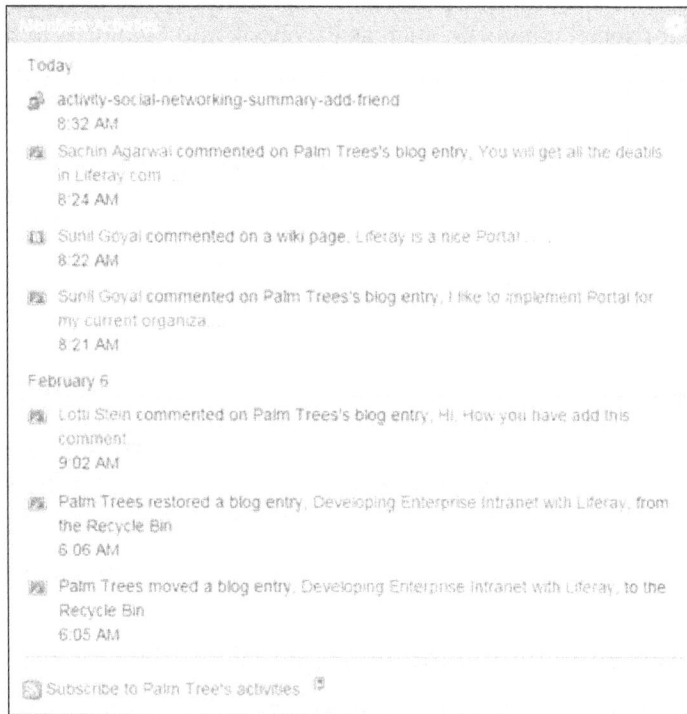

Figure 6.27: Member's activities

In the preceding screenshot, you can see that the site members' activities have been listed, for example, Sunil and Sachin have become friends. So, it will track all the activities done on the site.

There is one more Activities portlet, named Friends Activities portlet, which you can place in the users' public pages and track your friends' activities.

Managing a personal page with the Social Networking portlet

Liferay provides you with unique portlets, while allowing you to create user personal pages for social networks, such as Facebook and Google+. In the user's personal page, you can place few a portlets, as shown in the screenshot (*Figure 6.28*), such as **Summary**, **Request**, **Friends**, **Wall**, **Page Comments**, and **Friends' Activities**.

In the following screenshot, you can see Sunil Goyal's personal page (My Profile), where the Summary portlet provides the user's information with the user's full name, avatar (image), job title, about me, and the link to edit profile. **Edit Profile** allows users to edit **Job Title** and add **About Me** content. Even you can find the link for **My Account** inside the **Edit Profile** page from where you can change the user's details, such as password, e-mail address, and much more.

The Requests portlet allows you to get requests from friends, as shown in the following screenshot, where Rajeeva has requested for friendship with Sunil. Now the Request portlet shows the two options **Confirm** and **Ignore**. **Confirm** will add Rajeeva as a friend in Sunil's Friends portlet, while **Ignore** will reject the request.

The Friends portlet lists all the friends of users with the link to the profile. Once Sunil confirms Rajeeva as a friend, Rajeeva will be listed in the Friends portlet in the same way that Sachin was.

The Wall portlet allows the posting of the status on the user's page (wall). It allows users and their friends to put the status.

The Page Comments portlet allows users and their friends to comment on the status. You can subscribe to comments too.

The Friends Activities portlet lists all the activities done by his friends on the portal.

The following is the screenshot of the Social Networking site for individual users:

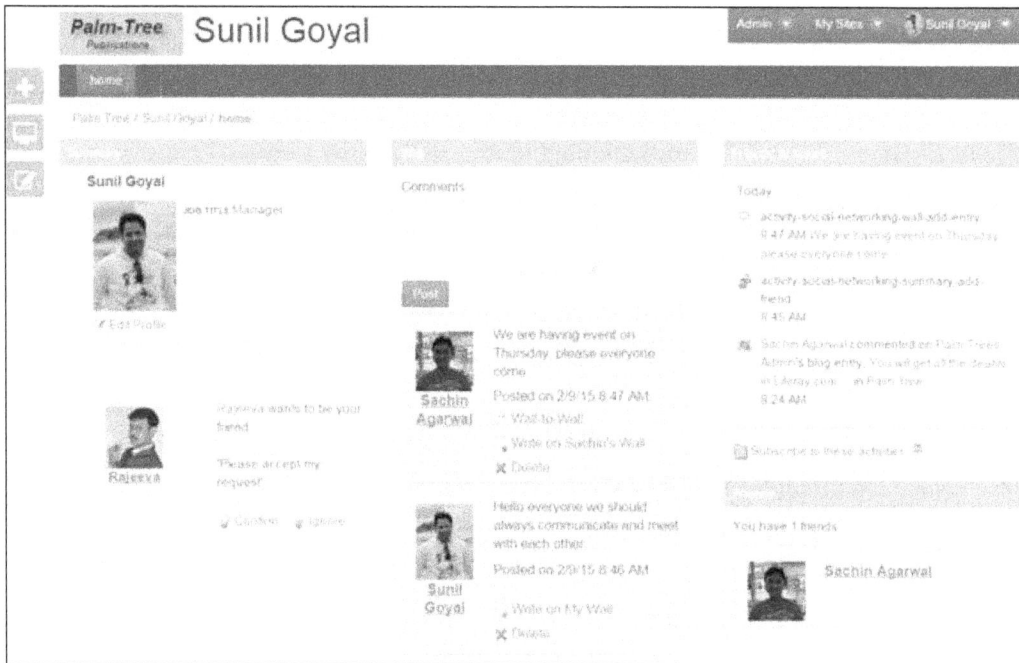

Figure 6.28: A user's personal page

You need to set up the portal for the user's personal page so that all the users have the same social networking features. To achieve this, the best way is to configure the portal in such a manner that pages with a specific portlet are automatically displayed for the personal page.

By using **User Groups**, we can get the portlets on the page so that all users have common features. Follow these steps to achieve this:

1. Create a user group first.
2. Assign the users to the group.
3. Then, create the pages by adding and arranging portlets on it.
4. Finally, map to the user's personal site.

You can do the setting for the User Groups site, where users can't modify pages and the administrator can change in the future. Using the portal settings, it is possible to set **Default User Associations** to have all users be members of a particular group while creating users.

In the User Groups template, you can enable propagation of changes from the site template, which allows managing the user's personal pages in a whole portal if the user is a member of that particular group.

The other way to achieve the same is by configuring portal properties. In the `portal-ext.properties` file, you can mention the default layout and portlets for the user's personal pages. This will be implemented in the user's entire personal page of the portal. **Default User Private Layouts** and **Default User Public Layouts** can be configured to set up the default template for the user's personal and private pages.

> Note that User Groups is the standard and easy way to create the personal page for the user.

Creating a template for Social Networking

Let's create a template with the name `Social Networking`, which we can map with User Groups:

1. Click on **Site Template** under the **Site** category of **Control Panel**.
2. Then, click on the **Add** button and enter a name for **New Site Template** in the **Name** input field (for example, **Social Networking**).
3. Enter the description of **Site Template**.
4. Leave the **Active** checkbox as default; uncheck **Allow Site Administrators to Modify the Pages Associated with This site Template**; by this, the administrator will not be able to modify the template.
5. Click on the **Save** button to save the input.

The following screenshot shows the Social Networking template creation.

Now, after you have created the site template, you need to manage pages for the particular template where you can place the portlets. Then, finally, you need to map the template with the user group and assign the users to that particular group so that all the users have the same personal or private pages.

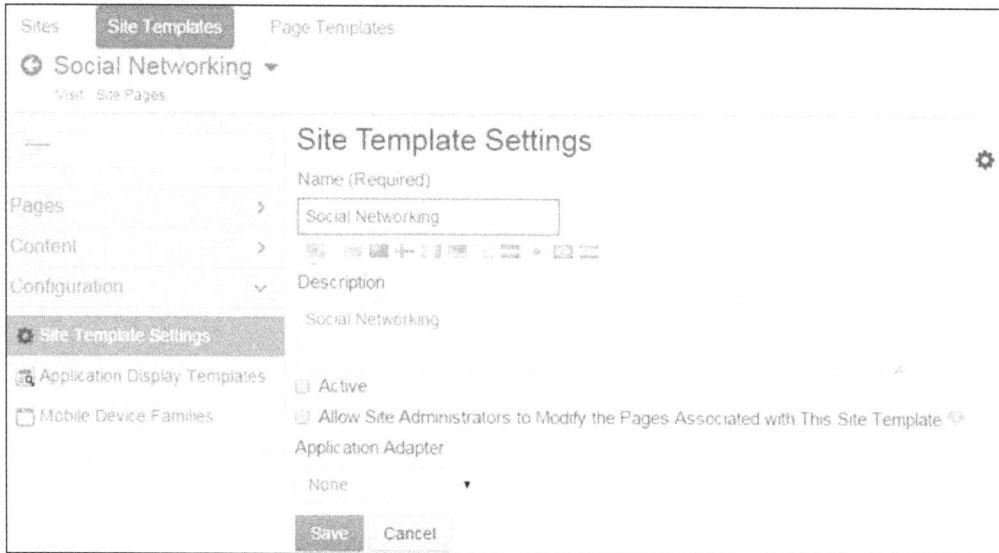

Figure 6.29: Site Templates

Now, let's create a page template to configure the portlets of a particular page for Social Networking:

1. Click on **Page Templates** under the **Site** category of **Control Panel**.
2. Then, click on the **Add** button and enter a name for the new page template in the **Name** input field (for example, Home).
3. Enter the description of the site template. Check the **Active** checkbox.
4. Click on the **Save** button to save the input.

You can use this page template for any page where you have placed the Social Networking portlet, which we have mentioned earlier.

After the creation of the page template, just click on **Edit** from the **Action** button and click on the configuration link, which will open a new window with the **Home** page.

Now, add the Social Networking portlet on the page; in other words, arrange the page as per *Figure 6.27*. The page template page will look somewhat similar to the following screenshot. Once it is mapped by any page, then all the portlets will be rendered properly.

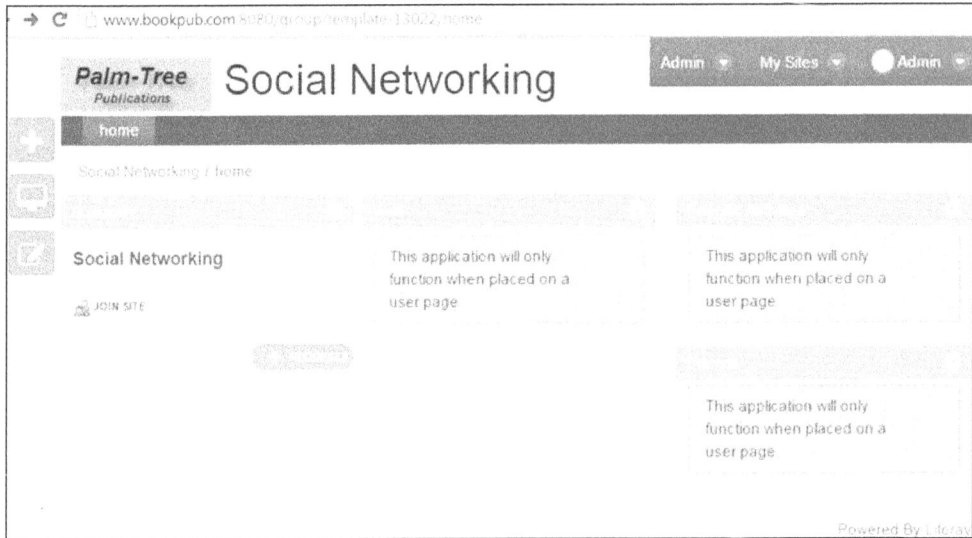

Figure 6.30: Page template for Social Networking

Once you've configured the page with the portlets, you just need to set the **Manage Pages** tab for Social Networking from the site templates. Let's do the settings:

1. Click on **Site Templates** under the **Portal** category of **Control Panel**.

2. It will list all **Site Templates**. Click on the **Action** button beside the **Social Networking Template** tab and select **Manage Pages**.

3. In **Manage Pages**, you'll able to manage the pages for the particular template. By default, the **Home** page is created under the parent page (pages).

> Note that you can directly place the Social Networking portlet under the **Home** page, which is already created by Liferay, or you can use the **Page Templates** feature to do so. **Page Templates** helps you to use the defined template for the page that has the proper design and placed portlets in it.

4. Let's use the **Page Templates** feature for this example. Delete the **Home** page, and create a new page by clicking on the **Add Child Page** button. You will get a popup to create a new **Child** page.

5. Fill the name, say Home, and select the template as **Home**, which you created earlier.

6. Click on the **Add Page** button.

Now, the page has been created, and your site template is mapped with the page template. So, if you modify or edit the page template, it will reflect everywhere you have used it.

Let's create a user group and select the public site template as a **Social Networking** group:

1. Click on **User Groups** under the **Users** category of **Control Panel**.

2. Then, click on the **Add** button. Enter a name for the new user group in the **Name** input field (for example, Social Networking).

3. Enter the description as Social Networking Group.

4. Enter the user group site details; for **Public Pages**, select **Social Networking Site**, and for **Private Pages**, select **Community Site**.

5. Check the **Enable propagation of changes from the site template** checkbox.

6. Finally, save it.

The members of this user group will have their public pages as the Social Networking page template. So, you have to assign the users to this group.

As mentioned earlier, you can configure the portal setting in such a way that whenever new users are created they will be assigned to the Social Networking user group.

Let's do the setting for the **Default Users Associations** tab:

1. Click on **Portal Settings** under the **Configuration** category of **Control Panel**.

2. Click on the **Users** link from the right-hand side panel, and select the **Default Users Associations** tab from the navigation.

3. Enter a name for the user group in the **User Groups Name** input field (for example, Social Networking).

4. Save it.

Now, whenever a new user is created, they will be associated with the Social Networking group.

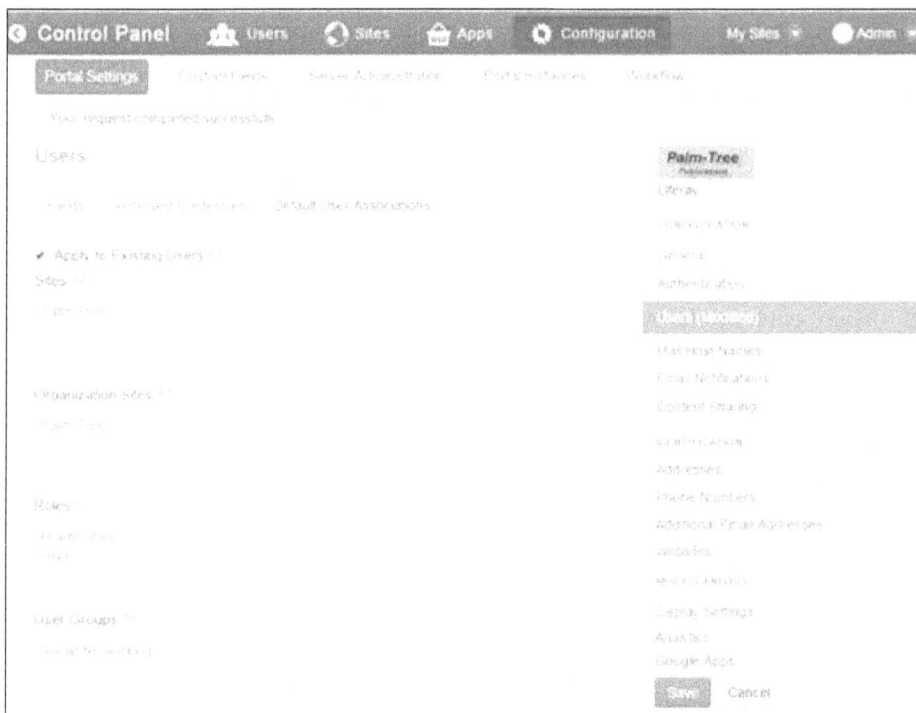

Figure 6.31: Portal setting—default user associations

Understanding how Liferay connects friends to friends using collaboration, we see that in Facebook and Google+, people are connected with each other and share theirs views because they have common interests. There are many ways to connect to users in social media, let's say if someone has posted something interesting, you add them as a friend.

The same thing happens in Liferay Social Networking—you will have many portlets, which always prompt you to find common interest people in portlets, such as the Friends, Activities, Members Activities, Calendar portlets, and many more portlets.

Liferay provides you with collaboration portlets, such as blogs, wikis, Message Boards, and Dynamic Data List. You can send a friend request to anyone when their idea or comments interests you and you have some common area of talk. Say you feel someone's wiki post is nice, and you want to be connected with that person, so you can simply send a friend request.

You can implement the social networking features in your custom portlets too using the Social Networking API—for instance, if you want to integrate social activity with custom portlets, you have to define `<social-activity-interpreter-class>` in liferay-`portal.xml`. There are a lot of things we can do with social networking.

Integrating social networking with Liferay

As we know, nowadays, social networking is very popular due to the likes of Facebook, Twitter, Google+, and LinkedIn. You might come across a situation where your portal content needs to be displayed on Facebook for some specific users. So, you need to integrate Facebook with Liferay.

Liferay provides a very easy way to integrate Facebook and other social networking sites. You can add a Liferay portlet on Facebook as an application, such as Message Boards, calenders, wikis, and other content on the portal available to Facebook users. For this, you must have a developer key. In all the portlets, you will find the Facebook tab in the portlet's configuration pop-up screen. Once you create an application on Facebook, get the developer key and also the Page URL from Facebook so that you can paste that URL in the portlet configuration under the Facebook tab. Now, you can find your application on the Facebook page.

Signing on with Facebook

We find lot of sites have sign on with Facebook. Let's try to create this sign on in Liferay Portal too. So, to sign on to the portal, you can use the Facebook username and password:

1. First, you need to have the Facebook application account to get a new account and follow the link `developers.facebook.com/docs/guides/web`.

2. Now, you have to edit settings under the **Web Site** tab. Fill in the **Site URL** text field and the **Site Domain** text field. If you're testing locally, you can set **Site URL** as `http://localhost:8080` and **Site Domain** to localhost. I've added an entry in my hosts file, so `bookpub.com` would hit my local Tomcat at port `8080`. Click on **Save** when you're done with your settings.

> Note that if you do change your domain, make sure you update all the relevant areas.

3. Log in as an administrator in Liferay Portal.

4. Go to the **Portal settings** tab under the **configuration** category in **Control Panel**.

5. Then, click on **Authentication** on the right-hand side menu and then click on the **Facebook** tab.

6. Check the checkbox to enable **Facebook SSO**. Next, fill in **Application ID**, which is a numeric ID (not to be confused with the application key) and **Application Secret** (don't tell/show anyone this), and then update the domain part of **Redirect URL** if you are not using localhost (I changed mine from localhost to `bookpub.com`).

7. Click on **Save** when you're finished.

Finally, you can see the Facebook link under the password field in the login portlet. Or if you are already logged in to Facebook in the same browser, it takes the same credentials to connect you.

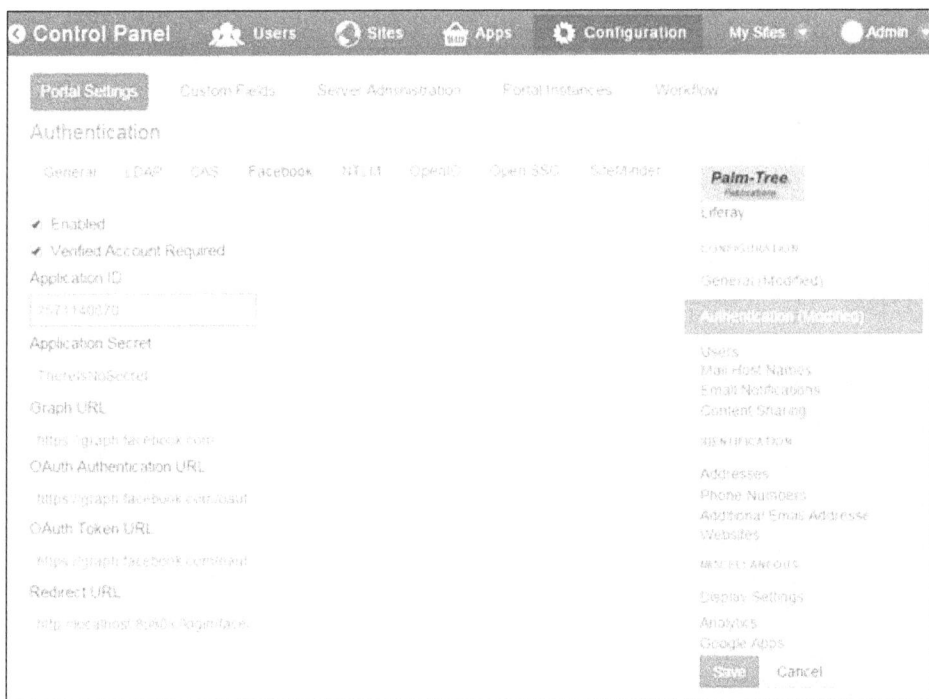

Figure 6.32: Facebook setting

Summary

This chapter introduced you to the WYSIWYG editor and gave a clear idea about how to install in CKEditor. It also introduced you to adding entries to blogs, managing (that is, to view, update, and delete) entries of blogs, and adding comments to a given entry of blogs first. Then, it discussed how to assign permissions on the Blogs portlet and entries of blogs. It also introduced the ways to publish blogs through the Recent Bloggers portlet and the Blogs Aggregator portlet and acquainted us with building blogs with the WYSIWYG editor CKEditor. Finally, it discussed RSS and other related portlets, such as the RSS portlet. You learned how to create a social networking environment in a portal, manage personal pages, and connect to friends. Also, we configured the sign on between Facebook and Liferay Portal.

In the next chapter, we will be learning about sites in detail.

7
Understanding Sites

In the intranet portal `bookpub.com` of the enterprise Palm Tree Publications, it would be nice to have the ability to build websites within a short time. Liferay 6.2 provides you with Site, where employees can share interests about the Book Street and Book Workshop sites and roll out to other teams. The sites provide teams with the ability to create and manage sites and enable their members to build different websites. The site has its own pages, which include public pages and private pages, content management systems, membership management, and permissions management. Each site maintains its own individual site scope.

Meanwhile, it would be nice if we could stage, schedule, and publish web content in our portal `bookpub.com` locally or remotely through workflow. As a content creator, you can update what you've created and publish it in a staging area. Then, other users can review and modify it in the staging area. Moreover, content editors can make a decision whether to publish web content from staging to live. Before going live, you can schedule web content as well. For publishing features, you can choose either local publishing or remote publishing; you can publish either the entire website or just a subset of pages.

This chapter will discuss how to manage sites. It will include a discussion on how to create and manage sites as well as how to create and manage the pages, teams, and members within a site. It will also introduce staging and publishing, workflow, scheduling, virtual hosting, and a set of site tools.

By the end of this chapter, you will have learned how to:

- Manage sites, pages, teams, and memberships of sites
- Apply site templates and page templates
- Virtual hosting, stage, preview, and publish websites

- Schedule and publish remotely
- Application Display Template (ADT), Social Activity, Workflow Configuration and Mobile Device Families

Site

As an administrator at the enterprise Palm Tree Publications, you would be required to provide an environment to roll out to other teams. Thus, you can provide an environment for users to manage the site, which includes managing pages (both public pages and private pages), managing teams, assigning members, assigning user roles, and so on.

What's a site? Loosely speaking, a site is a special group where users in the group share the same or similar interests. In general, a site is a collection of users who have a common interest. Both roles and users can be assigned to a site that are given exclusive access to specific pages or content.

Actually, sites are special groups that have a set of users or a set of user groups. Thus, a site may have a set of users associated. An organization can be associated and unassociated to an existing site whenever required for business needs.

As mentioned earlier, an organization is a special group too. So, you may ask: what's the difference between a site and an organization? When should you use sites instead of organizations?

There is a very thin line between both. Sites are mainly about pages, and organizations are about user management. Sites can have members and can be hierarchical too. Sites can be open, restricted, or private based on the privacy needs of the site, whereas organizations don't have such features; they are always considered to be centrally maintained.

Therefore, if you are planning to build a website and provide the ability to join and invite members and no user management is needed, then use sites. If you are planning to build a website and a hierarchical structure is required, then use organization.

> Note that sites can be managed hierarchically; whenever we create an organization, the hierarchy should match the site hierarchy so that the portal doesn't confuse the two.
>
> Basically, a hierarchical site makes the managing of site memberships and site content sharing much simpler.

In general, there are two portlets: the first portlet is Sites Admin (portlet ID `134`) in **Control Panel** and the second is My Sites (portlet ID `29`). "Why are there two portlets?" you may ask. The My Sites portlet provides a way to navigate from site to site and can be added to any page in the current portal instance. Let's discuss the Site Admin portlet first, followed by the My Sites portlet.

Adding a site

As we have discussed in previous chapters, **Control Panel** has different categories — **sites** is one of them. Under the sites category, there are site templates and page templates. The **Portal administrator** has the right to create and manage sites, site templates, and page templates from the control panel. The **Site administrator** can manage pages, users, content, and configuration of the site from the site administration panel.

In *Chapter 2, Setting Up a Home Page and Navigation Structure for the Intranet*, we saw how to create a site; let's create a site again and discuss it in detail:

1. Log in as a portal administrator.
2. Click on **Admin | Control Panel** from the dock bar menu.
3. Click on **Sites** under the **Sites** category of **Control Panel**.
4. Click on the **Add** button; a dropdown will appear (with **Blank Site**, **Community Site**, **Intranet Site**, and **Manage Sites Templates**). Select **Community Site**.
5. Fill in the site name, say `Book Street`, and the **Description**, check the **Active** checkbox (to make the site's state active), select the **Membership** type from the options — **Open**, **Restricted**, and **Private** — **Open** in this case. Select **Public pages** and **Enable** the propagation of changes from the site template.
6. If there is a site hierarchy, you can select the parent site, too. For this example, the site will be left as it is.
7. Finally, save the changes.

Creating a Site in Liferay is very simple and straightforward. The following screenshot illustrates the creation of the site with the name **Book Street**. Create another site called **Book Workshop**.

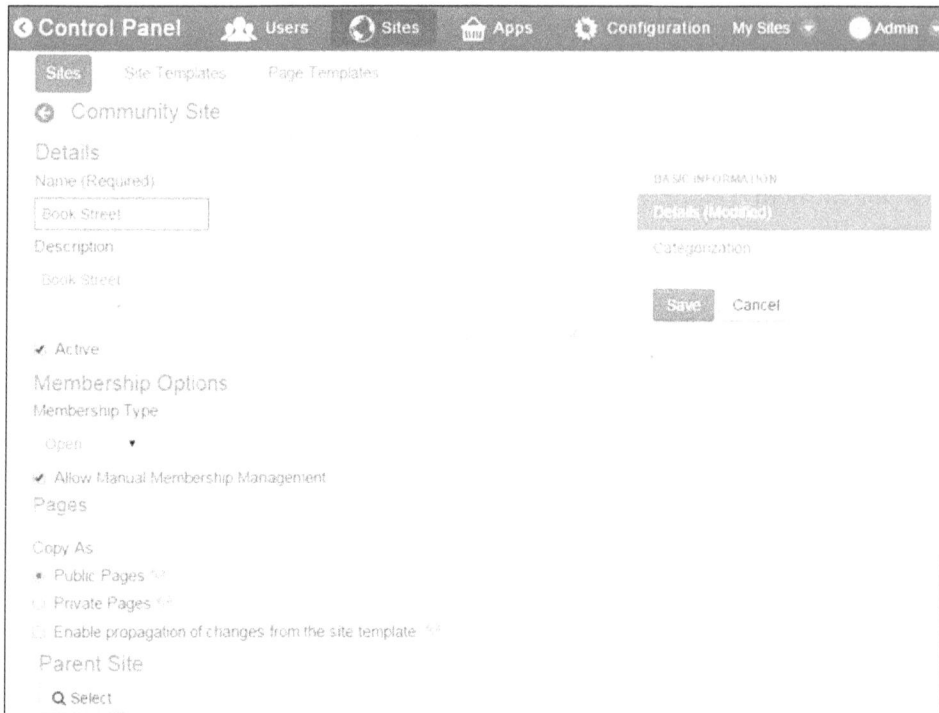

Figure 7.1: Site creation

In Liferay, sites allow the user to perform the task much easier and faster using predefined site templates. There are three types of Site templates provided by Liferay: **Blank Site**, **Community Site**, and **Internet Site**. You can create your own template whenever it is required.

If you have not created the site while creating the Organization, you can create the site separately and map the site with the organization manually. All users of the organization will be members of the site automatically. And the Site name and description will be automatically synced with those of the organization.

> Note that the **Active** checkbox allows you to make the site active and deactivate.

After saving the Site, you will be redirected to the Site settings page for a specific site. Follow this screenshot:

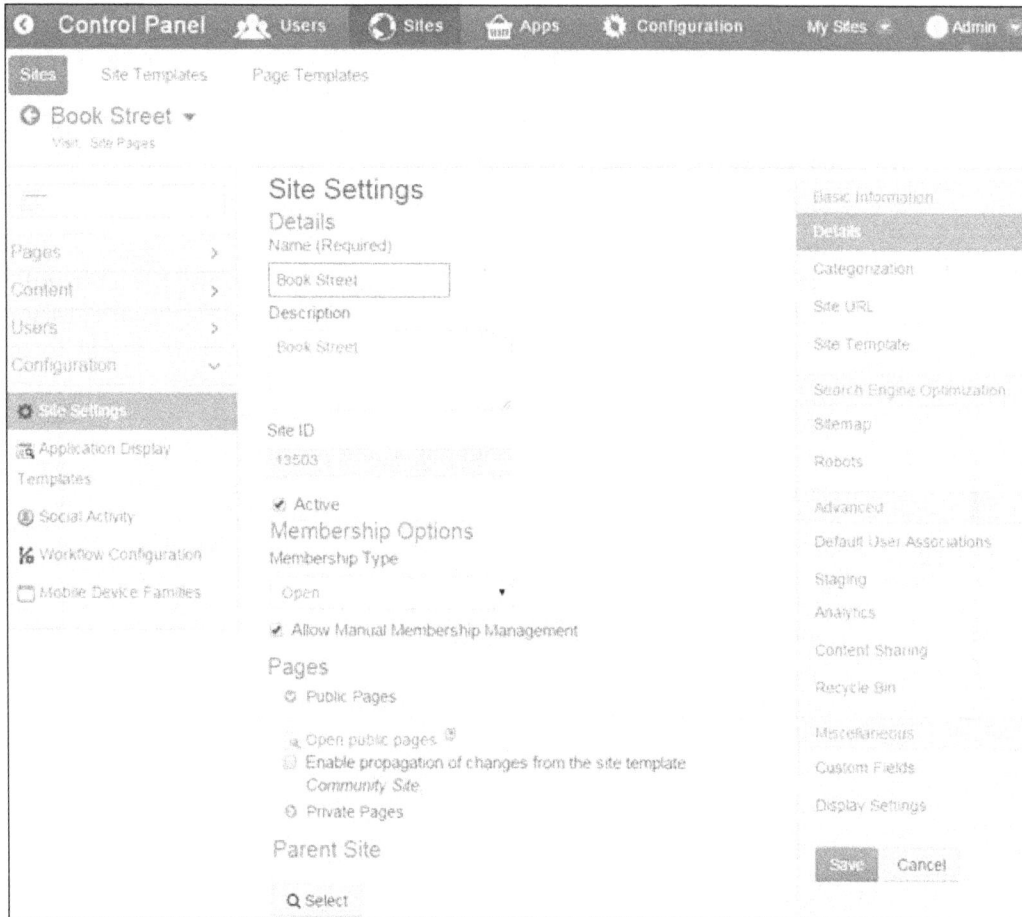

Figure 7.2: The Site Settings page

Site settings allows four main settings sections: Basic Information, Search Engine Optimization, Advanced, and Miscellaneous:

- **Basic Information**: **Details** (site information), **Categorization**, **Site URL**, and **Site Template**

- **Search Engine Optimization**: **Sitemap** and **Robots**

- **Advanced**: **Default User Association**, **Staging**, **Analytics**, **Content Sharing**, and **Recycle Bin**

- **Miscellaneous**: **Custom Fields** and **Display Settings**

Let's discuss each of these sections in brief.

- **Basic Information**:
    - ○ **Details**: This allows an administrator to change site settings, such as the description and membership type of a site, and also allows specifying private and public pages of a site. Even you can configure Application Adapter Template (ADT) and select the Parent site for the current site.
    - ○ **Categorization**: This allows an administrator to apply categories and tags to the site.
    - ○ **Site URL**: The administrator can set a friendly URL and/or a virtual host for the site. Also, the site administrator can enable the directory indexing for Documents and Media.

> A friendly URL helps you to manage the path of the site in the portal's URL. It is used for both public and private pages. For public pages, a friendly URL is appended to `http://localhost:8080/web`. For private pages, friendly URLs are appended to `http://localhost:8080/group`. A friendly URL is always unique as regards its name, and it should be friendly with respect to human readability, which helps in indexing bots and is critical to good search engine optimization.
>
> Virtual hosts help in easy web navigation for the end user by connecting a domain or subdomain to a site.

- ○ **Site Template**: When the site is created from a site template, it will display information about the association between the site template and the site.

- **Search Engine Optimization**:
    - ○ **Sitemap**: It allows the administrator to send the sitemap to search engines so that they can crawl your site. The administrator can view what is being sent to the search engines by clicking on the **Preview** link to see the generated XML.
    - ○ **Robots**: Before setting the robots.txt rule, you might have to set up virtual hosting for the site.

- **Advanced**:
    - ○ **Default User Associations**: The administrator can configure site roles and teams that newly assigned site members will have by default.

- ° **Staging**: When the administrator enables staging locally/remotely, it allows you to edit and revise a page before publishing. We will discuss staging more in detail later in this chapter.

- ° **Analytics**: An administrator can set the Google Analytics ID; this will get inserted in every page. Google Analytics provides services that let you do all kinds of traffic analyses on the site. An administrator can also configure piwik, which is a web analytics platform that can provide valuable information on your site's visitors. It is basically used for marketing campaigns.

- ° **Content Sharing**: This allows the administrator to configure the content sharing between the parent site and the child site. The default value here is "enabled".

- ° **Recycle Bin**: The administrator can set the option to enable/disable Recycle Bin for the site. The administrator can also set the trash entries' maximum age, that is, the number of days for which content can be stored in Recycle Bin until it is permanently deleted.

- **Miscellaneous**:
  - ° **Custom Fields**: It allows editing the custom fields, which administrators have already configured for the site resource. If it is not defined, the administrator can define in **Control Panel – Custom Fields** under **Configuration**.

  - ° **Display Settings**: The administrator can change the language for the site. There are options to use default language options or define a new default language.

Managing sites

After adding a set of sites, you can manage them easily. You can view sites and search, edit, and delete sites as well.

Viewing sites

To view the available sites, you need to have proper access rights. You can simply click on **Sites** under the **Sites** category **Control Panel**. Note that as a portal administrator, you will be able to see the entire **Sites** list in the current portal instance.

As shown in following screenshot, sites will appear with **Name**, **Type**, **Members**, **Active**, **Pending Request**, and **Tags** and the **Actions** button with a set of icons, such as **Site Administration**, **Add Child Site**, **Go to Public Page**, **Leave**, **Deactivate** (deactivate the site), and **Delete**.

- **Name**: The name of the Sites, link to the child sites (if there are any), an orderable column. In the screenshot, the Palm Tree site has five child sites.

- **Type**: This can be **Open**, **Restricted**, or **Private**.

- **Members**: This is the number of members and the number of organizations associated.

- **Active**: This can be either **Yes** or **No**.

- **Pending Requests**: This is the number of members who have requested for membership.

- **Tags**: These are the tags of sites.

The following screenshot displays all the sites in the portal. Palm Tree, with its five child sites, is also listed in the list that follows the screenshot:

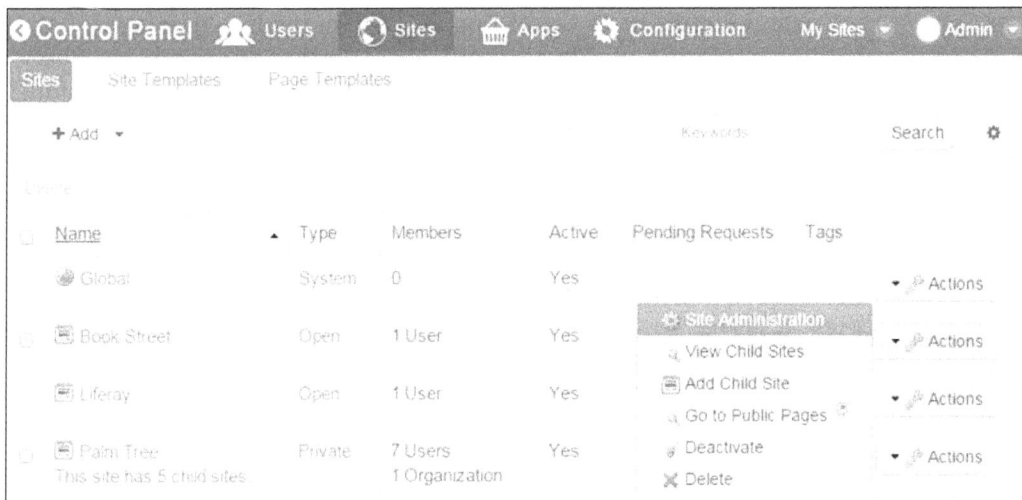

Figure: 7.3: View all sites

- **Site Administration**: This action will redirect you to the site administration panel (site settings) where you can update the current site
- **View Child Sites**: This action allows you to view child sites for a particular site
- **Add Child Site**: This allows you to add a child site for a particular site
- **Go to Public Pages**: This is a link to the public page of the site
- **Deactivate**: This will deactivate the site, and the site members will not able to access the site
- **Delete**: This allows you to delete a particular site

Searching sites

To search sites, you can simply type the search criteria in a search input field first. Then, click on the **Search** button. The portlet will list the search results, that is, a list of sites, where each site has columns such as **Name**, **Type**, **Members**, **Active**, **Pending Request**, **Tags**, and the **Actions** button with a set of icons.

Liferay 6.2 has the advanced search feature too; if you want to search for any specific site with respect to the name or description with all or any matches. It's very simple. You just need to click on the **Gear** icon beside the search button, input the name or description fields, and click on the search button. It will filter according to your search criteria.

Editing a site

Let's suppose that you want to update the description of the site "Book Street" with a new description, "A site for Book Street". As a portal administrator or site administrator, you will have the permission to update the site settings. As shown in *Figure 7.2*. From the site's setting page, you can simply set the new description A site for Book Street in the description field and save it.

> Note that Site Administration Panel has control over the whole site. Under **Configuration** | **Site**, settings allow the site administrator or portal administrator to update the site with all the possible settings provided.

Deleting a site

Let's suppose that the site "Book Street" doesn't exist anymore; you're going to delete it. The following are the simple steps to delete the "Book Workshop" site:

1. Click on **Site** under the **Sites** category of **Control Panel**.

2. Locate a site, let's say **Book Street**, that you want to delete.

3. Click on the **Delete** icon from the **Actions** button on the right-hand side of the **Book Street** site.

4. A screen will appear asking whether you want to delete the selected site. Click on the **OK** button to delete, or click on the **Cancel** button if you don't want to delete the selected site.

> Note that deleting a site will delete all pages that belong to the site. At the same time, the links of all users and roles assigned to the site will get released immediately.

Creating and managing pages

A site is just a shell that can contain a set of pages—both public pages and private pages. Via the site **Administration Page | Site** pages, you would be able to manage the pages of a given site if you have proper access rights.

Viewing pages

As a Site Administrator, you can navigate to the **Admin** tab in the dock bar and select **Site Administration | Pages**. It will redirect you to the **Site Administration** page, so now you can edit and configure the site pages.

For our example "Book Street" site, you have to log in as the portal administrator and select the "Book Street" site from the **My Sites** drop-down menu in the dock bar. Finally, select the **Site Administration** page from the **Admin** tab. Or you can go to **Control Panel | Sites** and click on **Site Administration** from the **Actions** tab on the right-hand side of the site. The pages that belong to the "Book Street" site are displayed in a tree structure on the left-hand side. Every page can have child pages, as shown in the following screenshot:

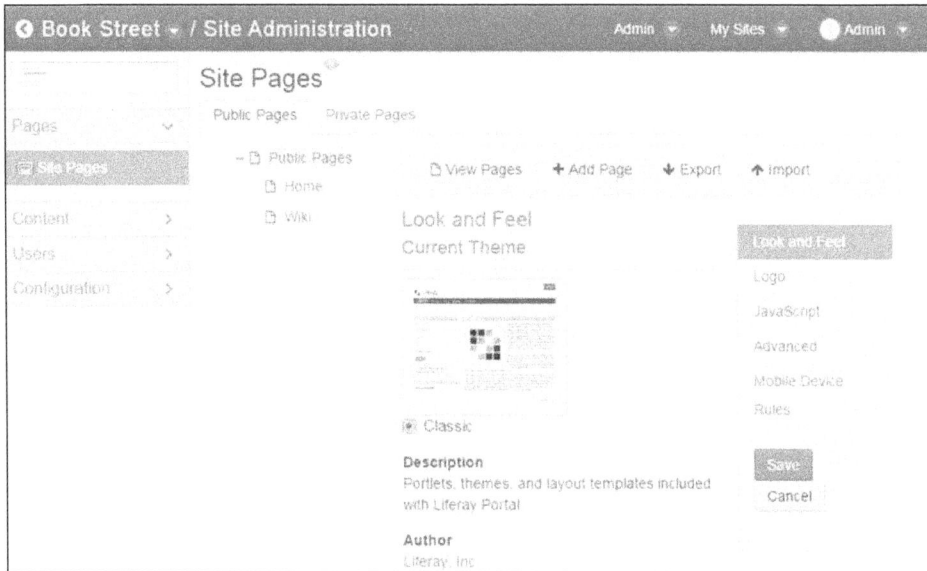

Figure 7.4: Site Pages

To view all the pages in public pages, simply click on the **Public Pages** tab. Similarly, to view all the pages in private pages, simply click on the **Private Pages** tab.

In *Chapter 2, Setting Up a Home Page and Navigation Structure for the Intranet*, we discussed the topics **Building pages** and **Setting up portal pages**. That will give you a clear idea about managing pages in a site. Let's discuss more advanced features of pages.

In brief, you can add, edit, and delete pages and assign permissions on individual pages. You can use the following functional items, but you are not limited by that. By the way, you can reorder pages by dragging and dropping pages. Thus, you can change the parent/child relation between pages:

- **Public Pages**: This is about managing public pages of the current site
- **Private Pages**: This is about managing private pages of the current site
- **View Pages**: This opens in a new tab with public pages or private pages displayed with full look and feel
- **Add Page**: This is about adding a new page to the current site
- **Export**: This is about exporting the current site pages, either public pages or private pages of the current site, to LAR files
- **Import**: This is about importing the current site pages, either public pages or private pages to the current site, as LAR files

- **Look and Feel**: This is about changing themes of either public pages or private pages
- **Logo**: This is about uploading a logo for public pages or private pages that will be used instead of the default enterprise logo
- **JavaScript**: This allows us to paste JavaScript code that will be executed at the bottom of the page
- **Advanced**: The advanced link provides the settings to merge the page
- **Mobile Device Rules**: This allows you to select mobile device families on the current page. A mobile device family is a set of rules configured for different mobile operating systems. See more details in the upcoming *Mobile Device Families* section of this chapter.

Note that once you select the page under public pages, you will get more control to manage an individual page.

- **Add Child Page**: This adds a new child page to the selected page
- **Permissions**: This sets permissions for the selected page
- **Delete**: This allows you to delete the selected page
- **Copy Applications**: This copies the portlets from a selected page to a different page

Site pages have public and private pages, which have different sets of pages and their settings. The following screenshot shows the public **Home** page settings details:

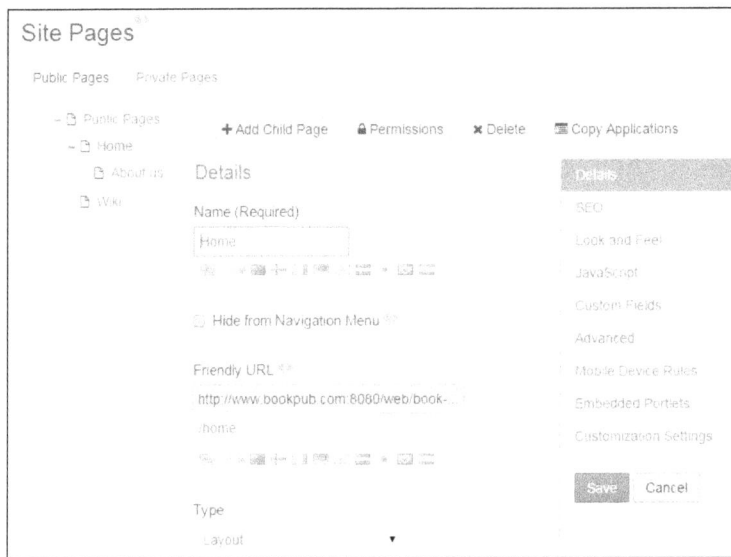

Figure 7.5: Site Pages

The following list explains the links in the right-hand side panel in the preceding screenshot:

- **Details**: This link provides page details, such as **Name, Hide page from Navigation Menu, Friendly URL**, and **Page Type**.

- **SEO**: The SEO link allows the setting of the HTML title, meta tags (**Description, Keywords, Robots**), and **Sitemap** (**Include, Page Priority, Change Frequency**).

- **Look and Feel**: This link allows changing themes of either public pages or private pages.

- **JavaScript**: This link allows us to paste JavaScript code that will be executed at the bottom of the page.

- **Custom Fields**: This link allows setting of the custom fields for the selected page.

- **Advance**: This link provides the settings for **Query String, Target**, and icon of the page.

- **Mobile Device Rules**: This allows settings of the same mobile device rules as that of the public page. It even allows the administrator to define specific mobile device rules for this current page.

- **Embedded Portlets**: This link allows embedding portlets in the page.

- **Categorization**: The administrator can set the categories and tags for this current page.

- **Customization Settings**: This link allows settings to customize the current page for the users selected. Users with the permission to customize this page will be able to customize those sections marked as customizable. It gives the option to select columns to make it customizable, based on the layout selected. This is about importing and exporting pages.

The export and import of data generally revolves around the concept of storing data outside the portal permanently or temporarily. The portal does this by handling the creation and interpretation of LAR files. The functions of data export and import are done portlet-wise. In the **Site Administration** page, you would be able to export all pages—either public pages or private pages of a given site—to a LAR file. What would you like to export? The following are possible items that you can include, but you are not limited to these:

- **Pages**: By default, you can select the required pages by clicking on change link. A pop-up window where you can select required pages will open. By default, it has **Site Pages** Settings, **Theme** settings, and **Logo**.

- **Application Configuration**: You have two choices: All Applications, Choose Applications. By default, this includes Setup, Archived Setup, User preferences, Data, and portlets, such as, Blogs, Web Content, Dynamic Data List, and so on.
  - ° **All Applications**: The configuration of all applications will be exported. The export of archived setups and user preferences can be disabled using the **Change** link option.
  - ° **Choose Applications**: Only the configuration of selected application will be exported.

- **Content**: You have two choices: **All Content** and **Choose Content**. By default, it has **Date Range, Categories, Document and Media**, and so on.
  - ° **All Content**: The content and metadata of all the applications will be exported.
  - ° **Choose Content**: Only the content and metadata of the selected applications will be exported using the change option to disable the export of the content and metadata for each application.

- **Permissions**: The permissions assigned to the exported pages and individual portlet windows will be included if this option is checked.

Now, let's export pages in a given site, for example, "Book Street", by following these steps:

1. Click on **Site Pages** under the category **Site Administrating panel**.

2. Select pages—either public pages or private pages. Let's say that you're going to export public pages; click on the **Public Pages** tab.

3. Click on the **Export** button. Now, it will export all pages (public pages in this example), their layouts, their configurations, their look and feel, and their permissions to a LAR file (Liferay Archive). On clicking on the **Export** button, a popup will appear, and you would be asked to export the selected data to the given LAR filename and select what you would like to export.

4. Click on the **Export** button. The **Current and Previous** tab will open where it will record the LAR file details. It will generate a LAR file and save it in the portal. Here, you will find the download link from where you can download the LAR file to save it locally.

Exporting the data to another Liferay instance is very simple using the LAR file. The following screenshot shows that the export of public pages into a LAR file:

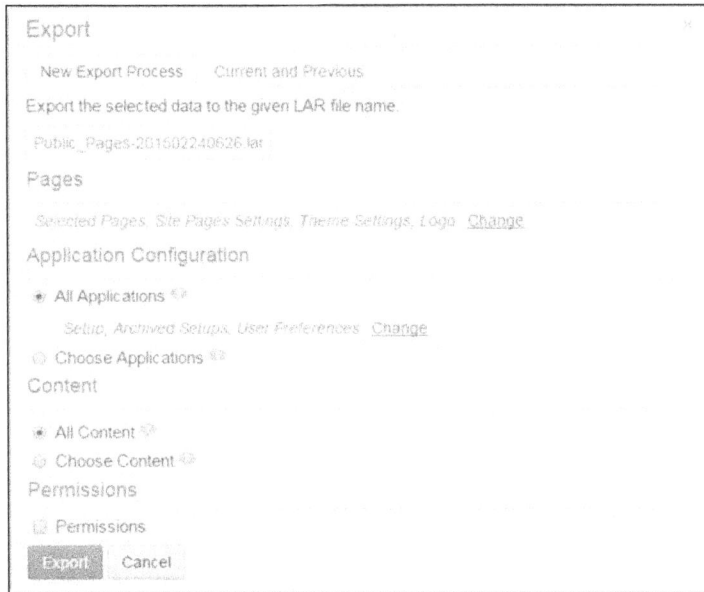

Figure 7.6: Site pages export

Of course, you would be able to export private pages too. To do so, first, click on the **Private Pages** tab, and then click on the **Export** button.

If necessary, you can import a LAR file into the current site by following these steps:

1. Select pages (either public pages or private pages). Let's say that you're going to import public pages. Click on the **Public Pages** tab.

2. Click on the **Import** button.

3. After clicking on the **Import** button, the import popup will appear and would be asked to import (upload) a LAR file. Once it's uploaded, the LAR file will ask for configuration steps. You can configure the import data and select what you would like to import, such as pages, applications, content, and permissions.

4. Click on the **Continue** button. Now, you have to set Update Data for the LAR file, such as **Mirror, Mirror with overwriting**, and **Copy as New**. The Author settings for the current content are as follows:

    ○ **Mirror**: All data and content inside the imported LAR file will be created as new the first time while maintaining a reference to the source. Subsequent imports from the same source will update the entries instead of creating new entries.

    ○ **Mirror with overwriting**: This shows the same behavior as the mirror strategy, but if a document or an image with the same name is found, it will overwrite it.

    ○ **Copy as New**: All data and content inside the imported LAR file will be created as new entries within the current site every time the LAR file is imported.

5. Click on the **Import** button. The portal will overwrite the selected data of the current site. The **Current and Previous** tab will open, where it will record the LAR file details.

Page Import always maintains the history of the **current and previous** imports of LAR made in public or private pages. The following screenshot shows the current and previous import list:

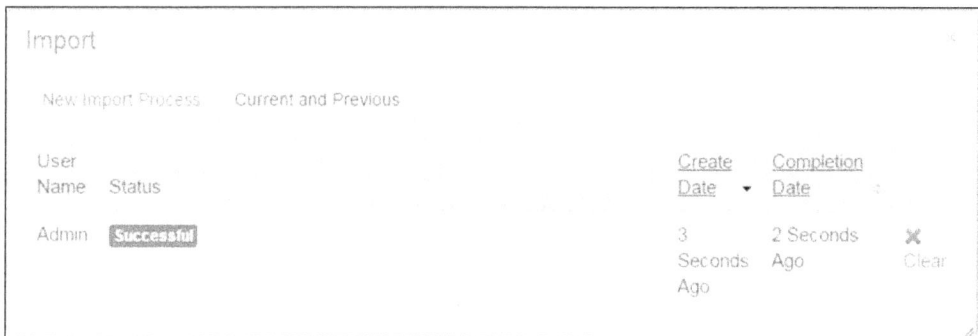

Figure 7.7: Site pages import

Of course, you will be able to import to private pages, too. To do so, first click on the **Private Pages** tab and click on the **Import** button. Moreover, you would have the ability to merge data and manage the ID of resources. A word of caution: you can export permissions on resources but not on users (not even roles). Therefore, roles and users have to be the same on the source as well as the target.

> Note that LAR is short for Liferay Archive. It includes all of the pages, their layouts, their configurations, their look and feel, their permissions, and so on. Importing a LAR file will overwrite any existing pages of a given site configured in the LAR file.

Updating the look and feel of pages

Besides the ability to export and/or import either private pages or public pages, you have the ability to change themes, that is, the look and feel of these pages as well. In general, each page must have a theme associated; all pages from either public pages or private pages can share the same theme.

Let's say that you are going to apply the theme "so-theme" on the public pages of the site "Book Street". There are two tasks you have to accomplish: firstly, deploy the theme "so-theme". Secondly, apply the theme "so-theme" on public pages. How to implement it? The following are the steps:

1. Drop WAR file `${so-theme-war}` to the folder `$LIFERAY_HOME/deploy`. The portal will deploy it automatically in the currently running Liferay Portal instance.

2. Select the "Book Street" site from **My Sites**, and then click on **Admin | Pages** from the dock bar, which will bring you to **Site Administration Panel**.

3. Select pages — either public pages or private pages. Let's say that you're going to apply a theme on a public page. Click on the **Public Pages** tab. Now, let's select **Public Pages**.

> Note that you can implement the theme at the parent level too. Implementing the theme to Public Pages will apply to all the pages. Even different themes can be applied to different pages.

4. Click on the **Look and Feel** link (by default, it's selected) and you would see the available themes, such as **Classic**.

5. Now, select your own theme, that is, `so-theme`. And finally **save** it.

As shown in this process, themes can be applied to either public or private pages. Of course, you would be able to apply a theme on an individual page. "How?" you may ask. Locate a page, say "Home", and click on it. You would see the **Look and Feel** link. By selecting the **Look and Feel** link, you would be able to apply themes to the current page individually.

Uploading a logo

As mentioned earlier, each site can have a logo as its enterprise logo. Thus, we can upload a logo as the enterprise logo of a site. If no logo has been uploaded, then the site would use the default enterprise logo for public and private pages.

Let's say that you are going to upload a logo called BookStreet_logo.png on the pages of the site "Book Street". You may be wondering about how to upload the logo. The following are the steps that you can take. They are shown in the following screenshot as well:

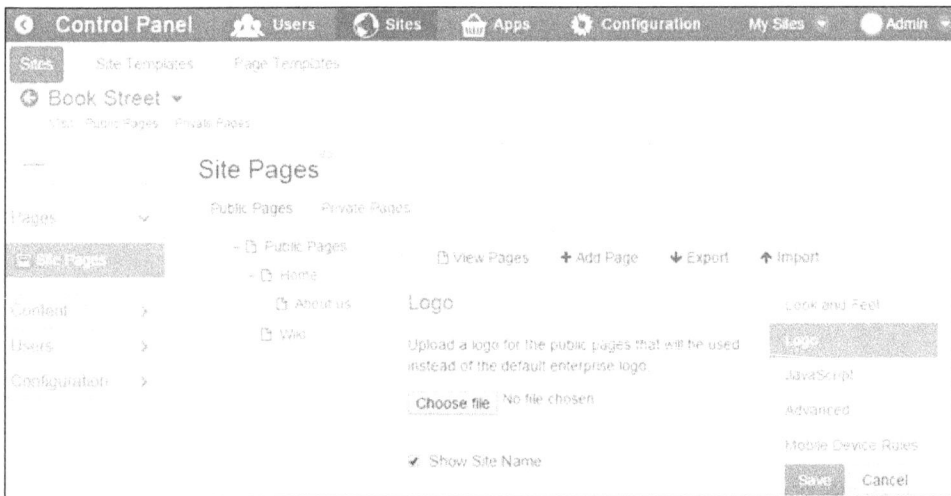

Figure 7.8: Site logo settings

1. As a site administrator, go to **Site Administrator Panel** of the Book Street site. Click on **Site Pages** under **Pages**.

2. Select the public or private page for which you want to change the logo. Select **Logo** from the right-hand side menu.

3. Upload the file BookStreet_logo.png by clicking on the button **Choose File**.

4. Now, you will have the choice to have a logo and a Site Name on the public page. You need to enable the checkbox **Show Site Name**. By default, the checkbox **Show Site Name** is checked.

5. Click on the **Save** button.

> Note that **Logo** can be applied for each site differently since logos are associated with public and private pages. For a site, public and private pages can have different logos too.

Merging pages

More interestingly, you would be able to configure the top-level public pages of the current site (any sites except the default one — **Liferay**) to merge with the top-level pages of the public pages of the Liferay site. Therefore, users can then navigate between the two sites more seamlessly.

Let's say that you need to merge the top-level public pages of the Liferay site into the public pages of the site "Book Street". You may ask, "how are we going to achieve it?" The following are the steps:

1. As a site administrator, go to **Site Administrator Panel** of the Book Street site. Click on **Site Pages** under Pages.

2. Select the **Public page | Advanced** link; you would see a checkbox **Merge Liferay public pages** — enable it.

3. Save the changes.

Note that you can merge only the top-level public pages of the Liferay site into the public pages of the Book Street site.

In fact, the pages of the public pages of the Liferay site aren't copied to a target site. Only a link called `mergeGuestPublicPages=true` in the column `typeSettings` of the table `Group_` was generated. When the link is set as `mergeGuestPublicPages=false`, the feature `mergeGuestPublicPages` would be disabled.

> This "merging" of pages is not a "hard merge". Let's say that the site administrator has merged ten different sites on one portal and all enabled the Merge default site's public page option. Now, the portals keep track of `currentscopeGroupId` (the ID of the current site) and the previous `scopeGroupId` (the ID of the previously visited site). If the Merge default site's public pages option is enabled for either the current site or the previous site, the pages of the default site are merged into the pages of the other site.

SEO

What is SEO?

"Search engine optimization (SEO) is the process of improving the volume or quality of traffic to a web site from search engines via "natural" or unpaid ("organic" or "algorithmic") search results."

`- wikipedia.org`

Liferay provides the settings to optimize the page data and allows the indexes that crawl the page. You have the option to set the various meta tags for **Description**, **Keywords**, and **Robots**. Separate Robots could be set in the **Robots** section that let you tell indexing robots how frequently the page is updated and how it should be prioritized. Let's suppose that the page is set to localize and that Liferay allows generating canonical links by language.

> In Liferay, each asset (web content article, blog entry, and so on) has a unique URL. From the search engine's point of view, this will make your pages rank higher since any references to variations of a specific URL will all be considered references to the same page.

How to customize SEO? The sitemap protocol allows us to set the following parameters for each page of the website:

- **Include**: Yes, No
- **Page Priority**: A number from 0.0 to 1.0 indicating the priority of the page relative to other pages of the website
- **Change Frequency**: **Always**, **Hourly**, **Daily**, **Weekly**, **Monthly**, **Yearly**, **Never**

Site templates and page templates

Site Templates and page Templates are another most wonderful feature in Liferay Portal. We have already discussed in *Chapter 2*, *Setting Up a Home Page and Navigation Structure for the Intranet*, and *Chapter 3*, *Bringing in Users*, about the site templates and page templates. Over here, we will look into it in more in detail. However, it is difficult for users who want to just create a site and start collaborating. They have to first create a theme, define layouts, and add portlets. **Site Templates** would be a good tool in this case when creating websites with preconfigured pages which include layouts, portlets, and themes. The portlet **Site Templates** allows the portal administrator to define a set of site templates as predefined websites that the users will be able to choose from to create new websites.

As you have seen, you don't need to create new pages as blank. Instead, you would be able to apply the layout and portlets of preconfigured pages on newly created pages. **Page Templates** allows the portal administrator to define a set of page templates as predefined pages that the users will be able to choose from to create new pages.

Creating page templates

As we know, a **page template** is only available to the portal administrator. Let's log in as a portal administrator. In the control panel, select **Page Templates** under **Sites**.

1. Click on the **Add** button to create a new page template.
2. Input the name, say **Publish Department**, and with a suitable description.
3. Enable the **Active** checkbox so that the page template is in active mode.
4. Finally, save the settings.

Now you will be able the see **Publish Department** in the page template list. Once page templates are available, you need to add the layout and the portlets to the page template. Click on **Publish Department** from the page template list. You will be able to see **Open Page Template** below **Configuration**. Click on **open page template**; it will open in a new tab. Now apply the layout and also place the required portlets on the page.

Assigning permissions

As you have seen, Page Templates is available only via **Control Panel**. Therefore, in order to view Page Templates, you need to have the **Access in Control Panel** permission first. Let's assign the **MB Topic Admin** role to access the page template in control panel where Lotti is associated as a member.

To set the permission entitlements for **Page Template**, portal administrators need to define permissions in **Roles**. Under the **Users** section, click on **Roles** in **Control Panel** and locate **MB Topic Admin**. Select **Define Permissions** from the **Action** button beside **MB Topic Admin**. Search for **Page Template**; you will get the entitlement settings for **Page Template**:

- **Control Panel | Sites | Page Templates**: General Permissions, Resource Permissions (Page Template)

Let discuss each of them in detail.

Control Panel | Sites | Page Templates: General Permissions

Action	Description
Access in Control Panel	This provides the ability to access the portlet in control panel
Configuration	This provides the ability to configure the portlets
Permission	This provides the ability to assign permissions
View	This provides the ability to view

As shown in the following implementation, the user "Lotti Stein" would be able to access the **Page Templates** portlet under the category **Sites** of **Control Panel**:

1. Log in as a portal administrator. Since roles is only accessible by the Portal admin.

2. Click on **Roles** under the category **Users** of **Control Panel**.

3. Then, locate a role, say **MB Topic Admin**.

4. Then, click on the **Define Permissions** icon from the **Actions** menu on the right-hand side of the role. Now, search for **Page Templates**.

5. Click on the **Control Panel**: **Site | Page Templates** link and enable the **Access** checkboxes in **Control Panel** and **View**.

6. Click on the **Save** button.

> Note that the **MB Topic Admin** role should be of the *regular* type.

After assigning general permissions on the portlet Page Templates, you can go deeper and assign permissions on page templates. The following table shows permissions on page templates. Generally, by default, this entitlement for page templates is assigned only to Portal Administrator. In our case, you can assign these entitlements to MB Topic Admin too.

Control Panel | Sites | Page Templates: Page Template

Action	Description
Delete	This provides the ability to delete the page template
Update	This provides the ability to update the page template
Permission	This provides the ability to assign permissions
View	This provides the ability to view

Applying page templates

Now you would be able to apply page templates when adding a new page (either a private page or a public page). When a page template has been applied, the page will have same page layout and portlets as that of the page template. How do we apply page templates? As shown in following set of steps and the screenshot, while adding a new page, page templates are available:

1. Click on the **Add** button from the dock bar menu, and select **Page** from the left-hand side panel.

2. Provide the **Page** name, say `publishing`, and then select **Type** (page type). You will be able to see different page types, for example, **Empty Page**, **Blogs**, **Wiki**, **Panel**, **Publish Department**, and so on. In our case, select **Publish Department**.

3. Finally, save the page.

Obviously, you can only apply page templates on new pages. In other words, page templates are unavailable for existing pages—neither public nor private pages.

Creating site templates

Site templates are preconfigured websites—either public pages or private pages with multiple pages, each with its own theme, layout template, portlets, and portlet configuration. Site templates can also contain content, document and media, recycle bin, and so on. Just as with any other sites, it has its own content scope. Fortunately, site templates change this scenario and reduce website creation time. In *Chapter 6*, *Blogs, WYSIWYG Editors, and Social Networking*, you created a Site Template for social networking. The Site Templates portlet allows the portal administrator to define new sites that are each created with the same default pages, portlets, and contents (both public pages and private pages). Site Templates are only accessed and managed by Portal administrator.

Let's create a Site Template called "Departments", as shown in the following steps.

1. Click on **Site Template** under the **Site** category of **Control Panel**.

2. Then, click on the **Add** button, enter a name for New Site Template in the **Name** input field (for example, **Department**).

3. Enter the description of the **Site Template**.

4. Leave the **Active** checkbox as default, uncheck **Allow Site Administrators to modify the pages Associated with This site Template**. By this, the administrator will not be able to modify the template.

5. Click on the **Save** button to save the inputs.

Managing site templates

Site templates are manageable. That is, you are able to add, delete, and update site templates to manage pages of site templates and, furthermore, to assign permissions if you have proper access rights. Similar to page templates, site templates are specified as a database table `LayoutSetPrototype` with the columns: `uuid_`, `layoutSetPrototypeId`, `companyId`, `create date`, `modified date`, `name`, `description`, `settings_`, and `active_`. How does it work? Let's have a deep look at the management of site templates.

The following figure displays the list of site templates with actions:

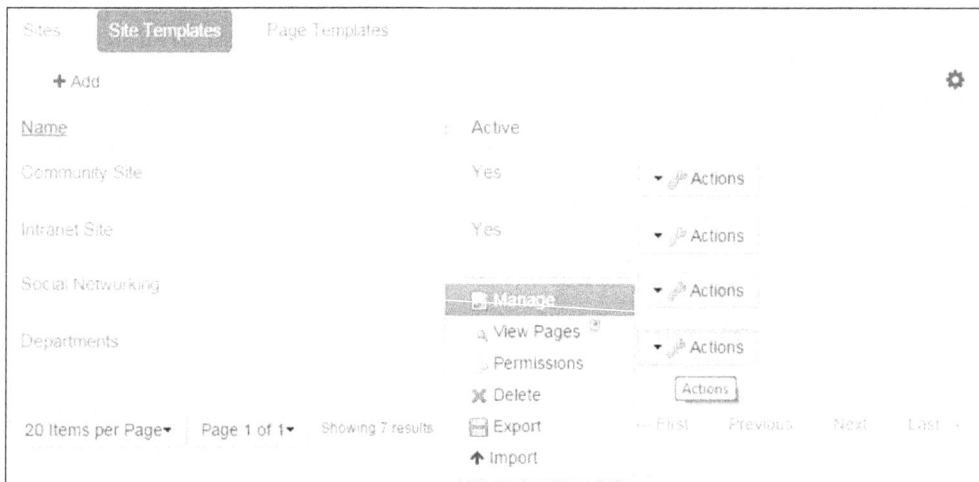

Figure 7.9: View Site Templates

As shown in the previous screenshot, you would be able to edit and delete site templates and also assign permissions on site templates. When updating a site template, you would have a chance to update the name and description. Moreover, you would also be able to disable the **Active** checkbox, making the site template invisible to end users. Note that only active site templates would be enabled for end users.

When editing a site template, you would see a link called **View Pages** under the **Configuration** title. On clicking on the link, a new window will open with a URL, such as `/group/template-id/home`. It will display the Site Template Name "**Department**", with the applied default classic theme of Liferay. On this page, you will be able to apply your theme, add portlets, update portlets, update the page layout, and so on. Note that `template-id` is a pattern, that is, the keyword **template + Id**, where the ID would be the value of the column `layoutSetPrototypeId`.

You can manage the site template by clicking on **Action | Manage**. It will redirect you to the site templates panel. The left-hand side panel menu contains the **Pages**, **Content**, and **Configuration** sections. The panel just likes a regular site. You can create pages of the site template into hierarchies, and when you create a site using the site template "department", all the pages and portlets in each page get copied from the site template to that site. By default, all the changes made in site templates get reflected on the site based on that template.

The following screenshot illustrates the **Site Template Settings** panel:

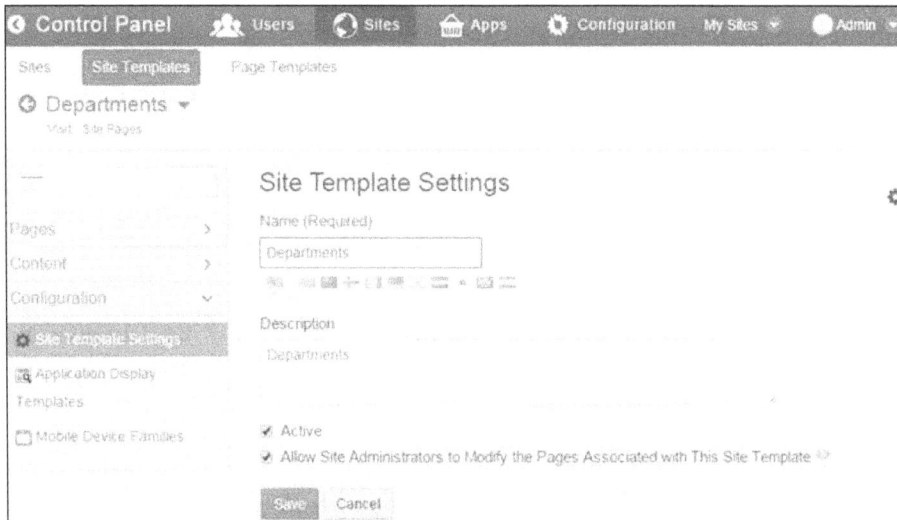

Figure 7.10: Site Template Settings

The **Content** section has a separate scope based on the site template. Any content that is created here is only available for that specific site template and the site associated with it. For example, when you create any web content inside the site template, it will be available inside the site template and the site using the same template.

The **Configuration** section allows you to set the settings for **Site Template**, **Application Display Templates** and **Mobile Device**.

Assigning permissions

As you have seen, Site Templates is available only via **Control Panel**. Therefore, in order to view Site Templates, you need to have the **Access in Control Panel** permission. Let's assign the **MB Topic Admin** role to access the site template in **Control Panel**, where Lotti is associated as a member.

To set the permission entitlements for **Site Template**, portal administrators need to define permissions in **Roles**. Under the **Users** section, click on **Roles** in **Control Panel** and locate **MB Topic Admin**. Select **Define Permissions** from the **Action** button beside **MB Topic Admin**. Search for **Site Template**; you will get the entitlement settings for **Site Template**:

- **Control Panel | Sites | Site Templates**: General Permissions, Resource Permissions (Site Template)
- **Site Administration | Configuration | Site Template Settings**: General Permissions

Let's discuss each of them in detail.

Control Panel | Sites | Site Templates: General Permissions

Action	Description
Access in Control Panel	This provides the ability to access the portlet in control panel
Configuration	This provides the ability to configure the portlets
Permission	This provides the ability to assign permissions
View	This provides the ability to view

As shown in the following implementation, the user "Lotti Stein" would be able to access the portlet Site Templates under the category **Sites** of **Control Panel**:

1. Log in as a portal administrator since Roles is only accessible by the Portal admin.
2. Click on **Roles** under the category **Users** of **Control Panel**.
3. Then, locate a role, say **MB Topic Admin**.
4. Then, click on the **Define Permissions** icon from the **Actions** menu on the right-hand side of the role. Now, search for **Site templates**.

5. Click on **Control Panel**: **Site** | **Site Templates** link, enable the **Access** checkboxes in **Control Panel** and **View**.

6. Click on the **Save** button.

> Note that the role of **MB Topic Admin** should be of the *regular* type.

After assigning general permissions on the portlet Site Templates, you can go deeper and assign permissions on page templates. The following table shows permissions on page templates. Generally, by default, this entitlement for the Site template is assigned only to Portal Administrator. In our case, you can assign these entitlements for MB Topic Admin, too.

Control Panel | Sites | Site Templates: Site Template

Action	Description
Delete	This provides the ability to delete the site template
Update	This provides the ability to update the site template
Permission	This provides the ability to assign permissions
View	This provides the ability to view

The preceding entitlements are for delete, update, permission, and view of site templates. Any role that has these entitlements will be able to delete and update the site templates. They can even set the permissions for the site templates. The **View** entitlement is for viewing the site templates.

Site Administration | Configuration | Site Template Settings: General Permissions

Action	Description
Access in Site Administration	This provides the ability to access the portlet in Site Administration
Add to Page	This provides the ability to add site template into the page
Configuration	This provides the ability to configure the portlets
Permission	This provides the ability to assign permissions
View	This provides the ability to view

The preceding entitlements are to access the configurations and see whether they can be viewed and accessed in **Control Panel** and **Site Administration**.

Applying a site template

Let's apply a site template while creating a site:

1. Go to **Sites** in **Control Panel**.
2. Click on the **Add** button and select "**Departments**".
3. Enter the name and description for the site, and, finally, save the settings.

The site will be created using the site template "**Departments**" with all the settings defined in site templates.

Bringing users into sites

As discussed earlier, you will have the ability to assign users to sites if you have proper access control. You will also be able to assign users to site roles for a given site. Moreover, users would have the ability to join or leave an open site. More interestingly, you would be able to request membership to a given site as a member, or you would be able to approve or deny membership requests as an owner of a given site. This section will bring users into sites.

Assigning users

The Liferay site allows the Site Administrator to manage user membership. A Site Administrator will able to assign individual users, groups, and organizations to the site. Let's use the user membership in our case study; for instance, the user "Lotti Stein" isn't a member of the site **Book Street** yet. Now, as a site administrator, you want to assign the user "Lotti Stein" to the site "Book Street", as shown in the following screenshot:

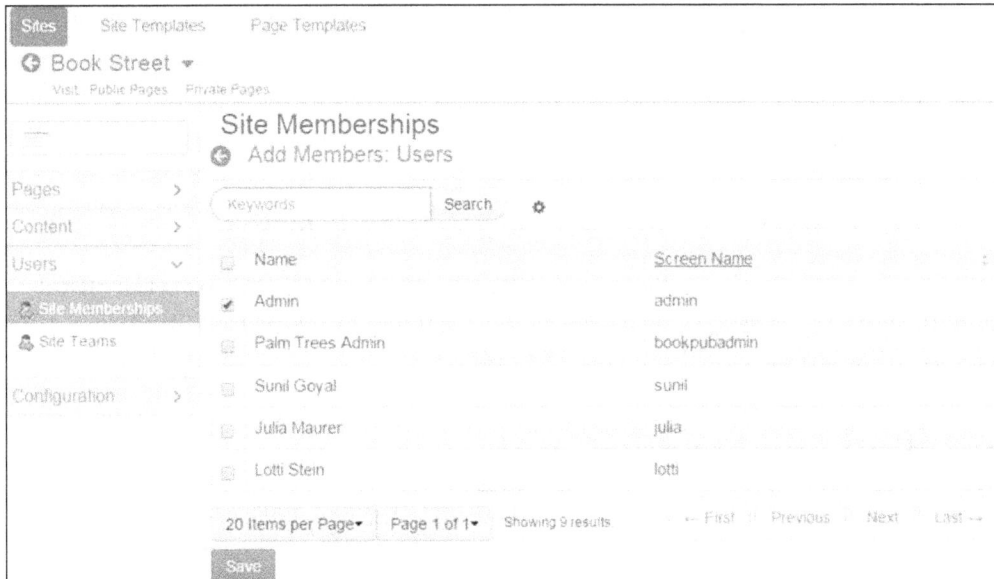

Figure 7.11: Site Memberships

1. Log in as the Site Administrator of the site "Book Street".

2. Click on **Admin | Users** under the dock bar menu. Default **Site Memberships** will open in the **Site Administrator** panel.

3. Check that the site content is selected as **Book Street**. If not, you can also select the site from the top dropdown in the dock bar menu.

4. Once you are in the **Membership** page, you will be able to see the list of users and organization for a particular site, that is, the **Summary** tab.

5. Select the **Users** tab. You will be able to see the list of users associated with Book Street. Now click on the **Assign Users** link at the bottom.

6. Now, you will be able to view the same screenshot as *Figure 7.11*. Just enable the checkbox beside "Lotti Stein".

7. Save the change.

Similarly, you would be able to assign users of organizations and/or user groups into a site indirectly.

- **Users**: This is about assigning individual selected users to a site
- **Organizations**: This is about assigning users of selected organizations to a site
- **User Groups**: This is about assigning users of selected user groups to a site

Note that if a user, say "Lotti Stein", has been assigned to a site via both Users and Organizations, only one record would be saved in the database. As you can see, this is a more flexible approach to assign users to a site.

Assigning an organization

An organization with public or private pages needs to have a site associated with it. A site administrator can assign any organization to the site. Let's see the example to assign the "Marketing Department" organization to the "Book Street" site.

1. Log in as a Site Administrator of' "Palm Tree".
2. Click on **Admin** | **Users** under the dock bar menu.

[Check that the site content is selected as Book Street.]

3. Upon selecting the Organization tab, you will be able to see the list of organizations associated with Book Street. Now, click on the **Assign Users** link at the bottom. You will get the list of organizations inside the portal.
4. Locate the organization that you would like to associate with Book Street, that is, Marketing Department. Now select the Marketing department organization.
5. Finally, save the settings.

Assigning organization to the "Book Street" site is simple; refer to the following screenshot to implement it:

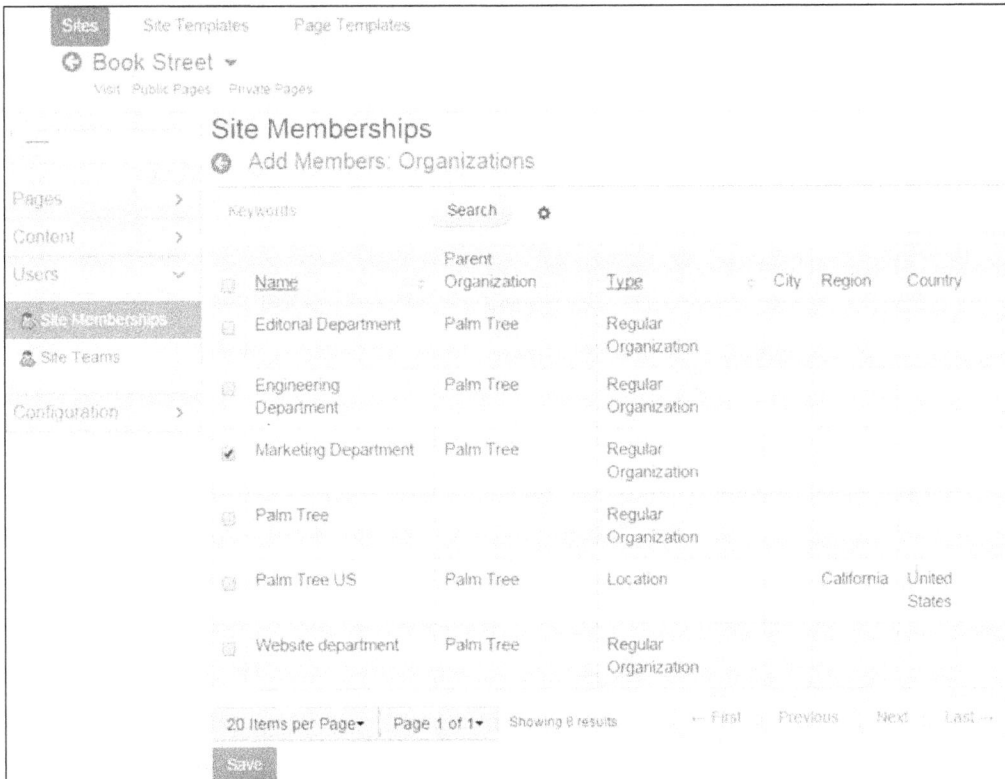

Figure 7.12: Assigning organizations

Assigning Groups

The site administrator can assign a group to the site. In some cases, you might have to assign a group in the site so that all the users of the group are assigned to the site. Let's assign the "**Managers**" group to the site "Book Street":

1. Log in as a Site Administrator of the site' Palm Tree.

2. Click on **Admin | Users** under the dock bar menu.

> Check that the site content is selected as Book Street.

3. Select the **User Groups** tab; you will be able to see the list of **User Groups** associated with Book Street. Now click on the **Assign User Groups** link at the bottom. You will get the list of user groups inside the portal.

4. Locate the users group that you would like to associate with Book Street, that is, manager, and select the checkbox.

5. Finally, save the settings.

To assign user groups to the site, refer to the following screenshot for the preceding example.

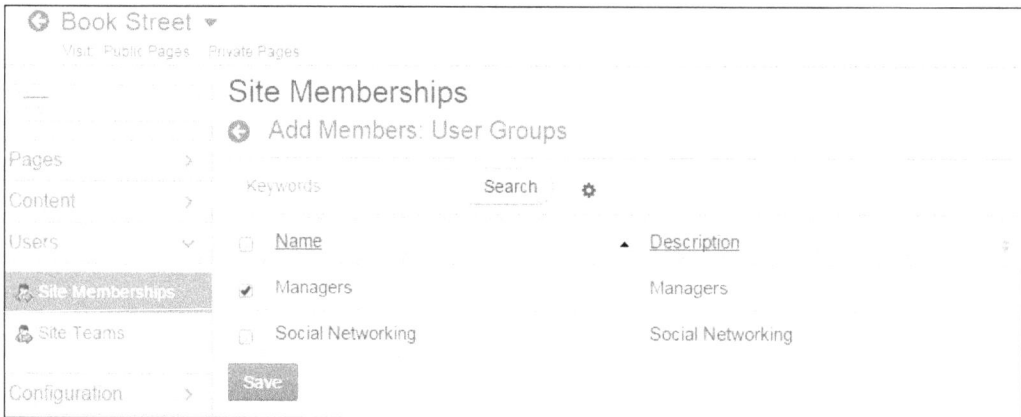

Figure 7.13: Assigning User Groups

Note that it's an advantage while implementing the enterprise intranet portal. You might be implementing the LDAP in which all the users are associated with some groups. While importing the users from LDAP, you just need to create user groups in the portal. Finally, map it with sites where you want all the users of that user's group to get access to that site.

Assigning site roles to Users and User Groups

As stated earlier, Assign User Roles allows us to assign site-scoped roles to users. By default, sites are created with three site-scoped roles: Site Administrator, Site Member, and Site Owner, as shown in *Figure 7.14*. In general, you can assign one or more of these roles to users in a site if you have proper access rights. The three roles are explained after this information box:

> Note that all members of a site will get the Site Member role.

- **Site Administrator**: They are super users of the site but cannot make other users into a Site Administrator
- **Site Owner**: They are super users of the site and can assign site roles to users
- **Site Member**: All the member of the site gets the site member role

Generally speaking, there are two steps to assign site roles to users and user groups — to choose a role and to assign site roles to users and user groups. For example, the user "Lotti Stein" is a member of the site "Book Street". Now, as an administrator, you want to assign the user "Lotti Stein" to the Site Owner site role. How can we implement it? The following are sample steps:

1. Log in as the Site Administrator of the site "Book Street".
2. Click on **Admin | Users** under the dock bar menu. The default **Site Memberships** will open in the **Site Administrator** panel.
3. Check that the site content is selected as **Book Street**. You can also select the site from the top drop-down menu in the dock bar menu.
4. Once you are in the **Membership** page, you will able to see the list of users and organizations for a particular site, that is, the **Summary** tab.
5. In the users list, locate "Lotti Stein", click on the **Action** button beside the name, and select **Assign Site Roles**.
6. Now you will be able to select the role for "Lotti Stein", as shown in *Figure 7.14*.
7. Enable the checkbox next to **site owner** and click on the **Update Associations** button.

After assigning the site role to the user with the preceding steps, the following screenshot displays the default roles for Site:

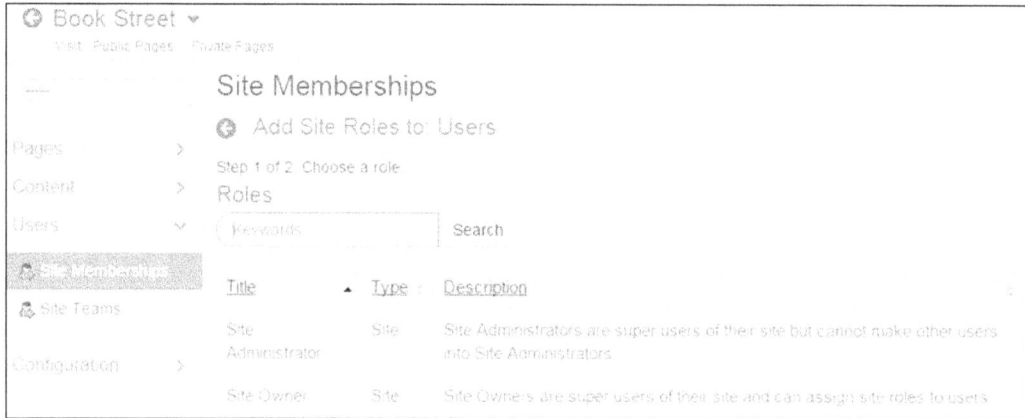

Figure 7.14: Site roles for users and user groups

Let's assign the roles to groups site-scoped in a different way.

1. Follow the preceding steps from 1–4.

2. Click on the **Add Site Role to** dropdown from the top tab. You will see two options: **Users** and **User Groups**.

3. Select **User Groups**, and you will land on the role page. Select the role, say **Site Owner**.

4. Now, you will be able to see the list of users who are assigned to the site owner under the **current** tab.

5. Click on the **Available** tab, which will list all the members of the site. From the list, enable the checkbox beside the user groups "**Managers**".

6. Finally click on the **Update Associations** button.

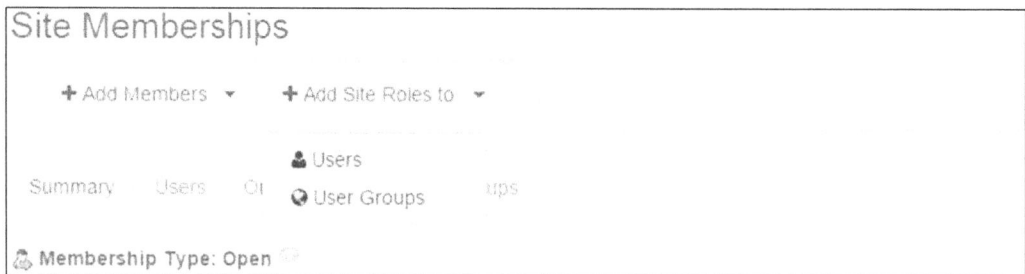

Figure 7.15: Adding site roles to User Groups

> Note that even you can assign the site-scoped Role to the users, from users and Organizations by clicking on the **Action** button next to the user and selecting **Edit**. Now select the role from the right-hand side control, and finally, choose the site-scoped role for a particular user.

Creating teams

A team provides great flexibility to the site administrator in creating various sets/teams of users and permissions for site-specific functions. Teams are ad hoc groups of a site's users that do the same set of tasks. It provides the feature of providing permission to specific sets of users for a particular functionality on the site. Teams can be scoped for collecting permission within a single site.

The list of functions to assign a Site Team includes:

- Moderating the site's Wiki content, Message Boards threads, and so on

- Editing a specific page on the site and writing blogs

So, the Site Administrator can create a team with the name Moderator, which will assign the Moderator job in Wiki and Message Board.

> Note that each site has its own scope. So, all the settings for a particular site will not be available to any other site. Also, the permissions defined for one site will not be available for other site settings.
>
> But it's not the same case for User Groups. Once you define the custom role to a user group, the role will be available at the portal level and the same specific permission defined by it would only apply within the scope of a designated site.

Let's create a team "Moderator" for the Book Street site, the permission defined for it will be only available to the Book Street site only and no other site can have same permission:

1. Log in as a Site Administrator of the site "Book Street".

2. Click on **Admin | Users** under the dock bar menu. Select **Site Teams** from the **Site Administrator** panel.

3. Check that the site content is selected as **Book Street**. You can also select the site from the top dropdown in the dock bar menu.

4. Click on the **Add Team** button. Enter the team details—the name **Moderator** and the description **Moderator Team**.

5. Finally, save the team by clicking on the save button.

Site Teams is created as shown in the following screenshot. Each site team has actions, such as **Edit**, **Permissions**, **Assign Members**, and **Delete**. Site Teams can be managed by the Site Administrator.

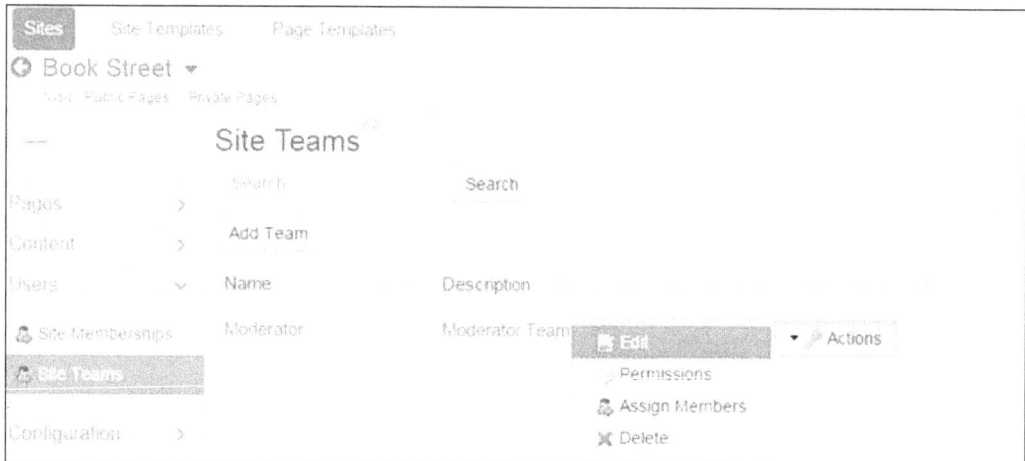

Figure 7.16: Creating a team

Assigning users to a team

The Moderator team might need to assign users who have common interests to the team. So, let's add member/users to the "Moderator" team:

1. Follow the preceding steps 1–3.

2. A list of teams that has been created will be displayed. Locate the team **Moderator** and click on the **Action** button next to that team. See *Figure 7.16*.

3. Click on **Assign Members** and you will find the list of members in this team. For our example, there is no member for this team.

4. Let's assign users by selecting the **Available** tab, which will list all the members assigned to the "**Book Street**" site.

5. Select the users from the list and click on the **Update Associates** button.

The following screenshot illustrates the user association with a site team:

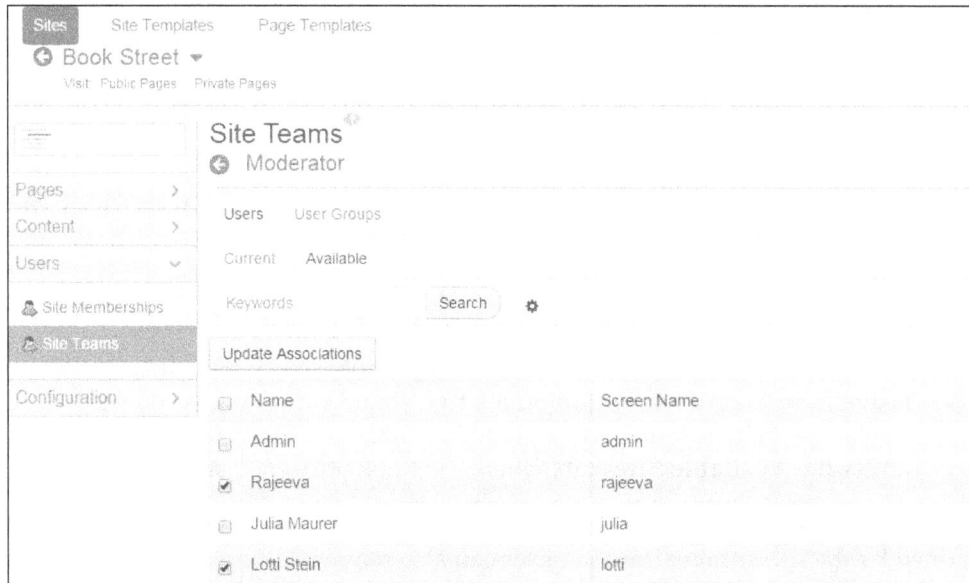

Figure 7.17: Assigning users to Site Memberships

> Note that you can assign **Users** and **User Groups** to the team. The users and user groups should be already added to the particular site and only then the available users and user groups will be listed.

Join

As mentioned in earlier chapters, the portal provides the ability to allow users to join an open site and become members of the site. For example, as a user, say "Lotti Stein", of the enterprise Palm Tree Publication, you're going to join the "Book Street" site. Let's simply do it in a sequence by following these steps:

1. Log in as a user, say "Lotti Stein".

2. Click on **Lotti Stein**, and from the drop-down menu, select **My Dashboard** under the dock bar menu.

3. In **My Dashboard**, you will find the **My Sites** portlet, with two tabs "**My Sites**" and "**Available Sites**", where you would see a list of sites.

4. Under the **Available Sites** tab, locate a site, say "Book Street", and click on the icon **Join** on the right-hand side of the site. You would see that the icon **Join** has now become the icon **Leave**.

Leave

Site members can also leave the site in which they are already a member. For example, as a user, say "Lotti Stein", of the enterprise Palm Tree Publications, you are a member of the site "Book Street". For some reasons, you may want to leave this site. How do we achieve it? Let's do it in sequence by following these steps:

1. Log in as a user, say "Lotti Stein".

2. Click on **Lotti Stein** and from the drop-down menu, select **My Dashboard** under the dock bar menu.

3. In **My Dashboard**, you will find the **My Sites** portlet, with two tabs "**My Sites**" and "**Available Sites**", where you would see a list of sites.

4. Under the "**My Sites**" tab, locate a site, say **Book Street**, and click on the icon **Leave** from the **Action** button on the right-hand side. You would see that the **Book Street** site is removed from the **My Sites** tab. The Site will be available under the **Available Sites** tab, where the Book Street site shows the icon **Join**.

Users can join and leave an open site at will. To join a restricted site, a user has to be added by the site administrator. A user can also request to be added through the **Sites** section of **Control Panel**. A private site is similar to a restricted site but doesn't appear in the **Sites** section of **Control Panel** for users who aren't members.

Requesting membership

In a restricted site, users can request for membership and the site owners of a given restricted site would be able to view membership requests of the restricted site and then approve or deny membership requests. Of course, these membership request processes are only available for **restricted** sites. How do they work?

Let's create a case study. The Book Street site is an open site, and we can change the settings of a site to a restricted site. Simply go to site settings and change **Member type** to **Restricted**.

Now, as a user, "Lotti Stein" of the enterprise Palm Tree Publications, wants to be a member of a restricted site "Book Street". How can we set this up? Let's do it by following these steps:

1. Log in as a user, say "Lotti Stein".

2. Click on **Lotti Stein**, and from the drop-down menu, select **My Dashboard** under the dock bar menu.

3. In **My Dashboard**, you will find the **My Sites** portlet with two tabs "**My Sites**" and "**Available Sites**", where you would see a list of sites.

4. Under the "**Available Sites**" tab, locate a site, let's say "**Book Street**", and click on the **Request Membership** icon on the right-hand side of the site.

5. Then, input comments, such as "my favorite website", and click on the **Save** button to save the changes. Your membership request is pending, and you would see the icon **Membership Requested** next on the right-hand side of the site.

Note that once this membership request gets approved, the user "Lotti Stein" would see the icon **Request Membership** become the icon **Leave**. The following screenshot displays the request for membership that was made:

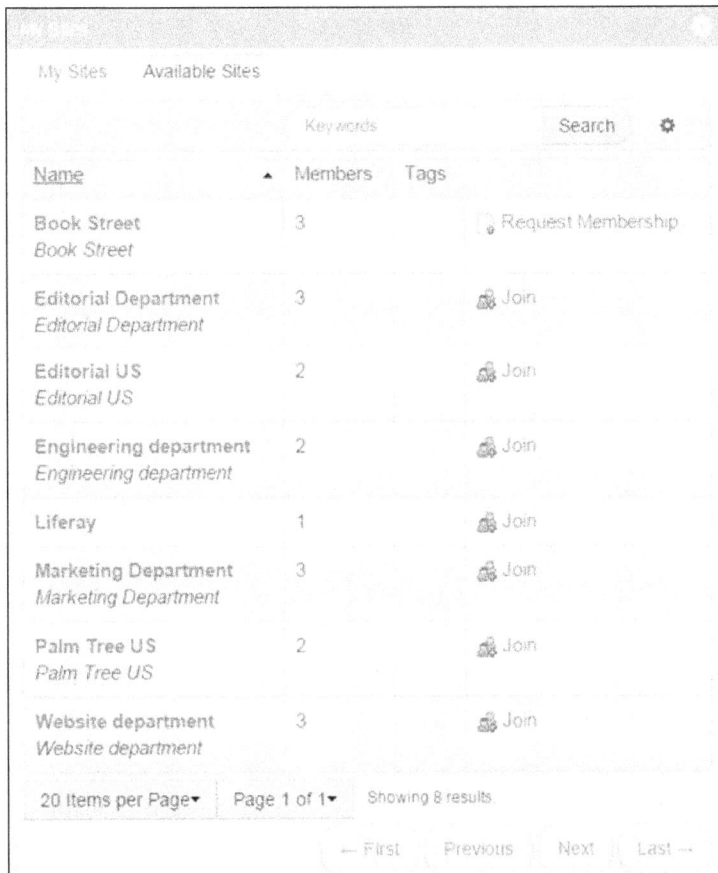

Figure 7.18: Requesting membership to a restricted site

Of course, any users could send membership requests on any restricted sites. The site owner would handle these membership requests. For instance, a site owner, such as "Book Street", is going to handle membership requests on the restricted site, such as "Book Street". How do we accomplish it? Let's do it by following these steps:

1. Log in as a Site Administrator of the site "Book Street".

2. Click on **Admin | Users** under the dock bar menu. The default **Site Memberships** will open in the Site Administrator panel.

3. Check that the site content is selected as **Book Street**. You can also select the site from the top dropdown in the dock bar menu.

4. Once you are on the **Membership** page, you will be able to see the list of users and organizations for a particular site, that is, the **Summary** tab. You will also be able to see the message "**There are 1 membership request pending.**" You can click on the link, or you would be able to see the **View Membership Requests** tab. Click on the tab and you can see a list of pending membership requests, if any, as shown in the following screenshot:

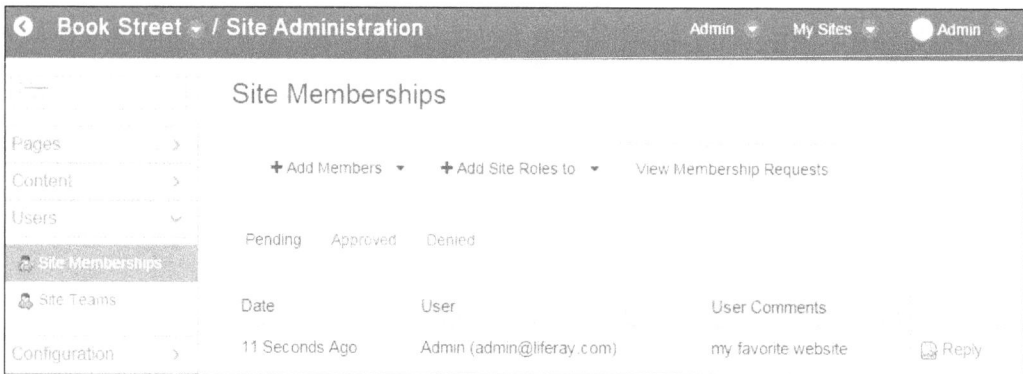

Figure 7.19: View membership requests

5. Locate a request, for example, "Lotti Stein", and click on the **Reply** icon on the right-hand side of the membership request.

6. Choose the status **Approve** or **Deny**. Let's say you selected **Approve** and input comments, say "Welcome".

7. Click on the **Save** button to save the inputs, or click on the **Cancel** button to discard inputs. You would be able to view the approved membership request or denied membership request.

> Note that only the site owner has the ability to view membership requests in a given restricted site.

The tabs details under **View Membership** requests are as follows:

- **Pending**: This is a set of pending membership requests with **Date**, **User**, **User Comments**, and a **Reply** icon. The site owner would be able to approve or deny membership requests.

- **Approved**: This is a set of approved membership requests with **Date**, **User**, **User Comments**, **Reply Date**, **Replier**, and **Reply Comments**.

- **Denied**: This is a set of denied membership requests with **Date**, **User**, **User Comments**, **Reply Date**, **Replier**, and **Reply Comments**.

As shown in the preceding code, all membership requests of a given restricted site will go to the **Pending** tab first. Once the request has been approved, it will go to the **Approval** tab, and the user will be a member of the restricted site. Otherwise, once the request gets denied, it will go to the **Denied** tab, and the user will not be a member of the currently restricted site.

What's happening?

As stated earlier, the Site is available in **Control Panel**. What's happening? When membership requests are approved or denied, e-mails are sent to requestors. "How to set it up?" you may ask.

Settings

The portal sets the following properties in `portal.properties` by default:

```
sites.email.from.name=Joe Bloggs
sites.email.from.address=test@liferay.com
sites.email.membership.reply.subject=com/liferay/portlet/sites/dep
    endencies/email_membership_reply_subject.tmpl
sites.email.membership.reply.body=com/liferay/portlet/sites/depend
    encies/email_membership_reply_body.tmpl
sites.email.membership.request.subject=com/liferay/portlet/sites/d
    ependencies/email_membership_request_subject.tmpl
sites.email.membership.request.body=com/liferay/portlet/sites/depe
    ndencies/email_membership_request_body.tmpl
```

This code sets the e-mail **FROM** name via the property `sites.email.from.name` and the e-mail **FROM** address via the property `sites.email.from.address`. Of course, you can override them in `portal-ext.properties`.

E-mail notification settings for membership requests and replies are configurable too. Thus, the subject and body of the membership reply and request are specified as TMPL files. Obviously, you can customize these setting by overriding TMPL files in `portal-ext.properties`.

Assigning permissions

As discussed earlier, site management is available only in the **Site Administration Panel**. If a user, such as "Lotti Stein", was a member of a site, such as "Palm Tree", in the current portal instance, then the user would be able to access the Site Administration Panel, and they would have the ability to manage the pages of the current site **Pages** from the left-hand side panel. It is convenient to access sites and manage pages of the site. This is not a standard approach. Normally, the sites should be accessed through the **Access in Control Panel** permission action, and pages of a site should be managed via permission **Pages**. In this section, we're going to discuss permissions on a portlet and permission in a site.

Let's assign the **MB Topic Admin** role to access the site in control panel, where Lotti is associated as a member.

To set the permission entitlements for **Site**, portal administrators need to define permissions in **Roles**. Under the **Users** section, click on **Roles** in **Control Panel** and locate **MB Topic Admin**. Select **Define Permissions** from the **Action** button beside **MB Topic Admin**. After that, search for **Site**; you will get the entitlement settings for **Site**:

- **Control Panel | Sites | Sites**: General Permissions, Resource Permissions (Site).

Let's discuss each of them in detail:

Control Panel | Sites | Sites: General Permissions

Action	Description
Access in Control Panel	This provides the ability to access the portlet in control panel
Configuration	This provides the ability to configure the portlets
Permission	This provides the ability to assign permissions.
View	This provides the ability to view

Let's say the user "Lotti Stein" is a member of the role "MB Topic Admin" and a member of the "Book Street" site. As a portal administrator, you are required to grant the **Access in Control Panel** permission to the user "Lotti Stein" and grant the **Add Pages** permission too. How do we accomplish this? We do it by following these steps:

1. Log in as a portal administrator since Roles is only accessible by the Portal admin.

2. Click on **Roles** under the category **Users** of **Control Panel**.

3. Then, locate a role, say **MB Topic Admin**.

4. Then, click on the **Define Permissions** icon from the **Actions** menu on the right-hand side of the role. Now, search for **Sites**.

5. Click on **Control Panel**: **Site** | **Site** link and enable the **Access** checkboxes in **Control Panel** and **View** under general permissions.

6. Finally, save the changes.

From now on, users and the members of the role "MB Topic Admin" will have access to the Site in **Control Panel**. Follow this section to add pages.

Control Panel | Sites | Sites: Resource Permissions | Site

The role Site Owner can set up all permissions: **Assign Members, Assign User Roles, Delete, Manage Announcements, Manage Archived Setups, Manage Pages, Manage Teams, Manage Staging, Permissions, Publish Staging, Update**, and **View**. All permission actions are unsupported for the role Guest. The following table shows entitlement permissions on a site:

Action	Description
Add Page	This provides the ability to add the portlet into the page
Add Page Variation	This provides the ability to add page variation on the page for staging
Add Site	This provides the ability to add site
Add Site Pages Variation	This provides the ability to add Site pages variation for staging
Assign Members	This provides the ability to assign members
Assign User Roles	This provides the ability to assign users to site roles
Configure Applications	This provides the ability to configure application
Delete	This provides the ability to delete the site
Export/Import Application Info	This provides the ability to export/import the application info
Export/Import Pages	This provides the ability to export/import the pages LAR
Go to Site Administration	This provides the ability to access Site Administration Panel
Manage Announcements	This provides the ability to manage announcements

Action	Description
Manage Archived Setups	This provides the ability to manage archived setups
Manage Pages	This provides the ability to manage pages
Manage Staging	This provides the ability to manage staging pages
Manage Subsites	This provides the ability to manage sub sites
Manage Teams	This provides the ability to manage teams
Permissions	This provides the ability to assign permissions on the site
Preview in Device	This provides the ability to preview in Devices
Publish Staging	This provides the ability to publish staging pages
Publish to Remote	This provides the ability to publish to remote
Update	This provides the ability to update the site
View	This provides the ability to view the site
View Members	This provides the ability to view members
View Staging	This provides the ability to view staging

Let's say the user "Lotti Stein" is a member of the role "MB Topic Admin" and a member of the "Book Street" site. As a portal administrator, you are required to grant permission to the user "Lotti Stein" and also grant the **Add Pages** and **Manage Pages** permissions. How do we accomplish this? We do it by following these steps:

1. Log in as a portal administrator since Roles is only accessible by Portal admin.

2. Click on **Roles** under the category **Users** of **Control Panel**.

3. Then, locate a role, say **MB Topic Admin**.

4. Then, click on the **Define Permissions** icon from the **Actions** menu on the right-hand side of the role. Now, search for **Sites**.

5. Enable the **Manage Pages** and **Add Pages** checkboxes.

6. Click on the **Save** button.

As shown in the preceding processes, it grants the **Manage Pages** permission for the role "MB Topic Admin" on all sites in the current portal instance. As a member of the role "MB Topic admin", "Lotti Stein" would see the **Add** icon in the dock bar menu, able to add pages to any site.

Advanced site settings

Whenever you build a portal, you need to configure a lot of settings so that it is easy for end users to trigger the portal URL and Sitemap for the search engine crawler and much more. Liferay provide advanced settings for the sites with many configuration features. Let's explore each of them one by one. All the advanced settings for the site are only accessible by the Site Administrator. So, log in as the Site Administrator of Palm Tree. Now, click on **configuration** under **Admin | Site Administration** from the dock bar menu. It will redirect you to the site settings page. You will be able to see links with different settings, which are described as follows:

- **Basic Information**: **Details**, **Categorization**, **Site URL**, and **Site Template**.

- **Search Engine Optimization**: **Sitemap** and **Robots**.

- **Advanced**: **Default User Associations**, **Staging**, **Analytics**, **Content Sharing**, and **Recycle Bin**

- **Miscellaneous**: **Custom Fields** and **Display Settings**

The following screenshot illustrates the Site settings; you will be able to see the right-hand side links, which are mentioned in the preceding list. We are going to describe each of them in detail.

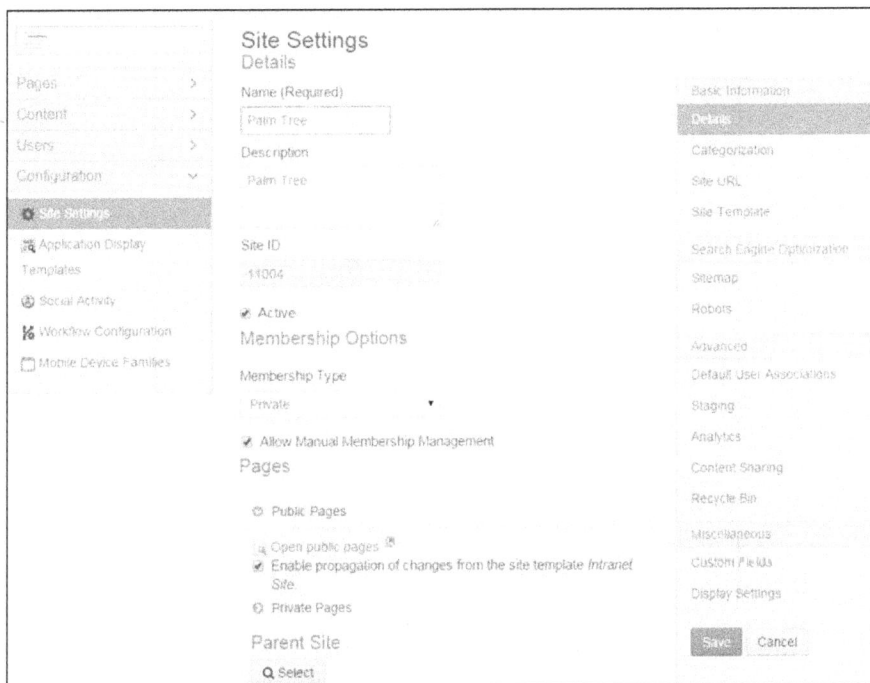

Figure 7.20: Site Settings

- **Details**: The Site Administrator will be able to change the Site name, descriptions, and membership type of a Site. They can also make the site active or inactive and also set the parent site.

- **Categorization**: The Site Administrator will be able to set the tags and categories for the site.

- **Site URL**: The Site Administrator will able to set the friendly URL and Virtual Hosts for the site. Let's discuss both in detail.

  ○ Friendly URL: It allows the site administrator to manage the path of the site in the intranet portal's URL. It can be implemented in both public and private pages. Basically, the friendly URL should be human-readable and easy to understand so that it raw boosts the search and helps the SEO understand the URLs. It should be unique too. Friendly URLs for public pages and private pages are appended to `http://localhost:8080/web` and `http://localhost:8080/group` respectively. In our "Palm Tree" example, it should append `/palmtree`. Therefore, the public URL becomes `http://localhost:8080/web/palmtree`, and the private URL becomes `http://localhost:8080/group/palmtree`.

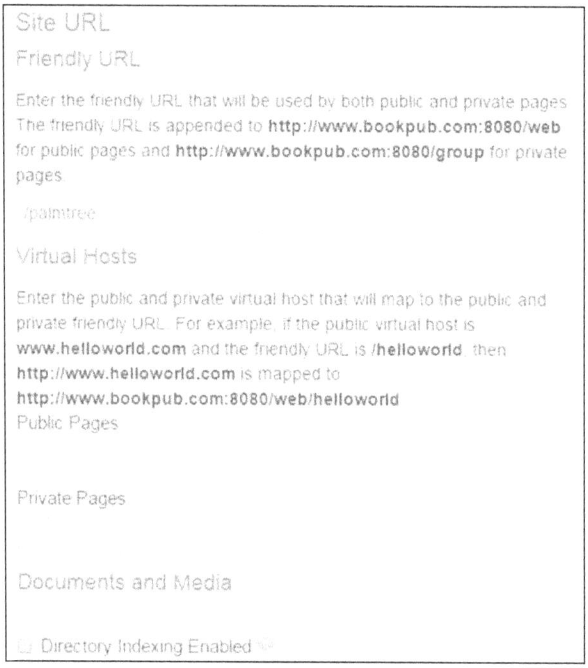

Figure 7.21: Site URL settings

- ○ Virtual Host: This allows the site administrator to define the domain name; it might be a full domain or subdomain. Basically, it helps users to navigate the portal easily. In Liferay, you can have multiple sites. Each site needs to set their virtual hosts to help the Liferay Portal server to understand and pick the site quickly.

For our example "Palm Tree", you need to create a domain name, say bookpub.com, and point it to the Liferay server. Now the DNS name bookpub.com needs to point to your portal's IP address. After that, you can enter bookpub.com:8080 in Virtual Host.

- **Site Template**:
  - ○ Whenever you use the site template in you site, you will be able to see the details of the site template and a link between the site template and the site. There will be two checkboxes for **Active**, and **Site template** allows modifications to the template, which is used whether or not modifications to the template pages are allowed.

- **Sitemap**:
  - ○ Liferay provides you with the unique feature of sitemap; it will generate the sitemap in one click. It uses the sitemap protocol to generate the sitemap. When you publish your site to the search engines provided (Google and Yahoo), their web crawlers will use the sitemap to index your site. This process is required to be done only once. The sitemap XML will be sent to the respective search engines and periodically crawl the sitemap once you have the initial request made. If you want to preview the sitemap XML, just click on the preview link for private pages and public pages.

- **Robots**:
  - ○ The Site Administrator will be able to configure robots.txt rules for the domain. Before doing this, you must configure Virtual Host for the site. It provides you with the option for both public and private pages.

- **Default User Associations**:
  - ○ The Site Administrator has the right to set default user associations for site roles and teams. It allows assigning new user members with default roles and teams for a particular site.

- **Staging**:
    - ◦ Liferay provides you with the staging feature of a site where the Site Administrator can enable it. Once it is enabled, you can edit and revise a page behind the scenes and then publish it live. We will discuss this further in later chapters.

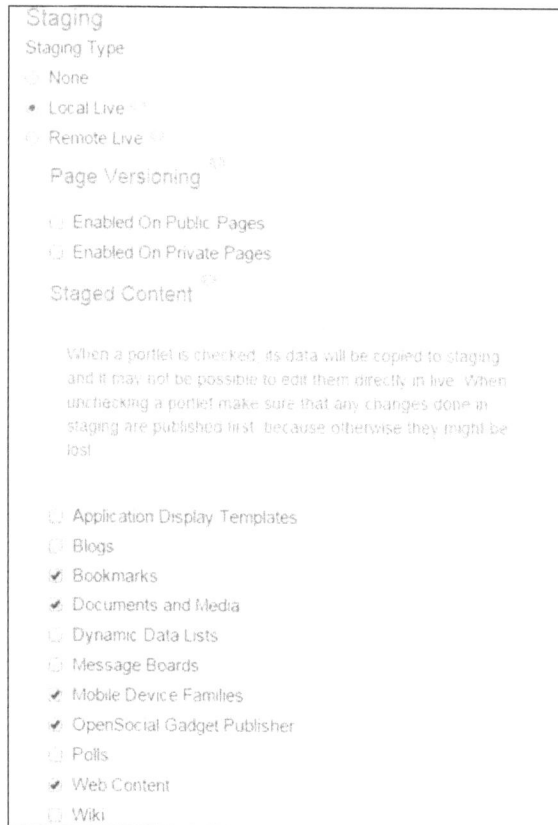

Figure 7.22: Staging settings

- **Analytics**:
    - ◦ The Site Administrator can set Google Analytics for the site. Liferay provides seamless integration with Google Analytics, which is a free service. Once the Site Administrator sets the Google Analytics ID and the piwik script on every page, this code get added. Google Analytics lets you to do all the traffic analysis on your site. It tells you who visited the site, where the visitors are from, and what pages they most often visited.

- **Content Sharing**:
    - ○ Content sharing gives the feature of sharing the content with subsites, which can display content from this site. By default, this value is enabled. You can change it to disable; once you do that, immediately revoke content sharing from all subsites.

- **Recycle Bin**:
    - ○ The Site Administrator has an option to enable/disable the Recycle Bin for your site. It even has an option to regulate the maximum age, that is, the number of days for which content can be stored in Recycle Bin until it is permanently deleted.

- **Custom Fields**:
    - ○ A custom field is a way to add an attribute to a site in the portal. The Site Administrator has the right to edit the custom fields, which are already configured for the site resources. Custom Fields can be configured from **Control Panel | Configuration | Custom Fields**, from where you can add custom fields to different resources.

- Display Settings:
    - ○ Display settings are there to configure the language options for your site. You can use the default language options, or you can define a custom default language.

Application Display Templates

Liferay 6.2 introduced a new feature, the **Application Display Templates** (ADT) framework. The ADT framework allows the portal administrator to override default templates, eliminating the limitations to the way your site's content is displayed. ADT helps with ways to define custom display templates used to render asset-centric applications. Say, for example, we need to display assets in the asset publisher in different sizes or different fashions.

You can get more benefits from the ADT with respect to different scenarios. Let's take one use case: if you want to include social media buttons in the Wiki portlet for Facebook or Twitter, you can create a custom template and configure with the portlet. The custom template wraps the skin of your portlet and provides you with unlimited control over its appearance and functionality in your portlet.

> Note that the ADT is always associated with the site where the custom template will reside. Set the ADT in the global context and make your template available across all sites. In the global context, you will have a sample ADT template for reference.

Let's create an ADT for the Palm Tree site. In the Site Administrator Panel, select **Application Display Templates** from the left-hand side menu.

1. On clicking on the **Add** button, a drop-down menu will appear with different resources, such as **Asset Publisher template**, **Blogs Template**, **Categories Navigation Template**, **Document and Media Template**, **Site Map Template**, **Tags Navigation Template**, and **Wiki Template**.

2. Select **Document and Media Template** and input the name "Carousel", the language "FreeMarker", and the description "Carousel for Home page".

3. In the right-hand side script box, paste the following code:

```
<#assign aui = taglibLiferayHash["/WEB-INF/tld/aui.tld"] />
<#assign liferay_portlet = taglibLiferayHash["/WEB-INF/tld/
liferay-portlet.tld"] />
<#if entries?has_content>
  <style>
    #<@liferay_portlet.namespace />carousel .carousel-item
    {
      background-color: #000;
      height: 250px;
      overflow: hidden;
      text-align: center;
      width: 700px;
    }
    #<@liferay_portlet.namespace />carousel .carousel-
      item img {
      max-height: 250px;
      max-width: 700px;
    }
  </style>
  <div id="<@liferay_portlet.namespace />carousel">
    <#assign imageMimeTypes = propsUtil.getArray("dl.file.
      entry.preview.image.mime.types") />
      <#list entries as entry>
        <#if imageMimeTypes?seq_contains(entry.getMime
          Type()) >
          <div class="carousel-item">
            <img src="${dlUtil.getPreviewURL(entry, entry.
              getFileVersion(), themeDisplay, "")}" />
```

```
            </div>
          </#if>
        </#list>
      </div>
    <@aui.script use="aui-carousel">
      new A.Carousel( {
        contentBox: '#<@liferay_portlet.namespace
          />carousel',
        height: 250,
        intervalTime: 2,
        width: 700
      }).render();
    </@aui.script>
  </#if>
```

4. Finally, save the ADT.

The following screenshot displays the ADT list in Palm Tree:

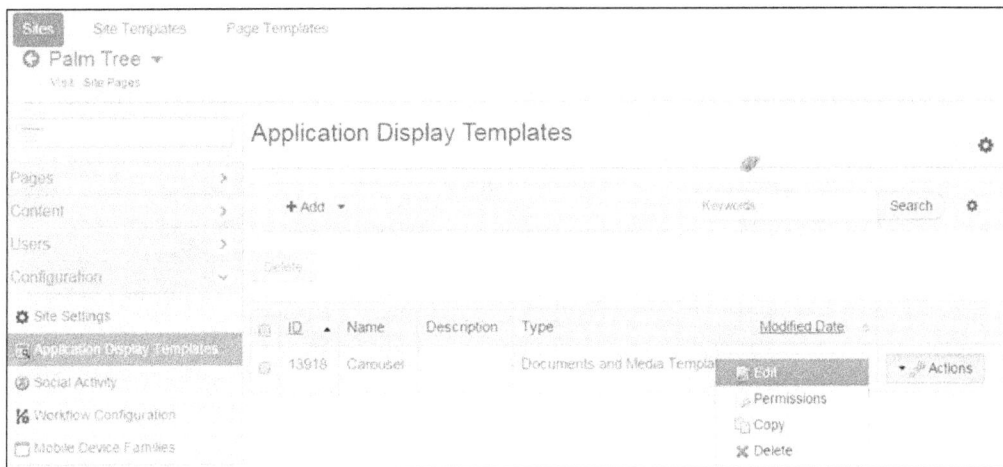

Figure 7.23: ADT settings

Once the ADT is saved, you can manage your ADT using the **Action** button:

- **Edit**: You can update the template
- **Permissions**: You can set the permissions from Delete, update permissions, and finally view for the ADT
- **Copy**: This lets you make a copy of the ADT
- **Delete**: This allows you to delete the ADT

Now, we need to enable the ADT for the portlet to configure our template. Let's place the Media Gallery portlet on the home page through **Add | Content and Applications | Applications | Content Management | Media Gallery**.

1. In the media gallery portlet, select **Configuration** from the **Gear** icon in the top-right corner of the portlet.

2. In **Configuration**, enable the **Show Action** and **Show Folder Menu** display settings. Disable **Show Navigation Links** and Show **Search** in display settings. Also, disable **Enable Ratings** and **Enable Comments ratings** in the ratings settings. Finally, save and close the popup.

3. Upload images in **Documents and Media**.

4. Finally, you will be able to see the carousel on the home page.

The following screenshot shows the carousel on the home page using the ADT framework in the Document and Media portlet:

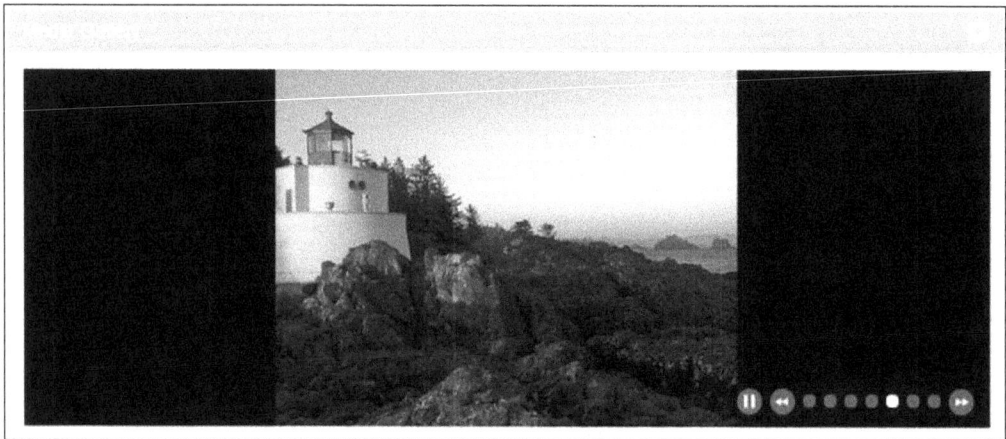

Figure 7.24: The ADT carousel slideshow

Finally, you created a carousel slideshow by transforming the Media Gallery portlet.

Liferay Social Activity

As we have seen, Liferay provides user interaction on your portal through different applications, such as Message Boards, Wikis, and Blogs. It's better to know which users are contributing value and which users are not. Liferay Social Activity allows you to tweak the measurements used to calculate user involvement within a site. Contribution and participation values determine the reward value of an action. Refer to the following screenshot for better understanding:

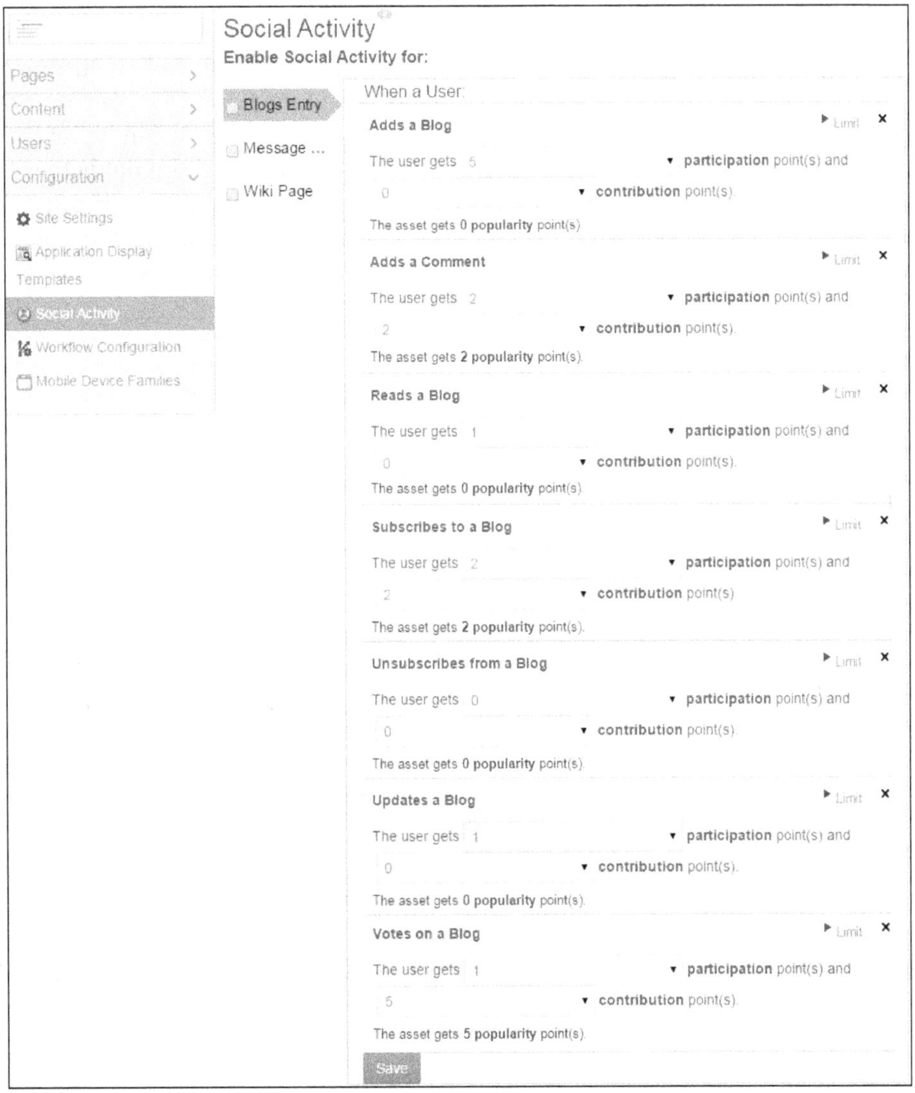

Figure 7.25:Social Activity

Different site instances can have separate Social Activity configurations. There are three type of track metrics provided by social activity, which helps us to determine the user involvement in the application, such as **Participation**, **Contribution**, and **Popularity** (for the asset involvement). The Site Administrator can enable social activity from **Site Administrator Panel | Configuration** section | **Social Activity**. Let's enable the **Blogs Entry** contents for social activity. Social Activity is set on the basics of the actions performed on the application by the user. In **Blogs Entry**, different actions, such as **Adds a Blog**, **Adds a Comments**, **Read a Blog**, **Subscribes to a Blogs**, **Unsubscribes from a Blog**, **Updates a Blog**, and last but not least **Votes on a Blog**. You need to set the point's values and limits on several actions for blogs. Refer to the following screenshot for **Adds a Comments** on blogs; when adding a comment, you can set two points for participation and two points for contribution. Points can be selected from the drop-down selection box. The limit can be set by clicking the limit link from the top-right, which provides a few more fields to set the limit for contribution and popularity. You can set the limit per asset for times a day, times, and times per period, which you can select from the dropdown. Even you can set the participation limit for an asset.

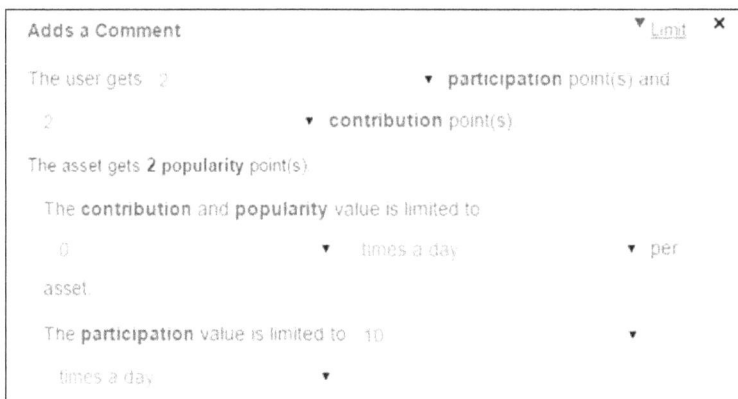

Figure 7.26:Social Activity

If you add the points for **Adds a Blog**, say something like two points for participation and five points for contribution, the asset popularity gets five points. When the users add a new blog entry, they receive five contribution points and the asset receives five popularity points. But in **Votes** on a Blog, blog entries benefit from all the contribution points, which go to the original asset creator, and all the popularity points go to the original assets since no creation action has taken place.

The primary purpose of Social Activity is to track the users who regularly contribute to the portal and participate in the discussion and recognize them. You can view the user's ranks in the **User Statistics** portlet. The user statistics portlet provides configuration to set the rankings with different checkboxes.

- **Rank by Contribution**: Ranks are calculated on the basis of the user's contribution score

- **Rank by Participation**: Ranks are calculated on the basis of the user's participation score

- **Show Header Text**: This allows you to define whether to show the title or only the rankings

- **Show Totals**: This toggles the display of the user's activity score.

- **Display Additional Activity Counters**: This provides other additional information next to the user's name—the number of comments on the assets, and so on

The Social Activity portlet is a robust application and is valuable for community-driven content creation. It's make it easier for us to recognize the users based on their activities.

Workflow Configuration

Liferay's Kaleo workflow engine is available in Marketplace for CE and EE versions of Liferay 6.2. It comes with Community Edition of the Tomcat bundle. Once you install it, it will provide you with a Workflow link under configuration. It comes with a sample workflow, that is, **Single Approver Workflow**. Refer to the following screenshot for better understanding.

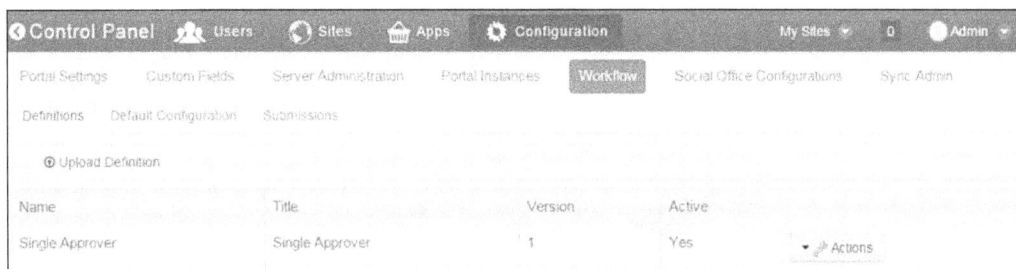

Figure 7.27: Workflow in Control Panel

In the preceding interface, you can upload a new workflow definition by clicking on the **Upload Definition** link. There are the following three tab views:

- **Definitions**: This lists all the uploaded workflows

- **Default Configuration**: This allows you to set the default workflow for different resources (**Page Revision**, **User**, **Blogs Entry**, **Web Content Article**, **Comments**, **Message Boards Message**, and **Wiki Page**) for a single portal instance

- **Submissions**: This provides a list of all the jobs pending and completed through the workflow

We will see Workflow Configuration in detail in *Chapter 10, Marketplace, Social Office, and Audience Targeting*.

The Site Administrator will also be able to configure the workflow from the Site Administrator panel by clicking on **Workflow Configuration** under the **Configuration** section in the left-hand side panel. Refer to the following screenshot to configure the workflow for Web Content Article:

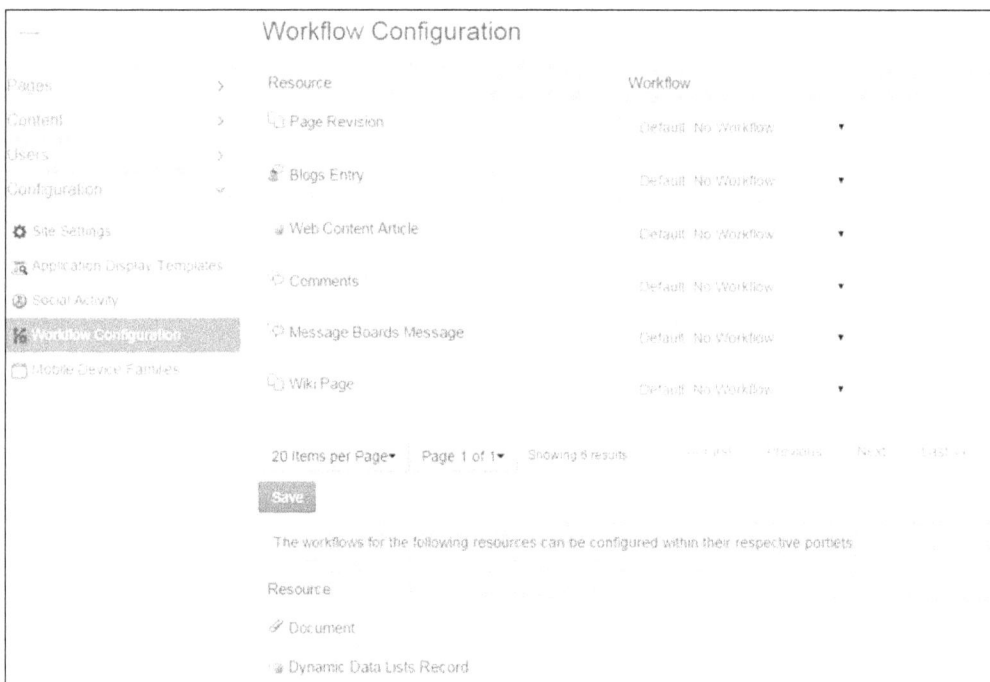

Figure 7.28: Workflow Configuration in Site Administration Panel

If you see the preceding screenshot, you can select the workflow for different resources for a site level. Now you can select the workflow for **Web Content Article** with **Single Approval Workflow** (the latest version copy).

> Note that the Kaleo workflow engine maintains the versioning of each workflow definition and creates a new copy whenever you do any changes in the file.

Once you have configured the workflow for the **Web Content Article** resource and saved it, the workflow will be implemented to **Web Content Article**.

Whenever you create any new web content article, you need to click on the **Submit for Publication** button, which will start the workflow. Approvers will get the notification and they need to approve it to allow the web content to be published.

Mobile Device Families

Mobile Device Families manages the configuration of the portal behaviors on different devices, such as mobile phones and tablets. The Site Administrator can configure the mobile device families with rules to alter the behavior of the portal on the different devices. It need to be configured at both the **Site** and **Page** levels with any number of mobile device families (all Android devices and all iOS tablets). Prioritization can be set on families to determine which one applies to a given page request.

Liferay Marketplace has a plugin called **Device Recognition**, which allows you to recognize devices. WURFL is integrated with the plugin, which basically has an open source database licensed with the AGPLv3 license. You need to have a mobile database deployed to make the mobile device rules get implemented.

> Note that if you want to make all the sites in the portal have mobile device rules set, then you can configure the Global Site. Navigate to **Control Panel | Sites | Global**.

Let's set the mobile device families for all the Android families by following these steps:

1. Log in as the site administrator, click on **Admin**, and select the configuration from the dropdown on the dock bar menu.
2. Select **Mobile Device Families** from the left-hand side panel.
3. Click on the **Add Device Family** button, which will open a form.

4. Fill in the name and description, say **All Android Families** and **All Android families smart phone** respectively.

5. Click on the **Save** button.

After you click on the **Save** button, you will see a new link, **Manage Classification Rules**, appear. Refer to the following screenshot:

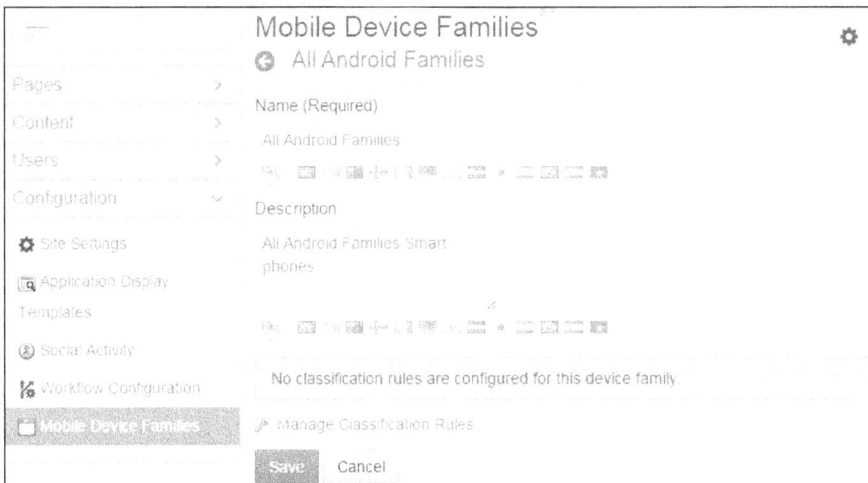

Figure 7.29: Mobile Device Families configuration in Site Administration Panel

Now, on clicking on Manage Classification Rules, you will be redirected to a page where you need to configure the rule for Android mobile phones. Refer to *Figure 7.30*. Input **name**, **description**, **Operating System**, and **Device Type** (select other devices since we are creating the rule for mobile phones and not for tablets). You need to input the device's **Physical Screen Size** and **Screen Resolution**. Finally, click on the **Save** button, and we are done with creating a rule for mobile devices.

> A classification rule specifies the characteristics of the devices that belong to a device family. Each family can have several classification rules.

If there is no device recognition provider installed, it will display the message at the top, saying **There is no device recognition provider installed. It will not be possible to determine the characteristics of the devices accessing the portal. Please contact the portal administrator or install it from the Liferay Marketplace**.

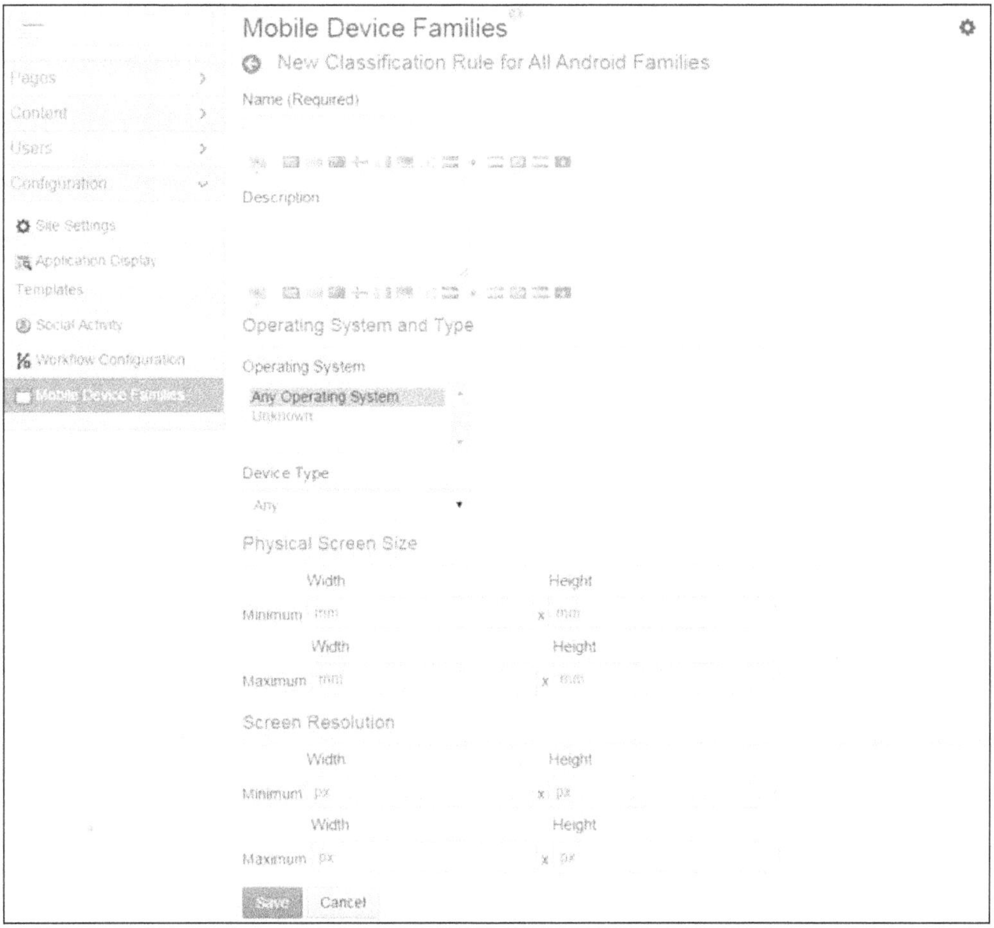

Figure 7.30: Manage classification rule for mobile device families in Site Administration Panel

Now we have to make the page redirect to our mobile device rule. Click on **Site Page** under **Pages** on the left-hand side panel. Click on **Mobile Device Rules** from the right-hand side panel, and then click on the **Select Device Family** button. A pop-up window will be open to allow you to choose **Device Families**, which we have created recently. Refer to the following screenshot to configure the page.

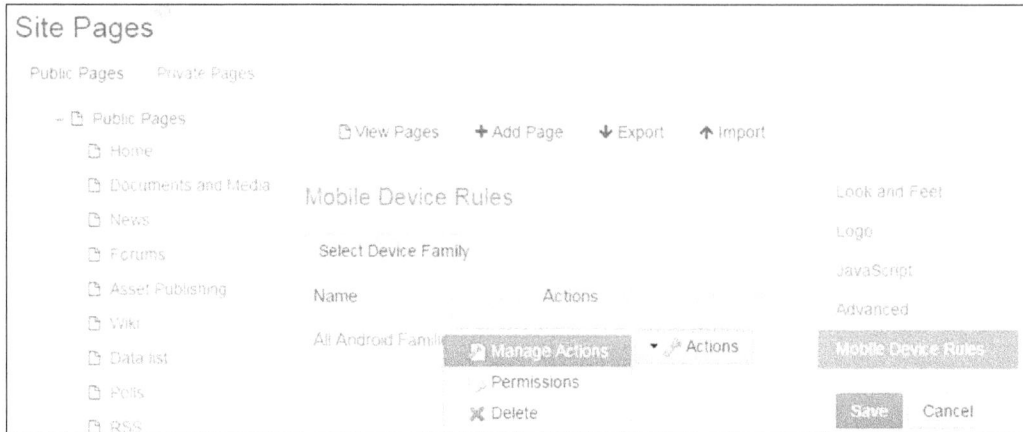

Figure 7.31: Mobile Device Rules in Site Pages settings

In the preceding screenshot, you selected the **All Android Families** device rule. Each rule will have Action associated, which is as follows:

- **Manage Actions**: This allows you to set the action for a particular device rule by creating the action and linking the type for the device rule, such as **Redirect to URL**, **Layout Template Modification**, **Theme Modification**, and **Redirect to Site**.

- **Permission**: This allows you to set the permissions for the device rule.

- **Delete**: This allows you to delete the device rule associated with a page.

Finally, when users access the site from their Android mobile, it will call **Mobile Device Rules** and proceed as per the actions defined.

Summary

This chapter introduced you to advanced settings of Site, managing site with different actions, such as editing, deleting, searching, and so on. It also helps us to understand the permissions settings for sites. You learned how to create Site Templates and Page Templates with the permissions settings too. You have seen how to assign the users in the site and set the roles for different users. Creating a team was a nice experience, which gave the Site Administrator more flexibility to work with the users and create a prefect group for an organization. You learned how to create work on the advanced settings of the sites, which we will see more in detail in the coming chapters. This chapter has also introduced you to the new feature of Liferay 6.2, the Application Display Templates (ADT) framework. Using the ADT, we completed one live example too. You also learned Social Activity to rank users based on their contribution toward different resources. You also saw how to enable the workflow configuration for the web content article resource. We have also done the configuration of Mobile Device Families for a particular site page. In the next chapter, you are going to learn about Document and Media and Liferay Sync.

8
Document and Media Management

In an organization, an intranet portal should have the feature of document management so that the organization can maintain the documents in the portal itself. In an intranet portal `bookpub.com` of the enterprise Palm Tree Publications, you are going to implement document management. In this chapter, you are going to learn how to use Documents and Media Library. Liferay 6.2 Documents and Media Library has the ability to sort files online using the same type of structure that you use to store locally. The best part is that you can use it to store files of any type, use it as virtual share drive, and even mount and browse external repositories. In this chapter, you will learn in detail about the **Documents and Media** portlet, **Media Gallery** portlet, and **Documents and Media Display** portlet.

The Document and Media Library has many other features and settings, which you will explore in this chapter, such as **Document Type and Metadata Sets**; **Alternative File Repository Options** using an **External Repositories** example (Alfresco repositories); **Microsoft Office Integration**; and **Automatic Previews and Metadata**. In Liferay 6.2, these document types and media settings have given excellent support to the whole documents and media portlet.

In this chapter, Liferay Sync will be discussed in detail. This is a unique feature in Liferay that allows you to automatically synchronize the entire document with your local filesystem.

This chapter will also discuss how to configure workflows with the documents and media portlet.

By the end of this chapter, you will have learned:

- How to set up the documents and media
- How to set up document types and metadata sets
- About the details of the Media Gallery portlet
- About the different settings in the documents and media portlet
- How to set up the workflow on documents and media
- How to install and configure Liferay Sync
- How to integrate Liferay with the Alfresco CMS

Documents and Media

The Documents and Media portlet (portlet id 20) is basically available in the Site Administration panel and in the dock bar too. The Documents and Media portlet is non-instanceable, which means that in a page, only one portlet can be hosted. In the same site scope, documents and media will have the same documents since it's sharing the same dataset.

As a site administrator, you would be able to explore the Documents and Media portlet in the Site Administrator panel. Let's log in as the Site Administrator and click on **content** in **Admin | Site Administration** from the dock bar and then select **Documents and Media**.

The following screenshot shows the Documents and Media portlet with images uploaded into it:

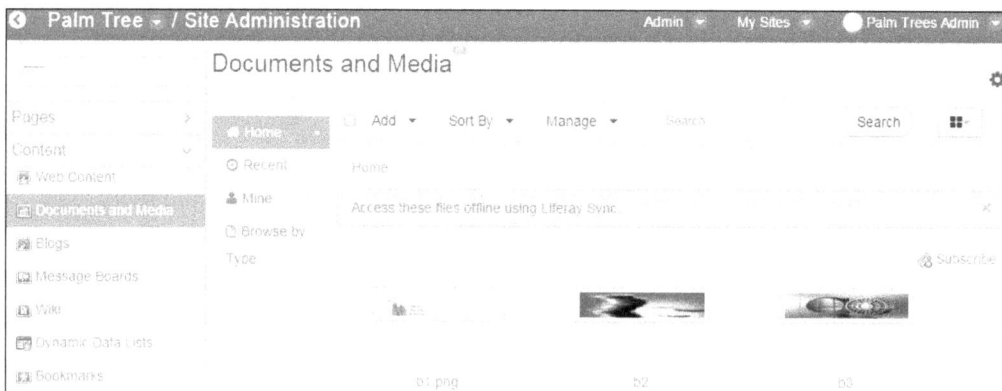

Figure 8.1: The Documents and Media portlet

The Documents and media portlet has the fine filtering feature for end user requirements.

Managing documents and media

Documents and media can be managed by the Site Administrator. Liferay 6.2 has made document management very user friendly and easy to maintain.

In the preceding screenshot, there is the links section with the names **Home**, **Recent**, **Mine**, and **Browse by Type**; these are all filters. **Home** is the default folder, which contains the folders and documents. **Recent** displays all documents that have been recently uploaded, edited, or downloaded. **Mine** displays all the documents uploaded by you. **Browse by Type** shows the options of the document type. If you select any document type, it will fetch all the documents related to that document type. Let's start to work with Documents and Media.

Let's discuss the menu at the top of the Documents and Media portlet that contains the **Add**, **Sort By**, and **Manage** buttons. Beside that, there is a **search** textbox with a search button, which allows you to search for a file from a list. There is also a button which allows you to switch the view for the listed documents. These views are **icon view**, **descriptive view**, and **list view**.

There is a **Subscribe** link in the top-right corner. It will be visible in all the folders. When you click on the **Subscribe** link, it subscribes you to the folder you are currently viewing, and you will receive e-mail notifications whenever any actions take place in the folder, say adding, editing, or deleting files.

The following are the options under the **Add** menu button:

- **Folder**: This allows you to create a new folder in your portlet's filesystem.
- **Shortcut**: This allows you to create a shortcut to any document that you have read access for. Also, you can specify who can access the original document through a shortcut.
- **Repository**: Liferay 6.1 introduced this new feature. It allows you to add an entirely new repository to your Documents and Media portlet. While creating the repository, you have to specify the repository type and choose an ID, even the AtomPub protocol, if you are using it.
- **Multiple Documents**: This allows you to upload multiple documents at one go.
- **Basic Documents**: This allows you to upload a single document. By default, basic documents are not described by any metadata sets.

The rest of the options in the Add menu are default document types, such as **Contract**, **Marketing Banner**, **Online Training**, **Sales Presentation**, and **Publisher document**, which are each described by a unique metadata set. Whenever you add a file associated with any document type, you will be provided with the file upload form with additional fields for metadata in a specific document type use case. Let's discuss the Contract document type for example.

Contract

The Contract document type is intended to be used to describe legal contracts. It has specific metadata for Contract documents, such as the **Effective Date**, **Expiration Date**, **Contract Type**, **Status**, **Legal reviewer**, **Signing Authority**, and **Deal Name** fields.

So, whenever you create any new document type for your use case, it will also appear under the Add menu. After that, when you want to upload a file using the specific document type, you need to fill in all the metadata.

> Liferay 6.2 provides you with the drag and drop upload feature. You can upload the file just by dragging it from your local filesystem to the Documents and Media folder location. It will upload the file with the same filename as the File Title and is available instantly.

Liferay Documents and Media provides you with a sort feature, which allows you to sort the listed document in different ways. The following are the options for sorting under the **Sort By** button:

- **Title**: This allows you to sort the document by title alphabetically
- **Create Date**: This allows you to sort the document by creation date
- **Modified Date**: This allows you to sort the document by the last time they were modified
- **Downloads**: This allows you to sort the document by the number of times they were downloaded
- **Size**: This allows you to sort the document by file size

After **Sort By**, you can see the **Manage** menu button. It allows you to view details of document types and metadata sets. Let's discuss it:

- **Document Types**: This allows the viewing of all the document types. Also, you can create a new Document Type.
- **Metadata Sets**: It displays a list of defined metadata sets as well as their portal IDs. You can also create new Metadata Sets.

We are going to discuss Document Type and Metadata Sets further in the coming sections.

Adding folders

In our filesystem, we generally maintain our files in different folder structures. In the same way, in intranet portals, different department folders can be maintained for their documents. In our use case, let's create a folder with the name `Editorial Department`, which will contain two subfolders with the names `Editorial Germany` and `Editorial US`:

1. Log in as the Site Administrator of the site Palm Tree.
2. Click on **Content** in **Admin | Site Administration** from the dock bar menu.
3. Select **Documents and Media** from the left-hand side panel.
4. In Documents and Media, select the folder from the **Add** dropdown.
5. Fill in the name `Editorial Department` and the description `Editorial department folder`.
6. Keep the default permission settings, that is, **Anyone Guest Role**. If you need to change the permission, click on the **More Options** link to do so.
7. Finally, **Save** it.

The folder with the name `Editorial Department` has been created. Now create a subfolder inside the `Editorial Department` folder. Click on the `Editorial Department` folder first, then:

1. Select the folder from the **Add** drop down.
2. Fill in the name `Editorial Germany` and the description `Editorial Germany folder`.
3. Keep the default permission settings, that is, **Anyone Guest Role**. If you need to change the permission, click on the **More Options** link to change the permission.
4. Finally, save it.

Follow the same steps for the `Editorial US` folder. The following screenshot shows the two folders **Editorial Germany** and **Editorial US** inside **Editorial Department**. Also, it shows the **Actions** dropdown in the folder too.

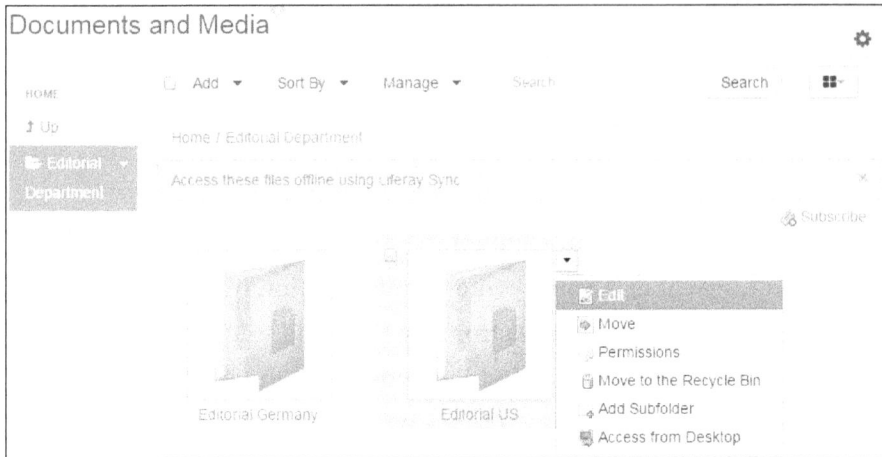

Figure 8.2: Folder and subfolders inside Documents and Media

In the preceding screenshot, you can see the folder structure with Editorial Department having two subfolders. Each folder has an **Action** dropdown with **Edit**, **Move**, **Permissions**, **Move to the Recycle Bin**, **Add Subfolder**, and **Access from Desktop**. Let's know each action in brief.

- **Edit**: This lets you edit the folder settings and also allows you to enable the workflow for documents and media. See the *Enabling the workflow in Documents and Media* section for more details.

- **Move**: This lets you move the folder to a new location.

- **Permissions**: This allows you to configure folder-specific permissions for the folder.

- **Move to the Recycle Bin**: This lets you remove the folder from the Documents and Media library.

- **Add Subfolder**: This allows you to create a subfolder for a particular folder without going into the folder.

- **Access from Desktop**: This allows you to access the folder directly from the explorer of your desktop operating system, basically using the WebDAV URL `http://localhost:8080/webdav/palmtree/document_library/Editorial%20Department/Editorial%20US`.

Editing folders

As mentioned earlier, we can edit the folder settings. Let's change the description of the `Editorial Germany` folder:

1. Click on the **Edit** action from the **Action** dropdown of the `Editorial Germany` folder.

2. Now you can change the description of the folder from `Editorial Germany folder` to `This folder is for Editorial Germany`..

3. Here, you will see **Document Type Restrictions and Workflow** settings too. These settings are used to restrict certain document types in the folder. Also, we can set the workflow configuration for the folder too. We will discuss this in detail in the coming section.

4. Finally, **save** the changes.

Editing a folder has a setting for workflow, which we will discuss in the coming section. The following screenshot shows the folder being edited:

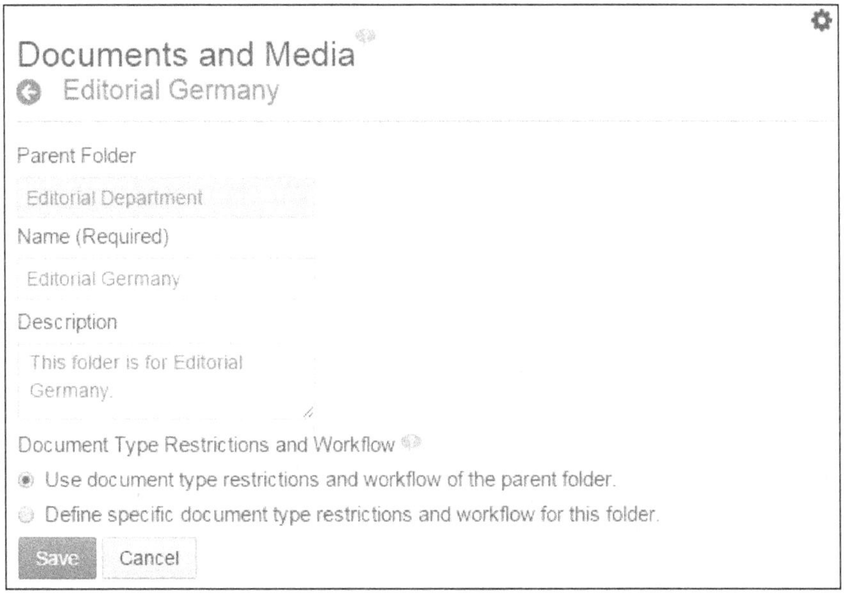

Figure 8.3: Editing a folder

Moving folders

Sometimes, users create folders wrongly, which need to be moved to their respective locations or removed completely. Liferay 6.2 has the feature to move the folder to its respective location. Let's see how we can move the folder to another location:

1. Click on the **Move** action from the **Action** dropdown of the `Editorial Germany` folder.

2. Now you can select the desired parent folder location by selecting the select button. You will get the pop-up window where you can choose the parent folder.

3. Finally, click on the **Move** button.

This is a nice feature for document management. The following screenshot shows the illustration of the moving of the `Editorial Germany` folder from `Editorial Department` to some other folder:

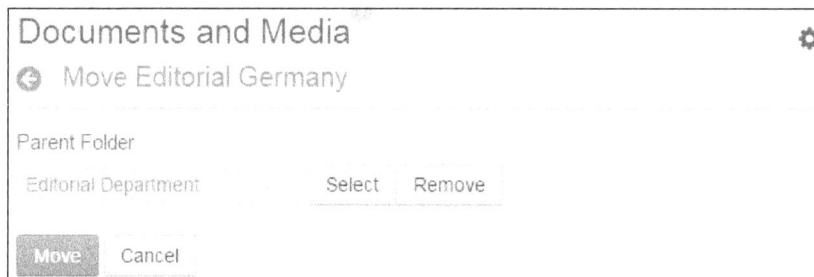

Figure 8.4: Moving folders

> Note that moving a folder also moves the files in that folder. You can move folders to any parent folder location for which you have the required permissions.

In the Palm Tree intranet portal, the users will upload the documents in their respective folders. Let's see the case study of adding files/documents to the `Editorial Germany` folder.

Adding files

In Liferay 6.2, we have the freedom to upload any kind of file extension. Liferay 6.2 reads most of them very easily and also allows the user to preview the document in the document preview panel. Let's upload an `Editorial Department.pdf` file into the Editorial Germany folder.

1. In **Documents and Media**, click on the **Editorial Germany** folder.
2. Click on **Basic Document** from the **Add** button.
3. A new document page will open. Here, you can select the document and publish it.
4. Choose the file from your local system.
5. Fill in the **Title** and **Description** of the document, say `Editorial Document` and `Editorial department document project`, respectively.
6. Set the **Categorization** and **Tags** for the document.
7. Leave the default **Related Assets** and **Permissions** settings.
8. Finally, publish the document by clicking on the **Publish** button.

You can see the following screenshot for uploading the file in the Documents and Media library:

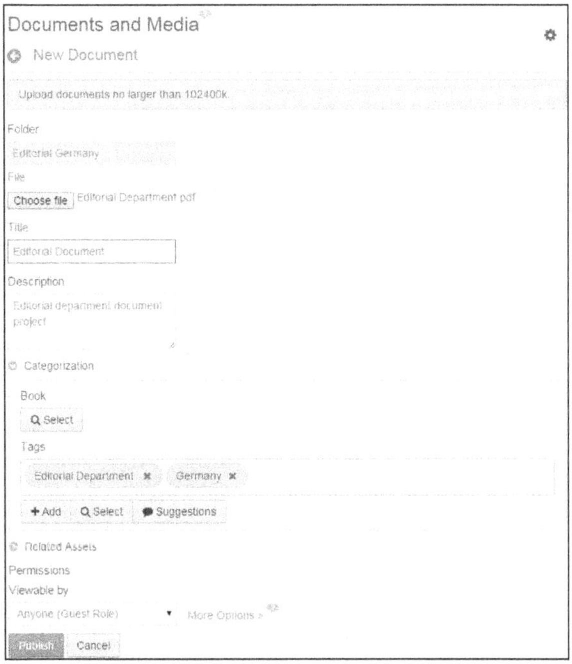

Figure 8.5: Adding a file

Once you publish the document, it creates the document in the Documents and Media library. After publishing, you will be able to view the document in **Documents and Media**. The following screenshot displays the document inside **Documents and Media** with the actions. Let's discuss the actions in brief:

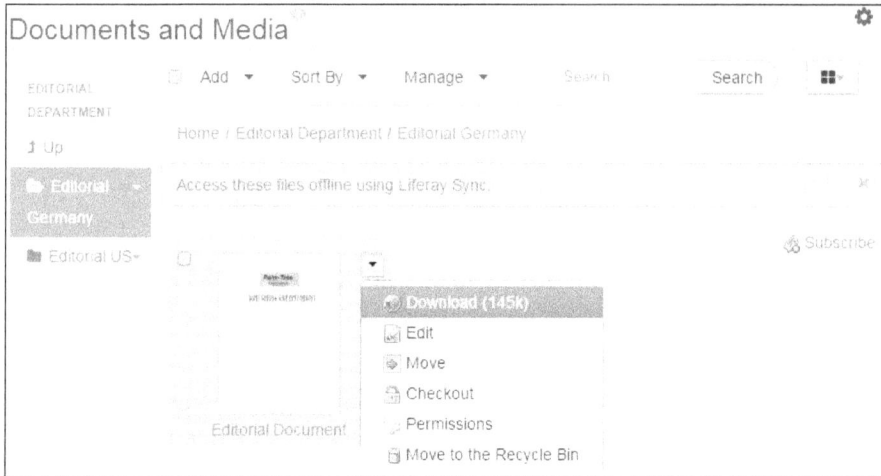

Figure 8.6: A file inside Documents and Media

All documents created in Documents and Media will have actions, which are used to update the document and its settings. In the preceding screenshot, the actions that you can perform on the documents are as follows:

- **Download**: This allows you to download the document.

- **Edit**: This allows you to change the content of a document; point it to a different file; change its title, description, or document type; or add tags, categories, or related assets.

- **Move**: This allows you to move the file to a desired location in the portal.

- **Checkout**: This allows you to safely work on the document while you are editing and prevent other users from modifying the same document. Once your work is done, you can check the document back in.

- **Permissions**: This allows you to set the file-specific permission on the document.

- **Move to the Recycle Bin**: This allows you to remove the documents from Documents and Media.

Now let's view the document by clicking on the document itself. You will be able to see that the document opens with a lot of details, such as its version number, version history, and status, and also who uploaded it and who last edited it. The following screenshot will describe all the fields clearly:

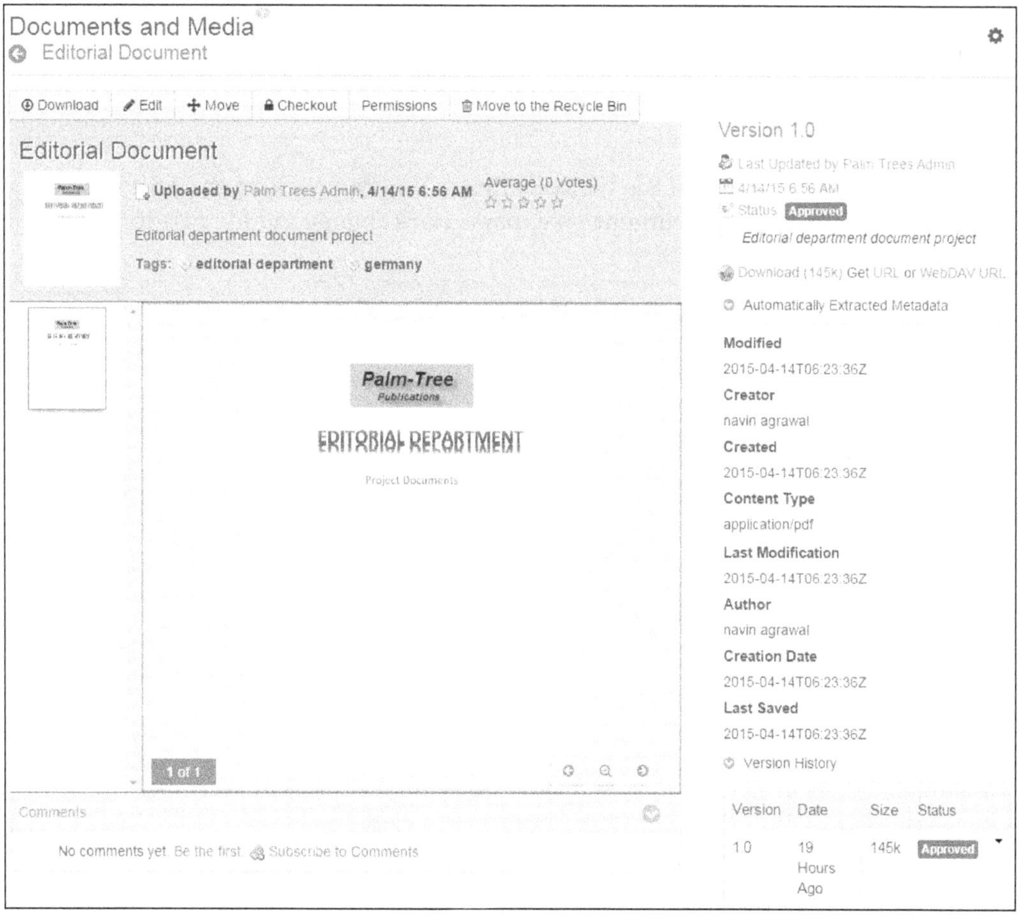

Figure 8.7: View a file

Liferay has the beauty of displaying the document inside Documents and Media. Most of the files are supported, such as `.pdf`, `.png`, `.txt`, `.doc`, `.xml`, and more. In the preceding screenshot, you will see details of the file and also its actions. We have already discussed the same actions. You will be able to see the document title, by which user the file got uploaded, and when it was uploaded. You can even put the rating/vote for the document by setting the **Averages** (stars); you can see the file description. The tags are also visible. The document view section can be zoomed in to read the file content clearly. If the comments section is enabled, you can view comments, add comments, or subscribe to comments.

> [✎ Note that **Comments** are enabled by default.]

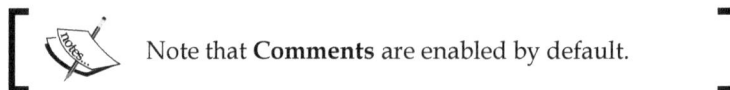

If you see the right-hand side information, it provides metadata of the document, such as versions, last updated by user, status, description of the file, download link, WebDAV URL, content type, author, last saved date, and version history.

Editing files

You might be required to edit the file sometimes. You can click on the **Edit** button from the top menu of the document view page. Let's change the file title to `Editorial project document`.

1. Click on the **Edit** button from the top menu of the document:

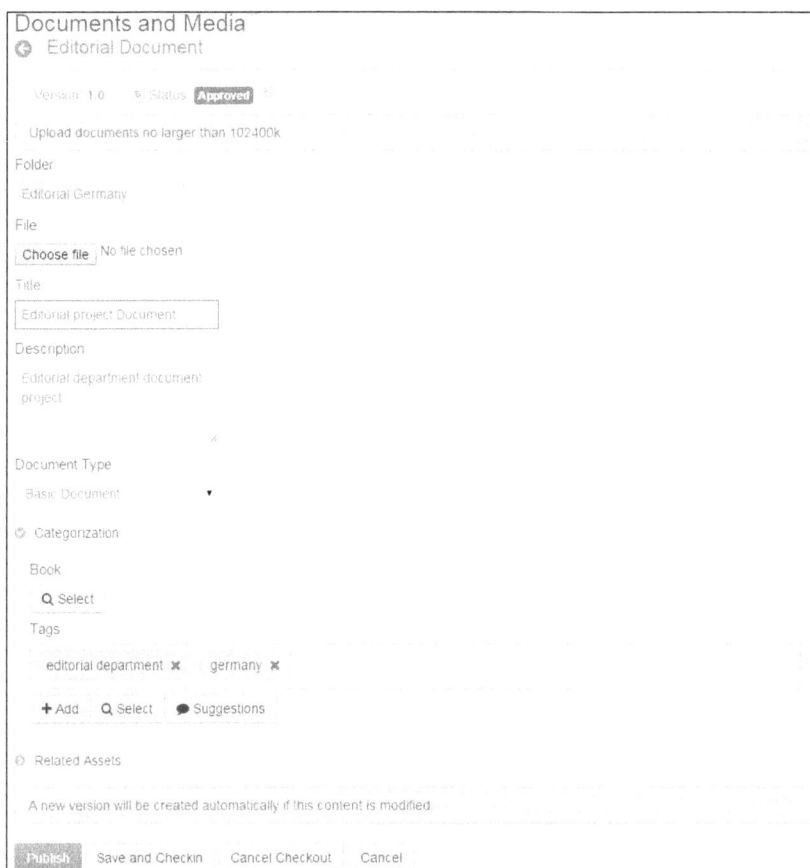

Figure 8.8: Edit File

2. The edit from page file will be open. Change the file's title to `Editorial project document`.

3. Finally, save it.

Once it's saved, you will see that the file's title has been changed to `Editorial project document`.

Checkout and checkin

In the document management system, checkout and checkin is an essential feature. Liferay provides us with the best implementation on the Document and Media library. Let's have a use case where the Palm Tree administrator wants to edit the `Editorial project document` file and doesn't want another user to overwrite the document on which they are working. Lotti Stein, at the same time, tries to access the document and also tries to edit it.

1. Log in as the Site Administrator of Palm Tree.

2. Click on **Content** from **Admin | Site Administration** from the dock bar menu.

3. Select **Documents and Media** from the left-hand side panel.

4. Navigate to the **Editorial Germany** folder and double-click on the document `Editorial project document`.

5. The document will open in the document view. Click on the **Checkout** button from the top menu.

6. After clicking on it, the message **You now have a lock on this document. No one else can edit this document until you unlock it. This lock will automatically expire in 1 day.** will be displayed.

7. Now you can edit and upload the new document. For the duration of time for which you are working on the document, no other user can work on the same document.

8. Let's log in as Lotti Stein and go to the **Document and Media** page from the navigation menu bar, which we created before.

9. The Document and Media portlet is already placed in the page.

10. Navigate to the **Editorial Germany** folder, and double-click on the document `Editorial project document`.

11. Lotti will also see an error (red) message **You cannot modify this document because it was locked by Palm Trees Admin on 4/16/15 7:36 AM.**. It totally depends on the permissions that Lotti has. If Lotti doesn't have the permission to edit the file, she will not get any message. If Lotti has the permission to do **Override Checkout**, she will see the same message that **Palm Tree Admin** received.

The checkout feature gave you the privilege to work on the file independently. Now once your work is completed on the file, you can click on the **Save and Checkin** button in the edits form. The following screenshot displays the document view after checkout:

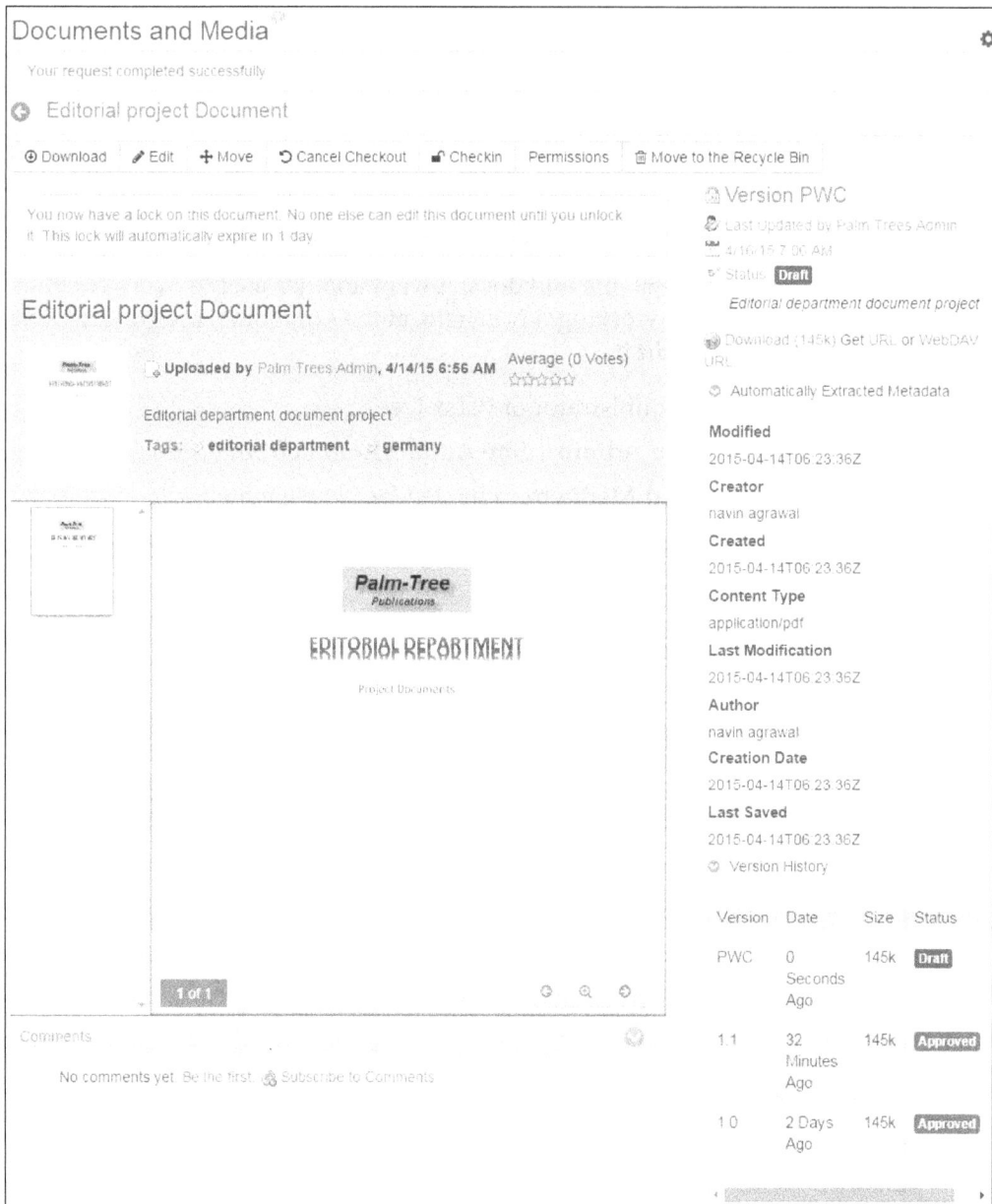

Figure 8.9: File checkout

The version of the document has changed to **Version PWC**. Liferay creates a draft copy of the file that is called **personal working copy (PWC)**.

> Note that you can cancel the checkout by simply clicking on the **Cancel Checkout** button.

Adding a shortcut

Liferay has a nice feature called Add Shortcut. You can add a document shortcut from different sites, but you should have the read access permission on the document. Let's create a shortcut document inside the Palm Tree site. We will access a document from the Editorial Germany site and create a shortcut for it:

1. Click on the **Add** button and select **Shortcut**.

2. You will be redirected to the **New File Shortcut** page; select the **Site** and **Document**:

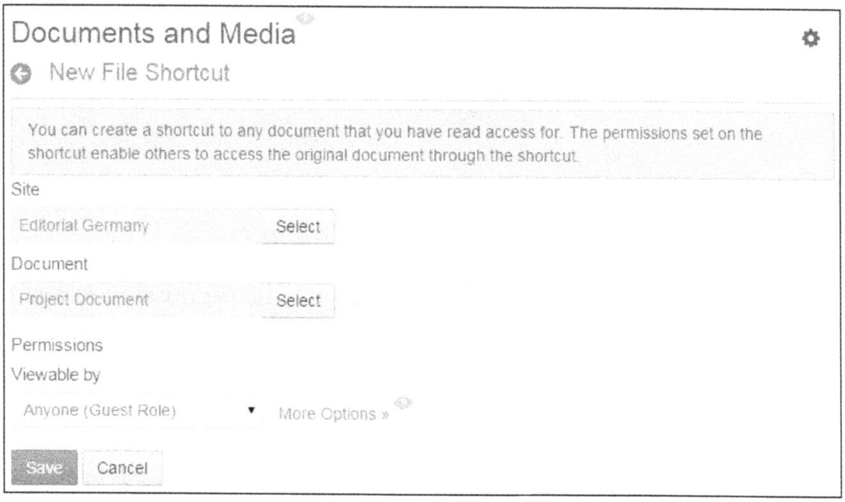

Documents and Media
New File Shortcut

You can create a shortcut to any document that you have read access for. The permissions set on the shortcut enable others to access the original document through the shortcut.

Site
Editorial Germany   Select

Document
Project Document   Select

Permissions
Viewable by
Anyone (Guest Role)   ▼   More Options »

Save   Cancel

Figure 8.10: Adding a shortcut

3. Finally, Save it.

> Note that the permission set on the shortcut enables others to access the original document through the shortcut.

Now you can see the shortcut file with the name `Project Document` has been created in the `Editorial Germany` folder under **Palm Tree | Document and Media**:

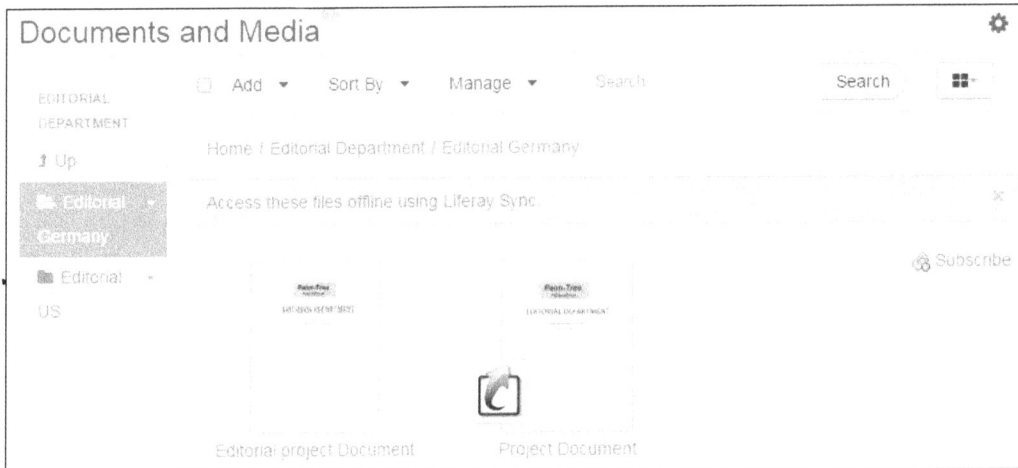

Figure 8.11: Adding a shortcut file

The shortcut feature adds value to document management. You can also set the permissions entitlements on the shortcut. In the next section, it will be discussed in detail.

Assigning permissions

The Document and Media portlet can be accessed inside **Site Administration Panel** and also outside (pages). The Site Member won't have the permission to add and edit files in the Document and Media portlet, but they may have access to view the file.

Let's provide the role entitlements for the **MB Topic Admin** role that allows the user to edit a document and where Lotti is associated as a member.

To set the permission entitlements for **Document and Media**, the portal administrator needs to define permissions in roles. Under the **User** section, click on **Roles** in **Control Panel** and locate **MB Topic Admin**. Select **Define Permissions** from the **Action** button beside **MB Topic Admin**. Search for documents and media. You will get the entitlements setting for documents and media.

Permissions for **Document and Media** can be assigned under **Site Administration |
Content** and **Site Administration | Applications**:

- **Site Administration | Content**: General Permissions, Resource Permissions
  (Documents), Document Folder, Document, Shortcut, and Document Type
- **Site Administration | Applications**: This has the same set of role entitlements

Let's discuss each of them in detail.

General Permissions

Action	Description
Access in Site Administration	This provides the ability to access the portlet in site administration panel
Add Display Template	This provides the ability to add display template
Add to Page	This provides the ability to add portlet to page
Configuration	This provides the ability to configure the portlets
Permission	This provides the ability to assign permissions
View	This provides the ability to view

General Permissions are defined as those that the users can enjoy most administrator
rights for a particular application in the portal. Access in Site Administration
entitlements are given to the users who have the Admin rights.

> Whenever you give entitlements for the specific portlets,
> you have to be clear about the users' roles.

Resource Permissions – documents

Resource Permissions defines what actions can be performed on resources displayed
or managed from the preceding application. Basically, resources are any user-facing
application in the portal, such as users, organization, sites, blogs, wikis, and so on.

Action	Description
Add Documents	This provides the ability to add documents
Add Documents Type	This provides the ability to add documents types
Add Folder	This provides the ability to add folders
Add Repository	This provides the ability to add repositories
Add Shortcut	This provides the ability to add shortcuts

Action	Description
Add Structure	This provides the ability to add structures
Permissions	This provides the ability to assign permissions
Subscribe	This provides the ability to subscribe
Update	This provides the ability to update the document
View	This provides the ability to view

Documents folder

Permissions entitlements for the Documents folder are to access the folder and add a file to that folder. Even other actions can be given:

Action	Description
Access	This provides the ability to access the document folder
Add Documents	This provides the ability to add documents
Add Shortcut	This provides the ability to add shortcuts
Add Subfolder	This provides the ability to add subfolders
Delete	This provides the ability to delete
Permissions	This provides the ability to assign permissions
Update	This provides the ability to update the document
View	This provides the ability to view

Access entitlements can be assigned to the role that needs to access the folder and needs the ability to add documents and subfolders.

Document

Permissions entitlements on the document are assigned from **Site Administration | Content | Document**. Also, discussions on the document entitlements can be assigned from here:

Action	Description
Add Discussion	This provides the ability to add discussions on the document
Delete	This provides the ability to delete
Delete Discussion	This provides the ability to delete discussions on the document
Override Checkout	This provides the ability to override checkout on the documents
Permissions	This provides the ability to assign permissions
Update	This provides the ability to update the document

Action	Description
Update Discussion	This provides the ability to update discussions on the document
View	This provides the ability to view

Let's say the user "Lotti Stein" is a member of the role "MB Topic Admin". As a portal administrator, you are required to grant the Update permission on the document for the user "Lotti Stein" and also grant the View permission. How do we accomplish this? We do it by following these steps:

1. Log in as a portal administrator since Roles are only accessible by the Portal admin.
2. Click on **Roles** under the category **Users** of **Control Panel**.
3. Then, locate a role, say **MB Topic Admin**.
4. Then, click on the **Define Permissions** icon from the **Actions** menu on the right-hand side of the role. Now, search for **Documents and Media**.
5. Click on **Documents and Media** from **Site Administration | Content** and enable the **Update** checkbox and **View** checkbox from the document.
6. Finally, save the changes.

From now on, users and members of the role "MB Topic Admin" will have the edit button enabled for documents.

Shortcut

Permission entitlements for shortcut files can be assigned to users to delete, update, view, and set the permission on the shortcut:

Action	Description
Delete	This provides the ability to delete the shortcut files
Permissions	This provides the ability to assign permissions
Update	This provides the ability to update the shortcut files
View	This provides the ability to view

Document type

Permission entitlements for document type can be assigned to the users to delete, update, and configure the permission on the document type.

Action	Description
Delete	This provides the ability to delete
Permissions	This provides the ability to assign permissions
Update	This provides the ability to update the document
View	This provides the ability to view

Documents and Media – configuration

As mentioned earlier, Documents and Media is available in **Control Panel** as well as Site Administration Panel. In both places, you will find the configuration for Documents and Media. In Site Administration Panel, select documents and media from the content. Select the **Gear** icon from the top-right corner and click on **Configuration**.

Even you can do the same configuration from the **Document and Media** portlet from any page by clicking on the **Gear** icon and selecting the configuration link.

Configuration has four tabs, **Display Settings**, **Email Form**, **Document Added Email**, and **Document Updated Email**.

Let's discuss Display Settings first. It has many settings, such as **Root folder**, **Show Search**, **Maximum Entries to Display**, **Enable Related Assets**, **Display Style Views**, **Entries Listing for List Display Style**, and **Ratings**. Let's discuss each of them:

- **Root folder**: This allows you to select the Root folder for documents and media.

- **Show Search**: You can enable and disable search in documents and media.

- **Maximum Entries to Display**: This allows you to set the maximum number of entries to display in the Documents and Media portlet.

- **Enable Related Assets**: This allows you to enable and disable related assets.

- **Display Style Views**: This allows multiple select for the display style views; currently, it has icon, descriptive, and list. You can deselect any one from them.

- **Entries Listings for List Display Style**: This allows multiple selects for the column headings for the documents listings display style. By default, Name, Size, Status, Downloads, and Action are set. You can also include Create Date and Modified Date.

- **Ratings**: You can enable the ratings and comment ratings for documents and media.

Refer to the following screenshot for display settings in the configuration popup:

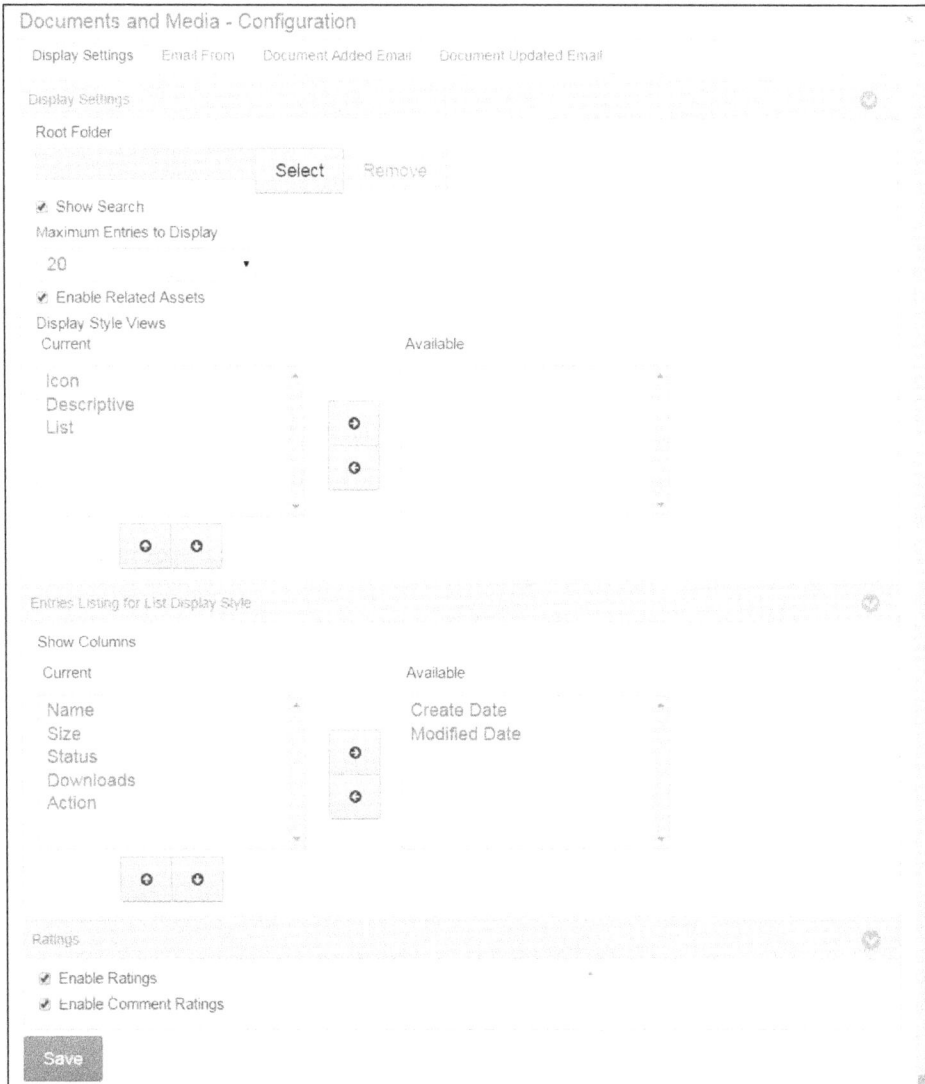

Figure 8.12: Documents and Media - Configuration | Display Settings

The **Email From** tab is for setting the e-mail sender name and the sender e-mail address. The following screenshot displays the **Email From** tab with definitions of terms. The **Definitions of Terms** are defined, which are used to get site names and so on and input into the text field.

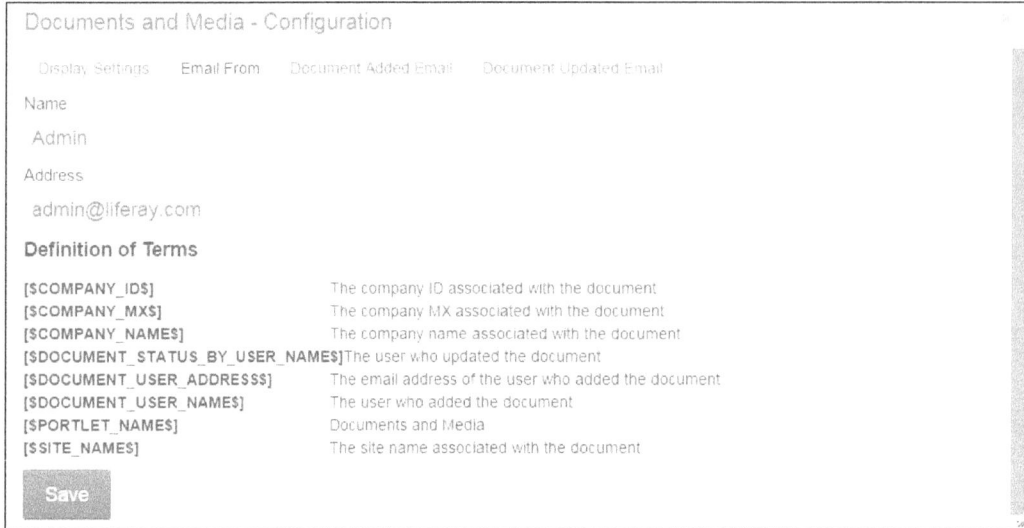

Documents and Media - Configuration

Display Settings   Email From   Document Added Email   Document Updated Email

Name

Admin

Address

admin@liferay.com

Definition of Terms

[$COMPANY_ID$]	The company ID associated with the document
[$COMPANY_MX$]	The company MX associated with the document
[$COMPANY_NAME$]	The company name associated with the document
[$DOCUMENT_STATUS_BY_USER_NAME$]	The user who updated the document
[$DOCUMENT_USER_ADDRESS$]	The email address of the user who added the document
[$DOCUMENT_USER_NAME$]	The user who added the document
[$PORTLET_NAME$]	Documents and Media
[$SITE_NAME$]	The site name associated with the document

Save

Figure 8.13: Documents and Media - Configuration | Email From

The **Document Added Email** settings are for sending notification e-mails while anyone is adding a file to an administrator. You can enable or disable the mail, change the mail subject, and change the mail body. You can use the definition of a team for the e-mail subject and body.

A **Document Added Email** settings screenshot is displayed here:

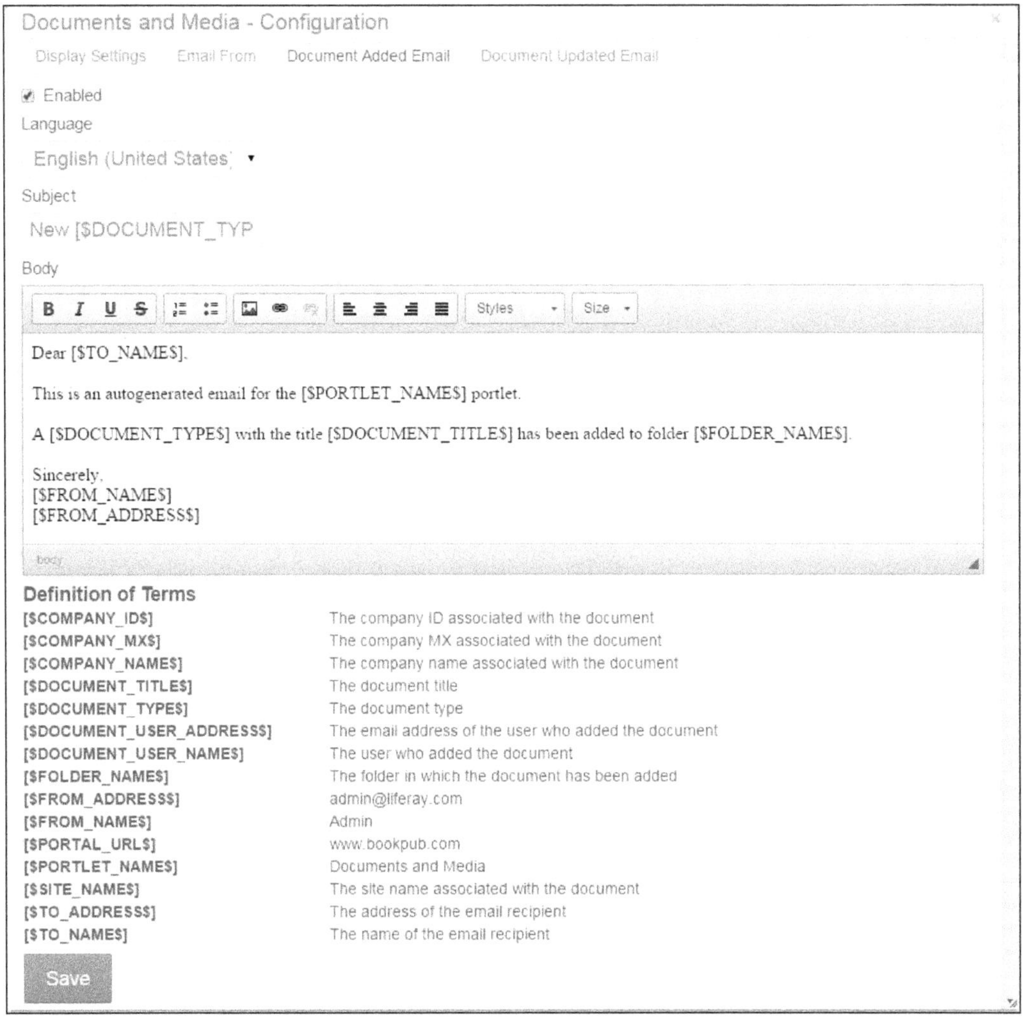

Documents and Media - Configuration

Display Settings   Email From   Document Added Email   Document Updated Email

☑ Enabled

Language

English (United States) ▼

Subject

New [$DOCUMENT_TYP

Body

| B | *I* | U̲ | S̶ | ⅠⅢ | ⅢⅢ | 🖼 | 🔗 | 🎨 | ≣ | ≣ | ≣ | ≣ | Styles ▾ | Size ▾ |

Dear [$TO_NAMES],

This is an autogenerated email for the [$PORTLET_NAMES] portlet.

A [$DOCUMENT_TYPES] with the title [$DOCUMENT_TITLES] has been added to folder [$FOLDER_NAMES].

Sincerely,
[$FROM_NAMES]
[$FROM_ADDRESSS]

body

Definition of Terms

[$COMPANY_IDS]	The company ID associated with the document
[$COMPANY_MXS]	The company MX associated with the document
[$COMPANY_NAMES]	The company name associated with the document
[$DOCUMENT_TITLES]	The document title
[$DOCUMENT_TYPES]	The document type
[$DOCUMENT_USER_ADDRESSS]	The email address of the user who added the document
[$DOCUMENT_USER_NAMES]	The user who added the document
[$FOLDER_NAMES]	The folder in which the document has been added
[$FROM_ADDRESSS]	admin@liferay.com
[$FROM_NAMES]	Admin
[$PORTAL_URLS]	www.bookpub.com
[$PORTLET_NAMES]	Documents and Media
[$SITE_NAMES]	The site name associated with the document
[$TO_ADDRESSS]	The address of the email recipient
[$TO_NAMES]	The name of the email recipient

Save

Figure 8.14: Documents and Media Configuration – Document Added Email

Document Updated Email is a mail notification to the administrator when a file has been updated. You can enable and disable the mail notification. Also, you can change the mail subject and body. The following screenshot shows **Document Updated Email**:

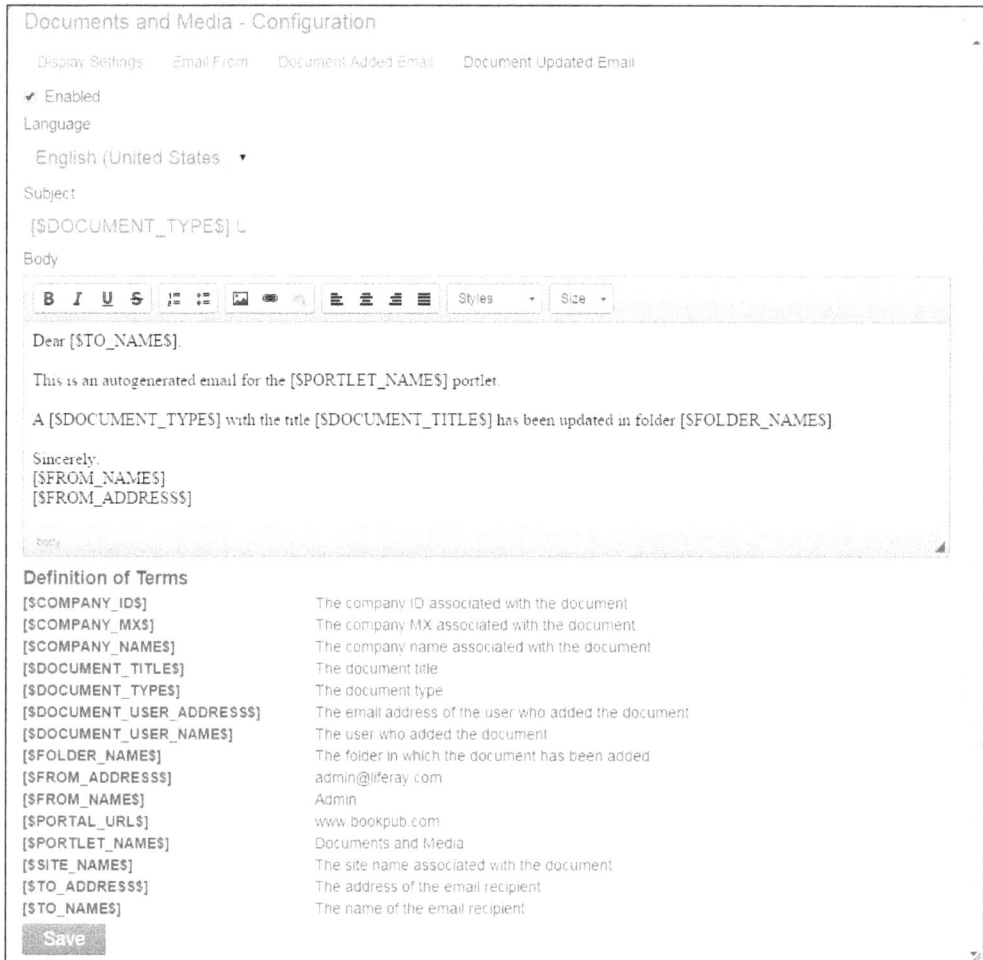

Figure 8.15: Documents and Media - Configuration | Document Updated Email

When you configure the Document and Media portlet from the page, it will provide more options tabs, such as **Setup**, **Permissions**, **Communication**, **Sharing**, and **Scope**. It also provides the **Archive/Restore Setup** link in the top-right corner of the pop-up window. Let's discuss the aforementioned tabs in detail:

- **Setup**: This allows you to set up the documents and media configuration.

- **Permissions**: This allows you to set up the permissions for a portlet.

- **Communication**: This allows you to map and share parameters, such as `categoryId`, `nodeId`, `tag`, `nodeName`, `resetCur`, and `title` for inter-portlet communication. Refer to *Chapter 5, Understanding Wikis, Dynamic Data Lists, and Polls*, for more details.

- **Sharing**: This allows you to share the portlet with social media and websites.

- **Scope**: This allows you to set the scope of the portlet. Refer to *Chapter 5, Understanding Wikis, Dynamic Data Lists, and Polls*, for more details.

- **Archive/Restore Setup**: This allows you to archive the documents and media data for future reference. Once you have archived it, you can restore it whenever required. For more details, refer to *Chapter 4, Forums, Categorization, and Asset Publishing*.

Understanding the import and export of documents

Liferay allows you to export and import portlet data for most of the out-of-the-box portlets, such as the Document and Media, Web Content, Blogs, Wiki, and Message Boards portlets. You can export and import data from a portlet by clicking on the **Gear** icon and selecting the **Export/Import** link. It will open a pop-up window for the **Export** and **Import** tabs. Let's discuss Export in detail.

Export has two tabs: **New Export Process** and **Current and Previous**.

- **New Export Process**: This allows you to export the `.lar` file, which includes all the configuration, content, and permissions on Documents and Media. Refer to the following screenshot for the Export interface.

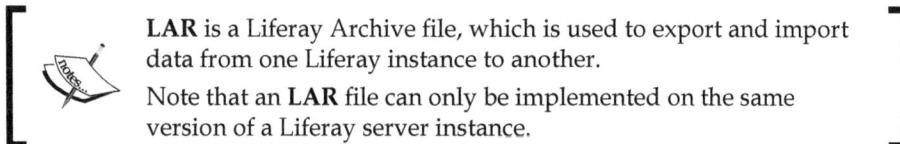

> LAR is a Liferay Archive file, which is used to export and import data from one Liferay instance to another.
>
> Note that an **LAR** file can only be implemented on the same version of a Liferay server instance.

- **Current and Previous**: This lists all the export `.lar` files generated currently and previously.

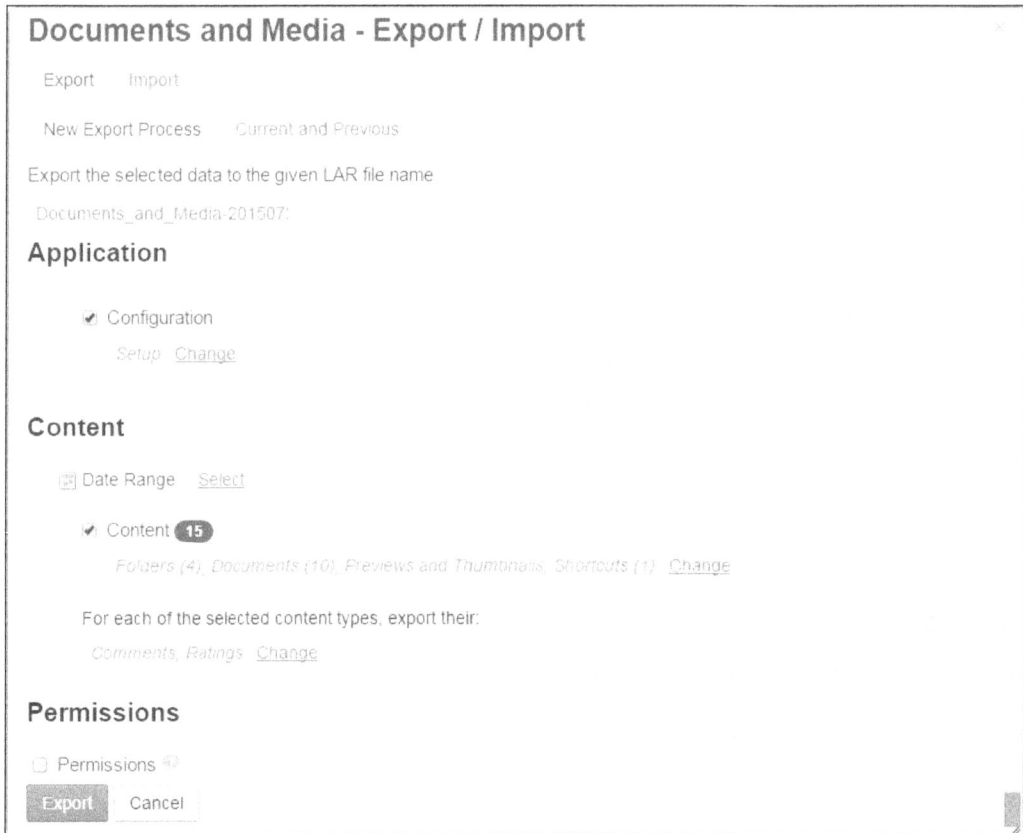

Figure 8.16: Documents and Media - Export

You can select the document by the date range, selecting the document folder, or individual documents.

Import also has two tabs: **New Import Process** and **Current and Previous**. Refer to the following screenshot. For importing, you can just drag and drop the `.lar` file or browse the `.lar` file from your local system. After selecting the LAR file, you will get a screen similar to the export screen. Select the appropriate content and permission and click on **Continue**.

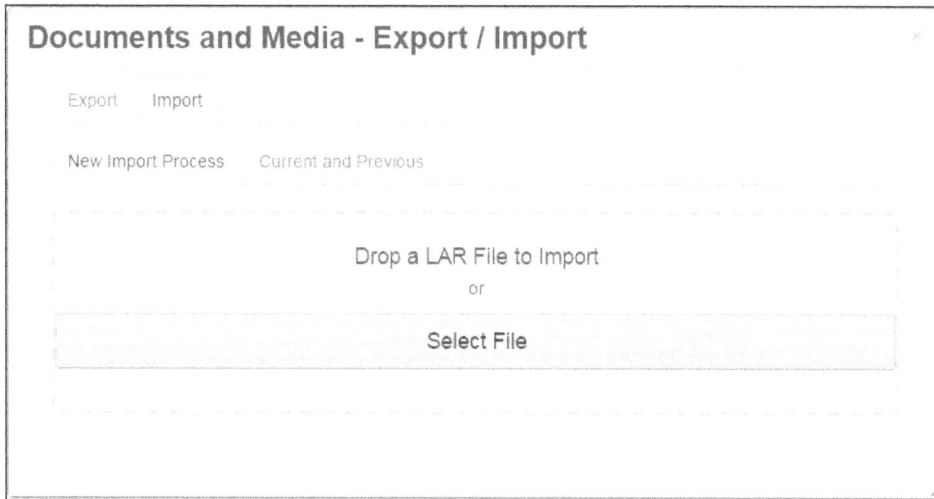

Documents and Media - Export / Import

Export   Import

New Import Process   Current and Previous

Drop a LAR File to Import

or

Select File

Figure 8.17: Documents and Media - Import

Finally, once done, it will be listed in the **Current and Previous** tab. You will find all the old and new import `.lar` file details in this tab.

Extra settings for the Documents and Media portlet

The Documents and Media library is so flexible that many settings are defined in `portal.properties`. As you saw earlier, the e-mail settings can also be set through `portal-ext.properties`.

Liferay has excellent portal configuration features, which allows you to do extensive customization for different applications/portlets:

```
dl.email.from.name=
dl.email.from.address=

dl.email.file.entry.added.enabled=true
dl.email.file.entry.added.subject=com/liferay/portlet/documentlibr
  ary/dependencies/email_file_entry_added_subject.tmpl
```

```
dl.email.file.entry.added.body=com/liferay/portlet/documentlibrary
  /dependencies/email_file_entry_added_body.tmpl
```

```
dl.email.file.entry.updated.enabled=true
dl.email.file.entry.updated.subject=com/liferay/portlet/documentli
  brary/dependencies/email_file_entry_updated_subject.tmpl
dl.email.file.entry.updated.body=com/liferay/portlet/documentlibra
  ry/dependencies/email_file_entry_updated_body.tmpl
```

The configuration settings for Email notification can be done in `portal-ext.` `properties`. As mentioned earlier, you can override these properties.

Liferay has a file storage system, which is mapped to the default folder; that is, `dl.store.file.system.root.dir=${liferay.home}/data/document_library`.

You can set the Amazon s3 bucket values too:

```
dl.store.s3.access.key=
dl.store.s3.secret.key=
dl.store.s3.bucket.name=
```

The Document library of Liferay is very strong, and you can override most of the settings through the UI as well as from the properties file. Document library file icons are also defined. If you want to add any icon, you need to override this key and add the image in the `doc.gif`:

```
dl.file.icons=.bmp,.css,.doc,.docx,.dot,.gif,.gz,.htm,.html,.jpeg,
  .jpg,.js,.lar,.odb,.odf,.odg,.odp,.ods,.odt,.pdf,.png,.ppt,
  .pptx,.rtf,.swf,.sxc,.sxi,.sxw,.tar,.tiff,.tgz,.txt,.vsd,.xls,
  .xlsx,.xml,.zip,.jrxml
```

File extensions defined as * will permit all the file extensions:

```
dl.file.extensions=*
```

The settings `dl.file.entry.open.in.ms.office.manual.check.` `in.required=true` are there to force users to perform a checkin via the Document Library user interface when using the *Open in MS Office* feature. If set to false, the settings allow users to automatically do a checkin to the file upon closing the appropriate MS Office applications. The following property is set for the document version number. Setting this to `0` forces all updates to file entries to result in a new version. By default, it is set to `1`.

```
dl.file.entry.version.policy=1
```

For image previews, the settings are as follows:

```
dl.file.entry.preview.image.mime.types=image/bmp,image/gif,image/j
    peg,image/pjpeg,image/png,image/tiff,image/x-citrix-
    jpeg,image/x-citrix-png,image/x-ms-bmp,image/x-png,image/x-tiff
```

There are many more settings that you can override using `portal-ext.properties`.

File repository

In documents and media, the files are stored in the filesystem of the server on which it's running. As mentioned previously, it is stored in the folder location of the server `dl.store.file.system.root.dir=${liferay.home}/data/document_library`.

You can overwrite the value to some other location in your server. Liferay also supports different ways of storing the documents and media files. The following is a list of these different ways:

- Advanced file system store
- **Content Management Interoperability Services (CMIS)** store
- **Database Storage (DBStore)**
- **Amazon Simple Storage (S3Store)**
- **Java Content Repository (JCRStore)**
- Filesystem store

You can store the document in the aforementioned Amazon Simple Storage (S3 bucket) configuration:

```
dl.store.s3.access.key=
dl.store.s3.secret.key=
dl.store.s3.bucket.name=
```

You can set the number of days that files should be left in the temporary directory before they are deleted:

```
dl.store.s3.temp.dir.clean.up.expunge=7
```

Set the number of calls to S3Store and get the file before triggering the cleanup process:

```
dl.store.s3.temp.dir.clean.up.frequency=100
```

By doing these settings, you can point the file repository to Amazon s3 storage.

Document types and metadata sets

As we discussed earlier, Liferay provides the document type and metadata set for Documents and Media. Using these document types or metadata sets, users can create their document, which will have extra fields for particular types of documents.

Let's take a use case for the document type. In an intranet of the Palm Tree Publications enterprise, Editorial Department needs to upload a document, which should have specific fields, such as publishing date, coauthor, document coordinator, and copyright. The metadata of the document helps the document to become searchable within the portal very easily. This helps users to search the document using the metadata value of the document.

> Note that Document types and Metadata sets are very useful to find the document easily through search.

Let's create a new document type for our use case:

1. Select **Manage | Document Type** from the top menu of Documents and Media.

2. Click on the **Add** button from the **Document Type** dialog box.

3. Fill in the name and description `Publisher document` for the document type.

4. Now you can define **Main Metadata Fields** or select **Additional Metadata Fields**.

5. **Main Metadata Fields** are directly tied to their document type and are not available to other document types. **Additional Metadata Fields** are defined independently, and they can be used by multiple document types.

6. In **Main Metadata Fields**, we need to create fields for the document type. The following screenshot shows the fields for the publisher document:

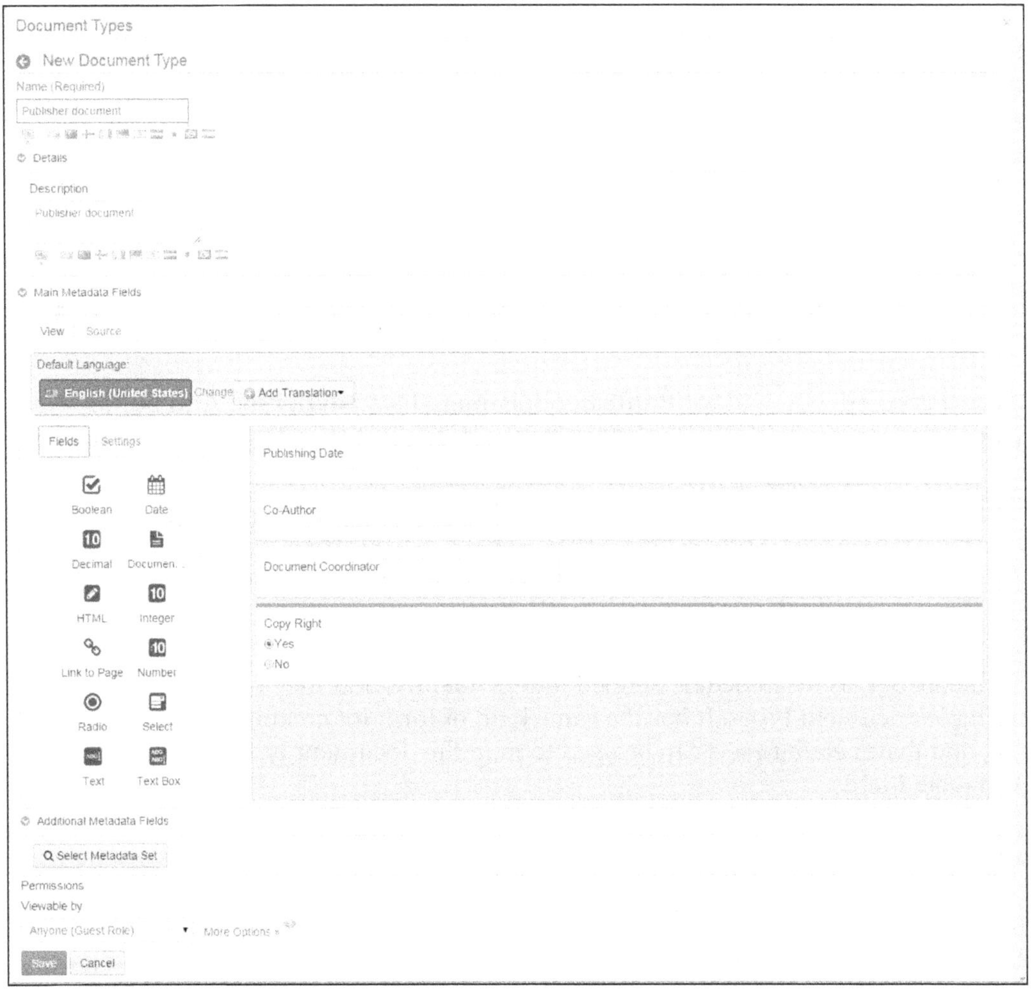

Figure 8.18: Document Types

In the **Main Metadata Fields** section, you can choose the fields to use from the area on the left-hand side and drag and drop them into the area on the right-hand side. The drag and drop interface allows nested fields, so you need to be careful about where you drop the fields. You can also do the settings for the default values, field labels, mouseover tips, required or not, widths, and other settings from the **Settings** tab. Configuring the fields settings, just click on the field from the area on the right-hand side, and then subsequently select the settings tab on the left-hand side for that particular field.

> Note that we need to create **Additional Metadata Fields** separately and map it with Document Type. We can also create **Additional Metadata Fields** while creating document type and map it before saving the document type.

Once it is saved, you will get **Publisher document** listed under the Add button. Now you are able to create the document using the document type **Publisher document**.

> This document type, that is, **Publisher document**, will only be available to the current site and not globally. If you want to have the document type throughout the site scope, you need to create the document type in the **Global** site scope.

Metadata Set, as discussed, is defined independently, and they can be used by multiple document types. It has the same kind of form for creating **Metadata Set**, and that metadata sets can be used to map the document type in **Additional Metadata Fields**.

The Media Gallery portlet

In the previous chapter, we created an image carousel using Media Gallery. The Media Gallery portlet (portlet ID 31) is used to display images to the end users in an arranged manner. The Media Gallery portlet can be configured in such a way that we can select a particular folder to display images. In the *Application Display Templates* section of *Chapter 7, Understanding Sites*, we used media gallery to create the carousel. In the same way, you can use it for different purposes. In the Palm Tree intranet portal, create a page with the name "Media Gallery" and place in it the Media Gallery portlet.

Once you place the portlet on the page, it displays only the images and video files from the Documents and Media portlet. For displaying a proper image gallery, you need to configure the portlet.

Click on the **Gear** icon from the top-right corner of the portlet. The **Media Gallery – Configuration** popup will open. It has different tabs: **Setup, Permissions, Communication, Sharing,** and **Scope**.

Setup will be open by default; it has different sections, **Display Settings, Folder settings,** and **Ratings**. Refer to the following screenshot.

Display settings has different checkboxes which are **Show Actions, Show Folder Menu, Show Navigation Links,** and **Show Search**:

- **Show Action**: This will have the files action on all the image files.

- **Show Folder Menu**: This will show the folder view inside Media Gallery.

- **Show Navigation Links**: This will show the navigation menu at the top with the **Home, Recent,** and **Mine** links.

- **Show Search**: Media Gallery has the **Show Search** text box and **Search** button.

- **Folder Listing**: This allows you to select the folder from where the image files need to be display in Media Gallery.

- **Ratings**: With this, you can enable rating for the images. Also, you can enable comment ratings too.

- **Show Media Type**: This is a multiselection for the media type, which file extensions need to be displayed inside Media Gallery.

- **Display Template**: You can select the Application Display Template (ADT). Refer to the *Application Display Templates* section of *Chapter 7, Understanding Sites*.

The following screenshot shows the **Media Gallery – Configuration** popup:

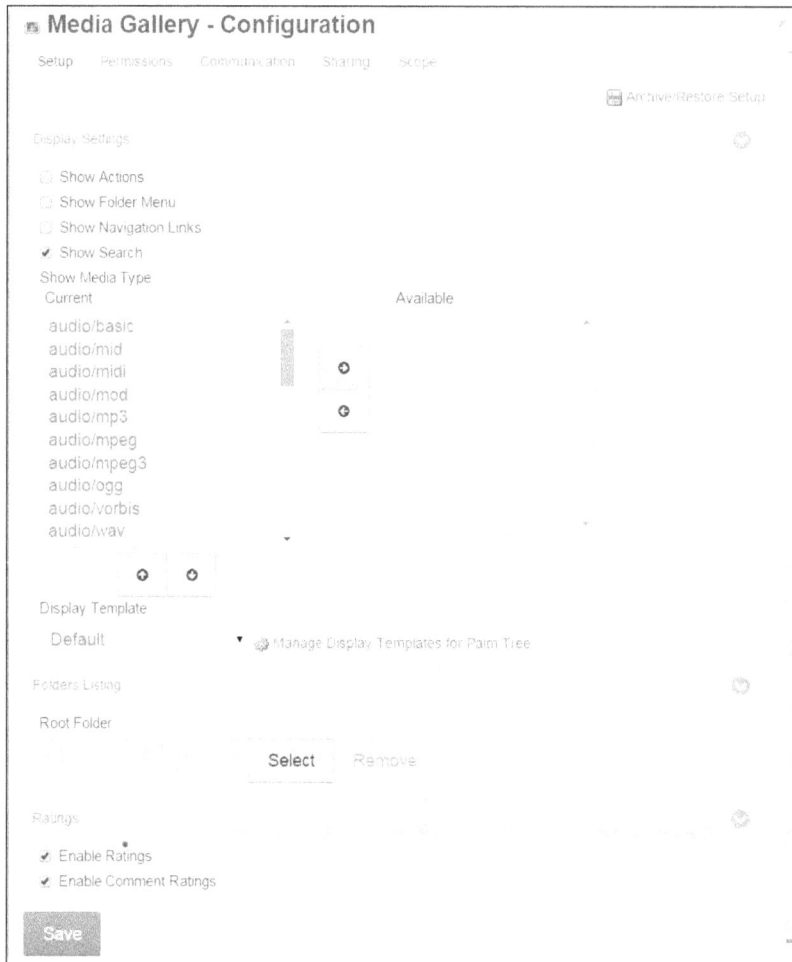

Figure 8.19: Media Gallery - Configuration settings

Enabling the workflow in Documents and Media

You can enable the workflow on the files of Documents and Media too. For Documents and Media, you need to configure the folder and enable the workflow. On doing this, only that particular folder will be enabled for the workflow. That means if you want to enable the workflow for a particular department, you need to enable the workflow for the top folder and the rest of the subfolders will have the workflow enabled.

Let's configure the default workflow (Single Approver) to the Editorial Department folder. Follow these steps:

1. Locate the `Editorial Department` folder and click on **Edit** from the **Action** dropdown.

2. In the **Document Type Restrictions and Workflow** option, select **Define specific document type restrictions and workflow for this folder.**.

3. Select the document type **Basic Document**. A new section will open to set the workflow.

4. Now, select the **Single Approval** workflow from the dropdown.

5. Finally, save it.

The following screenshot shows that the workflow is enabled for the Editorial Department folder:

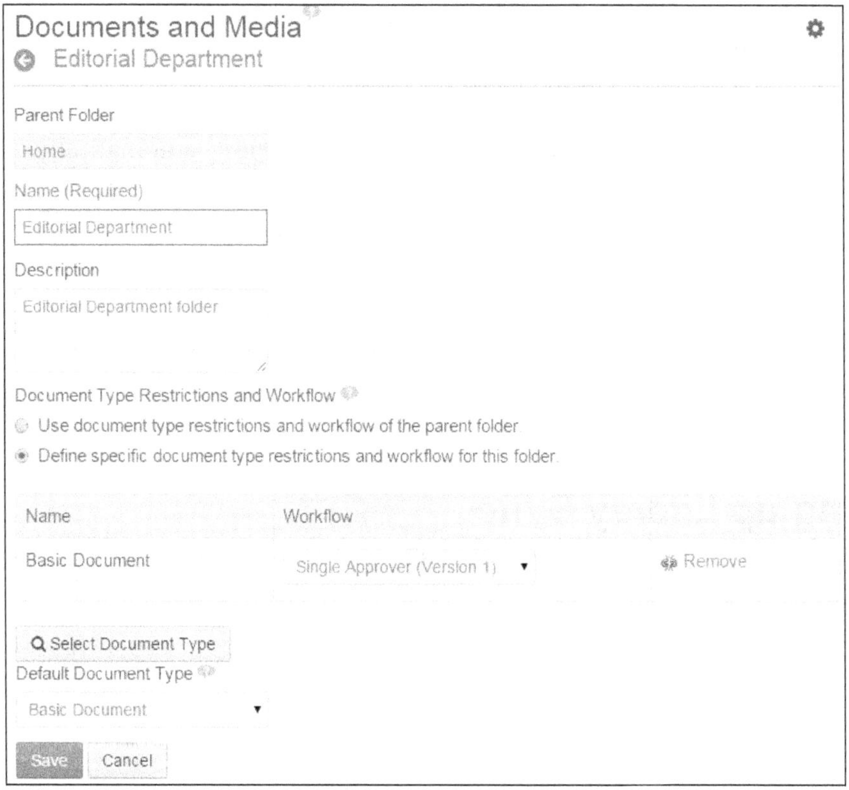

Figure 8.20: Documents and Media workflow settings

Now if you create any files under any subfolder of **Editorial Department**, you will observe that the **Publish** button for file creation has changed to the **Submit for Publication** button. Once the file is created, it will be in the pending state until Approver approves it.

Liferay Sync

Liferay Sync is an add-on application for Liferay 6.1 GA2 CE and EE and later versions. Liferay Sync allows you to synchronize files and folders from Liferay Portal, your local desktop, and even mobile environments. Users can publish, access, and share documents and files from their local environment without using the browser. Currently, most operating systems are supported by Liferay Sync for Mac and Windows (64-bit and 32-bit). Liferay Sync 1.2.3 GA3 and Liferay Sync 3.0 Beta have been released. Liferay Sync Beta for Linux is available. For mobile, Liferay Sync 3.0 Beta for Android and iOS are available. Whenever any users add, and collaborate on, files in Documents and Media, Liferay Sync synchronizes all the documents across all configured Sync clients. Liferay Sync is part of Liferay Platform. It's so well integrated that it takes care of the authentication, versioning, and social collaboration functions. Liferay Sync stores documents and files locally, while allowing you to work on the files offline. Once you are online, it reconnects automatically and synchronizes the files.

Liferay Sync makes the Liferay document management more robust and advanced, in line with today's market demand.

> Note that Liferay Sync is also designed to work with Liferay Social Office. You can sync one site from the Social Office CE as well as one site from the Liferay Portal CE.

Setting up Liferay Sync

As mentioned previously, Liferay Sync has two versions released, for Windows and Mac. Let's discuss the older and more stable version, Liferay Sync 1.2.3 GA3.

Older versions of Liferay Sync

You have to download the client application installer from `https://www.liferay.com/downloads/liferay-sync`. For Windows, the installer will be named `liferay-sync-<version>-<date>-x<bit>.msi`. For Mac, the installer will be named `liferay-sync-1.2.3-<version>-<date>.dmg`. For Linux, the installers will be named `liferay-sync-<version>-<date>-amd<bit>.deb` and `liferay-sync-<version>-<date>-i<bit>.rpm`.

In our case, you will install the Windows version. Once it's installed, you can see the Liferay Sync icon in your taskbar. Open the application with a double-click. To set up, you have to provide Liferay credentials. The following is the screenshot where you need to set the Sync Folder location, Server URL, and login credentials.

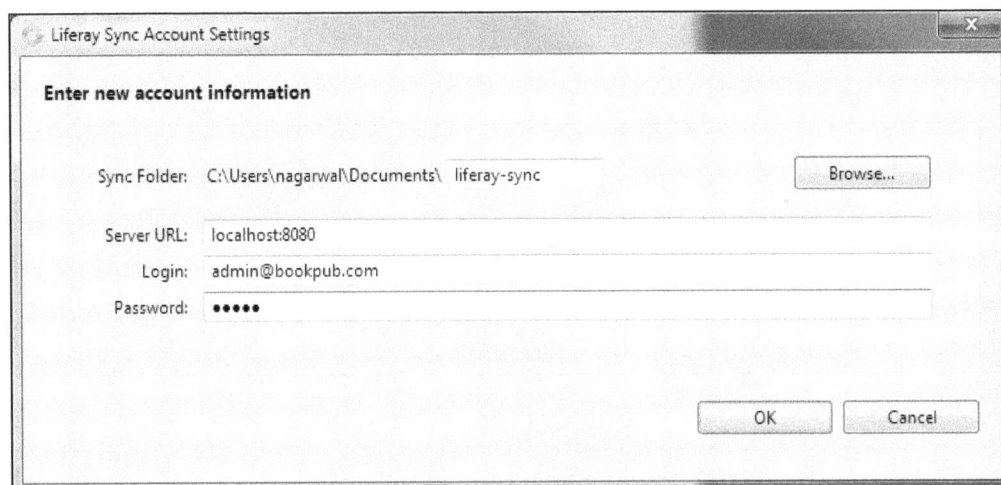

Figure 8.21: Liferay Sync client interface for creating an account

Now do the settings for a Liferay Sync account:

1. You can keep the default **Sync Folder** location as of now.
2. Set the **Server URL** to `http://localhost:8080`.
3. Provide the Liferay credentials and click on **OK**.

Now you need to configure the Site and the Documents and Media document folder. As you can see in the following screenshot, you can set the time interval in seconds for updating the document from Liferay Portal. Even you can change the connection settings. Finally, you need to select the sites for which you want to synchronize the Documents and Media files. After all the settings, click on **OK**.

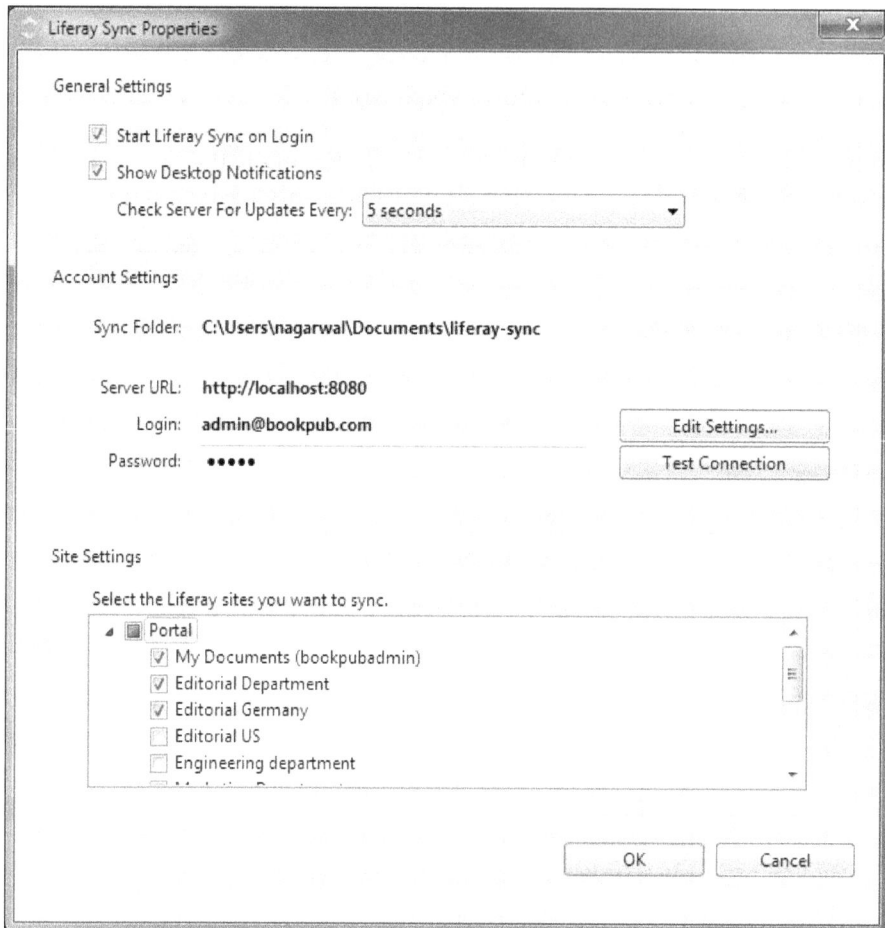

Figure 8.22: Liferay properties setting

You can set the following fields:

1. Check the checkbox for **Start Liferay Sync on Login**.
2. Check the checkbox for **Show Desktop Notifications**.
3. Select the option for **Check Server For Updates Every**. You can select the time interval in seconds.

4. Account Settings is for the local folder location, server URL, and login credentials. Here, you can change the settings by clicking on the **Edit Settings** button. Even you can test the connection.

5. Site Settings is for selecting the Liferay sites you want to sync.

When you are finally done with setting the fields, navigate to the folder in your local system, which is mentioned in settings. You will be able to see that the folder structure and the respective files of that particular site got synchronized from Liferay Portal.

Now, let's discuss the Liferay Sync 3.0 BETA version.

Liferay Sync 3.0 BETA

Liferay Sync 3.0 BETA is more advanced and robust. It is an add-on application for Liferay 6.2 CE and EE that synchronizes files between the Liferay server and the user's desktop and mobile environments. The Liferay 6.2 Documents and Media portlet contains all the logic used by Liferay Sync. To configure Liferay 6.2 with Liferay Sync, you need to install the Sync Connector Web plugin (sync-web). You can download Sync Connector and Client from `https://www.liferay.com/downloads/liferay-sync`. Check the requirements section under Liferay Sync 3.0 BETA and download the Sync Beta connector for CE or EE. Deploy the `.lpkg` file in the running Liferay server in the same way we deploy other Liferay plugins. By doing this, you will install sync-web and sync-admin-portlet. The Sync Admin portlet is controlled by portal administrators in **Control Panel** under the **Configuration** section.

> Note that Liferay sync-web and sync-admin are very new and don't come with the Liferay bundle. Also, you need to keep both the client and server sides (sync-web and sync-admin) up to date. Without this sync-web and sync-admin plugin, the portal administrator will not be able to enable Sync for any site.

Once the server-side plugin is installed, you need to configure the Sync in **Control Panel**. Follow these steps to configure the sync:

1. Log in as the portal administrator.

2. Click on **Control Panel** from the **Admin** dropdown (dock bar).

3. Under the **Configuration** section, click on **Sync Admin**; you will be able to see a screen similar to the following screenshot.

4. In the **General** tab, the portal administrator can control enabling and disabling the sync. The portal administrator can allow users access to personal sites, maximum connections, and poll intervals (setting the seconds for how often clients will poll the server for updates) in seconds.

5. For now, check the **Enabled** checkbox, input the value for maximum connection as 1, and input the value for poll interval as 5.

6. Finally, save it.

The **Sync Admin** screenshot for the **General** tab allows you to enable Liferay Sync for your portal:

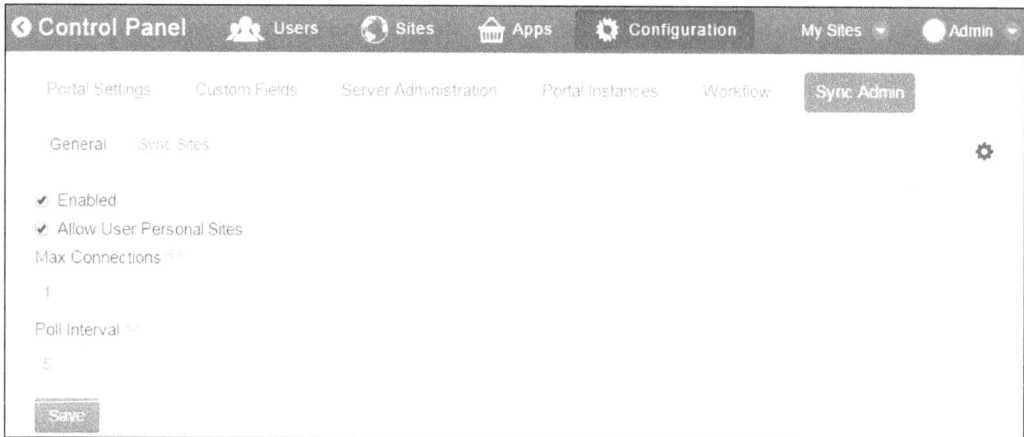

Figure 8.23: Liferay Sync Admin—the General tab in Control Panel

There is another tab, **Sync Site**, that has a list of all the sites in the portal, and each site has actions that are mentioned in the following screenshot:

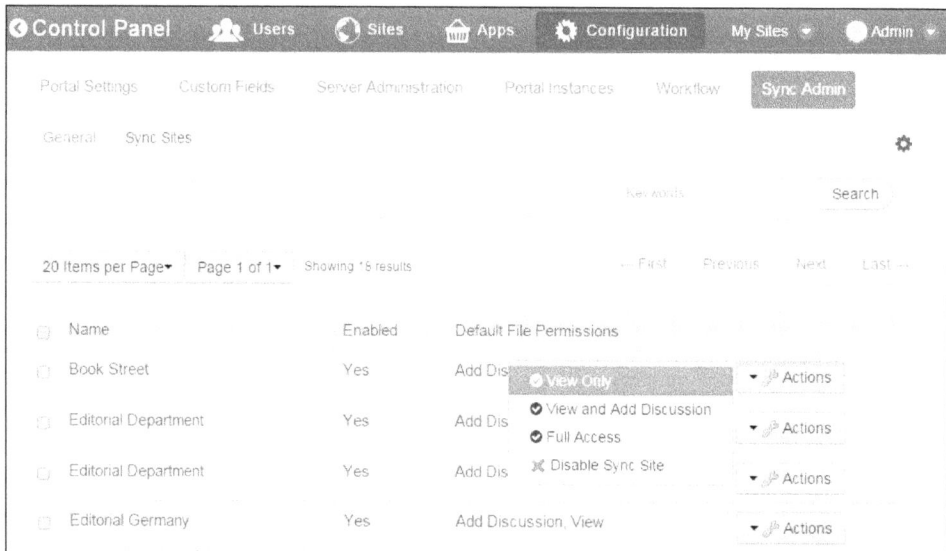

Figure 8.24: Liferay Sync Admin —the Sync Sites tab in Control Panel

Here's a brief description of the actions mentioned in the preceding screenshot:

- **View only**: This will give only the view permission for a particular site
- **View and Add Discussion**: This will give view and add discussion permissions for a particular site
- **Full Access**: This will give full permission for a particular site
- **Disable Sync Site**: This will disable the sync for a particular site

Once you are done with the configuration for Sync Admin in **Control Panel**, you have to download the **Liferay Sync 3.0 Beta** client from the URL mentioned previously. As of now, it's available only for Windows and Mac. Once it's installed, Liferay Sync will start, and it will pop up a login form; see the following screenshot:

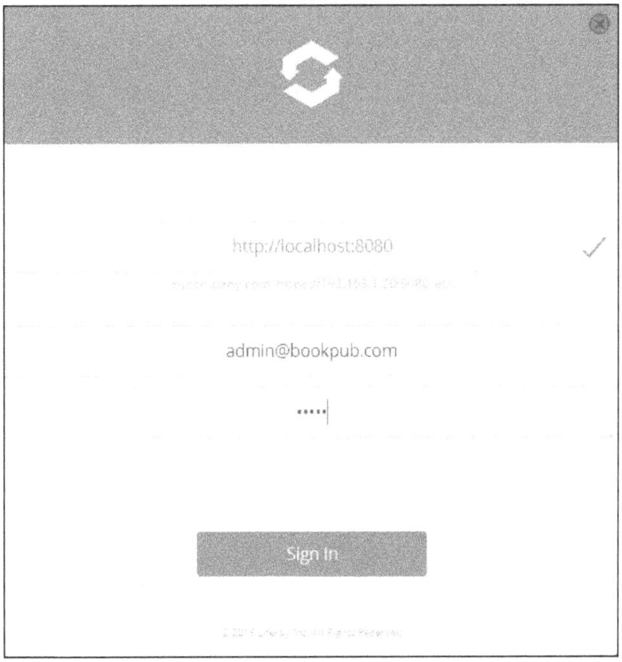

Figure 8.25: Liferay Sync 3.0 Beta Sign In

Provide **Server URL**. If the server is in a running state, it will put the tick and allow you to move further for login credentials. The login credentials are the same as those of the Liferay Portal server; finally, click on the **Sign In** button.

The next step is to select sites by checking the checkbox beside the sites. You can even search the sites that you want to select. Refer to the following screenshot.

Liferay Sync allows you to select multiple sites, for which you will synchronize all the documents and files in your local system.

After Sites are selected, click on the **Proceed** button for the next step. Refer to the following screenshot, which displays the site-selecting window:

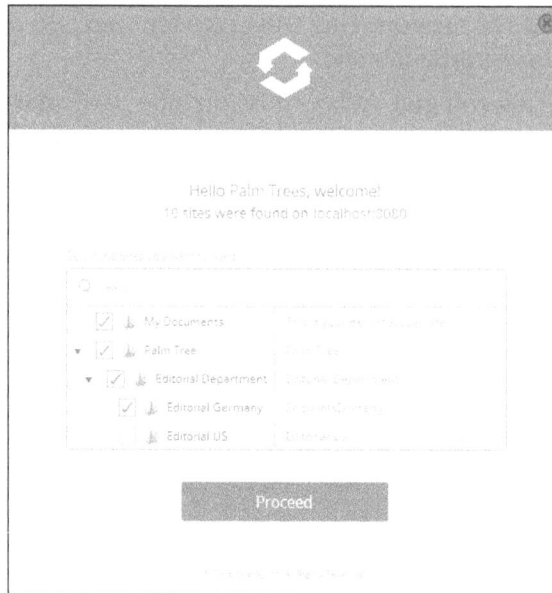

Figure 8.26: Site selecting in Liferay Sync 3.0 Beta

In the next step, provide your local sync folder's name and location, and then click on the **Start Syncing** button; refer to the following screenshot:

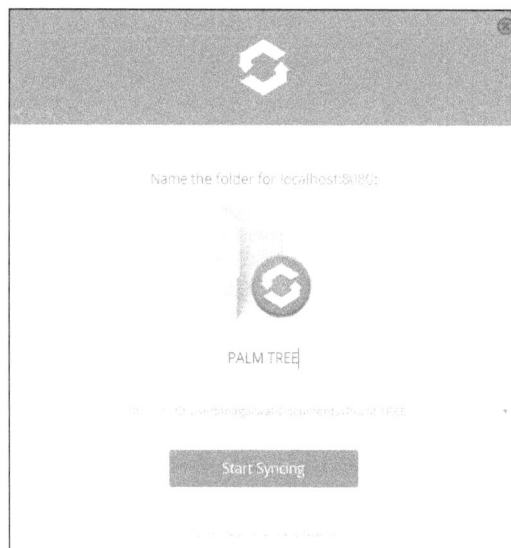

Figure 8.27: Liferay Sync 3.0 BETA

Finally, on clicking on the **Start Syncing** button, you will get the *Congratulations* message. The following screenshot shows the message with the **Open Folder** button:

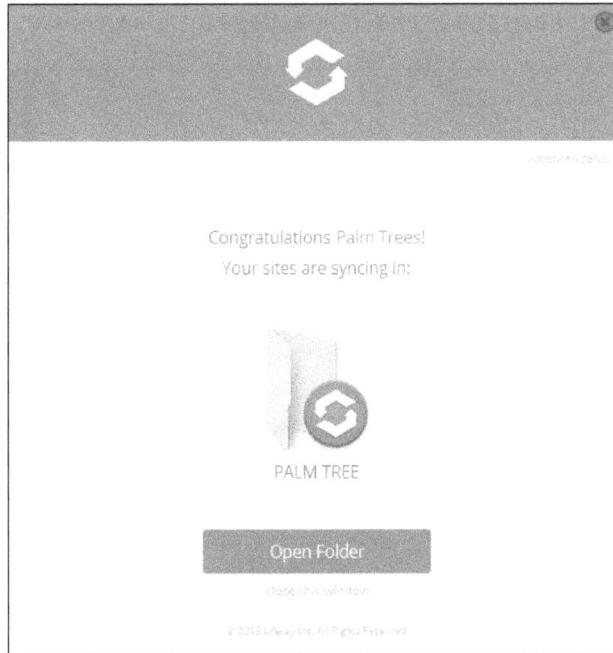

Figure 8.28: Congratulations, you've successfully set up Liferay Sync

Now, click on the **Open Folder** button; it will open the local folder location that you have specified. Note that the initial sync may take some time depending on the data (files) being transferred.

As we mentioned earlier, after installing Liferay Sync, an icon appears in the task bar. It allows you to reconfigure the settings (Preference), check which sites are synced, use the help button, open the Sync folder, and also stop the sync. The following screenshot illustrates Preference settings for Liferay Sync:

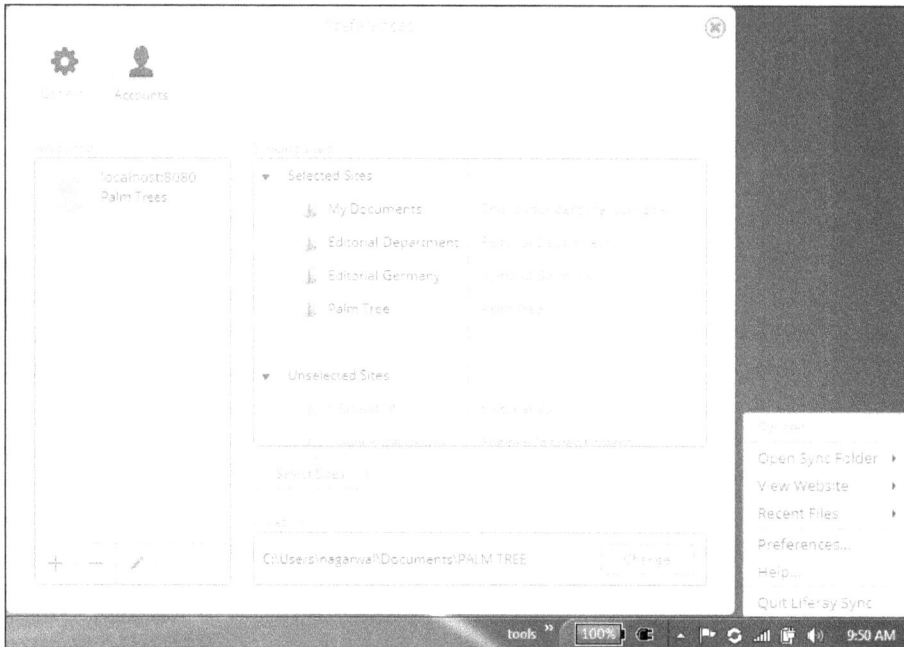

Figure 8.29: Preference settings for Liferay Sync – Accounts tab

In the preceding screenshot, Liferay Sync in the task bar has the following actions:

- **Open Sync Folder**: This opens the local folder location in which sync is configured
- **View Website**: This opens a specific site's Documents and Media page in the browser (login credentials are required)
- **Recent Files**: This shows the files that synced recently
- **Preference**: This opens the preference settings, where you can do the settings for Liferay Sync
- **Help**: This provides you with a step-by-step document on using Liferay Sync
- **Quit Liferay Sync**: This stops Liferay Sync in your desktop system. Sync will stop, and no data transfer will take place

Preference settings in the **Accounts** tab allow settings for connections, site selections, and local folder locations. You can have multiple connections for multiple Liferay Portals. Each connection will have a different set of sites and a different local folder location.

In the **Accounts** tab, under **Accounts**, you can create multiple connections using the plus (+) icon. If you want to delete the connection, you can click on the minus icon, and to edit, you can click on the pencil icon.

> Note that while deleting the connection, be cautious. It will delete the local folder location too.

> Before deleting the connection, change the local folder name.

All the sites for which you have the permissions will be listed on the right-hand side. Now select the required site that you want to sync by clicking on the **Select Site** button. A pop-up window will open. Here you can select the Sites; once you are done with selecting, click on **Confirm**. All the selected Sites will be listed under **Selected Sites** and the unselected ones will be listed under **Unselected Sites**.

> Note that deselecting the site also deletes its folder on your local system for those particular sites.

> Before deselecting the site, change the local folder location. Now if you deselect the sites, it will not find the old files in your local folder structure. So, there's no chance of losing data.

The General tab under Preferences has only three settings:

- **Launch Liferay Sync on startup**: Enabling this makes Liferay Sync on desktop start up
- **Show Desktop Notifications**: Enabling this makes Desktop Notifications when sync is completed
- **Automatically check for updates**: Enabling this checks for updates automatically

The following is a screenshot of the **General** tab settings of **Preferences**:

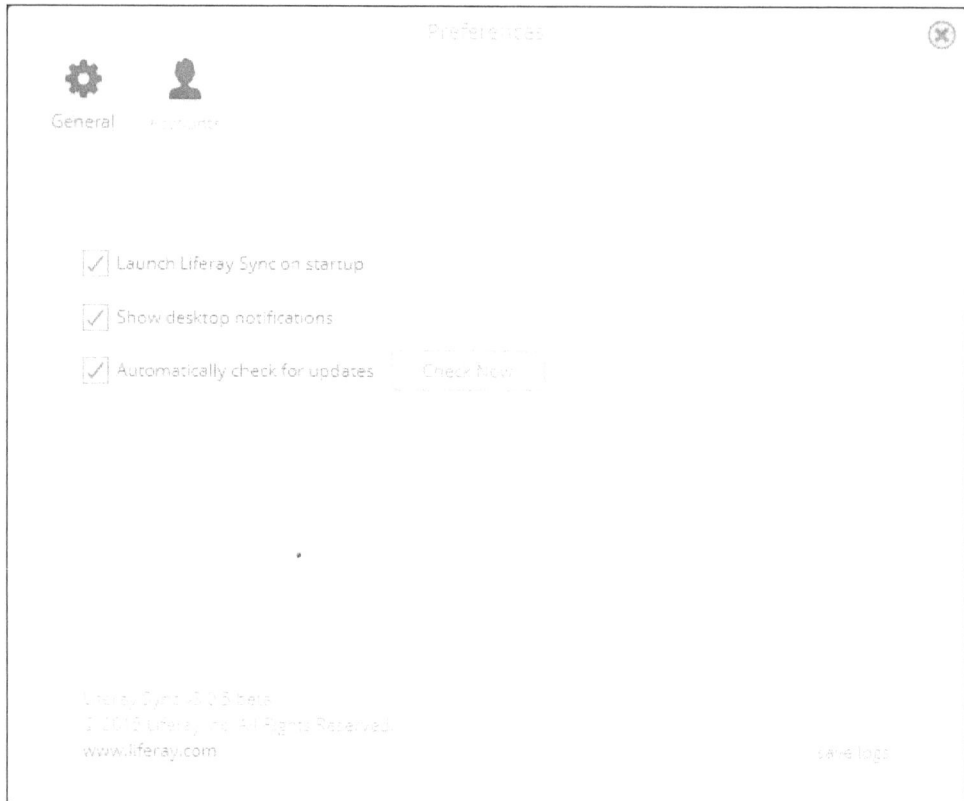

Figure 8.30: Preference settings for Liferay Sync – General tab

Even you can click on the **Check Now** button to sync the data from the portal instantly.

Files in the local folder

Now when you navigate to the local folder location, you will find a folder for each site, and each folder will have the folder structure with files in the same way as in the Documents and Media portlet. See the following screenshot; you will be able to see the `Editorial project Document.pdf` file:

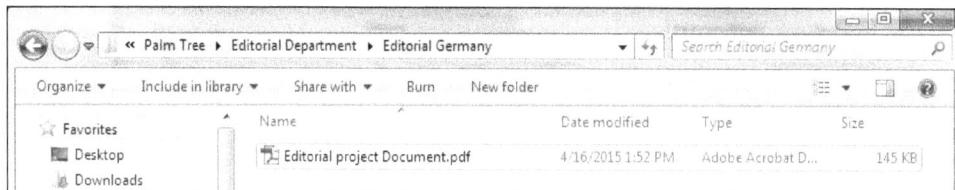

Figure 8.31: Local folder of Windows for Liferay Sync

From here, you can edit and update the file. If you delete the file, it will also be removed from the portal. You can recover it from the Recycle Bin portal if you want to get the file back.

> Make sure that the Recycle Bin portal is enabled all the time; by default, it is enabled. Otherwise, you will not be able to recover the file you have deleted.

Liferay Sync Client for mobile devices

Liferay Sync Client is also available for mobile (Android and iOS) devices. All the functionality of the desktop Sync is available in mobile devices too, but only one single account can be connected by a mobile device. Download the mobile version for Android and Mac from Play Store and iTunes apps store, respectively.

In Android, Liferay Sync is available through Play Store — install the app. After installing it, you will be able to see the following screen, which gives the welcome message, and what the Liferay Sync Mobile app provides you with:

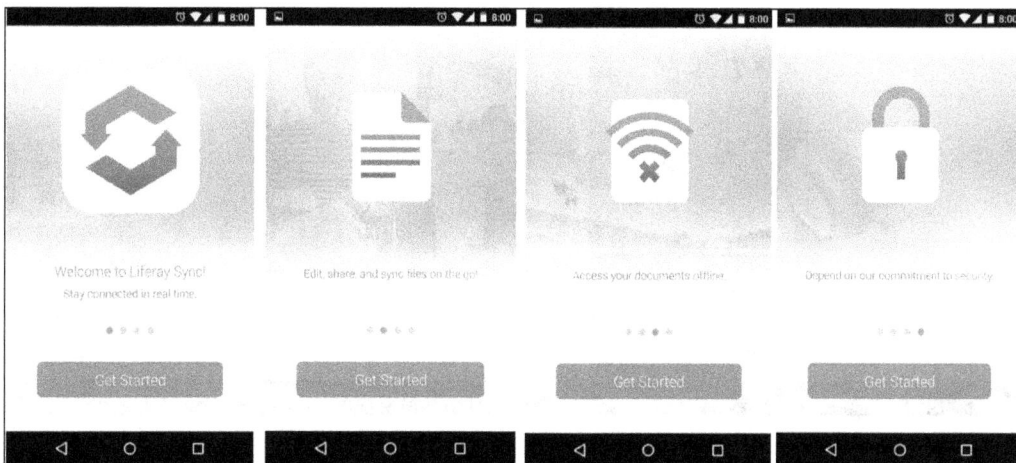

Figure 8.32: The Liferay Sync mobile welcome screen

Once you have installed the app in your mobile, let's explore some interesting features. The Liferay Sync Mobile app is dynamic and robust. The user gets the features of editing, sharing, and syncing files. The user can also access the document in the offline mode. Click on the **Get Started** button.

You need to use **Sign In** with the same credentials as for the portal. Also input the server URL and finally click on the **Sign In** button. Refer to the following screenshot with four mobile screens; you will see the second screen with the username and **Gear** icon for settings with the **My Sites**, **My Documents**, and **Favorites** links:

- **My Sites**: This lists all sites for which you have access permissions
- **My Documents**: This lists all documents that you have created/uploaded from a mobile device
- **Favorites**: This lists all the files and documents that are marked as favorites

In the same screen, you will see a list of all sites. Just slide the screen to the left-hand side and you will come to the third screen, **My Sites**. Now select the Editorial Germany Sites folder. It will open, and if it contains any folders or files, it displays them. Click on the plus (+) sign in the top-right corner of the screen to add a new folder, upload a file, upload a photo, or upload a video. Refer to the fourth screen to add files:

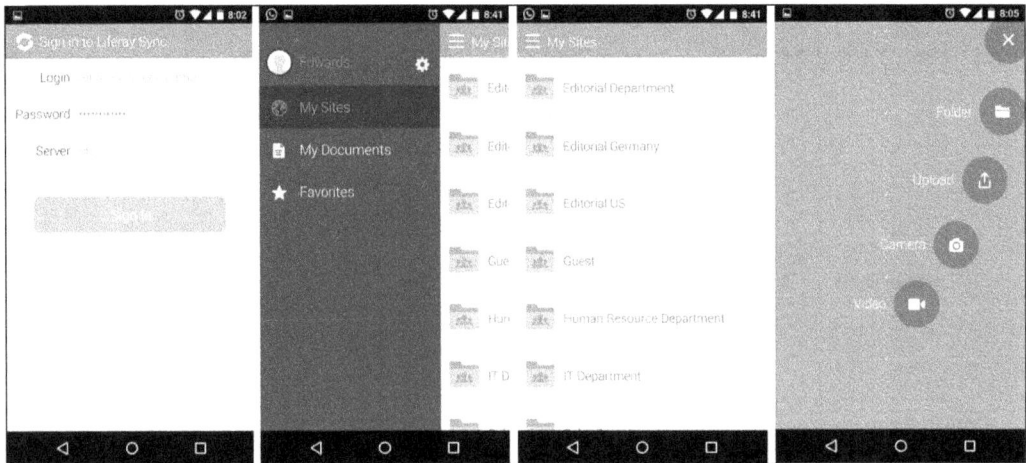

Figure 8.33: Liferay Sync mobile screens

Once you upload the files, it will be listed under that particular site or folder. Refer to the following screenshot—the first mobile screen. Editorial project document.pdf is shown with the date and file size. You can download the file on which you want to work.

> Mobile Sync does not automatically download all the files since mobile storage is limited; with this, you save your storage memory.

File editing is also permitted. You can see the dotted icon beside the file. Once you click on that, a slider screen will appear; refer to the second screen in the following image. In the top-left corner, start marking your favorite files. It shows the file version, filename, date of last modification, and size of the file in KB. There are four icons: **Share**, **Move**, **Rename**, and **Delete**. Let's discuss these in detail:

- **Share**: This allows you to share the file with other users
- **Move**: This allows you to move the file and folder to other sites or folder structures
- **Rename**: This allows you to rename the file and folder
- **Delete**: This allows you to delete the file and folder

The following image shows the two mobile screens of the file:

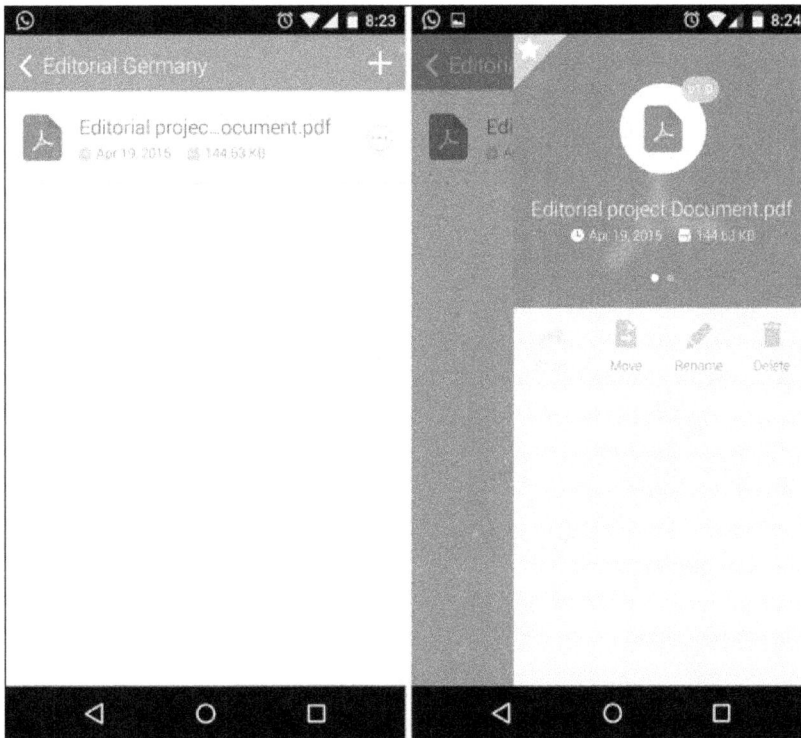

Figure 8.34: Liferay Sync mobile screens for files

Finally, Liferay Sync is set for all environments: portal, desktop, and mobile.

Liferay integration with Alfresco

In certain situations, we might have to integrate third-party software into our portal to make the portal more robust and to enable it to fit into our organization infrastructure.

Alfresco is another exciting open source alternative for enterprise content management and document management. For more information, you can visit `http://docs.alfresco.com/community/concepts/welcome-infocenter_community.html`.

Let's discuss a case study where the Palm Tree enterprise already has Alfresco set up for the employees and contains a huge amount of document data, which needs to be accessed in Liferay Portal by the end user.

> We are going to integrate Liferay 6.2 with the Alfresco 5.x repository through CMIS.

Basically, Liferay provides easy ways to integrate the Alfresco repository using **Content Management Interoperability Services** (**CMIS**). Both Liferay and Alfresco support the CMIS feature to integrate other content management repositories.

> The CMIS standard defines a domain model, web services, and Restful AtomPub bindings that can be used by applications to work with one or more content management repositories/systems. For more information, visit `http://docs.oasis-open.org/cmis/CMIS/v1.0/cmis-spec-v1.0.html`.

Let's look into an Alfresco application that shows the **User Homes** folder and that displays the list of uploaded documents. The following screenshot shows the Alfresco **My Files | Users Homes** folder and displays the list of documents in the right-hand side panel.

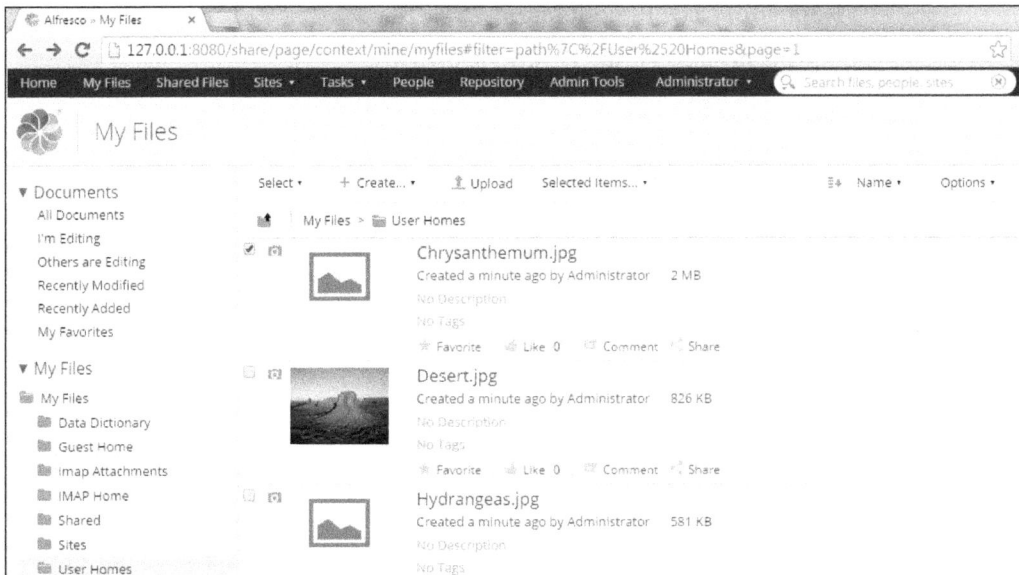

Figure 8.35: Alfresco My Files user interface—the User Homes folder
contains all the documents uploaded into it

Now we need to integrate the Alfresco repository into the Liferay Documents and Media portlet using the CMIS feature. Let's follow the steps mentioned here:

> If you are not using any SSO for either server, make sure that you create the same user admin/admin in Liferay. Doing this, you will have a common user in both environments.
>
> Make sure that both servers Liferay and Alfresco are running on different ports.

1. Log in with the admin portal user, click on **Content** from **Admin | Site Administration**.

2. Select **Documents and Media** from the left-hand side panel menu.

3. Select **Repository** from the **Add** dropdown.

4. The **New Repository** form will appear; fill up the form with the following data:

   ○ **Name**: Alfresco Repository

   ○ **Description**: Alfresco Repository

   ○ **Repository Type: CMIS Repository (AtomPub)**

   ○ **Repository URL**: http://localhost:8080/alfresco/api/-default-/public/cmis/versions/1.1/atom

- ° **Repository ID**: Keep it blank
- ° **Permission**: Keep the default settings

5. Finally, save the settings.

Refer to the following screenshot to create a new repository in Liferay Portal:

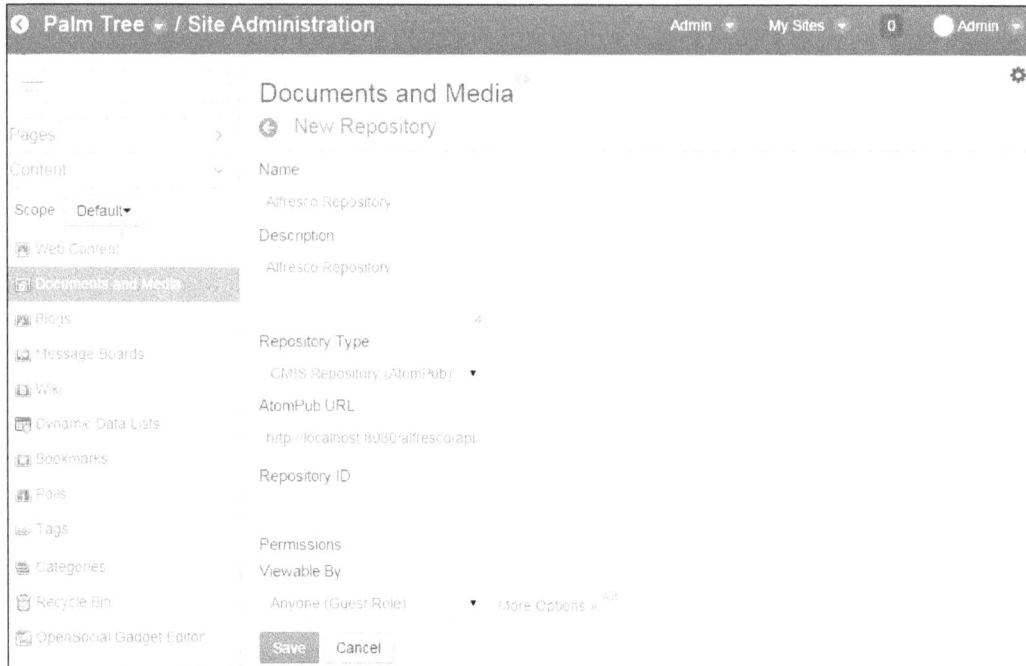

Figure 8.36: Liferay CMIS settings for Document and Media file repository

After saving the **New Repository** form, you will see **Alfresco Repository** inside the **Documents and Media** portlet.

Open Alfresco Repository by double-clicking on it, which will list all the folders and documents within it. The following screenshot shows a list of folders inside Alfresco Repository within the **Documents and Media** portlet:

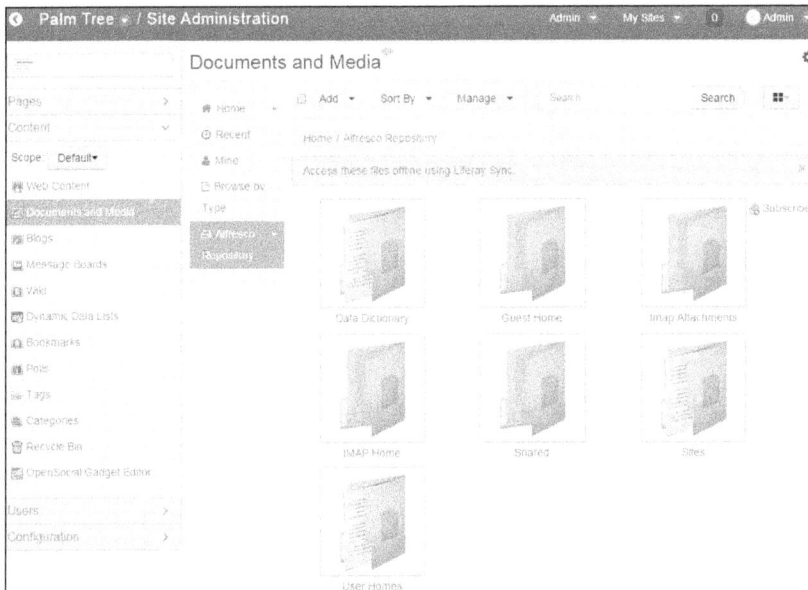

Figure 8.37: Synchronization of all folders from Alfresco busing CMIS

Select the **User Homes** folder, which has all the documents created by the user in the Alfresco application. Refer to the following screenshot, which displays the list of documents inside the **User Homes** folder:

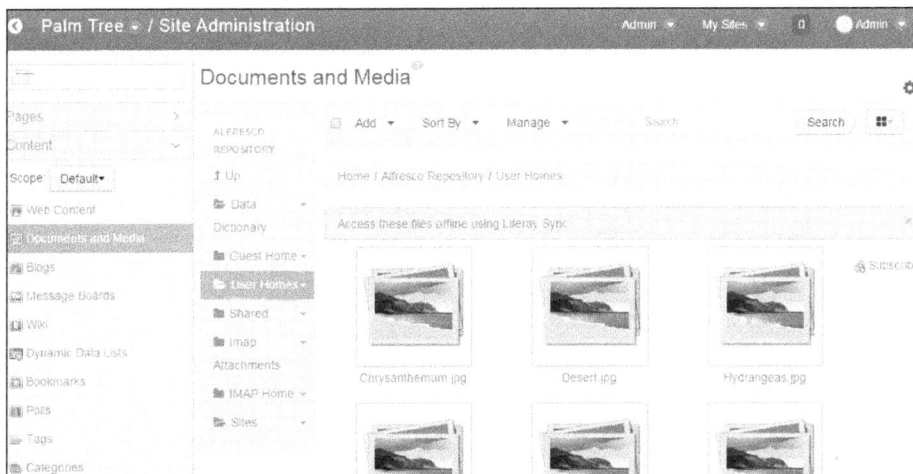

Figure 8.38: The User Homes folder of Alfresco with all the documents listed in the right hand-side panel

Finally, we have achieved the integration of Liferay 6.2 with Alfresco 5.0. In the same way, using CMIS, you can integrate other third-party CMSes with Liferay.

Now you can set the permission on the repository for different users to access and work on the documents.

> It's better to have SSO implemented so that the respective users can get proper permission entitlements.

Summary

Documents and Media Library is very robust. Liferay 6.2 has come up with more enhancements. In future versions, it will be stronger and advanced. In this chapter, you saw the different operations under documents and media: adding folders, files, and shortcuts. You learned about the edit folder and files with simple steps. The most used functions in document management are the checkout and checkin of the documents. This chapter also taught you how to set permissions to roles for documents and media. Generally, Liferay allows you to change the file repository to different storage systems. You saw how to enable the workflow for Documents and Media files. The chapter also taught you the best file syncing application for Liferay Documents and Media, Liferay Sync. The chapter helped you to get through the different environment settings for Liferay Sync. As discussed, Liferay Sync can be connected with desktop and mobile environments. You also learned how to integrate Alfresco CMS into Liferay using the CMIS feature.

In the next chapter, you are going to learn about Web Content Management System.

Web Content Management

9

Web Content Management (WCM) is either bundled or a web application with administration tools designed to allow users to create, manage, and store content on web pages. The intranet portal `bookpub.com` of Palm Tree Publications will have a lot of web content for different departments. To manage and publish this web content, Liferay 6.2 comes with Web Content Management System. It provides nontechnical end users with the ability to add and publish content to the portal website without having programming knowledge of any sort. For complex requirements, you can write the templates. These templates will be used by nontechnical users to create web content inside the portal.

In this chapter, you will learn to create and manage web content. In `bookpub.com` of Palm Tree Publications, we have multiple sites. As mentioned earlier, each site will have a different scope and contain a distinct set of users, content, and data. So, in our example, each site will have its web content and it only can be accessed by appropriate sets of users. Liferay Web Content Management provides a simple interface to manage the content for your portal so that nontechnical users can create, edit, stage, approve, and publish web content easily.

By the end of this chapter, you will learn how to:

- Create and publish Web Content
- Export and import Web Content
- Create and manage structures and templates
- Localize Web Content
- Schedule Web Content
- Stage page publication
- Implement workflow in Web Content

Web Content

The Liferay Web Content portlet (portlet ID 15) is available inside the site administration panel. Liferay Web Content is a very powerful and robust application, which allows users to create and manage web content very easily.

Let's explore the web content for the marketing department site. After that, we will complete a use case on web content using the workflow:

1. Now, log in as the site administrator of **Palm Tree** and click on **Admin | Site Administration | Content** from the dock bar menu. You will land on the **web content** portlet page inside **site administration panel**.

2. Once you have logged in as the site administrator, you can decide where the content needs to be created and in which site it should be displayed. You can even create the content in the global site so that the content is globally available across the portal's sites.

3. Change the **Palm Tree** site scope to the **marketing department** scope, where the content needs to be created.

4. For changing the scope, click on the down arrow button beside **Palm Tree** on the dock bar menu and select **Marketing Department** from the drop-down list. Like this, you made the portal change the scope for the content asset from the **Palm Tree** site to the **Marketing Department** site.

5. Follow this screenshot, which displays the Web Content portlet page and the change of scope of the site:

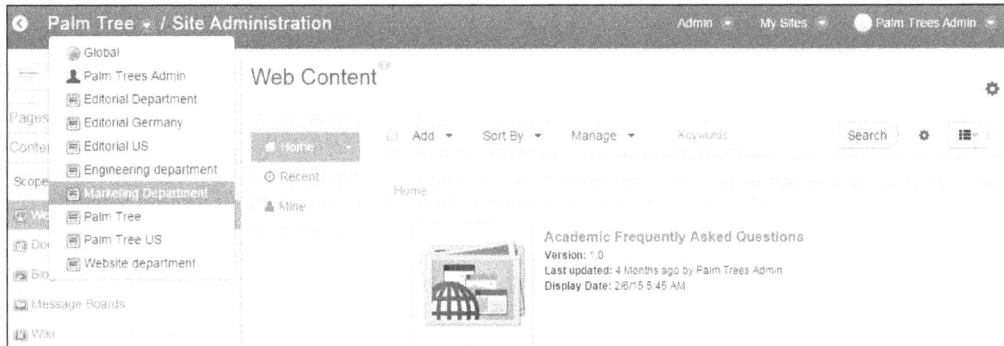

Figure 9.1: The Web Content portlet showing the change of site content scope

Managing Web Content

In the Web Content portlet, you will be able to see one vertical menu and one horizontal menu. Let's discuss this menu in detail. The vertical menu has **Home**, **Recent**, and **Mine**. The horizontal menu has **Add**, **Sort By**, **Manage**, **Search**, and **Switch the view**.

Let's discuss the vertical and horizontal menus' actions in detail:

- **Home**: This is a parent folder for web content. It displays the list of all the web content created under **Home**. Clicking on the down arrow beside the **Home** button displays a few actions, such as **Add Folder**, **Subscribe**, and **Permissions**.

- **Recent**: This displays all the recent web content created.

- **Mine**: This displays all the web content created by the user.

- **Browse by Structure**: This displays all the web content according to the structure.

Let's discuss the horizontal menu's actions in detail.

- **Add**: This allows you to add a new folder and create web content based on different structures. By default, Liferay provides the **Basic Web Content** structure.

- **Sort By**: This allows you to sort the web content list based on **Display Date** and **Modified Date**.

- **Manage**: You can create different structures, templates, and feeds for web content. Later in the chapter, we will discuss structures, templates, and feeds in detail.

- **Search**: This allows you to search the specific web content from the list of web content. If you see a **Gear** icon beside the **Search** button, that is the advanced search feature in Liferay 6.2. Once you click on the icon, a pop-up form appears, where you can search with the web content ID, title, description, content, type, and status.

- **Switch the view**: This allows you to switch the view of the web content list, whereby you can change the views with three different types: **Icon View**, **Descriptive View**, and **List View**.

Now let's create basic web content for our marketing department using the default basic structure and template.

Creating Web Content

In Liferay, creating and managing the web content is very easy for the end user. You can create web content using the workflow, or you can simply publish the content without workflow. Now, let's create content without workflow. Later in the chapter, we will enable the workflow and create web content based on that.

In the marketing department site scope, click on **web content** from the left-hand side panel menu and follow these steps:

1. Click on the **Add** button and select **Basic Web Content** from the drop-down.

2. The **New Web Content** page will appear; refer to the following screenshot:

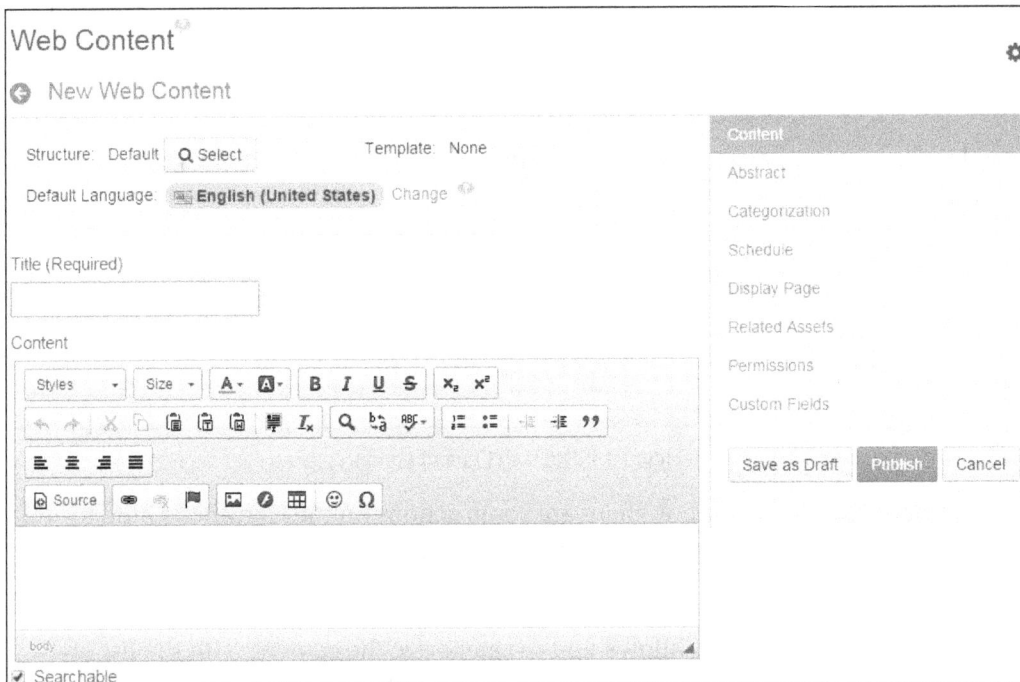

Figure 9.2: New Web Content

3. Fill in the **Title**, say `Marketing Strategy`, and **Content** (in the WYSIWYG editor), say `We are going to follow a new marketing strategy this year for sales`.

4. Finally, click on the **Publish** button.

The web content is created with a unique content ID. The following screenshot shows the **Marketing Strategy** web content in the list:

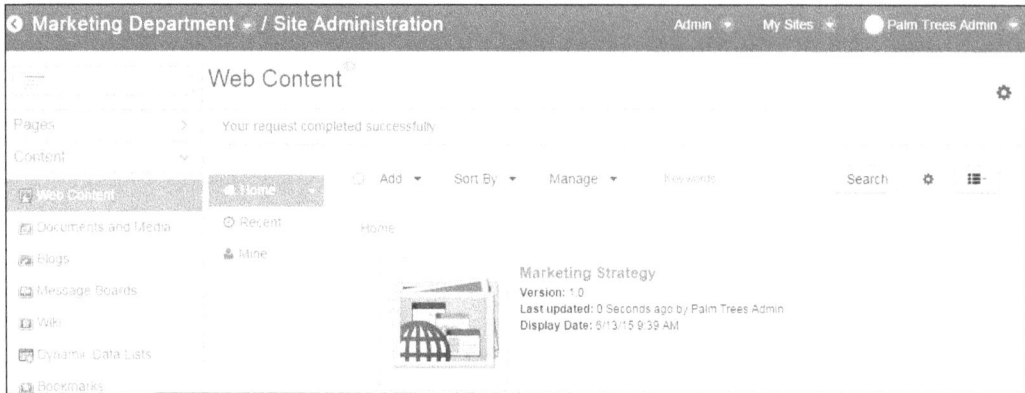

Figure 9.3: The Web Content portlet

While creating the web content, there are some actions on the right-hand side to customize web content; refer to *Figure 9.2*:

- **Abstract**: This allows you to describe the web content summary.

- **Categorization**: This allows you to categorize the content with the list of options provided. The list options are **Announcements**, **Blogs**, **General**, **News**, **Press Release**, and **Test**. To make your content searchable properly, you can even create tags.

- **Schedule**: This allows you to set the date and time after which your content publishes and/or expires.

- **Display Page**: This allows you to define the display page for your content. In a publication house, there will be different departments for different book types, say information technology books and literature books. The marketing department needs to manage the different categories of books on the website. They can use the display page feature. You can find the content display page template under **Page Template** in the **Sites** section of the control panel. Generally, the content display page template is configured with the **Asset Publisher**, **Tags Navigation**, and **Search** portlets.

- **Related Assets**: This allows you to map any number of assets with your content within a site or across the portal even if the assets are not tags and not in the same category. You can associate your content to a Blogs Entry, Message Boards Message, Web Content, Calendar Event, Bookmarks Entry, Documents and Media Document, and Wiki Page.

- **Permissions**: This allows you to set access permissions for your content. You can set limited viewable permissions for different roles by clicking on the **More** option.

- **Custom fields**: This allows you to set customized metadata about the web content. This custom field needs to be defined in the custom field section of the control panel.

To display the preceding content, you need to map the content with the **Web Content Display** portlet on the marketing department page.

Viewing Web Content

To view the **Marketing Strategy** web content on the marketing department site, follow these steps:

1. From the dock bar menu, select **My Sites | Marketing Department**.

2. In the **Marketing Department** site, create a new **Web Content** page and add the **Web Content Display** portlet. The following screenshot shows the Web Content Display portlet on the marketing department site page:

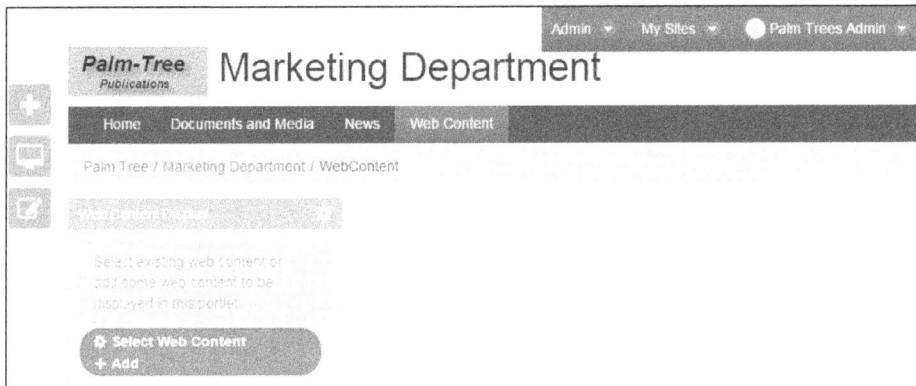

Figure 9.4: The Web Content Display portlet

3. Click on the **Gear** icon (**Select Web Content**) in the Web Content Display portlet, due to which a pop-up window will appear—select the **Marketing Strategy** content, and finally save it.

4. Refresh the page and you will see that the content is changed in the Web Content Display portlet. Change the **Title** of the Web Content portlet by double-clicking on the portlet title bar, and save the changes by clicking on the tick mark on the right-hand side; follow this screenshot:

Figure 9.5: The Web Content Display portlet—change of title

As mentioned earlier, Liferay provides a robust Web Content Management System. It also has the version managing feature. Whenever you edit the content, it creates a new version for the content. Let's edit the preceding content and publish it.

Editing Web Content

Liferay makes content editing easier for end users by providing them with two ways of editing, which are as follows:

- Users with appropriate permissions can edit the content from the site page itself within the Web Content Display portlet
- Users with appropriate permissions can edit the content from the site administration panel

Let's edit using the first approach for this example. In the Web Content Display portlet, you will find the **Edit** icon below the content. Refer to *Figure 9.4*. Click on the edit link, and the edit screen will appear; refer to the following screenshot.

In the Edit screen, you will find actions, such as **Basic Preview**, **Permissions**, and **View History**. **Basic Preview** is used to preview the web content before publishing it. **Permissions** allow you to set the access permission for the content. **View History** displays the version list of the content.

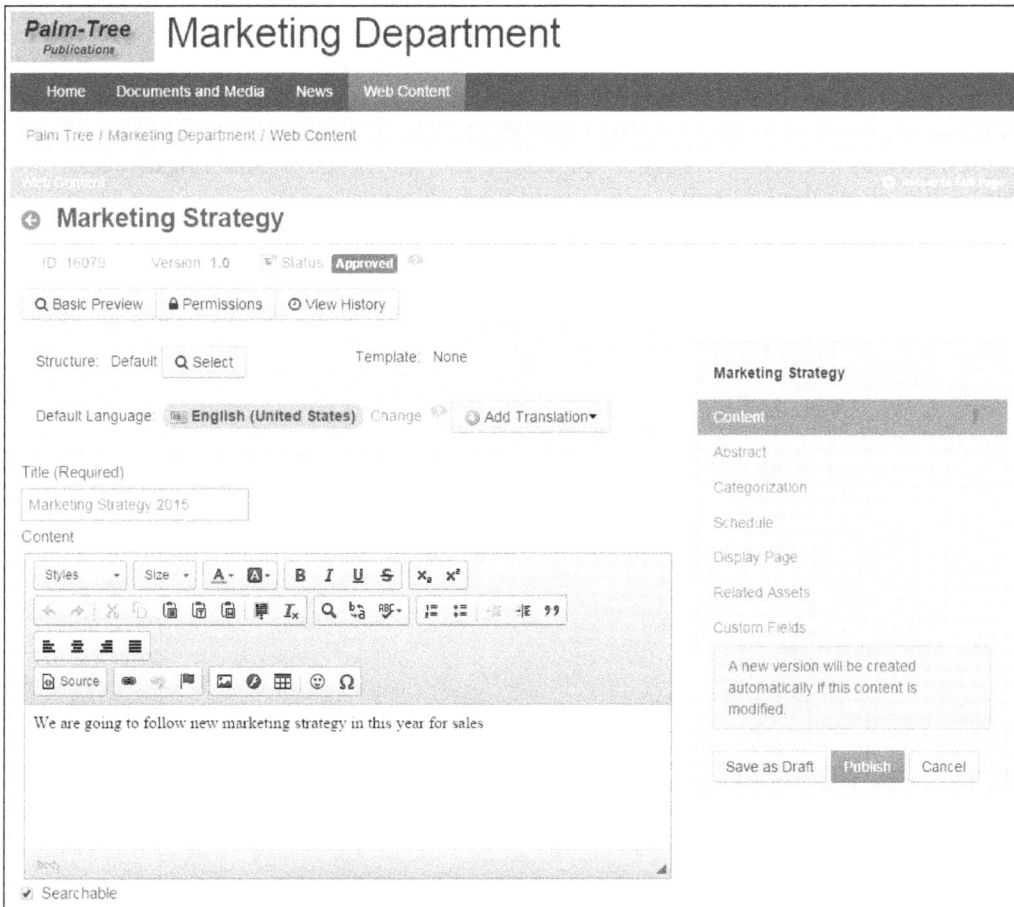

Figure 9.6: The Web Content Display portlet edit page

Now, change the title to `Marketing Strategy 2015`. Follow the preceding screenshot. Finally, click on the **Publish** button. The content title has been changed to **Marketing Strategy 2015**.

Localization

Liferay web content provides a very dynamic feature, that is, localization, so that you have the ability to choose a default language. Refer to the preceding screenshot, and you will find **Default Language is English (United State)**. Beside that, there is the **Add Translation** select button.

The following screenshot shows the languages available for translation. You can add languages from the portal settings in the control panel. You can even add languages in the `portal-ext.properties` file using the `locales.enabled` key with language values, such as `locales.enabled= en_US,ar_SA,hi_IN,nl_NL` for English USA, Arabic (Saudi Arabia), Hindi (India), and Dutch (Netherlands).

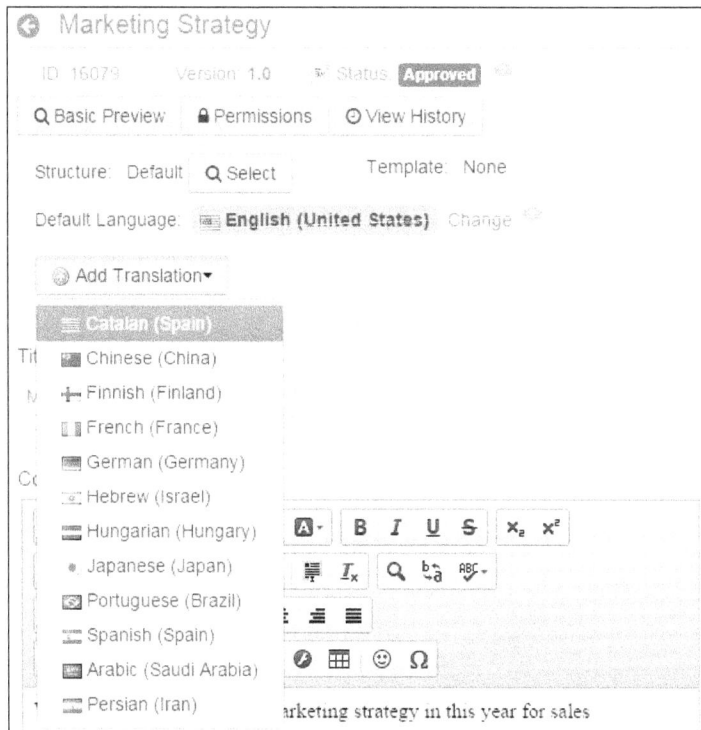

Figure 9.7: The Web Content edit mode—adding language translation

Let's suppose that you have selected the language German. A pop-up window will open to translate the content to the German language — fill in the title of the content and the main content in the German language and save it. Now, the web content has both English and German languages. When the portal language is changed to the German language, the Web Content Display portlet will display the German content.

If you want to remove the translation from the web content, simply open the translation and click on the **Remove Translation** button.

Adding folders

In web content, you can also add folders to differentiate different web content in the site scope. It's very simple — the same as creating folders in documents and media. Let's add one folder in the web content with the name **IT Books**:

1. Let's assume that you are in the **Web Content** portlet inside **Site Administration Panel**.

2. Click on the **Add** button and select the **Folder** link.

3. The **New Folder** page will open — fill the folder name **IT Books** and the description **Information Technology Book**. Keep the default permission settings.

4. Finally, click on the **Save** button.

The folder with **IT Books** has been created under the **Home** parent folder.

> Note that Liferay provides you with action on the folder too, such as **Edit**, **Move**, **Move to the Recycle Bin**, **Add Subfolder**, and **Permissions**.

Moving Web Content

Liferay provides the feature of moving web content from the folder to another in the same site scope. Let's suppose there is a requirement to move the **Computer science** web content to the **IT Book** folder. You will then need to perform the following steps:

1. Click on the **Move** action from the content action list. Refer to the following screenshot:

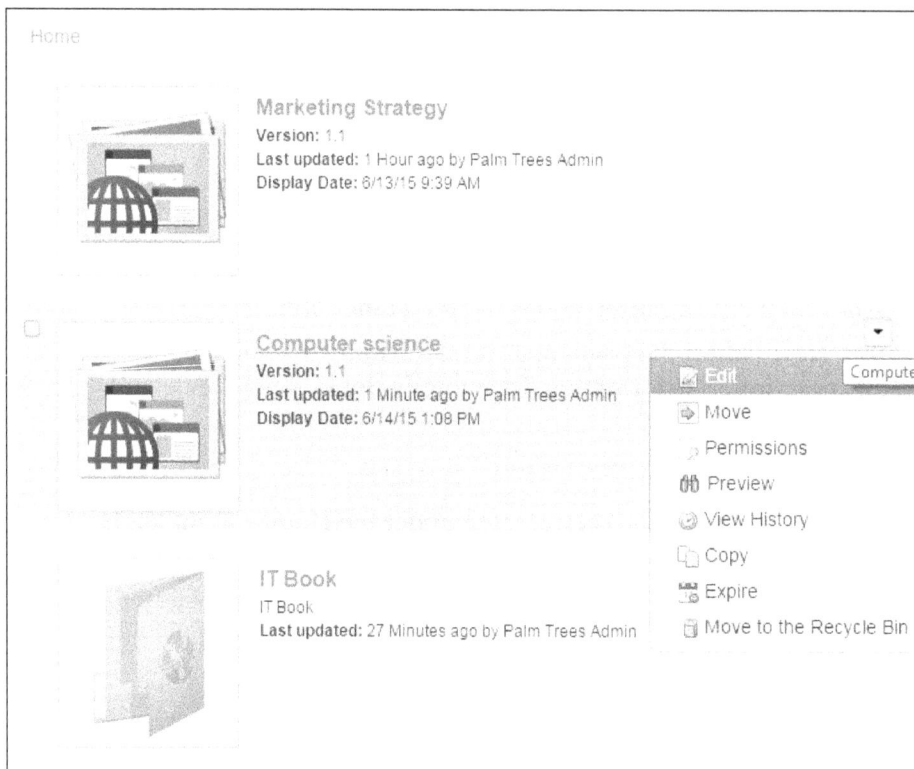

Figure 9.8: The Web Content list

2. After clicking on the **Move** action, the **Move** page will appear with **Current Folder** and the **New Folder** names.

3. You can select and browse the required folder where you want to move the **Computer science** web content. In our example, we need to move the content to the **IT Book** folder.

4. After selecting the **New Folder** name, click on the **Move** button.

Finally, the content will move to the **IT Book** folder.

Structures and templates

Liferay WCM comes with the unique feature of managing the content in a proper manner with the help of structures and templates. This allows the user the flexibility of handling the content more robustly and also controls the mishandling of the content. Web content is divided into two parts: the first part is structures and the second part is templates.

Structures

Structures are used to define the sets of fields in a form available to users when they create content. Each structure is mapped to templates that define the pattern of the content displayed to the end users.

The benefits of structures are as follows:

- This improves the manageability of content for the site administrator.
- This provides a format for the content to make users know what is needed to be entered to have a complete article. This makes it much easier for the end users to add content.

After getting the user input for the web content using the structure form, finally it can be formatted automatically using a mapped template.

Let's add a structure for our use case with **Title Tag line** (text), **Body** (HTML is WYSIWYG editor), **Book Sample Attachment** (Document and Media), **Author** (text), **Date Of Release** (date), and **Price** (decimal). To create the structure, you should have sufficient permissions. Follow these steps to create the structure:

1. In the **Site Administration** panel, select **Web Content** and then click on **Structures** from the **Manage** dropdown. The **Structure** interface pop-up window will open.
2. Click on the **Add** button, and the **New Structure** form will appear.
3. Fill in the structure name with `Book Structure` and click on the **Details** link to expand for filling the description `Structure` for the book's web content. Keep the parent structure default, that is, blank.

4. In the **View** tab, create the structure, as shown in the following screenshot:

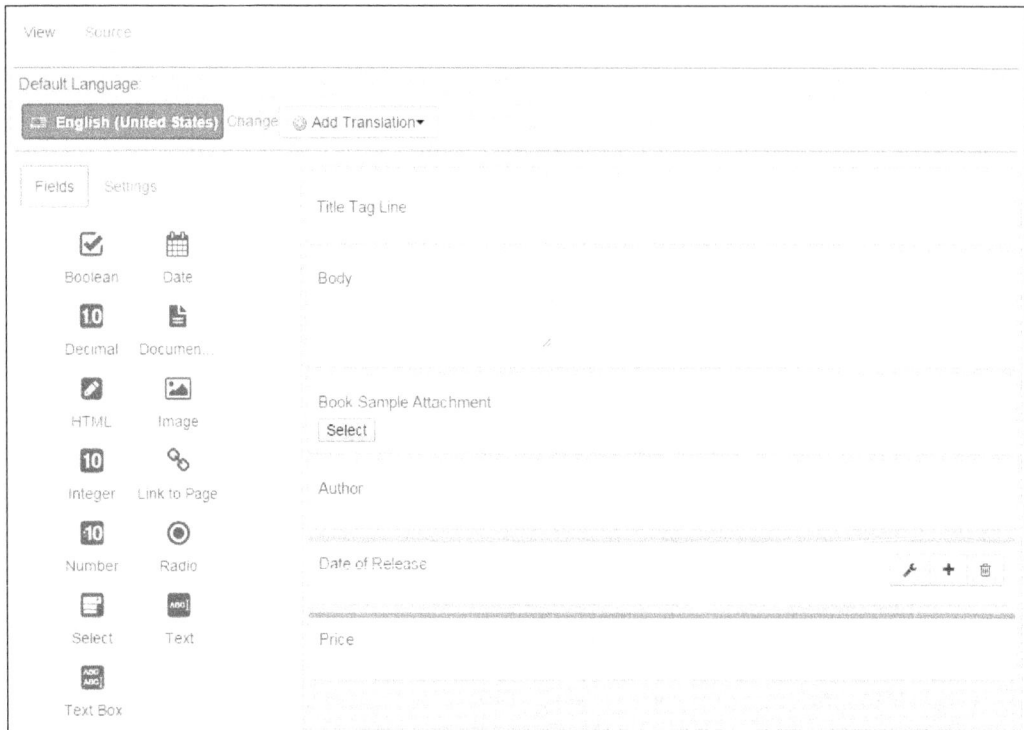

Figure 9.9: The Web Content structure

5. You can drag and drop the fields into the right-hand side box. After placing the field, you can set the field's settings to customize the field label, mark required, and so on, by clicking on the **Settings** tab.

6. In the preceding screenshot, you can see the **Source** tab, which provides the source for the structure.

7. Finally, click on the **Save** button to save the structure.

Here's a list of the fields to create the structure:

- **Boolean**: This adds a checkbox to your structure and has the value `true` for checked and `false` for unchecked.

- **Date**: This adds the date picker to your structure; the date picker helps the user with selecting the desired date in the proper format.

- **Decimal**: This adds the field that takes the number format value, including the decimal point.

- **Document and Media**: This adds a field with the browse button to select existing files from Documents and Media Library. It even allows us to upload files into the Document library.

- **HTML**: This adds the WYSIWYG editor for rich content.

- **Image**: This adds the field to browse images from Documents and Media.

- **Integer**: This adds a field that takes nonfractional number format values.

- **Link to Page**: This adds the field that allows you to link the page to the same site.

- **Number**: This adds a field that only allows number format values.

- **Radio**: This adds an option field onto your structure.

- **Select**: This adds a select drop-down box. With settings, you can make the box allow to select single and multiple values.

- **Text**: This adds a simple textbox for the title and the author name.

- **Text Box**: This adds the text area onto your structure to store long descriptions.

Structures provide a huge range of fields, which help you to gather the information from the users for web content.

After you click on the **Save** button, it will create a structure with the name **Book structure**. Once you visit the **Structure** pop-up window, you will find that **Book Structure** is listed with the following heading **ID**, **Name**, **Description**, **Modified Date**, and **Actions**. Each structure will have a few actions, which need to be managed. Refer to the following screenshot:

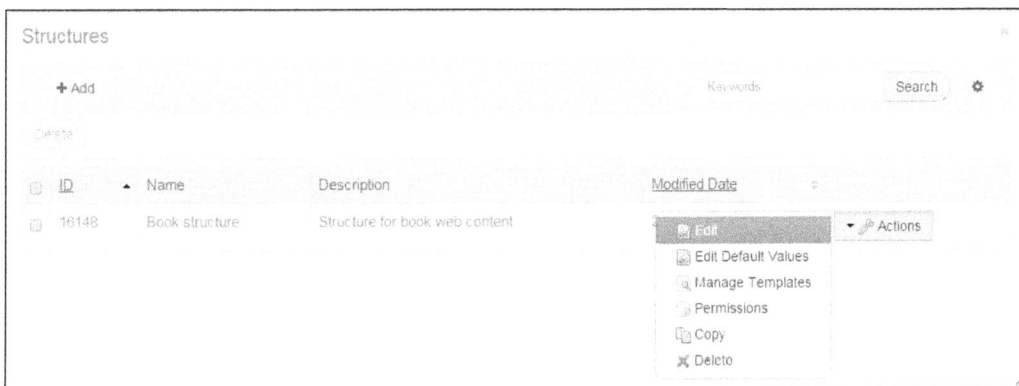

Figure 9.10: Web Content structure actions

The actions are as follows:

- **Edit**: This allows the user to edit the structure whenever needed.
- **Edit Default Values**: This allows the user to set the default values for the structure. These default values help the users with predefined values while creating the web content.
- **Manage Templates**: This allows you to create templates for the specific structure. Even you can create the template from the template pop-up window separately and only need to select the structure for mapping with the template. With **Manage Templates**, it automatically selects the respective structure.
- **Permissions**: With this, you can set the access permissions for the structure.
- **Copy**: With this, you can copy the structure to another by specifying the new structure name.
- **Delete**: With this, you can delete the structure forever.

As mentioned previously, default values for particular structures can be set. You can set most values, such as **Content**, **Abstract**, **Categorization**, **Display Page**, **Related Assets**, **Permissions**, and **Custom Fields**. When you create new web content, the default values will be right there. For example, you want to make sure that whenever the content is created using this structure, it should have **Information Technology** tags. You can set the **Tags** with **Information Technology** in **Categorization**. Now all the web content created based on this structure will always have **Information Technology** tags.

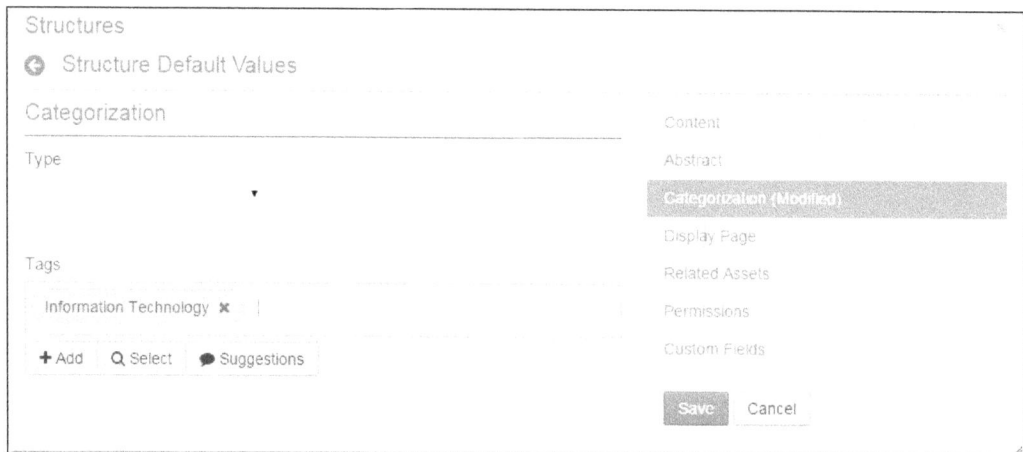

Figure 9.11: Web Content default values

Templates

Templates are the wrapper of look and feel over the content. All the input from the web content author will be used by a template and put all together with a nice design for the end user to view. Whenever developers make changes to the structure, they should also update the changes in the respective templates. In some scenarios, you can use generic templates that are not associated with any structure. Generic templates are free templates that can be reusable code importable into another template. Templates can be created in three languages: **FreeMarker** (`.ftl`), **Extensible Stylesheet Language** (`.xsl`), and **Velocity** (`.vm`).

- **FreeMarker template language**: This is one of the most popular languages to write templates. It is a *template engine* — a generic tool to generate text output (anything from HTML to autogenerated source code) based on templates. For more detail information, visit http://freemarker.org/.

- **Extensible Stylesheet language**: This is also used for templates to transform the underlying XML of a structure into HTML form for the browser.

- **Velocity macro**: It is a scripting language, which allows the developer to write logic within HTML. For more information visit `https://velocity.apache.org/engine/releases/velocity-1.5/`.

Now, let's create the template for the preceding structure. The template can be created in two ways, which are as follows:

- Firstly, you can directly create the template from the structure list action by using **Manage Templates**. This action will automatically associate the structure with the template.

- Secondly, you can go to the **Manage** button just as with structures and select the template from the dropdown.

In this example, we will go with the second approach; follow these steps to create templates:

1. Select **Template** from the **Manage** button dropdown of the web content section in **Site Administration Panel**.

2. The template pop-up window will appear; click on the **Add** button.

3. Fill in the template name `Book Template`, and click on the **Detail** link to expand a few fields. Select the structure for which the template is going to be created. Select the language in which you are going to create the template. We selected FreeMarker for our example. Also, fill in the description `Template for book content`. You can even select the small image for the template.

4. In the following screen, you can find the right-hand side script section, where you have to write the FreeMarker script. You can use the left-hand side panel to quickly add commonly used variables.

5. After completing the template code, you can save the template.

6. The following screenshot shows the script box with the left-hand side panel and the right-hand side panel. The left-hand side panel is to assist you while coding. And you have to write the script in the right-hand side panel.

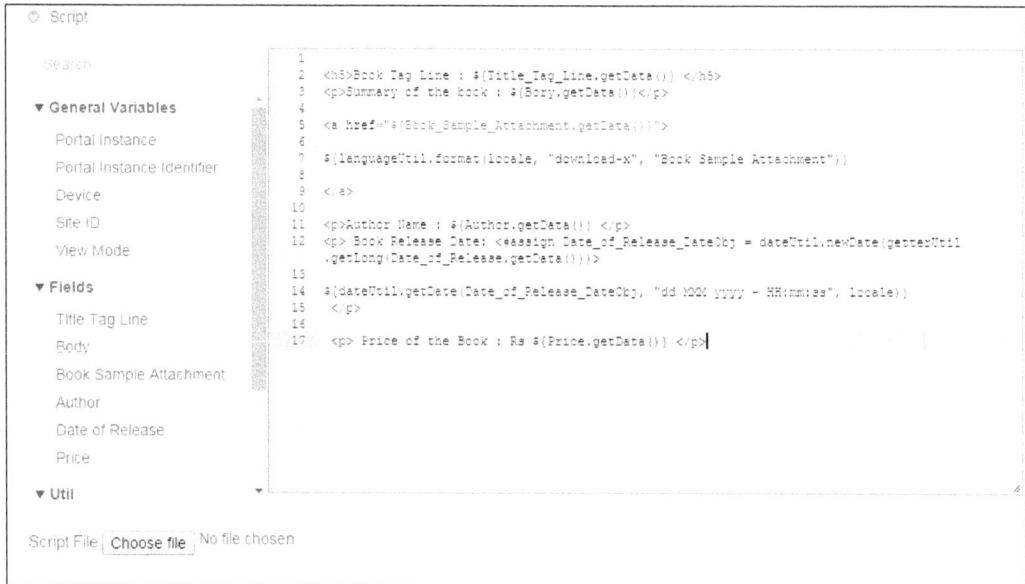

Figure 9.12: Template scripting with the FreeMarker language

In the preceding screenshot, you can see the choose file button; you can upload any script file in any format. The script code will be displayed in the right-hand side box.

After saving the template, it will be listed in the templates pop-up window with actions. The following screenshot shows the action associated with it.

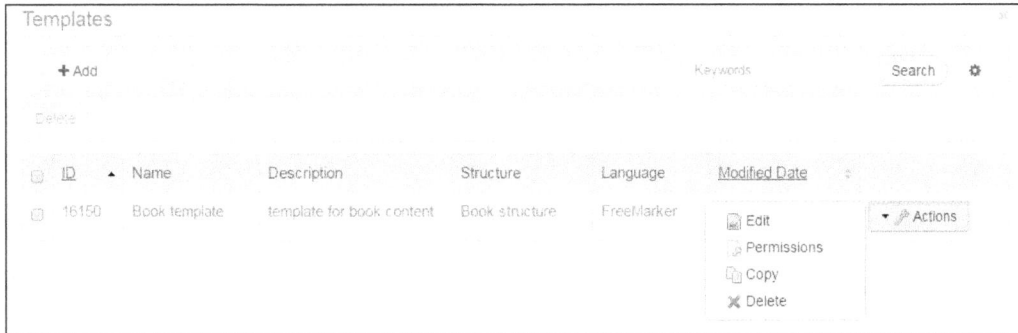

Figure 9.13: Structure and template Web Content

The actions on the template are as follows:

- **Edit**: This allows you to edit the template
- **Permissions**: This allows you to set the access permission for the template
- **Copy**: This makes a duplicate copy of the template
- **Delete**: This deletes the template forever

Finally, the structure and template are ready for the content. Now, you can create content using the book structure by following the steps:

1. Go to **Site Administration Panel** and select **Book Structure** from the **Add** button of the web content section.
2. A new web content page will appear; fill in the required data and publish it.
3. Go to the site page and in the Web Content Display portlet, select the web content.

The web content will be published as per the template design. The view of the web content is different than the previous one:

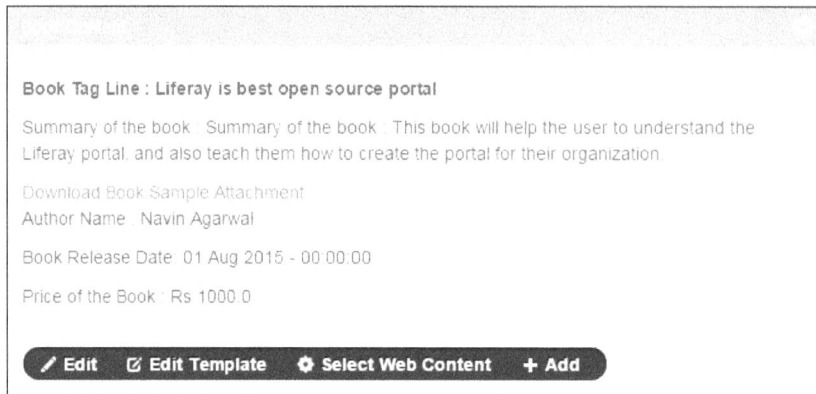

Book Tag Line : Liferay is best open source portal

Summary of the book : Summary of the book : This book will help the user to understand the Liferay portal. and also teach them how to create the portal for their organization.

Download Book Sample Attachment
Author Name : Navin Agarwal

Book Release Date : 01 Aug 2015 - 00:00:00

Price of the Book : Rs 1000.0

/ Edit   ☑ Edit Template   ✿ Select Web Content   + Add

Figure 9.14: Change effected in the web content look and feel after implementing the template

We have used a sample template without any CSS; you can use CSS and make the look and feel more attractive.

Assigning permissions

The Web Content portlet can be accessed inside **Site Administration Panel** too. A Site member won't have the permissions to add and edit web content on the Web Content portlet, but they might have access to view the content.

Let's provide the role entitlements for the **MB Topic Admin** role and allow the user to edit content, where Lotti is associated as a member.

To set the permission entitlements for the web content, the portal administrator needs to define permissions in roles. Under the **User** section, click on **Roles** in **Control Panel** and locate **MB Topic Admin**. Select **Define Permissions** from the **Action** button beside Mb Topic Admin and search for the web content. You will get the entitlements settings for the web content.

Permissions for **Web Content** can be assigned under **Site Administration | Content**:

- **Site Administration | Content**: General Permissions, Resource Permissions (Web Content), Web Content Folder, Web Content Article, Web Content Feed, Web Content Structure, and Web Content Template.

Let discuss each of them in detail.

General Permissions

General Permissions is defined as the permissions with which the users can enjoy most administrator rights for a particular application in the portal. Access to Site Administration entitlements are given to the users who have the access to create and edit the content:

Action	Description
Access to Site Administration	This provides the ability to access the portlet in the site administration panel
Configuration	This provides the ability to configure the portlets
Permission	This provides the ability to assign permissions
View	This provides the ability to view

Whenever you give entitlements for specific portlets, you have to be clear about the user roles.

Resource Permissions – Web Content

Resource Permissions defines what actions can be performed on resources displayed or managed from the application. Basically, resources are any user-facing application in the portal, such as uses, organization, sites, blogs, wikis, and so on:

Action	Description
Add Feed	This provides the ability to add feeds
Add Folder	This provides the ability to add folders
Add Structure	This provides the ability to add structures
Add Template	This provides the ability to add templates
Add Web Content	This provides the ability to add web content
Permissions	This provides the ability to assign permissions
Subscribe	This provides the ability to subscribe
View	This provides the ability to view

Let's say the user "Lotti Stein" is a member of the role "MB Topic Admin". As a portal administrator, you are required to provide the entitlement to add the web content and view for the user "Lotti Stein" and also provide the entitlements to access the Web Content portlet in the site administration panel. How do we accomplish this? We do it by following these steps:

1. Log in as a portal administrator since **Roles** is only accessible by the Portal admin.

2. Click on **Roles** under the category **Users** of **Control Panel**.

3. Then, locate a role, say **MB Topic Admin**.

4. Then, click on the **Define Permissions** icon from the **Actions** menu on the right-hand side of the role. Now, search for **Web Content**.

5. Click **Web Content** from **Site Administration | content**, enable the **Access in Site Administration** checkbox from **General permissions**, and use **Add Web Content** from **Web Content**.

6. Finally, save the changes.

From now on, users and members of the role "MB Topic Admin" will have the **Add Web Content** button to add the content.

Web Content folder

Permissions entitlements for web content folders are to access the folder and add the file to that folder:

Action	Description
Access	This provides the ability to access the web content folder
Add Subfolder	This provides the ability to add subfolders
Add Web Content	This provides the ability to add the web content
Delete	This provides the ability to delete
Permissions	This provides the ability to assign permissions
Update	This provides the ability to update
View	This provides the ability to view

Access entitlements can be assigned to the role that needs to access the folder and needs the ability to add the web content and subfolders.

Web Content articles

Permissions entitlements on web content articles are assigned for the user who has access to the web content related to discussions. The following are the entitlements listed for the discussions on the web content:

Action	Description
Add Discussion	This provides the ability to add discussions on the web content
Delete	This provides the ability to delete
Delete Discussion	This provides the ability to delete discussions on the web content
Expire	This provides the ability to expire the web content
Permissions	This provides the ability to assign permissions
Update	This provides the ability to update the web content
Update Discussion	This provides the ability to update discussions on the web content
View	This provides the ability to view

Web Content feeds

Permission entitlements for web content feeds can be assigned to the users to delete, update, view, and set the permission on the feed:

Action	Description
Delete	This provides the ability to delete feeds
Permissions	This provides the ability to assign permissions
Update	This provides the ability to update the feed
View	This provides the ability to view

Web Content structures

Permission entitlements for web content structures can be assigned to the users to delete, update, and configure the permission on the structure:

Action	Description
Delete	This provides the ability to delete
Permissions	This provides the ability to assign permissions
Update	This provides the ability to update the structure
View	This provides the ability to view

Web Content templates

Permission entitlements for web content templates can be assigned to the users to delete, update, and configure the permission on the template:

Action	Description
Delete	This provides the ability to delete templates
Permissions	This provides the ability to assign permissions
Update	This provides the ability to update the template
View	This provides the ability to view

Web Content configurations

As mentioned previously, the Web Content portlet is only available in **Site Administration Panel**. You can do the configuration for the Web Content portlet in **Site Administration Panel** by selecting web content from the left-hand side panel content scope. Select the **Gear** icon from the top-right corner and click on configuration.

Configuration has four tabs, which are **Email From**, **Web Content Added Email**, **Web Content review Email**, and **Web Content Updated Email**. Also, you will see the Archive/Restore Setup link, which allows you to archive the content and restore it again when required. Let's discuss each tab in detail.

The **Email From** tab is for setting the e-mail sender's name and the sender's e-mail address. The following screenshot displays the **Email From** tab:

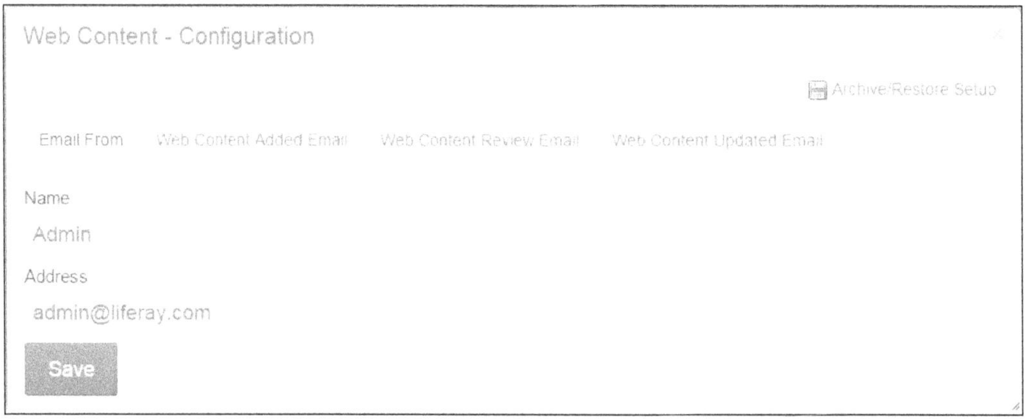

Web Content - Configuration

Archive/Restore Setup

Email From   Web Content Added Email   Web Content Review Email   Web Content Updated Email

Name

Admin

Address

admin@liferay.com

Save

Figure 9.15: Web Content - Configuration | Email From

The email tab to which the web content is added allows you the enable the mail feature to send mail when the new web content is added. The following screenshot displays the e-mail format for sending mail when new content is created:

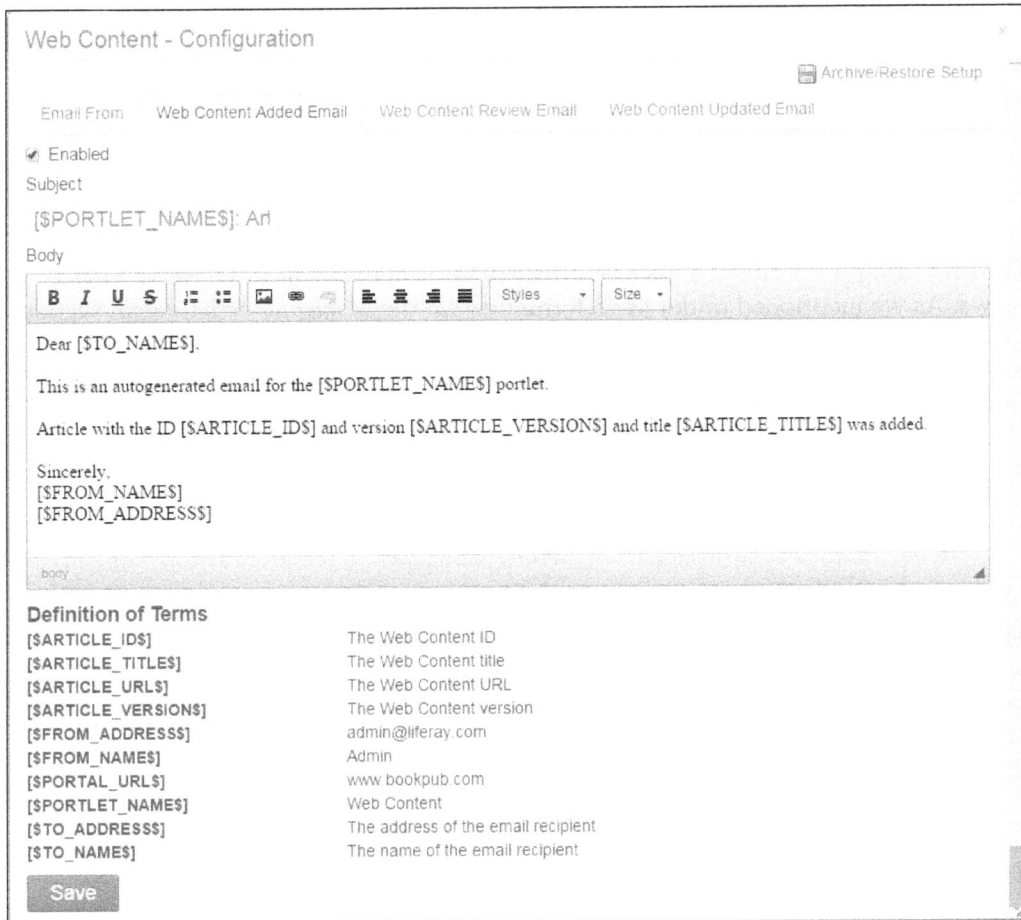

Figure 9.16: Web Content - Configuration | Web Content Added Email

You can enable or disable the mail and even change the mail subject and body. You can use the definition of team for the e-mail subject and body.

In the same way, in the other two tabs, **Web Content Review Email** and **Web Content Update Email**, you can enable or disable the mail and even change the mail subject and body.

Web Content Review Email is used for e-mail notifications to content reviewers when content is created. **Web Content Update Email** is used for the e-mail notification when content is updated.

Extra settings for Web Content

The Web Content portlet is so flexible that many settings are defined in `portal.properties`. As you saw earlier, the localization setting can also be set through `portal-ext.properties`.

Liferay has excellent portal configuration features, which allow you to do extensive customization for different applications/portlets. Let's have a look at the configurable items in the properties file:

```
journal.display.views=icon,descriptive,list
journal.default.display.view=icon
```

The preceding property, `journal.display.views`, allows you to set the display views. As we mentioned under **switch the** view in the *Managing Web Content* section, there are three different views: icon, descriptive, and list. The property `journal.default.display.view=icon` sets the default display as the icon. You can override this property in `portal-ext. properties`, for example, if you want to have list as the default view, just set the `journal.default.display.view=list` value:

```
journal.article.form.add=content,abstract,categorization,schedule,
    display-page,related-assets,permissions,custom-fields
journal.article.form.update=content,abstract,categorization,schedu
    le,display-page,related-assets,custom-fields
```

The preceding properties are for the right-hand side panel menu of the new web content page. The first one appears when we add new web content. And the second one appears when we update the existing web content:

```
journal.article.force.autogenerate.id=true
journal.article.types=announcements,blogs,general,news,press-
    release,test
```

The property `journal.article.force.autogenerate.id=true` is set to true to generate the content IDs automatically. In **Categorization**, you find the type drop-down list; it is mapped by `journal.article.types`, which has the announcements, blogs, general, news, press-release, and test values. If you want to remove the test, simply override this property in `portal-ext.properties`:

```
journal.article.view.permission.check.enabled=false
```

The preceding property is set to true to check whether a user has the view permission on the content. The default value is false so that the content is not checked for the user view permission:

```
journal.article.comments.enabled=true
```

Every bit of web content has the comments area for users; to remove the comments for web content, you just need to update the preceding property in `portal-ext.properties` with false.

```
journal.template.freemarker.restricted.variables=serviceLocator
journal.template.velocity.restricted.variables=serviceLocator
```

The preceding properties are set for the input of a comma-delimited list of variables, which are restricted from the context in FreeMarker- and Velocity-based content:

```
journal.image.extensions=.gif,.jpeg,.jpg,.png
```

The property is defined for image extension in the web content; you can add a few more extensions, or you can make an asterisk mark to permit all file extensions:

```
journal.publish.version.history.by.default=true
```

Set the preceding property to false when only the latest approved version of the web content should be published by default:

```
journal.email.from.name=
journal.email.from.address=
journal.email.article.added.enabled=true
journal.email.article.added.subject=com/liferay/portlet/journal/de
    pendencies/email_article_added_subject.tmpl
journal.email.article.added.body=com/liferay/portlet/journal/depen
    dencies/email_article_added_body.tmpl
```

The properties are for e-mail notification settings for the workflow. They map the workflow with e-mail templates for the web content. For each workflow action, notification templates are defined.

The export and import of Web Content

The export/import feature allows you to export the LAR file, which includes content, configuration, and permission settings of the Web Content portlet. The same LAR file can be imported in other Liferay instances, which have the same version of the Liferay server.

You can export the web content by following these steps:

1. In the Site Administration panel, click on the **Gear** icon and select the **Export/Import** link of the Web Content portlet.
2. You will get the **Export** form, which allows you to select the content by the date range or simply checking the **Content** checkbox. This also allows you to select the configuration and permissions of the web content. Refer to the following screenshot for the export form.

3. Finally, click on the **Export** button.

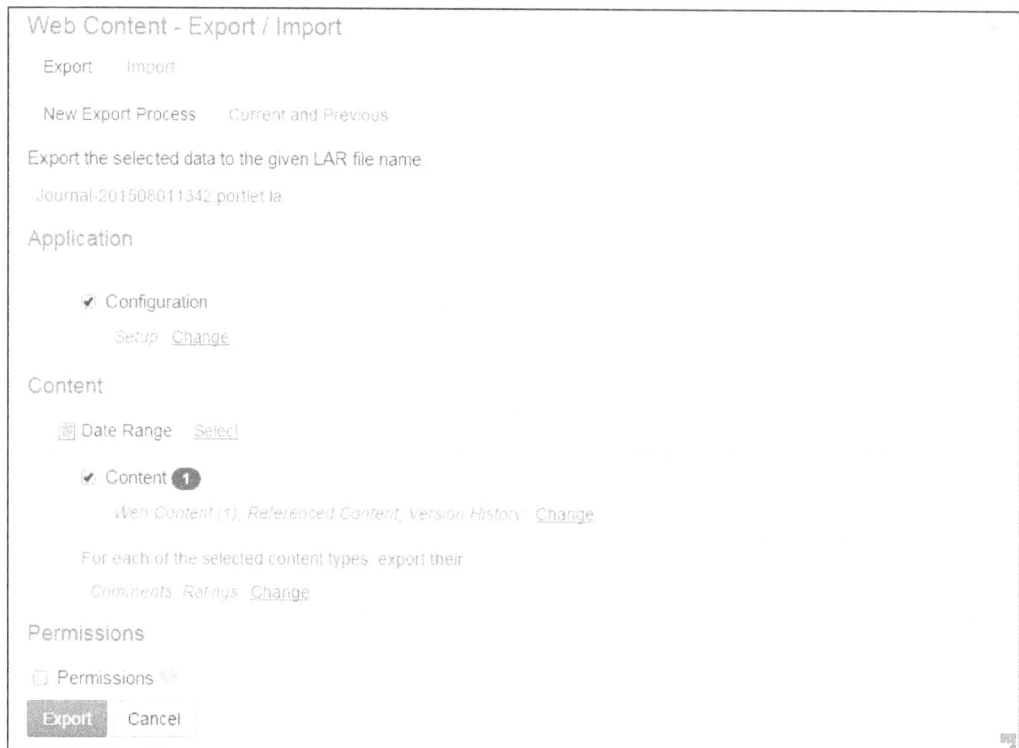

Figure 9.17: Web Content export

4. After you click on the **Export** button, it will start the export process and list it in the **Current and Previous** tab. The following screenshot shows the successful export of the LAR file. You can download the .lar file and import the LAR file to other Liferay instances.

> Note that a LAR file can only be imported in the same version of the Liferay server. For example, you can't import the LAR file of Liferay 6.2 CE to Liferay 6.2 EE.

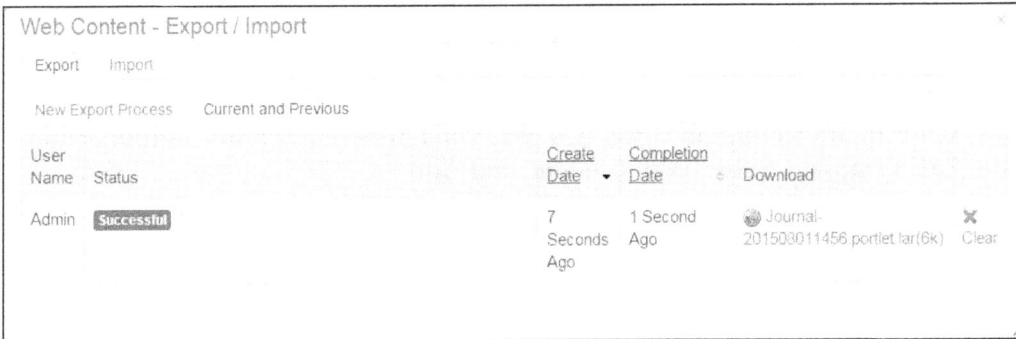

Figure 9.18: Web Content Export | Current and Previous

Importing the LAR file to the Web Content portlet is very easy. You just need to browse or drag and drop the .lar file within the dotted boundary inside the **New Import Process** tab; refer to the following screenshot:

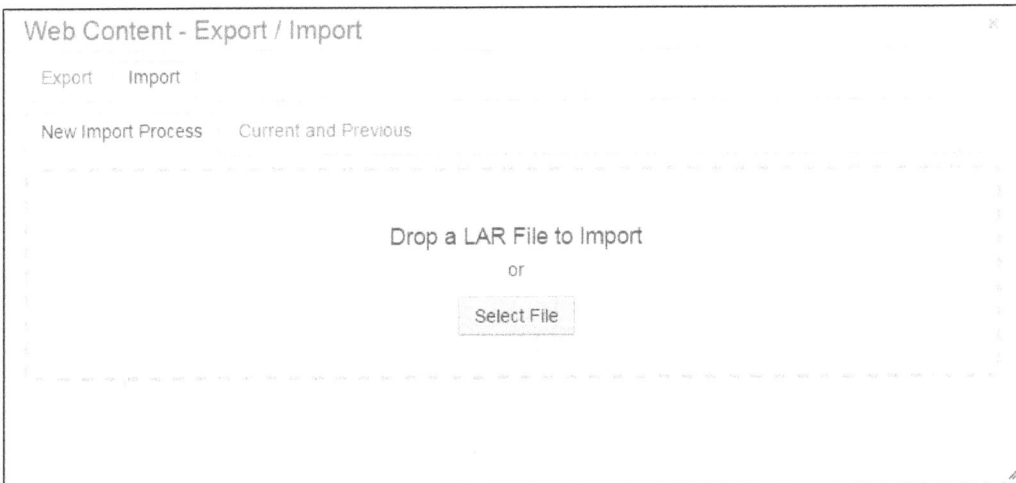

Figure 9.19: Web Content import

5. After you select the file, it will start the import process and list it in the **Current and Previous** tab.

The Web Content Display portlet

The **Web Content Display** portlet basically displays the web content on the site page, which we have already seen in the preceding sections. Here, we will explore it more in detail. If you refer to *Figure 9.14*, you will notice that it provides four actions: **Edit**, **Edit Template**, **Select Web Content**, and **Add**:

- **Edit**: This allows the user to edit the web content on the page itself. When **Edit** is clicked on, it opens the web content edit page and the user can directly edit the content.

- **Edit Template**: This allows users to edit templates. Once they click on the **Edit Template** link, it opens the template edit page and they can make changes in the template directly.

- **Select Web Content**: This allows the user to select the web content and do the required configuration settings, such as enable print, enable ratings, enable comments, and so on.

- **Add**: It allows the creation of new web content on the fly. Users need not visit the **Site Administrator Panel** to create the content. Once a user clicks on the **Add** link, a new web content page opens for the user.

The Web Content Display portlet also has configuration settings. Users can click on the **Gear** icon and select the **Configuration** link. Its opens the configuration pop-up window, with five tabs, which are **Setup**, **Supported Clients**, **Permissions**, **Sharing**, and **Scope**:

- **Setup**: It's similar to the **Select Web Content** link, which allows the user to configure **Web Content**, **Enable Print**, **Enable Related Assets**, **Enable Ratings**, and so on. Refer to the *Asset Publisher* section of *Chapter 4*, *Forums, Categorization, and Asset Publishing*, to know about the key words. Refer to the next screenshot for more details. Once you select the content, **Displaying Content** will display the selected content and then finally save the content.

- **Supported Clients**: This shows the portlet mode views Regular Browser and Mobile Device. You can enable and disable this as and when required.

- **Permissions**: This allows access permissions to be set for the Web Content portlet for different roles.

- **Sharing**: You can share the portlet with other social media and other websites. It provides tabs such as My Website, Facebook, OpenSocial Gadget, Netvibes, and Friends.

- **Scope**: Users can define the scope of the Web Content portlet globally.

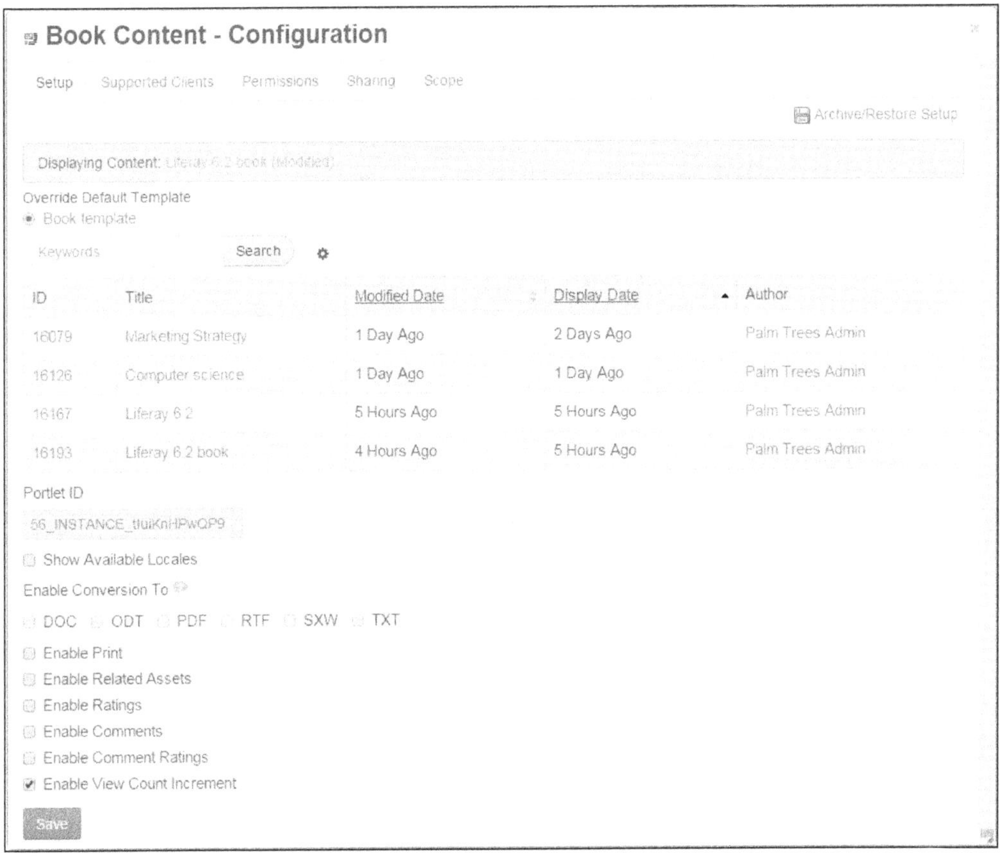

Figure 9.20: Book Content - Configuration | Setup

The Web Content Display configuration helps users to configure the portlet and view the content with extra enabled features.

The Web Content Search portlet

In an intranet portal, sometimes you might have to search the content all over the site. To search, you need to have a search engine that will find the content all over the site. Liferay provides you with the Web Content Search portlet, which allows you to do faceted searches. The Portal admin can place the Web Content Search portlet on the page. Now, the end user can search for the content over the site and get the required list of the search items.

The faceted search allows the search results to be narrowed down by applying a set of filters to the result of a search query. The Liferay Search portlet supports faceted searches.

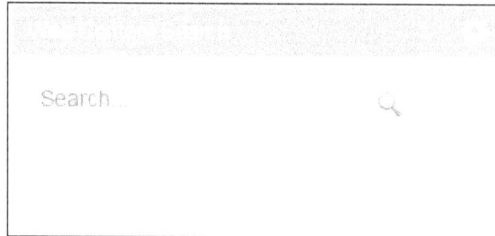

Figure 9.21: The Web Content Search portlet

If you do the search for a keyword, say portal, it finds the content over the site and provides the list of contents. The following screenshot shows the search result for content over the site:

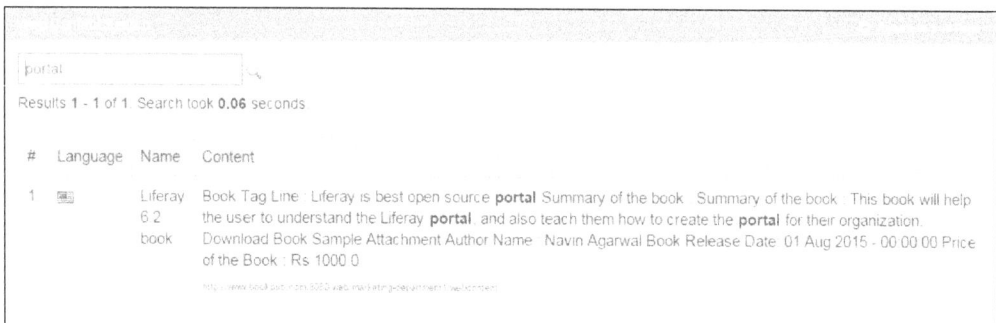

Fig 9.22: The Web Content Search portlet – Result

In the configuration, you can set the web content type. With this, you define the search behavior. For example, if you define the content type as **Blog**, the search will only be performed on blog type content. That means you are restricting the search on different content types. The options provided for different content types are **Announcements**, **Blogs**, **General**, **News**, **Press Release**, and **Test**. You can add new content types as per your requirement through `portal-ext.properties`:

```
journal.article.types=announcements,blogs,general,news,press-
    release,test
```

Scheduling Web Content

Liferay 6.2 has the unique feature of scheduling web content, whereby it allows users the flexibility of determining content displayed, expired and/or reviewed. This allows the author to make their content schedule while creating; it's a nice feature to keep the portal free from outdated content. The following screenshot displays the schedule for the content, with settings for display date, never expire, and never review.

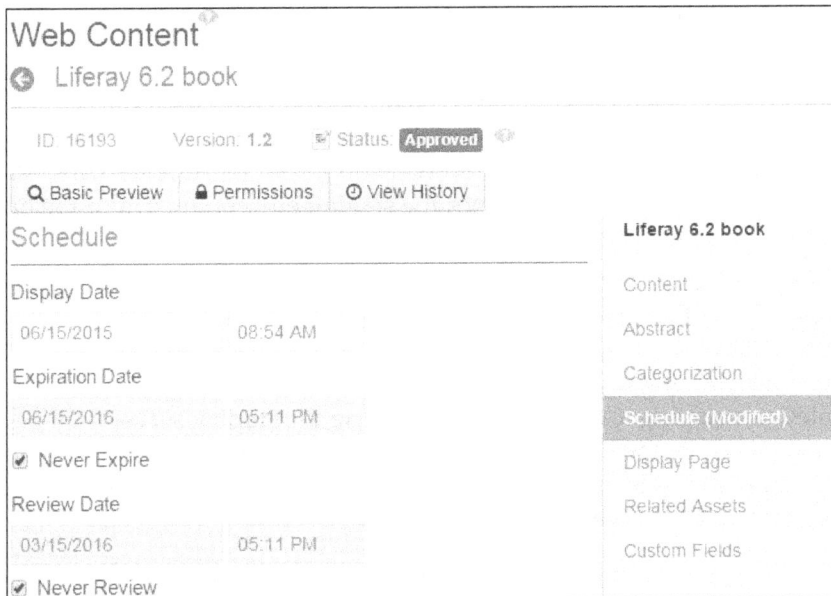

Figure 9.23: The Web Content schedule

The settings in the schedule are explained here:

- **Display Date**: This is set when the web content is displayed
- **Expiration Date**: This is set when the web content expires; the default date is 1 year
- **Never Expire**: This allows you to make the web content never expire
- **Review Date**: This sets the web content review date
- **Never Review**: This allows you to make the web content never be reviewed

Scheduling allows you control in managing when, and for how long, your web content is displayed on your website. You even have an ability to determine when your content should be reviewed for accuracy and/or relevance.

Staging page publication

Liferay have a very unique feature of staging page publication, which helps you to make the change on the pages behind the scenes and publish every change in one shot. Basically, it is a specialized staging area where you do the current changes to your site, without letting users know the changes are happening in backend. Once your update is finished, you can publish all the changes at once.

The site administrator can configure the staging in two ways:

- **Local Live**: In this, both the staging and local environments are hosted on the same server. Whenever Local Live staging is enabled for a site, a clone of the site is created containing copies of the entire site's existing pages. The portal data is also copied, depending on which portlets are selected when staging is enabled. The cloned site becomes the staging environment, and the original site becomes the live environment.

- **Remote Live**: When Remote Live staging is enabled for a site, a connection is established between the current site and another site on a remote Liferay server. The remote site becomes the live environment and the current site becomes the staging environment—an instance of Liferay Portal used solely for staging. Content creators can use the staging server to make their changes, while the live server handles the incoming user traffic. When changes to the site are ready to be published, they are pushed over the network to the Remote Live server.

Whether you enable Local Live staging or Remote Live staging, the interface for managing and publishing staged pages is the same.

Question come up, "when should Local Live staging be used and when should Remote Live staging be used?" The pros and cons of Local Live staging are as follows.

Pros	Cons
It allows you to publish site changes very quickly since the staged and live environments are on the same server	Since the staged content and the production content are stored in the same database, the content isn't well protected or backed up unlike Remote Live staging
It is easier and faster to switch between the staged and live environments	You can't install a new version of the portlet in a Local Live staging environment since only one version of a portlet can be installed at any given time on a single Liferay server

The pros and cons of Remote Live staging are as follows:

Pros	Cons
It can install two version of the portlet since there are two separate servers for the live and staging environments	Publishing is slower than in Local Live staging since data needs to be transferred over a network
Additionally, you can also use one Liferay instance as the staging server for multiple production servers	You need more hardware to run a separate staging server

> Liferay 6.2 also offers the Page Versioning feature. This feature works with both Local Live staging and Remote Live staging and allows site administrators to create multiple variations of staged pages.

Local Live staging

Local Live Staging can be enabled from the site settings. As a site administrator, you can go to the site administration panel, select the **Configuration** page, select **Site Settings** from the left-hand side menu, and click on **Staging** listed under Advanced on the right-hand side menu. The **Staging** settings page will appear, where you can select either **None, Local Live** or **Remote Live** from the options. After selecting any one option, it will display additional settings. Say you have selected **Local Live**, for which additional settings appear; refer to the next screenshot. Staging allows changes to be made in a staging environment so that work can be reviewed, possibly using a workflow, before it's published to a live site. Let's enable **Local Live** staging; select the Local Live staging option—additional options appear below, such as **Page Versioning** and **Staging Content**. Page versioning can be enabled on the site's public pages, private pages, both, or neither. It allows you to work in parallel on different versions of pages and maintains a history of all page modifications. The following screenshot shows the Local Live staging settings page:

1. Let's check the **Enable On Public Page** checkbox, select **Documents and Media** and **Web Content** from **Staged Content**, and **Save** it.

2. You will get a popup for confirmation, asking **Are you sure you want to activate local staging for Palm Tree?**. Click on **OK** to confirm or **Cancel** to cancel the settings.

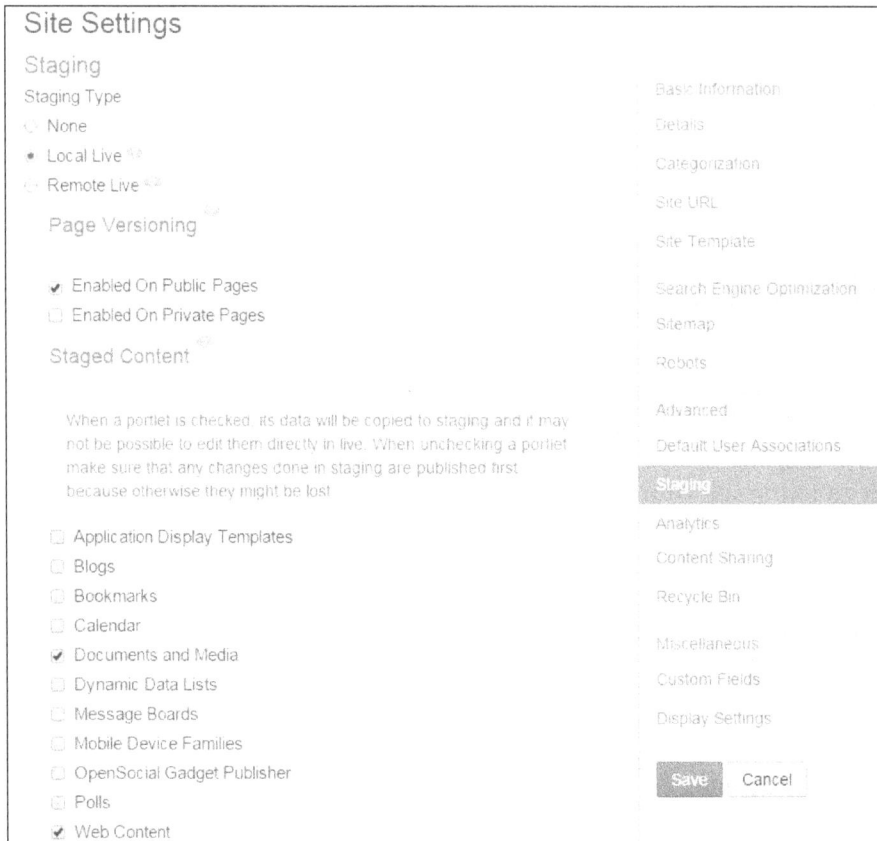

Figure 9.24: Staging—Local Live

3. After you enable **Local Live** staging and save the setting, you will find the **Staging** and **Live** buttons on the dock bar menu.

4. Click on the **Staging** button, which will open the staging public page for you, where you can make changes by placing the portlet and configuring it.

5. Clicking on the **Live** button will display the actual public page (production) without your changes made in the staging page.

6. Now, after you have made final changes to the **Staging** page, you can publish it to the **Live** site by simple clicking on the **Publish to Live** button, which appears after clicking on the arrow link beside the **Staging** button on the dock bar menu.

Refer to the next screenshot for the **Staging** and **Live** buttons on the dock bar menu.

There are a few settings (**Gear** icon) available on the staging bar, namely **Manage Site Pages Variations** and **Manage Page Variations**. Also, you will find the **History** icon and the **Undo** and **Redo** icon. Let's discuss each in brief:

○ **Manage Site Pages Variations**: This allows the site administrator to work in parallel on multiple versions of a staged site page.

○ **Manage Page Variations**: This allows the site administrator to work in parallel on multiple versions of a staged page.

○ **History**: This lists all the revisions of the page based on the publication dates. The site administrator will be able to review history and see how the pages looked at that point.

○ **Undo/Redo**: This allows us to undo and redo the changes on the page, which will save you the time required to manually add and remove the portlet on the page.

○ **Mark as Ready for Publication**: When you are done with making changes in the staged page, you can click on the **Mark as Ready for Publication** button, which will change the status from **Draft** to **Ready for Publication**. Now, you can click on the **Publish to Live** button.

> Note that the changes you have made before clicking on **Marked as Ready for Publication** will be published to the live site. The changes you made after clicking on **Marked as Ready for Publication** will not get effected.

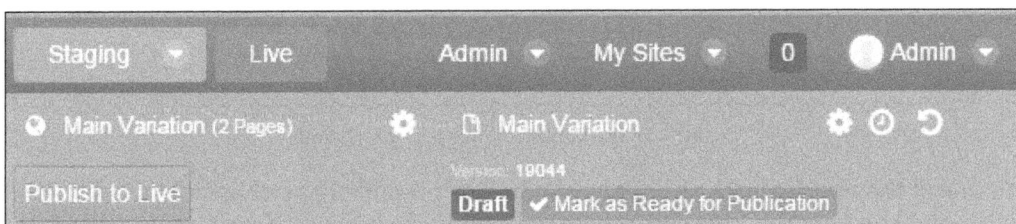

Figure 9.25: Staging in the dock bar menu — the Publish to Live button

7. After clicking on the **Publish to Live** button, a **Publish to Live** configuration pop-up window appears, which allows you to configure the staging content to move to the **Live** site page.

8. The following screenshot has different tabs: **New Publication Process**, **Current and Previous**, and **Scheduled**:

   ○ **New Publication Process**: This allows you to configure the staging content to move to the live site.

   ○ **Current and Previous**: This lists all the old and current published content through staging.

   ○ **Scheduled**: This lists the scheduled event for moving content from Staging to Live. This scheduled event can be created in **New Publication Process**.

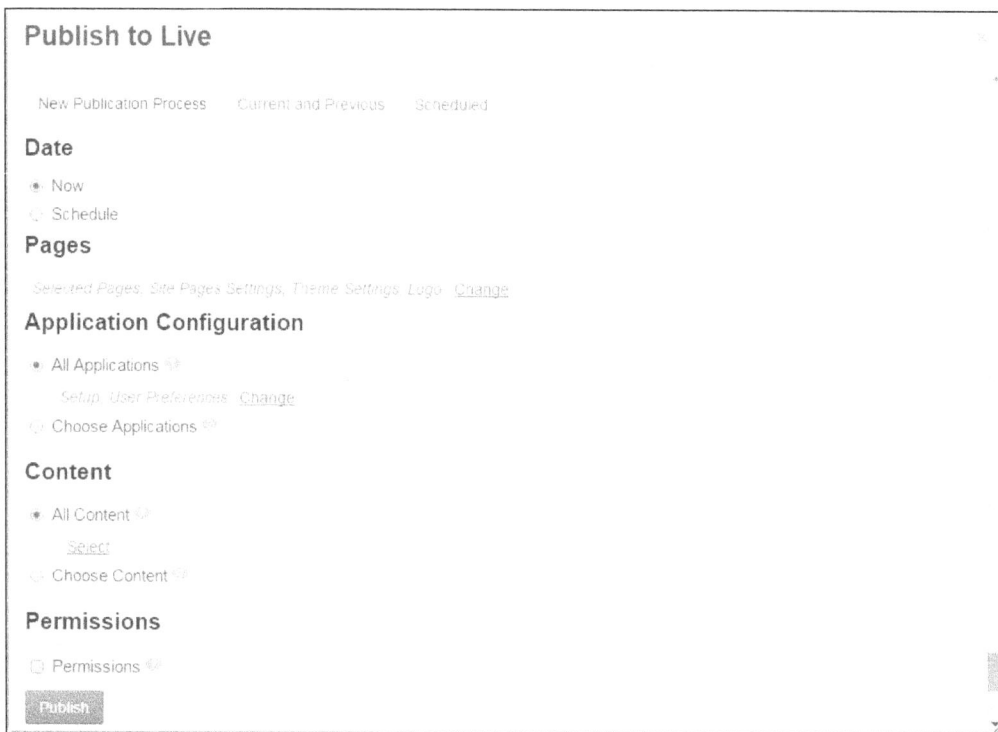

Figure 9.26: The Publish to Live pop-up window

It's one of the best features of Liferay that makes possible the publishing of content without disturbing the **Live** site, which maintains the history of content moved from staging to the **Live** site.

Let's see the **Remote Live** staging configuration.

Remote Live staging

Once you enable **Remote Live** staging, you get the additional settings for the remote host servers. The remote site becomes the live environment and the current site becomes the staging environment. Both remote and live Liferay servers should be separate systems, and even the databases should be separate. So, both servers will share the necessary information transferred over the network connection.

Before enabling **Remote Live** staging for the site, you need to add the remote **Liferay** server to the current Liferay server. Also, the current Liferay server needs to be added in the remote Liferay server. It makes a bridge between the two servers. The Liferay server's tunneling servlet authentication verifier checks both the servers. In portal-ext.properties, you have to set the following properties for the current server:

```
tunnel.servlet.hosts.allowed=127.0.0.1,SERVER_IP,[Remote server IP
address]
axis.servlet.hosts.allowed=127.0.0.1,SERVER_IP,192.168.0.16,[Remote
server IP address]
tunneling.servlet.shared.secret=[secret]
auth.verifier.TunnelingServletAuthVerifier.hosts.allowed=
```

Add the property in the remote Liferay server `portal-ext.properties` file:

```
tunnel.servlet.hosts.allowed=127.0.0.1,SERVER_IP,[Local server IP
address]
axis.servlet.hosts.allowed=127.0.0.1,SERVER_IP,192.168.0.16,[Local
server IP address]
tunneling.servlet.shared.secret=[secret]
auth.verifier.TunnelingServletAuthVerifier.hosts.allowed=
```

Liferay's use of a preshared key between your staging and production environments helps secure the remote publication process by removing the need to send the publishing user's password to the remote server for web service authentication. Using a preshared key allows the Liferay server to create an authorization context (permission checker) from the provided e-mail address, screen name, or user ID without the user's password. You can specify any value for the `tunneling.servlet.shared.secret` property, which should be matched with the remote server value. Finally, you need to restart both Liferay servers after making these portal properties update changes.

After restarting both servers, you can enable **Remote Live** staging. You also need to set your remote Liferay server IP address into the **Remote Host/IP** field. If in your case, the remote Liferay server is a cluster, then you need to set **Remote Host/IP** to the load-balanced IP address of the cluster in order to increase the availability of the publishing process. Next, input the port on which the remote Liferay instance is running into the **Remote Port** field. Now you only need to input Remote Path Context if a nonroot portal servlet context is being used on the remote Liferay server, and finally, input the site ID of the site on the remote Liferay server, which will be used for the Live environment. Check the remote Liferay server for the site ID. If a site hasn't already been created, then you need to log in to the remote Liferay server and create a new blank site. Note the Site ID after the site is created. Then, you can input it into the **Remote Site ID** field on your local Liferay server. Finally, it's best to check the **Use a Secure Network Connection** field to use HTTPS for the publication of pages from your local (staging) Liferay server to your remote (live) Liferay server.

The following screenshot shows the settings for Remote Live staging:

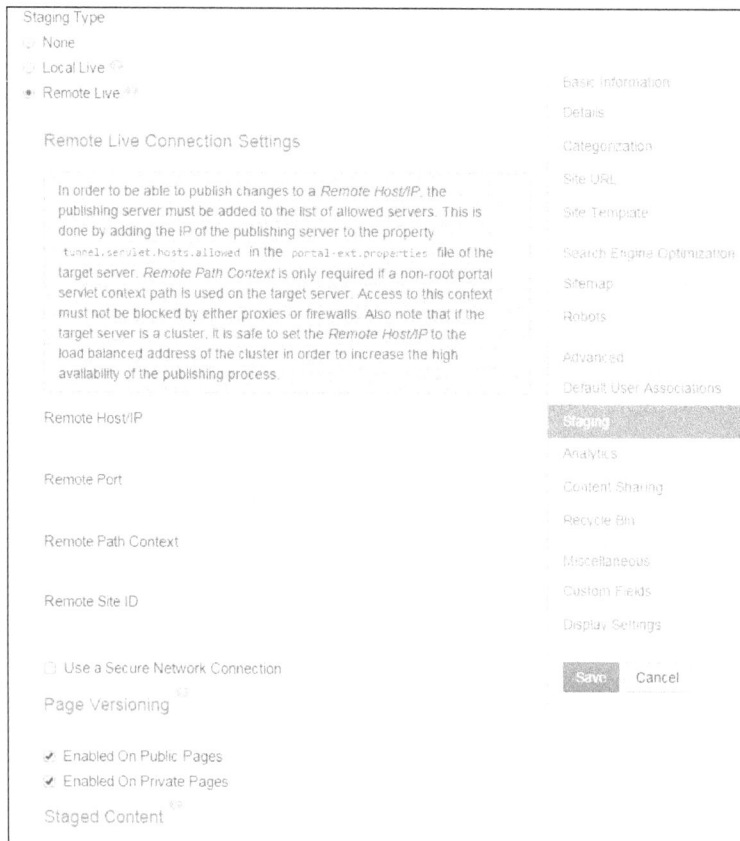

Figure 9.27: Staging—Remote Live

> Note that if you are unable to set the tunneling servlet shared secret or the values of these properties on your current and remote servers properly or the values don't match, then you won't be able to enable staging and an error message appears when you try to publish changes from the local (staging) server to the Remote (Live) server.
>
> Liferay passes the user's e-mail address, screen name, or user ID to the remote server to perform a permission check.

In order for a publishing operation to succeed, the operation must be performed by a user who has identical credentials and permissions on both the local (staging) and the remote (live) server. This is true regardless of whether the user attempts to publish the changes immediately or attempts to schedule the publication for later.

A workflow for Web Content

The Liferay Web Content portlet supports a workflow, which makes it more efficient and robust. In the web content, the workflow is used to make the web content pass through the review and approval process to achieve the content standard before publishing it on the site.

Liferay 6.2 CE is bundled with the Kaleo workflow beforehand, and for Liferay 6.2 EE, the Kaleo workflow can be installed too.

Making your content error-free and standard, you need to enable the workflow for Web Content Management System; it's very simple and straightforward. You need to design the workflow definition as per your requirement.

Let's take a case study for workflow definition in Palm Tree Organization, which has a simple workflow. The web content, when created, is passed through the workflow, where the reviewer (Editor) reviews the content and approves it. It again goes to the approver (Publisher), who reviews the content and approves it. If the reviewer or approver rejects the content, then the content goes back to the author and asks for a resubmit.

For this requirement, you need to create a workflow definition, which needs to be uploaded in **Control Panel | Configuration | Workflow**. In *Chapter 10, Marketplace, Social Office, and Audience Targeting,* you will learn how to upload the workflow definition in the control panel.

For now, let's imagine you have uploaded the workflow definition in the control panel. Now, you need to enable the workflow for the Palm Tree site, which you can achieve in a very simple way. We have already discussed this in the *Advance site settings* section of *Chapter 7, Understanding Sites*. Let's explore this again in detail.

The Site Administrator has the access permission to configure the workflow from the Site Administrator panel by clicking on **Workflow Configuration** under the **Configuration** section in the left-hand side panel. The workflow configuration will open, which allows the configuration of different resources, such as **Page Revision**, **Blogs Entry**, **Web content Article**, **Comments**, **Message Boards Message**, and **Wiki Page**. Select the workflow for **Web Content Article** from the selection box provided with the same name and version that you uploaded in the control panel. Refer to the following screenshot for the workflow configuration for the Palm Tree site:

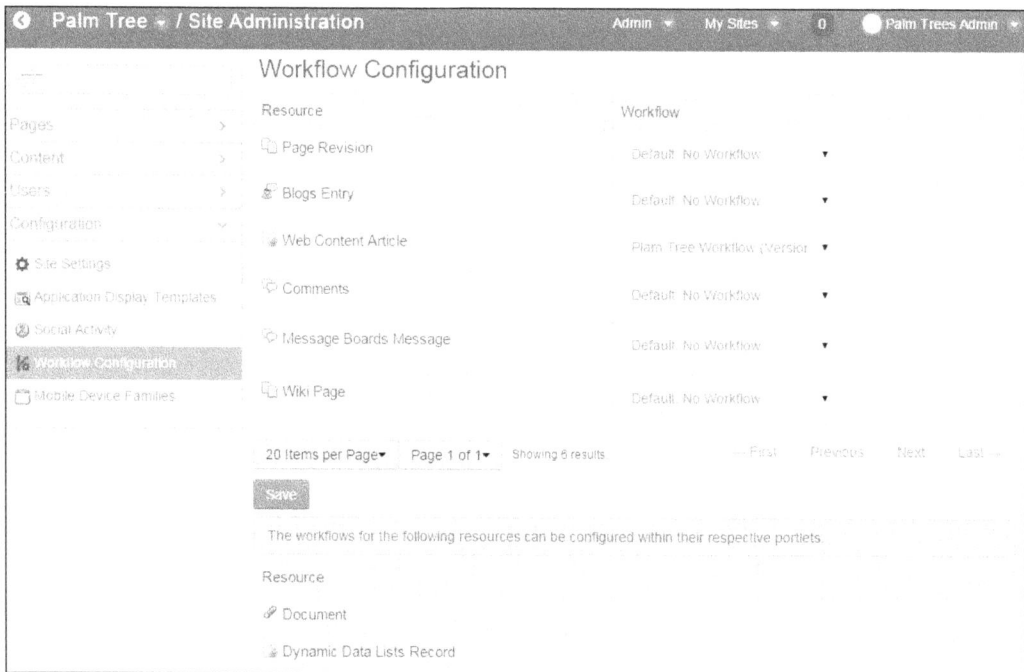

Figure 9.28: Palm Tree / Site Administration | Workflow Configuration

Once the workflow configuration is complete, you will able to see the **Submit for Publication** button instead of the **Publish** button while creating the web content:

> Note that different sites can be configured with different workflows as per their requirement.

Let's create basic web content inside the Palm Tree organization using the workflow. Refer to the following screenshot, which displays new web content creation with the **Submit for Publication** button:

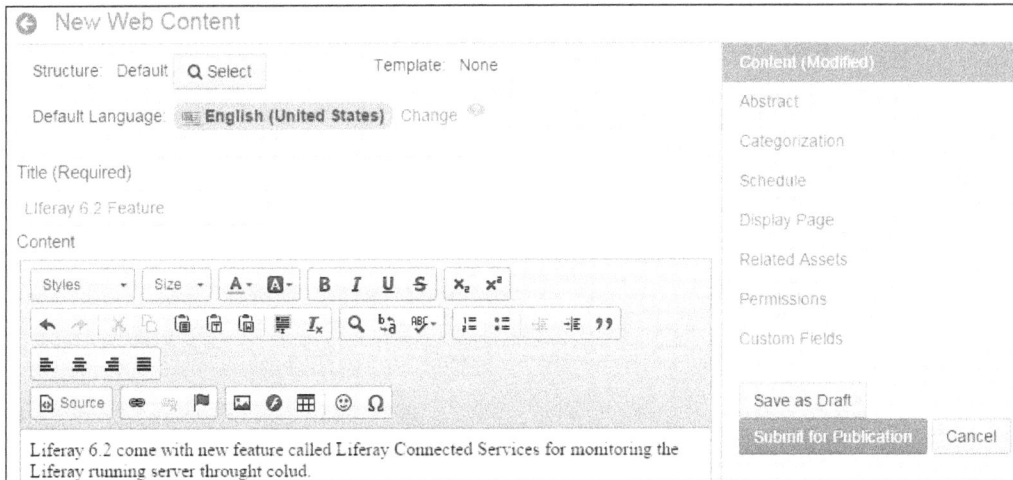

Figure 9.29: Creating Web Content using workflow

1. Once you click on the **Submit for Publication** button, it will send the e-mail notification to the reviewer, who also receives a notification in the dock bar menu displayed in the following screenshot:

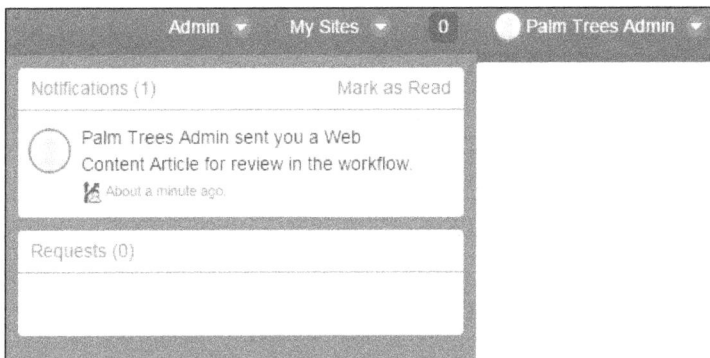

Figure 9.30: Reviewer notification in the dock bar menu

The reviewer can directly click on the notification, which will open a pop-up window for **My Workflow Task**. It will have details of the document and to whom the workflow is assigned. Also, it shows a preview of the content with the view link to make it easy for the reviewer to review the content directly by clicking on the view link; refer to the next screenshot.

2. On the right-hand side, you have three links, which are described as follows:

　◦ **Assign to Me**: This allows you to assign the workflow task in your name

　◦ **Assign to...**: This allows you to assign the workflow task to another reviewer

　◦ **Update Due Date**: This allows you to update the due date for the workflow task

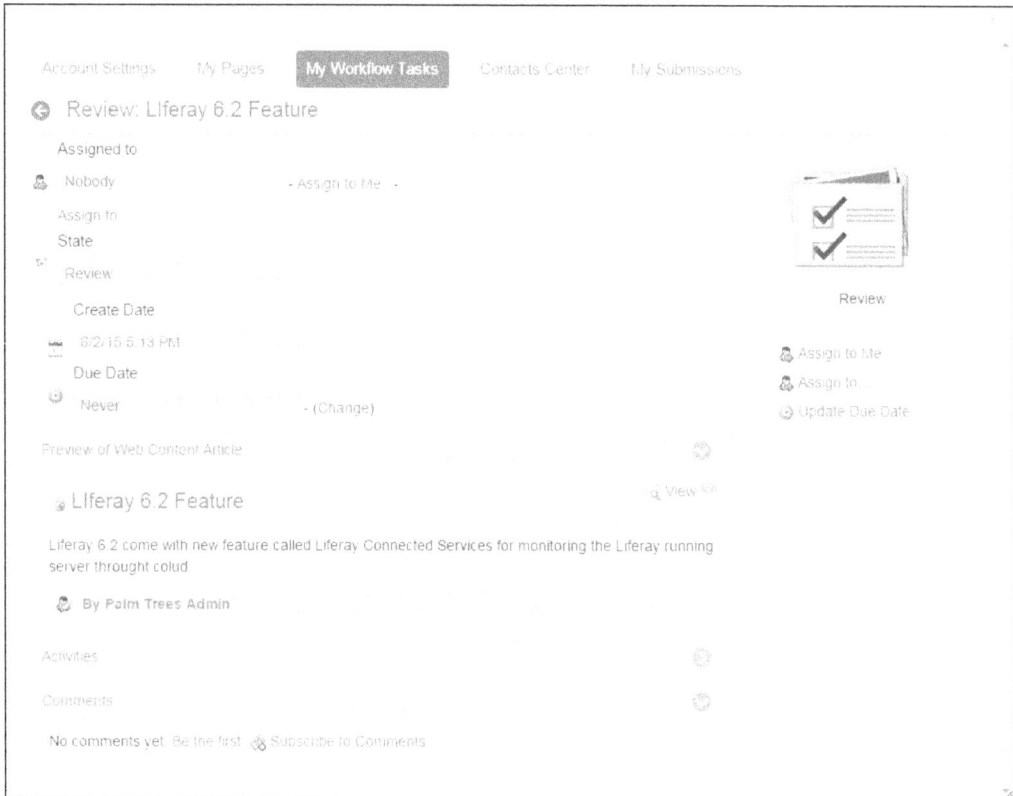

Figure 9.31: My Workflow Tasks — Assign to Me

3. Click on the **Assign to Me** link, which pops up a screen for comment input with the **OK** and **Cancel** buttons.

4. Input the comments, say **Assigned to me for Review** and click on the **OK** button.

5. After clicking on the **OK** button, the workflow task is assigned to you. The following screenshot displays the workflow task assigned to you, and by clicking on the approve link on the right-hand side, you can move the workflow to the second level:

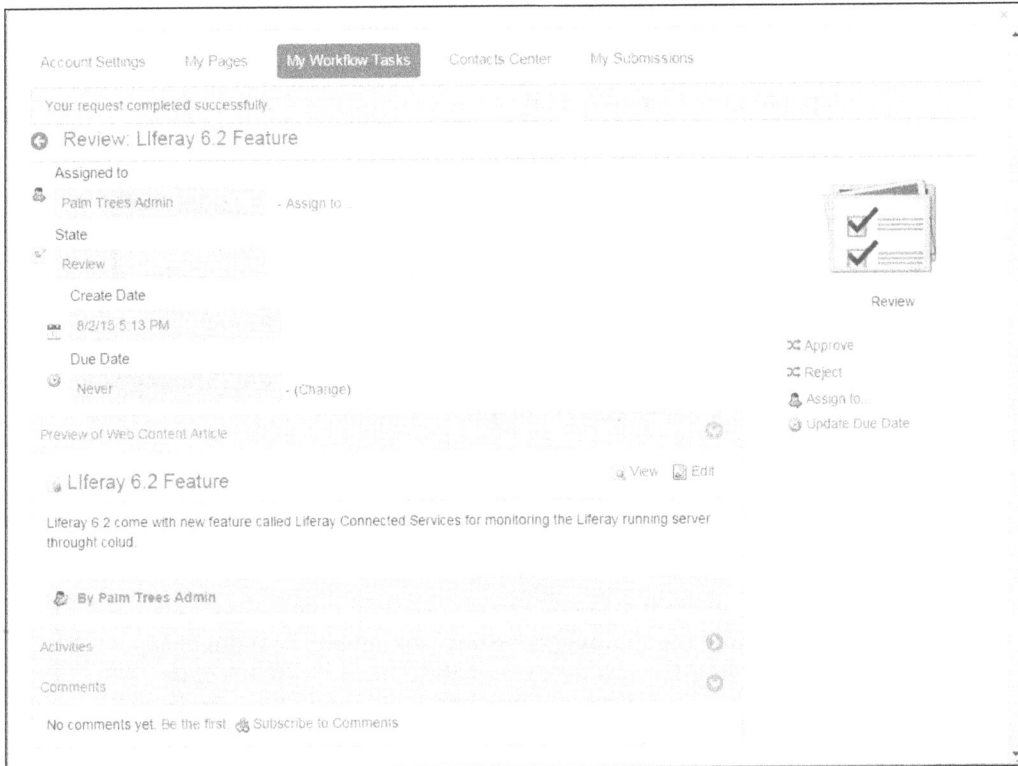

Figure 9.32: My Workflow Tasks—Review

In the preceding screenshot, you can see the workflow task is assigned to you and state of the workflow is the **review** mode.

6. In the **Preview of the web content Article** section, you will find the **view** and **Edit** links; by clicking on the **Edit** link, you can edit the content.

7. In the **Activities** section, you can see all the activities done in the particular workflow task. You can also give comments for the web content by clicking on the **Be the first** link in the **Comment** section.

8. On the right-hand side, you will find the following links:

   ° **Approve**: This allows you to approve the content for other levels

   ° **Reject**: This allows you to reject the content and send it back to the author for resubmitting it

   ° **Assign to...**: This allows you to assign the review step to other reviewers

   ° **Update Due Date**: This allows you to update the due date for the workflow task

> Note that the preceding links are part of your workflow definition. You can have different labels according to your workflow definition.

Once the Reviewer has approved the content after review, in the next step, it will be moved to the Approver (Publisher) status to review the content. The Approver (Publisher) will have the same screen as the preceding one to approve or reject the content.

Once the approver approves the content, it will be published to the site. The status of the content will be approved.

> The content is in the pending status until it is in the workflow engine. Once the approver approves the content, the status changes to **Approve**. If the approver rejects the content, the status of the content changes to **Reject**. If the author withdraws the submission, the status of the content changes to **Draft**.

The reviewer or approver can go to the **My Account** page from the **Users** dropdown in the dock bar menu. In the **My Account** pop-up window, you will find different links; select the **My Workflow Tasks** link, where you get the two tabs, **Pending** and **Completed**:

- **Pending**: Here, you will find two accordions with the names **Assigned to My Roles** and **Assign to Me**:

  ° **Assign to Me**: This lists all the workflow tasks assigned to you.

  ° **Assigned to My Roles**: This lists all the unassigned workflow tasks. From here, you can assign the workflow task to yourself or to other reviewers.

- **Completed**: This will list all the completed workflow jobs.

Refer to the next screenshot for the **My Workflow Tasks** pop-up window.

The entry of the workflow task in **Assign to Me** has some actions links: **Approve**, **Reject**, **Assign to…**, and **Update Due Date**. If you click on the workflow task entry link on **Task** and **Title**, a detail of the workflow task will open; refer to *Figure 9.32*. In the same way, when you click on the workflow task link from **Assigned to My Roles** accordion, it will open a detail of the workflow task for assigning; refer to *Figure 9.31*.

> You can do all the operations on the workflow task, such as **Approve**, **Reject**, **Assign to…**, and **Update Due Date** from **My Workflow Tasks** without going to the detail page of the workflow task.

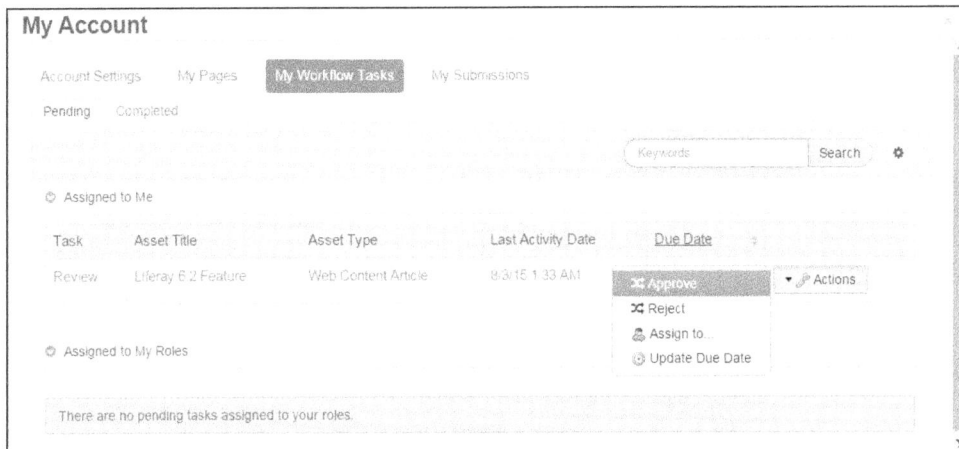

Figure 9.33: My Workflow Tasks inside My Account

Liferay also provides a feature from where you can withdraw your workflow submission. In the **My Account** pop-up window, you will find the **My Submissions** link beside **My Workflow Tasks**. Click on the **My Submissions** link to list all the workflow tasks submitted by logged-in users under the **Pending** tab. The following screenshot displays the list of workflow tasks submitted by the Palm Tree administrator.

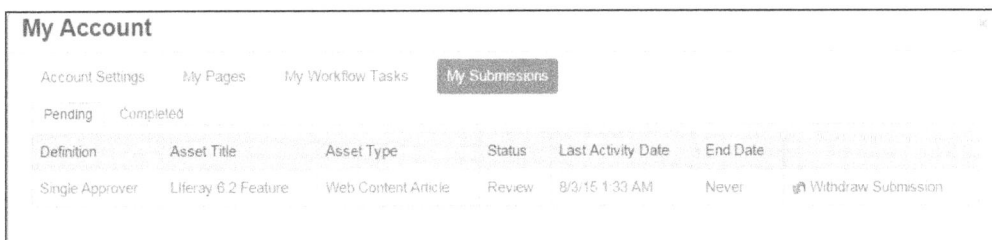

Figure 9.34: My Submissions inside My Account

Users can withdraw workflow submissions by clicking on the **Withdraw Submission** link. By this action, the content will be released from the workflow engine, and it will change the content status to **Draft**. The **Completed** tab displays the list of completed workflow task submitted by the logged-in user.

Summary

The Web Content Management (WCM) system is essential with any kind of portal and site development tool. Liferay provides one of the best WCMs in a portal technology. Web content helps users to create and manage content. In this chapter, you saw the best possible ways to create and manage the web content. You even learned how to create structures and templates for the best look and feel of the content. You learned how to assign permissions for roles to allow them to access the web content features. We even explored the Web Content Display portlet and the Web Content Search portlet in detail. Liferay WCM's best feature, scheduling, was also discussed. You learned how to hide the updating process of the content from the user by using the Liferay Staging feature. The Liferay workflow allows you to make the content more accurate and correct by reviewing the content at different levels. You learned in detail about the workflow implementation and its work through the web content.

In the next chapter, you are going to learn about Marketplace, Liferay Social Office, and Targeting Content to Audience in detail.

10
Marketplace, Social Office, and Audience Targeting

As mentioned earlier, Marketplace is a hub for all portlets and applications. Marketplace provides leverage to share and download Liferay-compatible portlets and applications. As per the new trend, what Play Store is to mobile, Liferay's Marketplace is to enterprise portals. Marketplace provides a unique platform for developers and software organizations to develop applications/portlets for other portal users.

In Marketplace, applications can be sold or kept for free. Liferay Social Office is an application available in Marketplace. It provides a shared workspace solution that helps office teams to work collaboratively using the tools. Liferay Social Office gives the features that organizations are using in their daily activities, such as sharing knowledge and communicating among the team. Each small and big team can keep them up to date and find the right people with the right knowledge using Social Office. Social Office helps to turn collective knowledge into collective action. It has a unique feature that allows everyone in the team to work in the right context and achieve the goal.

We are going to learn more in detail about Social Office in this chapter. Audience targeting is a new feature that Liferay has come up with, which allows you to divide audiences into user segments. It basically targets specific content and creates campaigns for different user segments. Audience Targeting also provides a tool to measure the effectiveness of your campaigns. We are also going to learn search in Liferay. Search places an important role in the content management system and portal.

By the end of this chapter, you will have learned about:

- Marketplace tool uses
- Marketplace plugins and management
- Installing apps and managing them
- The Liferay Social Office portal
- Audience targeting app uses
- User segment content listing and display
- Liferay Search

Marketplace

Liferay 6.2 Marketplace is a hub for sharing and downloading all Liferay-compatible applications. It acts as an application store—similar to what Play Store is to Google Android phones. Liferay made marketplace a one-stop site for the release and sharing of apps among users. The best part is that small organizations have started developing useful applications for users by paying little or even free of cost. The applications can be easily downloaded through the Liferay site and even through Liferay Portal.

Now, in our example, if the Palm Tree requirement matches one of the applications in Marketplace, then it's easy to use the application rather than building it from scratch. This is similar to what we did in *Chapter 6, Blogs, WYSIWYG Editors, and Social Networking*, where we downloaded a social networking application. Please refer to *Chapter 6, Blogs, WYSIWYG Editors, and Social Networking*, to search for an application and install the application in Liferay Portal.

> Marketplace apps are validated by the Liferay team before they are released in Marketplace.

As mentioned earlier, Liferay Marketplace can be browsed over the site `https://liferay.com/marketplace` without signing into the Liferay site; refer to the following screenshot.

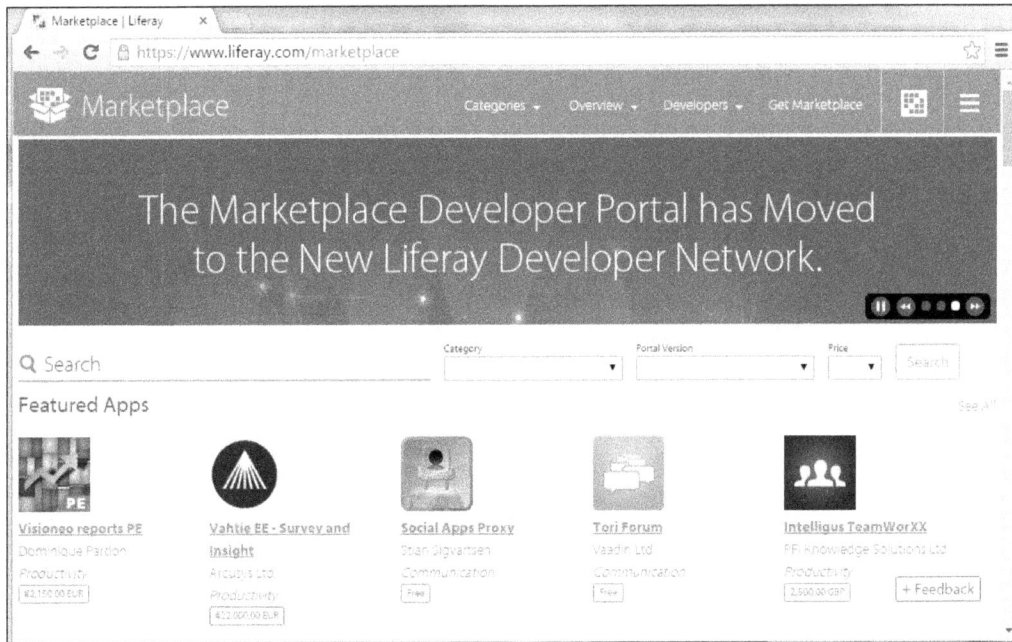

Figure 10.1: Marketplace view on the Liferay site

If you want to purchase and download the apps, you need to log in to the liferay. com site. Once you purchase the app through the Liferay site, you will get an `.lpkg` file, which can be directly copied to the deploy folder in your Liferay server. After deploying the application, it will get installed in your Liferay instance. It's easier to download and install apps from Marketplace through a running Liferay instance. Once you have purchased the app, you just need to install it by clicking on the **Install** button, similar to what we did in *Chapter 6, Blogs, WYSIWYG Editors, and Social Networking*, for downloading the social networking app.

In Marketplace, you will find lots of apps from Liferay as well as from different organizations and users, and some apps are available free of cost or can be purchased by paying a small amount. You can purchase an app in your name or a company's name from liferay.com. Once you have purchased an app, you're free to download and install any available version of the app whenever required.

> Accessing Marketplace always needs the log in to the liferay.com domain. If you don't have an account, you need to sign up for liferay.com and create an account.

Exploring Marketplace in the Liferay site

Let's have a look at the Marketplace site page. In the preceding screenshot, you will be able to see **Search bar**, **Category**, **Portal Version**, and **Price** with a **Search** button. You will see a categorized list of apps. Now, if you want to search a particular application, say **Web Form** of **Liferay 6.2 CE GA** of the portal version. That is very simple. Just input **Web Form** in the search bar, select the category as **Productivity** from the dropdown, select **Liferay Portal version**, and finally click on the **Search** button. You can even select **Price (Free/Paid)**. Follow this screenshot:

Figure 10.2: Marketplace searching application

After searching, you will get the results page with a list of applications. Click on one of the applications, say **Web Form CE**. It will open a Web Form detail page, where every bit of information about **Web Form CE** is mentioned. Refer to the following screenshot:

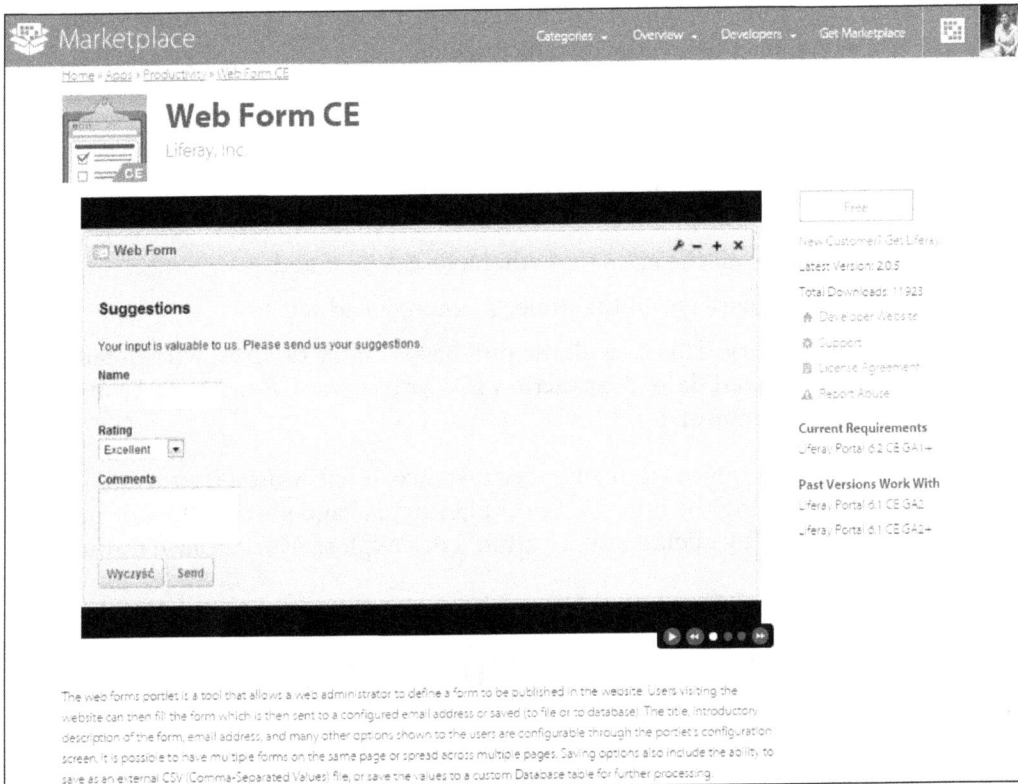

Figure 10.3: Marketplace profile page

As you click on the **Free/Buy** button from the right-hand side panel, the purchase window will appear. After that, select **New Project** or select **For Personal Use Only**, check the agreement checkbox, and click on **Purchase**.

After purchasing the app, the purchase page will open, from where you can download the app by clicking on the **App** button. This will provide you with the `.lpkg` file, which you can deploy to your Liferay instance.

The **Purchase** page also provides you with the left-hand side navigation menu. This menu consists of actions, such as **Account Settings**, **License**, **Apps**, **Projects**, and **Purchase History**. Let's discuss the actions in detail:

- **Account Settings**: This allows you to change your account settings for `liferay.com`

- **License**: This lists all the licenses that you have purchased for the enterprise version

- **Apps**: This lists all the apps that you have downloaded

- **Projects**: This displays all the projects you have added

- **Purchase History**: This lists all the purchase history of apps, with details such as **Purchased date**, **Transaction ID**, **App** (name), **Purchased From**, **Project**, and **Amount**.

When we access Marketplace from a Liferay instance, it has a similar process. Rather than downloading the app as `.lpkg` (Liferay package file), it allows you to install the app directly by clicking on a button. Let's explore Marketplace through a Liferay instance.

Exploring Marketplace through a Liferay instance

Liferay 6.2, as we have mentioned in previous chapters, is divided into sections, such as **Users**, **Sites**, **Apps**, and **Configuration**, which you can see in the control panel. Under the **Apps** section, you can see tools to manage applications. The actions listed under the **Apps** section are **App Manager**, **Store**, **Purchased**, **Plugins Configuration**, and **License Manager**.

Let discuss each in detail:

- **App Manager**: This allows you to access information about the apps you've installed.

- **Store**: This allows you to access Marketplace after logging in using Liferay credentials.

- **Purchased**: This lists all the apps that you have purchased from Marketplace.

- **Plugin Configurations**: This allows you to configure the apps that are installed in the Liferay instance. Here, you can make the app/portlet active or inactive, and you can also set the access permission for roles.

- **License Manager**: This maintains the license for Liferay Enterprise Edition and also provides the server information for Community Edition. It even allows registering the application using the order ID.

In the following screenshot, you can see the **Apps** section inside **Control Panel**:

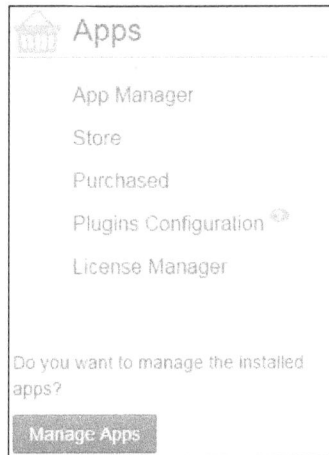

Figure 10.4: Apps section in Control Panel

Marketplace can be accessed through **Store** by entering the **Liferay.com** credentials, which will link to this administrator's account. After logging in to `liferay.com` through **Store**, you will land in the Marketplace site of Liferay. Now, you can browse and search for any applications. The following screenshot displays the login form to access Marketplace.

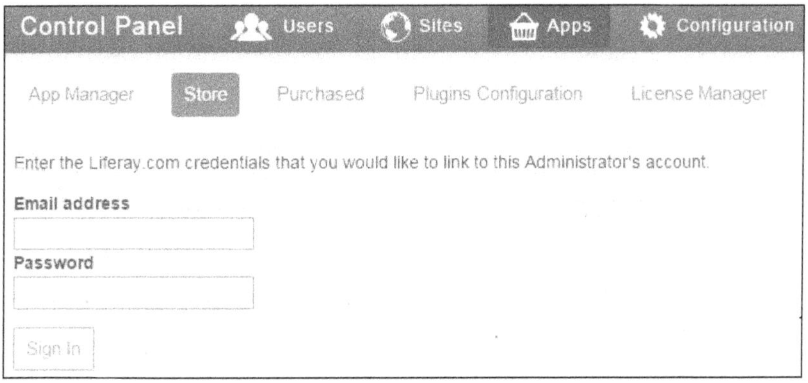

Figure 10.5: Login form to access Marketplace inside Control Panel

After successful login, you will be able to access the same Marketplace web page inside Apps Store, and you can browse and search for the Web Form app. Then, click on the app name (Web Form) – the Marketplace profile page will open. Clicking on the **Free** button allows you to navigate to the purchase page, where you can mention the **Project Name** or select the **For Personal Use** checkbox, check the agreement, and finally click on the **Purchase** button. Once you have done the purchase of the app, it will be listed in the **Purchase** tab. You can click on the **Purchase** tab, search for the respective app in the list, and click on the **Install** button. It will take a while to install. After installation is done, the button will be renamed as uninstall. If you want to uninstall the app, you can simply click on the **Uninstall** button, which will remove the app from the current Liferay instance. Sometimes, you download an app that is not compatible with the current Liferay instance, and then it shows the **Not Compatible** message. Refer to the following screenshot:

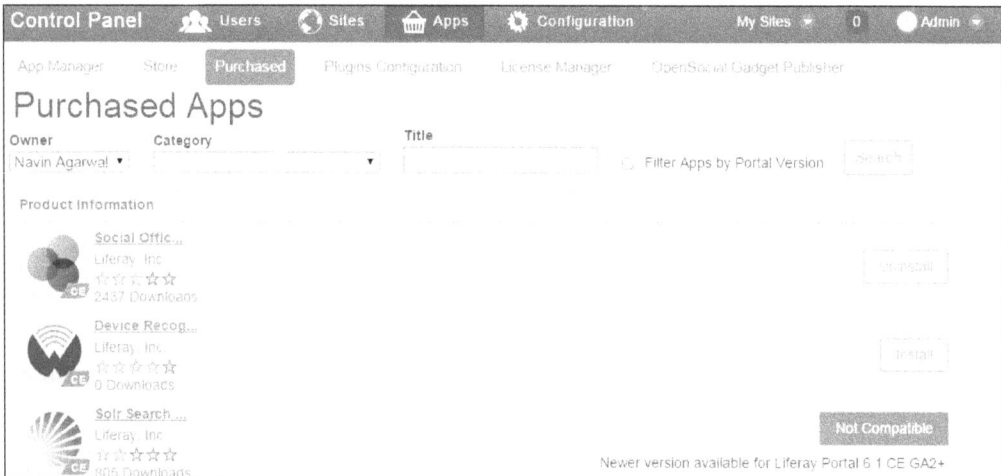

Figure 10.6: Purchased Apps inside Control Panel

In the preceding screenshot, you can see that the Social Office app is installed and that the Device Reorganization app is not installed. The Solr Search app is not compatible with the current Liferay instance, hence it's showing the **Not Compatible** message.

Creating and uploading apps in Marketplace

Liferay provides you with the tools to create apps for Marketplace. It's purely in development mode, which involves the code to be written. To create an app for Marketplace, you can go through `https://www.liferay.com/documentation/liferay-portal/6.2/development/-/ai/liferay-marketplace-liferay-portal-6-2-dev-guide-11-en`.

To create the app, you can create portlets, themes, layouts templates, hook plugins, web plugins, and OSGi bundles. Let's describe each of them in brief.

Portlets

Portlets are web applications that run on the portlet life cycle in the portal. The main functionality in the portal is its portlet application that runs on it. The portlet resides in the portlet container and performs the job until the life cycle ends. You can develop portlets using the Model-View-Controller design pattern, which is basically provided by many frameworks. You need to use the Liferay software development toolkit to develop your own portlet plugin.

Themes

Themes are also plugins and can hot deploy into the Liferay instance. Themes are mainly for the look and feel of the portal — we can say it's a wrapper of design over the portal. You can create your own theme plugin using the Liferay software development tool kit.

Layout templates

Layout templates make your portlets arranged properly on the portal page. It's a kind of structure of the page that makes a placeholder for the portlets. In this placeholder, you can drag and drop your portlets.

Hook plugins

Hook plugins are used to modify the exiting code by slightly tuning it as per our requirements. The Hook plugin allows you to change the eventing system, model listeners, portal properties, language properties, and even Liferay's core JSPs. It proves very helpful in developing portals by changing the Liferay code JSPs that does not cause migration issues in the future. Also, hooks are hot deployable.

Web plugins

Web plugins are Java EE web modules that can be integrated into Liferay. Liferay supports third-party integration very smoothly with the help of **Enterprise Service Bus (ESB)**.

OSGi bundles

Liferay 6.2 has come up with a new framework, **Open Services Gateway initiative (OSGi)**, to develop modular Java applications. It's similar to regular web Java applications, but it should include additional metadata so that it is capable of running in an OSGi framework. Liferay is going to release an app based on the OSGi framework shortly.

App Manager

As mentioned earlier, **App Manager** lists all the applications that are installed in the current Liferay instance. It has two tabs: **Manage** and **Install**. **Manage** lists all the applications installed in the current running Liferay instance in different categories. **Install** allows you to install portlets and apps by uploading the LPKG or WAR files. Refer to the following screenshot:

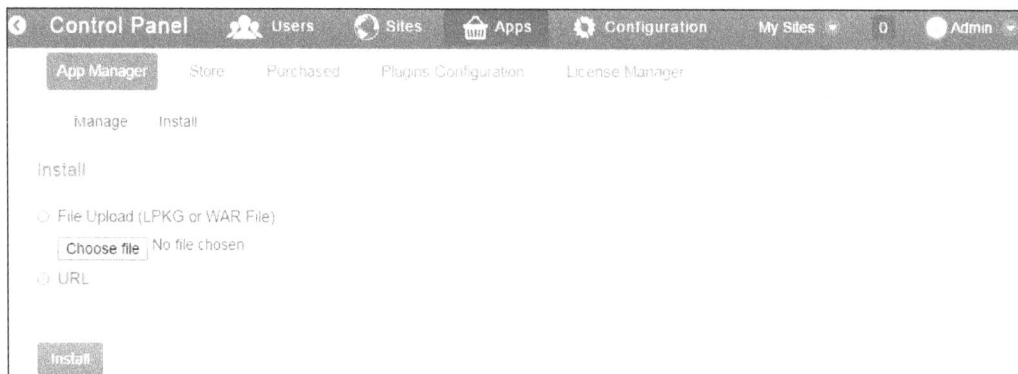

Figure 10.7: Installing apps through App Manager

You can choose the LPKG or WAR file and click on the install button. It will install the app in the currently running Liferay instance.

Liferay Social Office

Liferay Social Office is a social collaboration solution for the organization that makes communication easier, saves time, and builds teams among the employees, and it also helps in raising productivity. Let's point out the features of Social Office:

* Enhancing your existing personal workflow with social tools
* Keeping your team up to date with information
* Getting skilled persons for the right task
* Transforming collective knowledge into collective action

Social Office provides the team with tools and applications to enhance work, share knowledge among the team, and increase productivity. Moreover, the user interface is intuitive, with familiar and convenient desktop conventions that won't require a steep learning curve or any at all. It provides visibility to the team activity so that each user's correspondence and relationships happen in the context of a shared collaborative effort. Not only does this cut down on the time needed for daily syncing up and make time for more meaningful conversation, this makes the team members' focus change from their own task to the bigger picture objectives of the project. Social Office also allows teams members to work on the right context using the tools for document sharing, knowledge sharing, and collaboration tools – all seamlessly integrated.

Social Office is also an app on Liferay Marketplace that you can install into your current Liferay instance. Follow the preceding Marketplace steps to install the Social Office app into your Liferay instance. After installing **Liferay Social Office**, you will get two site templates under the **Sites** section in **Control Panel**. As you know, the site template can be used to create a new site, and it can also be mapped to the user's private or public pages, also known as **personal site**.

Under **Site Template**, two templates are created with the names **Social Office User Home** and **Social Office User Profile**, respectively. Using these site templates, map the user's **Public** page and **Private** page with the **Social Office User Profile** site template and the **Social Office User Home** site template, respectively. Whenever you click on **My Profile** from the dock bar, the **Social office User Profile** page opens in the same way as when you click on **My dashboard** from the dock bar, **Social Office User Dashboard** opens.

> Map the user's **Public** page with **Social Office User Profile**, which is nothing but the **My Profile** link in the dock bar. Map the user's **Private** page with **Social Office User Home**, which is nothing but the **My Dashboard** link in the dock bar.
>
> The other way of using Social Office in the portal is by creating sites for different site templates. This site will be common to all users. Create sites by using the **Social Office User Home** and **Social Office User Profile** site templates. After creating the sites, you can assign the users, organization, and user group for **Control Panel** | **Configuration** | **Social Office Configuration**. You can set the roles and sites settings for the site type.

Let's explore this scenario with an example.

My Profile

My Profile is the public page that basically has the user's information. Other portal users can access this page to get information about the user and their activities on the portal.

Click on the **My Profile** link in the dock bar, which will open the public page of the user. My Profile is now Social Office user profile, which has a different theme and layout; refer to the following screenshot. It also has the prefect arrangement of portlets that makes Social Office easy to use for the end user.

Observe the following screenshot. It's a My Profile page of Vishal Gupta. It has the left-hand side navigation menu bar with different pages, such as **Profile**, **Contacts**, **Microblogs**, and **Home**. In the middle column, you will able to see the user's status message, information about the user, and their projects. In the right-most column, **Sites** details and **Tags** of the user are listed.

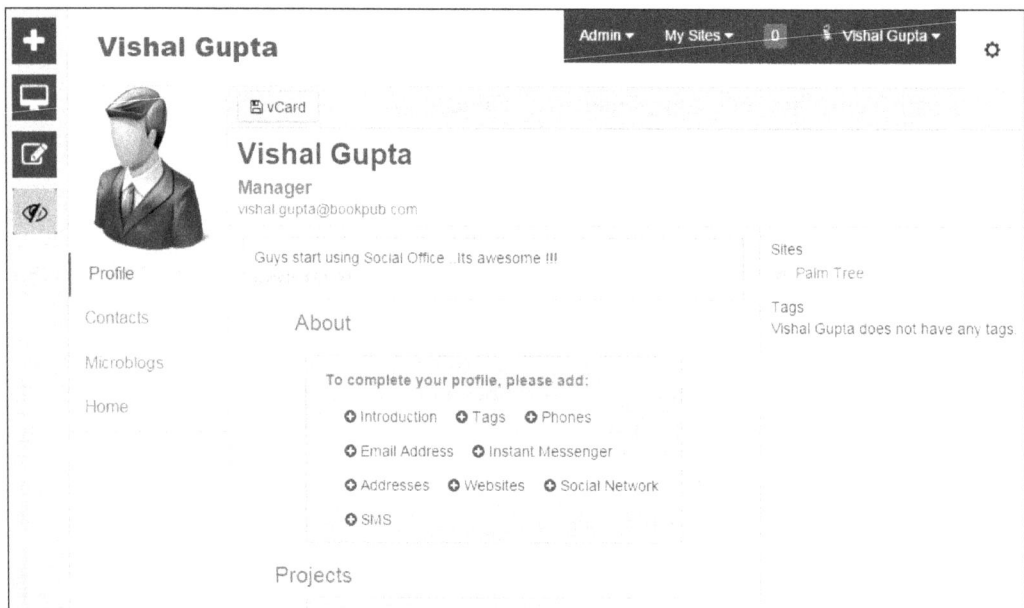

Figure 10.8: My Profile page as a Social Office user profile

In the preceding screenshot, you can see the dock bar on the left-most side that allows you to add pages and applications to the page. You can even modify the layouts as required by changing certain properties:

Let's understand the different pages in brief:

- **Profile**: This provides user information, with all the details and activities the user has performed. Refer to the preceding screenshot.

- **Contacts**: This lists all the contacts you are connected to. It's a kind of phone directory with extra actions on each contact, such as **Disconnect**, **Follow**, **Block**, **Message**, and **vCard**. Refer to the following screenshot:

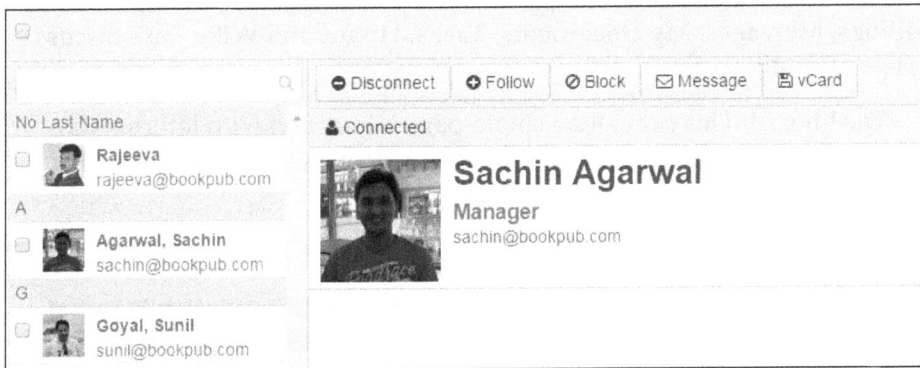

Figure 10.9: Contacts in My Profile page

When a user from your contacts, say Sachin Agarwal, views your profile page, they can view your contacts with the same action for each contact, by which they can extend their contact list by sending connect requests. This is similar to any social media site.

- **Microblogs**: Here, you can update you micro status and share with the teams easily. Refer to *Figure 10.8*. The status **Guys start using Social Office .. Its awesome !!!** is a microblog.

- **Home**: This is a normal Liferay page link.

My Dashboard

My Dashboard is the user's private page that is mapped with the Social Office user's home page. Clicking on **My Dashboard** from the dock bar menu will redirect your user's dashboard page. The next screenshot shows the user's dashboard.

The dashboard allows the users to interact with the system easily. It provides the user with all the information in one place. Here too, users get the most of the information in one page, such as announcements, activities, upcoming tasks, and events. These applications make the user's dashboard very useful when each individual wants to get an update every second in the team.

My Dashboard comes with several pages, such as **Dashboard**, **Contacts Center**, **Microblogs**, **Messages**, **My Documents**, **Tasks**, **Home**, and **Wiki**. Let's discuss each page in detail:

- **Dashboard**: This provides a single-page interaction with information on the page for the user. The following screenshot shows the dashboard of Vishal Gupta:

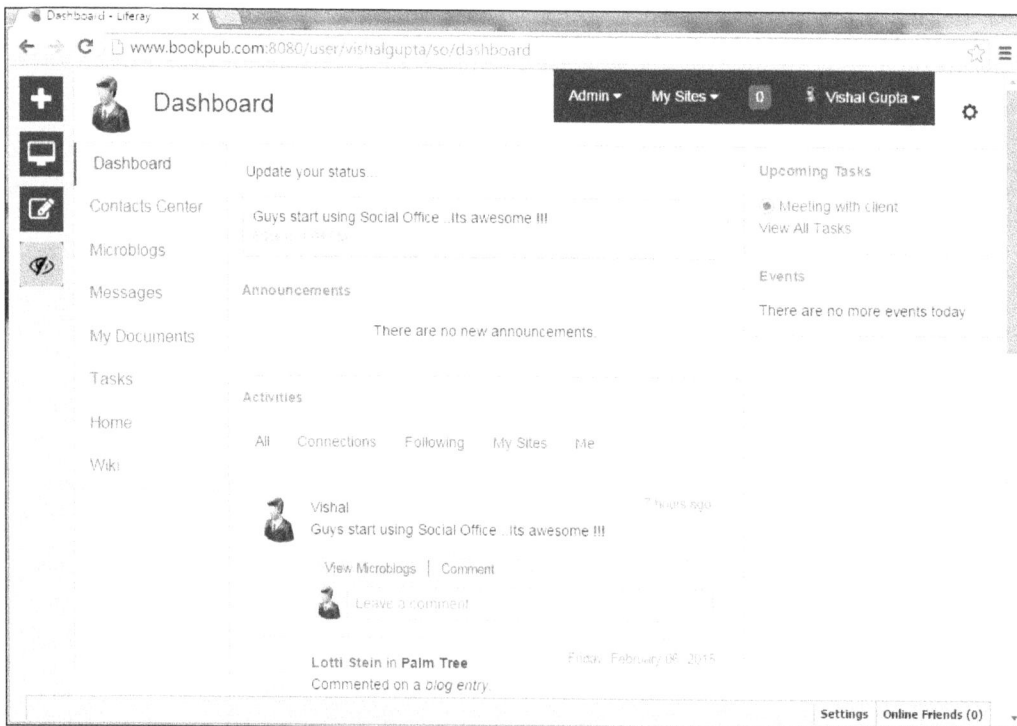

Figure 10.10: Social Office user home as Dashboard

The preceding screenshot shows the activities of different tabs, such as **All**, **Connections**, **Followings**, **My Sites**, and **Me**.

- **Contacts Center**: This provides you with the user's directory: you can find on the left-hand side a list of the user contacts and the user's details on the right-hand side panel of whoever is a member of this site (next screenshot). You can even directly send the connect request, follow the contact, block the contact, and message the contact.

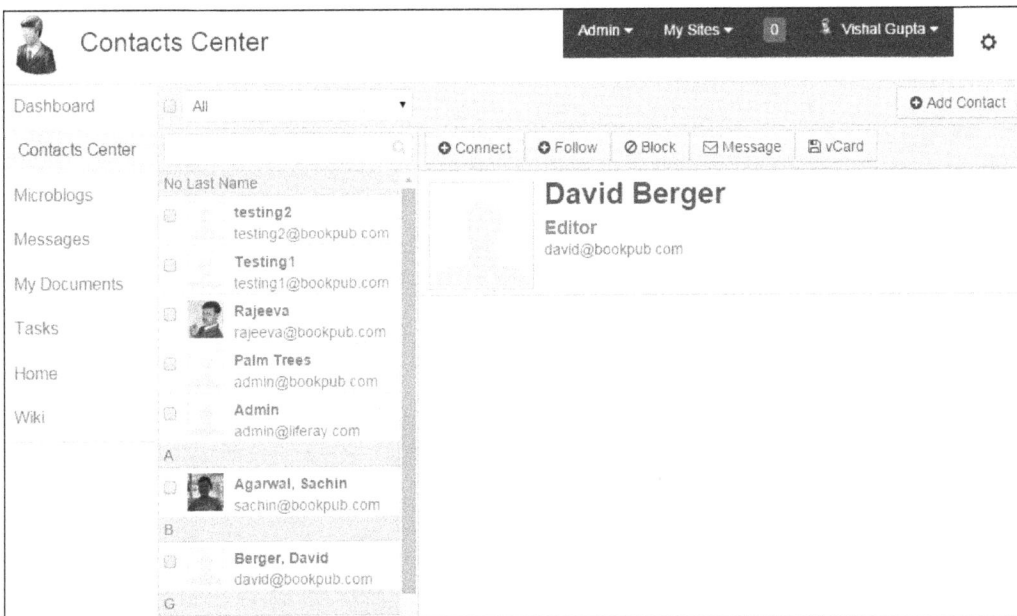

Figure 10.11: Contacts Center

Also, you can download the vCard of the contact, that is, the `.vcf` file, and save the contact in a third-party software.

- **Microblogs**: Here, you can update you micro status and share it with the teams easily.

- **Message**: This lists all the messages you received from your contacts. You can even send the new message to your contact.

- **My Documents**: Here, the Documents and Media portlet is placed, which helps the users to upload their personal documents and media files. It stores the documents and files in the user's personal site scope. Basically, a user can maintain their personal documents and media.

- **Tasks**: This provides users the ability to create to-do lists with due dates. This is displayed in their **Profile** page and **Dashboard** page. See the following screenshot for tasks:

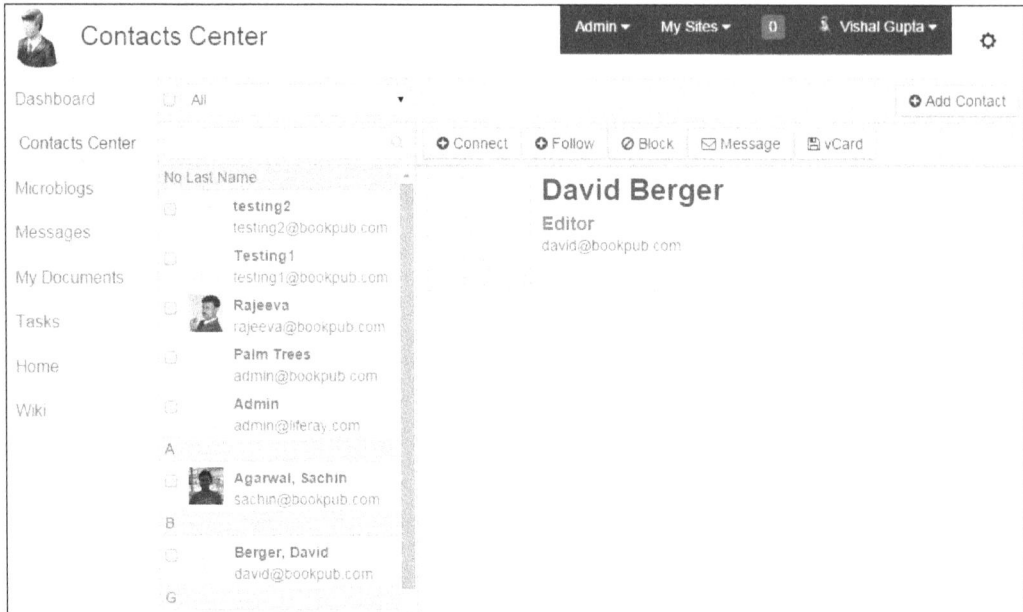

Figure 10.11: Users Tasks

Users can create tasks and assign them to other contacts too. This makes it easier among the team to be updated about the task assigned by your superiors.

- **Home**: This is a normal Liferay page containing portlets such as Message Boards, search, user statistics, and upcoming events.

- **Wiki**: This is again a normal Liferay page that contains the wiki and tag cloud portlets.

Social Office Configurations

When we install the **Social Office** app, it also creates a configuration interface for the portal administrator under **Social Office Configurations**. This configuration interface allows the portal administrator to set the Social Office users, organizations, and user groups. It also allows the setting of **Roles** for **Social Office Users** and **Sites** for different types of sites.

When you create a separate Social Office site for all the users, then the configurations settings can be done appropriately for users, organizations, and user groups.

Let's do Social Office configurations for a site that has a **Public** page **Social Office User Profile** and a **Private** page **Social Office User Home**. Social Office Configurations has two tabs: **Assign Social Office** and **General**. The following screenshot displays **Social Office Configurations**:

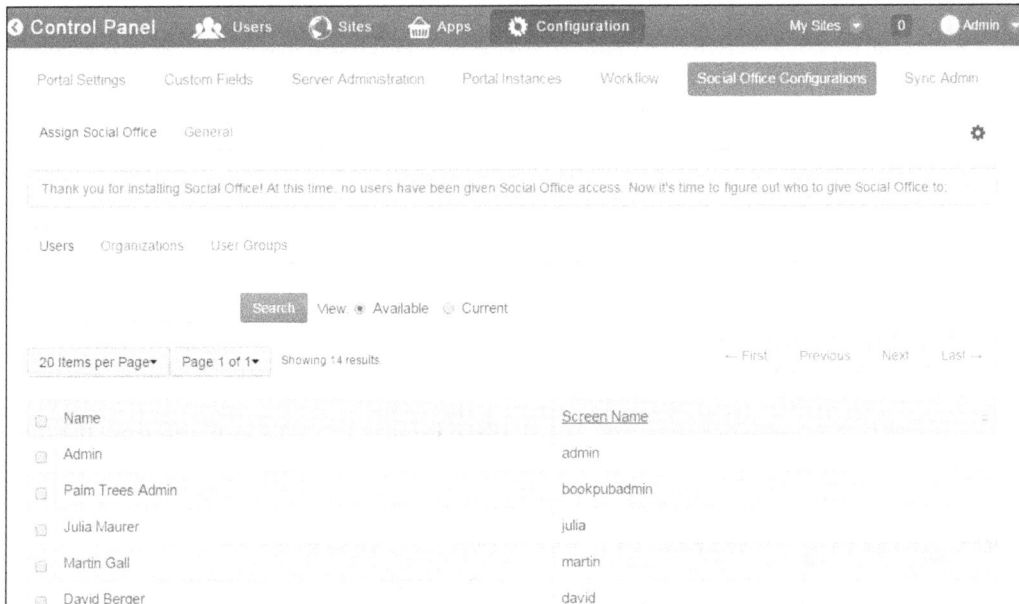

Figure 10.13: Social Office Configurations — Assign Social Office

As you can see in the preceding screenshot, the Assign Social Office tab is selected, which prompts you to assign **Users**, **Organizations**, and **User Groups** for **Social Office**. You can just search for the users in the list, select it by checking the checkbox, and finally click on the **Save** button. In the same way, you can assign **Organizations** and **User Groups**.

General settings are basically for **Role** and **Sites**. It allows you to set the Social Office users role for Add Sites. You can select the site type, which can be added by default through the Sites application at the time of creating the site. The options for site type are **Open**, **Public Restricted**, **Private Restricted**, and **Private**. The following screenshot provides the Social Office Configurations screen:

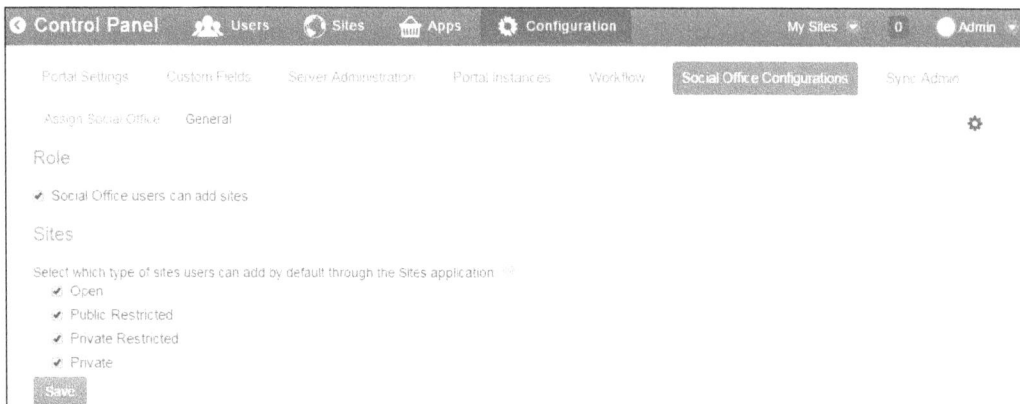

Figure 10.14: Social Office Configurations — General settings

In the preceding screenshot, you can see that we have set the default site type for all.

Targeting content to audiences

Targeting content to audience is a robust application for the end user to experience. It's a new app feature by Liferay 6.2 known as Audience Targeting. The Liferay Audience Targeting app is available to both community and enterprise editions in Marketplace. This app allows you to divide your audience into user segments and target specific content to specific user segments. You can also create campaigns for different user segments. It also allows you to analyze the campaigns very effectively with the analytics program. You can configure user segments by setting the website to display different assets to different users. Campaigns allow you to set specific content to be displayed to different user segments for fixed time periods. It also allows you to extend the communication to the targeted user segments with the selected content.

Let's say that in Palm Tree Publications, the marketing team needs to target the online customer by publishing the advertisement content. To increase the sale, the marketing department needs to target the customer on the basis of their interest, say advertisements related to Java books will be targeted only at the *developer* user segment and advertisements related to management books will be targeted only at the *manager* user segment. This will help the marketing team to achieve its goal. You can create multiple user segments for different types of audiences, which are defined by multiple rules based on session attributes, profile attributes, behavior, and information from social networking. You can write your own custom rules and rule types with minimal coding. After installing the Audience Targeting app, it adds an **Audience Targeting** section to the **Configuration** section of **Site Administration Panel** of **Control Panel** and also add an audience targeting simulator to the dock bar. The app also provide a few more applications to work with.

It also provides a few more applications: **User Segment Content Display**, **User Segment Content List**, and **Campaign Content Display**. Now you can add these applications to any page to display the content. After that, you can configure it through **Site Administrator Panel** | **Configuration** | **Audience Targeting**.

Installing and uninstalling the Audience Targeting app

As mentioned, you can install it from **Marketplace**, which has **Community Edition** and **Enterprise Edition** for Liferay 6.2. Simply follow the preceding steps to install apps from Marketplace.

To uninstall Audience Targeting from the Tomcat server, follow these steps:

1. Delete the `Work` and `Temp` folders from the currently running Liferay instance of your server. The folder locations are `[Liferay Home]/tomcat-[version]/work` and `[Liferay Home]/tomcat-[version]/temp`.

2. Delete OSGi folder from the following location: `[Liferay Home]/data/osgi`.

3. Restart the server.

Finally, the Audience Targeting app will not get initiated when the server starts.

User segment management

Audience Targeting is focused on specific sites. When the user visits a particular site, Audience Targeting activates and performs its operation on the content based on the rule defined for the user segment. In **Site Administration Panel | Configuration | Audience Targeting,** you will be able to manage the user segments and campaigns.

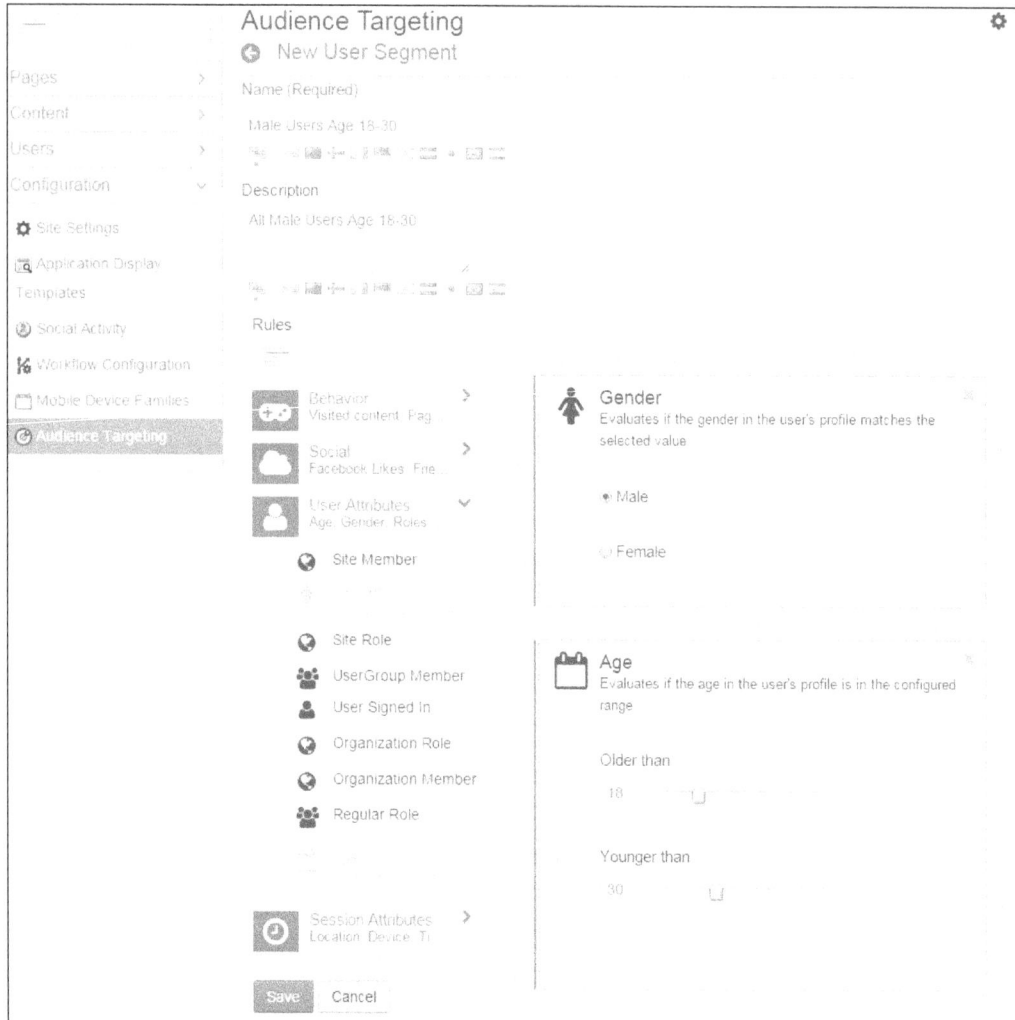

Figure 10.15: Audience Targeting — Creating User Segments

User segments address mainly the portal users in the database (logged in or not). The user segment is defined by one or more rules, one of which the user has to match in order to belong to the specific user segment.

To add a new user segment to Audience Targeting, follow these steps:

1. Log in as Site Administrator.
2. Click on **Audience Targeting** from the left panel, which is under the **Configuration** section.
3. The **Audience Targeting** page will open listing all the **User Segments** created for this particular site.
4. Click on the **Add User Segment** link; it will open up the form similar to the previous screenshot.
5. Now, fill in the **Name** and **Description**.
6. All the rules deployed appear under the **Rules** heading, which you can drag and drop on the right-hand side to apply the rule to the user segment.
7. Now after applying the rule, configure the rule's parameters, just as you applied the gender rule to select **Male** or **Female**, to complete the rule.
8. After configuring the rules, set the permissions for the user segment. For now, keep the default permissions.
9. Finally, save the user segment by clicking on the **Save** button.

The following screenshot displays the list for the **User Segment** list:

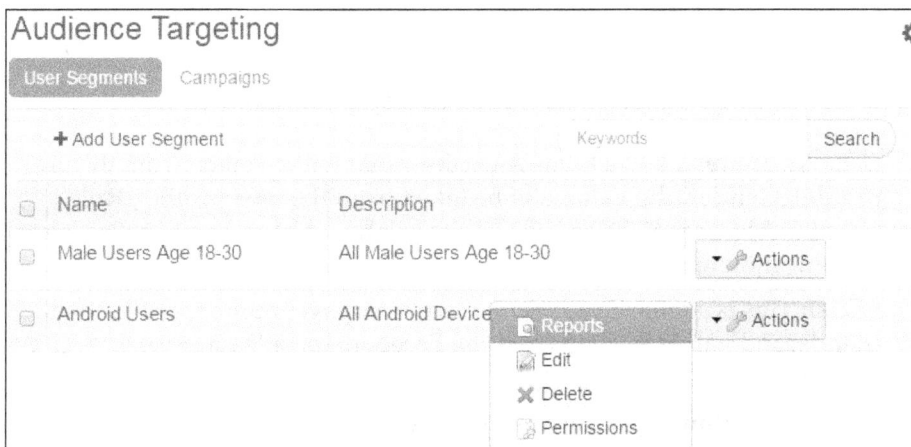

Figure 10.16: Audience Targeting — list of User Segments

> Note that if you configure Audience Targeting in Global Scope, then all the sites will inherit it and the user segments and campaigns will be available to all. In the same way, when you configure Audience Targeting in the parent site, all the child sites will inherit it and the user segment and campaigns will be available to all.

Liferay has provided certain default user segment rules that are included with the app:

- **User Attribute**: This is basically for the user attributes, defined as age, gender, role, and membership

- **Social**: This is basically for social media, which is defined as a specific Facebook page, number of Facebook friends, city, age, gender, education, and other data taken from the Facebook profile page

- **Session Attributes**: This is basically based on the geographical location (obtained from the IP address), browser, device, operating system, and finally time

- **Behavior**: This is based on the viewed page or content and the score points rule

You can create your own custom rules developed as an OSGi plugin, which you can deploy in the server.

Understanding User Segment rules

Liferay has enabled developers to create their own custom rules deployed as OSGi plugins.

The rules that are available to create user segments are as follows:

- **User Attribute**: This includes **Age** (the value will be taken from the user profile), **Gender** (the value will be taken from the user profile), **Role** (regular role, organization role, or site role), and **Membership** (Site member, Organization member, User Group member)

- **Social**: This is similar to a specific Facebook page, number of Facebook friends, and values fetched from the Facebook profile page, such as city, age, gender, education, and so on

- **Session Attributes**: This obtains your location from the IP address, browser, device, operating system, and time

- **Behavior**: This is the viewed page or content and the score points rule

Liferay Audience Targeting provides you with two **Select** buttons in the page section. After selecting the page, you will see **User Segments** and **User Segment (Global)** in categorization and assets settings. Using this button, you will able to set one or more site scopes or global user segments to the content.

Managing campaigns

Liferay provides a feature with which you can manage campaigns. A campaign is defined as an effort to expose a set of assets to a certain user segment within a specific period of time. Let's add **Campaign** to our site by following these steps:

1. In Site Administration Panel, select **Audience Targeting**, and click on the **Campaign** link.

2. Click on the **Add Campaign** link and fill in **Name** and **Description** (optional).

3. Then, select the user segment to target a start date and an end date.

4. Indicate whether the campaign is active or inactive.

5. Finally, save the campaign.

> There can be multiple campaigns active at the same time that target the same user segment. It takes the priority attribute of the campaigns, that is, which campaign takes precedence.

You can also deactivate the campaign whenever you want. Deactivating a campaign is similar to deleting the campaign except that a deactivated campaign can be reactivated later.

You can also manage campaign priorities when multiple campaigns are running at the same time on your portal site.

Finally, you will have a **Campaign** report, which will show you the details as to how many times the content has been displayed to users.

The Liferay Audience Targeting application provides different display portlets for the purposes of displaying content to the targeted users of the site. The portlets are available with their names as follows:

- **User Segment Content Display**
- **User Segment Content List**
- **Campaign Content Display**

All these portlets are instanceable and support Application Display Templates (ADTs) for the look and feel of the content. You can configure these portlets to display content according to the rules that you have defined for **User Segment** and **Campaign**.

Search

The Search Liferay 6.2 bundle is integrated with the Lucene search framework, which provides the search and indexing functionality for the whole portal. Lucene search converts the searchable entities into documents that are custom objects corresponding to searchable entities. So, whenever the Lucene index is searched, a hits object is returned that contains pointers to the documents that match the search query. Searching for any query using an index will be much faster than searching for entities in the database if an indexed document contains the data as per your requirement.

The Lucene search mechanism totally depends on the index documents. First, it finds an indexed document with specific fields for specific values. Once you get the matching document in the index, it makes it easy for you to retrieve the values of any other fields of the matching documents. Moreover, if you need to, run the database query to retrieve the entities that correspond to the indexed documents. This query will be less expensive than the database query done without indexed documents.

Let's understand some search and indexing keywords:

- The Search index contains a collection of documents that are Java-based objects that represent entities that has been saved to the database.

- Each document contains a collection of fields and their values. Fields represent the metadata about each document link title, content, description, created date, tags, and so on.

- Fields can be single-valued or multi-valued. A single-valued field can have only one term, and a multi-valued field can have multiple terms. A term is defined as a single, non-whitespaced value that can be searched easily.

- A phrase is a series of terms separated by spaces. You can use a phrase as a term in a search by surrounding it with double quotes.

- The result of a search is a collection of hits, which generally are pointers to documents that match the search query.

You can implement the Lucene search and indexing in your custom portlet using the Apache Lucene APIs. Follow these steps for implementing search and indexer in your custom portlet.

1. In your custom portlet, create the `Indexer` class and make an entry in the `liferay-portlet.xml` file. Something similar to the following line of code for the class `AssetIndexer` inside Asset Publisher portlet needs to be entered:

```
<indexer-class>com.liferay.portlet.assetpublisher.
   util.AssetIndexer</indexer-class>
```

2. Run the service builder to update the entity service layer to make sure that the index is updated with the creation, modification, or deletion of an entity.

3. Now, in the JSP, you need to create a search bar, and in another JSP, you should have the result page. You can even configure the Liferay default search portlet with your custom portlet.

You will find many Liferay out-of-the box portlets where the Search portlet allows the searching of Liferay assets, the list of which is as follows: Users, Blog posts, Document and Media folders, Document and Media files, Web Content folders, Web Content files, Message Board Messages, Wiki pages, and so on.

Faceted search

Faceted search is a search mechanism that allows you to set the filter on the search query to narrow down the search result. It's faster and easier for the user to locate their desired result at the top. Liferay's Search portlet is created based on faceted search, which contains several facets, such as **Site**, **Asset Type**, **Tag**, **Category**, **User**, **Folder**, and **Modified Date**. When you do the search in the Liferay Search portlet for any search term, it displays the result set. The following screenshot displays the search result set with the left-hand side panel, which allows you to refine your search by clicking on one or more facets to apply a search filter.

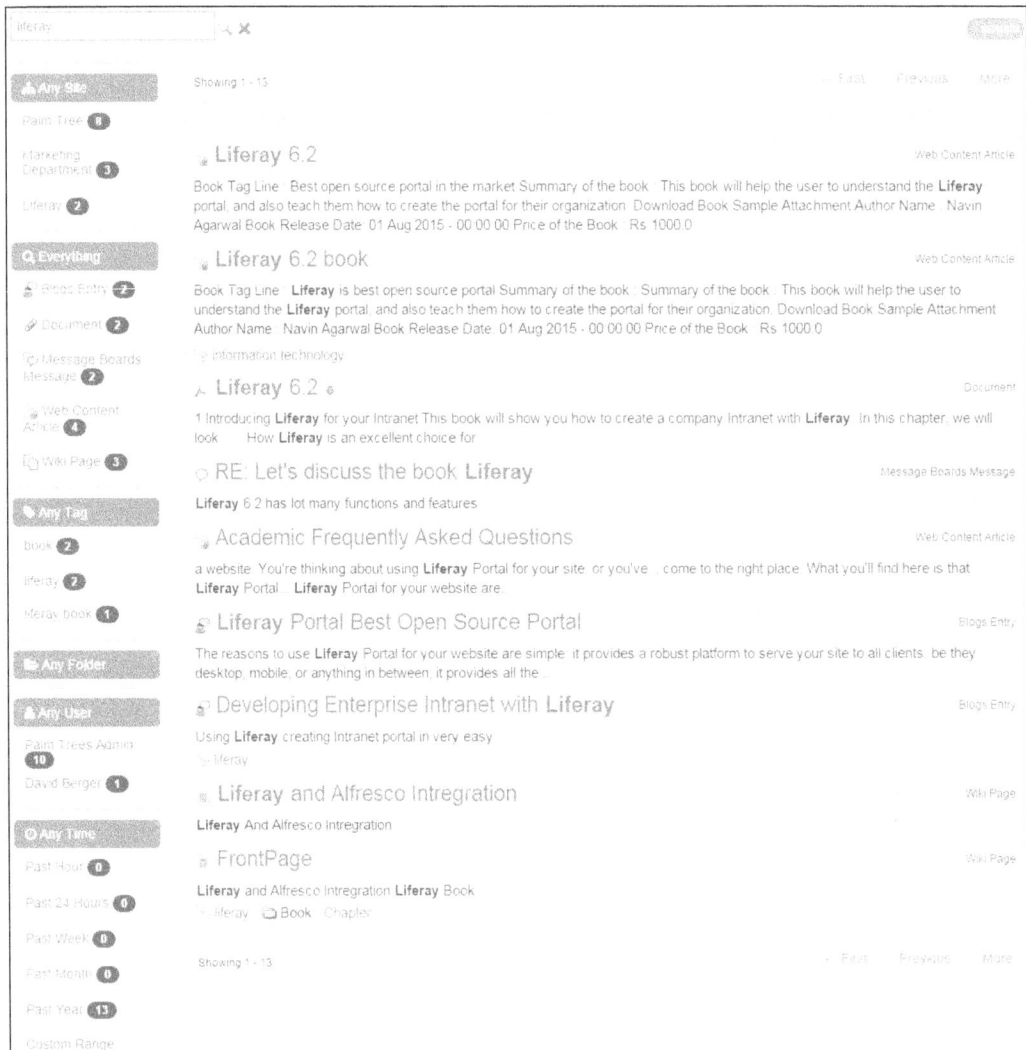

Figure 10.17: Search portlet result page

If you see the preceding search result, it searches the term throughout entire sites. You can do the filter for a particular site by selecting the site facets, say "Palm Tree". The result will be filtered based on the Palm Tree site.

> Note that each facet in the left-hand side panel has a number beside it, which is nothing but the number of search result values for a particular search term.

For a better understanding of faceted search, you should need to know the terms associated with faceted search:

- **Facet**: This is a group of information bits about specific indexed fields, their terms, and their frequencies.

- **Frequency**: This is used when a term appears within a set of documents multiple times.

- **Term Result List**: This is a list of information bits about a specific facet.

- **Frequency Threshold**: This is the minimum value for a frequency required for a term to display in the search-result list. If the frequency threshold of a facet is set to 4, then a term should be appearing more than 4 times; otherwise, the result list won't be displayed.

- **Max Terms**: This keeps the search results under control by setting the value for the maximum number of terms to be shown in the result list regardless of the total larger list.

- **Order**: This displays the result list in ascending order and descending order.

- **Range**: This defines the range for the search term matching frequencies. For example, if you define a range for a search term, that is, a modified date range between the years 2010 and 2015, it will display that search list for the modified date of the same range.

Configuration of the Search portlet

Administrators can configure the Search portlet as per their requirements. It provides full control for the left facet menu panel, which comes under Basic settings, where you can include and exclude any facets you want. It also allows you to enable **Spelling Check** features, **Display Related Queries**, and Add **New Related Queries Based on Successful Queries**. Even in other settings, the administrator can enable and disable **Display Results in Document Form**, **View in Context**, **Display Main Query**, and **Display Open Search Results**.

You even have an option for Advanced settings for facets, where you need to modify the JSON as per your requirement. The following screenshot displays the Search portlet's configuration settings:

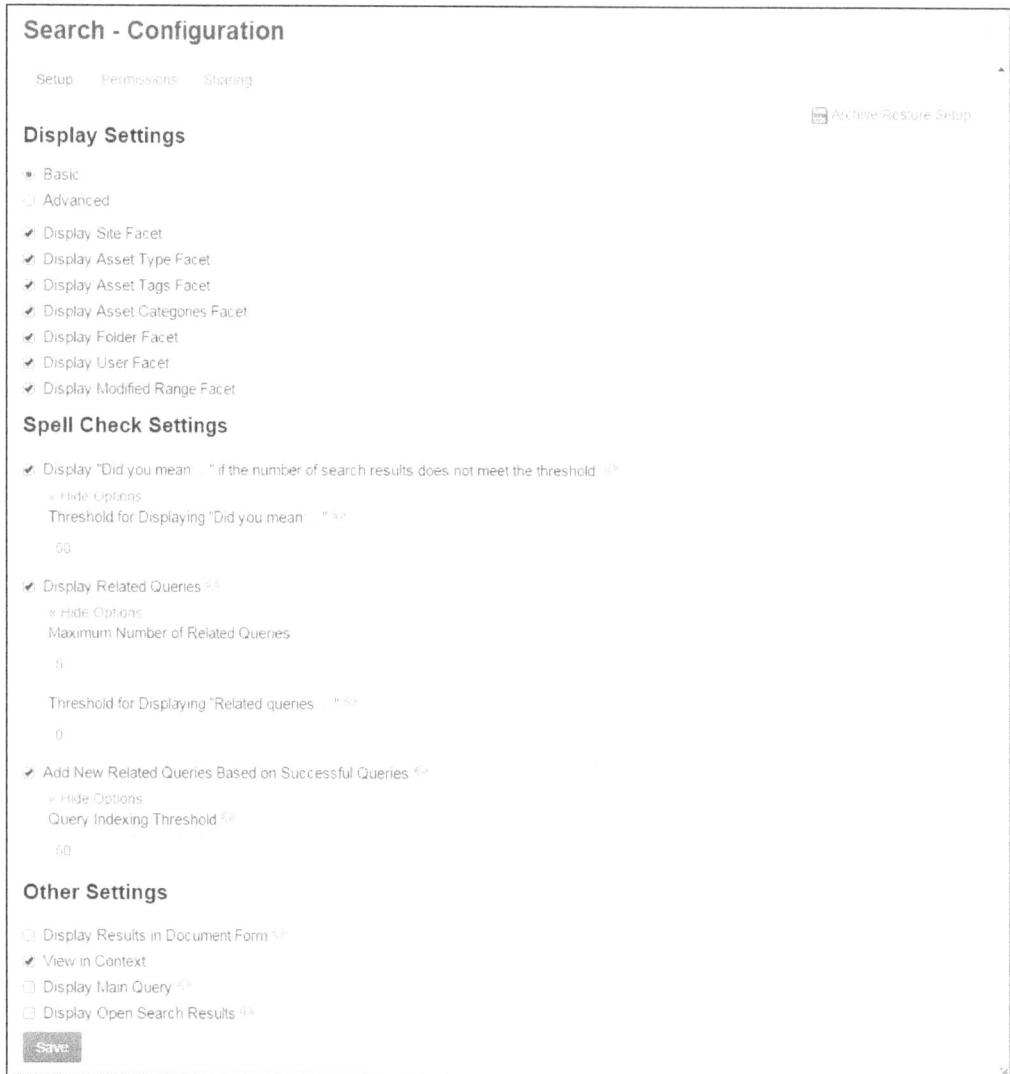

Figure 10.18: Search portlet configuration

Summary

Marketplace is a one-stop hub for apps. You can find apps related to the community and enterprise editions for different servers. Apps from Liferay and different organizations are available in Marketplace; even individual developers can upload apps. Installing apps from Marketplace is very convenient for end users. Liferay Social Office is also available in Marketplace. It is a good collaboration interface for the team in one organization. Liferay Social Office will help team growth and productivity. It provides robust features for the team to grow in an organization. Social Office, when integrated with Liferay Portal, makes the members involved in communication. This is the best product to help managers to assign work to team members. The Audience Targeting app is a new feature from Liferay. This app allows you to divide your audience into user segments, target specific content to specific user segments, and also create campaigns for different user segments. It also allows you to analyze the campaigns very effectively with the analytics program. You can configure user segments by setting the website to display different assets to different users. Campaigns allow you to set specific content to be displayed to different user segments for fixed time periods.

In the next chapter, we will look at the server administrator area. In the next chapter, you will learn about Liferay Server Administration, Performance Tuning, Liferay Connected Services, and Updates of Liferay 7.0.

11
Server Administration

Liferay Server Administration allows you to handle the Liferay Portal server by monitoring different areas within the server. The Liferay Portal server is so huge that the administrator needs to monitor it and configure it with the required settings to keep the portal server running smoothly. Apart from the other tools that the server administrator uses, such as **JProfile**, or any Java performance-monitoring tool to monitor the memory for JDK, they need to keep an eye on the logs and Liferay properties that are configured. The Liferay bundle itself comes integrated with a lot of programs that are required to be monitored.

The server administrator's responsibility towards the Liferay Portal server is to handle the server performance, configure the Liferay Portal server settings, monitor the server through Liferay Cloud Services, create a Liferay Cluster environment, and so on. In this chapter, we are going to discuss the server administration part, which will allow the administrator to handle the server properly and keep it healthy always so that the users never face performance issues while accessing the portal.

By the end of this chapter, you will learn how to:

- Set up the Liferay administrator
- Configure the server properties, data migration, and set the properties for uploading a file
- Set up e-mail configuration and set up external services
- Create multiple portal instances
- Do performance tuning of your JDK to improve the server performance
- Set the Content Delivery Network for your server
- Explore Liferay Cloud Services
- Create multiple Liferay cluster environments
- Get new updates about the Liferay 7 portal

Liferay server administrator

Liferay Portal provides an interface to handle the server resources. You can perform various tasks related to the portal server. In **Control Panel** under **Configuration**, you will find **Server Administration**, which allows you to define settings and execute commands on the server. Under **Server Administration**, there are a few tabs with the names **Resources**, **Log Levels**, **Properties**, **CAPTCHA**, **Data Migration**, **File uploads**, **Mail**, **External Services**, **Script**, and **Shutdown**. Now, let's discuss each of them in detail.

Resources

Resources provides you with different actions on the server that only the portal administrator can execute. Refer to the next screenshot and the actions that administrators execute to improve portal performance:

- **Run the garbage collector to free up memory.**: This allows you to send requests to the JVM to call the garbage collection task.

- **Clear content cached by this VM.**: This allows you to send requests to the JVM to clear content stored in the local cache.

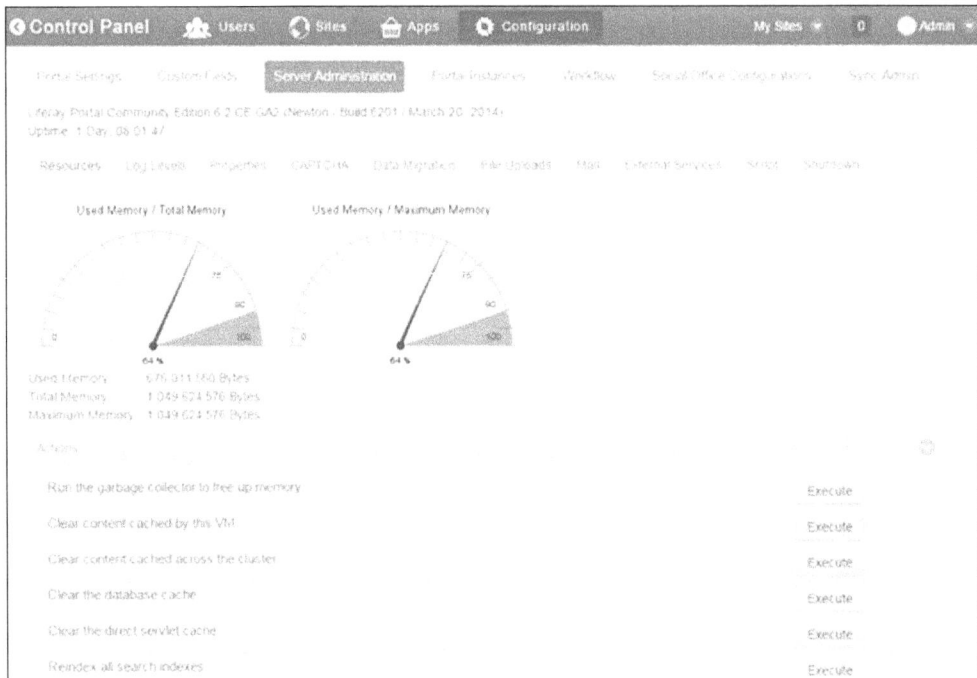

Figure 11.1: Server Administration in Control Panel — Resources

- **Clear content cached across the cluster.**: This allows you to send requests to the JVM to clear the content cached across the entire cluster.

- **Clear the database cache.**: This allows you to send a request to the JVM to clear the database cache. This action only clears the database result cache.

- **Clear the direct servlet cache.**: This allows you to send a request to the JVM to clear the direct servlet cache. The direct servlet cache is a feature that optimizes JSP serving performance by caching and accessing the servlets generated directly instead of accessing them over the application server's dispatcher chain.

- **Reindex all search indexes.**: This allows you to send a request to regenerate all search indexes. It will impact the portal performance if you are not using the Solr search server, so try to do this at nonpeak times.

- **Reindex all spell check indexes**: This allows you to send a request to regenerate all spellcheck indexes.

- **Reset preview and thumbnail files for the Documents and Media portlet.**: This allows you to send a request to reset the thumbnail and preview files for each item in your portal's Documents and Media libraries.

- **Generate thread dump.**: This allows you to take a thread dump to examine later and determine whether there is any kind of deadlock.

- **Verify database tables of all plugins.**: For the accuracy of data retrieval, you can check all the tables against their indexes.

- **Verify Membership Policies.**: This allows you to correct the membership policies for all the users in the site. Suppose that someone has manually changed the Liferay database, resulting in a user being assigned to a site in violation of a site membership policy. When you execute the action, it verifies methods of all the site membership policies that have been implemented. It checks that all the site membership is in accordance with site membership policies; otherwise, the necessary changes are made.

- **Clean up Permissions.**: This process removes the assignment of some permissions on the Guest, User, and Power User roles to simplify the management of "User Customizable Pages". Notably, the "Add To Page" permissions are removed from the Guest and User roles for all portlets. Likewise, the same permission is reduced in scope for Power Users from a portal-wide scope to "User Personal Site".

Log Levels

Log Levels allows you to dynamically change the log levels for any class hierarchy in the portal. To add a new or custom class hierarchy, you can simply add it through the **Add Category** tab. Once you change the log level of the top-level class hierarchy, it will be implemented to all the classes under that hierarchy. It makes the developer's life easy while developing any application. The developer can enable the log levels for their custom classes to find out the issues. The following screenshot shows the log level for the different classes:

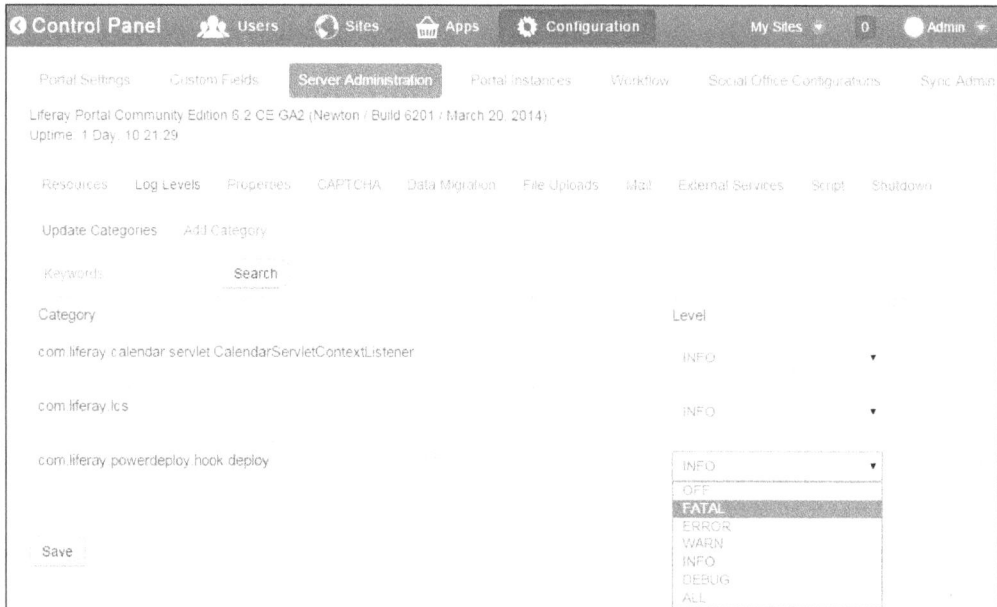

Figure 11.2: Server Administration in Control Panel—Log Levels

In the preceding screenshot, each class has a different category of log level, such as **OFF**, **FATAL**, **ERROR**, **WARN**, **INFO**, **DEBUG**, and **ALL**. If you want to change the log level of any class, just choose the log category and click on the **Save** button.

The **Add Category** tab allows you to add the category and its level, for example, you need to set the custom class with the full package name (com.<companyDomain>.<projectName>.<action>.<ClassName>) in the first textbox, select the level, and finally save the settings. After saving the settings, it will be listed in the updated **Category** list.

Chapter 11

Properties

Liferay and JVM define many settings as properties. There are two properties tabs: one is System Properties and the other one is Portal Properties.

The System Properties tab displays the list of System Properties for the JVM as well as Liferay System Properties; refer to the following screenshot:

Figure 11.3: Server Administration in Control Panel—System Properties

The Portal Properties tab lists all the portal properties of Liferay Portal; refer to the following screenshot. These properties can be changed in `portal-ext.properties`.

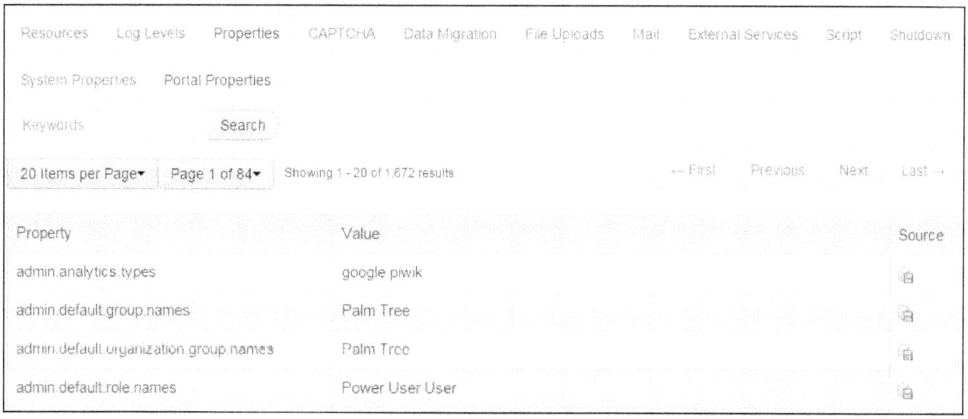

Figure 11.4: Server Administration in Control Panel—Portal Properties

The information about properties is provided to be used while debugging or checking the configuration of the currently running Liferay Portal.

CAPTCHA

Liferay provides a simple **CAPTCHA** service that is designed to thwart bots from registering for accounts on sites. You can also choose to use the Google **reCAPTCHA** service. You can enable these settings by providing public and private keys for **reCAPTCHA**. The portal will use the new **reCAPTCHA** rather than Liferay's simple **CAPTCHA**. Refer to the following screenshot to set reCAPTCHA:

Figure 11.5: Server Administration in Control Panel—CAPTCHA

Data Migration

This tab is used to migrate data from one system to another. Liferay makes it easier for the administrator to migrate data without any script.

In the following screenshot, you can see that it's divided into two sections. The first section allows you to specify database settings and copy the entire Liferay database that is running.

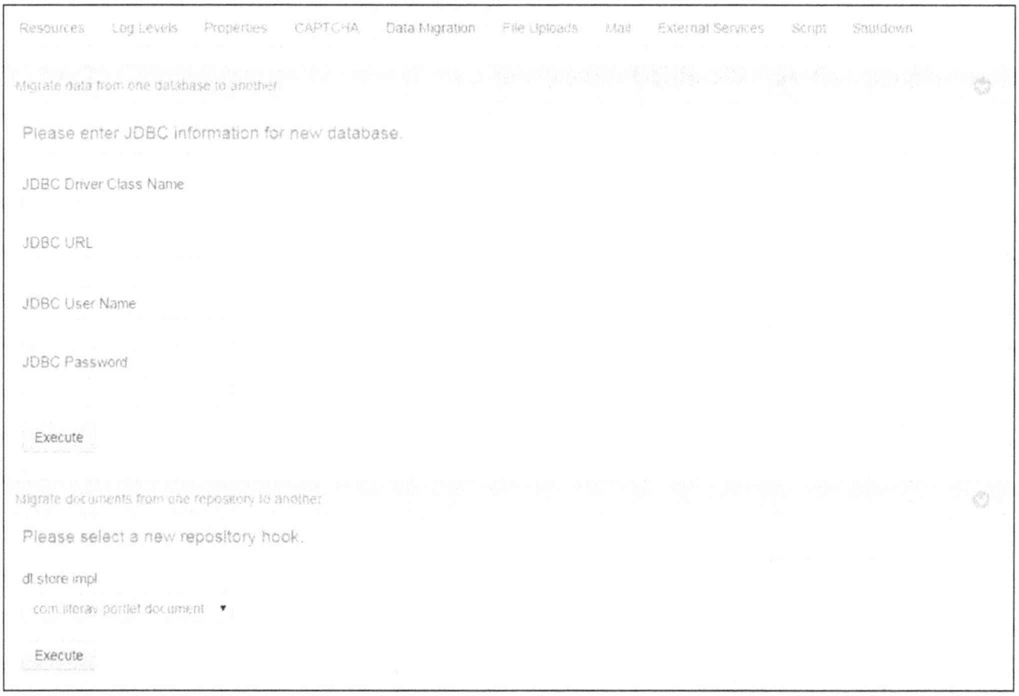

| Resources | Log Levels | Properties | CAPTCHA | Data Migration | File Uploads | Mail | External Services | Script | Shutdown |

Migrate data from one database to another

Please enter JDBC information for new database.

JDBC Driver Class Name

JDBC URL

JDBC User Name

JDBC Password

Execute

Migrate documents from one repository to another

Please select a new repository hook.

dl.store.impl

com.liferay.portlet.document ▾

Execute

Figure 11.6: Server Administration in Control Panel—Data Migration

Now, let's migrate your documents in the next section. It provides you with different options to move your documents and media, such as **Advance File System Store**, **CMI Store**, **DB Store**, **JCR Store**, and **S3 Store**. You even need to set up the portal-ext.properties file so that the hook is properly configured before running this migration. In the Document Library hook, set the location to which you want your documents to be migrated and then click on **Execute**. Your document will be migrated to the new repository. Shut down the server, make the new repository the default in the portal-ext.properties file, and finally restart the server.

File Uploads

The **File Uploads** tab allows you to define the settings' overall maximum file size and then override the size for specific applications within Liferay Portal. Here, you can also restrict the file type and its size. Here's the list of applications for which file upload settings are used: **Document and Media**, **Web Content Images**, **Shopping Cart Images**, **Software Catalog Images**, and **User Images**. You can also limit the allowed file extensions for the entire portal or for individual applications. Portal Administration has a lot of flexibility for setting up the file upload and managing files within Liferay Portal.

Mail

Liferay provides the flexibility to the portal administrator to configure the mail settings in **Control Panel** as well as in the `portal-ext.properties` file. Defining settings for mail configuration inside **Control Panel** is better rather than doing it in the `portal-ext.properties` file. Mail settings can be done for POP servers (incoming mails) and SMTP servers (outgoing mails).

External services

External services enable the portal administrator to configure third-party tools, such as ImageMagick, OpenOffice, and Xuggler. Whenever users upload the file to Documents and Media, the preview of certain types of documents is generated automatically since Liferay comes with PDFBox by default. To improve the preview that provides higher quality, you can configure ImageMagick, OpenOffice, and Xuggler. Using these tools, you can generate automatic previews for several types of files including text files, office suite files, PDFs, images, audio files and video files.

For Liferay 6.2, it's better to install the latest stable version of Open Office `https://www.openoffice.org`, ImageMagick `http://www.imagemagick.org/script/index.php`, and Xuggler `http://www.xuggle.com/xuggler`. Xuggler can be installed from the external services interface of **Control Panel**. After you have installed these tools, you can proceed with the configuration of external services.

Configuring ImageMagick

Installing ImageMagick on your operating system includes the installation of Ghostscript; now you need to configure Liferay to use ImageMagick. Liferay provides you the option to do the configuration either in `portal-ext.properties` or from **Control Panel**.

In the `portal-ext properties` file, add the following lines of configurations. Make sure that the search points to the directories for the ImageMagick and Ghostscript executables:

```
imagemagick.enabled=true
imagemagick.global.search.path[apple]=/opt/local/bin:/opt/local/sh
   are/ghostscript/fonts:/opt/local/share/fonts/urw-fonts
imagemagick.global.search.path[unix]=/usr/local/bin:/usr/local/sha
   re/ghostscript/fonts:/usr/local/share/fonts/urw-fonts
imagemagick.global.search.path[windows]=C:\\Program Files\\ImageMagick
```

In **Control Panel**, navigate to **External Service** under **Server Administration**, check in to enable ImageMagick, and input the correct path for the ImageMagick and Ghostscript executables.

Configuring OpenOfiice and LibreOffice

OpenOffice and LibreOffice are both open source applications that allow you to run in server mode, thus allowing you to convert documents to and from of all the different types. After configuration, Liferay uses these features to automatically convert content on the fly. Installation of OpenOffice or LibreOffice can be done to the same machine in which Liferay is running, or you can even have a separate host.

When you've installed OpenOffice or LibreOffice on the same machine where Liferay is running, you can start it in server mode by following this command:

```
soffice -headless -accept="socket,host=127.0.0.1,port=8100;urp;" -
   nofirststartwizard
```

Once OpenOffice or LibreOffice has started in server mode, you can configure from the Liferay **Control Panel** or by setting the properties in `portal-ext.properties`.

Set the following property in the `portal-ext.properties` file to enable OpenOffice:

```
openoffice.server.enable=true
```

Set the server host and port of OpenOffice or LibreOffice even if it is running in the same server:

```
openoffice.server.host=127.0.0.1
openoffice.server.port=8100
```

When OpenOffice or LibreOffice is integrated with Liferay, it uses the caching mechanism to store the converted document. Liferay also uses it when the user tries to convert the same document again. When a request comes for a fresh document, it directly generates it; otherwise, it checks in the cache memory temp folder and returns it to the user. You can disable the cache by setting the following property in the `portal-ext.properties` file:

```
openoffice.cache.enabled=false
```

You can define the same settings in **Control Panel | Server Administration | External Services**.

Configuring Xuggler

Xuggler helps you to play audio and video files in Documents and Media. You can install and configure it through **Control Panel** under **External Services** of **Server Administration**. Select the specific `Xuggler.jar` file that matches your operating system and then click on **Install**.

After installing Xuggler, restart your server, and then enable Xuggler from **Control Panel**, or set the property in the `portal-ext.properties` file:

```
xuggler.enabled=true
```

Script

Liferay provides you with the scripting console, which allows administrators to execute migration or management code instantly with one click. This scripting console is capable of running several scripting languages, such as **Ruby**, **Python**, **Groovy**, **JavaScript**, and **Beanshell**. Refer to the following screenshot for the scripting console:

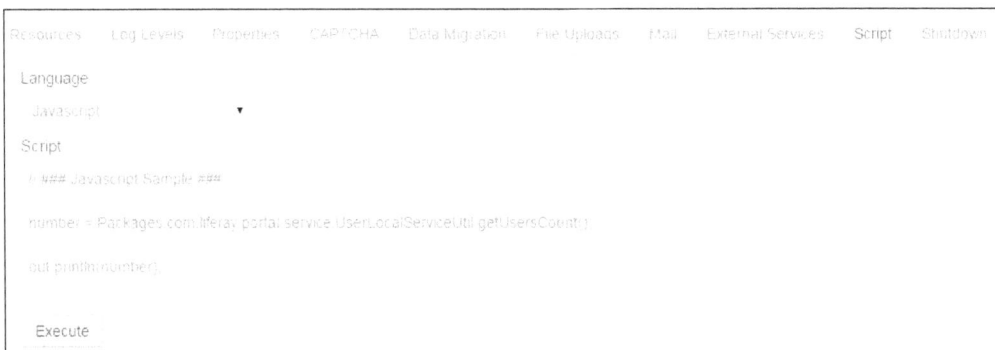

Figure 11.7: Server Administration in Control Panel—Script

The code in the preceding screenshot prints the number of users available within the portal. If you want to update each user in the system to set their `agreedToTermsOfUse` attribute to false and skip the default user, follow this code:

```
import com.liferay.portal.service.UserLocalServiceUtil
userCount = UserLocalServiceUtil.getUsersCount()
users = UserLocalServiceUtil.getUsers(0, userCount)
for (user in users){
  if(!user.isDefaultUser() &&
  !user.getEmailAddress().equalsIgnoreCase("test@liferay.com")) {
    user.setAgreedToTermsOfUse(false)
    UserLocalServiceUtil.updateUser(user)
  }
}
```

Note that when the script code accesses Liferay Service Layer, you should be alert and keep a few points in mind while working with the script console:

- There is no preview or undo
- Scripts run synchronously; be careful with scripts that might take a while to execute
- While using the Local Service, no permission checks are enforced

> You can use the script console to test your code while developing any portlet.

Shutdown

Liferay provides a simple way in which you can shut down your Liferay Portal server while users are logged in. The Shutdown tab allows you to set the number of minutes until shutdown and a custom message that will be displayed.

Once the Server Administrator clicks on the shutdown button after defining the two fields, logged in users will be able to see the message at the top of their portal pages. When the given time expires, all the pages in the portal will display a message saying the portal has been shut down.

Portal Instances

Liferay Portal allows you to configure and run multiple portal instances on a single server. The data of each portal instance is kept separately in the same database. Each portal instance should have its own domain name with which Liferay directs users to the proper instance based on this domain name. So, you need to configure the domain name before configuring or adding an instance. The following screenshot displays the list of portal instances created in the currently running Liferay Portal server.

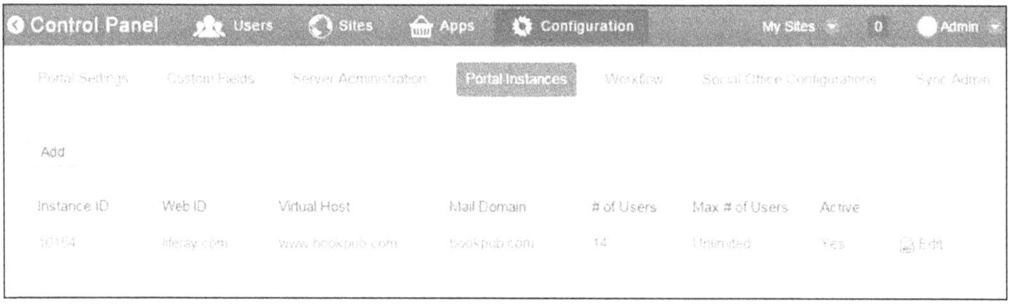

Figure 11.8: Portal Instances in Control Panel

You can add a new instance by clicking on the Add button. After that, you need to define four fields and a checkbox:

- **Web ID**: Add the domain name; it's generally a user-generated ID for an instance.

- **Virtual Host**: Use the domain name that you have configured in your network. When users are directed to the Liferay server via this domain name, Liferay Server will be able to send them to the proper portal instance.

- **Mail Domain**: Settings to send mail notifications from the portal enter the domain name for the mail host for this instance.

- **Max # of Users**: Use the maximum numbers of user accounts the portal instance should support.

- **Active**: Check the checkbox to make the instance active or inactive.

After filling in the fields, finally save it. Now you can trigger the new domain URL that you configured; you will see that a fresh Liferay instance opens up.

Custom Fields

Liferay Portal allows the administrator to add additional custom fields to many different types of assets and resources. Custom fields are added from the **Control Panel | Configuration** section. Suppose you want to have a custom field for the Users resource, say the Department field, for all the users, you just need to click on the **Edit** link beside User and add new custom fields with the key and type of fields. The following screenshot displays the list of resources where custom fields can be implemented:

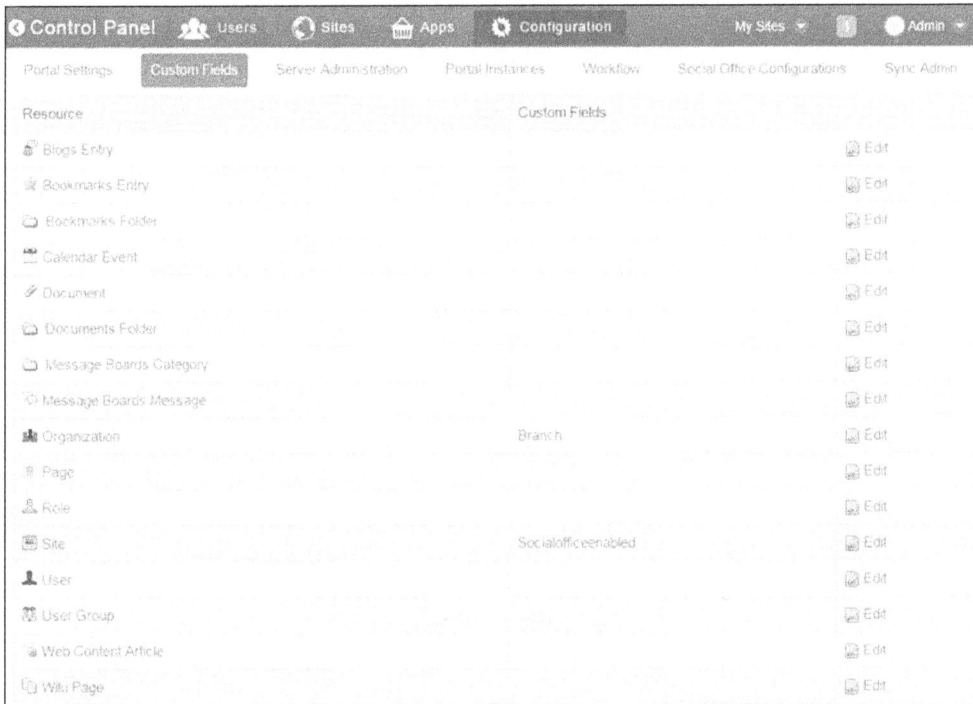

Figure 11.9: Custom Fields in Control Panel

In the preceding screenshot the **Site** and **Organization** resources already have the custom fields **Branch** and **Socialofficeenabled**. Let's add a new custom field for the **User** resource by following these steps:

1. Click on the **Edit** link next to the **User** resource.
2. Click on the **Add Custom Field** button to add a custom field.
3. Input the **Key**, that is, the field name that is going to be displayed to the user, say **Department**.

4. Select the type of field for the respective fields. Liferay provides different options for the field's type. Refer to the following screenshot for the field's type:

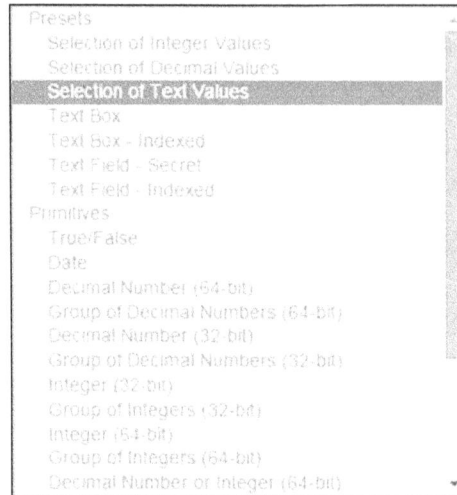

Figure 11.10: Custom Fields types

5. Finally, **Save** the new custom field.

The new **Department** custom field has been created for the User resource with the selection box. Under the User resource, you will find the list of custom fields created. Now, you need to set up the values for the selection box. Click on the **Department** custom field, which allows you to edit the custom field detail. In the **Values** textbox, input the values for the departments, such as **Human Resource**, **Marketing**, and so on. Also, change the value for **Display Type**, that is, **Selection List**. Finally, click on **Save** to save the **Department** custom field detail form.

Now, if you go to the individual user's detail page in **Control Panel | Users** section and click on **Custom Field** from the right-hand side menu. You will be able to see the new **Department** custom field with the selection box having the values **Marketing** and **Human Resource**.

Performance tuning

Every application is required to be tuned to improve the performance, especially when the users have increased and the site winds up generating more traffic than you anticipated. You can improve the Liferay Portal performance by changing settings in some properties files and improving the in-memory capacity.

Memory

It's a vital area for improving system performance. Whenever there is a need to optimize performance, you should first check the amount of memory space for JVM heap. There should be sufficient memory in your server, and your JVM is tuned to use it to avoid the impact due any disk swapping.

Java provides you with a few JVM command properties that control the amount of memory in the Java heap:

- `-Xms`: This sets the initial Java heap size
- `-Xmx`: This sets the maximum Java heap size
- `-XX:MaxPermSize`: This sets the permanent generation space

The preceding three settings allow you to control the memory in the Java heap. The initial heap size and maximum heap size should be set to the same value, which prevents the JVM from having to reallocate memory when the application needs more while it's running. This also helps JVM to create the maximum amount of memory at the initial start time:

```
-Xms1024m -Xmx1024m -XX:MaxPermSize=256m
```

These settings create Java JVM 1024 MB for its regular heap size and creates a PermGen space of 256 MB, which is perfectly fine for machines nowadays or a developer machine. Whenever you face performance problems and the profiler shows that a lot of garbage collection is going on, firstly, you need to check the increase in memory available to the JVM. Monitor the profiler (NetBeans, YourKit, or JProfiler) on the server to look into memory issues. You might need to increase the memory with the **garbage collection** (**GC**) running frequently.

The moderate machines nowadays, especially with 64-bit systems, have huge memory; you can allocate large JVM memory space.

> Note that a very large JVM memory allocation will take more time than it takes for garbage collection to take place. So, you should not create JVMs of more than 2 GB in size. The best way to achieve higher amounts of memory on a single system is by running multiple JVMs in a single Liferay instance.

The performance may also get affected by the PermGen space since it contains long-lived classes interned strings (immutable string objects that are kept around for a long time to increase the string's processing performance). While increasing the JVM memory space, you might have to increase the PermGen space accordingly.

Garbage collection

The system creates various Java objects while running and storing in heap memory. Some objects are alive and have a link reference, while others are not. Garbage collection is the process of cleaning the heap memory by identifying the objects that are not in use. Note these points about garbage collection:

- Used objects or reference objects are those that have active pointers by the running program

- Unused objects or dereferenced objects are no longer referenced by any running program

The unused objects fill up the heap memory space until JVM calls garbage collection.

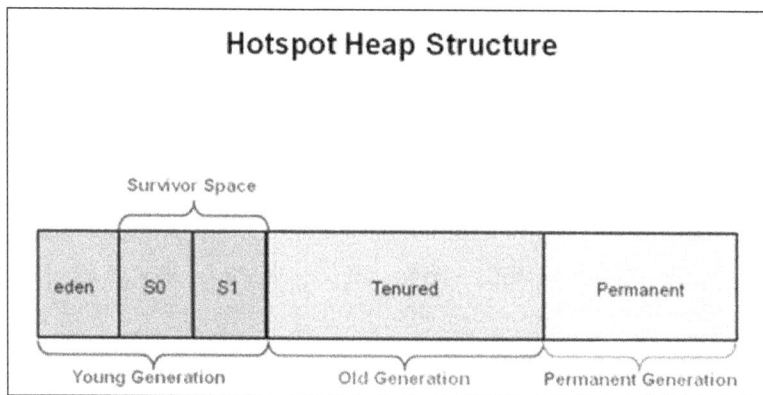

Figure 11.11: Java garbage collection

The preceding image has been referred from `http://www.oracle.com/webfolder/technetwork/tutorials/obe/java/gc01/index.html`.

The heap memory is divided into three sections: young generation, old generation, and permanent generation. The young generation is divided into three sections: Eden (where new objects are created) and two "survivor spaces", which can be named S0 and S1 spaces. In the young generation, all new objects are allocated and aged. When the young generation fills up, this causes a *minor garbage collection*. Minor collections can be optimized by assuming a high object mortality rate. Garbage collection runs in the young generation. Eden is swept for the object that is no longer referenced. The rest of the objects are moved to the S1 survivor space, and S0 survivor space is swept. If any other objects in the space, which still has a reference, are moved to the S1 space, the S0 space is cleared out altogether. Now, S0 and S1 swap roles and processing is freed up again until the next time the JVM calls garbage collection.

A young generation full of dead objects is collected very quickly. A few of the surviving objects are aged and eventually move to the old generation. Similarly, after a predetermined number of generations of garbage collection in the old generation, the surviving objects can be moved to the permanent generation.

JDK processes the sequence of serial garbage collectors to achieve this. This perfectly works for small and shortlived desktop Java-based applications, but it might not perform in the same way in server-based applications, such as Liferay Portal. To make our server-based application run perfectly, you may need to use the **Concurrent-Mark-Sweep (CMS)** collector.

The concurrent mark sweep collector is targeted at applications that are sensitive to garbage collection pauses. It performs most garbage collection activities *concurrently*, that is, while the application threads are running, to keep garbage collection-induced pauses short.

Then, it allows the application to run while it marks all objects that are reachable from the set it marked. Finally, it adds another phase called the remark phase, which finalizes marking by revisiting any objects modified while the application was running. It then sweeps through and collects garbage. Java can be tuned in every aspect in the way memory management design is done.

If you want to experiment with Java tuning, just follow the profiling tool and change the settings to improve server performance:

- **NewSize, MaxNewSize**: You can set the initial size and the maximum size of the new and young generations.
- **+UseParNewGC**: This makes garbage collection happen in parallel using multiple CPUs. This increases the application speed and also shortens the garbage collection process.

- **+UseConcMarkSweepGC**: This allows the use of Concurrent Mark-Sweep Garbage Collector, which improves the performance of larger applications by making applications pause for a while and calls the garbage collector.
- **CMSParallelRemarkEnabled**: This enables the garbage collector to use multiple threads during the CMS remarks phase. This decreases the pauses during this phase.
- **SurvivorRatio**: This controls the size of the two survivor spaces. It's a ratio between the survivor space size and Eden. The default is 25.
- **ParallelGCThreads**: This is the number of threads to use for parallel garbage collection. This should be equal to the number of CPU cores in your server.

A sample configuration using the preceding parameters might look similar to this:

```
JAVA_OPTS="$JAVA_OPTS -XX:NewSize=700m -XX:MaxNewSize=700m -
    Xms2048m
-Xmx2048m -XX:MaxPermSize=128m -XX:+UseParNewGC -
    XX:+UseConcMarkSweepGC
-XX:+CMSParallelRemarkEnabled -XX:SurvivorRatio=20
-XX:ParallelGCThreads=8"
```

> Note that you should be careful while following the procedure of adjusting the settings of garbage collections, testing under-load environments, and adjusting again.

Let's make changes in the Liferay Properties files to improve server performance.

Properties file changes

Liferay allows you to set the properties values in the `portal-ext.properties` file to improve the server performance.

You can set the property that allows you to load the theme-merged CSS files for faster loading. You can even disable loading by setting the URL parameter `css_fast_load` to 0:

```
theme.css.fast.load=true
```

To load the JavaScript files into one compacted file you can set the property in `portal-ext.properties` file, which will improve the performance:

```
Javascript.fast.load=true
```

All these settings in the `portal-ext.properties` file will improve the performance by loading the theme and JavaScript faster.

Now, let's have a look at servlets filters and disable the unused ones to improve the performance.

Disabling unused servlet filters

Liferay, as a portal application, comes with a number of servlet filters enabled and running. Most likely for your installation, you might not need all of them since servlet filters intercept the HTTP request and do some processing on it before the Liferay Server starts building the page while running. You can improve performance by disabling the unused servlet filters by setting the properties in the `portal-ext.properties` file.

You can copy the servlet filter section from the original `portal.properties` file into `portal-ext.properties` and then go through the list and disable the unrequired servlet filters by setting them to false. For example, if there is no requirement for CAS for single sign-on, simply disable it by setting it to false. In the same way, you can set the properties for NTLM if you are not using single sign-on features. The following are the two properties that you can make false:

```
com.liferay.portal.servlet.filters.sso.cas.CASFilter=true
com.liferay.portal.servlet.filters.sso.ntlm.NtlmFilter=true
```

There are many servlet filters defined, which you need to check and disable. The fewer the servlet filters running, the less are the processing time and power needed for each request.

So, finally, you have achieved the goal of improving the Liferay Portal server performance by defining the preceding settings.

> Note that after doing the settings, you should do the load testing of the portal. There might be a chance of a performance issue occurring in a custom-portlet application that's doing something it shouldn't do.
>
> Make it a practice to do load testing of the application before putting it into production. It's the best way to find out potential performance issues.

Now, have a look at the configuration of Content Delivery Network, which may also help with improving portal performance.

Content Delivery Network

Content Delivery Network (CDN) is a large distributed system of servers deployed in multiple data centers across the Internet. It serves content to end users with high availability and high performance. The static content (images, JavaScript, CSS, and so on) is stored on multiple servers, and while retrieving the content, it pulls from the nearest server (closest to the users).

CDN functions as a caching proxy, which means the static content is copied to a local server in a cache for fast and easy retrieval of content. By this process, you improve the latency time since the browsers are so much more capable of downloading static content from the local server cache. When the users request the server for content, it generally triggers an algorithm and locates the content closest to the user. It reduces waiting time for the request and load on the application server. This process also improves the portal performance.

Liferay has some restrictions on using CDN as it allows only the dynamically retrieving request content.

> Note that you should make sure from the CDN provider that you don't have to upload the content directly to CDN as it should fetch the content itself.

You can configure CDN in Liferay Portal by very simple steps; there are two ways to set CDN. Let's explore them:

1. By setting properties in the `portal-ext.properties` file.
2. By setting through **Control Panel**.

In the `portal-ext.properties` file, you need to set the properties for CDN, which are given here:

```
cdn.host.http=
cdn.host.https=
cdn.dynamic.resources.enabled=true
```

The first one, `cdn.host.http`, allows you to set the hostname that will be used to serve static content for requests made over the HTTP protocol. The other one is `cnd.host.https`, which allows you to set the hostname that will be used to serve static content for requests made over the HTTPS protocol. You can disable both properties dynamically at runtime by setting the URL parameter `cdn_enable` to `0`.

Last but not least, `cdn.dynamic.resources.enable=true` enables you to serve, by dynamically generated CSS, images, and JavaScript. If set to `false`, it allows the usage of CDN, which does not support lazy loading of content.

Now, let's have a look at the same setting in **Control Panel**. Follow these steps to set CDN:

1. Log in as Portal Administrator.

2. Navigate to **Control Panel** and select **Portal Settings** under the **Configuration** section.

3. Now look for CDN settings in the page; refer to the following screenshot marked with the red box.

4. Set the settings, and finally save it.

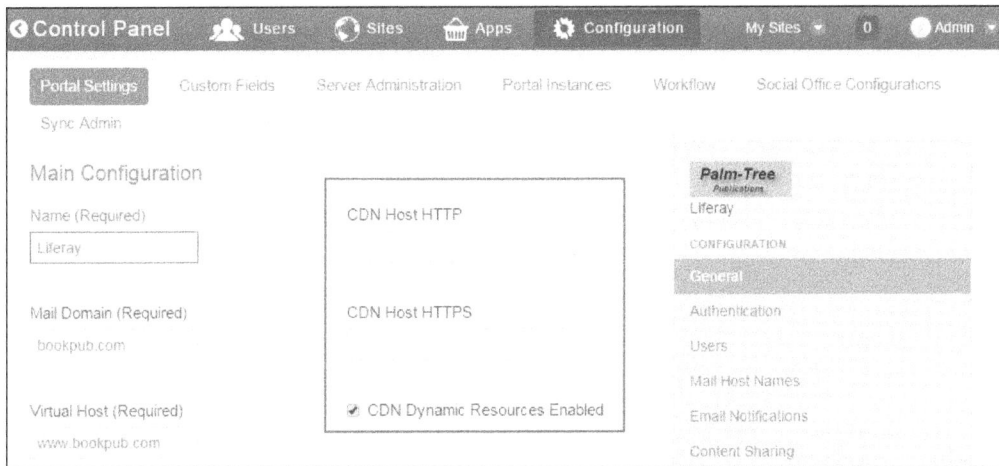

Figure 11.12: Content Delivery Network (CDN) in Control Panel

By defining the preceding settings for CDN, latency time will be reduced and your overall portal performance will be improved.

Liferay Connected Services

Liferay Connected Services (**LCS**) is a set of tools and services that lets you manage and monitor your Liferay installations. LCS allows you to install fix packs for your server seamlessly over the cloud. LCS won't install anything that you don't specifically choose for installation. It provides you with one-click downloading and updating. It also monitors your Liferay server performance with the help of tools such as data on pages, portlets, memory usage, JVM performance, and many more. The best part is that LCS works regardless of whether your Liferay instance is on a single discreet server or in a cluster environment. LCS supports Liferay Portal 6.1 GA 3 or 6.2 GA 1 and higher. LCS is available for both community and enterprise editions. For Enterprise Edition, LCS provides the fix patch and other updates over the cloud.

LCS is cloud-based; you need to have an account to access it. First, create an account in `http://liferay.com`, and then set up an LCS account at `https://lcs.liferay.com`. While creating an LCS account, you will be asked to download the **Liferay Connected Services Client** application; you can refer to the following screenshot:

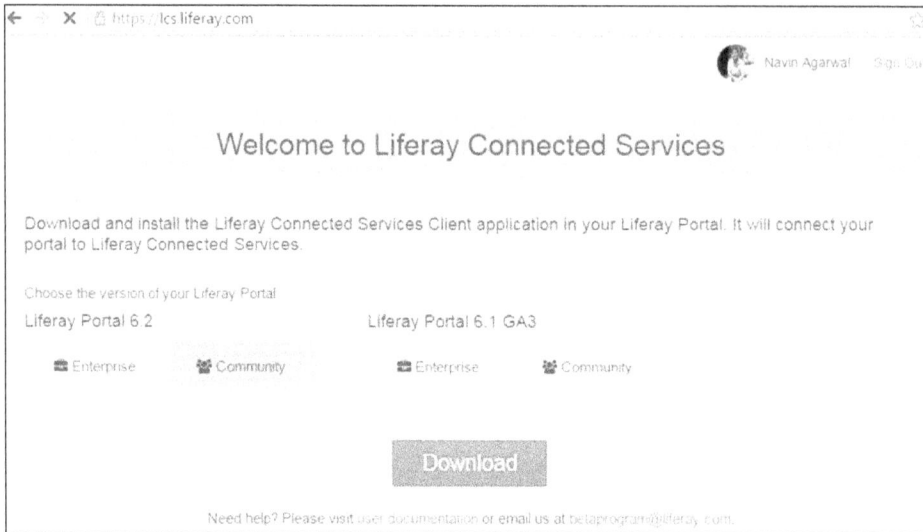

Figure 11.13: The LCS screen for downloading the Liferay Connected Services Client application

After you download the `.war` file, it will provide steps to do to get connected; the following screenshot shows this:

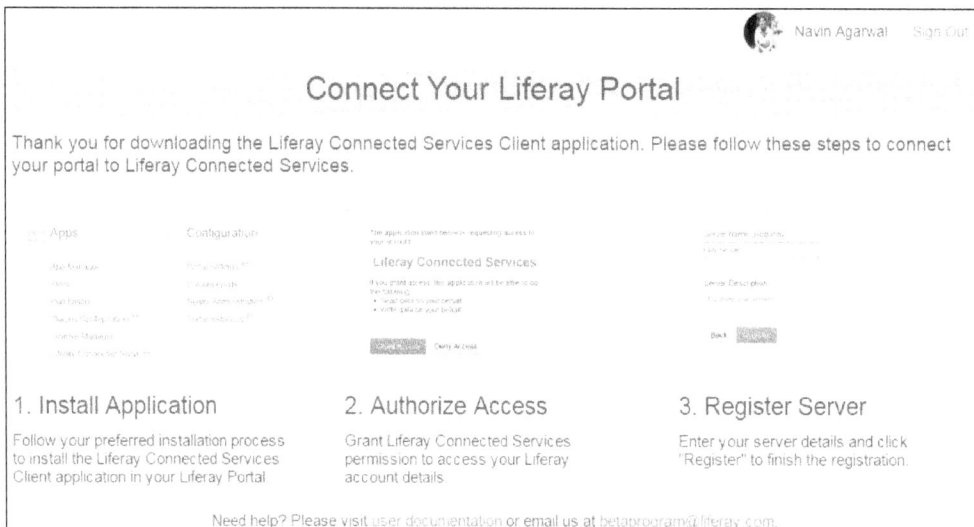

Figure 11.14: The LCS instructions for installing the Liferay Connected Services Client application

If your server accesses the Web through a proxy, you need to set the properties in the `portal-ext.properties` file, which resides inside the WAR file of the LCS client portlet:

1. Open the WAR file of the LCS client portlet using the WinRAR software and locate the `portal-ext.properties` file in the location `WEB-INF/classes/portlet-ext.properties`.

2. Add properties at the end of the file with the values `proxy.host.name=` and `proxy.host.port=`.

3. After you save the `portal-ext.properties` file in the WAR file, simply deploy it.

> If there is no proxy used to access your server, you don't need to add properties to the `portal-ext.properties` file.

You can deploy the LCS `.war` file to your Liferay instance. After installing the `.war` file in Liferay Portal, a new service called **Liferay Connected Service** will appear under the **Apps** section in **Control Panel**. Click on the **Authorize Access** button to authorize **Liferay Connected Services** to start receiving your portal metrics data from **Liferay Connected Services** under **Apps** in **Control Panel**. You can refer to the following screenshot:

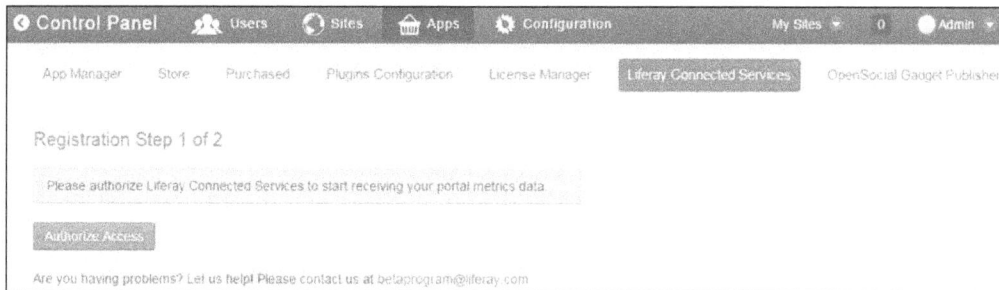

Figure 11.15: The Liferay Connected Services Client application in Control Panel

Next, log in to liferay.com using the Liferay credentials, and click on the **Grant** button to provide permission to access your Liferay account details; refer to the following screenshot:

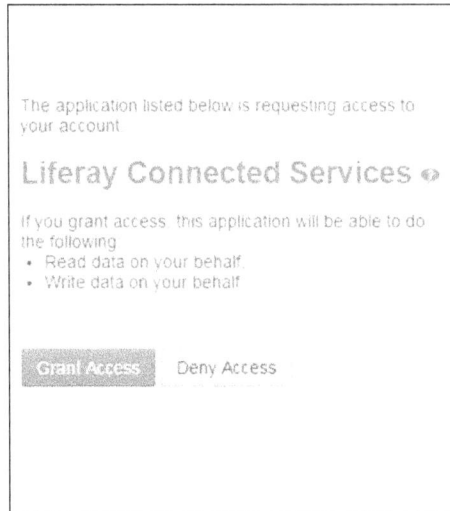

Figure 11.16: Grant Access to the Liferay Connected Services Client application to access your Liferay account

After giving the grant access permission, you need to register your server details with LCS by filling out the form.

> Information required for the following terms that you need to know:
> - **Project**: This generally represents a group of users below a company or organization who are working together on a common project
> - **Environment**: This represents a cluster of servers or a virtual aggregation of servers
> - **Server**: This represents a concrete portal instance, which can be a standalone server or a cluster node

Let's describe the fields to make it easier when filling them in:

- **Project**: Select the project from the drop-down menu
- **Environment**: Select an environment or create a new one by clicking on the **Edit New Environment** button; a pop-up window will open to fill its **Name**, **Location**, and **Description**
- **Server Name**: Provide your server name so that you can differentiate in the LCS account

- **Server Location**: Input your city, office building, or anyplace else that lets you know where the server resides
- **Server Description**: Input the server description by which you can differentiate the servers in LCS

Finally, you can click on **Register**; follow this screenshot:

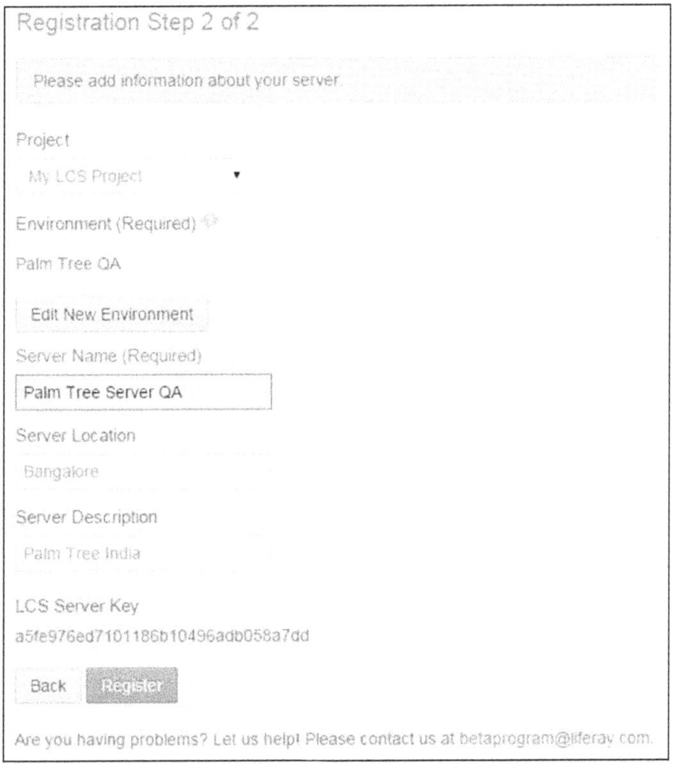

Figure 11.17: The Liferay Connected Services Client application form for registration of the server

After you register the server, you need to synchronize it with LCS:

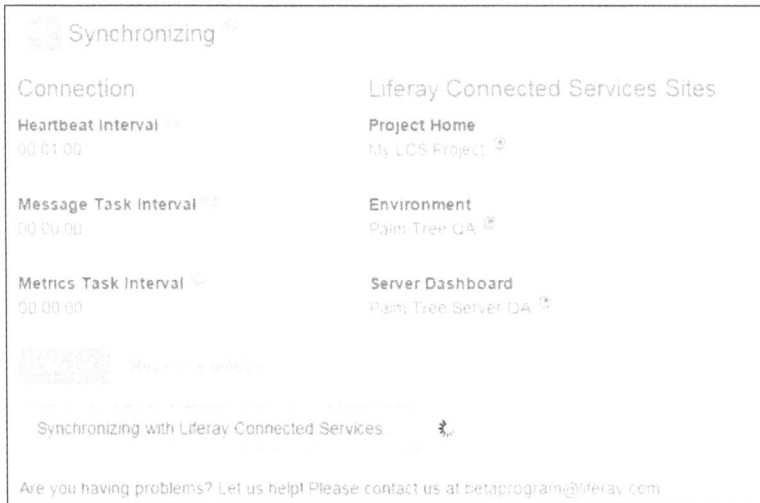

Figure 11.18: The Liferay Connected Services Client application form for the registration of the server

Let's have a look at LCS sites in detail.

Managing the server through the LCS site

Once you open **My LCS Project** in the LCS site, it lists all the available fix packs available across a cluster; refer to the following screenshot for the **Dashboard** view. LCS downloads and installs fix packs simultaneously across all nodes; you don't have to handle each one individually.

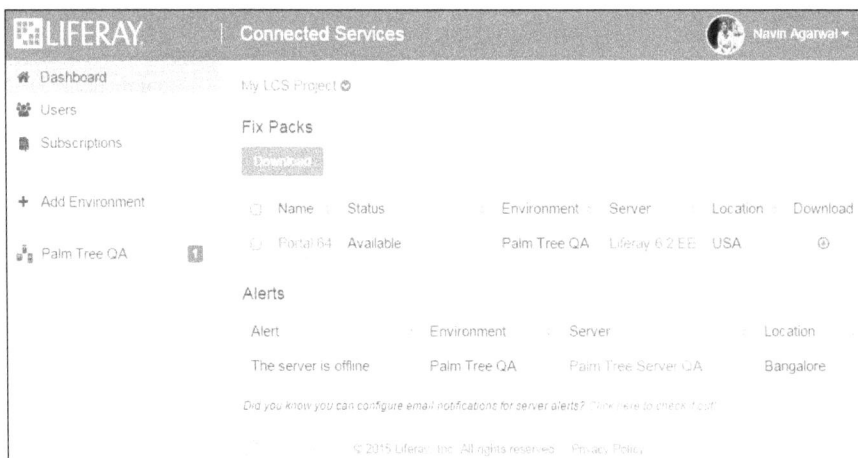

Figure 11.19: The Liferay Connected Services (LCS) Dashboard view

In the preceding screenshot, you will be able to see the **Fix Packs** and **Alerts** tables. The **Fix Packs** table generally lists the available fix packs for the running servers. The **Alerts** table generally lists many other kinds of messages, such as **the server is offline**, **monitoring is unavailable**, and so on. In the left-hand side menu panel, you will be able to manage the users and even add new environments. The following screenshot displays the **Users** details. As an administrator, you can invite other users and manage them too.

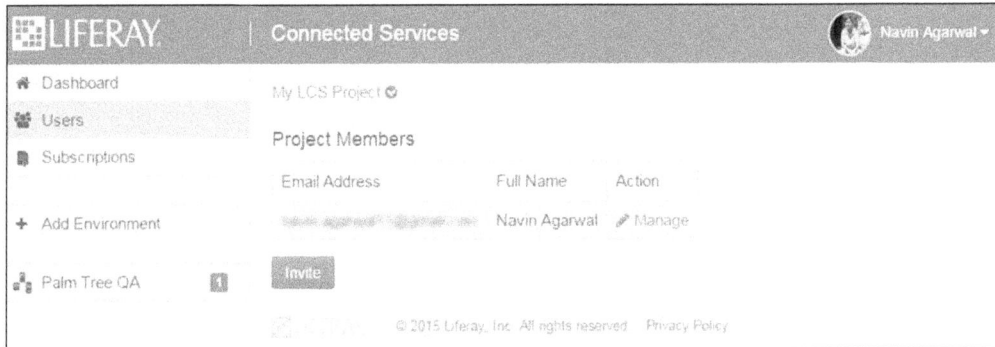

Figure 11.20: Liferay Connected Services (LCS) Users view

You can also see the subscription of environments by clicking on the **Subscription** link from the left-hand side panel, and if required, you can regenerate the token of the listed environment by clicking on the **Regenerate** link from the **Actions** button.

The LCS site allows you to add new environments by clicking on the **Add Environment** button from the left-hand side panel. After clicking on **Add Environment**, you get the form with the Name, Description, and Location fields. After filling in the details, finally click on the create button to create the new environment entry.

To view **Environment Details**, you need to click on the environment, that is, **Palm Tree QA** in our example, which you can click from the left-hand side panel. Refer to the following screenshot, which shows the details of the server in LCS:

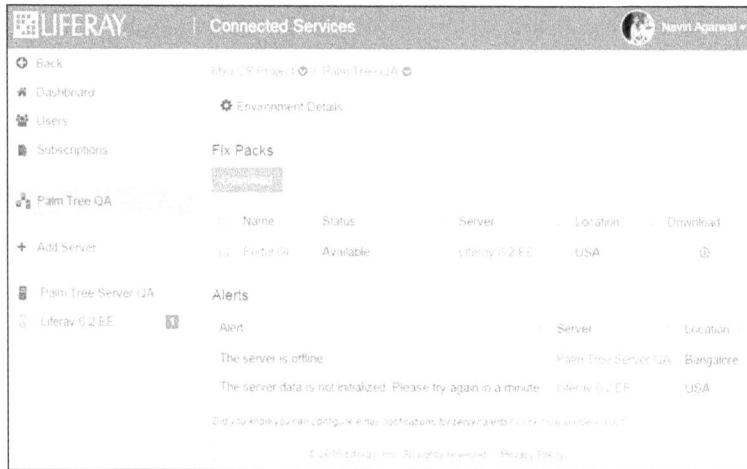

Figure 11.21: Liferay Connected Services (LCS) environment view

If you notice, there are two servers registered, which are **Palm Tree Server QA** and **Liferay 6.2 EE**. Once you select the server instance, it will display the fix packs under the **Available** tab for that particular server. Even you can monitor your server performance and other details from here. Refer to the following screenshot, which displays the server details along with other controls features:

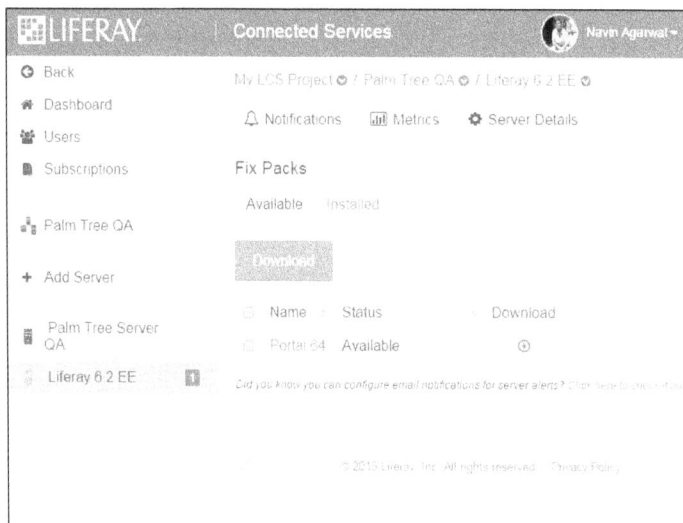

Figure 11.22: Liferay Connected Services (LCS) server view

You can click on the download button, which will download all the fix packs available, or you can simply select a particular fix pack from the list and click on the download icon next to it. Once the fix pack is downloaded and the server restart is done, the fix pack will be installed into your server automatically and will be listed under the **Installed** tab. Cluster environments also work in the same manner.

There are three buttons at the top, which are as follows:

- **Notifications**: This displays the available fix packs for the particular server instance.

- **Metrics**: This displays the different metrics and statistics of the server performance. This has three different categories defined; let's discuss them in detail:

    ° **Application**: This has three other categories defined within it:

    Pages: This lists the page load time along with the frequency with which specific pages are loaded.

    Portlets: This lists the portlet load time, along with their frequency for specific portlets in your server. Refer to the following screenshot; if you notice, the dock bar frequency is 23, and the average loading time is 5208 milliseconds:

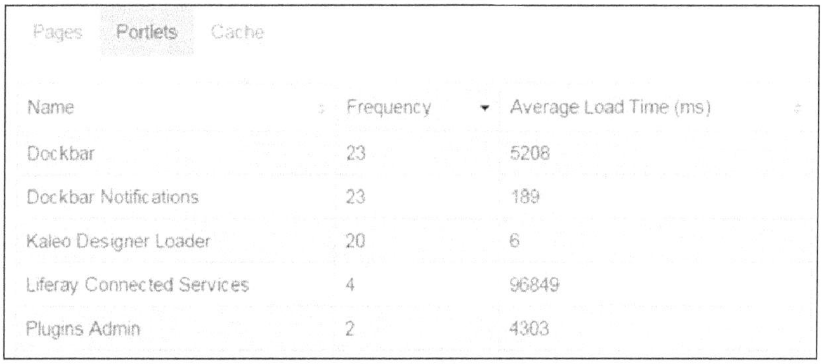

Pages	Portlets	Cache

Name	Frequency ▾	Average Load Time (ms)
Dockbar	23	5208
Dockbar Notifications	23	189
Kaleo Designer Loader	20	6
Liferay Connected Services	4	96849
Plugins Admin	2	4303

Figure 11.23: Liferay Connected Services (LCS) application | Portlets

Cache: This lists the Liferay Single VM metrics and Hibernate metrics tables; refer to the following screenshot:

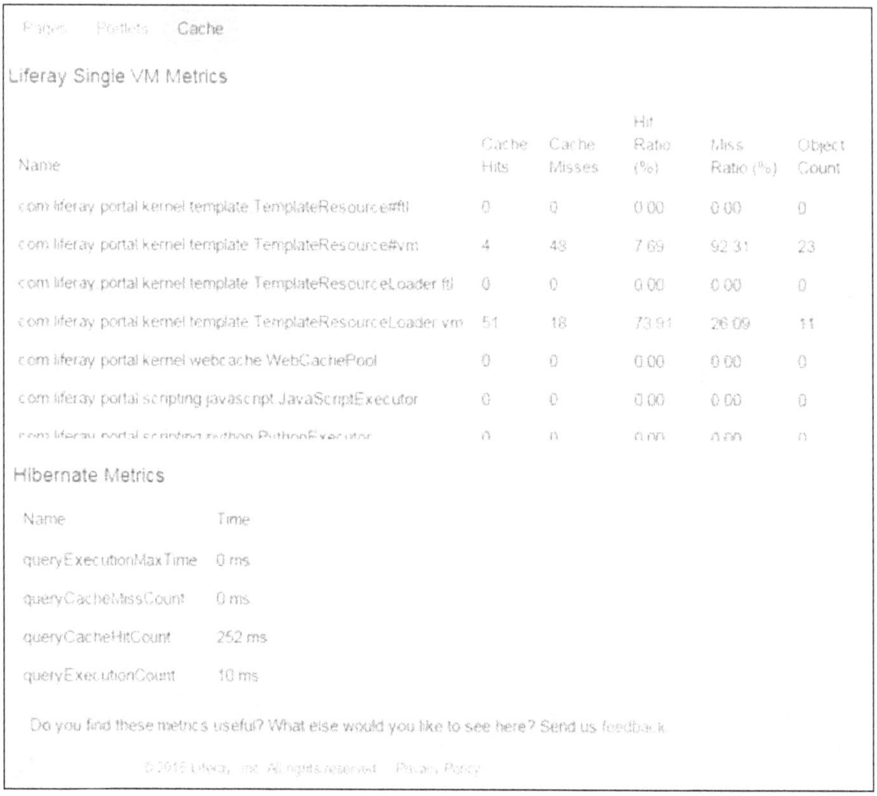

	Cache Hits	Cache Misses	Hit Ratio (%)	Miss Ratio (%)	Object Count
Liferay Single VM Metrics					
Name					
com.liferay.portal.kernel.template.TemplateResource#ftl	0	0	0.00	0.00	0
com.liferay.portal.kernel.template.TemplateResource#vm	4	48	7.69	92.31	23
com.liferay.portal.kernel.template.TemplateResourceLoader.ftl	0	0	0.00	0.00	0
com.liferay.portal.kernel.template.TemplateResourceLoader.vm	51	18	73.91	26.09	11
com.liferay.portal.kernel.webcache.WebCachePool	0	0	0.00	0.00	0
com.liferay.portal.scripting.javascript.JavaScriptExecutor	0	0	0.00	0.00	0
com.liferay.portal.scripting.python.PythonExecutor	0	0	0.00	0.00	0

Hibernate Metrics

Name	Time
queryExecutionMaxTime	0 ms
queryCacheMissCount	0 ms
queryCacheHitCount	252 ms
queryExecutionCount	10 ms

Do you find these metrics useful? What else would you like to see here? Send us feedback

© 2015 Liferay, Inc. All rights reserved. Privacy Policy

Figure 11.24: Liferay Connected Services (LCS) application | Cache

- ° **JVM**: This displays the statistics about the JVM running on your server, including **Garbage Collector Metrics** and **Memory Metrics**; refer to the following screenshot:

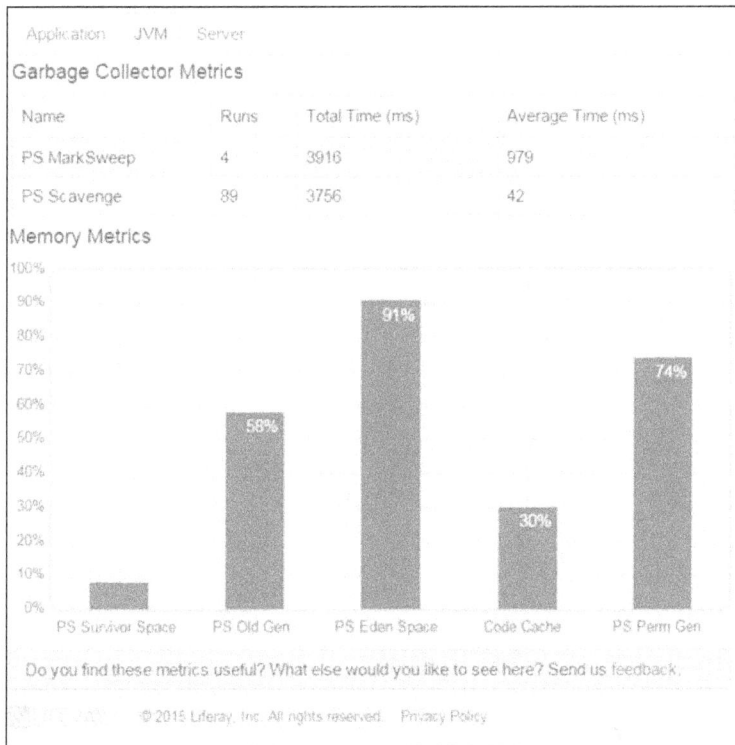

Figure 11.25: The Liferay Connected Services (LCS) JVM metrics view

JVM metrics are very useful from a server performance point of view. They display the usage of **PS Survivor Space**, **PS Old Gen**, **PS Eden Space**, **Code Cache**, and **PS Perm Gen**.

○ **Server**: This displays the horizontal bar graph that shows the number of **Current Threads** and **JDBC Connection Pools** that are running on your server.

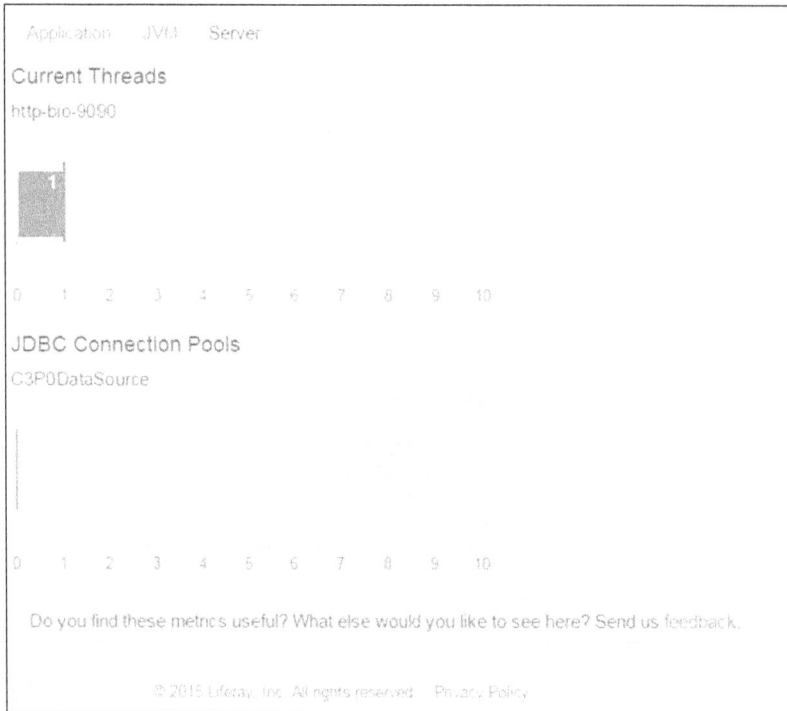

Figure 11.26: The Liferay Connected Services (LCS) Server metrics view

• **Server Details**: This displays the server details and also allows you to edit and unregister your server from LCS. It has two tabs—**Server Settings** and **Server Properties**:

○ **Server Settings**: This allows you to edit the server name, description, and location. You can even unregister your server from LCS by clicking on the **Unregister** button.

- ° **Server Properties**: This displays general information about your Liferay server and hardware. See the following screenshot for server properties:

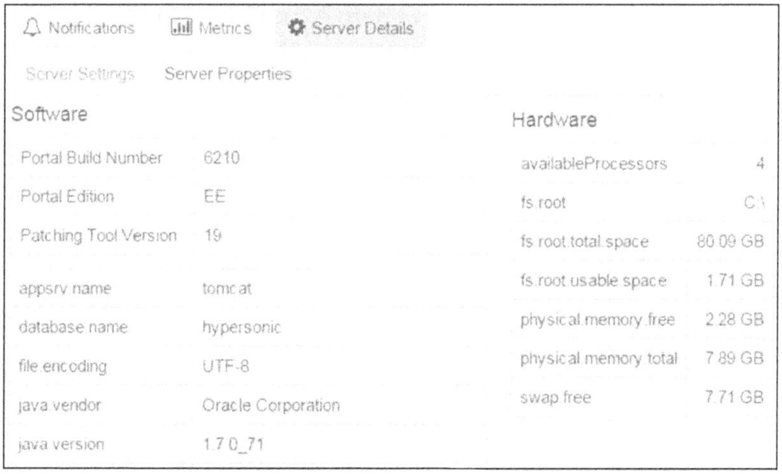

Figure 11.27: Liferay Connected Services (LCS) Server Properties view

LCS is a very powerful tool that greatly simplifies the fix pack update process and also gives you extensive information on your running server.

Now you will learn about Liferay clustering.

Liferay clustering

Liferay Portal is configured for a single-server environment, which comes out of the box. When your site traffic starts increasing, you need to increase your server size as per the requirement. Here comes the Liferay Portal cluster design, which allows you to route the site traffic in different servers.

Liferay Portal works perfectly in a cluster of multiple machines—a horizontal cluster or in clusters of multiple VMs on a single machine, that is, a vertical cluster or a mixture of the two.

Let's take a scenario where you have installed Liferay on different server nodes. Now to make the cluster environment, you need to define several optimizations and configurations.

- All the server nodes should be pointed to the same Liferay database or database cluster
- All nodes of the clusters should have the access to Documents and Media repositories
- For a cluster environment, you should configure a search for replication or use a separate search server
- The cache mechanism should replicate across all nodes of the cluster
- If you are using server farms, you must configure the hot deployment folders for each node

> A server farms configuration is done via a script, which helps you to deploy normally to any node's deploy folder, and the farm script will sync the deployment to all nodes.

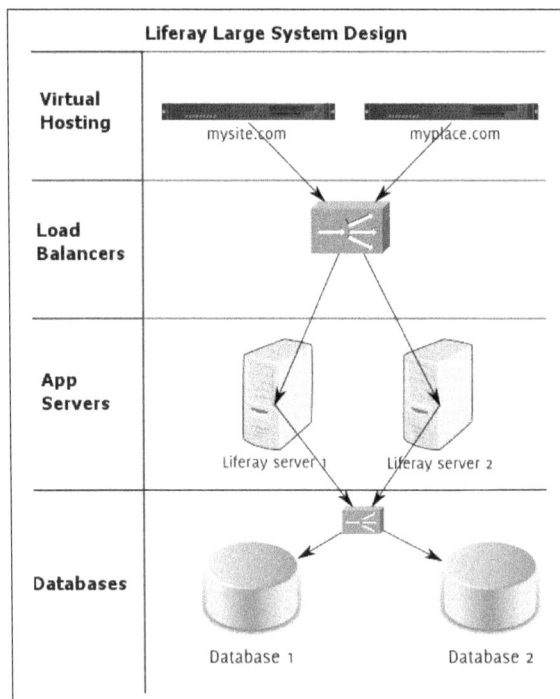

Figure 11.28: Liferay Large System Design

Let's discuss each of the preceding points in detail to configure a cluster environment.

A common database for multiple nodes

Each node in the cluster should be configured with a data source that points to one Liferay database (or a database cluster) that all the nodes will share. You should not use the embedded HSQL database that comes along with the Liferay bundle; instead, you should use a different database. To optimize your database, there are two options: a read-writer database configuration and sharding.

The read-writer database configuration

Liferay Portal supports two different data sources to read and write, which helps you split your database infrastructure into two different sets: one optimized for reading and another optimized for writing. By doing this, it makes the databases sync in a much faster manner than a single data source that handles everything.

Now, you need to set up the properties in `portal-ext.properties` files to enable a read-writer database:

```
jdbc.read.driverClassName=com.mysql.jdbc.Driver
jdbc.read.url=jdbc:mysql://databaseread.com/lportal?useUnicode=tru
    e&characterEncoding=UTF-8\&useFastDateParsing=false
jdbc.read.username=<user name>
jdbc.read.password=<password>

jdbc.write.driverClassName=com.mysql.jdbc.Driver
jdbc.write.url=jdbc:mysql://databasewrite.com/lportal?useUnicode=true&
characterEncoding=UTF-8\&useFastDateParsing=false
jdbc.write.username=<user name>
jdbc.write.password=<password>
```

The preceding code is for the read-writer for the database configuration. Specify the user name and password for each database configuration.

Now you need to enable the read-writer database configuration by uncommenting the Spring property, that is, `#META-INF/dynamic-data-source-spring.xml,\` in the `portal-ext.properties` file:

```
spring.configs=\
  META-INF/base-spring.xml,\
  META-INF/hibernate-spring.xml,\
  META-INF/infrastructure-spring.xml,\
  META-INF/management-spring.xml,\
  META-INF/util-spring.xml,\
  META-INF/jpa-spring.xml,\
  META-INF/executor-spring.xml,\
  META-INF/audit-spring.xml,\
```

```
    META-INF/cluster-spring.xml,\
    META-INF/editor-spring.xml,\
    META-INF/jcr-spring.xml,\
    META-INF/ldap-spring.xml,\
    META-INF/messaging-core-spring.xml,\
    META-INF/messaging-misc-spring.xml,\
    META-INF/mobile-device-spring.xml,\
    META-INF/monitoring-spring.xml,\
    META-INF/notifications-spring.xml,\
    META-INF/poller-spring.xml,\
    META-INF/rules-spring.xml,\
    META-INF/scheduler-spring.xml,\
    META-INF/scripting-spring.xml,\
    META-INF/search-spring.xml,\
    META-INF/workflow-spring.xml,\
    META-INF/counter-spring.xml,\
    META-INF/mail-spring.xml,\
    META-INF/portal-spring.xml,\
    META-INF/portlet-container-spring.xml,\
    META-INF/staging-spring.xml,\
    META-INF/virtual-layouts-spring.xml,\
    #META-INF/dynamic-data-source-spring.xml,\
    #META-INF/shard-data-source-spring.xml,\
    #META-INF/memcached-spring.xml,\
    classpath*:META-INF/ext-spring.xml
```

After setting the properties for two databases for replication and enabling the `dynamic-data-source-spring.xml` in `portal-ext.properties`, you need to restart the server.

Database sharding

Sharding is a type of database partitioning that separates very large databases into smaller, faster, more easily managed parts called data shards. It is also used to describe an extremely high-scalability configuration for the systems with massive numbers of users.

This helps you to split up the database by different types of data stored in it. For example, implementing database sharding helps you to split up the database with respect to the user's last name: the ones that begin with A to F go in one database, G to L go into another database, and so on. Whenever the user logs in, it identifies the user's last name and directs them to the application that is connected to the database corresponding to their last name.

In different portal instances, you can configure sharding properties using the com.
liferay.portal.dao.shard.RoundRobinShardSelector class. In this class, the
default algorithm for sharding has been implemented in Liferay, which helps Liferay
to select different portal instances and eventually distributes the data across them.

Liferay provides you with an alternative by which you can use the com.liferay.
portal.dao.shard.ManualShardSelector class. For this, you'd need to configure
your shards manually in **Control Panel**.

You can also develop and implement your own sharding algorithm and configure it
in the portal-ext.properties file:

```
shard.selector=com.liferay.portal.dao.shard.RoundRobinShardSelecto
    r
#shard.selector=com.liferay.portal.dao.shard.ManualShardSelector
#shard.selector=[your implementation here]
```

After you have enabled sharding, you need to make sure that you are using the
Liferay data source implementation instead of your application server. Set the
database properties in portal-ext.properties:

```
jdbc.default.driverClassName=com.mysql.jdbc.Driver
jdbc.default.url=jdbc:mysql://localhost/lportal?useUnicode=true&ch
    aracterEncoding=UTF-8\&useFastDateParsing=false
jdbc.default.username=
jdbc.default.password=
jdbc.one.driverClassName=com.mysql.jdbc.Driver
jdbc.one.url=jdbc:mysql://localhost/lportal1?useUnicode=true&chara
    cterEncoding=UTF-8\&useFastDateParsing=false
jdbc.one.username=
jdbc.one.password=
jdbc.two.driverClassName=com.mysql.jdbc.Driver
jdbc.two.url=jdbc:mysql://localhost/lportal2?useUnicode=true&chara
    cterEncoding=UTF-8\&useFastDateParsing=false
jdbc.two.username=
jdbc.two.password=
shard.available.names=default,one,two
```

After you set the preceding properties, you can set up the DNS for the domain names
pointing to a different Liferay installation. Now, go to **Control Panel**, click on **Portal
Instances** under the **Configuration** section, and create two or three instances bound
to the DNS names that you have configured.

> Note that when using the `RoundRodinShardSelector` class, Liferay automatically enters data into each instance one by one. If you're using the `ManualShardSelector` class, then you have to specify a shard for each instance from the Portal Instance add interface in the **Control Panel | Configuration section**.

Finally, you need to modify the `spring.configs` section of your `portal-ext.properties` file to enable the sharding configuration, that is, `META-INF/shard-data-source-spring.xml`.

After doing all the settings and configuration, your database for a large installation is complete.

Documents and Media Library for all nodes

Liferay Portal has a unique feature in Document and Media Library, which allows you to mount several other repositories. If you have a separate repository that you have mounted, all nodes of the cluster should point to this repository. Now you should focus on improving performance. At this point, it is good to cluster your third-party repository by going through the documentation for the repository you have used. If you don't have any third-party repository, you can configure the Liferay repository to perform perfectly in a cluster configuration.

Now, we need to configure the Liferay Document and Media Library stores files and check whether all the files have the proper and same access to each file for every other node. In the `portal-ext.properties` file, there are several configuration properties that allow you to configure the file storage with the `dl.store.impl=` property:

```
#dl.store.impl=com.liferay.portlet.documentlibrary.store.AdvancedF
  ileSystemStore
#dl.store.impl=com.liferay.portlet.documentlibrary.store.CMISStore
#dl.store.impl=com.liferay.portlet.documentlibrary.store.DBStore
dl.store.impl=com.liferay.portlet.documentlibrary.store.FileSystem
  Store
#dl.store.impl=com.liferay.portlet.documentlibrary.store.JCRStore
dl.store.impl=com.liferay.portlet.documentlibrary.store.S3Store
```

The preceding properties allow the Liferay Document Library server to use this to persist documents and files. If you notice in the preceding code, except for the `FileSystemStore` entry, the other entries are commented. That means Liferay will store the documents in your local filesystem.

Understanding the filesystem store

As you have seen in the preceding code, this is a default store for Liferay. This uses your local filesystem folder to store files. The filesystem can be used for a clustered environment, but we need to use a storage area network or a clustered filesystem to handle concurrent requests and file locking.

The filesystem store is tightly bound with the Liferay database; as per the default settings, documents are stored in the `document_library` subfolder of the data folder in the Liferay bundle. The path of the folder can be changed by changing the property value with a new folder path location:

```
dl.store.file.system.root.dir=${liferay.home}/data/document_librar
    y
```

Let's look at the following image for the filesystem storage folder structure, which is created based on primary keys in the Liferay database:

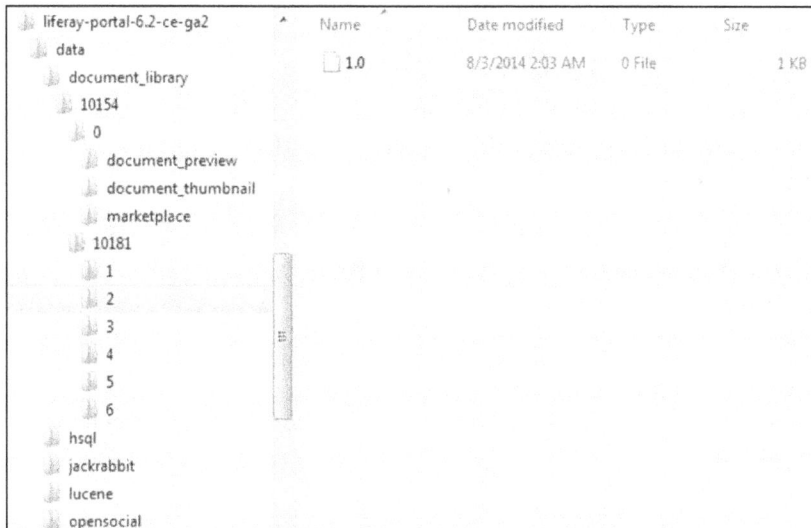

Figure 11.29: Liferay filesystem storage

The format to create a folder path to store any documents is this:

```
/companyId/folderId/numericFileEntryName/versionNumber
```

The first folder name is the company ID to which the site belongs and the second folder name is the ID of the Document and Media folder within which the document resides. The third folder name is the numeric file entry name of the document itself, and finally, the fourth folder is the version number, which is used to store multiple versions of the document.

Filesystem storage is bound with Liferay so closely and tightly that document and media files are stored according to their folder structure.

Understanding the Liferay Advanced filesystem store

The Liferay Advanced filesystem store is similar to the default filesystem store. It also stores the files in the local filesystem. The main difference is that many operating systems do not allow creating a number of files that can be stored in a particular folder. To overcome this, the advanced filesystem programmatically creates a structure that can be expanded to millions of files by alphabetically nesting the files in folders.

To make the cluster environment, you need to point the store to a network-mounted filesystem, which supports concurrent request and file locking; it should allow access to all the nodes.

Understanding the CMIS store

Liferay Portal has a feature that allows you to mount different repositories using **Content Management Interoperability Services** (**CMIS**) within the Document and Media Library.

You can mount the Liferay repository connected to a clustered CMIS repository by configuring the properties files. In portal-ext. properties, you can set the following properties for the CMIS repository:

```
dl.store.cmis.credentials.username=<userName>
dl.store.cmis.credentials.password=<password>
dl.store.cmis.repository.url=http://localhost:8080/alfresco/servic
  e/api/cmis
dl.store.cmis.system.root.dir=Liferay Home
```

After configuring the preceding properties and restarting, the server is done. Liferay repositories are connected to CMIS via the CMIS store. The CMIS protocol prevents multiple file access from causing data corruption.

Understanding JCR Store

The **Java Content Repository** (**JCR**) standard is implemented in Liferay Portal to store data. Liferay comes with jackrabbit, a project from Apache as it's a JSR-170 compliant document repository. Jackrabbit is used to store the documents on the local filesystem by default. If you notice the preceding screenshot, jackrabbit is a subfolder under the data folder, which has a configuration file called `repository.xml`.

It's this `repository.xml` that you can configure to store files in a database that can be accessed by all the nodes, and which operates as a cluster within a Liferay cluster. Even you can move the default repository location to a shared folder; then, there is no need to edit jackrabbit's `repository.xml` file. Instead, you can change the following property value in the `portal-ext.properties` file, which points to a shared folder location that all the nodes can access:

```
jcr.jackrabbit.repository.root=${liferay.home}/data/jackrabbit
```

In the shared location, a new configuration file will be generated, which you can modify to do jackrabbit's configuration.

> Note that best practice is to configure jackrabbit in a cluster. You should redirect jackrabbit into your database of choice. This will have the capability of handling concurrency and file locking.

Now you need to uncomment the section to move the jackrabbit configuration to a new repository.xml file in a database. It is done to make it simpler for the administrator to comment out the sections related to the filesystem and uncomment the section related to the database. You can configure any database as per your requirement; by default, the MySQL database is configured.

For more information about configuring jackrabbit, see the documentation at `http://jackrabbit.apache.org`.

Understanding Amazon Simple Storage Service

Amazon Simple Storage Service (S3) is a cloud-based storage solution, which you can use with Liferay Portal. You can store your documents from all the nodes in one location seamlessly. You should have an amazon s3 account to configure it. In the `portal-ext properties` file, you need to configure the following properties:

```
dl.store.s3.access.key=
dl.store.s3.secret.key=
dl.store.s3.bucket.name=
```

After you configure the preceding properties, set your store implementation to S3Store:

```
dl.store.impl=com.liferay.portlet.documentlibrary.store.S3Store
```

Refer to the Amazon simple storage documentation for additional details on using Amazon's service.

Liferay 7 updates

Liferay Portal is growing with time and adopting new technologies emerging in the field of user experience. Currently, Liferay Portal is ranked at the second position in the Gartner Magic Quadrant for Horizontal Portals. It's the only open source portal on the market. As the open source portal demand increases, Liferay Portal also keeps itself updated with new technologies. Liferay Portal 7 is coming with new technologies for better end user experience for universal devices. Liferay 7 has a lot of new features to make it the best portal on the market.

Now, developing an advanced website using Liferay will be very easy for the developer.

Let's have a look at the new features in Liferay 7:

- User engagement (interaction platform) by User Personas
- Single-page Application to improve performance
- Audience Targeting by user segments, suggested content, and analytics
- Power user productivity center
- Integrated forms and workflow
- Building modern websites is easier
- Improved developer experience by making it true modular architecture.
- Liferay Mobile SDK to create collaboration and productivity on the go
- Liferay Connected Services for monitoring servers

User Personas

Personas help to focus decisions surrounding site components by adding a layer of real-world consideration to the conversation:

- This helps in representing a major user group for your site
- This expresses and focuses on the major needs and expectations of the most important user group
- This gives a clear picture of the user's expectations and how they are likely to use the site
- This aids in uncovering universal features and functionality
- This describes real people with backgrounds, goals, and values

The following screenshot displays User Personas for the portal:

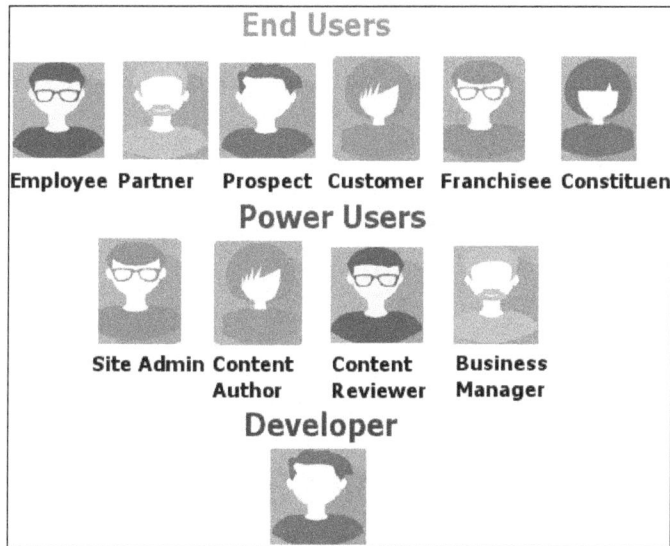

Figure 11.30: Liferay 7 User Personas

The purpose of personas is to create reliable and realistic representations of your key audience segments for reference.

Single-page Applications

A **Single-page Application (SPA)** is a web application or website that fits on a single web page with the goal of providing a more fluid user experience akin to a desktop application. It helps in improving the page loading time as compared to the older version. As the user clicks on links and interacts with the page, subsequent content is loaded dynamically. The application will often update the URL in the address bar to emulate traditional page navigation, but another full page request is never made.

The Audience Targeting application

Audience Targeting is a new feature in both Liferay 6.2 and Liferay 7. It raises the engagement experience of your portal to a whole new level. Liferay provides the Audience Targeting application in Marketplace. This app allows you to segment your audience, target specific content to different user segments, and create campaigns to target content to user segments. It also allows you to track user actions and generate reports that provide insight into the effectiveness of your campaigns. We discussed this in the preceding chapter in detail.

The developer experience

Liferay has come up with broader perspectives for different users, such as the end user experience, power user experience, and developer experience. Liferay tried to make the developer experience better by making Liferay 7 True Modular Architecture with the following advantages:

- Improved maintenance
- Better release process
- Lightweight
- More flexibility
- Micro-service oriented
- Makes everything independent and extensible

Advanced Liferay Mobile SDK

The Liferay Mobile SDK plugin for Eclipse simplifies developing Android apps that use Liferay. You can configure Mobile SDKs manually to use with Android apps and/or iOS apps. Once configured, you can invoke Liferay services from your app. The Liferay Mobile SDK bridges the gap between your native app and Liferay's services.

Liferay Connected Services

Liferay Connected Services was released for Liferay 6.2 too, which we discussed in previous sections.

Summary

Server Administration is essential for maintaining the server and keeps it healthy for end users to use. In this chapter, you saw how to handle the server administrator in the control panel by reindexing the database and searches. You also saw how to enable the CAPTCHA and make data migration databases easier. This chapter also taught you how to improve the server performance by setting the properties for JDK and Liferay. Content Delivery Network increases the performance of the server by keeping the static content in the local cache for fast access. LCS is a new feature that helps you to monitor the server and trigger the fixes from the cloud. It saves time and improves the server performance too. You also came to know about the new features of Liferay 7, which is going to be a major release from Liferay.

Index

Symbol

$PORTAL_ROOT_HOME folders
dtd 59
errors 59
html 59
layouttpl 59
wap 59
WEB-INF 59

A

Access Control List (ACL) 235
Activities portlets 19
Advanced filesystem store 566
advanced site settings 377-381
Alfresco
Liferay, integrating with 444-448
URL 444
Amazon Simple Storage Service (S3) 567
announcements and alerts, RSS
about 287
Announcements portlet, configuring 291
Announcements portlet, features 290
entries, managing 287-289
Application Display Templates (ADT)
about 306, 381
creating 382-384
App Manager 506
architecture, Liferay Portal
Frontend layer 10
Persistence layer 10
Service layer 10
Web services API layer 10

Asset Publisher
about 200
Asset Renderer Framework 208
assets, selecting dynamically 206, 207
assets, selecting manually 202-204
configuration 201
customization 207, 208
features 200
velocity templates, adding 208
assets
tagging 191, 192
Audience Targeting app
about 514, 569
faceted search 522, 523
installing 515
Search portlet, configuring 523
uninstalling 515
user segment management 516-520
authentication
about 81, 129
auto login 131
configuration 129, 130
general settings 139
LDAP authentication 131-133
OpenID authentication 137
Open SSO authentication 137, 138
SSO authentication 135, 136
authorization
about 81, 143
permission 143, 144
permission algorithms, setting 147, 148
permission, defining on role 144-146

[PACKT] PUBLISHING | open source*
community experience distilled

Thank you for buying
Liferay Portal 6.2 Enterprise Intranets

About Packt Publishing

Packt, pronounced 'packed', published its first book, *Mastering phpMyAdmin for Effective MySQL Management*, in April 2004, and subsequently continued to specialize in publishing highly focused books on specific technologies and solutions.

Our books and publications share the experiences of your fellow IT professionals in adapting and customizing today's systems, applications, and frameworks. Our solution-based books give you the knowledge and power to customize the software and technologies you're using to get the job done. Packt books are more specific and less general than the IT books you have seen in the past. Our unique business model allows us to bring you more focused information, giving you more of what you need to know, and less of what you don't.

Packt is a modern yet unique publishing company that focuses on producing quality, cutting-edge books for communities of developers, administrators, and newbies alike. For more information, please visit our website at www.packtpub.com.

About Packt Open Source

In 2010, Packt launched two new brands, Packt Open Source and Packt Enterprise, in order to continue its focus on specialization. This book is part of the Packt Open Source brand, home to books published on software built around open source licenses, and offering information to anybody from advanced developers to budding web designers. The Open Source brand also runs Packt's Open Source Royalty Scheme, by which Packt gives a royalty to each open source project about whose software a book is sold.

Writing for Packt

We welcome all inquiries from people who are interested in authoring. Book proposals should be sent to author@packtpub.com. If your book idea is still at an early stage and you would like to discuss it first before writing a formal book proposal, then please contact us; one of our commissioning editors will get in touch with you.

We're not just looking for published authors; if you have strong technical skills but no writing experience, our experienced editors can help you develop a writing career, or simply get some additional reward for your expertise.

[PACKT] open source
community experience distilled
PUBLISHING

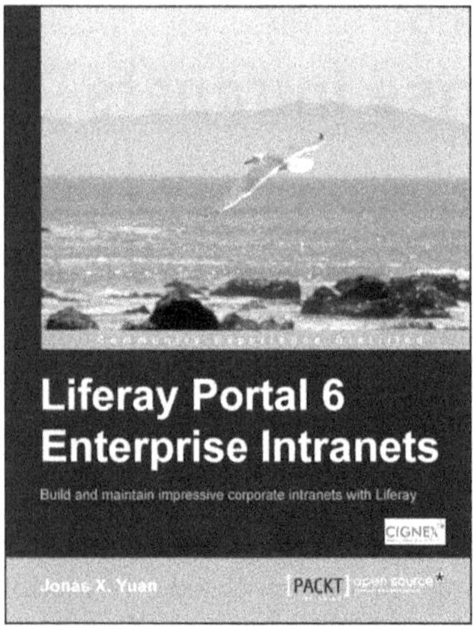

Liferay Portal 6 Enterprise Intranets

ISBN: 978-1-84951-038-7 Paperback: 692 pages

Build and maintain impressive corporate intranets with Liferay

1. Develop a professional Intranet using Liferay's practical functionality, usability, and technical innovation.
2. Enhance your Intranet using your innovation and Liferay Portal's out-of-the-box portlets.
3. Maximize your existing and future IT investments by optimizing your usage of Liferay Portal.

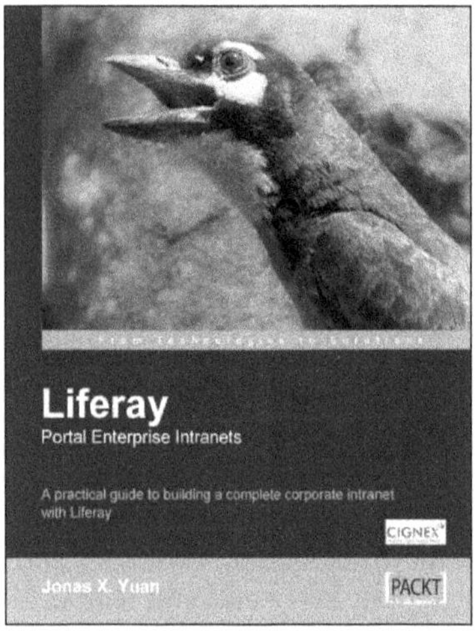

Liferay Portal Enterprise Intranets

ISBN: 978-1-84719-272-1 Paperback: 408 pages

A practical guide to building a complete corporate intranet with Liferay

1. Install, set up, and use a corporate intranet with Liferay—complete guide.
2. Discussions, document management, collaboration, blogs, and more.
3. Clear, step-by-step instructions, practical examples, and straightforward explanation.

Please check **www.PacktPub.com** for information on our titles